# The Gallup Poll

Public Opinion 1984

GEORGE H. GALLUP
(1901–1984)
Founder and Chairman of The Gallup Poll

# The Gallup Poll

## Public Opinion 1984

*George Gallup, Jr.*

SR Scholarly Resources Inc.
Wilmington, Delaware

# ACKNOWLEDGMENTS

The preparation of this volume has involved the entire staff of The Gallup Poll and their contributions are gratefully acknowledged. I particularly wish to thank James Shriver, III, managing editor of The Gallup Poll; and Professor Fred L. Israel of the City College of New York, who has been the principal coordinator of this volume and of the eleven volumes that preceded it.

G.G.

© 1985 by The Gallup Poll
All rights reserved
First published 1985
Printed in the United States of America

Scholarly Resources Inc.
104 Greenhill Avenue
Wilmington, DE  19805

Library of Congress Catalog Card Number: 79-56557
International Standard Serial Number: 0195-962X
International Standard Book Number: 0-8420-2234-1

# CONTENTS

# FOREWORD

Nineteen hundred eighty-five marks the fiftieth year of the Gallup Poll, a milestone its founder did not live to see, for Dr. George H. Gallup died on July 27, 1984 at his summer home in Switzerland. During his lifetime, however, Dr. Gallup saw scientific polling, which he helped pioneer, spread to all corners of the globe.

Many years ago Lord Bryce saw the great obstacle to an informed democracy to be the absence of a way to measure public opinion accurately and continuously; democracy then was an exercise in guesswork. Dr. Gallup helped overcome this obstacle in 1935 when he founded the Gallup Poll. In the succeeding five decades, more than 2 million Americans have been interviewed through both the Gallup Poll and the Gallup Organization Inc. In addition, Gallup International, founded in 1947, now includes thirty-six affiliated companies conducting research in eighty-six nations on five continents.

George Gallup was born in Jefferson, Iowa, on November 18, 1901. After earning his undergraduate, master's, and Ph.D. degrees at the University of Iowa, he taught eighteen college courses in three academic disciplines, from Freshman English to the Psychology of Advertising to Newspaper Management, in four universities. He also began to apply survey research procedures to a wide variety of fields, devising the "reading and noting" research techniques for determining newspaper readership and conducting the first national survey of magazines to determine which ads attract the most attention.

In 1932 he joined the New York advertising firm of Young and Rubicam as head of its marketing and copy research departments. There he carried on his research into print media and established the first nationwide radio audience measurement, using the coincidental method, a technique he originated; later he developed the impact method, a recall procedure now widely used to measure television and print advertising effectiveness. About his fifteen years in advertising, Dr. Gallup once said in a Young and Rubicam newsletter: "I look back on my days at Y&R with the greatest of pleasure. I can honestly say that I never spent a dull day there. And the professional standards and practices were as high as those I had encountered in my university teaching days. The people with whom I was associated were talented, bright, and witty."

In the early 1930s, while still at Young and Rubicam, Dr. Gallup began his work in the field of public opinion and election forecasting, inspired in part by the desire to help his mother-in-law win election and then reelection as secretary of state of Iowa; she was the first woman to hold that office. In the same decade, Dr. Gallup also developed a complete research program for Hollywood movie studios—measuring the appeal of story ideas, the box-office draw of stars, publicity penetration, and preview reaction—which culminated in forecasts of the box-office receipts of specific films. He worked with David O. Selznick, Walt Disney, Samuel Goldwyn, and others. Not coincidentally, one of the most researched pictures in movie history, *The Best of Our Lives*, won ten Oscars.

This fascination with research led Dr. Gallup into his primary concern: the Gallup Poll. For a half century, Gallup-affiliated organizations here and abroad have assessed public opinion on an extraordinary variety of political, social, and economic issues, including the hopes and fears of people around the globe, their leisure-time activities, morals and manners, and religious beliefs.

The topics covered by the Gallup Poll over the last fifty years have closely reflected the turbulent events of this period. Many of the questions have dealt with change and reform in different areas of life, for Dr. Gallup was an apostle of change, and his strictly objective approach to measuring public opinion belied the passionate soul of a reformer. He sought the public's views on reform in education, in the criminal system, and in politics, including a better way of seeking out the ablest men and women for high political office; improvements in election campaigns; and the opportunity for the people to express their views more directly on important national issues, by means of the initiative and referendum.

In the case of many legislative issues and proposals, Dr. Gallup believed that the people were often years ahead of their legislative leaders and sought to prove it. To use his own words: "Through nearly five decades of polling, we have found the collective judgment of the people to be extraordinarily sound, especially on issues which come within the scope of the typical person's experience. Often the people are actually ahead of their elected leaders in accepting innovations and radical changes."

During his long career, Dr. Gallup explored many dimensions of human life and society. He thought that the next great development in medicine would come through exploration of environmental factors associated with illness; to prove his point he conducted a landmark survey dealing with infantile paralysis in the era before the Salk vaccine. Another survey dealt with factors related to old age, a study that included interviews with nearly 700 persons over the age of 95 in the United States and Great Britain. Still another pioneering study in the 1940s dealt with psychological well-being; in short, personal happiness.

Among his most ambitious projects was a global survey conducted in 1976 to determine the quality of life in all areas of the world, a study that sampled populations embracing two-thirds of the world's 4 billion inhabitants. More recently, the international values study dealt with the social, moral, and religious attitudes of the peoples of most of the major countries in Europe, including the Eastern bloc, and around the world.

Dr. Gallup had many interests beyond public opinion polling. For example, he had founded in 1926 Quill and Scroll, an honor society for high-school journalists which now has 11,000 chapters here and abroad. His lifelong concern for education, however, led him to initiate annual surveys of the people's attitudes on the public schools. The editors of the *Journal for High School and Middle School Administrators* wrote in tribute to his contributions: "Gallup's death leaves American schools with one less friend and supporter. He started his annual poll about American education in 1969. He believed that alerting education's decision makers to the public's thinking about the issues was extremely important. He was right. Knowing the public's perceptions of our work is certainly one good measure of our effectiveness. We owe much to Gallup for helping to establish a national benchmark for American education."

Columnist Neal R. Pierce saw Dr. Gallup as "a democratic man, a fervid believer in the wisdom of the common men and women and how polling could and should let them influence haughty, distant government. He was also a civil activist encouraging people to do for themselves in their communities." And the *National Civil Review* reported: "Gallup's interest in finding out what citizens thought was matched only by his dedication to finding ways for citizens—particularly young people—to make those thoughts come alive in action to improve their state and local governments. The National Municipal League was the beneficiary of his insights and unflagging vitality over four decades, in several official capacities and as long-time foreman of the All-Americans Cities Jury."

More than a century ago, Ralph Waldo Emerson wrote: "Every institution is but the lengthened shadow of a single man." Certainly this phrase applies to Dr. Gallup and the worldwide survey operation he started. He always had the talent of surrounding himself with bright and creative people and, indeed, such people were inevitably drawn to him; but essentially it was his own energy, creativity, and integrity that have been the driving forces behind Gallup survey research around the globe.

Perhaps the most fitting tribute to Dr. Gallup's long and illustrious career is found in the poll itself: on November 6 the vote for the presidential candidates exactly matched the final Gallup preelection survey results, making this forecast the most accurate one in the long history of the Gallup Poll.

*George Gallup, Jr.*
*Princeton, New Jersey*

# PREFACE

[This introductory essay by Dr. George Gallup is excerpted from a section entitled "How Polls Operate" from his book *The Sophisticated Poll Watcher's Guide.*]

## THE CROSS-SECTION

The most puzzling aspect of modern polls to the layman is the cross-section or sample. How, for example, is it possible to interview 1,000 or 2,000 persons out of a present electorate of about 150 million and be sure that the relatively few selected will reflect accurately the attitudes, interests, and behavior of the entire population of voting age?

Unless the poll watcher understands the nature of sampling and the steps that must be taken to assure its representativeness, the whole operation of scientific polling is likely to have little meaning, and even less significance, to him.

With the goal in mind of making the process understandable, and at the risk of being too elementary, I have decided to start with some simple facts about the nature of sampling—a procedure, I might add, that is as old as man himself.

When a housewife wants to test the quality of the soup she is making, she tastes only a teaspoonful or two. She knows that if the soup is thoroughly stirred, one teaspoonful is enough to tell her whether she has the right mixture of ingredients.

In somewhat the same manner, a bacteriologist tests the quality of water in a reservoir by taking a few samples, maybe not more than a few drops from a half-dozen different points. He knows that pollutants of a chemical or bacteriological nature will disperse widely and evenly throughout a body of water. He can be certain that his tiny sample will accurately reflect the presence of harmful bacteria or other pollutants in the whole body of water.

Perhaps a more dramatic example is to be found in the blood tests given routinely in clinics and hospitals. The medical technician requires only a few drops of blood to discover abnormal conditions. He does not have to draw a quart of blood to be sure that his sample is representative.

These examples, of course, deal with the physical world. People are not as much alike as drops of water, or of blood. If they were, then the world of individuals could be sampled by selecting only a half-dozen persons anywhere. People are widely different because their experiences are widely different.

Interestingly, this in itself comes about largely through a sampling process. Every human being gathers his views about people and about life by his own sampling. And, it should be added, he almost invariably ends with a distorted picture because his experience is unique. For example, he draws conclusions about "California" by looking out of his car or airplane window, by observing the people he meets at the airport or on the streets, and by his treatment in restaurants, hotels, and other places. This individual has no hesitancy in telling his friends back home what California is really like—although his views, obviously, are based upon very limited sampling.

The Black man, living his life in the ghetto, working under conditions that are often unpleasant and for wages that are likely to be less than those of the white man who lives in the suburban community, arrives at his own views about racial equality. His sample, likewise, is unrepresentative even though it may be typical of fellow Blacks living under the same conditions. By the same token, well-to-do whites living in the suburbs with the advantages of a college education and travel have equally distorted views of equality. These distortions come about because their sampling, likewise, is based upon atypical experiences.

Although every individual on the face of the earth is completely unique, in the mass he does conform to certain patterns of behavior. No one has expressed this better than A. Conan Doyle, author of the Sherlock Holmes series. He has one of his characters make this observation:

> While the individual man is an insoluble puzzle, in the aggregate he becomes a mathematical certainty. You can never foretell what any one man will do, but you can say with precision what an average number will be up to. Individuals vary, but averages remain constant.

Whenever the range of differences is great—either in nature or man—the sampling process must be conducted with great care to make certain that all major variations or departures from the norm are embraced.

Since some differences that exist may be unknown to the researcher, his best procedure to be sure of representativeness is to select samples from the population by a chance or random process. Only if he follows this procedure can he be reasonably certain that he has covered all major variations that exist.

This principle can be illustrated in the following manner. Suppose that a government agency, such as the Bureau of the Census, maintained an up-to-date alphabetical list of the names of all persons living in the United States eighteen years of age and older. Such a file, at the present time, would include approximately 148 million names.

Now suppose that a survey organization wished to draw a representative sample of this entire group, a sample, say of 10,000 persons. Such a representative sample could be selected by dividing 150,000,000 by 10,000—which produces a figure of 15,000. If the researcher goes systematically through the entire file and records the name of every 15,000th listed, he can be sure that his sample is representative.

The researcher will find that this chance selection, in the manner described, has produced almost the right percentage of Catholics and Protestants, the proper proportion of persons in each age and educational level. The distribution of persons by occupation, sex, race, and income should be broadly representative and consistent with the best available census data. It is important, however, to emphasize the words "broadly representative." The sample—even of 10,000—most likely would not include a single person belonging to the Fox Indian tribe or a single resident of Magnolia, Arkansas. It might not include a single citizen of Afghanistan heritage or a single Zoroastrian.

For the purposes served by polls, a sample normally needs to be only broadly representative. A study could be designed to discover the attitudes of American Indians, in which case the Fox Indians should be properly represented. And a specially designed study of Arkansas would likely embrace interviews with residents of Magnolia.

But for all practical purposes, individuals making up these groups constitute such a small part of the whole population of the United States that their inclusion, or exclusion, makes virtually no difference in reaching conclusions about the total population or even of important segments of the population.

Unfortunately, there is no master file in the United States of persons over the age of eighteen that is available to the researcher. Moreover, even a few weeks after the decennial census such a file would be out of date. Some citizens would have died, some would have moved, and still others would have reached the age of eighteen.

Unlike some European countries, no attempt is made in the United States to keep voter registration lists complete and up to date. Because of this failure to maintain accurate lists of citizens and of registered voters, survey organizations are forced to devise their own systems to select samples that are representative of the population to be surveyed.

Any number of sampling systems can be invented so long as one all-important goal is kept in mind. Whatever the system, the end result of its use must be to give every individual an equal opportunity of being selected. Actually, not every individual will have an equal chance, since some persons will be hospitalized, some in mental or penal institutions, and some in the armed forces in foreign lands. But while these individuals help make up the total United States citizenry, most are disenfranchised by the voting laws of the various states or find difficulty in implementing their opinions at election time. Typically, therefore, they are not included in survey cross-sections.

The Gallup Poll has designed its sample by choosing at random not individuals as described previously, but small districts such as census tracts, census enumeration districts, and townships. A random selection of these small geographical areas provides a good starting point for building a national sample.

The United States population is first arranged by states in geographical order and then within the individual states by districts, also in geographical order. A sampling interval number is determined by dividing the total population of the nation by the number of interviewing locations deemed adequate for a general purpose sample of the population eighteen years of age and older. In the case of the Gallup Poll sample, the number of locations, so selected, is approximately 300.

At the time of this writing, the population of the United States eighteen years and older is approximately 150,000,000. Dividing 150,000,000 by 300 yields a sampling interval of 500,000. A random starting number is then chosen between 1 and 500,000 in order to select the first location. The remaining 299 locations are determined by the simple process of adding 500,000 successively until all 300 locations are chosen throughout the nation.

A geographical sampling unit having been designated, the process of selection is continued by choosing at random a given number of individuals within each unit. Suppose that the sampling unit is a census tract in Scranton, Pennsylvania. Using block statistics, published by the Census Bureau for cities of this size, a block, or a group of blocks, within the tract is chosen by a random method analogous to the procedure used to select the location.

Within a block or groups of blocks so selected, the interviewer is given a random starting point. Proceeding from this point, the interviewer meets his assignment by taking every successive occupied dwelling. Or, as an alternative procedure, he can be instructed to take every third or every fifth or every tenth dwelling unit and to conduct interviews in these designated homes.

In this systematic selection plan, the choice of the dwelling is taken out of the hands of the interviewer. As a reminder to the reader, it should be pointed out that the area or district has been selected by a random procedure; next, the dwelling within the district has been chosen at random. All that now remains is to select, at random, the individual to be interviewed within the household.

This can be done in several ways. A list can be compiled by the interviewer of all persons of voting age residing within each home. From such a household list, he can then select individuals to be interviewed by a random method. Ingenious methods are employed to accomplish this end. One survey organization in Europe, for example, instructs the interviewer to talk to the person in the household whose birthday falls on the nearest date.

Now the process is complete. The district has been selected at random; the dwelling unit within the district has been selected at random; and the individual within the dwelling unit has been selected at random. The end result is that every individual in the nation of voting age has had an equal chance of being selected.

This is the theory. In actual practice, problems arise, particularly in respect to the last stage of the process. The dwelling unit chosen may be vacant, the individual selected within a household may not be at home when the interviewer calls. Of course, the interviewer can return the next day; in fact, he or she can make a half-dozen call backs without finding the person. Each call back adds that much to the cost of the survey and adds, likewise, to the time required to complete the study.

Even with a dozen call backs, some individuals are never found and are never interviewed. They may be in the hospital, visiting relatives, on vacation, on a business trip, not at home except at very late hours, too old or too ill to be interviewed—and a few may even refuse to be interviewed.

Since no nationwide survey has ever reached every person designated by any random selection procedure, special measures must be employed to deal with this situation. In the early 1950s, the Gallup Poll introduced a system called Time-Place interviewing. After an intensive study of the time of day when different members of a household are at home, an interviewing plan was devised that enabled interviewers to reach the highest proportion of persons at the time of their first call.

Since most persons are employed outside the home, interviewing normally must be done in the late afternoon and evening hours, and on weekends. These are the times when men, and especially younger men, are likely to be at home and therefore available to be interviewed.

In various nations, survey organizations are working out new ways to meet this problem of the individual selected for the sample who is not at home. These new procedures may meet more perfectly the ideal requirements of random sampling.

Many ardent advocates of the procedure described as "quota sampling" are still to be found. This, it should be pointed out, was the system generally employed by the leading survey organizations in the pre-1948 era.

The quota system is simplicity itself. If the state of New York has 10% of the total population of the United States, then 10% of all interviews must come from this state. In the case of a national sample of 10,000, this would mean 1,000 interviews.

Going one step further, since New York City contains roughly 40% of the population of the state, then 40% of the 1,000 interviews must be allocated to New York City, or 400. And since Brooklyn has roughly a third of the total population of New York City, a third of the 400 interviews, or 133, must be made in this borough. In similar fashion, all of the 1,000 interviews made in the state of New York can be distributed among the various cities, towns, and rural areas. Other states are dealt with in similar fashion.

Making still further use of census data, the interviews to be made in each city, town, or rural areas can be assigned on an occupational basis: so many white-collar workers, so many blue-collar workers, so many farmers, so many business and professional people, so many retired persons, and so many on the welfare rolls. The allocation can also be made on the basis of rents paid. The interviewer, for example, may be given a "quota" of calls to be made in residential areas with the highest rental values, in areas with medium priced rentals, and in low rental areas.

Typically, in the quota sampling system, the survey organization predetermines the number of men and women and the age, the income, the occupation, and the race of the individuals assigned to each interviewer.

In setting such quotas, however, important factors may be overlooked. In 1960, for example, a quota sample that failed to assign the right proportion of Catholic voters would have miscalculated John Kennedy's political strength. An individual's religious beliefs, obviously, cannot be ascertained by his appearance or by the place where he dwells; this applies to other factors as well.

Not only do theoretical considerations fault the quota system but so do the problems that face the interviewer. When the selection of individuals is left to him, he tends to seek out the easiest-to-interview respondents. He is prone to avoid the worst slum areas, and consequently he turns up with interviews that are likely to be skewed on the high income and educational side. Typically, a quick look at the results of quota sampling will reveal too many persons with a college education, too many persons with average and above average incomes, and in political polls, too many Republicans. Therefore, one of the many advantages of the random procedure is that the selection of respondents is taken out of the hands of the interviewer. In the random method, the interviewer is told exactly where to go and when to go.

Another consideration with cross-sections is keeping them up to date. Although America's population is highly mobile, fortunately for polltakers the basic structure of society changes little. Perhaps the greatest change in America in recent years has been the rising level of education. In 1935, when the Gallup Poll first published poll results, only 7.2% of the adult population had attended college for one year or more. Today that figure is 27%.

How does a research organization know that the sample it has designed meets proper standards? Normally, examination of the socioeconomic data gathered by the interviewer at the end of each interview provides the answer. As the completed interview forms are returned from the field to the Princeton office of the Gallup Poll, the facts from each are punched into IBM cards. In addition to the questions that have dealt with issues and other matters of interest, the interviewer has asked each person to state his occupation, age, how far he went in school, his religious preference, whether he owns or rents his dwelling, and many other questions of a factual nature.

Since the Census Bureau Current Population Surveys provide data on each one of these factors, even a hasty examination will tell whether the cross-section is fairly accurate—that is, whether the important factors line up properly with the known facts, specifically:
—the educational level of those interviewed
—the age level
—the income level
—the proportion of males to females
—the distribution by occupations

—the proportion of whites to nonwhites
—the geographical distribution of cases
—the city-size distribution.

Typically, when the educational level is correct (that is, when the sample has included the right proportion of those who have attended college, high school, grade school, or no school), when the geographical distribution is right and all areas of the nation have been covered in the correct proportion, when the right proportion of those in each income level has been reached, and the right percentages of whites and nonwhites and of men and women are included—then usually other factors tend to fall in line. These include such factors as religious preference, political party preference, and most other factors that bear upon voting behavior, buying behavior, tastes, interests, and the like.

After checking all of the above "controls," it would be unusual to find that every group making up the total population is represented in the sample in the exact percentage that it should be. Some groups may be slightly larger or smaller than they should be. The nonwhite population eighteen years and older, which makes up 11% of the total population, may be found to be less, or more, than this percentage of the returned interviews. Those who have attended high school in the obtained interviews may number 58%, when actually the true figure should be 54%.

Ways have been developed to correct situations such as these that arise out of the over-representation or under-representation of given groups. The sample can be balanced, that is, corrected so that each group is included in the proportion it represents in the total population. When this procedure is followed, the assumption is made that persons within each group who are interviewed are representative of the group in question. But there are obvious limitations to this. If only a few persons are found in a given category, then the danger is always present that they may not be typical or representative of the people who make up this particular group or cell.

On the whole, experience has shown that this process of weighting by the computer actually does produce more accurate samples. Normally, results are changed by only negligible amounts—seldom by more than 1 or 2 percentage points.

A persistent misconception about polling procedures is that a new sample must be designed for measuring each major issue. Actually, Gallup Poll cross-sections are always based upon samples of the entire voting age population. Every citizen has a right to voice his opinion on every issue and to have it recorded. For this reason, all surveys of public opinion seek to reach a representative cross-section of the entire population of voting age.

Some people ask if we go back to the same persons with different polls. The answer, in the case of the Gallup Poll, is "no"; the same person is not interviewed again. Some survey research is based upon fixed cross-sections or "panels." The same persons are reinterviewed from time to time to measure shifts in opinion.

There are certain advantages to this system—it is possible to determine to what extent overall changes cloak individual changes. But a practical disadvantage is that the size of the sample remains fixed. Unless the panel is very large, reliable information cannot be produced for smaller subgroups. In the case of the Gallup Poll, the same question can be placed on any number of surveys and the total sample expanded accordingly, since the same persons are not reinterviewed.

Panels have other limitations. One has to do with determining the level of knowledge. Having asked a citizen what he knows about a certain issue in the first interview, he may very well take the trouble to read about it when he sees an article later in his newspaper or magazine. There is, moreover, a widespread feeling among researchers that the repeated interviewing of the same person tends to make him a "pro" and to render him atypical for this reason. But the evidence is not clear-cut on this point. The greatest weakness, perhaps, is that panels tend to fall apart; persons change their place of residence and cannot be found for a second or subsequent measurement; some refuse to participate more than once and must be replaced by substitutes.

## THE SIZE OF SAMPLES

When the subject of public-opinion polls comes up, many people are quick to say that they do not know of anyone who has ever been polled.

The likelihood of any single individual, eighteen years of age or older, being polled in a sample of 1,500 persons is about one chance in 90,000. With samples of this size, and with the frequency that surveys are scheduled by the Gallup Poll, the chance that any single individual will be interviewed—even during a period of two decades—is less than one in 200.

An early experience of mine illustrates dramatically the relative unimportance of numbers in achieving accuracy in polls and the vital importance of reaching a true cross-section of the population sampled.

In the decade preceding the 1936 presidential election, the *Literary Digest* conducted straw polls during elections, with a fair measure of success. The *Literary Digest*'s polling procedure consisted of mailing out millions of postcard ballots to persons whose names were found in telephone directories or on lists of automobile owners.

The system worked so long as voters in average and above-average income groups were as likely to vote Democratic as Republican; and conversely, those in the lower income brackets—the have-nots—were as likely to vote for either party's candidate for the presidency.

With the advent of the New Deal, however, the American electorate became sharply stratified, with many persons in the above average income groups who had been Democrats shifting to the Republican banner, and those below average to the Democratic.

Obviously, a polling system that reached telephone subscribers and automobile owners—the perquisites of the better-off in this era—was certain to overestimate Republican strength in the 1936 election. And that is precisely what did happen. The *Literary Digest*'s final preelection poll showed Landon winning by 57% and Franklin D. Roosevelt losing with 43% of the two-party popular vote.

Landon did not win, as everyone knows. In fact, Roosevelt won by a whopping majority—62.5% to Landon's 37.5%. The error, more than 19 percentage points, was one of the greatest in polling history.

The outcome of the election spelled disaster for the *Literary Digest*'s method of polling, and was a boon to the new type of scientific sampling that was introduced for the first time in that presidential election by my organization, Elmo Roper's, and Archibald Crossley's.

The *Literary Digest* had mailed out 10,000,000 postcard ballots—enough to reach approximately one family in every three at that point in history. A total of 2,376,523 persons took the trouble to mark their postcard ballots and return them.

Experiments with new sampling techniques had been undertaken by my organization as early as 1933. By 1935 the evidence was clear-cut that an important change had come about in the party orientation of voters—that the process of polarization had shifted higher income voters to the right, lower income voters to the left.

When the presidential campaign opened in 1936, it was apparent that the *Literary Digest*'s polling method would produce an inaccurate figure. Tests indicated that a large majority of individuals who were telephone subscribers preferred Landon to FDR, while only 18% of those persons on relief rolls favored Landon.

To warn the public of the likely failure of the *Literary Digest,* I prepared a special newspaper article that was widely printed on July 12, 1936—at the beginning of the campaign. The article stated that the *Literary Digest* would be wrong in its predictions and that it would probably show Landon winning with 56% of the popular vote to 44% for Roosevelt. The reasons why the poll would go wrong were spelled out in detail.

Outraged, the *Literary Digest* editor wrote: "Never before has anyone foretold what our poll was going to show even before it started . . . Our fine statistical friend (George Gallup) should be advised that the Digest would carry on with those old fashioned methods that have produced correct forecasts exactly one hundred percent of the time."

When the election had taken place, our early assessment of what the *Literary Digest* poll would find proved to be almost a perfect prediction of the *Digest*'s final results—actually within 1 percentage point. While this may seem to have been a foolhardy stunt, actually there was little risk. A sample of only 3,000 postcard ballots had been mailed by my office to the same lists of persons who received the

*Literary Digest* ballot. Because of the workings of the laws of probability, that 3,000 sample should have provided virtually the same result as the *Literary Digest*'s 2,376,523 which, in fact, it did.

Through its own polling, based upon modern sampling procedures, the Gallup Poll, in the 1936 election, reported that the only sure states for Landon were Maine, Vermont, and New Hampshire. The final results showed Roosevelt with 56% of the popular vote to 44% for Landon. The error was 6.8 percentage points, the largest ever made by the Gallup Poll. But because it was on the "right" side, the public gave us full credit, actually more than we deserved.

The *Literary Digest* is not the only poll that has found itself to be on the "wrong" side. All polls, at one time or another, find themselves in this awkward position, including the Gallup Poll in the election of 1948. Ironically, the error in 1936—a deviation of 6.8 percentage points from the true figure—was greater than the error in 1948—5.4 percentage points. But the public's reaction was vastly different.

The failure of polls to have the winning candidate ahead in final results is seldom due to the failure of the poll to include enough persons in its sample. Other factors are likely to prove to be far more important, as will be pointed out later.

Examination of probability tables quickly reveals why polling organizations can use relatively small samples. But first the reader should be reminded that sampling human beings can never produce findings that are *absolutely* accurate except by mere chance, or luck. The aim of the researcher is to come as close as possible to absolute accuracy.

Since money and time are always important considerations in survey operations, the goal is to arrive at sample sizes that will produce results within acceptable margins of error. Fortunately, reasonably accurate findings can be obtained with surprisingly small samples.

Again, it is essential to distinguish between theory and practice. Probability tables are based upon mathematical theory. In actual survey work, these tables provide an important guide, but they can't be applied too literally.

With this qualification in mind, the size of samples to be used in national surveys can now be described. Suppose, for example, that a sample comprises only 600 individuals. What is the theoretical margin of error? If the sample is a perfectly drawn random sample, then the chances are 95 in 100 that the results of a poll of 600 in which those interviewed divide 60% in favor, 40% opposed (or the reverse) will be within 4 percentage points of the true figure; that is, the division in the population is somewhere between 56% and 64% in favor. The odds are even that the error will be less than 2 percentage points—between 58% and 62% in favor, 42% to 38% opposed.

What this means, in the example cited above, is that the odds are 19 to 1 that in repeated samplings the figure for the issue would vary in the case of those favoring the issue from 56% to 64%; the percentage of those opposed would vary between 44% and 36% in repeated samples. So, on the basis of a national sample of only 600 cases, one could say that the odds are great that the addition of many cases—

even millions of cases—would not likely change the majority side to the minority side.

Now, if this sample is doubled in size—from 600 to 1,200—the error factor using the 95 in 100 criterion or confidence level is decreased from 4 percentage points to 2.8 percentage points; if it is doubled again—from 1,200 to 2,400—there is a further decrease—from 2.8 to 2.0, always assuming a mathematically random sample.

Even if a poll were to embrace a total of 2,000,000 individuals, there would still be a chance of error, although tiny. Most survey organizations try to operate within an error range of 4 percentage points at the 95 in 100 confidence level. Accuracy greater than this is not demanded on most issues, nor in most elections, except, of course, those that are extremely close.

Obviously, in many fields an error factor as large as 4 percentage points would be completely unacceptable. In fact, in measuring the rate of unemployment, the government and the press place significance on a change as small as 0.1%. At present, unemployment figures are based upon nationwide samples carried out by the U.S. Bureau of Labor Statistics in the same general manner as polls are conducted. The government bases its findings on samples of some 50,000 persons. But samples even of this size are not sufficient to warrant placing confidence in a change as small as 0.1%. And yet such a change is often headlined on the front pages as indicating a real and significant change in the employment status of the nation.

Even if one were totally unfamiliar with the laws of probability, empirical evidence would suffice to demonstrate that the amassing of thousands of cases does not change results except to a minor extent.

An experiment conducted early in the Gallup Poll's history will illustrate this point. At the time—in the middle 1930s—the National Recovery Act (N.R.A.) was a hotly debated issue. Survey results were tabulated as the ballots from all areas of the United States were returned. The figures below are those actually obtained as each lot of new ballots was tabulated.

| NUMBER OF RETURNED BALLOTS | PERCENT VOTING IN FAVOR OF THE N.R.A. |
|---|---|
| First 500 | 54.9% |
| First 1,000 | 53.9 |
| First 5,000 | 55.4 |
| First 10,000 | 55.4 |
| First 30,000 | 55.5 |

From these results it can be seen that if only 500 ballots had been received, the figure would have differed little from the final result. In fact the greatest difference found in the whole series is only 1.6 percentage points from the final result.

This example represents a typical experience of researchers in this field. But one precaution needs to be observed. The returns must come from a representative sample of the population being surveyed; otherwise they could be as misleading as trying to project the results of a national election from the vote registered late in the afternoon of election day in a New Hampshire village.

The theoretical error, as noted earlier, can be used only as a guide. The expected errors in most surveys are usually somewhat larger. In actual survey practice, some sample design elements tend to reduce the range of error, as stratification does; some tend to increase the range of error as, for example, clustering. But these are technical matters to be dealt with in textbooks on statistics.

Survey organizations should, on the basis of their intimate knowledge of their sampling procedures and the analysis of their data, draw up their own tables of suggested tolerances to enable laymen to interpret their survey findings intelligently.

The normal sampling unit of the Gallup Poll consists of 1,500 individuals of voting age, that is, eighteen years and over. A sample of this size gives reasonable assurance that the margin of error for results representing the entire country will be less than 3 percentage points based on the factor of size alone.

The margin for sampling error is obviously greater for subgroups. For example, the views of individuals who have attended college are frequently reported. Since about one-fourth of all persons over eighteen years have attended college, the margin of error must be computed on the basis of one-fourth the total sample of 1,500, or 375. Instead of a margin of error of 3 percentage points, the error factor increases to 6 or 7 percentage points in the typical cluster sample.

In dealing with some issues, interest focuses on the views of subgroups such as Blacks, labor union members, Catholics, or young voters—all representing rather small segments of the total population. Significant findings for these subgroups are possible only by building up the size of the total sample.

This can be done in the case of the Gallup Poll by including the same question or questions in successive surveys. Since different, but comparable, persons are interviewed in each study, subgroup samples can be enlarged accordingly. Thus, in a single survey approximately 165 Blacks and other nonwhites would be interviewed in a sample of 1,500, since they constitute 11% of the total voting-age population. On three successive surveys a total of 495 would be reached—enough to provide a reasonably stable base to indicate their views on important political and social issues.

Since much interest before and after elections is directed toward the way different groups in the population vote, it has been the practice of the Gallup Poll to increase the size of its samples during the final month before election day to be in a position to report the political preferences of the many groups that make up the total population—information that cannot be obtained by analyzing the actual election returns. Election results, for example, do not reveal how women voted as opposed to men, how the different age groups voted, how different religious groups voted, how different income levels voted. Many other facts about the public's voting habits can be obtained only through the survey method.

During the heat of election campaigns, critics have asserted on occasion that the Gallup Poll increases its sample size solely to make more certain of being "right." Examination of trend figures effectively answers this criticism. The results reported on the basis of the standard sampling unit have not varied, on the average, more than 1 or 2 percentage points from the first enlarged sample in all of the national elections of the last two decades, and this, of course, is within the margin of error expected.

Persons unfamiliar with the laws of probability invariably assume that the size of the sample must bear a fixed relationship to the size of the "universe" sampled. For example, such individuals are likely to assume that if a polling organization is sampling opinions of the whole United States, a far larger sample is necessary than if the same kind of survey is to be conducted in a single state, or in a single city. Or, to put this in another way, the assumption is that since the population of the United States is roughly ten times that of New York State, then the sample of the United States should be ten times as large.

The laws of probability, however, do not work in this fashion. Whenever the population to be surveyed is many times the size of the sample (which it typically is), the size of samples must be almost the same. If one were conducting a poll in Baton Rouge, Louisiana, on a mayoralty race, the size of the sample should be virtually the same as for the whole United States. The same principle applies to a state.

Two examples, drawn from everyday life, may help to explain this rather mystifying fact. Suppose that a hotel cook has two kinds of soup on the stove—one in a very large pot, another in a small pot. After thoroughly stirring the soup in both pots, the cook need not take a greater number of spoonsful from the large pot or fewer spoonsful from the small pot to taste the quality of the soup, since the quality should be the same.

The second example, taken from the statistician's world, may shed further light on this phenomenon. Assume that 100,000 black and white balls are placed in a large cask. The white balls number 70,000; the black balls, 30,000. Into another cask, a much smaller one, are placed 1,000 balls, divided in exactly the same proportion: 700 white balls, 300 black balls.

Now the balls in each cask are thoroughly mixed and a person, blindfolded, is asked to draw out of each cask exactly 100 balls. The likelihood of drawing 70 white balls and 30 black balls is virtually the same, despite the fact that one cask contains 100 times as many balls as the other.

If this principle were understood then hours of Senate floor time could have been saved in recent years. Senator Albert Gore, of Tennessee, a few years ago, had this to say about the Gallup Poll's sampling unit of 1,500—as reported in the *Congressional Record*:

As a layman I would question that a straw poll of less than 1 per cent of the people could under any reasonable circumstance be regarded as a fair and meaningful cross-section. This would be something more than 500 times as large a sample as Dr. Gallup takes.

In the same discussion on the Senate floor, Senator Russell Long of Lousiana added these remarks:

I believe one reason why the poll information could not be an accurate reflection of what the people are thinking is depicted in this example. Suppose we should try to find how many persons should be polled in a city the size of New Orleans in order to determine how an election should go. In a city that size, about 600,000 people, a number of 1,000 would be an appropriate number to sample to see how the election was likely to go. . . . In my home town of Baton Rouge, Lousiana, I might very well sample perhaps 300 or 400 people and come up with a fairly accurate guess as to how the city or the parish would go, especially if a scientific principle were used. But if I were to sample only a single person or two or three in that entire city, the chances are slim that I would come up with an accurate guess.

If the reader has followed the explanation of the workings of the laws of probability, and of earlier statements about the size of samples, he will be aware of two errors in the senator's reasoning. Since both cities, New Orleans and Baton Rouge, have populations many times the size of the sample he suggested, both require samples of the same size. The second is his assumption that any good researcher would possibly attempt to draw conclusions about either city on the basis of "a single person or two."

The size of the "universe" to be sampled is typically very great in the case of most surveys; in fact, it is usually many times the size of the samples to be obtained. A different principle applies when the "universe" is small. The size of a sample needed to assess opinions of the residents of a community of 1,000 voters is obviously different from that required for a city that is much larger. A sample of 1,000 in such a town would not be a sample; it would be a complete canvass.

## DEVELOPING POLL QUESTIONS

Nothing is so difficult, nor so important, as the selection and wording of poll questions. In fact, most of my time and effort in the field of polling has been devoted to this problem.

The questions included in a national survey of public opinion should meet many tests: they must deal with the vital issues of the day, they must be worded in a way to get at the heart of these issues, they must be stated in language understandable to the least well educated, and finally, they must be strictly impartial in presenting the issue.

If any reader thinks this is easy, let him try to word questions on any present-day issue. It is a tough and trying mental task. And even years of experience do not make the problem less onerous.

One rule must always be followed. No question, no matter how simple, must reach the interviewing stage without first having gone through a thorough pretesting procedure. Many tests must be applied to see that each question meets required standards.

Every survey organization has its own methods of testing the wording of questions. Here it will suffice to describe in some detail how the Gallup Poll goes about this task.

Pretesting of questions dealing with complicated issues is carried on in the Interviewing Center maintained in Hopewell, New Jersey, by the Gallup organizations. Formerly, this center was a motion-picture theater. In the early 1950s it was converted into an interviewing center. The town of Hopewell is located in the middle of an area with a total population of 500,000—an area that includes the cities of Trenton and Princeton, suburban communities, small towns, and rural districts. Consequently, people from many walks of life are available for interviewing.

Pretesting procedures normally start with "in-depth" interviews with a dozen or more individuals invited to come to the center. The purpose of these interviews is to find out how much thought each participant has given to the issue under consideration, the level of his or her knowledge about the issue, and the important facets that must be probed. Most of the questions asked in these sessions are "open" questions—that is, questions which ask: "What do you know about the XX problem? What do you think about it? What should the government do about it?" and so forth.

In conversations evoked by questions of this type, it is possible, in an unhurried manner, to discover how much knowledge average persons have of a given issue, the range of views regarding it, and the special aspects of the issue that need to be probed if a series of questions is to be developed.

The next step is to try out the questions, devised at this first stage, on a new group of respondents, to see if the questions are understandable and convey the meaning intended. A simple test for this can be employed. After reading the question, the respondent is asked to "play back" what it says to him. The answer quickly reveals whether the person being interviewed understands the language used and whether he grasps the main point of the question. This approach can also reveal, to the trained interviewer, any unsuspected biases in the wording of the question. When the language in which a question is stated is not clear to the interviewee, his typical reaction is: "Will you read that question again?" If questions have to be repeated, this is unmistakable evidence that they should be worded in a simpler and more understandable manner.

Another procedure that has proved valuable in testing questions is the self-administered interview. The respondent, without the benefit of an interviewer, writes out the answers to the questions. The advantages of this procedure are many. Answers show whether the individual has given real thought to the issue and reveal, also, the degree of his interest. If he has no opinion, he will typically leave the question blank. If he has a keen interest in the issue, he will spell out his views in some detail. And if he is misinformed, this becomes apparent in what he writes.

Self-administered questionnaires can be filled out in one's own home, or privately in an interviewing center. Since the interviewer is not at hand, many issues, such as those dealing with sex, drug addiction, alcoholism, and other personal matters, can be covered in this manner. The interviewer's function is merely to drop off the questionnaire, and pick it up in a sealed envelope the next day—or the respondent can mail it directly to the Princeton office.

Even with all of these precautions, faulty question wordings do sometimes find their way onto the survey interviewing form. Checks for internal consistency, made when the ballots are returned and are tabulated, usually bring to light these shortcomings.

Most important, the reader himself must be the final judge. The Gallup Poll, from its establishment in 1935, has followed the practice of including the exact wording of questions, when this is important, in the report of the poll findings. The reader is thus in a position to decide whether the question is worded impartially and whether the interpretation of the results, based upon the question asked, is fair and objective.

A United States senator has brought up another point about questions:

How do pollsters like yourself determine what questions to ask from time to time? It seems to me that pollsters can affect public opinion simply by asking the question. The results could be pro or anti the president depending upon the questions asked and the president's relation to it.

To be sure, a series of questions could be asked that would prove awkward to the administration, even though worded impartially, and interpreted objectively. But this would be self-defeating because it would soon become apparent to readers and commentators that the survey organization was not engaged solely in fact-finding but was trying to promote a cause.

One way to prevent unintentional biases from creeping into survey operations is to have a staff that is composed of persons representing the different shades of political belief—from right to left. If not only the questions but also the written reports dealing with the results have to run this gamut—as is the practice in the Gallup office—the dangers of unintentional bias are decreased accordingly.

Still one more safeguard in dealing with biases of any type comes about through the financial support of a poll. If sponsors represent all shades of political belief, then economic pressures alone help to keep a poll on the straight and narrow path.

So much for bias in the wording and selection of questions. This still does not answer the question posed by some who wish to know what standards or practices are followed in deciding what issues to present to the public.

Since the chief aim of a modern public opinion poll is to assess public opinion on the important issues of the day and to chart the trend of sentiment, it follows that most subjects chosen for investigation must deal with current national and international issues, and particularly those that have an immediate concern for the typical citizen. Newspapers, magazine, and the broadcast media are all useful sources of ideas for polls. Suggestions for poll subjects come from individuals and institutions—from members of Congress, editors, public officials, and foundations. Every few weeks the public itself is questioned about the most important problems facing the nation, as they see them. Their answers to this question establish priorities, and provide an up-to-date list of areas to explore through polling.

A widely held assumption is that questions can be twisted to get any answer you want. In the words of one publisher: "If you word a question one way you get a result which may differ substantially from the result you get if you word the question in a different way."

It's not that easy. Questions can be worded in a manner to bring confusing and misleading results. But the loaded question is usually self-defeating because it is obvious that it is biased.

Hundreds of experiments with a research procedure known as the split-ballot technique (one-half the cross-section gets Question A, the other half Question B) have proved that even a wide variation in question wordings did not bring substantially different results if the basic meaning or substance of the question remained the same.

Change the basic meaning of the question, add or leave out an essential part, and the results will change accordingly, as they should. Were people insensitive to words—if they were unable to distinguish between one concept and another—then the whole *raison d'être* of polling would vanish.

Often the interpreters of poll findings draw inferences that are not warranted or make assumptions that a close reading of the question does not support. Consider, for example, these two questions:

"Do you feel the United States should have gotten involved in Vietnam in the first place?"

"Do you feel the United States should have helped South Vietnam to defend itself?"

While at first glance these questions seem to deal with the same point—America's involvement—actually they are probing widely different aspects of involvement. In the first case, the respondent can read in that we helped Vietnam "with our own troops"; in the second question, that our help would have been limited to materials. Many polls have shown that the American people are willing to give military supplies to almost any nation in the world that is endangered by the communists, but they are unwilling to send troops.

If the two questions cited above did not bring substantially different results, then all the other poll results dealing with this issue would be misleading.

Questions must be stated in words that everyone understands, and results are likely to be misleading to the extent that the words are not fully understood. Ask people whether they are disturbed about the amount of pornography in their magazines and newspapers and you will get one answer; if you talk about the amount of smut you will get another.

Word specialists may insist that every word in the language conveys a slightly different connotation to every individual. While this may be true, the world (and polls) must operate on the principle that commonly used words convey approximately the same meaning to the vast majority. And this fact can easily be established in the pretesting of questions. When a question is read to a respondent and he is then asked to "play it back" in his own words, it becomes quickly evident whether he has understood the words, and in fact, what they mean to him.

Some questions that pass this test can still be faulty. The sophisticated poll watcher should be on the alert for the "desirable goal" question. This type of question ties together a desirable goal with a proposal for reaching this end. The respondent typically reacts to the goal as well as to the means. Here are some examples of desirable goal questions:

"To win the war quickly in Vietnam, would you favor all-out bombing of North Vietnam?"

"To reduce crime in the cities, would you favor increasing jail and prison sentences?"

"In order to improve the quality of education in the United States, should teachers be paid higher salaries?"

These questions, which present widely accepted goals accompanied by the tacit assumption that the means suggested will bring about the desired end, produce results biased on the favorable side.

The more specific questions are, the better. One of the classic arguments between newspapers and television has centered around a question that asks the public: "Where do you get most of your news about what's going on in the world today—from the newspaper, or radio, or television, or magazines, or talking to people, or where?" The answers show TV ahead of daily newspapers. But when this question is asked in a way to differentiate between international news, and local and state news, TV wins on international news, but the daily newspaper has a big lead on local news. A simple explanation is that the phrase, "What is going on in the *world?*" is interpreted by the average citizen to mean in the faraway places—not his home city.

People are extremely literal minded. A farmer in Ontario, interviewed by the Canadian Gallup Poll, was asked at the close of the interview how long he had lived in the same house; specifically, the length of his residence there. The answer that came back was "Twenty-six feet and six inches."

Whenever it is possible, the questions asked should state both sides of the issue. Realistic alternatives should be offered, or implied.

Looking back through more than four decades of polling, this aspect of question wording warrants the greatest criticism. There is probably little need to state the other side, or offer an alternative, in a question such as this: "Should the voting age be lowered to include those eighteen years of age?" The alternative implied is to leave the situation as it is.

An excellent observation has been made by a political scientist on the faculty of a New England college:

> Somehow more realism must be introduced into polls. . . . People often affirm abstract principles but will not be willing to pay the price of their concrete application. For example, would you be willing to pay more for each box of soap you buy in order to reduce ground pollution—or $200 more for your next car in order to reduce air pollution, etc.?

This type of question is similar to the desirable goal question. The public wants to clear the slums, wants better medical care, improved racial relations, better schools, better housing. The real issue is one of priorities and costs. The role of the public opinion poll in this situation is to shed light on the public's concern about each major problem, establish priorities, and then discover whether the people are willing to foot the bill.

The well-informed person is likely to think of the costs involved by legislation that proposes to deal with these social problems. But to the typical citizen there is no immediate or direct relationship between legislation and the amount he has to pay in taxes. Congress usually tries to disguise costs by failing to tie taxes or costs to large appropriations, leaving John Doe with the impression that someone else will pay the bill.

Still another type of question that is suspect has to do with good intentions. Questions of this type have meaning only when controls are used and when the results are interpreted with a full understanding of their shortcomings.

Examples of questions that fall into this category are those asking people if they "plan to go to church," "read a book," "listen to good music," "vote in the coming election," and so forth.

To the typical American the word "intend" or "plan" connotes many things, such as "Do I think this is a good idea?" "Would I like to do it?" "Would it be good for me?" "Would it be good for other people?" These and similar questions of a prestige nature reveal attitudes, but they are a poor guide to action.

Behavior is always the best guide. The person who attended church last Sunday is likely to go next Sunday, if he says he plans to. The citizen who voted in the last election and whose name is now on the registration books is far more likely to vote than the person who hasn't bothered to vote or to register, even though he insists that he "plans" to do both.

Probably the most difficult of all questions to word is the type that offers the respondent several alternatives. Not only is it hard to find alternatives that are mutually exclusive; it is equally difficult to find a series that covers the entire range of opinions. Added to this is the problem of wording each alternative in a way that doesn't give it a special advantage. And finally, in any series of alternatives that ranges from one extreme of opinion to the other, the typical citizen has a strong inclination to choose one in the middle.

As a working principle it can be stated that the more words included in a question, either by way of explanation or in stating alternatives, the greater the possibilities that the question wording itself will influence answers.

A member of the editorial staff of a newsmagazine voiced a common reaction when he observed:

> On more than a few occasions I have found that I could not, were I asked, answer a poll with a "yes" or "no." More likely my answer would be "yes, but" or "yes, if." I wonder whether pollsters can't or just don't want to measure nuances of feeling.

Obviously it is the desire of a polling organization to produce a full and accurate account of the public's views on any given issue, nuances and all.

First, however, it should be pointed out that there are two main categories of questions serving two different purposes—one to *measure* public opinion, the other to *describe* public opinion. The first category has to do with the "referendum" type of question. Since the early years of polling, heavy emphasis has been placed upon this type of question, which serves in effect as an unofficial national referendum on a given issue, actually providing the same results, within a small margin of error, that an official nationwide referendum would if it were held at the same time and on the same issue.

At some point in the decision process, whether it be concerned with an important issue before Congress, a new law before the state legislature, or a school bond issue in Central City, the time comes for a simple "yes" or "no" vote. Fortunately, or unfortunately, there is no lever on a voting machine that permits the voter to register a "yes, if" or a "yes, but" vote. While discussion can and should proceed at length, the only way to determine majority opinion is by a simple count of noses.

If polling organizations limited themselves to the referendum type of question they would severely restrict their usefulness. They can and should use their machinery to reveal the many facets of public opinion of any issue, and to shed light on the reasons why the people hold the views they do; in short, to explore the "why" behind public opinion.

More and more attention is being paid to this diagnostic approach and the greatest improvements in the field of public opinion research in the future are likely to deal with this aspect of polling.

One of the important developments in question technique was the development in the late 1940s of a new kind of question design that permits the investigation of views on any issue of a complex nature.

This design, developed by the Gallup Poll, has been described as the "quintamensional approach" since it probes five aspects of opinion:

xxx

1. the respondent's awareness and general knowledge about it,
2. his overall opinions,
3. the reasons why he holds his views,
4. his specific views on specific aspects of the problem,
5. the intensity with which he hold his opinions.

This question design quickly sorts out those who have no knowledge of a given issue—an important function in successful public opinion polling. And it can even reveal the extent or level of knowledge of the interviewee about the issue.

This is how the system works. The first question put to the person being interviewed (on any problem or issue no matter how complex) is this: "Have you heard or read about the XXX problem (proposal or issue)?"

The person being interviewed can answer either "yes" or "no" to this question, or he can add, "I'm not sure." If he answers in the negative, experience covering many years indicates that he is being entirely truthful. If he answers "yes" or "I'm not sure" he is then asked: "Please tell me in your own words what the debate (or the proposal or issue) is about." At this point the person interviewed must produce evidence that reveals whether he has some knowledge of the problem or issue.

The reader might imagine himself in this interviewing situation. You are called upon by an interviewer and in the course of the interview are asked if you have "heard or read about the Bronson proposal to reorganize the Security Council of the United Nations." The answer is likely to be "no." Possibly you might say: "I seem to have heard about it somewhere." Or suppose that, just to impress the interviewer (something that rarely happens) you fall into the trap of saying "yes."

The next question puts you neatly and delicately on the spot. It asks you to describe in your own words what the Bronson proposal is. You have to admit at this point that you do not know, or come up with an answer that immediately indicates you do not know what it is.

At this stage the questioning can be expanded to discover just how well informed you are. If it is an issue or proposal, then you can be asked to give the main arguments for and the main arguments against the plan or issue. In short, by adding questions at this stage, the *level* of knowledge of the respondent can be determined.

The next question in the design is an "open" question that asks simply: "What do you think should be done about this proposal?" or "How do you think this issue should be resolved?" This type of question permits the person being interviewed to give his views without any specifics being mentioned. Answers, of course, are recorded by the interviewer as nearly as possible in the exact words of the respondent.

The third category of questions seeks to find out the "why" behind the respondent's views. This can be done with a simple question asking: "Why do you feel that way?" or variations of this, along with "nondirective" probes such as "What else?" or "Can you explain that in greater detail?"

The fourth category in the design poses specific issues that can be answered in "yes" or "no" fashion. At this fourth stage it is possible to go back to those who were excluded by the first two questions: those who said they had not heard or read about the issue in question or proved, after the second question, that they were uninformed.

By explaining in neutral language to this group what the problem or issue is and the specific proposals that have been made for dealing with it, the uninformed can voice their opinions, which later can be compared with those of the already informed group.

The fifth category attempts to get at the intensity with which opinions are held. How strongly does each side hold to its views? What action is each individual willing to take to see that his opinion prevails? What chance is there that he may change his mind?

This, then, is the quintamensional approach. And its special merit is that it can quickly sort out the informed from the uninformed. The views of the well informed can be compared not only with the less well informed but with those who are learning about the issue for the first time. Moreover, through cross-tabulations, it is possible to show how special kinds of knowledge are related to certain opinions.

The filtering process may screen out nearly all individuals in the sample because they are uninformed, but it is often of interest and importance to know how the few informed individuals divide on a complex issue. When the best informed individuals favor a proposal or issue, experience indicates that their view tends to be accepted by lower echelons as information and knowledge become more widespread.

But this is not the invariable pattern. In the case of Vietnam, it was the best educated and the best informed who reversed their views as the war went on. The least well educated were always more against the war in Vietnam.

It is now proper to ask why, with all of its obvious merits, this question design is not used more often. The answer is that polling organizations generally avoid technical and complex issues, preferring to deal with those on which the vast majority of Americans have knowledge and opinions. Often the design is shortened to embrace only the filter question that seeks to find out if the individual has read or heard about a given issue, and omits the other questions.

In the field of public opinion research, one finds two schools of thought: one is made up largely of those in academic circles who believe that research on public attitudes should be almost entirely descriptive or diagnostic; the other, made up largely of persons in political life or in journalism or allied fields, who want to know the "score." It is the task of the polling organization to satisfy both groups. And to do this, both categories of questions must be included in the surveys conducted at regular intervals.

The long experience of the Gallup Poll points to the importance of reporting trends of opinion on all the continuing problems, the beliefs, the wishes of the people.

In fact, about four out of every ten questions included in a typical survey are for the purpose of measuring trends. Simple "yes" and "no" questions are far better suited to this purpose than "open-ended" questions, and this accounts chiefly for the high percentage of this type of question in the field of polling.

## INTERVIEWERS AND INTERVIEWING PROBLEMS

Since the reliability of poll results depends so much on the integrity of interviewers, polling organizations must go to great lengths to see that interviewers follow instructions conscientiously.

A professor at an Ivy League college sums up the problems that have to do with interviewers in this question: "How do you insure quality control over your interviewers, preventing them from either influencing the answers, mis-recording them, or filling in the forms themselves?"

Before these specific points are dealt with, the reader may wish to know who the interviewers are and how they are selected and trained.

Women make the best interviewers, not only in the United States but in virtually every nation where public opinion survey organizations are established. Generally, they are more conscientious and more likely to follow instructions than men. Perhaps the nature of the work makes interviewing more appealing to them. The fact that the work is part-time is another reason why women prefer it.

Most interviewers are women of middle age, with high-school or college education. Most are married and have children.

Very few interviewers devote full time to this work. In fact, this is not recommended. Interviewing is mentally exhausting and the interviewer who works day after day at this task is likely to lose her zeal, with a consequent drop in the quality of her work.

When an area is drawn for the national cross-section, the interviewing department of the polling organization finds a suitable person to serve as the interviewer in this particular district. All the usual methods of seeking individuals who can meet the requirements are utilized, including such sources as school superintendents, newspaper editors, members of the clergy, and the classified columns of the local press.

Training for this kind of work can be accomplished by means of an instruction manual, by a supervisor, or by training sessions. The best training consists of a kind of trial-by-fire process. The interviewer is given test interviews to do after she has completed her study of the instruction manual. The trial interviews prove whether she can do the work in a satisfactory manner; more important, making these interviews enables the interviewer to discover if she really likes this kind of work. Her interviews are carefully inspected and investigated. Telephone conversations often straighten out procedures and clear up any misunderstandings about them.

Special questions added to the interviewing form and internal checks on consistency can be used to detect dishonesty. Also, a regular program of contacting persons who have been interviewed—to see if they in fact have been interviewed—is commonly employed by the best survey organizations.

It would be foolhardy to insist that every case of dishonesty can be detected in this manner, but awareness of the existence of these many ways of checking honesty removes most if not all of the temptation for the interviewers to fill in the answers themselves.

Experience of many years indicates that the temptation to "fudge" answers is related to the size of the work load given to the interviewer. If too many interviews are required in too short a time, the interviewer may hurry through the assignment, being less careful than she otherwise would be and, on occasion, not above the temptation to fill in a last few details.

To lessen this pressure, the assignment of interviews given to Gallup Poll interviewers has been constantly reduced through the years. At the present time, an assignment consists of only five or six interviews, and assignments come at least a week apart. This policy increases the cost per interview but it also keeps the interviewer from being subjected to too great pressure.

In the case of open questions that require the interviewer to record the exact words of the respondent, the difficulties mount. The interviewer must attempt to record the main thought of the respondent as the respondent is talking, and usually without benefit of shorthand. The addition of "probe" questions to the original open-end questions helps to organize the response in a more meaningful way. In certain circumstances, the use of small tape recorders, carried by the interviewer, is highly recommended.

So much for the interviewer's side of this situation. What about the person being interviewed? How honest is he?

While there is no certain way of telling whether a given individual is answering truthfully, the evidence from thousands of surveys is that people are remarkably honest and frank when asked their views in a situation that is properly structured— that is, when the respondent knows the purpose of the interview and is told that his name will not be attached to any of the things he says, and when the questions are properly worded.

It is important to point out that persons reached in a public opinion survey normally do not know the interviewer personally. For this reason, there is little or no reason to try to impress her. And, contrary to a widely held view, people are not inclined to "sound off" on subjects they know little about. In fact, many persons entitled, on the basis of their knowledge, to hold an opinion about a given problem or issue often hesitate to do so. In the development of the quintamensional procedure, described earlier, it was discovered that the opening question could not be stated: "Have you *followed* the discussion about the XX issue?" Far too many said they hadn't. And for this reason the approach had to be changed to ask: "Have you *heard or read* about the XX issue?"

The interviewer is instructed to read the question exactly as it is worded, and not try to explain it or amplify it. If the interviewee says, "Would you repeat that?" (incidentally, this is always the mark of a bad question), the interviewer repeats the question, and if on the second reading the person does not understand or get the point of the question, the interviewer checks the "no opinion" box and goes on to the next question.

But don't people often change their minds? This is a question often asked of poll-takers. The answer is, "Of course." Interviewed on Saturday, some persons may have a different opinion on Sunday. But this is another instance when the law of averages comes to the rescue. Those who shift their views in one direction will almost certainly be counterbalanced by those who change in the opposite direction. The net result is to show no change in the overall results.

Polls can only reflect people as they are—sometimes inconsistent, often uninformed. Democracy, however, does not require that every individual, every voter, be a philosopher. Democracy requires only that the sum total of individual views—the collective judgment—add up to something that makes sense. Fortunately, there now exists some forty years of polling evidence to prove the soundness of the collective judgment of the people.

How many persons refuse to be interviewed? The percentage is very small, seldom more than 10% of all those contacted. Interestingly, this same figure is found in all the nations where public opinion polls are conducted. Refusals are chiefly a function of lack of interviewing skill. Top interviewers are rarely turned down. This does not mean that a man who must get back to work immediately or a woman who has a cake in the oven will take thirty to forty-five minutes to discuss issues of the day. These situations are to be avoided. And that is why the Time-Place interviewing plan was developed by the Gallup Poll.

Readers may wonder how polls allow for the possible embarrassment or guilty conscience factor that might figure in an interviewee's answers to some questions. For example, while a voter might be prepared to vote for a third-party candidate like George Wallace, he might be uneasy about saying so to a stranger sitting in his living room.

When interviews and the interviewing situation are properly structured, however, this does not happen. In the 1968 election campaign, to follow the same example, the Gallup Poll found Wallace receiving at one point as much as 19% of the total vote. Later his popularity declined. The final poll result showed him with 15% of the vote; he actually received 14%. If there had been any embarrassment about admitting being for Wallace, his vote would obviously have been underestimated by a sizable amount.

Properly approached, people are not reluctant to discuss even personal matters—their private problems, their religion, sex. By using an interesting technique developed in Sweden, even the most revealing facts about the sex life of an individual can be obtained. And the same type of approach is found to be highly successful in finding out the extent of drug use by college students. Many studies about the religious beliefs of individuals have been conducted by the Gallup Poll without meeting interviewing difficulties.

The desire to have one's voice heard on issues of the day is almost universal. An interviewer called upon an elderly man and found him working in his garden. After he had offered his views on many subjects included in the poll, he called to the interviewer who had started for her car, and said: "You know, two of the most important things in my life have happened this week. First, I was asked to serve on a jury, and now I have been asked to give my views in a public opinion poll."

## MEASURING INTENSITY

To the legislator or administrator the intensity with which certain voters or groups of voters hold their opinions has special significance. If people feel strongly enough about a given issue they will likely do something about it—write letters, work for a candidate who holds a contrary view, contribute money to a campaign, try to win other voters to their candidate. To cite an example: Citizens who oppose any kind of gun control laws, though constituting a minority of the public, feel so strongly about this issue that they will do anything they can to defeat such legislation. As a result, they have succeeded in keeping strict gun laws from being adopted in most states and by the federal government.

Since most legislation calls for more money, a practical measure of the intensity of feeling about a given piece of legislation is the willingness to have taxes increased to meet the costs.

One politician made this criticism of polling efforts: "Issue polling often fails to differentiate between hard and soft opinion. If the issue is national health insurance, then the real test is not whether the individual favors it but how much more per year he is willing to pay in taxes for such a program."

This is a merited criticism of polls and, as stated earlier, one that points to the need for greater attention on the part of polling organizations. The action that an individual is willing to take—the sacrifice he is willing to undergo—to see that his side of an issue prevails is one of the best ways of sorting out hard from soft opinion.

Questions put to respondents about "how strongly" they feel, "how important it is to them," and "how much they care" all yield added insights into the intensity of opinions held by the public. The fact, however, that they are used as seldom as they are in the regular polls, here and abroad, indicates that the added information gained does not compensate for the time and the difficulties encountered by the survey interviewer. Most attitude scales are, in fact, better suited to the classroom with students as captive subjects than to the face-to-face interviews undertaken by most survey organizations.

The best hope, in my opinion, lies in the development of new questions that are behavior- or action-oriented. Here, then, is an important area where both academicians and practitioners can work together in the improvement of present research procedures.

The specific complaint mentioned above—that of providing a more realistic presentation of an issue—can probably be dealt with best in the question wording, as noted earlier.

While verbal scales to measure intensity can be usefully employed in many situations, two nonverbal scales have gained wide acceptance and use throughout the world. Since they do not depend upon words, language is no barrier to their use in any nation. Moreover, they can be employed in normal interviewing situations, and on a host of problems.

The scales were devised by Jan Stapel of the Netherlands Institute of Public Opinion and by Hadley Cantril and a colleague, F. P. Kilpatrick. While the scales seem to be similar, each has its own special merits.

The Stapel scale consists of a column of ten boxes. The five at the top are white, the five at the bottom black.

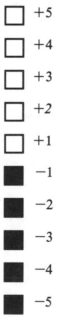

The boxes are numbered from +5 to −5. The interviewer carries a reproduction of this scale and at the appropriate time in the interview hands it to the respondent. The interviewer explains the scale in these or similar words: "You will notice that the boxes on this card go from the highest position of plus 5—something you like very much—all the way down to the lowest position of minus 5—or something you dislike very much. Now, how far up the scale, or how far down the scale, would you rate the following?"

After this explanation, the interviewer asks the respondent how far up or down the scale he would rate an individual, political party, product, company, proposal, or almost anything at issue. The person is told "put your finger on the box" that best represents his point of view; or, in other situations, to call off the number opposite the box. The interviewer duly records this number on his interviewing form.

One of the merits of the Stapel Scalometer is that it permits the person being interviewed to answer two questions with one response: whether he has a positive or a negative feeling toward the person or party or institution being rated, and at the same time the degree of his liking or disliking. By simply calling off a number he indicates that he has a favorable or unfavorable opinion of the F.B.I., of Jimmy Carter, or of the Equal Rights Amendment, and how much he likes or dislikes each. In actual use, researchers have found the extreme positions on the scale are most indicative and most sensitive to change. These are the +4 and +5 positions on the favorable side and the −4 and −5 positions on the negative side. Normally these two positions are combined to provide a "highly favorable" or a "highly unfavorable" rating.

Scale ratings thus obtained are remarkably consistent and remarkably reliable in ranking candidates and parties. In fact, the ratings given to the two major-party candidates have paralleled the relative standings of the candidates in elections, especially when the party ratings are averaged with the candidate ratings.

Cantril and Kilpatrick devised the "Self-Anchoring Scale."* Cantril and his associate, Lloyd Free, used this scale to measure the aspirations and fears of people in different nations of the world—both those living in highly developed countries and those in the least developed. They sought "to get an overall picture of the reality worlds in which people lived, a picture expressed by individuals in their own terms and to do this in such a way . . . as to enable meaningful comparisons to be made between different individuals, groups of individuals, and societies."

The Self-Anchoring scale is so simple that it can be used with illiterates and with people without any kind of formal education. A multination survey in which this measuring instrument was employed included nations as diverse in their educational and living standards as Nigeria, India, the United States, West Germany, Cuba, Israel, Japan, Poland, Panama, Yugoslavia, Philippines, Brazil, and the Dominican Republic.

---

*F. P. Kilpatrick and Hadley Cantril, "Self-Anchoring Scale." *Journal of Individual Psychology,* November 1960.

The scale makes use of a ladder device.

```
——— 10 ———
——— 9 ———
——— 8 ———
——— 7 ———
——— 6 ———
——— 5 ———
——— 4 ———
——— 3 ———
——— 2 ———
——— 1 ———
——— 0 ———
```

The person being interviewed describes his own wishes and hopes, the realization of which would constitute the best possible life. This is the top anchoring point of the scale. At the other extreme, the same individual describes his worries and fears embodied in the worst possible life he can imagine. With the use of this device, he is asked where he thinks he stands on the ladder today. Then he is asked where he thinks he stood in the past, and where he thinks he will stand in the future.

This same procedure was used by Albert Cantril and Charles Roll in a survey called *Hopes and Fears of the American People*—a revealing study of the mood of the American people in the spring of 1971.

Use of this scale would be extremely helpful in pursuing the goal set forth by Alvin Toffler in his book *Future Shock.* He writes:

The time has come for a dramatic reassessment of the directions of change, a reassessment made not by the politicians or the sociologists or the clergy or the elitist revolutionaries, not by technicians or college presidents, but by the people themselves. We need, quite literally, to "go to the people" with a question that is almost never asked of them: *"What kind of a world do you want 10, 20, or 30 years from now?"* We need to initiate, in short, a continuing plebiscite on the future. Toffler points out that "the voter may be polled about specific issues, but not about the general shape of the preferable future."

This is true to a great extent. With the exception of the Cantril-Free studies, this area has been largely overlooked by polling organizations. Toffler advocates a continuing plebiscite in which millions of persons would participate. From a practical point of view, however, sampling offers the best opportunity to discover just what the public's ideas of the future are—and more particularly, the kind of world they want ten years, twenty years, or thirty years from now.

## REPORTING AND INTERPRETING POLL FINDINGS

Public opinion polls throughout the world have been sponsored by the media of communication—newspapers, magazines, television, and radio. It is quite proper, therefore, to answer this question: "How well do the various media report and evaluate the results of a given poll?"

Since October 1935, Gallup Poll reports have appeared weekly in American newspapers in virtually all of the major cities. During this period, I am happy to report, no newspaper has changed the wording of poll releases sent to them to make the findings fit the newspaper's editorial or political views. Editors, however, are permitted to write their own headlines because of their own special type and format policies; they can shorten articles or, in fact, omit them if news columns are filled by other and more pressing material.

Since the funds for the Gallup Poll come from this source and since the sponsoring newspapers represent all shades of political belief, the need for strict objectivity in the writing and interpretation of poll results becomes an economic as well as a scientific necessity.

At various stages in the history of the Gallup Poll, charges have been made that the poll has a Republican bias, and at other times, a Democratic bias, largely dependent upon whether the political tide is swinging toward one side or the other. Even a cursory examination of the findings dealing with issues of the day, and of election survey results, will disprove this.

The Gallup Poll is a fact-finding organization, or looked at in another way, a kind of scorekeeper in the political world.

When poll findings are not to the liking of critics there is always a great temptation to try to discredit the poll by claiming that it is "biased," that it makes "secret adjustments" and that it manipulates the figures to suit its fancy, and that it is interfering with "democratic dialogue." Such charges were heard often in earlier years, but time has largely stilled this kind of attack on the poll's integrity.

Limitations of space, in the case of newspapers, and of time in the case of television and radio, impose restrictions on the amount of detail and analysis that can be included in any one report. The news media have a strong preference for "hard" news, the kind that reports the most recent score on candidate or party strength, or the division of opinion on highly controversial subjects. This type of news, it should be added, makes up the bulk of their news budgets.

These space and time requirements do require a different kind of poll report form from one that would be written to satisfy those who prefer a full and detailed description of public opinion.

A political writer for a large metropolitan newspaper has raised this point: "Is it not more accurate to report a point spread instead of a simple single figure? . . . If so, would it not be more responsible to state it that way, even though it would take away some of the sharpness in published reports?"

A degree of error is inherent in all sampling and it is important that this fact be understood by those who follow poll findings. The question is how best to achieve this end. One way, of course, is to educate the public to look at all survey results not as fixed realities or absolutes but as reliable estimates only.

The best examples, as noted earlier, are the monthly figures on unemployment and the cost of living. Should these be published showing a point spread or the margin of error? If they were, then the monthly index of unemployment, based as it is on a sample of 50,000, would read, at a given point in time, not 8.8%, but 8.5% to 9.1%. Reporting the cost of living index in such fashion would almost certainly cause trouble, since many labor contracts are based upon changes as small as 0.1%.

In reporting the trend of opinion, especially on issues, the inclusion of a point spread would make poll reports rather meaningless, particularly if the trend were not a sharp one. The character of the trend curve itself normally offers evidence of the variations due to sample size.

In the case of elections, the reporting of the margin of error can, on occasion, be misleading to the reader. The reason is that polling errors come from many sources, and often the least of these in importance is the size of the sample. Yet, the statistical margin of error relates solely to this one factor.

An example may help to shed light on this point. A telephone poll taken in a mayoralty race in a large eastern city, reported the standings of the candidates and added that they were accurate within "a possible error margin of 3.8%." In short, the newspaper in which the results were published and the polling organization assured readers that the results perforce had to be right within this margin, based upon the laws or probability. Actually, the poll figure was 14 percentage points short on the winning candidate. Factors other than the size of the sample were responsible for this wide deviation.

The best guide to a poll's accuracy is its record. If allowance is to be made for variation in the poll's reported figures, then perhaps the best suggestion, to be reasonably certain that the error will not exceed a stated amount in a national election, is to multiply by 2.5 the average deviation of the poll in its last three or four elections.

Still another way to remind readers and viewers of the presence of some degree of error in all survey findings is to find a word or words that convey this fact. A growing practice among statisticians in dealing with sampling data is to refer to results as "estimates." Unfortunately, this word conveys to some the impression that subjective judgments have entered into the process. A better word needs to be found that removes some of the certainty that is too often attached to poll percentages without, at the same time, erring in the opposite direction. The word "assessment" has been adopted by some survey researchers and it is hoped that it will come into general use in the future.

# DESIGN OF THE SAMPLE

The design of the sample used in the Gallup Poll is that of a replicated probability sample down to the block level in the case of urban areas and to segments of townships in the case of rural areas.

After stratifying the nation geographically and by size of community in order to insure conformity of the sample with the latest available estimates by the Census Bureau of the distribution of the adult population, about 350 different sampling locations or areas are selected on a strictly random basis. The interviewers have no choice whatsoever concerning the part of the city or county in which they conduct their interviews.

Interviewers are given maps of the area to which they are assigned, with a starting point indicated, and are required to follow a specified direction. At each occupied dwelling unit, interviewers are instructed to select respondents by following a prescribed systematic method. This procedure is followed until the assigned number of interviews is completed. The standard sample size for most Gallup Polls is 1500 interviews. This is augmented in specific instances where greater survey accuracy is considered desirable.

Since this sampling procedure is designed to produce a sample that approximates the adult civilian population (18 and older) living in private households in the United States (that is, excluding those in prisons and hospitals, hotels, religious institutions, and on military reservations), the survey results can be applied to this population for the purpose of projecting percentages into numbers of people. The manner in which the sample is drawn also produces a sample that approximates the population of private households in the United States. Therefore, survey results also can be projected in terms of numbers of households when appropriate.

## SAMPLING TOLERANCES

It should be remembered that all sample surveys are subject to sampling error; that is, the extent to which the results may differ from what would be obtained if the whole population surveyed had been interviewed. The size of such a sampling error depends largely on the number of interviews. Increasing the sample size lessens the magnitude of possible error and vice versa.

The following tables may be used in estimating sampling error. The computed allowances (the standard deviation) have taken into account the effect of the sample design upon sampling error. They may be interpreted as indicating the range (plus or minus the figure shown) within which the results of repeated samplings in the same time period could be expected to vary, 95 percent of the time (or at a confidence level of .5), assuming the same sampling procedure, the same interviewers, and the same questionnaire.

Table A shows how much allowance should be made for the sampling error of a percentage. The table would be used in the following manner: Say a reported percentage is 33 for a group that includes 1500 respondents. Go to the row "percentage near 30" in the table and then to the column headed "1500." The number at this point is three, which means that the 33 percent obtained in the sample is subject to a sampling error of plus or minus 3 points. Another way of saying it is that very probably (95 chances out of 100) the average of repeated samplings would be somewhere between 30 and 36, with the most likely figure being the 33 obtained.

In comparing survey results in two subsamples, such as men and woman, the question arises as to how large must a difference between them be before one can be reasonably sure that it reflects a statistically significant difference. In Table B and C, the number of points that must be allowed for, in such comparisons, is indicated.

For percentages near 20 or 80, use Table B; for those near 50, Table C. For percentages in between, the error to be allowed for is between that shown in the two tables.

Here is an example of how the tables should be used: Say 50 percent of men and 40 percent of women respond the same way to a question—a difference of 10 percentage points. Can it be said with any assurance that the ten-point difference reflects a significant difference between men and women on the question? (Samples, unless otherwise noted, contain approximately 750 men and 750 women.)

Because the percentages are near 50, consult Table C. Since the two samples are about 750 persons each, look for the place in the table where the column and row labeled "750" converge. The number six appears there. This means the allowance for error should be 6 points, and the conclusion that the percentage among men is somewhere between 4 and 16 points higher than the percentage among women would be wrong only about 5 percent of the time. In other words, there is a considerable likelihood that a difference exists in the direction observed and that it amounts to at least 4 percentage points.

If, in another case, male responses amount to 22 percent, and female to 24 percent, consult Table B because these percentages are near 20. The column and row labeled "750" converge on the number five. Obviously, then, the two-point difference is inconclusive.

## TABLE A

### Recommended Allowance for Sampling Error of a Percentage

**In Percentage Points**
**(at 95 in 100 confidence level)\***
**Size of the Sample**

|                      | 3000 | 1500 | 1000 | 750 | 600 | 400 | 200 | 100 |
|----------------------|------|------|------|-----|-----|-----|-----|-----|
| Percentages near 10  | 2    | 2    | 2    | 3   | 4   | 4   | 5   | 7   |
| Percentages near 20  | 2    | 3    | 3    | 4   | 4   | 5   | 7   | 9   |
| Percentages near 30  | 2    | 3    | 4    | 4   | 4   | 6   | 8   | 10  |
| Percentages near 40  | 3    | 3    | 4    | 4   | 5   | 6   | 9   | 11  |
| Percentages near 50  | 3    | 3    | 4    | 4   | 5   | 6   | 9   | 11  |
| Percentages near 60  | 3    | 3    | 4    | 4   | 5   | 6   | 9   | 11  |
| Percentages near 70  | 2    | 3    | 4    | 4   | 4   | 6   | 8   | 10  |
| Percentages near 80  | 2    | 3    | 3    | 4   | 4   | 5   | 7   | 9   |
| Percentages near 90  | 2    | 2    | 2    | 3   | 4   | 4   | 5   | 7   |

\*The chances are 95 in 100 that the sampling error is not larger than the figures shown.

## TABLE B

### Recommended Allowance for Sampling Error of the Difference Between Two Subsamples

**In Percentage Points**
**(at 95 in 100 confidence level)\***

**Percentages near 20 or percentages near 80**

|                    | 1500 | 750 | 600 | 400 | 200 |
|--------------------|------|-----|-----|-----|-----|
| Size of the Sample |      |     |     |     |     |
| 1500               | 3    |     |     |     |     |
| 750                | 4    | 5   |     |     |     |
| 600                | 5    | 6   | 6   |     |     |
| 400                | 6    | 7   | 7   | 7   |     |
| 200                | 8    | 8   | 8   | 9   | 10  |

## TABLE C

**Percentages near 50**

|                    | 1500 | 750 | 600 | 400 | 200 |
|--------------------|------|-----|-----|-----|-----|
| Size of the Sample |      |     |     |     |     |
| 1500               | 4    |     |     |     |     |
| 750                | 5    | 6   |     |     |     |
| 600                | 6    | 8   | 8   |     |     |
| 400                | 7    | 8   | 8   | 9   |     |
| 200                | 10   | 10  | 11  | 11  | 13  |

\*The chances are 95 in 100 that the sampling error is not larger than the figures shown.

# RECORD OF
# GALLUP POLL ACCURACY

| Year | Gallup<br>Final Survey* | | Election Result* | |
|------|------|------|------|------|
| 1984 | 59.0% | Reagan | 59.2% | Reagan |
| 1982 | 55.0 | Democratic | 55.8 | Democratic |
| 1980 | 47.0 | Reagan | 50.8 | Reagan |
| 1978 | 55.0 | Democratic | 54.0 | Democratic |
| 1976 | 48.0 | Carter | 50.0 | Carter |
| 1974 | 60.0 | Democratic | 58.9 | Democratic |
| 1972 | 62.0 | Nixon | 61.8 | Nixon |
| 1970 | 53.0 | Democratic | 54.3 | Democratic |
| 1968 | 43.0 | Nixon | 43.5 | Nixon |
| 1966 | 52.5 | Democratic | 51.9 | Democratic |
| 1964 | 64.0 | Johnson | 61.3 | Johnson |
| 1962 | 55.5 | Democratic | 52.7 | Democratic |
| 1960 | 51.0 | Kennedy | 50.1 | Kennedy |
| 1958 | 57.0 | Democratic | 56.5 | Democratic |
| 1956 | 59.5 | Eisenhower | 57.8 | Eisenhower |
| 1954 | 51.5 | Democratic | 52.7 | Democratic |
| 1952 | 51.0 | Eisenhower | 55.4 | Eisenhower |
| 1950 | 51.0 | Democratic | 50.3 | Democratic |
| 1948 | 44.5 | Truman | 49.9 | Truman |
| 1946 | 58.0 | Republican | 54.3 | Republican |
| 1944 | 51.5 | Roosevelt | 53.3** | Roosevelt |
| 1942 | 52.0 | Democratic | 48.0 | Democratic |
| 1940 | 52.0 | Roosevelt | 55.0 | Roosevelt |
| 1938 | 54.0 | Democratic | 50.8 | Democratic |
| 1936 | 55.7 | Roosevelt | 62.5 | Roosevelt |

*The figure shown is the winner's percentage of the Democratic-Republican vote except in the elections of 1948, 1968, and 1976. Because the Thurmond and Wallace voters in 1948 were largely split-offs from the normally Democratic vote, they were made a part of the final Gallup Poll preelection.

**Civilian vote 53.3, Roosevelt soldier vote 0.5 = 53.8% Roosevelt. Gallup final survey based on civilian vote.

estimate of the division of the vote. In 1968 Wallace's candidacy was supported by such a large minority that he was clearly a major candidate, and the 1968 percents are based on the total Nixon-Humphrey-Wallace vote. In 1976, because of interest in McCarthy's candidacy and its potential effect on the Carter vote, the final Gallup Poll estimate included Carter, Ford, McCarthy, and all other candidates as a group.

Average Deviation for 24
   National Elections ........................... 2.3 percentage points

Average Deviation for 17
   National Elections
   Since 1950, inclusive ........................ 1.5 percentage points

### Trend in Deviation Reduction

| Elections | Average Error |
|-----------|---------------|
| 1936–48 | 4.0 |
| 1950–58 | 1.7 |
| 1960–68 | 1.5 |
| 1970–82 | 1.4 |
| 1966–82 | 1.2 |
| 1972–84 | 1.2 |

# CHRONOLOGY

The chronology is provided to enable the reader to relate poll results to specific events or series of events that may have influenced public opinion.

**1983**

| | |
|---|---|
| December 2 | The unemployment rate dropped to 8.4% in November, a two-year low. |
| December 4 | Targets in Syria are bombed by U.S. planes. Two aircraft are shot down, and an American naval flier, Robert Goodman, is taken prisoner by the Syrians. |
| December 12 | The U.S. embassy in Kuwait is attacked; seven persons are killed and more than sixty are injured. |
| December 13 | American ships attack Syrian positions near Beirut. |
| | A presidential commission urges twenty-one as the national drinking age. |
| December 15 | The Reagan administration agrees to give Israel $1.4 billion in military aid during 1984. |
| | The last American combat troops leave Grenada. |
| December 17 | Members of the Palestine Liberation Organization begin evacuation from Tripoli on Italian ships. |
| December 29 | The United States formally announces its intention to withdraw from the United Nations Educational, Scientific and Cultural Organization. |

**1984**

January 3          The Federal Deposit Insurance Corporation reports that forty-eight federally insured banks failed in 1983, the highest total since 1939.

Jesse Jackson obtains the release of the captured naval flier whose plane was shot down over Syria.

January 5          Commerce Department figures show that all but one of the nation's largest retailers gained 10% or more in sales during December 1983, compared with December 1982. Sears, Roebuck and Company, the largest U.S. retailer, reported an increase of 17.5%.

Sales of automobiles in 1983, including imports, increased by 15.1% over 1982.

January 6          The Labor Department announces that the unemployment rate continued downward to 8.1% in December.

January 11         The Kissinger Commission endorses most of the Reagan policies in Central America.

January 12         The United States and China sign agreements on industrial cooperation.

January 13         The Labor Department announces that prices paid by producers for finished goods rose only 0.6% in 1983, the smallest increase since 1964. Credit was given to the sharp decline in energy prices.

The Federal Reserve Board reports that industrial production averaged 6.5% higher in 1983 than in 1982.

January 16         President Ronald Reagan calls for the resumption of arms talks with the Soviet Union.

January 18         The Commerce Department discloses that housing starts in 1983 increased 60.3% from 1982's depressed level.

January 19         Real personal income, adjusted for inflation, rose 3.2% in 1983, while the Gross National Product (GNP) climbed to an annual rate of 4.5% during the fourth quarter.

The National Urban League reports that the economic circumstances of black Americans declined in 1983, stating that black unemployment was more than twice as much as white unemployment, that 42% of black families were headed by single mothers, and that one-third of all blacks were living in poverty.

| | |
|---|---|
| January 29 | President Reagan announces that he will seek reelection in 1984 and also asks for the renomination of Vice-President George Bush. |
| February 1 | The president submits a $925.5-billion budget to Congress which was $180.4 billion out of balance. The budget for the 1985 fiscal year beginning October 1, 1984 included a proposed 14.5% increase in defense spending. |
| February 3 | The Labor Department reports that the unemployment rate in January fell to 7.9%. |
| February 8 | The growing deficit problem is credited to a 10% decline in the Dow-Jones Industrial Average. |
| February 9 | Soviet leader Yuri Andropov dies. Konstantin Chernenko replaces him. |
| February 17 | President Reagan proposes increased American aid to U.S.-supported governments in Central America. |
| February 21 | The president begins to remove U.S. Marines from Beirut and to place them on ships offshore. Reagan acted as the position of President Amin Gemayel deteriorated and his army crumbled. |
| February 28 | Senator Gary Hart upsets former Vice-President Walter Mondale in the New Hampshire primary. President Reagan receives 86% of the votes in the Republican primary. |
| February 29 | Senator Alan Cranston withdraws from the race for the Democratic presidential nomination. |
| March 1 | Senator Ernest Hollings and former Governor Reuben Askew withdraw from the race for the Democratic presidential nomination. |
| March 5 | The United States says that Iraq is using chemical weapons in its war against Iran. |
| March 9 | Unemployment in February declined to 7.7%. |

| | |
|---|---|
| March 13 | Senator Hart wins Democratic primaries in Massachusetts, Rhode Island, and Florida, while Mondale wins in Georgia and Alabama. The results force Senator John Glenn and former Senator George McGovern to withdraw from the race. Jackson finishes third in Georgia and Florida, saying he will remain in the race. |
| March 15 | The Senate rejects an amendment to permit silent prayer in public schools. |
| | The Federal Reserve Board states that industrial production rose by 1.2% in February, while housing starts jumped 11.2%. |
| March 17 | Mondale wins the Michigan caucuses. |
| March 19 | The U.S. balance of payments, a measure of the nation's trade with other nations, showed a record deficit of $40 billion in 1983. |
| March 20 | Mondale wins the Illinois primary. |
| March 27 | Hart takes the Connecticut primary. |
| March 30 | President Reagan formally ends U.S. participation in the multination Lebanese peace-keeping force. |
| March 31 | With 1,967 delegates needed for the Democratic nomination, Mondale has about 700, Hart 400, Jackson 100, and 400 are uncommitted. |
| April 3 | Mondale wins the New York primary, with Hart second and Jackson a close third. |
| April 5 | Major banks increase their prime lending rate from 11.5% to 12%, the highest level since October 1982. |
| | The Senate approves additional military aid to El Salvador and for the anti-Sandinista rebels in Nicaragua. |
| April 6 | Unemployment for March was 7.7%, virtually unchanged from recent months. |
| | Reports surface that the Central Intelligence Agency has participated in the mining of Nicaraguan harbors. |
| April 7 | Mondale wins the Pennsylvania primary, and Jackson carries Philadelphia. |

| April 9 | Nicaragua asks the International Court of Justice to order the United States to halt the mining. The Reagan administration says it will not accept the court's jurisdiction on disputes involving Latin America for two years. |
| --- | --- |
| April 10 | Administration economists estimate that the real GNP will grow by 5% in 1984. |
| April 11 | Reports appear that President Reagan has approved the decision to mine Nicaraguan ports. |
| April 19 | The Commerce Department discloses that the economy grew at an annual rate of 8.3% during the first quarter of 1984, a sharp increase from the 5% rate in the previous quarter. |
| April 26 | President Reagan begins a five-day visit to China. |
| April 30 | With 1,967 votes needed to nominate, Mondale has 1,075, Hart 575, Jackson 150; 275 support others or are uncommitted. |
| May 1 | Jackson wins the District of Columbia primary and Mondale takes Tennessee. |
| May 4 | Unemployment held steady at 7.7% in April. |
| May 5 | Jackson wins the Louisiana primary, while Mondale scores a big victory in Texas. |
| May 7 | Hart wins the Colorado caucuses. |
| | José Napoleón Duarte, a political moderate, is elected president of El Salvador. |
| May 8 | Hart wins the Ohio and Indiana primaries, and Mondale takes North Carolina and Maryland. |
| | The Soviet Union announces it will not participate in the summer Olympic Games in Los Angeles. |
| | Major banks boost their prime lending rate from 12% to 12.5%. |
| May 15 | Hart wins the Nebraska and Oregon primaries. |
| May 17 | The Senate supports the Reagan administration's plan to cut federal budget deficits. |

| | |
|---|---|
| May 19 | Duarte begins a four-day visit to the United States to meet President Reagan and members of Congress. He appeals for additional military aid and pledges to end death squad activities in El Salvador. |
| May 20 | Soviet Defense Minister Dimitri Ustinov announces that the USSR has increased the number of submarines carrying nuclear missiles off the coasts of the United States as a countermeasure to the deployment of U.S. missiles in Europe. |
| May 28 | President Reagan leads a Memorial Day tribute to an unidentified U.S. serviceman killed in the Vietnam War. |
| May 30 | U.S. trade deficit set another record in April at $12.2 billion. |
| June 1 | Unemployment fell to 7.4% in April. |
| June 2 | President Reagan visits Ireland. |
| June 5 | Mondale wins the key New Jersey primary and also West Virginia; Hart carries the California, New Mexico, and South Dakota primaries. Mondale claims that he has enough delegates to win a first ballot victory at the Democratic convention. |
| June 6 | A long period of rising tensions between Sikh extremists and the government of India in the state of Punjab culminates in a day-long battle, leaving more than 300 dead. |
| | Leaders of eight nations participate in ceremonies commemorating the fortieth anniversary of D-day. |
| June 15 | The Federal Reserve Board reports that industrial production advanced 0.4% in May. |
| June 25 | Major banks raise their prime interest rate from 12.5% to 13%. The U.S. dollar sets or approaches record highs in relation to major foreign currencies. |
| June 27 | Jackson succeeds in persuading Cuba to release twenty-two Americans from its jails. |
| June 28 | Congress approves a plan to bring pressure on the states to raise the legal drinking age to twenty-one. |
| July 6 | Unemployment fell to 7.0% in June. |

| July 12 | Mondale announces that he has asked Representative Geraldine Ferraro to be the Democratic candidate for vice-president. Never before has a major party nominated a woman for such a high office. By announcing his choice before the convention, Mondale broke another precedent. |

July 18    The Democratic convention nominates Mondale as its presidential candidate.

July 19    The Democratic convention nominates Ferraro as its candidate for vice-president. Mondale calls for a "new realism" in public life and warns that taxes will have to go up.

July 23    The Commerce Department says that the GNP rose by an impressive 7.5% during the second quarter of 1984.

July 24    President Reagan announces he has no plans to raise taxes.

July 26    George H. Gallup, founder of The Gallup Poll and a pioneer in public opinion polling, dies at age eighty-two.

July 28    The Olympic Games open in Los Angeles.

August 2    The Census Bureau reports that the nation's poverty rate edged upward to 15.3% in 1983, the highest level since 1965, and that the number of poor people totaled 35.3 million.

August 3    The unemployment rate for July rose slightly to 7.4%.

The stock market concludes the week with the heaviest trading volume ever. The Dow Jones average rose 87.46 points, setting another record.

August 4    President Reagan charges that Mondale, if elected, will raise taxes by $1500 per household. The president proposes no personal tax increases if reelected.

August 7    The House Ethics Committee is asked by the Washington Legal Foundation to investigate Representative Ferraro for her allegedly improper failure to provide details of her husband's finances as prescribed by the Ethics in Government Act.

August 8    Congress approves additional economic and military aid for Central America.

| | |
|---|---|
| August 11 | While testing a radio microphone, President Reagan jokes about outlawing the Soviet Union, saying that "we begin bombing in five minutes." |
| | The president signs into law an act to prohibit public high schools from barring students who wish to assemble for religious or political activities outside school hours. |
| August 12 | The Olympic Games close, showing a financial profit and a record number of gold medals for American athletes. |
| August 20 | Ferraro releases personal financial records, revealing that she and her husband have a net worth of almost $4 million. |
| August 21 | In a ninety-minute news conference before more than 200 reporters, Ferraro denies any wrongdoing with respect to her financial disclosure statements. |
| August 22 | Reagan and Bush are renominated by the Republican convention. |
| September 3 | Democratic candidates Mondale and Ferraro formally begin their campaign with a Labor Day march up New York City's Fifth Avenue, only to be greeted by mostly empty sidewalks. |
| | In southern California, President Reagan starts his campaign by saying that, if reelected, America's message to the world would be: "You ain't seen nothing yet." |
| September 7 | The unemployment rate continued at 7.4% in August. |
| September 10 | Mondale unveils his proposals for cutting the federal deficit by increasing taxes. |
| | Ferraro seeks to settle a controversy with New York Archbishop John O'Connor who says that she has misrepresented the position of the Roman Catholic Church on abortion. The archbishop believes that the teaching of the church on abortion is not divided, as Ferraro has asserted, but rather united in opposition; the controversy will continue throughout the campaign. |
| September 12 | The House Ethics Committee votes unanimously to investigate charges that Ferraro has violated congressional standards by claiming an exemption from the requirement that she disclose her spouse's finances. |

Reagan declares that Mondale's plan to cut budget deficits will increase taxes for "working families all across America" and adds that, whereas "we see an America where every day is the Fourth of July, they see an America where every day is April 15."

September 17    Mondale says he will make war and peace a major issue and charges that Reagan has made the world more dangerous.

September 20    The Commerce Department announces that the third quarter GNP rose 3.6%, about one-half the rate for the second quarter.

A suicide bomber drives a stationwagon to the front of the U.S. embassy annex in Beirut and detonates about 400 pounds of TNT. The explosion kills two Americans and scores of Lebanese.

September 28    For the first time as president, Reagan meets with a major Soviet leader—Foreign Minister Andrei Gromyko—at the White House. No known progress is made on issues dividing the superpowers.

October 2    Raymond Donovan, secretary of labor, pleads not guilty to a 137-count indictment charging him in an attempt to defraud the New York City Transit Authority

October 5    The unemployment rate remained at 7.3% for September.

October 7    Reagan and Mondale meet in Louisville, Kentucky, for their first televised debate, consisting of responses to questions posed by journalists.

October 11    Bush and Ferraro debate in Philadelphia.

October 21    With foreign affairs the subject, Reagan and Mondale hold their second debate, this time in Kansas City.

October 31    Prime Minister Indira Gandhi of India is assassinated in New Delhi.

November 6    President Reagan wins a record-breaking reelection victory, carrying forty-nine states and receiving 525 electoral votes. He wins 59% of the popular vote to 41% for Mondale.

November 21    The United States and the Soviet Union agree to send high-level disarmament teams to Geneva in early 1985.

U.S.-Nicaraguan talks aimed at reducing tensions end. No positive results are reported.

November 27     Secretary of the Treasury Donald Regan announces plans for a complete revision of the income tax law, the most encompassing since 1913.

November 28     Senator Robert Dole is elected Senate Majority Leader.

November 29     Secretary of Defense Caspar Weinberger says U.S. military forces will not be drawn gradually into combat in Central America, but, if American forces are committed anywhere, it would be with the clear intention of winning.

December 20     Prices at the consumer level rose two-tenths of 1% during November, the smallest increase since June. With only the December report to come, 1984 is almost certain to be the third consecutive year in which inflation was held to about 4%. By contrast, the Consumer Price Index averaged an 11.5% annual increase for the years 1979–1981.

## JANUARY 1
## CHURCH ATTENDANCE

Interviewing Date: Five Selected Weeks During 1983
Various Surveys

*Did you, yourself, happen to attend church or synagogue in the last seven days?*

| | Yes |
|---|---|
| National | 40% |

### By Religion

| | |
|---|---|
| Protestants | 39% |
| Catholics | 51 |

### Selected National Trend

| | |
|---|---|
| 1982 | 41% |
| 1981 | 41 |
| 1980 | 40 |
| 1979 | 40 |
| 1978 | 41 |
| 1977 | 41 |
| 1972 | 40 |
| 1969 | 42 |
| 1967 | 43 |
| 1958 | 49 |
| 1957 | 47 |
| 1955 | 49 |
| 1954 | 46 |
| 1950 | 39 |
| 1940 | 37 |
| 1939 | 41 |

*Do you happen to be a member of a church or synagogue?*

| | Yes |
|---|---|
| National | 69% |

### Selected National Trend

| | |
|---|---|
| 1982 | 67%* |
| 1981 | 68 |
| 1980 | 69 |
| 1978 | 68 |
| 1976 | 71 |
| 1965 | 73 |
| 1952 | 73 |
| 1947 | 76 |
| 1942 | 75 |
| 1939 | 72 |
| 1937 | 73 |

*Seven-survey average

Note: Four adults in every ten (40%) attended church or synagogue in a typical week in 1983, statistically matching the figure recorded for 1982. Churchgoing has remained remarkably constant since 1969, after having declined from the high points of 49% recorded in 1955 and 1958. Attendance has not varied by more than 2 percentage points since 1969.

The rate of churchgoing is higher among women than men and among older persons than younger. Attendance is highest in the East, where the greatest proportion of Catholics is found, and is lowest in the West. In 1983, 51% of Catholics nationwide attended Mass in a typical week, compared to 39% of churchgoing Protestants, figures that closely approximate those from the 1982 audit.

Since 1958, a peak year for church attendance, the decline in churchgoing has been sharpest among Catholics. Attendance at Mass has fallen 23 points since 1958, while Protestant churchgoing has remained remarkably stable during the same time period.

The proportion of adults who says they are church members also has changed little in recent years, with almost seven in ten Americans (69%) now claiming membership in a church or synagogue. The highest level of church membership

(76%) was found in 1947, close to the 73% recorded in the first Gallup audit in 1937.

It is important to bear in mind that the membership figures reported here are self-classifications, representing the proportions of people who say they are members of a church or synagogue, and may include some who are not actually on the rolls of local churches. It also should be stressed that adherents of certain faiths—for example, the Roman Catholic and Eastern Orthodox churches—are considered members at birth.

## JANUARY 5
## PREDICTIONS FOR 1984

Interviewing Date: 11/11–12/4/83
Special Telephone Survey

*So far as you are concerned, do you think that 1984 will be better or worse than 1983?*

Better ............................70%
Worse ............................15
Same (volunteered) .................. 7
Don't know ........................ 8

### Selected National Trend

| | Better | Worse | Same | Don't know |
|---|---|---|---|---|
| 1983 ........... | 50% | 32% | 10% | 8% |
| 1982 .......... | 41 | 44 | 11 | 4 |
| 1981 .......... | 49 | 26 | 19 | 6 |
| 1980 .......... | 31 | 56 | * | 13 |
| 1979 .......... | 33 | 55 | * | 12 |
| 1978 .......... | 45 | 30 | 18 | 7 |
| 1972 .......... | 57 | 22 | * | 21 |
| 1960 .......... | 56 | 7 | 28 | 9 |

*"Same" responses recorded with "don't know."

The following figures are the current survey results for member organizations of the Gallup International Research Institute, grouped by developing and industrial nations and ranked from most to least optimistic:*

| | Better | Worse | Same | Don't know |
|---|---|---|---|---|
| **Developing Nations** | | | | |
| Argentina ....... | 83% | 2% | 9% | 6% |
| Korea .......... | 66 | 5 | 25 | 5 |
| Venezuela ...... | 42 | 10 | 19 | 29 |
| India .......... | 42 | 40 | 11 | 7 |
| Brazil .......... | 40 | 40 | 11 | 9 |
| Costa Rica ...... | 26 | 48 | 23 | 3 |
| Uruguay ........ | 25 | 20 | 32 | 23 |
| Bolivia ......... | 24 | 59 | 15 | 2 |
| Chile .......... | 23 | 13 | 13 | 51 |
| Philippines ...... | 13 | 60 | 14 | 13 |
| Average ...... | 38 | 30 | 17 | 15 |
| **Industrial Nations** | | | | |
| United States .... | 70% | 15% | 7% | 8% |
| Canada ......... | 59 | 14 | 23 | 4 |
| Australia ........ | 57 | 19 | 17 | 7 |
| Greece ......... | 50 | 27 | 15 | 8 |
| Spain .......... | 37 | 25 | 26 | 12 |
| Sweden** ....... | 36 | 47 | 13 | 3 |
| Finland ......... | 35 | 21 | 43 | 1 |
| United Kingdom | 35 | 36 | 22 | 7 |
| Italy .......... | 32 | 41 | 24 | 3 |
| Switzerland ..... | 27 | 18 | 52 | 3 |
| Denmark ....... | 27 | 19 | 47 | 7 |
| Norway ........ | 23 | 14 | 62 | 1 |
| Japan .......... | 20 | 10 | 46 | 24 |
| West Germany ... | 20 | 16 | 52 | 12 |
| Ireland** ....... | 19 | 55 | 19 | 6 |
| France ......... | 18 | 45 | 31 | 6 |
| Netherlands ..... | 18 | 45 | 34 | 3 |
| Luxembourg ..... | 18 | 30 | 50 | 2 |
| Portugal ........ | 13 | 40 | 15 | 32 |
| Austria ......... | 10 | 42 | 42 | 6 |
| Belgium ........ | 8 | 53 | 33 | 6 |
| Average ...... | 30 | 30 | 32 | 8 |

*Interviews were conducted in these thirty-one nations during the last weeks of 1983.
**Total does not add to 100% due to rounding.

Note: Despite concern over international tensions, Americans are more optimistic in their outlook for the year 1984 than at any other time in the last quarter century. Although current expectations are relative to one's assessment of the year just past, no fewer than seven in ten predict that 1984 will be better than 1983 in terms of their own personal lives, while only 15% say worse and another 7% anticipate little change.

Americans today are more upbeat about the coming twelve months than they have been since the start of 1960. They also are more optimistic than all but the people of Argentina in a recent thirty-one-nation Gallup International Survey, in which more than 30,000 representative citizens were interviewed. The figure for Argentina undoubtedly reflects the hopeful response of the public to the election of a Democratic government that promises sweeping reforms of past excesses.

In addition to the Americans and the Argentinians, the Koreans, Canadians, and Australians are the most optimistic in their outlook for the coming twelve months. Among the most pessimistic are the Belgians and also the Filipinos, whose nation has been wracked by internal unrest following the assassination of Benigno Aquino. The twenty-one-nation total for the industrial countries shows pessimism matching optimism, while the ten-nation total for the developing countries shows optimism outweighing pessimism by a 4-to-3 ratio.

## JANUARY 8
## PRESIDENTIAL TRIAL HEATS/ DEMOCRATIC PRESIDENTIAL CANDIDATES

Interviewing Date: 12/9–12/83
Survey #228-G

*Asked of registered voters: Suppose the 1984 presidential election were being held today. If President Ronald Reagan were the Republican candidate and Walter Mondale were the Democratic candidate, which would you like to see win? [Those who were undecided were then asked: As of today, do you lean more to Reagan, the Republican, or to Mondale, the Democrat?]*

Reagan . . . . . . . . . . . . . . . . . . . . . . . . . . . .51%
Mondale . . . . . . . . . . . . . . . . . . . . . . . . . .44
Other; undecided . . . . . . . . . . . . . . . . . . . . 5

### By Sex
#### Male

Reagan . . . . . . . . . . . . . . . . . . . . . . . . . . . .57%
Mondale . . . . . . . . . . . . . . . . . . . . . . . . . .40
Other; undecided . . . . . . . . . . . . . . . . . . . . 3

#### Female

Reagan . . . . . . . . . . . . . . . . . . . . . . . . . . . .45%
Mondale . . . . . . . . . . . . . . . . . . . . . . . . . .48
Other; undecided . . . . . . . . . . . . . . . . . . . . 7

### By Ethnic Background
#### White

Reagan . . . . . . . . . . . . . . . . . . . . . . . . . . . .56%
Mondale . . . . . . . . . . . . . . . . . . . . . . . . . .39
Other; undecided . . . . . . . . . . . . . . . . . . . . 5

#### Nonwhite

Reagan . . . . . . . . . . . . . . . . . . . . . . . . . . . .12%
Mondale . . . . . . . . . . . . . . . . . . . . . . . . . .82
Other; undecided . . . . . . . . . . . . . . . . . . . . 6

#### Black

Reagan . . . . . . . . . . . . . . . . . . . . . . . . . . . .11%
Mondale . . . . . . . . . . . . . . . . . . . . . . . . . .84
Other; undecided . . . . . . . . . . . . . . . . . . . . 5

### By Education
#### College Graduate

Reagan . . . . . . . . . . . . . . . . . . . . . . . . . . . .50%
Mondale . . . . . . . . . . . . . . . . . . . . . . . . . .47
Other; undecided . . . . . . . . . . . . . . . . . . . . 3

#### College Incomplete

Reagan . . . . . . . . . . . . . . . . . . . . . . . . . . . .57%
Mondale . . . . . . . . . . . . . . . . . . . . . . . . . .37
Other; undecided . . . . . . . . . . . . . . . . . . . . 6

### High-School Graduate

Reagan ............................53%
Mondale ...........................43
Other; undecided ..................4

### Less Than High-School Graduate

Reagan ............................41%
Mondale ...........................51
Other; undecided ..................8

## By Region
### East

Reagan ............................49%
Mondale ...........................46
Other; undecided ..................5

### Midwest

Reagan ............................57%
Mondale ...........................40
Other; undecided ..................3

### South

Reagan ............................48%
Mondale ...........................46
Other; undecided ..................6

### West

Reagan ............................50%
Mondale ...........................44
Other; undecided ..................6

## By Age
### 18–29 Years

Reagan ............................50%
Mondale ...........................47
Other; undecided ..................3

### 30–49 Years

Reagan ............................51%
Mondale ...........................43
Other; undecided ..................6

### 50–64 Years

Reagan ............................52%
Mondale ...........................45
Other; undecided ..................3

### 65 Years and Over

Reagan ............................50%
Mondale ...........................42
Other; undecided ..................8

## By Income
### $40,000 and Over

Reagan ............................63%
Mondale ...........................34
Other; undecided ..................3

### $30,000–$39,999

Reagan ............................60%
Mondale ...........................38
Other; undecided ..................2

### $20,000–$29,999

Reagan ............................56%
Mondale ...........................39
Other; undecided ..................5

### $10,000–$19,999

Reagan ............................49%
Mondale ...........................44
Other; undecided ..................7

### Under $10,000

Reagan ............................33%
Mondale ...........................61
Other; undecided ..................6

## By Politics
### Republicans

Reagan ............................89%
Mondale ...........................9
Other; undecided ..................2

### Democrats

Reagan ............................22%
Mondale ...........................72
Other; undecided ................. 6

### Independents

Reagan ............................54%
Mondale ...........................39
Other; undecided ................. 7

### Selected National Trend

|  | Reagan | Mondale | Other; undecided |
|---|---|---|---|
| **1983** | | | |
| December 9–12 | 51% | 44% | 5% |
| November 18–21 | 47 | 48 | 5 |
| October 7–10 | 44 | 50 | 6 |
| September 16–19 | 47 | 44 | 9 |
| August 12–15 | 44 | 43 | 13 |
| June | 41 | 50 | 9 |
| April–May | 43 | 49 | 8 |
| February | 41 | 47 | 12 |
| **1982** | | | |
| December | 40 | 52 | 8 |
| October | 47 | 44 | 9 |
| April | 46 | 46 | 8 |

*Asked of registered voters: Suppose the 1984 presidential election were being held today. If President Ronald Reagan were the Republican candidate and Senator John Glenn were the Democratic candidate, which would you like to see win? [Those who were undecided were then asked: As of today, do you lean more to Reagan, the Republican, or to Glenn, the Democrat?]*

Reagan ............................49%
Glenn .............................44
Other; undecided ................. 7

### By Sex
#### Male

Reagan ............................55%
Glenn .............................40
Other; undecided ................. 5

### Female

Reagan ............................44%
Glenn .............................48
Other; undecided ................. 8

### By Ethnic Background
#### White

Reagan ............................54%
Glenn .............................40
Other; undecided ................. 6

### Nonwhite

Reagan ............................13%
Glenn .............................75
Other; undecided ................12

### Black

Reagan ............................14%
Glenn .............................73
Other; undecided ................13

### By Education
#### College Graduate

Reagan ............................48%
Glenn .............................48
Other; undecided ................. 4

### College Incomplete

Reagan ............................58%
Glenn .............................38
Other; undecided ................. 4

### High-School Graduate

Reagan ............................49%
Glenn .............................45
Other; undecided ................. 6

### Less Than High-School Graduate

Reagan ............................42%
Glenn .............................47
Other; undecided ................11

## By Region
### East
Reagan ...........................48%
Glenn ...........................45
Other; undecided .................. 7

### Midwest
Reagan ...........................56%
Glenn ...........................39
Other; undecided .................. 5

### South
Reagan ...........................43%
Glenn ...........................49
Other; undecided .................. 8

### West
Reagan ...........................51%
Glenn ...........................45
Other; undecided .................. 4

## By Age
### 18–29 Years
Reagan ...........................49%
Glenn ...........................43
Other; undecided .................. 8

### 30–49 Years
Reagan ...........................48%
Glenn ...........................47
Other; undecided .................. 5

### 50–64 Years
Reagan ...........................50%
Glenn ...........................46
Other; undecided .................. 4

### 65 Years and Over
Reagan ...........................51%
Glenn ...........................40
Other; undecided .................. 9

## By Income
### $40,000 and Over
Reagan ...........................61%
Glenn ...........................35
Other; undecided .................. 4

### $30,000–$39,999
Reagan ...........................59%
Glenn ...........................39
Other; undecided .................. 2

### $20,000–$29,999
Reagan ...........................54%
Glenn ...........................42
Other; undecided .................. 4

### $10,000–$19,999
Reagan ...........................47%
Glenn ...........................43
Other; undecided .................10

### Under $10,000
Reagan ...........................32%
Glenn ...........................61
Other; undecided .................. 7

## By Politics
### Republicans
Reagan ...........................86%
Glenn ...........................11
Other; undecided .................. 3

### Democrats
Reagan ...........................25%
Glenn ...........................68
Other; undecided .................. 7

### Independents
Reagan ...........................49%
Glenn ...........................42
Other; undecided .................. 9

## Selected National Trend

|  | Reagan | Glenn | Other; undecided |
|---|---|---|---|
| 1983 | | | |
| December 9–12 | 49% | 44% | 7% |
| November 18–21 | 47 | 47 | 6 |
| October 7–10 | 42 | 49 | 9 |
| September 16–19 | 42 | 48 | 10 |
| August 12–15 | 40 | 46 | 14 |
| June | 38 | 53 | 9 |
| April–May | 37 | 54 | 9 |
| February | 40 | 45 | 15 |
| 1982 | | | |
| December | 39 | 54 | 7 |

*Asked of Democrats and independents: Which one of the persons on this card would you like to see nominated as the Democratic party's candidate for president in 1984?\**

### Choice of Democrats**

| | |
|---|---|
| Walter Mondale | 40% |
| John Glenn | 24 |
| Jesse Jackson | 9 |
| George McGovern | 8 |
| Gary Hart | 3 |
| Alan Cranston | 3 |
| Ernest Hollings | 1 |
| Reubin Askew | 1 |
| None; don't know | 11 |

### Choice of Independents

| | |
|---|---|
| Glenn | 28% |
| Mondale | 26 |
| McGovern | 10 |
| Jackson | 6 |
| Cranston | 5 |
| Hart | 3 |
| Hollings | 1 |
| Askew | 1 |
| None; don't know | 20 |

*This survey was conducted before Jesse Jackson's successful efforts to gain the release of Lieutenant Robert Goodman, the American navy pilot who was captured by the Syrian government after his plane was shot down.

**The results of the five most recent surveys show considerable volatility in the race between Mondale and Glenn, characteristic of contests in which voters are not strongly committed to their choice of candidates. Consistent with earlier findings, none of the six other candidates on the list has proven to be a serious challenge to either Mondale or Glenn.

*Asked of Democrats: Suppose the choice for president in the Democratic convention in 1984 narrows down to Walter Mondale and John Glenn. Which would you prefer to have the Democratic convention select?*

### Choice of Democrats

| | |
|---|---|
| Mondale | 57% |
| Glenn | 34 |
| Undecided | 9 |

The following percentages represent the findings by strength of support:

### By Democrats

| | Mondale supporters | Glenn supporters |
|---|---|---|
| Strongly support | 35% | 27% |
| Moderately support | 61 | 64 |
| Can't say | 4 | 9 |

Note: The 1984 presidential election year opens on a cheerful political note for President Ronald Reagan who makes his best showing to date in test races against his chief Democratic rivals, Walter Mondale and John Glenn. Reagan leads Mondale 51% to 44% among registered voters. His best previous race, since these tests were started on a regular basis in 1982, was in September when the two men were in a statistical tie. The president leads Glenn by a 49% to 44% vote, a margin that is small enough to be a statistical tie. Reagan's best previous showing against Glenn was in November when they each received the support of 47% of registered voters.

Analysis of the strength of support given Mondale and Glenn shows a similar lack of commitment to either Democratic hopeful. In the case of both Mondale and Glenn, those who support them strongly are outnumbered 2 to 1 by those who only moderately back them in test races against Reagan. In contrast, Reagan backers are twice as likely to support the president strongly than they are moderately.

## JANUARY 12
## MOST ADMIRED WOMAN

Interviewing Date: 12/9–12/83
Survey #228-G

> *What woman that you have heard or read about, living today in any part of the world, do you admire the most? Who is your second choice?*

The following are listed in order of frequency of mention with first and second choices combined:

Margaret Thatcher
Mother Teresa of Calcutta
Nancy Reagan
Betty Ford
Jacqueline Kennedy Onassis
Barbara Walters
Sandra Day O'Connor
Princess Diana
Indira Gandhi
Queen Elizabeth II

Note: All but two of this year's ten most admired women appeared in the 1982 list as well. Absent from last year's ranking were Indira Gandhi and Jacqueline Kennedy Onassis.

Receiving frequent mention in the 1983 survey but not included in the top ten were former First Lady Rosalynn Carter, actresses Jane Fonda and Katharine Hepburn, former U.S. congresswoman Barbara Jordan, and civil rights activist Coretta King. The latter two women owe at least part of their high ranking to the votes of blacks, among whom Mrs. King ranks first and Mrs. Jordan third. Blacks awarded second place to another former congresswoman, Shirley Chisholm.

For the most part, men and women tend to admire the same individuals, but their ranking frequently differs. For example, Rosalynn Carter was ranked fifth by men but failed to make the top ten list among women. The top five choices of the men surveyed were Margaret Thatcher, Mother Teresa, Nancy Reagan, Barbara Walters, and Rosalynn Carter. In comparison, Mother Teresa, Nancy Reagan, Margaret Thatcher, Betty Ford, and Jacqueline Onassis were the corresponding choices among the women.

Survey respondents in these studies, which the Gallup Poll has conducted for more than three decades, are asked to give their choices without the aid of a prearranged list of names. This procedure, while opening the field to all possible choices, tends to favor those who are currently or have recently been in the news.

## JANUARY 15
## MOST ADMIRED MAN

Interviewing Date: 12/9–12/83
Survey #228-G

> *What man that you have heard or read about, living today in any part of the world, do you admire the most? Who is your second choice?*

The following are listed in order of frequency of mention with first and second choices combined:

Ronald Reagan
Pope John Paul II
Lech Walesa
Reverend Billy Graham
Edward Kennedy
Jimmy Carter ⎫
Jesse Jackson ⎭ tie
John Glenn
Henry Kissinger
Walter Mondale

Note: All but two of the men in the 1983 top ten also appeared in the 1982 audit. The two newcomers are Democratic candidates John Glenn and Walter Mondale. Lech Walesa, the Polish labor union leader and 1983 winner of the Nobel Peace Prize, moved up to third place in the latest audit, from sixth place in 1982. Jesse Jackson* advanced from ninth place to a tie for sixth.

Survey respondents in these studies, which have been conducted for more than three decades, are asked to give their choices without a list of names. This procedure, while opening the field to all possible choices, tends to favor those who are currently in the news.

*This survey was conducted before Jackson obtained the release of the downed American navy pilot.


## JANUARY 16
## REAGAN'S DEPTH OF SUPPORT UNMATCHED BY DEMOCRATIC HOPEFULS*

At the end of this month President Ronald Reagan is expected to announce that he will seek a second term. The latest results from the national polling organizations suggest that he has a slightly better than even chance of being reelected. A closer look at these polls indicates that, if anything, they may understate the president's political strength at this time.

While Reagan runs an even race against either Walter Mondale or John Glenn in the latest Gallup, *Washington Post*/ABC, and *Los Angeles Times* polls, Reagan's hard-core support is more than double that of Glenn or Mondale. As the president's approval ratings have improved over the past six months, opposition to the administration has failed to coalesce around either of the Democratic front-runners. The successful invasion of Grenada in October served to catalyze public

*This Gallup analysis was written by Andrew Kohut, president of the Gallup Organization, Inc.

opinion about the president. However, Reagan's ratings had been steadily improving throughout 1983 as the country began to shake off the effects of the recession.

In Gallup's first 1983 rating, 37% approved of the way Reagan was handling his presidential duties. By the end of the year, the proportion approving of his performance had increased to over 50%. Reagan's dramatically improved ratings are not the sole cause for Republican optimism. The president continues to have significant problems with blacks, women, union members, and others who either believe they have been dealt with unfairly by the administration or who worry about Reagan's foreign policy.

The Democrats themselves have given the president much to cheer about. Neither Mondale nor Glenn has been able to generate much public enthusiasm. In the most recent Gallup Poll, registered voters were asked how strongly they felt about their expressed preferences in this fall's election. As the following shows, those who were strongly committed to the president far outnumbered those strongly committed to Mondale or Glenn, even though the overall levels of support were about equal in each contest:

### Reagan Versus Glenn*

| | |
|---|---|
| Reagan | 49% |
| Strongly support | 31 |
| Moderately support | 18 |
| Glenn | 44 |
| Strongly support | 14 |
| Moderately support | 30 |
| Other; undecided | 7 |

### Reagan Versus Mondale*

| | |
|---|---|
| Reagan | 51% |
| Strongly support | 32 |
| Moderately support | 19 |
| Mondale | 44 |
| Strongly support | 16 |
| Moderately support | 28 |
| Other; undecided | 5 |

*Based on registered voters, December 9–12, 1983

The Democrats have a large base of anti-Reagan voters from which to draw support. Reagan has evoked more intense feelings, negative as well as positive, than any other president in the recent past. Yet neither Glenn nor Mondale seems to be able to make much of an impression on the large number of voters who do not want to see Reagan reelected.

In August the *Washington Post*/ABC poll asked supporters of Reagan, Glenn, and Mondale why they responded as they did. Over 70% of Reagan supporters said they chose the president because of their positive opinions of him. Only about one-third of Mondale's backing and a similar proportion of Glenn's support was positive. Most said they chose a Democratic candidate because of negative opinions about Reagan. The *Washington Post*/ABC pollsters repeated the question in December and came up with exactly the same findings. The Democratic candidates clearly have failed, so far, to give people reasons to vote for them except as an antidote to Reagan.

As the campaign progresses, Democrats will surely rally around their party's candidate, but neither front-runner has been able to capture the attention of voters. For months, voter preference between Glenn and Mondale has see-sawed, as only a minority of voters have strong convictions about their choice for the Democratic nomination.

Perhaps even more than most incumbent presidents Reagan's advantage is that he is the center of national attention. The success of Grenada, coming at a time when the recovery hit its full stride, combined to increase the president's stature, dwarfing his opponents by comparison.

Public opinion, however, tends to run in cycles. Reagan, at least for now, has the momentum, but there is still substantial opportunity for the Democrats. Whether they can capitalize on the issues of growing public dissatisfaction with the status quo in Lebanon and Central America, lasting pain and suffering from the recession, and lingering perceptions of the present administration's insensitivity to women and minority groups will ultimately decide the election.

## JANUARY 17
## DEMOCRATIC PRESIDENTIAL CANDIDATES

Interviewing Date: 1/13–16/84
Survey #229-G

*Asked of Democrats and independents: Which one of the persons on this card would you like to see nominated as the Democratic party's candidate for president this year?*

### Choice of Democrats

|  | Jan. 13–16, 1984 | Dec. 9–12, 1983 | Nov. 18–21, 1983 |
|---|---|---|---|
| Mondale | 47% | 40% | 47% |
| Glenn | 16 | 24 | 19 |
| Jackson | 9 | 10 | 7 |
| McGovern | 4 | 8 | 7 |
| Cranston | 4 | 3 | 3 |
| Hart | 3 | 3 | 2 |
| Askew | 1 | 1 | 3 |
| Hollings | 1 | 1 | 1 |
| None; don't know | 15 | 10 | 11 |

### Choice of Independents

|  | Jan. 13–16, 1984 | Dec. 9–12, 1983 | Nov. 18–21, 1983 |
|---|---|---|---|
| Mondale | 30% | 26% | 27% |
| Glenn | 24 | 28 | 27 |
| Jackson | 9 | 6 | 6 |
| McGovern | 8 | 10 | 9 |
| Cranston | 3 | 5 | 2 |
| Hart | 2 | 3 | 3 |
| Askew | 1 | 1 | 2 |
| Hollings | 1 | 1 | 3 |
| None; don't know | 22 | 20 | 21 |

*Asked of Democrats and independents: Suppose the choice for president in the Democratic convention this year narrows down to Walter Mondale and John Glenn. Which one would you prefer to have the Democratic convention select? Do you strongly support him, or do you only moderately support him?*

## Choice of Democrats

*Jan. 13–16, 1984*

Mondale . . . . . . . . . . . . . . . . . . . . . . . . . 67%
  Strongly support . . . . . . . . . . . . . .26
  Moderately support . . . . . . . . . . . .40
  Can't say . . . . . . . . . . . . . . . . . . . 1
Glenn . . . . . . . . . . . . . . . . . . . . . . . . . .25
  Strongly support . . . . . . . . . . . . . . 8
  Moderately support . . . . . . . . . . . .16
  Can't say . . . . . . . . . . . . . . . . . . . 1
Undecided . . . . . . . . . . . . . . . . . . . . . . 8

*Dec. 9–12, 1983*

Mondale . . . . . . . . . . . . . . . . . . . . . . . . . 57%
  Strongly support . . . . . . . . . . . . . .20
  Moderately support . . . . . . . . . . . .37
Glenn . . . . . . . . . . . . . . . . . . . . . . . . . .34
  Strongly support . . . . . . . . . . . . . . 9
  Moderately support . . . . . . . . . . . .25
Undecided . . . . . . . . . . . . . . . . . . . . . . 9

### Selected National Trend

| | Mondale | Glenn | Undecided |
|---|---|---|---|
| *1984* | | | |
| January 13–16 | 67% | 25% | 8% |
| *1983* | | | |
| December 9–12 | 57 | 34 | 9 |
| November 18–21 | 64 | 29 | 7 |
| August | 49 | 30 | 21 |
| June | 57 | 31 | 12 |
| February | 52 | 30 | 18 |
| *1982* | | | |
| December | 59 | 28 | 13 |

### Choice of Independents

*Jan. 13–16, 1984*

Mondale . . . . . . . . . . . . . . . . . . . . . . . . . 45%
  Strongly support . . . . . . . . . . . . . . 9
  Moderately support . . . . . . . . . . . .34
  Can't say . . . . . . . . . . . . . . . . . . . 2
Glenn . . . . . . . . . . . . . . . . . . . . . . . . . .42
  Strongly support . . . . . . . . . . . . . . 8
  Moderately support . . . . . . . . . . . .31
  Can't say . . . . . . . . . . . . . . . . . . . 3
Undecided . . . . . . . . . . . . . . . . . . . . . .13

*Dec. 9–12, 1983*

Mondale . . . . . . . . . . . . . . . . . . . . . . . . . 44%
  Strongly support . . . . . . . . . . . . . . 7
  Moderately support . . . . . . . . . . . . 37
Glenn . . . . . . . . . . . . . . . . . . . . . . . . . .42
  Strongly support . . . . . . . . . . . . . . 7
  Moderately support . . . . . . . . . . . . 35
Undecided . . . . . . . . . . . . . . . . . . . . . .14

### Selected National Trend

| | Mondale | Glenn | Undecided |
|---|---|---|---|
| *1984* | | | |
| January 13–16 | 45% | 42% | 13% |
| *1983* | | | |
| December 9–12 | 44 | 42 | 14 |
| November 18–21 | 42 | 42 | 16 |
| August | 34 | 39 | 27 |
| June | 38 | 43 | 19 |
| February | 42 | 35 | 23 |
| *1982* | | | |
| December | 41 | 40 | 19 |

Note: Former Vice-President Walter Mondale has forged into his largest lead to date over Senator John Glenn for the Democratic presidential nomination. In the latest national Gallup survey, Mondale received 47% of the nomination votes of Democrats to 16% for runner-up Glenn, a 31-percentage point margin. In the previous December contest, Mondale led Glenn 40% to 24%. The most recent survey was completed on the evening of January 16; thus, some interviews were conducted before and after the candidates' debate. However, this number is not large enough to affect materially the survey findings.

The Reverend Jesse Jackson placed third in the latest poll, with 9% of Democrats' support. This percentage is statistically unchanged from the 10% he received in December prior to his successful mission to obtain the release of the downed U.S. Navy flier from his Syrian captors.

The results of a nomination contest pitting the two front-runners against each other show Mondale now has a huge 42-point margin over Glenn (67% to 25%) among Democrats. In six earlier matches conducted in 1982 and 1983, Mondale's lead has ranged from a low of 19 points last August to a high of 35 points in November.

Not only does Mondale currently enjoy almost a 3-to-1 lead over Glenn among Democrats but also a substantially greater proportion of Mondale than Glenn backers says they strongly support their nomination candidate. Virtually all of Mondale's gain between the two most recent surveys among Democrats can be traced to a net increase in the percentage who strongly support him, from 20% in December to 26% in January. On the other hand, Glenn's attrition stems mainly from a 9-point decrease in the proportion of Democrats who back him only moderately—from 25% in December to 16% at present—while his strong supporters have stayed about the same in numbers (9% and 8% in December and January, respectively). In earlier surveys, changes in each candidate's standing were more closely related to increases and decreases in the undecided vote, a hallmark of contests in which voters are not strongly committed to their choice of candidates.

As consistently has been the case, the nomination race is much closer among political independents, who represent approximately one-third of the nation's voters and who may vote in states with "open" primaries and caucuses. In the current survey, Mondale receives 30% of independents' votes for the Democratic nomination, followed by Glenn with 24%, Jackson with 9%, and McGovern with 8%. There has been little movement in either the head-to-head matches among independents or in the strength of each rival's recent support.

## JANUARY 22
## PRESIDENTIAL TRIAL HEATS

Interviewing Date: 1/13–16/84
Survey #229-G

*Asked of registered voters: Suppose the 1984 presidential election were being held today. If President Ronald Reagan were the Republican candidate and Walter Mondale were the Democratic candidate, which would you like to see win? [Those who were undecided were then asked: As of today, do you lean more to Reagan, the Republican, or to Mondale, the Democrat?]*

Reagan . . . . . . . . . . . . . . . . . . . . . . . . . .48%
Mondale . . . . . . . . . . . . . . . . . . . . . . . . . .47
Other; undecided . . . . . . . . . . . . . . . . . . . . 5

### By Sex
#### *Male*

Reagan . . . . . . . . . . . . . . . . . . . . . . . . . .54%
Mondale . . . . . . . . . . . . . . . . . . . . . . . . . .41
Other; undecided . . . . . . . . . . . . . . . . . . . . 5

#### *Female*

Reagan . . . . . . . . . . . . . . . . . . . . . . . . . .43%
Mondale . . . . . . . . . . . . . . . . . . . . . . . . . .52
Other; undecided . . . . . . . . . . . . . . . . . . . . 5

### By Ethnic Background
#### *White*

Reagan . . . . . . . . . . . . . . . . . . . . . . . . . .53%
Mondale . . . . . . . . . . . . . . . . . . . . . . . . . .42
Other; undecided . . . . . . . . . . . . . . . . . . . . 5

#### *Nonwhite*

Reagan . . . . . . . . . . . . . . . . . . . . . . . . . . 8%
Mondale . . . . . . . . . . . . . . . . . . . . . . . . . .84
Other; undecided . . . . . . . . . . . . . . . . . . . . 7

#### *Black*

Reagan . . . . . . . . . . . . . . . . . . . . . . . . . . 7%
Mondale . . . . . . . . . . . . . . . . . . . . . . . . . .85
Other; undecided . . . . . . . . . . . . . . . . . . . . 8

### By Education
#### *College Graduate*

Reagan . . . . . . . . . . . . . . . . . . . . . . . . . .57%
Mondale . . . . . . . . . . . . . . . . . . . . . . . . . .40
Other; undecided . . . . . . . . . . . . . . . . . . . . 3

#### *College Incomplete*

Reagan . . . . . . . . . . . . . . . . . . . . . . . . . .57%
Mondale . . . . . . . . . . . . . . . . . . . . . . . . . .39
Other; undecided . . . . . . . . . . . . . . . . . . . . 4

### High-School Graduate

Reagan ............................46%
Mondale ..........................47
Other; undecided ................. 7

### Less Than High-School Graduate

Reagan ............................33%
Mondale ..........................61
Other; undecided ................. 6

## By Region
### East

Reagan ............................48%
Mondale ..........................48
Other; undecided ................. 4

### Midwest

Reagan ............................50%
Mondale ..........................44
Other; undecided ................. 6

### South

Reagan ............................47%
Mondale ..........................47
Other; undecided ................. 6

### West

Reagan ............................46%
Mondale ..........................50
Other; undecided ................. 4

## By Politics
### Republicans

Reagan ............................85%
Mondale ..........................14
Other; undecided ................. 1

### Democrats

Reagan ............................21%
Mondale ..........................74
Other; undecided ................. 5

### Independents

Reagan ............................47%
Mondale ..........................43
Other; undecided ................10

*Asked of registered voters: Suppose the 1984
presidential election were being held today.
If President Ronald Reagan were the Republican candidate and Senator John Glenn were
the Democratic candidate, which would you
like to see win? [Those who were undecided
were then asked: As of today, do you lean
more to Reagan, the Republican, or to Glenn,
the Democrat?]*

Reagan ............................47%
Glenn ............................45
Other; undecided ................. 8

## By Sex
### Male

Reagan ............................51%
Glenn ............................43
Other; undecided ................. 6

### Female

Reagan ............................43%
Glenn ............................47
Other; undecided ................. 9

## By Ethnic Background
### White

Reagan ............................52%
Glenn ............................41
Other; undecided ................. 7

### Nonwhite

Reagan ............................10%
Glenn ............................77
Other; undecided ................13

### Black

Reagan ............................ 9%
Glenn ............................78
Other; undecided ................14

## By Education
### College Graduate
Reagan ............................49%
Glenn ............................48
Other; undecided ................... 3

### College Incomplete
Reagan ............................56%
Glenn ............................39
Other; undecided ................... 5

### High-School Graduate
Reagan ............................35%
Glenn ............................57
Other; undecided ................... 8

### Less Than High-School Graduate
Reagan ............................35%
Glenn ............................57
Other; undecided ................... 8

## By Region
### East
Reagan ............................48%
Glenn ............................44
Other; undecided ................... 9

### Midwest
Reagan ............................45%
Glenn ............................48
Other; undecided ................... 7

### South
Reagan ............................49%
Glenn ............................43
Other; undecided ................... 8

### West
Reagan ............................46%
Glenn ............................49
Other; undecided ................... 6

## By Politics
### Republicans
Reagan ............................83%
Glenn ............................13
Other; undecided ................... 4

### Democrats
Reagan ............................23%
Glenn ............................68
Other; undecided ................... 9

### Independents
Reagan ............................43%
Glenn ............................47
Other; undecided ..................10

*Asked of registered voters: Suppose the 1984 presidential election were being held today. If President Ronald Reagan were the Republican candidate and the Reverend Jesse Jackson were the Democratic candidate, which would you like to see win? [Those who were undecided were then asked: As of today, do you lean more to Reagan, the Republican, or to Jackson, the Democrat?]*

Reagan ............................68%
Jackson ............................23
Other; undecided ................... 9

## By Sex
### Male
Reagan ............................72%
Jackson ............................21
Other; undecided ................... 7

### Female
Reagan ............................64%
Jackson ............................26
Other; undecided ..................10

## By Ethnic Background
### White
Reagan . . . . . . . . . . . . . . . . . . . . . . . . . . . . .75%
Jackson . . . . . . . . . . . . . . . . . . . . . . . . . . . .16
Other; undecided . . . . . . . . . . . . . . . . . . . 9

### Nonwhite
Reagan . . . . . . . . . . . . . . . . . . . . . . . . . . . .10%
Jackson . . . . . . . . . . . . . . . . . . . . . . . . . . . .82
Other; undecided . . . . . . . . . . . . . . . . . . . 8

### Black
Reagan . . . . . . . . . . . . . . . . . . . . . . . . . . . . 5%
Jackson . . . . . . . . . . . . . . . . . . . . . . . . . . . .88
Other; undecided . . . . . . . . . . . . . . . . . . . 7

## By Education
### College Graduate
Reagan . . . . . . . . . . . . . . . . . . . . . . . . . . . .73%
Jackson . . . . . . . . . . . . . . . . . . . . . . . . . . . .21
Other; undecided . . . . . . . . . . . . . . . . . . . 6

### College Incomplete
Reagan . . . . . . . . . . . . . . . . . . . . . . . . . . . .73%
Jackson . . . . . . . . . . . . . . . . . . . . . . . . . . . .21
Other; undecided . . . . . . . . . . . . . . . . . . . 6

### High-School Graduate
Reagan . . . . . . . . . . . . . . . . . . . . . . . . . . . .66%
Jackson . . . . . . . . . . . . . . . . . . . . . . . . . . . .23
Other; undecided . . . . . . . . . . . . . . . . . . .11

### Less Than High-School Graduate
Reagan . . . . . . . . . . . . . . . . . . . . . . . . . . . .61%
Jackson . . . . . . . . . . . . . . . . . . . . . . . . . . . .29
Other; undecided . . . . . . . . . . . . . . . . . . .10

## By Region
### East
Reagan . . . . . . . . . . . . . . . . . . . . . . . . . . . .70%
Jackson . . . . . . . . . . . . . . . . . . . . . . . . . . . .22
Other; undecided . . . . . . . . . . . . . . . . . . . 8

### Midwest
Reagan . . . . . . . . . . . . . . . . . . . . . . . . . . . .70%
Jackson . . . . . . . . . . . . . . . . . . . . . . . . . . . .21
Other; undecided . . . . . . . . . . . . . . . . . . . 9

### South
Reagan . . . . . . . . . . . . . . . . . . . . . . . . . . . .64%
Jackson . . . . . . . . . . . . . . . . . . . . . . . . . . . .25
Other; undecided . . . . . . . . . . . . . . . . . . .11

### West
Reagan . . . . . . . . . . . . . . . . . . . . . . . . . . . .67%
Jackson . . . . . . . . . . . . . . . . . . . . . . . . . . . .27
Other; undecided . . . . . . . . . . . . . . . . . . . 6

## By Age
### 18–24 Years
Reagan . . . . . . . . . . . . . . . . . . . . . . . . . . . .65%
Jackson . . . . . . . . . . . . . . . . . . . . . . . . . . . .32
Other; undecided . . . . . . . . . . . . . . . . . . . 3

### 25–29 Years
Reagan . . . . . . . . . . . . . . . . . . . . . . . . . . . .63%
Jackson . . . . . . . . . . . . . . . . . . . . . . . . . . . .30
Other; undecided . . . . . . . . . . . . . . . . . . . 7

### 30–49 Years
Reagan . . . . . . . . . . . . . . . . . . . . . . . . . . . .67%
Jackson . . . . . . . . . . . . . . . . . . . . . . . . . . . .23
Other; undecided . . . . . . . . . . . . . . . . . . .10

### 50–64 Years
Reagan . . . . . . . . . . . . . . . . . . . . . . . . . . . .70%
Jackson . . . . . . . . . . . . . . . . . . . . . . . . . . . .22
Other; undecided . . . . . . . . . . . . . . . . . . . 8

### 65 Years and Over
Reagan . . . . . . . . . . . . . . . . . . . . . . . . . . . .71%
Jackson . . . . . . . . . . . . . . . . . . . . . . . . . . . .17
Other; undecided . . . . . . . . . . . . . . . . . . .12

## By Income

### $40,000 and Over

Reagan ...........................81%
Jackson ...........................15
Other; undecided .................. 4

### $30,000–$39,999

Reagan ...........................74%
Jackson ...........................19
Other; undecided .................. 7

### $20,000–$29,999

Reagan ...........................76%
Jackson ...........................17
Other; undecided .................. 7

### $10,000–$19,999

Reagan ...........................65%
Jackson ...........................27
Other; undecided .................. 8

### Under $10,000

Reagan ...........................54%
Jackson ...........................34
Other; undecided .................11

## By Politics

### Republicans

Reagan ...........................93%
Jackson ........................... 4
Other; undecided .................. 3

### Democrats

Reagan ...........................50%
Jackson ...........................38
Other; undecided .................12

### Independents

Reagan ...........................69%
Jackson ...........................22
Other; undecided .................. 9

## By Religion

### Protestants

Reagan ...........................68%
Jackson ...........................23
Other; undecided .................. 9

### Catholics

Reagan ...........................71%
Jackson ...........................19
Other; undecided .................10

## By Occupation

### Professional and Business

Reagan ...........................75%
Jackson ...........................19
Other; undecided .................. 6

### Clerical and Sales

Reagan ...........................70%
Jackson ...........................26
Other; undecided .................. 4

### Manual Workers

Reagan ...........................64%
Jackson ...........................27
Other; undecided .................. 9

### Nonlabor Force

Reagan ...........................66%
Jackson ...........................22
Other; undecided .................12

## By Community Size

### One Million and Over

Reagan ...........................63%
Jackson ...........................28
Other; undecided .................. 9

### 500,000–999,999

Reagan ...........................66%
Jackson ...........................31
Other; undecided .................. 3

### 50,000–499,999

Reagan ............................72%
Jackson ...........................21
Other; undecided ................. 7

### 2,500–49,999

Reagan ............................75%
Jackson ...........................16
Other; undecided ................. 9

### Under 2,500; Rural

Reagan ............................68%
Jackson ...........................20
Other; undecided .................12

### Labor Union Families

Reagan ............................65%
Jackson ...........................23
Other; undecided .................12

### Nonlabor Union Families

Reagan ............................69%
Jackson ...........................24
Other; undecided ................. 7

### Selected National Trend

|  | Reagan | Jackson | Other; undecided |
|---|---|---|---|
| **1984** |  |  |  |
| January 13–16 | 68% | 23% | 9% |
| **1983** |  |  |  |
| November 18–21 | 70 | 20 | 10 |
| October | 64 | 24 | 12 |
| July–August | 61 | 22 | 17 |

*Asked of registered voters: Suppose the 1984 presidential election were being held today. If President Ronald Reagan were the Republican candidate and George McGovern were the Democratic candidate, which would you like to see win? [Those who were undecided were then asked: As of today, do you lean more to Reagan, the Republican, or to McGovern, the Democrat?]*

Reagan ............................60%
McGovern .........................33
Other; undecided ................. 7

### By Sex
#### Male

Reagan ............................65%
McGovern .........................28
Other; undecided ................. 7

#### Female

Reagan ............................54%
McGovern .........................38
Other; undecided ................. 8

### By Ethnic Background
#### White

Reagan ............................65%
McGovern .........................28
Other; undecided ................. 7

#### Nonwhite

Reagan ............................15%
McGovern .........................73
Other; undecided .................12

#### Black

Reagan ............................11%
McGovern .........................77
Other; undecided .................12

### By Education
#### College Graduate

Reagan ............................69%
McGovern .........................27
Other; undecided ................. 4

#### College Incomplete

Reagan ............................67%
McGovern .........................27
Other; undecided ................. 6

### High-School Graduate

Reagan ..............................58%
McGovern ...........................33
Other; undecided ................... 9

### Less Than High-School Graduate

Reagan ..............................47%
McGovern ...........................44
Other; undecided ................... 9

## By Region
### East

Reagan ..............................62%
McGovern ...........................32
Other; undecided ................... 6

### Midwest

Reagan ..............................59%
McGovern ...........................32
Other; undecided ................... 9

### South

Reagan ..............................58%
McGovern ...........................33
Other; undecided ................... 9

### West

Reagan ..............................59%
McGovern ...........................36
Other; undecided ................... 5

## By Age
### 18–24 Years

Reagan ..............................62%
McGovern ...........................33
Other; undecided ................... 5

### 25–29 Years

Reagan ..............................57%
McGovern ...........................39
Other; undecided ................... 4

### 30–49 Years

Reagan ..............................60%
McGovern ...........................32
Other; undecided ................... 8

### 50–64 Years

Reagan ..............................59%
McGovern ...........................34
Other; undecided ................... 7

### 65 Years and Over

Reagan ..............................58%
McGovern ...........................32
Other; undecided ................... 9

## By Politics
### Republicans

Reagan ..............................92%
McGovern ........................... 6
Other; undecided ................... 2

### Democrats

Reagan ..............................35%
McGovern ...........................55
Other; undecided ...................10

### Independents

Reagan ..............................61%
McGovern ...........................29
Other; undecided ...................10

Gallup Poll history indicates that the candidate ahead in test races early in an election year usually prevails in November. In 1980, however, Ronald Reagan was only the second candidate in Gallup Poll history to reverse the trend; John Kennedy in 1960 was the first.

### January 1980

Jimmy Carter ......................62%
Ronald Reagan .....................33*
Undecided ......................... 5

### March 1976

Jimmy Carter . . . . . . . . . . . . . . . . . . . . . . . 47%*
Gerald Ford . . . . . . . . . . . . . . . . . . . . . . 42
Undecided . . . . . . . . . . . . . . . . . . . . . . . 11

### February 1972

Richard Nixon . . . . . . . . . . . . . . . . . . . . . 49%*
George McGovern . . . . . . . . . . . . . . . . . . . 34
George Wallace . . . . . . . . . . . . . . . . . . . . 11
Undecided . . . . . . . . . . . . . . . . . . . . . . . 6

### April 1968

Richard Nixon . . . . . . . . . . . . . . . . . . . . . 43%*
Hubert Humphrey . . . . . . . . . . . . . . . . . . . 34
George Wallace . . . . . . . . . . . . . . . . . . . . 9
Undecided . . . . . . . . . . . . . . . . . . . . . . . 14

### January 1964

Lyndon Johnson . . . . . . . . . . . . . . . . . . . . 75%*
Barry Goldwater . . . . . . . . . . . . . . . . . . . . 18
Undecided . . . . . . . . . . . . . . . . . . . . . . . 7

### January 1960

Richard Nixon . . . . . . . . . . . . . . . . . . . . . 48%
John Kennedy . . . . . . . . . . . . . . . . . . . . . 43*
Undecided . . . . . . . . . . . . . . . . . . . . . . . 9

### January 1956

Dwight Eisenhower . . . . . . . . . . . . . . . . . . 61%*
Adlai Stevenson . . . . . . . . . . . . . . . . . . . . 35
Undecided . . . . . . . . . . . . . . . . . . . . . . . 4

### June 1952

Dwight Eisenhower . . . . . . . . . . . . . . . . . . 59%*
Adlai Stevenson . . . . . . . . . . . . . . . . . . . . 31
Undecided . . . . . . . . . . . . . . . . . . . . . . . 10

### January 1948

Harry Truman . . . . . . . . . . . . . . . . . . . . . 46%*
Thomas Dewey . . . . . . . . . . . . . . . . . . . . 41
Henry Wallace . . . . . . . . . . . . . . . . . . . . . 7
Undecided . . . . . . . . . . . . . . . . . . . . . . . 6

### April–May 1944

Franklin Roosevelt . . . . . . . . . . . . . . . . . . 47%*
Thomas Dewey . . . . . . . . . . . . . . . . . . . . 40
Undecided . . . . . . . . . . . . . . . . . . . . . . . 13

### July 1940

Franklin Roosevelt . . . . . . . . . . . . . . . . . . 48%*
Wendell Willkie . . . . . . . . . . . . . . . . . . . . 42
Undecided . . . . . . . . . . . . . . . . . . . . . . . 10

### July 1936

Franklin Roosevelt . . . . . . . . . . . . . . . . . . 49%*
Alfred Landon . . . . . . . . . . . . . . . . . . . . . 45
Undecided . . . . . . . . . . . . . . . . . . . . . . . 6

*Winner in November

## JANUARY 26
## LEBANON SITUATION

Interviewing Date: 1/13–16/84
Survey #229-G

*Do you think the United States should withdraw its troops from Lebanon at this time, or not?*

Should . . . . . . . . . . . . . . . . . . . . . . . . . . 57%
Should not . . . . . . . . . . . . . . . . . . . . . . . 34
No opinion . . . . . . . . . . . . . . . . . . . . . . . 9

### By Sex
#### Male

Should . . . . . . . . . . . . . . . . . . . . . . . . . . 54%
Should not . . . . . . . . . . . . . . . . . . . . . . . 40
No opinion . . . . . . . . . . . . . . . . . . . . . . . 6

#### Female

Should . . . . . . . . . . . . . . . . . . . . . . . . . . 60%
Should not . . . . . . . . . . . . . . . . . . . . . . . 29
No opinion . . . . . . . . . . . . . . . . . . . . . . . 11

## By Ethnic Background
### White
Should . . . . . . . . . . . . . . . . . . . . . . . . . . . .56%
Should not . . . . . . . . . . . . . . . . . . . . . . . .36
No opinion . . . . . . . . . . . . . . . . . . . . . . . 8

### Nonwhite
Should . . . . . . . . . . . . . . . . . . . . . . . . . . . .68%
Should not . . . . . . . . . . . . . . . . . . . . . . . .19
No opinion . . . . . . . . . . . . . . . . . . . . . . . .13

### Black
Should . . . . . . . . . . . . . . . . . . . . . . . . . . . .71%
Should not . . . . . . . . . . . . . . . . . . . . . . . .17
No opinion . . . . . . . . . . . . . . . . . . . . . . . .12

## By Education
### College Graduate
Should . . . . . . . . . . . . . . . . . . . . . . . . . . . .58%
Should not . . . . . . . . . . . . . . . . . . . . . . . .36
No opinion . . . . . . . . . . . . . . . . . . . . . . . 6

### College Incomplete
Should . . . . . . . . . . . . . . . . . . . . . . . . . . . .55%
Should not . . . . . . . . . . . . . . . . . . . . . . . .37
No opinion . . . . . . . . . . . . . . . . . . . . . . . 8

### High-School Graduate
Should . . . . . . . . . . . . . . . . . . . . . . . . . . . .56%
Should not . . . . . . . . . . . . . . . . . . . . . . . .35
No opinion . . . . . . . . . . . . . . . . . . . . . . . 9

### Less Than High-School Graduate
Should . . . . . . . . . . . . . . . . . . . . . . . . . . . .61%
Should not . . . . . . . . . . . . . . . . . . . . . . . .29
No opinion . . . . . . . . . . . . . . . . . . . . . . . .10

## By Region
### East
Should . . . . . . . . . . . . . . . . . . . . . . . . . . . .61%
Should not . . . . . . . . . . . . . . . . . . . . . . . .30
No opinion . . . . . . . . . . . . . . . . . . . . . . . 9

### Midwest
Should . . . . . . . . . . . . . . . . . . . . . . . . . . . .57%
Should not . . . . . . . . . . . . . . . . . . . . . . . .36
No opinion . . . . . . . . . . . . . . . . . . . . . . . 7

### South
Should . . . . . . . . . . . . . . . . . . . . . . . . . . . .52%
Should not . . . . . . . . . . . . . . . . . . . . . . . .37
No opinion . . . . . . . . . . . . . . . . . . . . . . . .11

### West
Should . . . . . . . . . . . . . . . . . . . . . . . . . . . .62%
Should not . . . . . . . . . . . . . . . . . . . . . . . .32
No opinion . . . . . . . . . . . . . . . . . . . . . . . 6

## By Age
### 18–24 Years
Should . . . . . . . . . . . . . . . . . . . . . . . . . . . .51%
Should not . . . . . . . . . . . . . . . . . . . . . . . .42
No opinion . . . . . . . . . . . . . . . . . . . . . . . 7

### 25–29 Years
Should . . . . . . . . . . . . . . . . . . . . . . . . . . . .63%
Should not . . . . . . . . . . . . . . . . . . . . . . . .29
No opinion . . . . . . . . . . . . . . . . . . . . . . . 8

### 30–49 Years
Should . . . . . . . . . . . . . . . . . . . . . . . . . . . .53%
Should not . . . . . . . . . . . . . . . . . . . . . . . .40
No opinion . . . . . . . . . . . . . . . . . . . . . . . 7

### 50 Years and Over
Should . . . . . . . . . . . . . . . . . . . . . . . . . . . .62%
Should not . . . . . . . . . . . . . . . . . . . . . . . .26
No opinion . . . . . . . . . . . . . . . . . . . . . . . .11

## By Politics
### Republicans
Should . . . . . . . . . . . . . . . . . . . . . . . . . . . .42%
Should not . . . . . . . . . . . . . . . . . . . . . . . .49
No opinion . . . . . . . . . . . . . . . . . . . . . . . 9

### Democrats

Approve .........................69%
Disapprove ......................24
No opinion ...................... 7

### Independents

Approve .........................58%
Disapprove ......................34
No opinion ...................... 8

*Do you think the United States made a mis-*
*take in sending the marines to Lebanon, or*
*not?*

Yes ............................52%
No .............................39
No opinion ...................... 9

## By Sex
### Male

Yes ............................50%
No .............................44
No opinion ...................... 6

### Female

Yes ............................54%
No .............................34
No opinion .....................12

## By Ethnic Background
### White

Yes ............................50%
No .............................41
No opinion ...................... 9

### Nonwhite

Yes ............................68%
No .............................20
No opinion .....................12

### Black

Yes ............................72%
No .............................17
No opinion .....................11

## By Education
### College Graduate

Yes ............................53%
No .............................40
No opinion ...................... 7

### College Incomplete

Yes ............................47%
No .............................45
No opinion ...................... 8

### High-School Graduate

Yes ............................51%
No .............................41
No opinion ...................... 8

### Less Than High-School Graduate

Yes ............................58%
No .............................29
No opinion .....................13

## By Region
### East

Yes ............................57%
No .............................35
No opinion ...................... 8

### Midwest

Yes ............................48%
No .............................43
No opinion ...................... 9

### South

Yes ............................48%
No .............................40
No opinion .....................12

### West

Yes ............................57%
No .............................36
No opinion ...................... 7

## By Age

### 18–24 Years

Yes ............................46%
No .............................47
No opinion ........................ 7

### 25–29 Years

Yes ............................57%
No .............................33
No opinion ........................10

### 30–49 Years

Yes ............................48%
No .............................45
No opinion ........................ 7

### 50 Years and Over

Yes ............................57%
No .............................31
No opinion ........................12

## By Politics

### Republicans

Yes ............................35%
No .............................56
No opinion ........................ 9

### Democrats

Yes ............................63%
No .............................29
No opinion ........................ 8

### Independents

Yes ............................55%
No .............................36
No opinion ........................ 9

## Selected National Trend

| | Yes | No | No opinion |
|---|---|---|---|
| *1984* | | | |
| January 13–16 | 52% | 39% | 9% |
| *1983* | | | |
| December | 47 | 44 | 9 |
| November | 45 | 45 | 10 |
| October | 51 | 37 | 12 |

As would be expected, a large majority (85%) of those who think we made a mistake sending troops to Lebanon want them brought home. Of particular interest is the fact that fully one-fourth (26%) of those who think we did not make a mistake nevertheless want our men to be withdrawn, as seen in the following table:

### Mistake Sending Troops?

| | Total | Yes (52%) | No (39%) |
|---|---|---|---|
| Withdraw troops? | | | |
| Yes ........... | 57% | 85% | 26% |
| No ........... | 34 | 11 | 68 |
| No opinion ..... | 9 | 4 | 6 |

Note: A majority of Americans today (57%) wants the United States to withdraw its troops from Lebanon. The same survey shows 52% saying the United States made a mistake in sending troops to that part of the world, an increase of 7 percentage points since a November survey.

The current findings suggest that the public's positive reaction to the successful operation in Grenada may be beginning to wear off. As reflected in the November survey, opposition to our involvement in Lebanon lessened as the public rallied around President Ronald Reagan at the time of the Grenada invasion.

The partisan nature of the debate on these issues between the Democratic presidential candidates and the Reagan forces is reflected in the views of the electorate. Two-thirds (69%) of Democrats compared to 42% of Republicans favor withdrawing our troops from Lebanon. In addition, 63% of Democrats and 35% of Republicans think we were wrong to send U.S. military forces there in the first place.

## JANUARY 29
## PRESIDENT REAGAN

Interviewing Date: 1/13–16/84
Survey #229-G

*Do you approve or disapprove of the way Ronald Reagan is handling his job as president?*

Approve ........................... 52%
Disapprove ......................... 38
No opinion ......................... 10

### Reagan Approval Ratings

#### *(Two-Survey Average)*

| | December–January 1983–84 | 1982–83 | Point difference |
|---|---|---|---|
| National | 53% | 39% | +14 |
| **By Sex** | | | |
| Male | 58% | 44% | +14 |
| Female | 48 | 33 | +15 |
| **By Race** | | | |
| White | 58% | 43% | +15 |
| Black | 14 | 10 | +4 |
| **By Education** | | | |
| College | 59% | 48% | +11 |
| High school | 52 | 38 | +14 |
| Grade school | 39 | 23 | +16 |
| **By Region** | | | |
| East | 50% | 35% | +15 |
| Midwest | 57 | 43 | +14 |
| South | 54 | 37 | +17 |
| West | 51 | 41 | +10 |
| **By Age** | | | |
| 18–29 years | 52% | 42% | +10 |
| 30–49 years | 56 | 39 | +17 |
| 50 years and over | 52 | 36 | +16 |
| **By Politics** | | | |
| Republicans | 83% | 72% | +11 |
| Democrats | 33 | 19 | +14 |
| Independents | 56 | 42 | +14 |

### Presidential Approval Ratings*

| | Jan. 4th year | Average for Year 3rd year | 2nd year | 1st year |
|---|---|---|---|---|
| Ronald Reagan | 52% | 44% | 44% | 58% |
| Jimmy Carter | 56 | 38 | 46 | 62 |
| Richard Nixon | 49 | 50 | 57 | 61 |
| Dwight Eisenhower | 76 | 71 | 65 | 69 |

*This table shows Reagan's approval rating averages for his first three years in office and those for his elected predecessors at comparable points in their tenure. Also shown are the approval ratings each received at the start of his fourth year.

### Selected National Trend
#### *(Reagan Performance Ratings)*

| | Approve | Dis-approve | No opinion |
|---|---|---|---|
| **1984** | | | |
| January 13–16 ...... | 52% | 38% | 10% |
| **1983** | | | |
| December ......... | 54 | 38 | 8 |
| November ......... | 53 | 37 | 10 |
| October ........... | 45 | 44 | 11 |
| September ........ | 47 | 42 | 11 |
| August ............ | 44 | 46 | 10 |
| July .............. | 42 | 47 | 11 |
| June .............. | 43 | 45 | 12 |
| May .............. | 43 | 45 | 12 |
| April ............. | 41 | 49 | 10 |
| March ............ | 41 | 49 | 10 |
| February ......... | 40 | 50 | 10 |
| January ........... | 35 | 56 | 9 |

Note: As the nation awaits President Ronald Reagan's decision on whether or not he will seek a second term, he is in a stronger position for a reelection bid than has been the case in at least two years. Reagan's strength at the start of his fourth year in office is reflected in two key Gallup measurements. First, his overall standing with the American people is as high today as it has been at any point in over two years. Second, the president's renewed popularity is reflected in his recent stronger performance in test elections against potential Democratic challengers Walter Mondale and John Glenn.

In the latest survey (mid-January), 52% approve of Reagan's handling of his presidential duties while 38% disapprove. The last time Reagan had a significantly higher job performance rating was in August 1981, when 60% approved and 29% disapproved. His highest approval rating of 68% was recorded in May 1981 shortly after he took office. The 35% shown for January 1983 represents his lowest rating to date.

The president's improved performance ratings since last year are found in all major population groups. Reagan consistently has received lower approval ratings from women and blacks. Although these differences are still apparent in the latest surveys, he clearly has made progress compared to findings one year earlier.

## FEBRUARY 2
## INFLATION AND UNEMPLOYMENT

Interviewing Date: 12/9–12/83
Survey #228-G

*The inflation rate is now running at about 5%. By this time next year, what do you think the inflation rate will be?*

|  | Dec. 1983* | Nov. 1982** | June 1982† |
|---|---|---|---|
| 9% or higher .... | 15% | 24% | 39% |
| 8% ............ | 10 | 16 | 11 |
| 7% ............ | 15 | 9 | 16 |
| 6% ............ | 12 | 17 | 10 |
| 5% ............ | 22 | 10 | 9 |
| 4% or lower ..... | 16 | 8 | 3 |
| No opinion ...... | 10 | 16 | 12 |
| Median average | 6.1% | 7.3% | 7.9% |

*The current unemployment rate is now 8.4%. By this time next year, what do you think the unemployment rate will be?*

|  | Dec. 1983* | Nov. 1982** | June 1982† |
|---|---|---|---|
| 10% or higher ... | 17% | 58% | 63% |
| 9% ............ | 9 | 12 | 12 |
| 8% ............ | 21 | 10 | 9 |
| 7% ............ | 16 | 4 | 5 |
| 6% ............ | 9 | 2 | 1 |
| 5% or lower ..... | 19 | 1 | 1 |
| No opinion ...... | 9 | 13 | 9 |
| Median average | 7.6% | 10.1% | 10.6% |

*Inflation rate at the end of 1984
**Inflation rate at the end of 1983
†Inflation rate at the end of 1982

## Inflation/Unemployment Forecasts

|  | Inflation 6% or lower | Unemploy- ment 7% or lower |
|---|---|---|
| National . . . . . . . . . . | 50% | 44% |

### By Sex

|  |  |  |
|---|---|---|
| Male . . . . . . . . . . . . | 54% | 45% |
| Female . . . . . . . . . . . | 45 | 43 |

### By Ethnic Background

|  |  |  |
|---|---|---|
| White . . . . . . . . . . . . | 53% | 45% |
| Nonwhite . . . . . . . . . | 30 | 33 |
| Black . . . . . . . . . . . . | 30 | 38 |

### By Education

|  |  |  |
|---|---|---|
| College . . . . . . . . . . | 62% | 48% |
| High school or less . . | 42 | 41 |

### By Region

|  |  |  |
|---|---|---|
| East . . . . . . . . . . . . . | 51% | 42% |
| Midwest . . . . . . . . . . | 46 | 47 |
| South . . . . . . . . . . . . | 44 | 45 |
| West . . . . . . . . . . . . | 49 | 38 |

### By Age

|  |  |  |
|---|---|---|
| 18–29 years . . . . . . . . | 45% | 44% |
| 30–49 years . . . . . . . . | 54 | 43 |
| 50 years and over . . . | 50 | 44 |

### By Income

|  |  |  |
|---|---|---|
| $20,000 and over . . . | 58% | 45% |
| Under $20,000 . . . . . | 42 | 43 |

### By Politics

| | | |
|---|---|---|
| Republicans . . . . . . . | 68% | 53% |
| Democrats . . . . . . . . | 42 | 40 |
| Independents . . . . . . | 47 | 43 |

Note: President Ronald Reagan's newly launched reelection campaign may benefit from a sharply lower "misery index," an economic barometer created in 1976 by presidential candidate Jimmy Carter to dramatize the failure of the Ford administration to improve the economy. Reagan, in turn, found the index an effective political weapon to use against President Carter during the 1980 campaign. The index—a combination of the public's forecasts of the inflation and unemployment rates—now stands at 13.7% compared to 20.7% recorded soon after the 1980 election. The current index is the most optimistic since this measurement began.

The public's projections of the inflation and unemployment rates for the end of 1983—obtained in November 1982 at the depth of the recession—combined to produce a misery index of 17.4%. This turned out to be far more pessimistic than the actual government figures of 3.8% inflation and 8.2% unemployment, indicating a misery index of only 12%. In earlier surveys a closer correlation was found between the public's misery index projections and subsequent government statistics.

### Misery Index Trend

| Survey dates | Year-end forecasts | Median Averages | | Total |
|---|---|---|---|---|
| | | Inflation rate | Unemploy- ment rate | |
| Dec. 1983 | 1984 | 6.1% | 7.6% | 13.7% |
| Nov. 1982 | 1983 | 7.3 | 10.1 | 17.4 |
| June 1982 | 1982 | 7.9 | 10.6 | 18.5 |
| Jan. 1982 | 1982 | 10.2 | 9.4 | 19.6 |
| Mar. 1981 | 1981 | 13.5 | 8.4 | 21.7 |
| Nov. 1980 | 1981 | 13.6 | 7.1 | 20.7 |

To a considerable extent, the public's current views of the twin economic problems of inflation and unemployment are colored by their political allegiance, with 68% of Republicans, but only 42% of Democrats, predicting an inflation rate of 6% or lower a year from now. The same pattern holds for unemployment, with Republicans more sanguine than Democrats about the jobless rate. Nationally, 44% of the public believes that the unemployment rate will be 7% or lower at this time next year. The same sentiment is expressed by 53% of Republicans but by only 40% of Democrats.

Republicans, whites, and persons from the upper-income and college-educated strata are more optimistic on both the inflation and unemployment fronts than are persons from population groups with a Democratic orientation.

## FEBRUARY 5
## GEORGE ORWELL'S "1984" PREDICTIONS—I

Interviewing Date: 12/9–12/83 (U.S. only)
Survey #228-G

*Have you read the book* 1984 *by George Orwell? Have you ever seen a movie or television version of George Orwell's* 1984?

| | Read book | Saw movie or television version |
|---|---|---|
| National . . . . . . . . . . . . | 22% | 10% |

### By Sex

| | | |
|---|---|---|
| Male . . . . . . . . . . . . . . | 24% | 12% |
| Female . . . . . . . . . . . . | 21 | 7 |

### By Ethnic Background

| | | |
|---|---|---|
| White . . . . . . . . . . . . . . | 24% | 9% |
| Nonwhite . . . . . . . . . . . | 12 | 12 |
| Black . . . . . . . . . . . . . . | 9 | 10 |

### By Education

| | | |
|---|---|---|
| College graduate . . . . . . | 56% | 21% |
| College incomplete . . . . | 30 | 12 |
| High-school graduate . . . | 13 | 7 |
| Less than high-school graduate . . . . . . . . . . | 4 | 1 |

### By Age

| | | |
|---|---|---|
| 18–29 years | 25% | 8% |
| 30–49 years | 33 | 16 |
| 50 years and over | 11 | 4 |

### By Other Countries in Survey

| | | |
|---|---|---|
| Brazil | 2% | 3% |
| Canada | 15 | 6 |
| Germany (West) | 13 | 9 |
| Great Britain | 24 | 21 |
| Switzerland | 11 | 4 |

*As you may recall, 1984 was written by George Orwell in 1948. The author pictured the world in 1984 as a place in which people lost all of their freedom. Thinking about the United States only, please tell me for each of these predictions if you think it is already happening, very likely to happen some day, only somewhat likely to happen, or not at all likely to happen in the United States:*

*There is no real privacy because the government can learn anything it wants about you?*

| | |
|---|---|
| Already happening | 47% |
| Very likely | 19 |
| Somewhat likely | 17 |
| Not at all likely | 9 |
| No opinion | 8 |

### By Sex
#### Male

| | |
|---|---|
| Already happening | 46% |
| Very likely | 19 |
| Somewhat likely | 19 |
| Not at all likely | 10 |
| No opinion | 6 |

#### Female

| | |
|---|---|
| Already happening | 47% |
| Very likely | 20 |
| Somewhat likely | 16 |
| Not at all likely | 8 |
| No opinion | 9 |

### By Ethnic Background
#### White

| | |
|---|---|
| Already happening | 47% |
| Very likely | 18 |
| Somewhat likely | 19 |
| Not at all likely | 9 |
| No opinion | 7 |

#### Nonwhite

| | |
|---|---|
| Already happening | 45% |
| Very likely | 24 |
| Somewhat likely | 11 |
| Not at all likely | 7 |
| No opinion | 13 |

#### Black

| | |
|---|---|
| Already happening | 47% |
| Very likely | 23 |
| Somewhat likely | 7 |
| Not at all likely | 9 |
| No opinion | 14 |

### By Education
#### College Graduate

| | |
|---|---|
| Already happening | 36% |
| Very likely | 21 |
| Somewhat likely | 31 |
| Not at all likely | 7 |
| No opinion | 5 |

#### College Incomplete

| | |
|---|---|
| Already happening | 43% |
| Very likely | 22 |
| Somewhat likely | 22 |
| Not at all likely | 9 |
| No opinion | 4 |

#### High-School Graduate

| | |
|---|---|
| Already happening | 55% |
| Very likely | 17 |
| Somewhat likely | 12 |
| Not at all likely | 10 |
| No opinion | 6 |

### Less Than High-School Graduate

Already happening . . . . . . . . . . . . . . . . . . .47%
Very likely . . . . . . . . . . . . . . . . . . . . . . .18
Somewhat likely . . . . . . . . . . . . . . . . . . . .11
Not at all likely . . . . . . . . . . . . . . . . . . . .10
No opinion . . . . . . . . . . . . . . . . . . . . . . . .15

## By Age
### 18–29 Years

Already happening . . . . . . . . . . . . . . . . . . .46%
Very likely . . . . . . . . . . . . . . . . . . . . . . .18
Somewhat likely . . . . . . . . . . . . . . . . . . . .19
Not at all likely . . . . . . . . . . . . . . . . . . . . 8
No opinion . . . . . . . . . . . . . . . . . . . . . . . . 8

### 30–49 Years

Already happening . . . . . . . . . . . . . . . . . . .47%
Very likely . . . . . . . . . . . . . . . . . . . . . . .22
Somewhat likely . . . . . . . . . . . . . . . . . . . .18
Not at all likely . . . . . . . . . . . . . . . . . . . . 7
No opinion . . . . . . . . . . . . . . . . . . . . . . . . 6

### 50 Years and Over

Already happening . . . . . . . . . . . . . . . . . . .47%
Very likely . . . . . . . . . . . . . . . . . . . . . . .17
Somewhat likely . . . . . . . . . . . . . . . . . . . .16
Not at all likely . . . . . . . . . . . . . . . . . . . .11
No opinion . . . . . . . . . . . . . . . . . . . . . . . . 9

## Other Countries

|  | Already happening responses only* |
|---|---|
| Brazil . . . . . . . . . . . . . . . . . . . . . . . | 43% |
| Canada . . . . . . . . . . . . . . . . . . . . . | 68 |
| Germany (West) . . . . . . . . . . . . . . | 18 |
| Great Britain . . . . . . . . . . . . . . . . | 59 |
| Switzerland . . . . . . . . . . . . . . . . . | 18 |

*Responses refer to internal conditions within each country.

*Poor people think their only chance to get ahead in life is to win a lottery?*

Already happening . . . . . . . . . . . . . . . . . . .20%
Very likely . . . . . . . . . . . . . . . . . . . . . . .16
Somewhat likely . . . . . . . . . . . . . . . . . . . .25
Not at all likely . . . . . . . . . . . . . . . . . . . .32
No opinion . . . . . . . . . . . . . . . . . . . . . . . . 7

## By Sex
### Male

Already happening . . . . . . . . . . . . . . . . . . .20%
Very likely . . . . . . . . . . . . . . . . . . . . . . .16
Somewhat likely . . . . . . . . . . . . . . . . . . . .24
Not at all likely . . . . . . . . . . . . . . . . . . . .35
No opinion . . . . . . . . . . . . . . . . . . . . . . . . 5

### Female

Already happening . . . . . . . . . . . . . . . . . . .20%
Very likely . . . . . . . . . . . . . . . . . . . . . . .16
Somewhat likely . . . . . . . . . . . . . . . . . . . .26
Not at all likely . . . . . . . . . . . . . . . . . . . .30
No opinion . . . . . . . . . . . . . . . . . . . . . . . . 8

## By Ethnic Background
### White

Already happening . . . . . . . . . . . . . . . . . . .19%
Very likely . . . . . . . . . . . . . . . . . . . . . . .15
Somewhat likely . . . . . . . . . . . . . . . . . . . .26
Not at all likely . . . . . . . . . . . . . . . . . . . .34
No opinion . . . . . . . . . . . . . . . . . . . . . . . . 6

### Nonwhite

Already happening . . . . . . . . . . . . . . . . . . .27%
Very likely . . . . . . . . . . . . . . . . . . . . . . .20
Somewhat likely . . . . . . . . . . . . . . . . . . . .22
Not at all likely . . . . . . . . . . . . . . . . . . . .21
No opinion . . . . . . . . . . . . . . . . . . . . . . . .10

### Black

Already happening . . . . . . . . . . . . . . . . . . .28%
Very likely . . . . . . . . . . . . . . . . . . . . . . .19
Somewhat likely . . . . . . . . . . . . . . . . . . . .21
Not at all likely . . . . . . . . . . . . . . . . . . . .20
No opinion . . . . . . . . . . . . . . . . . . . . . . . .12

## By Education

### College Graduate

Already happening . . . . . . . . . . . . . . . . . . .16%
Very likely . . . . . . . . . . . . . . . . . . . . . . . .12
Somewhat likely . . . . . . . . . . . . . . . . . . . .37
Not at all likely . . . . . . . . . . . . . . . . . . . . .32
No opinion . . . . . . . . . . . . . . . . . . . . . . . . 3

### College Incomplete

Already happening . . . . . . . . . . . . . . . . . . .18%
Very likely . . . . . . . . . . . . . . . . . . . . . . . .18
Somewhat likely . . . . . . . . . . . . . . . . . . . .24
Not at all likely . . . . . . . . . . . . . . . . . . . . .34
No opinion . . . . . . . . . . . . . . . . . . . . . . . . 6

### High-School Graduate

Already happening . . . . . . . . . . . . . . . . . . .23%
Very likely . . . . . . . . . . . . . . . . . . . . . . . .16
Somewhat likely . . . . . . . . . . . . . . . . . . . .25
Not at all likely . . . . . . . . . . . . . . . . . . . . .31
No opinion . . . . . . . . . . . . . . . . . . . . . . . . 5

### Less Than High-School Graduate

Already happening . . . . . . . . . . . . . . . . . . .20%
Very likely . . . . . . . . . . . . . . . . . . . . . . . .16
Somewhat likely . . . . . . . . . . . . . . . . . . . .19
Not at all likely . . . . . . . . . . . . . . . . . . . . .33
No opinion . . . . . . . . . . . . . . . . . . . . . . . .13

## By Age

### 18–29 Years

Already happening . . . . . . . . . . . . . . . . . . .22%
Very likely . . . . . . . . . . . . . . . . . . . . . . . .14
Somewhat likely . . . . . . . . . . . . . . . . . . . .29
Not at all likely . . . . . . . . . . . . . . . . . . . . .28
No opinion . . . . . . . . . . . . . . . . . . . . . . . . 7

### 30–49 Years

Already happening . . . . . . . . . . . . . . . . . . .20%
Very likely . . . . . . . . . . . . . . . . . . . . . . . .17
Somewhat likely . . . . . . . . . . . . . . . . . . . .26
Not at all likely . . . . . . . . . . . . . . . . . . . . .32
No opinion . . . . . . . . . . . . . . . . . . . . . . . . 5

### 50 Years and Over

Already happening . . . . . . . . . . . . . . . . . . .17%
Very likely . . . . . . . . . . . . . . . . . . . . . . . .16
Somewhat likely . . . . . . . . . . . . . . . . . . . .22
Not at all likely . . . . . . . . . . . . . . . . . . . . .36
No opinion . . . . . . . . . . . . . . . . . . . . . . . . 9

## Other Countries

|  | Already happening responses only |
| --- | --- |
| Brazil . . . . . . . . . . . . . . . . . . . . . . . . | 60% |
| Canada . . . . . . . . . . . . . . . . . . . | 32 |
| Germany (West) . . . . . . . . . . . . . . . | 30 |
| Great Britain . . . . . . . . . . . . . . . . . . | 39 |
| Switzerland . . . . . . . . . . . . . . . . . . . | 29 |

*The government urges citizens to hate people in other countries?*

Already happening . . . . . . . . . . . . . . . . . . . 9%
Very likely . . . . . . . . . . . . . . . . . . . . . . . . 6
Somewhat likely . . . . . . . . . . . . . . . . . . . .17
Not at all likely . . . . . . . . . . . . . . . . . . . . .62
No opinion . . . . . . . . . . . . . . . . . . . . . . . . 6

## By Sex

### Male

Already happening . . . . . . . . . . . . . . . . . . .11%
Very likely . . . . . . . . . . . . . . . . . . . . . . . . 7
Somewhat likely . . . . . . . . . . . . . . . . . . . .14
Not at all likely . . . . . . . . . . . . . . . . . . . . .62
No opinion . . . . . . . . . . . . . . . . . . . . . . . . 6

### Female

Already happening . . . . . . . . . . . . . . . . . . . 8%
Very likely . . . . . . . . . . . . . . . . . . . . . . . . 5
Somewhat likely . . . . . . . . . . . . . . . . . . . .18
Not at all likely . . . . . . . . . . . . . . . . . . . . .62
No opinion . . . . . . . . . . . . . . . . . . . . . . . . 7

## By Ethnic Background

### White

Already happening . . . . . . . . . . . . . . . . . . . 8%
Very likely . . . . . . . . . . . . . . . . . . . . . . 5
Somewhat likely . . . . . . . . . . . . . . . . . . . 16
Not at all likely . . . . . . . . . . . . . . . . . . . . 65
No opinion . . . . . . . . . . . . . . . . . . . . . . . 5

### Nonwhite

Already happening . . . . . . . . . . . . . . . . . . . 17%
Very likely . . . . . . . . . . . . . . . . . . . . . . 11
Somewhat likely . . . . . . . . . . . . . . . . . . . 17
Not at all likely . . . . . . . . . . . . . . . . . . . . 40
No opinion . . . . . . . . . . . . . . . . . . . . . . . 15

### Black

Already happening . . . . . . . . . . . . . . . . . . . 17%
Very likely . . . . . . . . . . . . . . . . . . . . . . 11
Somewhat likely . . . . . . . . . . . . . . . . . . . 18
Not at all likely . . . . . . . . . . . . . . . . . . . . 38
No opinion . . . . . . . . . . . . . . . . . . . . . . . 16

## By Education

### College Graduate

Already happening . . . . . . . . . . . . . . . . . . . 14%
Very likely . . . . . . . . . . . . . . . . . . . . . . 7
Somewhat likely . . . . . . . . . . . . . . . . . . . 22
Not at all likely . . . . . . . . . . . . . . . . . . . . 54
No opinion . . . . . . . . . . . . . . . . . . . . . . . 3

### College Incomplete

Already happening . . . . . . . . . . . . . . . . . . . 7%
Very likely . . . . . . . . . . . . . . . . . . . . . . 8
Somewhat likely . . . . . . . . . . . . . . . . . . . 18
Not at all likely . . . . . . . . . . . . . . . . . . . . 62
No opinion . . . . . . . . . . . . . . . . . . . . . . . 6

### High-School Graduate

Already happening . . . . . . . . . . . . . . . . . . . 8%
Very likely . . . . . . . . . . . . . . . . . . . . . . 4
Somewhat likely . . . . . . . . . . . . . . . . . . . 16
Not at all likely . . . . . . . . . . . . . . . . . . . . 67
No opinion . . . . . . . . . . . . . . . . . . . . . . . 5

### Less Than High-School Graduate

Already happening . . . . . . . . . . . . . . . . . . . 9%
Very likely . . . . . . . . . . . . . . . . . . . . . . 5
Somewhat likely . . . . . . . . . . . . . . . . . . . 12
Not at all likely . . . . . . . . . . . . . . . . . . . . 63
No opinion . . . . . . . . . . . . . . . . . . . . . . . 11

## By Age

### 18–29 Years

Already happening . . . . . . . . . . . . . . . . . . . 14%
Very likely . . . . . . . . . . . . . . . . . . . . . . 4
Somewhat likely . . . . . . . . . . . . . . . . . . . 23
Not at all likely . . . . . . . . . . . . . . . . . . . . 51
No opinion . . . . . . . . . . . . . . . . . . . . . . . 7

### 30–49 Years

Already happening . . . . . . . . . . . . . . . . . . . 10%
Very likely . . . . . . . . . . . . . . . . . . . . . . 8
Somewhat likely . . . . . . . . . . . . . . . . . . . 16
Not at all likely . . . . . . . . . . . . . . . . . . . . 62
No opinion . . . . . . . . . . . . . . . . . . . . . . . 4

### 50 Years and Over

Already happening . . . . . . . . . . . . . . . . . . . 4%
Very likely . . . . . . . . . . . . . . . . . . . . . . 5
Somewhat likely . . . . . . . . . . . . . . . . . . . 12
Not at all likely . . . . . . . . . . . . . . . . . . . . 71
No opinion . . . . . . . . . . . . . . . . . . . . . . . 8

## Other Countries

|  | *Already happening responses only* |
|---|---|
| Brazil . . . . . . . . . . . . . . . . . . . . . . . . | 17% |
| Canada . . . . . . . . . . . . . . . . . . . | 7 |
| Germany (West) . . . . . . . . . . . . . . . . . | 5 |
| Great Britain . . . . . . . . . . . . . . . . . . . | 8 |
| Switzerland . . . . . . . . . . . . . . . . . . . | 9 |

*Anybody who criticizes the government is severely punished?*

Already happening ..................... 4%
Very likely .......................... 6
Somewhat likely ....................18
Not at all likely .....................66
No opinion ......................... 6

## By Sex
### Male

Already happening ..................... 4%
Very likely .......................... 7
Somewhat likely ....................18
Not at all likely .....................66
No opinion ......................... 5

### Female

Already happening ..................... 3%
Very likely .......................... 5
Somewhat likely ....................18
Not at all likely .....................65
No opinion ......................... 9

## By Ethnic Background
### White

Already happening ..................... 3%
Very likely .......................... 6
Somewhat likely ....................17
Not at all likely .....................68
No opinion ......................... 6

### Nonwhite

Already happening ..................... 5%
Very likely .........................12
Somewhat likely ....................24
Not at all likely .....................46
No opinion .........................13

### Black

Already happening ..................... 6%
Very likely .........................10
Somewhat likely ....................26
Not at all likely .....................46
No opinion .........................12

## By Education
### College Graduate

Already happening ..................... 5%
Very likely .......................... 2
Somewhat likely ....................29
Not at all likely .....................61
No opinion ......................... 3

### College Incomplete

Already happening ..................... 2%
Very likely .......................... 8
Somewhat likely ....................16
Not at all likely .....................70
No opinion ......................... 4

### High-School Graduate

Already happening ..................... 4%
Very likely .......................... 6
Somewhat likely ....................16
Not at all likely .....................68
No opinion ......................... 6

### Less Than High-School Graduate

Already happening ..................... 4%
Very likely .......................... 8
Somewhat likely ....................14
Not at all likely .....................62
No opinion .........................12

## By Age
### 18–29 Years

Already happening ..................... 3%
Very likely .......................... 7
Somewhat likely ....................20
Not at all likely .....................62
No opinion ......................... 8

### 30–49 Years

Already happening ..................... 4%
Very likely .......................... 7
Somewhat likely ....................18
Not at all likely .....................66
No opinion ......................... 5

### 50 Years and Over

Already happening ................... 4%
Very likely ......................... 5
Somewhat likely ..................... 16
Not at all likely ..................... 68
No opinion .......................... 7

### Other Countries

|  | *Already happening responses only* |
|---|---|
| Brazil ......................... | 42% |
| Canada ....................... | 3 |
| Germany (West) ................ | 5 |
| Great Britain .................. | 4 |
| Switzerland ................... | 4 |

*The government says the only way we can have peace is by waging war?*

Already happening ................... 13%
Very likely ......................... 14
Somewhat likely ..................... 24
Not at all likely ..................... 44
No opinion .......................... 5

### By Sex
#### Male

Already happening ................... 13%
Very likely ......................... 12
Somewhat likely ..................... 25
Not at all likely ..................... 47
No opinion .......................... 3

#### Female

Already happening ................... 12%
Very likely ......................... 16
Somewhat likely ..................... 22
Not at all likely ..................... 42
No opinion .......................... 8

### By Ethnic Background
#### White

Already happening ................... 12%
Very likely ......................... 14
Somewhat likely ..................... 24
Not at all likely ..................... 46
No opinion .......................... 4

#### Nonwhite

Already happening ................... 20%
Very likely ......................... 14
Somewhat likely ..................... 19
Not at all likely ..................... 32
No opinion .......................... 15

#### Black

Already happening ................... 18%
Very likely ......................... 13
Somewhat likely ..................... 20
Not at all likely ..................... 34
No opinion .......................... 15

### By Education
#### College Graduate

Already happening ................... 18%
Very likely ......................... 15
Somewhat likely ..................... 29
Not at all likely ..................... 37
No opinion .......................... 1

#### College Incomplete

Already happening ................... 11%
Very likely ......................... 14
Somewhat likely ..................... 28
Not at all likely ..................... 45
No opinion .......................... 2

#### High-School Graduate

Already happening ................... 11%
Very likely ......................... 14
Somewhat likely ..................... 24
Not at all likely ..................... 47
No opinion .......................... 4

### Less Than High-School Graduate

Already happening . . . . . . . . . . . . . . . . . . . .12%
Very likely . . . . . . . . . . . . . . . . . . . . . . .13
Somewhat likely . . . . . . . . . . . . . . . . . . . .16
Not at all likely . . . . . . . . . . . . . . . . . . . .46
No opinion . . . . . . . . . . . . . . . . . . . . . . . .13

## By Age
### 18–29 Years

Already happening . . . . . . . . . . . . . . . . . . . .15%
Very likely . . . . . . . . . . . . . . . . . . . . . . .17
Somewhat likely . . . . . . . . . . . . . . . . . . . .28
Not at all likely . . . . . . . . . . . . . . . . . . . .34
No opinion . . . . . . . . . . . . . . . . . . . . . . . . 6

### 30–49 Years

Already happening . . . . . . . . . . . . . . . . . . . .13%
Very likely . . . . . . . . . . . . . . . . . . . . . . .14
Somewhat likely . . . . . . . . . . . . . . . . . . . .27
Not at all likely . . . . . . . . . . . . . . . . . . . .43
No opinion . . . . . . . . . . . . . . . . . . . . . . . . 3

### 50 Years and Over

Already happening . . . . . . . . . . . . . . . . . . . .11%
Very likely . . . . . . . . . . . . . . . . . . . . . . .11
Somewhat likely . . . . . . . . . . . . . . . . . . . .17
Not at all likely . . . . . . . . . . . . . . . . . . . .53
No opinion . . . . . . . . . . . . . . . . . . . . . . . . 8

## Other Countries

| | *Already happening responses only* |
|---|---|
| Brazil | 13% |
| Canada | 3 |
| Germany (West) | 5 |
| Great Britain | 7 |
| Switzerland | 5 |

*The government urges people to surrender freedom in order to gain greater security?*

Already happening . . . . . . . . . . . . . . . . . . . .11%
Very likely . . . . . . . . . . . . . . . . . . . . . . .10
Somewhat likely . . . . . . . . . . . . . . . . . . . .21
Not at all likely . . . . . . . . . . . . . . . . . . . .51
No opinion . . . . . . . . . . . . . . . . . . . . . . . . 7

## By Sex
### Male

Already happening . . . . . . . . . . . . . . . . . . . .13%
Very likely . . . . . . . . . . . . . . . . . . . . . . .10
Somewhat likely . . . . . . . . . . . . . . . . . . . .20
Not at all likely . . . . . . . . . . . . . . . . . . . .52
No opinion . . . . . . . . . . . . . . . . . . . . . . . . 5

### Female

Already happening . . . . . . . . . . . . . . . . . . . . 8%
Very likely . . . . . . . . . . . . . . . . . . . . . . .11
Somewhat likely . . . . . . . . . . . . . . . . . . . .22
Not at all likely . . . . . . . . . . . . . . . . . . . .49
No opinion . . . . . . . . . . . . . . . . . . . . . . . .10

## By Ethnic Background
### White

Already happening . . . . . . . . . . . . . . . . . . . .10%
Very likely . . . . . . . . . . . . . . . . . . . . . . .10
Somewhat likely . . . . . . . . . . . . . . . . . . . .21
Not at all likely . . . . . . . . . . . . . . . . . . . .53
No opinion . . . . . . . . . . . . . . . . . . . . . . . . 6

### Nonwhite

Already happening . . . . . . . . . . . . . . . . . . . .14%
Very likely . . . . . . . . . . . . . . . . . . . . . . .12
Somewhat likely . . . . . . . . . . . . . . . . . . . .21
Not at all likely . . . . . . . . . . . . . . . . . . . .32
No opinion . . . . . . . . . . . . . . . . . . . . . . . .19

### Black

Already happening . . . . . . . . . . . . . . . . . . . .15%
Very likely . . . . . . . . . . . . . . . . . . . . . . .11
Somewhat likely . . . . . . . . . . . . . . . . . . . .22
Not at all likely . . . . . . . . . . . . . . . . . . . .32
No opinion . . . . . . . . . . . . . . . . . . . . . . . .20

## By Education
### College Graduate

| | |
|---|---|
| Already happening | 15% |
| Very likely | 10 |
| Somewhat likely | 31 |
| Not at all likely | 43 |
| No opinion | 1 |

### College Incomplete

| | |
|---|---|
| Already happening | 9% |
| Very likely | 13 |
| Somewhat likely | 20 |
| Not at all likely | 54 |
| No opinion | 4 |

### High-School Graduate

| | |
|---|---|
| Already happening | 9% |
| Very likely | 10 |
| Somewhat likely | 19 |
| Not at all likely | 55 |
| No opinion | 7 |

### Less Than High-School Graduate

| | |
|---|---|
| Already happening | 11% |
| Very likely | 8 |
| Somewhat likely | 17 |
| Not at all likely | 48 |
| No opinion | 16 |

## By Age
### 18–29 Years

| | |
|---|---|
| Already happening | 12% |
| Very likely | 10 |
| Somewhat likely | 25 |
| Not at all likely | 45 |
| No opinion | 8 |

### 30–49 Years

| | |
|---|---|
| Already happening | 11% |
| Very likely | 11 |
| Somewhat likely | 24 |
| Not at all likely | 48 |
| No opinion | 6 |

### 50 Years and Over

| | |
|---|---|
| Already happening | 10% |
| Very likely | 10 |
| Somewhat likely | 15 |
| Not at all likely | 57 |
| No opinion | 9 |

## Other Countries

| | Already happening responses only |
|---|---|
| Brazil | 35% |
| Canada | 12 |
| Germany (West) | 8 |
| Great Britain | 11 |
| Switzerland | 6 |

*People are asked to make great economic sacrifices but government officials themselves live in luxury?*

| | |
|---|---|
| Already happening | 51% |
| Very likely | 16 |
| Somewhat likely | 19 |
| Not at all likely | 10 |
| No opinion | 4 |

## By Sex
### Male

| | |
|---|---|
| Already happening | 50% |
| Very likely | 17 |
| Somewhat likely | 19 |
| Not at all likely | 11 |
| No opinion | 3 |

### Female

| | |
|---|---|
| Already happening | 51% |
| Very likely | 16 |
| Somewhat likely | 18 |
| Not at all likely | 10 |
| No opinion | 5 |

## By Ethnic Background
### White

Already happening . . . . . . . . . . . . . . . . . . . .50%
Very likely . . . . . . . . . . . . . . . . . . . . . . . . .17
Somewhat likely . . . . . . . . . . . . . . . . . . . . .19
Not at all likely . . . . . . . . . . . . . . . . . . . . . .11
No opinion . . . . . . . . . . . . . . . . . . . . . . . . . 3

### Nonwhite

Already happening . . . . . . . . . . . . . . . . . . . .57%
Very likely . . . . . . . . . . . . . . . . . . . . . . . . .12
Somewhat likely . . . . . . . . . . . . . . . . . . . . .12
Not at all likely . . . . . . . . . . . . . . . . . . . . . . 8
No opinion . . . . . . . . . . . . . . . . . . . . . . . . .11

### Black

Already happening . . . . . . . . . . . . . . . . . . . .58%
Very likely . . . . . . . . . . . . . . . . . . . . . . . . .10
Somewhat likely . . . . . . . . . . . . . . . . . . . . .13
Not at all likely . . . . . . . . . . . . . . . . . . . . . .10
No opinion . . . . . . . . . . . . . . . . . . . . . . . . . 9

## By Education
### College Graduate

Already happening . . . . . . . . . . . . . . . . . . . .44%
Very likely . . . . . . . . . . . . . . . . . . . . . . . . .14
Somewhat likely . . . . . . . . . . . . . . . . . . . . .28
Not at all likely . . . . . . . . . . . . . . . . . . . . . .13
No opinion . . . . . . . . . . . . . . . . . . . . . . . . . 1

### College Incomplete

Already happening . . . . . . . . . . . . . . . . . . . .48%
Very likely . . . . . . . . . . . . . . . . . . . . . . . . .19
Somewhat likely . . . . . . . . . . . . . . . . . . . . .18
Not at all likely . . . . . . . . . . . . . . . . . . . . . .13
No opinion . . . . . . . . . . . . . . . . . . . . . . . . . 2

### High-School Graduate

Already happening . . . . . . . . . . . . . . . . . . . .55%
Very likely . . . . . . . . . . . . . . . . . . . . . . . . .17
Somewhat likely . . . . . . . . . . . . . . . . . . . . .17
Not at all likely . . . . . . . . . . . . . . . . . . . . . . 7
No opinion . . . . . . . . . . . . . . . . . . . . . . . . . 3

### Less Than High-School Graduate

Already happening . . . . . . . . . . . . . . . . . . . .52%
Very likely . . . . . . . . . . . . . . . . . . . . . . . . .13
Somewhat likely . . . . . . . . . . . . . . . . . . . . .15
Not at all likely . . . . . . . . . . . . . . . . . . . . . .12
No opinion . . . . . . . . . . . . . . . . . . . . . . . . . 8

## By Age
### 18–29 Years

Already happening . . . . . . . . . . . . . . . . . . . .53%
Very likely . . . . . . . . . . . . . . . . . . . . . . . . .17
Somewhat likely . . . . . . . . . . . . . . . . . . . . .19
Not at all likely . . . . . . . . . . . . . . . . . . . . . . 6
No opinion . . . . . . . . . . . . . . . . . . . . . . . . . 5

### 30–49 Years

Already happening . . . . . . . . . . . . . . . . . . . .52%
Very likely . . . . . . . . . . . . . . . . . . . . . . . . .19
Somewhat likely . . . . . . . . . . . . . . . . . . . . .18
Not at all likely . . . . . . . . . . . . . . . . . . . . . . 9
No opinion . . . . . . . . . . . . . . . . . . . . . . . . . 2

### 50 Years and Over

Already happening . . . . . . . . . . . . . . . . . . . .48%
Very likely . . . . . . . . . . . . . . . . . . . . . . . . .13
Somewhat likely . . . . . . . . . . . . . . . . . . . . .19
Not at all likely . . . . . . . . . . . . . . . . . . . . . .15
No opinion . . . . . . . . . . . . . . . . . . . . . . . . . 5

## Other Countries

| | Already happening responses only |
|---|---|
| Brazil . . . . . . . . . . . . . . . . . . . . . . . . | 84% |
| Canada . . . . . . . . . . . . . . . . . . | 70 |
| Germany (West) . . . . . . . . . . . . . . . . . | 32 |
| Great Britain . . . . . . . . . . . . . . . . . . | 59 |
| Switzerland . . . . . . . . . . . . . . . . . . . . | 15 |

*The government uses false words and statistics to hide bad news about the economy and quality of life?*

Already happening . . . . . . . . . . . . . . . . . . . 40%
Very likely . . . . . . . . . . . . . . . . . . . . 17
Somewhat likely . . . . . . . . . . . . . . . . 23
Not at all likely . . . . . . . . . . . . . . . . 14
No opinion . . . . . . . . . . . . . . . . . . . . . 6

## By Sex

### Male

Already happening . . . . . . . . . . . . . . . . . . . 38%
Very likely . . . . . . . . . . . . . . . . . . . . 18
Somewhat likely . . . . . . . . . . . . . . . . 24
Not at all likely . . . . . . . . . . . . . . . . 15
No opinion . . . . . . . . . . . . . . . . . . . . . 5

### Female

Already happening . . . . . . . . . . . . . . . . . . . 42%
Very likely . . . . . . . . . . . . . . . . . . . . 16
Somewhat likely . . . . . . . . . . . . . . . . 22
Not at all likely . . . . . . . . . . . . . . . . 13
No opinion . . . . . . . . . . . . . . . . . . . . . 7

## By Ethnic Background

### White

Already happening . . . . . . . . . . . . . . . . . . . 39%
Very likely . . . . . . . . . . . . . . . . . . . . 17
Somewhat likely . . . . . . . . . . . . . . . . 25
Not at all likely . . . . . . . . . . . . . . . . 14
No opinion . . . . . . . . . . . . . . . . . . . . . 5

### Nonwhite

Already happening . . . . . . . . . . . . . . . . . . . 44%
Very likely . . . . . . . . . . . . . . . . . . . . 17
Somewhat likely . . . . . . . . . . . . . . . . 11
Not at all likely . . . . . . . . . . . . . . . . 12
No opinion . . . . . . . . . . . . . . . . . . . . . 16

### Black

Already happening . . . . . . . . . . . . . . . . . . . 47%
Very likely . . . . . . . . . . . . . . . . . . . . 17
Somewhat likely . . . . . . . . . . . . . . . . 10
Not at all likely . . . . . . . . . . . . . . . . 12
No opinion . . . . . . . . . . . . . . . . . . . . . 14

## By Education

### College Graduate

Already happening . . . . . . . . . . . . . . . . . . . 40%
Very likely . . . . . . . . . . . . . . . . . . . . 15
Somewhat likely . . . . . . . . . . . . . . . . 30
Not at all likely . . . . . . . . . . . . . . . . 14
No opinion . . . . . . . . . . . . . . . . . . . . . 1

### College Incomplete

Already happening . . . . . . . . . . . . . . . . . . . 35%
Very likely . . . . . . . . . . . . . . . . . . . . 22
Somewhat likely . . . . . . . . . . . . . . . . 25
Not at all likely . . . . . . . . . . . . . . . . 14
No opinion . . . . . . . . . . . . . . . . . . . . . 3

### High-School Graduate

Already happening . . . . . . . . . . . . . . . . . . . 42%
Very likely . . . . . . . . . . . . . . . . . . . . 18
Somewhat likely . . . . . . . . . . . . . . . . 22
Not at all likely . . . . . . . . . . . . . . . . 13
No opinion . . . . . . . . . . . . . . . . . . . . . 5

### Less Than High-School Graduate

Already happening . . . . . . . . . . . . . . . . . . . 41%
Very likely . . . . . . . . . . . . . . . . . . . . 14
Somewhat likely . . . . . . . . . . . . . . . . 16
Not at all likely . . . . . . . . . . . . . . . . 15
No opinion . . . . . . . . . . . . . . . . . . . . . 14

## By Age

### 18–29 Years

Already happening . . . . . . . . . . . . . . . . . . . 40%
Very likely . . . . . . . . . . . . . . . . . . . . 20
Somewhat likely . . . . . . . . . . . . . . . . 23
Not at all likely . . . . . . . . . . . . . . . . 11
No opinion . . . . . . . . . . . . . . . . . . . . . 6

### 30–49 Years

Already happening . . . . . . . . . . . . . . . . . . . 42%
Very likely . . . . . . . . . . . . . . . . . . . . 17
Somewhat likely . . . . . . . . . . . . . . . . 25
Not at all likely . . . . . . . . . . . . . . . . 12
No opinion . . . . . . . . . . . . . . . . . . . . . 4

### 50 Years and Over

Already happening . . . . . . . . . . . . . . . . . . . .38%
Very likely . . . . . . . . . . . . . . . . . . . . . . . . .16
Somewhat likely . . . . . . . . . . . . . . . . . . . .20
Not at all likely . . . . . . . . . . . . . . . . . . . . .18
No opinion . . . . . . . . . . . . . . . . . . . . . . . . . 8

### Other Countries

|  | *Already happening responses only* |
| --- | --- |
| Brazil . . . . . . . . . . . . . . . . . . . . . . . . . | 72% |
| Canada . . . . . . . . . . . . . . . . . . . . . | 53 |
| Germany (West) . . . . . . . . . . . . . . . . | 12 |
| Great Britain . . . . . . . . . . . . . . . . . | 57 |
| Switzerland . . . . . . . . . . . . . . . . . . . | 13 |

*The government hopes that some day all children will be produced by artificial insemination?*

Already happening . . . . . . . . . . . . . . . . . . . 3%
Very likely . . . . . . . . . . . . . . . . . . . . . . . . . 5
Somewhat likely . . . . . . . . . . . . . . . . . . . .10
Not at all likely . . . . . . . . . . . . . . . . . . . . .74
No opinion . . . . . . . . . . . . . . . . . . . . . . . . . 8

### By Sex
#### Male

Already happening . . . . . . . . . . . . . . . . . . . 1%
Very likely . . . . . . . . . . . . . . . . . . . . . . . . . 5
Somewhat likely . . . . . . . . . . . . . . . . . . . .10
Not at all likely . . . . . . . . . . . . . . . . . . . . .76
No opinion . . . . . . . . . . . . . . . . . . . . . . . . . 8

#### Female

Already happening . . . . . . . . . . . . . . . . . . . 4%
Very likely . . . . . . . . . . . . . . . . . . . . . . . . . 4
Somewhat likely . . . . . . . . . . . . . . . . . . . .11
Not at all likely . . . . . . . . . . . . . . . . . . . . .72
No opinion . . . . . . . . . . . . . . . . . . . . . . . . . 9

### By Ethnic Background
#### White

Already happening . . . . . . . . . . . . . . . . . . . 2%
Very likely . . . . . . . . . . . . . . . . . . . . . . . . . 4
Somewhat likely . . . . . . . . . . . . . . . . . . . . 9
Not at all likely . . . . . . . . . . . . . . . . . . . . .78
No opinion . . . . . . . . . . . . . . . . . . . . . . . . . 7

#### Nonwhite

Already happening . . . . . . . . . . . . . . . . . . . 6%
Very likely . . . . . . . . . . . . . . . . . . . . . . . . .11
Somewhat likely . . . . . . . . . . . . . . . . . . . .18
Not at all likely . . . . . . . . . . . . . . . . . . . . .45
No opinion . . . . . . . . . . . . . . . . . . . . . . . . .20

#### Black

Already happening . . . . . . . . . . . . . . . . . . . 6%
Very likely . . . . . . . . . . . . . . . . . . . . . . . . .10
Somewhat likely . . . . . . . . . . . . . . . . . . . .18
Not at all likely . . . . . . . . . . . . . . . . . . . . .45
No opinion . . . . . . . . . . . . . . . . . . . . . . . . .21

### By Education
#### College Graduate

Already happening . . . . . . . . . . . . . . . . . . . 1%
Very likely . . . . . . . . . . . . . . . . . . . . . . . . . 1
Somewhat likely . . . . . . . . . . . . . . . . . . . . 7
Not at all likely . . . . . . . . . . . . . . . . . . . . .89
No opinion . . . . . . . . . . . . . . . . . . . . . . . . . 1

#### College Incomplete

Already happening . . . . . . . . . . . . . . . . . . . 2%
Very likely . . . . . . . . . . . . . . . . . . . . . . . . . 4
Somewhat likely . . . . . . . . . . . . . . . . . . . .10
Not at all likely . . . . . . . . . . . . . . . . . . . . .78
No opinion . . . . . . . . . . . . . . . . . . . . . . . . . 6

#### High-School Graduate

Already happening . . . . . . . . . . . . . . . . . . . 3%
Very likely . . . . . . . . . . . . . . . . . . . . . . . . . 6
Somewhat likely . . . . . . . . . . . . . . . . . . . .11
Not at all likely . . . . . . . . . . . . . . . . . . . . .72
No opinion . . . . . . . . . . . . . . . . . . . . . . . . . 8

### Less Than High-School Graduate

Already happening . . . . . . . . . . . . . . . . . . 3%
Very likely . . . . . . . . . . . . . . . . . . . . . . 6
Somewhat likely . . . . . . . . . . . . . . . . . .13
Not at all likely . . . . . . . . . . . . . . . . . . .62
No opinion . . . . . . . . . . . . . . . . . . . . . . .16

## By Age
### 18–29 Years

Already happening . . . . . . . . . . . . . . . . . . 4%
Very likely . . . . . . . . . . . . . . . . . . . . . . 5
Somewhat likely . . . . . . . . . . . . . . . . . .13
Not at all likely . . . . . . . . . . . . . . . . . . .68
No opinion . . . . . . . . . . . . . . . . . . . . . . . 9

### 30–49 Years

Already happening . . . . . . . . . . . . . . . . . . 3%
Very likely . . . . . . . . . . . . . . . . . . . . . . 5
Somewhat likely . . . . . . . . . . . . . . . . . . 9
Not at all likely . . . . . . . . . . . . . . . . . . .78
No opinion . . . . . . . . . . . . . . . . . . . . . . . 5

### 50 Years and Over

Already happening . . . . . . . . . . . . . . . . . . 1%
Very likely . . . . . . . . . . . . . . . . . . . . . . 4
Somewhat likely . . . . . . . . . . . . . . . . . . 9
Not at all likely . . . . . . . . . . . . . . . . . . .75
No opinion . . . . . . . . . . . . . . . . . . . . . . .11

## Other Countries

|  | Already happening responses only |
| --- | --- |
| Brazil . . . . . . . . . . . . . . . . . . . . . | 16% |
| Canada . . . . . . . . . . . . . . . . . . | 2 |
| Germany (West) . . . . . . . . . . . . . . . . | 2 |
| Great Britain . . . . . . . . . . . . . . . . . | 2 |
| Switzerland . . . . . . . . . . . . . . . . . | 17 |

*The country is ruled by a dictator?*

Already happening . . . . . . . . . . . . . . . . . . 3%
Very likely . . . . . . . . . . . . . . . . . . . . . . 6
Somewhat likely . . . . . . . . . . . . . . . . . .14
Not at all likely . . . . . . . . . . . . . . . . . . .72
No opinion . . . . . . . . . . . . . . . . . . . . . . . 5

## By Sex
### Male

Already happening . . . . . . . . . . . . . . . . . . 3%
Very likely . . . . . . . . . . . . . . . . . . . . . . 6
Somewhat likely . . . . . . . . . . . . . . . . . .14
Not at all likely . . . . . . . . . . . . . . . . . . .73
No opinion . . . . . . . . . . . . . . . . . . . . . . . 5

### Female

Already happening . . . . . . . . . . . . . . . . . . 3%
Very likely . . . . . . . . . . . . . . . . . . . . . . 6
Somewhat likely . . . . . . . . . . . . . . . . . .15
Not at all likely . . . . . . . . . . . . . . . . . . .70
No opinion . . . . . . . . . . . . . . . . . . . . . . . 6

## By Ethnic Background
### White

Already happening . . . . . . . . . . . . . . . . . . 2%
Very likely . . . . . . . . . . . . . . . . . . . . . . 6
Somewhat likely . . . . . . . . . . . . . . . . . .14
Not at all likely . . . . . . . . . . . . . . . . . . .74
No opinion . . . . . . . . . . . . . . . . . . . . . . . 4

### Nonwhite

Already happening . . . . . . . . . . . . . . . . . . 5%
Very likely . . . . . . . . . . . . . . . . . . . . . . 7
Somewhat likely . . . . . . . . . . . . . . . . . .19
Not at all likely . . . . . . . . . . . . . . . . . . .51
No opinion . . . . . . . . . . . . . . . . . . . . . . .18

### Black

Already happening . . . . . . . . . . . . . . . . . . 6%
Very likely . . . . . . . . . . . . . . . . . . . . . . 9
Somewhat likely . . . . . . . . . . . . . . . . . .19
Not at all likely . . . . . . . . . . . . . . . . . . .50
No opinion . . . . . . . . . . . . . . . . . . . . . . .16

## By Education

### College Graduate

Already happening ................... 1%
Very likely ......................... 2
Somewhat likely .....................15
Not at all likely ....................81
No opinion .......................... 1

### College Incomplete

Already happening ................... 2%
Very likely ......................... 3
Somewhat likely .....................15
Not at all likely ....................76
No opinion .......................... 3

### High-School Graduate

Already happening ................... 3%
Very likely ......................... 9
Somewhat likely .....................15
Not at all likely ....................68
No opinion .......................... 5

### Less Than High-School Graduate

Already happening ................... 4%
Very likely ......................... 9
Somewhat likely .....................12
Not at all likely ....................65
No opinion ..........................10

## By Age

### 18–29 Years

Already happening ................... 5%
Very likely ......................... 7
Somewhat likely .....................16
Not at all likely ....................68
No opinion .......................... 4

### 30–49 Years

Already happening ................... 2%
Very likely ......................... 7
Somewhat likely .....................16
Not at all likely ....................71
No opinion .......................... 4

### 50 Years and Over

Already happening ................... 2%
Very likely ......................... 5
Somewhat likely .....................12
Not at all likely ....................74
No opinion .......................... 7

## Other Countries

| | Already happening responses only |
|---|---|
| Brazil | 34% |
| Canada | 13 |
| Germany (West) | 3 |
| Great Britain | 16 |
| Switzerland | 2 |

Note: In the opinion of many Americans and the people of five other nations, few of the grim visions depicted in George Orwell's classic novel *1984* have come true. Large majorities in each country, for example, see no evidence that their lands are ruled by dictators who use political torture, hatred, war, or dissolution of family ties as official government policy. Nevertheless, two of Orwell's visions—loss of privacy and economic deprivation—are judged by many in the survey to constitute a real threat presently to their personal freedom.

Nearly one-half the Americans (47%) believe they now have little or no privacy because our government can learn anything it wants about them. An additional 19% say it is very likely we may lose the right of privacy. The Canadians (68%) and British (59%) express even greater belief that they have lost the right to privacy in their countries. Brazilians at 43% are not far behind, but only 18% each of the people of West Germany and Switzerland believes the government is looking over their shoulder.

Despite the loss of privacy, only 3% of Americans believe this country now has a dictatorial leader, and 72% see no likelihood of this ever occurring. Similar opinions are found in Germany and Switzerland, but surprisingly 16% of the British and 13% of the Canadians characterize their current leaders as dictators. One in three of the Brazilians (34%) says that their nation's leader is a dictator. Many Brazilians (42%) also fear that criticism of their government would result in severe punishment, but only 3% to 5% each of the people of the United States and the other industrialized nations shares this view.

In Orwell's *1984* the party elite lived in luxury while others were asked to make increasingly greater economic sacrifices; this is now happening according to 84% of the Brazilians. Canada's economic woes may seem minor in comparison to Brazil's, but seven in ten Canadians (70%) complain of government officials' hypocrisy, and about six in ten British (59%) share this view. Despite economic recovery, one-half the Americans (51%) say there is a dual standard of economic morality. One in three West Germans (32%) agrees, but only 15% of the Swiss believe this is happening in their country.

Compounding the problem, 72% of the Brazilians, 57% of the British, and 53% of the Canadians say their governments use the "doublespeak" of economic jargon and statistics to hide economic woes. This view is shared by four in ten Americans (40%) but by only 12% of the West Germans and 13% of the Swiss.

Orwell called the poor "proles" and depicted them as believing that their only chance to get ahead in life was to win a lottery. Only two in ten Americans (20%) believe we have reached this state of affairs. The people of other nations are less sanguine about the lottery, with 60% of the Brazilians, 39% British, 32% Canadians, 30% West Germans, and 29% of the Swiss seeing their poor population believing that picking a winning number is their only chance to get ahead.

Only 13% of Americans believe our government tells us our only avenue to peace is by waging war, and even fewer (9%) say that hatred of people in other countries is a matter of government policy. Brazilians share these views of their country at about the same level as Americans, but even fewer Canadians, British, West Germans, and Swiss see their government as promoting war.

About one in ten Americans (11%), Canadians (12%), and British (11%) says he is being asked to surrender freedom to gain greater security.

Slightly fewer West Germans (8%) and Swiss (6%) see this as the case, while about one in three (35%) Brazilians believes he is now asked to give up his freedom to gain security.

Nearly one in four Americans (22%) and British (24%) says he has read Orwell's *1984*, and one in ten Americans has seen a movie or television version of the novel. In England, where the story has been featured extensively on television in recent months, 21% say they have seen a televised or movie version. Slightly fewer Canadians (15%), West Germans (13%), and Swiss (11%) have read *1984*; among Brazilians the figure is only 2%.

## FEBRUARY 6
## GEORGE ORWELL'S *"1984"*
## PREDICTIONS—II

Interviewing Date: 12/9–12/83 (U.S. only)
Survey #228-G

*For each of the following countries please tell me if you think the people of that country now have a great deal of freedom, only some freedom, very little freedom, or no freedom at all:*

*United States?*

| | |
|---|---|
| Great deal | 80% |
| Only some | 11 |
| Very little | 1 |
| None at all | * |
| No opinion | 8 |

### By Sex
#### Male

| | |
|---|---|
| Great deal | 81% |
| Only some | 10 |
| Very little | 1 |
| None at all | * |
| No opinion | 8 |

### Female

| | |
|---|---|
| Great deal | 79% |
| Only some | 11 |
| Very little | 1 |
| None at all | * |
| No opinion | 9 |

## By Ethnic Background
### White

| | |
|---|---|
| Great deal | 81% |
| Only some | 10 |
| Very little | 1 |
| None at all | * |
| No opinion | 8 |

### Nonwhite

| | |
|---|---|
| Great deal | 71% |
| Only some | 19 |
| Very little | 4 |
| None at all | * |
| No opinion | 6 |

### Black

| | |
|---|---|
| Great deal | 71% |
| Only some | 18 |
| Very little | 4 |
| None at all | * |
| No opinion | 7 |

## By Education
### College Graduate

| | |
|---|---|
| Great deal | 85% |
| Only some | 8 |
| Very little | 1 |
| None at all | * |
| No opinion | 6 |

### College Incomplete

| | |
|---|---|
| Great deal | 83% |
| Only some | 10 |
| Very little | * |
| None at all | * |
| No opinion | 7 |

### High-School Graduate

| | |
|---|---|
| Great deal | 80% |
| Only some | 12 |
| Very little | 1 |
| None at all | * |
| No opinion | 7 |

### Less Than High-School Graduate

| | |
|---|---|
| Great deal | 74% |
| Only some | 13 |
| Very little | 2 |
| None at all | * |
| No opinion | 11 |

## By Age
### 18–29 Years

| | |
|---|---|
| Great deal | 77% |
| Only some | 12 |
| Very little | 1 |
| None at all | * |
| No opinion | 10 |

### 30–49 Years

| | |
|---|---|
| Great deal | 82% |
| Only some | 10 |
| Very little | 1 |
| None at all | * |
| No opinion | 7 |

### 50 Years and Over

| | |
|---|---|
| Great deal | 80% |
| Only some | 11 |
| Very little | 1 |
| None at all | * |
| No opinion | 8 |

*Less than 1%

## Other Countries in Survey

| | Great deal responses only* | Very little and none at all responses only* |
|---|---|---|
| Brazil ............. | 41% | 13% |
| Canada ............ | 83 | 2 |
| Germany (West) ..... | 85 | 2 |
| Great Britain ........ | 73 | 3 |
| Switzerland ........ | 81 | 4 |

*Responses refer to the degree of freedom in the United States.

### Great Britain?

| | |
|---|---|
| Great deal ......................... | 60% |
| Only some ........................ | 24 |
| Very little ........................ | 4 |
| None at all ....................... | 1 |
| No opinion ........................ | 11 |

## Other Countries

| | Great deal responses only | Very little and none at all responses only |
|---|---|---|
| Brazil ............. | 27% | 18% |
| Canada ............ | 69 | 4 |
| Germany (West) ..... | 73 | 3 |
| Great Britain ........ | 73 | 4 |
| Switzerland ........ | 73 | 3 |

### France?

| | |
|---|---|
| Great deal ......................... | 44% |
| Only some ........................ | 33 |
| Very little ........................ | 6 |
| None at all ....................... | * |
| No opinion ........................ | 16 |

*Less than 1%

## Other Countries

| | Great deal responses only | Very little and none at all responses only |
|---|---|---|
| Brazil ............. | 24% | 18% |
| Canada ............ | 56 | 6 |
| Germany (West) ..... | 69 | 4 |
| Great Britain ........ | 49 | 6 |
| Switzerland ........ | 77 | 3 |

### West Germany?

| | |
|---|---|
| Great deal ......................... | 33% |
| Only some ........................ | 35 |
| Very little ........................ | 17 |
| None at all ....................... | 3 |
| No opinion ........................ | 12 |

## Other Countries

| | Great deal responses only | Very little and none at all responses only |
|---|---|---|
| Brazil ............. | 13% | 31% |
| Canada ............ | 37 | 23 |
| Germany (West) ..... | 69 | 4 |
| Great Britain ........ | 41 | 12 |
| Switzerland ........ | 78 | 5 |

### East Germany?

| | |
|---|---|
| Great deal ......................... | 3% |
| Only some ........................ | 14 |
| Very little ........................ | 42 |
| None at all ....................... | 30 |
| No opinion ........................ | 11 |

## Other Countries

| | Great deal responses only | Very little and none at all responses only |
|---|---|---|
| Brazil ............. | 9% | 37% |
| Canada ............ | 2 | 72 |
| Germany (West) ..... | 1 | 83 |
| Great Britain ........ | 1 | 75 |
| Switzerland ........ | 3 | 76 |

## Poland?

| | |
|---|---|
| Great deal | 1% |
| Only some | 8 |
| Very little | 42 |
| None at all | 39 |
| No opinion | 10 |

### Other Countries

| | Great deal responses only | Very little and none at all responses only |
|---|---|---|
| Brazil | 8% | 44% |
| Canada | * | 83 |
| Germany (West) | * | 89 |
| Great Britain | * | 89 |
| Switzerland | 2 | 86 |

*Less than 1%

## Soviet Union?

| | |
|---|---|
| Great deal | 1% |
| Only some | 5 |
| Very little | 33 |
| None at all | 53 |
| No opinion | 8 |

### Other Countries

| | Great deal responses only | Very little and none at all responses only |
|---|---|---|
| Brazil | 9% | 51% |
| Canada | 1 | 88 |
| Germany (West) | * | 86 |
| Great Britain | 1 | 87 |
| Switzerland | 1 | 85 |

*Less than 1%

## Red China?

| | |
|---|---|
| Great deal | 2% |
| Only some | 13 |
| Very little | 40 |
| None at all | 38 |
| No opinion | 8 |

### Other Countries

| | Great deal responses only | Very little and none at all responses only |
|---|---|---|
| Brazil | 17% | 52% |
| Canada | 1 | 75 |
| Germany (West) | 1 | 70 |
| Great Britain | 2 | 62 |
| Switzerland | 4 | 63 |

## Japan?

| | |
|---|---|
| Great deal | 37% |
| Only some | 36 |
| Very little | 16 |
| None at all | 3 |
| No opinion | 7 |

### Other Countries

| | Great deal responses only | Very little and none at all responses only |
|---|---|---|
| Brazil | 23% | 19% |
| Canada | 36 | 24 |
| Germany (West) | 40 | 18 |
| Great Britain | 26 | 19 |
| Switzerland | 47 | 18 |

## Italy?

| | |
|---|---|
| Great deal | 31% |
| Only some | 41 |
| Very little | 13 |
| None at all | 1 |
| No opinion | 14 |

### Other Countries

| | Great deal responses only | Very little and none at all responses only |
|---|---|---|
| Brazil | 23% | 16% |
| Canada | 39 | 13 |
| Germany (West) | 56 | 7 |
| Great Britain | 31 | 8 |
| Switzerland | 70 | 5 |

## Canada?

| | |
|---|---|
| Great deal | 78% |
| Only some | 13 |
| Very little | 2 |
| None at all | 1 |
| No opinion | 6 |

### Other Countries

| | Great deal responses only | Very little and none at all responses only |
|---|---|---|
| Brazil | 22% | 19% |
| Canada | 85 | 2 |
| Germany (West) | 75 | 5 |
| Great Britain | 76 | 1 |
| Switzerland | 83 | 2 |

## Mexico?

| | |
|---|---|
| Great deal | 26% |
| Only some | 43 |
| Very little | 19 |
| None at all | 3 |
| No opinion | 10 |

### Other Countries

| | Great deal responses only | Very little and none at all responses only |
|---|---|---|
| Brazil | 20% | 18% |
| Canada | 21 | 22 |
| Germany (West) | 26 | 30 |
| Great Britain | 9 | 29 |
| Switzerland | 25 | 27 |

## India?

| | |
|---|---|
| Great deal | 9% |
| Only some | 31 |
| Very little | 34 |
| None at all | 8 |
| No opinion | 18 |

### Other Countries

| | Great deal responses only | Very little and none at all responses only |
|---|---|---|
| Brazil | 11% | 31% |
| Canada | 10 | 40 |
| Germany (West) | 8 | 52 |
| Great Britain | 8 | 44 |
| Switzerland | 11 | 44 |

## Iran?

| | |
|---|---|
| Great deal | 1% |
| Only some | 9 |
| Very little | 35 |
| None at all | 45 |
| No opinion | 10 |

### Other Countries

| | Great deal responses only | Very little and none at all responses only |
|---|---|---|
| Brazil | 5% | 55% |
| Canada | * | 81 |
| Germany (West) | * | 82 |
| Great Britain | 1 | 83 |
| Switzerland | 2 | 83 |

*Less than 1%

Note: While most Americans say they enjoy a great deal of freedom, they have serious doubts about the degree of freedom in many other nations of the world, including some of our closest allies. Eight in ten U.S. citizens (80%) say Americans have a great deal of freedom, but far fewer (60%) say this about the British and even less (44%) think the French people have a great deal of freedom. The Canadians (78%) are the only people thought by Americans to have a level of freedom comparable to their own.

These findings are from a six-nation survey conducted late last year by Gallup International in the United States, Brazil, Canada, Switzerland, the United Kingdom, and West Germany. Survey respondents in the six countries are nearly unanimous in their opinion that in the Communist nations, as well as in Iran, the people have little freedom or none at all. Perceptions of the levels of freedom in the other nations tested varied widely.

This report is the second in a two-part series on public opinion based on George Orwell's novel *1984*. While survey respondents in each of the six nations say few of Orwell's pessimistic predictions have come true, they nevertheless see the loss of privacy and economic deprivation as serious threats to their personal freedom.

Orwell wrote *1984* amidst the despair of postwar Europe and might be bemused today by the irony of seven in ten West Germans (69%) rating themselves on a par with the French and British as possessing a great deal of freedom. The Swiss, untouched by World War II, rate West Germany very highly, but in English-speaking nations West Germany is seen as enjoying great freedom by only 41% of the British, 37% of the Canadians, and 33% of the Americans. The West Germans and other Western nations look askance at affairs in East Germany, with 3% or fewer believing East Germans possess a great deal of freedom, and with 72% or more—83% in West Germany—saying they have little or no freedom.

Fewer West Germans see Japan (40%) and Italy (56%) as having freedom than they believe is true in their own country. The Swiss are more generous in their opinions, but other nations are less sure about the degree of freedom enjoyed by the Japanese and Italians.

Mexico is believed by about only one person in four in the nations surveyed (except in Britain) to possess a great deal of freedom, and about the same proportion say Mexicans enjoy little or no freedom.

India may be the land of Indira Gandhi, but only about one in ten of the people surveyed in other nations believes Indians enjoy a great deal of freedom. Conversely, about four in ten say the people of India have little or no freedom.

Survey respondents in the West see very little or no freedom in the USSR or Poland, with over eight in ten respondents in the industrialized West giving this opinion. Red China, perhaps as a result of its publicized liberalization in recent years, fares only slightly better.

# FEBRUARY 9
# PRESIDENT REAGAN

Interviewing Date: 1/13–16/84
Survey #229-G

> *Now let me ask you about some specific problems. As I read off each problem, would you tell me whether you approve or disapprove of the way President Ronald Reagan is handling that problem:*

*Economic conditions in this country?*

Approve . . . . . . . . . . . . . . . . . . . . . . . . .48%
Disapprove . . . . . . . . . . . . . . . . . . . . . . .43
No opinion . . . . . . . . . . . . . . . . . . . . . . . 9

## By Sex
### Male

Approve . . . . . . . . . . . . . . . . . . . . . . . . .56%
Disapprove . . . . . . . . . . . . . . . . . . . . . . .39
No opinion . . . . . . . . . . . . . . . . . . . . . . . 5

### Female

Approve . . . . . . . . . . . . . . . . . . . . . . . . .41%
Disapprove . . . . . . . . . . . . . . . . . . . . . . .47
No opinion . . . . . . . . . . . . . . . . . . . . . . .12

## By Ethnic Background
### White

Approve . . . . . . . . . . . . . . . . . . . . . . . . .53%
Disapprove . . . . . . . . . . . . . . . . . . . . . . .39
No opinion . . . . . . . . . . . . . . . . . . . . . . . 8

### Nonwhite

Approve . . . . . . . . . . . . . . . . . . . . . . . . .17%
Disapprove . . . . . . . . . . . . . . . . . . . . . . .72
No opinion . . . . . . . . . . . . . . . . . . . . . . .11

### Black

Approve . . . . . . . . . . . . . . . . . . . . . . . . .12%
Disapprove . . . . . . . . . . . . . . . . . . . . . . .76
No opinion . . . . . . . . . . . . . . . . . . . . . . .12

## By Education
### College Graduate
Approve . . . . . . . . . . . . . . . . . . . . . . . . . . .62%
Disapprove . . . . . . . . . . . . . . . . . . . . . .33
No opinion . . . . . . . . . . . . . . . . . . . . . 5

### College Incomplete
Approve . . . . . . . . . . . . . . . . . . . . . . . . . .56%
Disapprove . . . . . . . . . . . . . . . . . . . . . .38
No opinion . . . . . . . . . . . . . . . . . . . . . 6

### High-School Graduate
Approve . . . . . . . . . . . . . . . . . . . . . . . . . .48%
Disapprove . . . . . . . . . . . . . . . . . . . . . .43
No opinion . . . . . . . . . . . . . . . . . . . . . 9

### Less Than High-School Graduate
Approve . . . . . . . . . . . . . . . . . . . . . . . . . .30%
Disapprove . . . . . . . . . . . . . . . . . . . . . .56
No opinion . . . . . . . . . . . . . . . . . . . . .14

## By Region
### East
Approve . . . . . . . . . . . . . . . . . . . . . . . . . .48%
Disapprove . . . . . . . . . . . . . . . . . . . . . .44
No opinion . . . . . . . . . . . . . . . . . . . . . 8

### Midwest
Approve . . . . . . . . . . . . . . . . . . . . . . . . . .48%
Disapprove . . . . . . . . . . . . . . . . . . . . . .45
No opinion . . . . . . . . . . . . . . . . . . . . . 7

### South
Approve . . . . . . . . . . . . . . . . . . . . . . . . . .49%
Disapprove . . . . . . . . . . . . . . . . . . . . . .41
No opinion . . . . . . . . . . . . . . . . . . . . .10

### West
Approve . . . . . . . . . . . . . . . . . . . . . . . . . .48%
Disapprove . . . . . . . . . . . . . . . . . . . . . .44
No opinion . . . . . . . . . . . . . . . . . . . . . 8

## By Age
### 18–29 Years
Approve . . . . . . . . . . . . . . . . . . . . . . . . . .46%
Disapprove . . . . . . . . . . . . . . . . . . . . . .45
No opinion . . . . . . . . . . . . . . . . . . . . . 9

### 30–49 Years
Approve . . . . . . . . . . . . . . . . . . . . . . . . . .53%
Disapprove . . . . . . . . . . . . . . . . . . . . . .42
No opinion . . . . . . . . . . . . . . . . . . . . . 5

### 50 Years and Over
Approve . . . . . . . . . . . . . . . . . . . . . . . . . .45%
Disapprove . . . . . . . . . . . . . . . . . . . . . .44
No opinion . . . . . . . . . . . . . . . . . . . . .11

## By Politics
### Republicans
Approve . . . . . . . . . . . . . . . . . . . . . . . . . .79%
Disapprove . . . . . . . . . . . . . . . . . . . . . .14
No opinion . . . . . . . . . . . . . . . . . . . . . 7

### Democrats
Approve . . . . . . . . . . . . . . . . . . . . . . . . . .29%
Disapprove . . . . . . . . . . . . . . . . . . . . . .64
No opinion . . . . . . . . . . . . . . . . . . . . . 7

### Independents
Approve . . . . . . . . . . . . . . . . . . . . . . . . . .48%
Disapprove . . . . . . . . . . . . . . . . . . . . . .41
No opinion . . . . . . . . . . . . . . . . . . . . .11

### Foreign policy?
Approve . . . . . . . . . . . . . . . . . . . . . . . . . .38%
Disapprove . . . . . . . . . . . . . . . . . . . . . .49
No opinion . . . . . . . . . . . . . . . . . . . . .13

## By Sex
### Male
Approve . . . . . . . . . . . . . . . . . . . . . . . . . .42%
Disapprove . . . . . . . . . . . . . . . . . . . . . .50
No opinion . . . . . . . . . . . . . . . . . . . . . 8

### Female

Approve ...........................34%
Disapprove .......................48
No opinion .......................18

### By Ethnic Background
#### White

Approve ...........................41%
Disapprove .......................46
No opinion .......................13

#### Nonwhite

Approve ...........................17%
Disapprove .......................68
No opinion .......................15

#### Black

Approve ...........................12%
Disapprove .......................71
No opinion .......................17

### By Education
#### College Graduate

Approve ...........................38%
Disapprove .......................55
No opinion ....................... 7

#### College Incomplete

Approve ...........................46%
Disapprove .......................22
No opinion .......................12

#### High-School Graduate

Approve ...........................40%
Disapprove .......................47
No opinion .......................13

#### Less Than High-School Graduate

Approve ...........................28%
Disapprove .......................53
No opinion .......................19

### By Region
#### East

Approve ...........................34%
Disapprove .......................50
No opinion .......................16

#### Midwest

Approve ...........................36%
Disapprove .......................53
No opinion .......................11

#### South

Approve ...........................43%
Disapprove .......................43
No opinion .......................14

#### West

Approve ...........................38%
Disapprove .......................50
No opinion .......................12

### By Age
#### 18–29 Years

Approve ...........................39%
Disapprove .......................49
No opinion .......................12

#### 30–49 Years

Approve ...........................43%
Disapprove .......................47
No opinion .......................10

#### 50 Years and Over

Approve ...........................32%
Disapprove .......................51
No opinion .......................17

### By Politics
#### Republicans

Approve ...........................63%
Disapprove .......................24
No opinion .......................13

### Democrats

Approve . . . . . . . . . . . . . . . . . . . . . . . . . .24%
Disapprove . . . . . . . . . . . . . . . . . . . . . .64
No opinion . . . . . . . . . . . . . . . . . . . . . .12

### Independents

Approve . . . . . . . . . . . . . . . . . . . . . . . . . .34%
Disapprove . . . . . . . . . . . . . . . . . . . . . .52
No opinion . . . . . . . . . . . . . . . . . . . . . .14

### Situation in Lebanon?

Approve . . . . . . . . . . . . . . . . . . . . . . . . . .28%
Disapprove . . . . . . . . . . . . . . . . . . . . . .59
No opinion . . . . . . . . . . . . . . . . . . . . . .13

## By Sex
### Male

Approve . . . . . . . . . . . . . . . . . . . . . . . . . .31%
Disapprove . . . . . . . . . . . . . . . . . . . . . .59
No opinion . . . . . . . . . . . . . . . . . . . . . .10

### Female

Approve . . . . . . . . . . . . . . . . . . . . . . . . . .25%
Disapprove . . . . . . . . . . . . . . . . . . . . . .59
No opinion . . . . . . . . . . . . . . . . . . . . . .16

## By Ethnic Background
### White

Approve . . . . . . . . . . . . . . . . . . . . . . . . . .30%
Disapprove . . . . . . . . . . . . . . . . . . . . . .57
No opinion . . . . . . . . . . . . . . . . . . . . . .13

### Nonwhite

Approve . . . . . . . . . . . . . . . . . . . . . . . . . .13%
Disapprove . . . . . . . . . . . . . . . . . . . . . .74
No opinion . . . . . . . . . . . . . . . . . . . . . .13

### Black

Approve . . . . . . . . . . . . . . . . . . . . . . . . . .10%
Disapprove . . . . . . . . . . . . . . . . . . . . . .77
No opinion . . . . . . . . . . . . . . . . . . . . . .13

## By Education
### College Graduate

Approve . . . . . . . . . . . . . . . . . . . . . . . . . .30%
Disapprove . . . . . . . . . . . . . . . . . . . . . .62
No opinion . . . . . . . . . . . . . . . . . . . . . . 8

### College Incomplete

Approve . . . . . . . . . . . . . . . . . . . . . . . . . .26%
Disapprove . . . . . . . . . . . . . . . . . . . . . .59
No opinion . . . . . . . . . . . . . . . . . . . . . .15

### High-School Graduate

Approve . . . . . . . . . . . . . . . . . . . . . . . . . .30%
Disapprove . . . . . . . . . . . . . . . . . . . . . .58
No opinion . . . . . . . . . . . . . . . . . . . . . .12

### Less Than High-School Graduate

Approve . . . . . . . . . . . . . . . . . . . . . . . . . .24%
Disapprove . . . . . . . . . . . . . . . . . . . . . .58
No opinion . . . . . . . . . . . . . . . . . . . . . .18

## By Region
### East

Approve . . . . . . . . . . . . . . . . . . . . . . . . . .24%
Disapprove . . . . . . . . . . . . . . . . . . . . . .64
No opinion . . . . . . . . . . . . . . . . . . . . . .12

### Midwest

Approve . . . . . . . . . . . . . . . . . . . . . . . . . .25%
Disapprove . . . . . . . . . . . . . . . . . . . . . .63
No opinion . . . . . . . . . . . . . . . . . . . . . .12

### South

Approve . . . . . . . . . . . . . . . . . . . . . . . . . .32%
Disapprove . . . . . . . . . . . . . . . . . . . . . .52
No opinion . . . . . . . . . . . . . . . . . . . . . .16

### West

Approve ...........................30%
Disapprove .........................58
No opinion .........................12

### By Age
#### 18–29 Years

Approve ...........................29%
Disapprove .........................58
No opinion .........................13

#### 30–49 Years

Approve ...........................32%
Disapprove .........................57
No opinion .........................11

#### 50 Years and Over

Approve ...........................23%
Disapprove .........................62
No opinion .........................15

### By Politics
#### Republicans

Approve ...........................45%
Disapprove .........................41
No opinion .........................14

#### Democrats

Approve ...........................18%
Disapprove .........................71
No opinion .........................11

#### Independents

Approve ...........................25%
Disapprove .........................60
No opinion .........................15

### Situation in Central America?

Approve ...........................28%
Disapprove .........................49
No opinion .........................23

### By Sex
#### Male

Approve ...........................34%
Disapprove .........................48
No opinion .........................18

#### Female

Approve ...........................22%
Disapprove .........................51
No opinion .........................27

### By Ethnic Background
#### White

Approve ...........................30%
Disapprove .........................47
No opinion .........................23

#### Nonwhite

Approve ...........................11%
Disapprove .........................67
No opinion .........................22

#### Black

Approve ........................... 9%
Disapprove .........................68
No opinion .........................23

### By Education
#### College Graduate

Approve ...........................30%
Disapprove .........................56
No opinion .........................14

#### College Incomplete

Approve ...........................30%
Disapprove .........................49
No opinion .........................21

### High-School Graduate

Approve ...........................31%
Disapprove ......................47
No opinion ......................22

### Less Than High-School Graduate

Approve ...........................20%
Disapprove ......................49
No opinion ......................31

## By Region
### East

Approve ...........................25%
Disapprove ......................55
No opinion ......................20

### Midwest

Approve ...........................28%
Disapprove ......................49
No opinion ......................23

### South

Approve ...........................32%
Disapprove ......................42
No opinion ......................26

### West

Approve ...........................25%
Disapprove ......................55
No opinion ......................20

## By Age
### 18–29 Years

Approve ...........................26%
Disapprove ......................47
No opinion ......................27

### 30–49 Years

Approve ...........................33%
Disapprove ......................48
No opinion ......................19

### 50 Years and Over

Approve ...........................24%
Disapprove ......................53
No opinion ......................23

## By Politics
### Republicans

Approve ...........................40%
Disapprove ......................37
No opinion ......................23

### Democrats

Approve ...........................20%
Disapprove ......................61
No opinion ......................19

### Independents

Approve ...........................27%
Disapprove ......................47
No opinion ......................26

Note: President Ronald Reagan's political standing is enhanced by steadily growing public approval for his handling of the economy. However, he appears to be increasingly vulnerable on foreign policy issues at a time when Americans' concern over the threat of war has grown to its highest point since the Vietnam War.

The latest survey shows 48% approving and 43% disapproving of Reagan's handling of economic conditions. In August the figures were 37% approval and 54% disapproval. On his handling of foreign policy, fewer approve (38%) than disapprove (49%) of Reagan's performance, a drop of 8 points in approval since a survey conducted soon after the successful Grenada action last fall.

Approval is also falling for Reagan's handling of the situation in Lebanon and Central America. Currently, 28% approve and 59% disapprove of Reagan's handling of the Lebanese situation; in November the figures were 34% and 52%, respectively.

On Central America, 28% approve and 49% disapprove, a downturn since November when 36% approved of his handling of the situation there and 44% disapproved.

The public's latest appraisals of the president's performance on the domestic and foreign fronts should be examined in the context of their key concerns today. For the first time since the Vietnam War, international tensions and the threat of war are named by the American people as the top problems facing the United States. This marks a sharp departure from surveys conducted between 1973 and 1983 when economic problems were paramount. A total of 37% now name the threat of war, followed closely by unemployment named by 32%, as the number one problem.

The public's views on the president's handling of specific problems depend in considerable measure on their political affiliation, with far more Republicans than either Democrats or independents approving of Reagan's actions.

## FEBRUARY 12
## NATIONAL SERVICE AND GOVERNMENT BENEFITS

Interviewing Date: 12/9–12/83
Survey #228-G

*It has been proposed that all young men and women be required to give one year of national service, either in the armed forces or in civilian social work. In return, they would receive government benefits to help cover the cost of their college education. Does this proposal sound like a good idea or a poor idea to you?*

Good idea . . . . . . . . . . . . . . . . . . . . . . . . . .65%
Poor idea . . . . . . . . . . . . . . . . . . . . . . . . . .30
No opinion . . . . . . . . . . . . . . . . . . . . . . . . 5

### By Sex
#### Male

Good idea . . . . . . . . . . . . . . . . . . . . . . . . . .65%
Poor idea . . . . . . . . . . . . . . . . . . . . . . . . . .30
No opinion . . . . . . . . . . . . . . . . . . . . . . . . 5

#### Female

Good idea . . . . . . . . . . . . . . . . . . . . . . . . . .64%
Poor idea . . . . . . . . . . . . . . . . . . . . . . . . . .31
No opinion . . . . . . . . . . . . . . . . . . . . . . . . 5

### By Ethnic Background
#### White

Good idea . . . . . . . . . . . . . . . . . . . . . . . . . .64%
Poor idea . . . . . . . . . . . . . . . . . . . . . . . . . .31
No opinion . . . . . . . . . . . . . . . . . . . . . . . . 5

#### Nonwhite

Good idea . . . . . . . . . . . . . . . . . . . . . . . . . .66%
Poor idea . . . . . . . . . . . . . . . . . . . . . . . . . .25
No opinion . . . . . . . . . . . . . . . . . . . . . . . . 9

#### Black

Good idea . . . . . . . . . . . . . . . . . . . . . . . . . .66%
Poor idea . . . . . . . . . . . . . . . . . . . . . . . . . .24
No opinion . . . . . . . . . . . . . . . . . . . . . . . . 10

### By Education
#### College Graduate

Good idea . . . . . . . . . . . . . . . . . . . . . . . . . .74%
Poor idea . . . . . . . . . . . . . . . . . . . . . . . . . .24
No opinion . . . . . . . . . . . . . . . . . . . . . . . . 2

#### College Incomplete

Good idea . . . . . . . . . . . . . . . . . . . . . . . . . .61%
Poor idea . . . . . . . . . . . . . . . . . . . . . . . . . .34
No opinion . . . . . . . . . . . . . . . . . . . . . . . . 5

#### High-School Graduate

Good idea . . . . . . . . . . . . . . . . . . . . . . . . . .63%
Poor idea . . . . . . . . . . . . . . . . . . . . . . . . . .32
No opinion . . . . . . . . . . . . . . . . . . . . . . . . 5

#### Less Than High-School Graduate

Good idea . . . . . . . . . . . . . . . . . . . . . . . . . .63%
Poor idea . . . . . . . . . . . . . . . . . . . . . . . . . .30
No opinion . . . . . . . . . . . . . . . . . . . . . . . . 7

## By Age

### 18–24 Years

Good idea ......................... 58%
Poor idea ......................... 38
No opinion ........................ 4

### 25–29 Years

Good idea ......................... 60%
Poor idea ......................... 34
No opinion ........................ 6

### 30–49 Years

Good idea ......................... 66%
Poor idea ......................... 30
No opinion ........................ 4

### 50 Years and Over

Good idea ......................... 67%
Poor idea ......................... 27
No opinion ........................ 6

## By Politics

### Republicans

Good idea ......................... 62%
Poor idea ......................... 35
No opinion ........................ 3

### Democrats

Good idea ......................... 68%
Poor idea ......................... 26
No opinion ........................ 6

### Independents

Good idea ......................... 64%
Poor idea ......................... 30
No opinion ........................ 6

Note: The American people have long favored a national program of voluntary youth service, recently proposed by Senator John Glenn, but they would go farther than the Democratic presidential candidate suggested and make such a program mandatory. A recent Gallup survey shows that two-thirds (65%) of the American people favor a national service plan requiring all young men and women to give one year of national service, either in the armed forces or in nonmilitary social work. In return they would receive government benefits to help cover the cost of their college education, as stipulated in the Glenn proposal. Such a program also meets with the support of 58% of young adults (18 to 24) who would be most affected if such a plan were launched. The views of men and women are virtually identical.

The idea of tying national service to college benefits was advanced by David S. Saxon, chairman of M.I.T., who recommended in a speech last November that "we examine thoroughly the potential of a program of universal service coupled with an analogous universal 'G.I. Bill' for education." Saxon's plan would cover all young people, men and women alike; encourage military service and a variety of socially valuable activities; permit no deferments except for extreme hardship or disability; ensure that all service activities are integrated ethnically, racially, sexually, and socioeconomically; and provide access to higher education or to alternative postsecondary training for all persons in the program.

Proponents of national service believe that such a program should be part of the educational process, enabling young persons to experience the real world. Others favor it as a way to provide special training to those who do not plan to go on to college. Still others like the concept because they think it would give all young people a better and more realistic view of the social problems of America, while offering them an opportunity to find solutions. Still others note that national service could meet head on one of the most basic and intractable problems of U.S. society: youth unemployment.

Earlier surveys have shown that the following areas are among those in nonmilitary service that potential volunteers would find of greatest interest: conservation work in national forests and parks, tutoring low-achieving students, day care for young children, assistance for the elderly, help in floods and natural disasters, hospital work, and rehabilitating run-down housing.

## FEBRUARY 16
## DEMOCRATIC PRESIDENTIAL CANDIDATES

Interviewing Date: 2/10–13/84
Survey #231-G

*Asked of Democrats and independents: Which one of the persons on this card would you like to see nominated as the Democratic party's candidate for president this year?*

### Choice of Democrats

|  | Feb. 10–13 | Jan. 27–30 | Jan. 13–16 |
|---|---|---|---|
| Walter Mondale ...... | 49% | 47% | 47% |
| Jesse Jackson ........ | 13 | 11 | 9 |
| John Glenn .......... | 13 | 15 | 16 |
| George McGovern .... | 5 | 7 | 4 |
| Reubin Askew ....... | 2 | 2 | 1 |
| Alan Cranston ....... | 3 | 3 | 4 |
| Gary Hart ........... | 3 | 2 | 3 |
| Ernest Hollings ...... | 1 | 1 | 1 |
| None; don't know .... | 11 | 12 | 15 |

### Choice of Independents

|  | Feb. 10–13 | Jan. 27–30 | Jan. 13–16 |
|---|---|---|---|
| Mondale ........... | 33% | 32% | 30% |
| Jackson ........... | 9 | 8 | 9 |
| Glenn ............. | 22 | 18 | 24 |
| McGovern .......... | 7 | 7 | 8 |
| Askew ............ | 2 | 3 | 1 |
| Cranston ........... | 3 | 4 | 3 |
| Hart .............. | 3 | 6 | 2 |
| Hollings ........... | 3 | 1 | 1 |
| None; don't know .... | 18 | 21 | 22 |

*Asked of Democrats and independents: Suppose the choice for president in the Democratic convention this year narows down to Walter Mondale and John Glenn. Which one would you prefer to have the Democratic convention select?*

### Choice of Democrats

| Mondale | 70% |
|---|---|
| Glenn | 22 |
| Undecided | 8 |

### Selected National Trend

|  | Mondale | Glenn | Undecided |
|---|---|---|---|
| *1984* | | | |
| January 13–16 .... | 67% | 25% | 8% |
| *1983* | | | |
| December ........ | 57 | 34 | 9 |
| August .......... | 49 | 30 | 21 |
| February ......... | 52 | 30 | 18 |
| *1982* | | | |
| December ........ | 59 | 28 | 13 |

### Choice of Independents

| Mondale | 52% |
|---|---|
| Glenn | 33 |
| Undecided | 15 |

### Selected National Trend

|  | Mondale | Glenn | Undecided |
|---|---|---|---|
| *1984* | | | |
| January 13–16 .... | 45% | 42% | 13% |
| *1983* | | | |
| December ........ | 44 | 42 | 14 |
| August .......... | 34 | 39 | 27 |
| February ......... | 42 | 35 | 23 |
| *1982* | | | |
| December ........ | 41 | 40 | 19 |

Note: The Reverend Jesse Jackson has moved into a statistical tie with Senator John Glenn for second place as the choice of Democratic voters for their party's presidential nomination. Winning the vote of 49% of Democrats interviewed, former Vice-President Walter Mondale continues to have a solid hold on first place, as determined by a national in-person survey completed on February 13.

Jackson's move into a tie for second is due to his own growing appeal—up 6 points since November—as well as Glenn's loss of support—down 6 points. Although Glenn has slipped among Democratic voters, he is holding his own among independents but still trails Mondale 22% to 32% with this group.

When Mondale and Glenn are pitted head to head, Mondale holds more than a 3-to-1 lead over his rival among Democrats. Among independents, however, the race is a much closer 52% to 33%, with Mondale the favorite.

## FEBRUARY 19
## PRESIDENTIAL TRIAL HEATS

Interviewing Date: 2/10–13/84
Survey #231-G

*Asked of registered voters: Suppose the 1984 presidential election were being held today. If President Ronald Reagan were the Republican candidate and Walter Mondale were the Democratic candidate, which would you like to see win? [Those who were undecided were then asked: As of today, do you lean more to Reagan, the Republican, or to Mondale, the Democrat?]*

Reagan . . . . . . . . . . . . . . . . . . . . . . . . . . .52%
Mondale . . . . . . . . . . . . . . . . . . . . . . . . . .42
Other; undecided . . . . . . . . . . . . . . . . . . 6

### By Sex
#### Male

Reagan . . . . . . . . . . . . . . . . . . . . . . . . . . .55%
Mondale . . . . . . . . . . . . . . . . . . . . . . . . . .39
Other; undecided . . . . . . . . . . . . . . . . . . 6

#### Female

Reagan . . . . . . . . . . . . . . . . . . . . . . . . . . .49%
Mondale . . . . . . . . . . . . . . . . . . . . . . . . . .45
Other; undecided . . . . . . . . . . . . . . . . . . 6

### By Ethnic Background
#### White

Reagan . . . . . . . . . . . . . . . . . . . . . . . . . . .57%
Mondale . . . . . . . . . . . . . . . . . . . . . . . . . .37
Other; undecided . . . . . . . . . . . . . . . . . . 6

#### Nonwhite

Reagan . . . . . . . . . . . . . . . . . . . . . . . . . . .15%
Mondale . . . . . . . . . . . . . . . . . . . . . . . . . .77
Other; undecided . . . . . . . . . . . . . . . . . . 8

#### Black

Reagan . . . . . . . . . . . . . . . . . . . . . . . . . . .10%
Mondale . . . . . . . . . . . . . . . . . . . . . . . . . .81
Other; undecided . . . . . . . . . . . . . . . . . . 9

### By Education
#### College Graduate

Reagan . . . . . . . . . . . . . . . . . . . . . . . . . . .65%
Mondale . . . . . . . . . . . . . . . . . . . . . . . . . .31
Other; undecided . . . . . . . . . . . . . . . . . . 4

#### College Incomplete

Reagan . . . . . . . . . . . . . . . . . . . . . . . . . . .58%
Mondale . . . . . . . . . . . . . . . . . . . . . . . . . .36
Other; undecided . . . . . . . . . . . . . . . . . . 6

#### High-School Graduate

Reagan . . . . . . . . . . . . . . . . . . . . . . . . . . .50%
Mondale . . . . . . . . . . . . . . . . . . . . . . . . . .45
Other; undecided . . . . . . . . . . . . . . . . . . 5

#### Less Than High-School Graduate

Reagan . . . . . . . . . . . . . . . . . . . . . . . . . . .38%
Mondale . . . . . . . . . . . . . . . . . . . . . . . . . .54
Other; undecided . . . . . . . . . . . . . . . . . . 8

### By Region
#### East

Reagan . . . . . . . . . . . . . . . . . . . . . . . . . . .52%
Mondale . . . . . . . . . . . . . . . . . . . . . . . . . .43
Other; undecided . . . . . . . . . . . . . . . . . . 5

#### Midwest

Reagan . . . . . . . . . . . . . . . . . . . . . . . . . . .51%
Mondale . . . . . . . . . . . . . . . . . . . . . . . . . .44
Other; undecided . . . . . . . . . . . . . . . . . . 5

#### South

Reagan . . . . . . . . : . . . . . . . . . . . . . . . . . .54%
Mondale . . . . . . . . . . . . . . . . . . . . . . . . . .39
Other; undecided . . . . . . . . . . . . . . . . . . 7

### West

| | |
|---|---|
| Reagan | 51% |
| Mondale | 44 |
| Other; undecided | 5 |

## By Age
### 18–29 Years

| | |
|---|---|
| Reagan | 52% |
| Mondale | 45 |
| Other; undecided | 3 |

### 30–49 Years

| | |
|---|---|
| Reagan | 55% |
| Mondale | 40 |
| Other; undecided | 5 |

### 50 Years and Over

| | |
|---|---|
| Reagan | 55% |
| Mondale | 39 |
| Other; undecided | 6 |

## By Income
### $40,000 and Over

| | |
|---|---|
| Reagan | 70% |
| Mondale | 27 |
| Other; undecided | 3 |

### $30,000–$39,999

| | |
|---|---|
| Reagan | 58% |
| Mondale | 39 |
| Other; undecided | 3 |

### $20,000–$29,999

| | |
|---|---|
| Reagan | 52% |
| Mondale | 42 |
| Other; undecided | 6 |

### $10,000–$19,999

| | |
|---|---|
| Reagan | 47% |
| Mondale | 49 |
| Other; undecided | 4 |

### Under $10,000

| | |
|---|---|
| Reagan | 37% |
| Mondale | 53 |
| Other; undecided | 10 |

## By Politics
### Republicans

| | |
|---|---|
| Reagan | 87% |
| Mondale | 10 |
| Other; undecided | 3 |

### Democrats

| | |
|---|---|
| Reagan | 24% |
| Mondale | 72 |
| Other; undecided | 4 |

### Independents

| | |
|---|---|
| Reagan | 56% |
| Mondale | 35 |
| Other; undecided | 9 |

### Selected National Trend

| | Reagan | Mondale | Other; undecided |
|---|---|---|---|
| 1984 | | | |
| February 10–13 ... | 52% | 42% | 6% |
| January 27–30 .... | 53 | 43 | 4 |
| January 13–16 .... | 48 | 47 | 5 |
| 1983 | | | |
| December ........ | 51 | 44 | 5 |
| October ........ | 44 | 50 | 6 |
| August ......... | 44 | 43 | 13 |
| June ........... | 41 | 50 | 9 |
| April–May ....... | 43 | 49 | 8 |
| February ........ | 41 | 47 | 12 |
| 1982 | | | |
| December ........ | 40 | 52 | 8 |
| October ........ | 47 | 44 | 9 |

*Asked of registered voters: Suppose the 1984 presidential election were being held today. If President Ronald Reagan were the Republican candidate and Senator John Glenn were the Democratic candidate, which would you like to see win? [Those who were undecided were then asked: As of today, do you lean more to Reagan, the Republican, or to Glenn, the Democrat?]*

Reagan . . . . . . . . . . . . . . . . . . . . . . .53%
Glenn . . . . . . . . . . . . . . . . . . . . . . . .41
Other; undecided . . . . . . . . . . . . . . . . . . 6

## By Sex
### Male

Reagan . . . . . . . . . . . . . . . . . . . . . . .55%
Glenn . . . . . . . . . . . . . . . . . . . . . . . .39
Other; undecided . . . . . . . . . . . . . . . . . . 6

### Female

Reagan . . . . . . . . . . . . . . . . . . . . . . .52%
Glenn . . . . . . . . . . . . . . . . . . . . . . . .42
Other; undecided . . . . . . . . . . . . . . . . . . 6

## By Ethnic Background
### White

Reagan . . . . . . . . . . . . . . . . . . . . . . .58%
Glenn . . . . . . . . . . . . . . . . . . . . . . . .36
Other; undecided . . . . . . . . . . . . . . . . . . 6

### Nonwhite

Reagan . . . . . . . . . . . . . . . . . . . . . . .21%
Glenn . . . . . . . . . . . . . . . . . . . . . . . .70
Other; undecided . . . . . . . . . . . . . . . . . . 9

### Black

Reagan . . . . . . . . . . . . . . . . . . . . . . .15%
Glenn . . . . . . . . . . . . . . . . . . . . . . . .74
Other; undecided . . . . . . . . . . . . . . . . . .11

## By Education
### College Graduate

Reagan . . . . . . . . . . . . . . . . . . . . . . .62%
Glenn . . . . . . . . . . . . . . . . . . . . . . . .34
Other; undecided . . . . . . . . . . . . . . . . . . 4

### College Incomplete

Reagan . . . . . . . . . . . . . . . . . . . . . . .61%
Glenn . . . . . . . . . . . . . . . . . . . . . . . .34
Other; undecided . . . . . . . . . . . . . . . . . . 5

### High-School Graduate

Reagan . . . . . . . . . . . . . . . . . . . . . . .51%
Glenn . . . . . . . . . . . . . . . . . . . . . . . .42
Other; undecided . . . . . . . . . . . . . . . . . . 7

### Less Than High-School Graduate

Reagan . . . . . . . . . . . . . . . . . . . . . . .39%
Glenn . . . . . . . . . . . . . . . . . . . . . . . .52
Other; undecided . . . . . . . . . . . . . . . . . . 9

## By Region
### East

Reagan . . . . . . . . . . . . . . . . . . . . . . .55%
Glenn . . . . . . . . . . . . . . . . . . . . . . . .40
Other; undecided . . . . . . . . . . . . . . . . . . 5

### Midwest

Reagan . . . . . . . . . . . . . . . . . . . . . . .49%
Glenn . . . . . . . . . . . . . . . . . . . . . . . .45
Other; undecided . . . . . . . . . . . . . . . . . . 6

### South

Reagan . . . . . . . . . . . . . . . . . . . . . . .56%
Glenn . . . . . . . . . . . . . . . . . . . . . . . .36
Other; undecided . . . . . . . . . . . . . . . . . . 8

### West

Reagan . . . . . . . . . . . . . . . . . . . . . . .52%
Glenn . . . . . . . . . . . . . . . . . . . . . . . .42
Other; undecided . . . . . . . . . . . . . . . . . . 6

## By Age
### 18–29 Years

Reagan . . . . . . . . . . . . . . . . . . . . . . .48%
Glenn . . . . . . . . . . . . . . . . . . . . . . . .47
Other; undecided . . . . . . . . . . . . . . . . . . 5

### 30–49 Years

Reagan . . . . . . . . . . . . . . . . . . . . . . .59%
Glenn . . . . . . . . . . . . . . . . . . . . . . . .35
Other; undecided . . . . . . . . . . . . . . . . . . 6

### 50 Years and Over

Reagan ............................55%
Glenn .............................39
Other; undecided ..................6

## By Income

### $40,000 and Over

Reagan ............................70%
Glenn .............................27
Other; undecided ..................3

### $30,000–$39,999

Reagan ............................59%
Glenn .............................35
Other; undecided ..................6

### $20,000–$29,999

Reagan ............................54%
Glenn .............................39
Other; undecided ..................7

### $10,000–$19,999

Reagan ............................47%
Glenn .............................48
Other; undecided ..................5

### Under $10,000

Reagan ............................40%
Glenn .............................50
Other; undecided ..................10

## By Politics

### Republicans

Reagan ............................87%
Glenn .............................10
Other; undecided ..................3

### Democrats

Reagan ............................27%
Glenn .............................67
Other; undecided ..................6

### Independents

Reagan ............................55%
Glenn .............................35
Other; undecided ..................10

## Selected National Trend

|  | Reagan | Glenn | Other; undecided |
|---|---|---|---|
| **1984** | | | |
| February 10–13 ... | 53% | 41% | 6% |
| January 27–30 .... | 57 | 38 | 5 |
| January 13–16 .... | 47 | 45 | 8 |
| **1983** | | | |
| December ........ | 49 | 45 | 6 |
| October ......... | 42 | 49 | 9 |
| August .......... | 40 | 46 | 14 |
| June ............ | 38 | 53 | 9 |
| April–May ....... | 37 | 54 | 9 |
| February ........ | 40 | 45 | 15 |
| **1982** | | | |
| December ........ | 39 | 54 | 7 |

Note: In the aftermath of the momentous foreign events of the past few weeks, President Ronald Reagan holds modest leads over Walter Mondale and John Glenn, two of his most likely Democratic opponents in this fall's presidential election. In the latest Gallup survey, conducted soon after the president's February 7 order to redeploy American marines from their Beirut outpost to U.S. Navy ships offshore and the February 9 death of Soviet leader Yuri Andropov, Reagan edges out Mondale 52% to 42%, with 6% undecided. The president currently tops Glenn by 12 points, 53% to 41%, with 6% undecided. Thus, Glenn displays almost as much voter strength against Reagan as does Mondale, despite the fact that the Ohio senator is far behind Mondale as the nomination choice of Democrats.

In a previously unreported test election taken between January 27 and 30, Reagan scored a 53%-to-43% victory over Mondale, representing the president's strongest showing against Mondale in over two years. In mid-January the two men were statistically tied, with Reagan winning 48% of the vote to Mondale's 47%.

In the late January test election, Reagan was the 57% to 38% winner over Glenn, his best record to date against the Ohio senator. The mid-January contest ended in a statistical deadlock—47% to 45%, respectively.

## FEBRUARY 23
## PRESIDENT REAGAN

Interviewing Date: 2/10–13/84
Survey #231-G

*Do you approve or disapprove of the way Ronald Reagan is handling his job as president?*

Approve ...........................55%
Disapprove .......................36
No opinion ...................... 9

### By Sex
#### Male

Approve ...........................60%
Disapprove .......................33
No opinion ...................... 7

#### Female

Approve ...........................51%
Disapprove .......................38
No opinion ......................11

### By Ethnic Background
#### White

Approve ...........................60%
Disapprove .......................32
No opinion ...................... 8

#### Nonwhite

Approve ...........................25%
Disapprove .......................64
No opinion ......................11

#### Black

Approve ...........................21%
Disapprove .......................67
No opinion ......................12

### By Education
#### College Graduate

Approve ...........................66%
Disapprove .......................31
No opinion ...................... 3

#### College Incomplete

Approve ...........................63%
Disapprove .......................31
No opinion ...................... 6

#### High-School Graduate

Approve ...........................58%
Disapprove .......................33
No opinion ...................... 9

#### Less Than High-School Graduate

Approve ...........................39%
Disapprove .......................47
No opinion ......................14

### By Region
#### East

Approve ...........................52%
Disapprove .......................40
No opinion ...................... 8

#### Midwest

Approve ...........................55%
Disapprove .......................36
No opinion ...................... 9

#### South

Approve ...........................61%
Disapprove .......................29
No opinion ......................10

#### West

Approve ...........................53%
Disapprove .......................40
No opinion ...................... 7

## By Age

### 18–29 Years

Approve ........................... 55%
Disapprove ......................... 36
No opinion ......................... 9

### 30–49 Years

Approve ........................... 58%
Disapprove ......................... 33
No opinion ......................... 9

### 50 Years and Over

Approve ........................... 57%
Disapprove ......................... 34
No opinion ......................... 9

## By Politics

### Republicans

Approve ........................... 86%
Disapprove ......................... 11
No opinion ......................... 3

### Democrats

Approve ........................... 33%
Disapprove ......................... 60
No opinion ......................... 7

### Independents

Approve ........................... 56%
Disapprove ......................... 32
No opinion ......................... 12

### Selected National Trend

|  | Approve | Dis-approve | No opinion |
|---|---|---|---|
| *1984* | | | |
| February 10–13 ..... | 55% | 36% | 9% |
| January 27–30 ...... | 55 | 37 | 8 |
| January 13–16 ...... | 52 | 38 | 10 |
| *1983* | | | |
| December ......... | 54 | 38 | 8 |
| October .......... | 45 | 44 | 11 |
| August ........... | 44 | 46 | 10 |
| June ............. | 43 | 45 | 12 |
| May ............. | 43 | 45 | 12 |
| March ........... | 41 | 49 | 10 |
| January ......... | 35 | 56 | 9 |

Note: President Ronald Reagan's standing with the American people continues the strong upward momentum that began one year ago, paralleling the economic recovery. His current job performance rating of 55% approval represents an unprecedented 20-percentage point improvement over the 35% approval rating recorded in late January 1983, his lowest showing to date. Not since mid-1981, during his "honeymoon" in office, has Reagan received significantly higher job ratings than at present.

Reagan's well-publicized "gender gap" still exists; 60% of men compared to 51% of women approve of his performance in office. Nevertheless, the fact that a majority of women approves—for the first time since the fall of 1981—is indicative of the general upward trend in the president's popularity.

## FEBRUARY 23
## LEBANON SITUATION

Interviewing Date: 2/10–13/84*
Survey #231-G

*Do you think the United States made a mistake in sending the marines to Lebanon, or not?*

Yes ............................... 58%
No ................................ 33
Don't know ........................ 9

## By Sex
### Male

Yes ............................... 58%
No ................................ 36
Don't know ........................ 6

*On February 7, President Ronald Reagan decided to withdraw American troops from Lebanon.

### Female

| | |
|---|---|
| Yes | 58% |
| No | 29 |
| Don't know | 13 |

### By Race

#### White

| | |
|---|---|
| Yes | 56% |
| No | 35 |
| Don't know | 9 |

#### Nonwhite

| | |
|---|---|
| Yes | 70% |
| No | 17 |
| Don't know | 13 |

#### Black

| | |
|---|---|
| Yes | 74% |
| No | 14 |
| Don't know | 12 |

### By Education

#### College Graduate

| | |
|---|---|
| Yes | 61% |
| No | 35 |
| Don't know | 4 |

#### College Incomplete

| | |
|---|---|
| Yes | 51% |
| No | 42 |
| Don't know | 7 |

#### High-School Graduate

| | |
|---|---|
| Yes | 56% |
| No | 35 |
| Don't know | 9 |

#### Less Than High-School Graduate

| | |
|---|---|
| Yes | 64% |
| No | 20 |
| Don't know | 16 |

### By Region

#### East

| | |
|---|---|
| Yes | 59% |
| No | 32 |
| Don't know | 9 |

#### Midwest

| | |
|---|---|
| Yes | 61% |
| No | 31 |
| Don't know | 8 |

#### South

| | |
|---|---|
| Yes | 53% |
| No | 35 |
| Don't know | 12 |

#### West

| | |
|---|---|
| Yes | 61% |
| No | 32 |
| Don't know | 7 |

### By Age

#### 18–24 Years

| | |
|---|---|
| Yes | 56% |
| No | 36 |
| Don't know | 8 |

#### 25–29 Years

| | |
|---|---|
| Yes | 66% |
| No | 19 |
| Don't know | 15 |

#### 30–49 Years

| | |
|---|---|
| Yes | 56% |
| No | 36 |
| Don't know | 8 |

#### 50 Years and Over

| | |
|---|---|
| Yes | 57% |
| No | 33 |
| Don't know | 10 |

## By Politics
### Republicans

Yes ...............................44%
No ...............................46
Don't know .......................10

### Democrats

Yes ...............................69%
No ...............................23
Don't know ...................... 8

### Independents

Yes ...............................58%
No ...............................35
Don't know ...................... 7

## Selected National Trend

|  | Yes | No | Don't know |
|---|---|---|---|
| **1984** | | | |
| February 10–13 ....... | 58% | 33% | 9% |
| January 13–16 ........ | 52 | 39 | 9 |
| **1983** | | | |
| December ........... | 47 | 44 | 9 |
| November ........... | 45 | 45 | 10 |
| October ............. | 51 | 37 | 12 |

*Do you think the United States should withdraw its troops from Lebanon at the present time, or not?*

Should ...........................74%
Should not .......................17
Don't know ...................... 9

## By Sex
### Male

Should ...........................73%
Should not .......................21
Don't know ...................... 6

### Female

Should ...........................74%
Should not .......................14
Don't know ......................12

## By Ethnic Background
### White

Should ...........................73%
Should not .......................18
Don't know ...................... 9

### Nonwhite

Should ...........................78%
Should not .......................12
Don't know ......................10

### Black

Should ...........................78%
Should not .......................11
Don't know ......................11

## By Education
### College Graduate

Should ...........................77%
Should not .......................19
Don't know ...................... 4

### College Incomplete

Should ...........................70%
Should not .......................21
Don't know ...................... 9

### High-School Graduate

Should ...........................72%
Should not .......................18
Don't know ......................10

### Less Than High-School Graduate

Should ...........................76%
Should not .......................11
Don't know ......................13

## By Region
### East

Should ...........................77%
Should not .......................16
Don't know ...................... 7

### Midwest

Should ............................78%
Should not ........................15
Don't know .......................  7

### South

Should ............................65%
Should not ........................21
Don't know .......................14

### West

Should ............................75%
Should not ........................17
Don't know .......................  8

## By Age
### 18–24 Years

Should ............................80%
Should not ........................14
Don't know .......................  6

### 25–29 Years

Should ............................86%
Should not ........................  7
Don't know .......................  7

### 30–49 Years

Should ............................72%
Should not ........................20
Don't know .......................  8

### 50 Years and Over

Should ............................72%
Should not ........................17
Don't know .......................11

## By Politics
### Republicans

Should ............................68%
Should not ........................22
Don't know .......................10

### Democrats

Should ............................80%
Should not ........................13
Don't know .......................  7

### Independents

Should ............................71%
Should not ........................19
Don't know .......................10

Note: The proportion of Americans who now think that sending the marines to Lebanon was a mistake rose to 58% in the latest survey, representing the highest proportion to hold this view since measurements began in October 1983. In response to a companion question, an overwhelming 74% of Americans believe the United States should withdraw its marines from Lebanon; in the January 1984 survey, the figure was 57%.

## FEBRUARY 26
## CANDIDATE BETTER FOR PEACE AND PROSPERITY

Interviewing Date: 1/27–30/84
Survey #230-G

*Which man, if elected president in November, do you think would be more likely to keep the United States out of World War III— Ronald Reagan or Walter Mondale?*

Reagan ...........................35%
Mondale ..........................44
Same (volunteered) ................11
No opinion .......................10

## By Politics
### Republicans

Reagan ...........................67%
Mondale ..........................15
Same (volunteered) ................  9
No opinion .......................  9

### Democrats

| | |
|---|---|
| Reagan | 17% |
| Mondale | 64 |
| Same (volunteered) | 11 |
| No opinion | 8 |

### Independents

| | |
|---|---|
| Reagan | 32% |
| Mondale | 45 |
| Same (volunteered) | 11 |
| No opinion | 12 |

*Now which man would do a better job of keeping the country prosperous—Ronald Reagan or Walter Mondale?*

| | |
|---|---|
| Reagan | 50% |
| Mondale | 34 |
| Same (volunteered) | 6 |
| No opinion | 10 |

### By Politics
#### Republicans

| | |
|---|---|
| Reagan | 84% |
| Mondale | 8 |
| Same (volunteered) | 4 |
| No opinion | 4 |

#### Democrats

| | |
|---|---|
| Reagan | 26% |
| Mondale | 55 |
| Same (volunteered) | 7 |
| No opinion | 12 |

#### Independents

| | |
|---|---|
| Reagan | 57% |
| Mondale | 28 |
| Same (volunteered) | 7 |
| No opinion | 8 |

Note: A plurality of American voters (44%) believes that Democratic front-runner Walter Mondale is more likely than Ronald Reagan to keep the United States out of World War III. However, the president is favored over Mondale by a much larger margin—50% to 34%—as better able to keep the country prosperous.

The issues of peace and prosperity have been crucial in virtually all of the presidential elections of the last half century. Gallup Poll analyses consistently have shown that President Reagan's political support has been more strongly tied to perceptions of his ability to manage the economy. However, in recent months foreign affairs have become more important to the public; nonetheless, they still play a secondary role to economic evaluations.

As would be expected, Republicans overwhelmingly back Reagan on these two issues. Democrats give their wholehearted support to Mondale on the peace issue, but only a 55% majority of Democrats thinks the former vice-president could do a better job than Reagan in keeping the nation prosperous. The real battleground though is among independent voters, who represent more than one-fourth of the electorate. Independents lean heavily toward Reagan on prosperity but vote decisively for Mondale on the issue of peace.

### MARCH 1
### LEBANON SITUATION

Interviewing Date: 2/10–13/84
Survey #231-G

*Do you approve or disapprove of the way President Ronald Reagan is handling the situation in Lebanon?*

| | |
|---|---|
| Approve | 28% |
| Disapprove | 60 |
| No opinion | 12 |

Interviewing Date: 2/13–19/84
Special Telephone Survey

*Do you think all the U.S. forces, including the navy's ships, should be withdrawn from the Lebanon area, or do you feel the United States should maintain a presence in the area?*

Withdraw forces . . . . . . . . . . . . . . . . . . . . . .44%
Maintain presence . . . . . . . . . . . . . . . . . . . .41
Don't know . . . . . . . . . . . . . . . . . . . . . . . .15

Note: The American people are closely divided on the question of whether the United States should withdraw all its forces, including its navy's ships, from the Lebanese area, or continue to maintain a presence there. A total of 44% favors a complete withdrawal from the area, while 41% think we should continue to keep our forces in the Middle East. These findings demonstrate the extent to which the Lebanese issue has become politicized. By a 2-to-1 ratio Republicans believe the United States should maintain a presence in Lebanon, while Democrats, by almost as large a margin, think that we should withdraw all our forces there.

Amid widespread public confusion and concern over the future role of the United States in the Middle East, a growing majority of Americans expresses disapproval of the way President Ronald Reagan is handling the situation in Lebanon. Currently, 60% disapprove while 28% approve; in November, 52% disapproved and 34% approved.

During this period of growing disapproval, the proportion of Americans who believed we made a mistake in sending troops to Lebanon reached 58%, as reflected in a survey conducted just after Reagan's February 7 announcement that the United States would withdraw its forces from Beirut. In addition, the number of Americans who wanted troops withdrawn from Beirut climbed from 57% in January to 74% in the February 10–13 survey.

## MARCH 1
## UNITED STATES/SOVIET UNION RELATIONS

Interviewing Date: 2/13–19/84
Special Telephone Survey

*Have you heard or read about the death of Soviet leader Yuri Andropov?*

Yes . . . . . . . . . . . . . . . . . . . . . . . . . . . . . . .93%
No . . . . . . . . . . . . . . . . . . . . . . . . . . . . . . . 7

*Asked of those who responded in the affirmative: Under the new Soviet leadership, do you think relations between the United States and the Soviet Union will get better or get worse during the next five years?*

Better . . . . . . . . . . . . . . . . . . . . . . . . . . . . .33%
Worse . . . . . . . . . . . . . . . . . . . . . . . . . . . . .17
Same (volunteered) . . . . . . . . . . . . . . . . . . . .15
No opinion . . . . . . . . . . . . . . . . . . . . . . . . . .35

## MARCH 4
## PRESIDENT REAGAN

Interviewing Date: 2/10–13/84
Survey #231-G

*Now let me ask you about some specific problems. As I read off each problem, would you tell me whether you approve or disapprove of the way President Ronald Reagan is handling that problem:*

*Economic conditions in this country?*

Approve . . . . . . . . . . . . . . . . . . . . . . . . . . . .49%
Disapprove . . . . . . . . . . . . . . . . . . . . . . . . .44
No opinion . . . . . . . . . . . . . . . . . . . . . . . . . 7

### By Politics
#### Republicans

Approve . . . . . . . . . . . . . . . . . . . . . . . . . . . .77%
Disapprove . . . . . . . . . . . . . . . . . . . . . . . . .18
No opinion . . . . . . . . . . . . . . . . . . . . . . . . . 5

#### Democrats

Approve . . . . . . . . . . . . . . . . . . . . . . . . . . . .28%
Disapprove . . . . . . . . . . . . . . . . . . . . . . . . .67
No opinion . . . . . . . . . . . . . . . . . . . . . . . . . 5

#### Independents

Approve . . . . . . . . . . . . . . . . . . . . . . . . . . . .51%
Disapprove . . . . . . . . . . . . . . . . . . . . . . . . .41
No opinion . . . . . . . . . . . . . . . . . . . . . . . . . 8

## Selected National Trend

| | Percent approving |
|---|---|
| *1984* | |
| February .................... | 49% |
| January .................... | 48 |
| *1983* | |
| November .................... | 48 |
| August .................... | 37 |

### *Unemployment?*

Approve ........................42%
Disapprove ......................50
No opinion ..................... 8

## By Politics
### *Republicans*

Approve ........................66%
Disapprove ......................26
No opinion ..................... 8

### *Democrats*

Approve ........................24%
Disapprove ......................70
No opinion ..................... 6

### *Independents*

Approve ........................42%
Disapprove ......................49
No opinion ..................... 9

## Selected National Trend

| | Percent approving |
|---|---|
| February 1984 .................. | 42% |
| August 1983 .................. | 28 |

### *Federal government's budget deficit?*

Approve ........................22%
Disapprove ......................62
No opinion ......................16

## By Politics
### *Republicans*

Approve ........................35%
Disapprove ......................51
No opinion ......................14

### *Democrats*

Approve ........................12%
Disapprove ......................74
No opinion ......................14

### *Independents*

Approve ........................23%
Disapprove ......................61
No opinion ......................16

### *Foreign policy?*

Approve ........................40%
Disapprove ......................46
No opinion ......................14

## By Politics
### *Republicans*

Approve ........................59%
Disapprove ......................26
No opinion ......................15

### *Democrats*

Approve ........................24%
Disapprove ......................64
No opinion ......................12

### *Independents*

Approve ........................40%
Disapprove ......................46
No opinion ......................14

## Selected National Trend

| | Percent approving |
|---|---|
| *1984* | |
| February .................... | 40% |
| January .................... | 38 |

*1983*
November ...................... 46
October ....................... 44
August ........................ 31

### Relations with the Soviet Union?

Approve .........................43%
Disapprove ......................42
No opinion ......................15

## By Politics
### Republicans

Approve ..........................61%
Disapprove .......................27
No opinion .......................12

### Democrats

Approve ..........................28%
Disapprove .......................58
No opinion .......................14

### Independents

Approve ..........................46%
Disapprove .......................39
No opinion .......................15

## Selected National Trend

|  | *Percent approving* |
|---|---|
| *1984* | |
| February ...................... | 43% |
| *1983* | |
| November ...................... | 46 |
| October ....................... | 44 |
| August ........................ | 41 |

### Situation in Central America?

Approve ..........................29%
Disapprove .......................48
No opinion .......................23

## By Politics
### Republicans

Approve ..........................44%
Disapprove .......................24
No opinion .......................22

### Democrats

Approve ..........................21%
Disapprove .......................59
No opinion .......................20

### Independents

Approve ..........................26%
Disapprove .......................49
No opinion .......................25

## Selected National Trend

|  | *Percent approving* |
|---|---|
| *1984* | |
| February ...................... | 29% |
| January ....................... | 28 |
| *1983* | |
| November ...................... | 36 |
| October ....................... | 27 |
| August ........................ | 24 |

### Situation in Lebanon?

Approve ..........................28%
Disapprove .......................60
No opinion .......................12

## By Politics
### Republicans

Approve ..........................45%
Disapprove .......................44
No opinion .......................11

### Democrats

Approve ..........................17%
Disapprove .......................74
No opinion ....................... 9

Approve ...........................28%
Disapprove .........................59
No opinion ........................13

## Selected National Trend

|  | Percent approving |
|---|---|
| *1984* | |
| February ..................... | 28% |
| January ..................... | 28 |
| *1983* | |
| November ..................... | 34 |
| October ..................... | 28 |

Note: President Ronald Reagan's gradual rise in popularity has been achieved despite low public approval of his foreign policy in general and his handling of the situations in Central America and Lebanon, specifically. Instead, his approval rating is more closely related to favorable assessments of his handling of domestic economic conditions.

Not only does the president receive a higher overall rating (49% approval) for his economic accomplishments than for other aspects of his job, but also the trend—up 12 points since August—is matched only by a 14-point improvement for his handling of unemployment. Reagan receives the lowest rating (22% approval) for his handling of the federal government's budget deficits, a category not included in earlier surveys.

Reagan's mid-February performance rating of 55% approval represents a 20-percentage point improvement over the 35% approval rating recorded at a similar period in 1983. Such a strong upward trend on the part of an incumbent president seeking reelection is without precedent in Gallup's fifty years of polling experience. At the same time, however, a smaller proportion in the latest survey approves (40%) than disapproves (46%) of the president's handling of foreign policy; as recently as last November, following the Grenada invasion, 46% approved and 41% disapproved.

The latest survey, conducted soon after the death of Soviet leader Yuri Andropov, also shows no significant change in Americans' perceptions of President Reagan's handling of relations with the Soviet Union. Currently, 43% approve and 42% disapprove of his performance in that area.

Approval is also falling for Reagan's actions in Lebanon and Central America, with 28% approving and 60% disapproving of his handling of the Lebanese situation; in November the figures were 34% and 52%, respectively. On Central America, 29% approve and 48% disapprove, also representing a decline since November when 36% approved of Reagan's handling of the situation there and 44% disapproved.

The public's views on the president's handling of specific problems depend in considerable measure on their political affiliation. Far more Republicans than either Democrats or independents approve of Reagan's actions.

## MARCH 7

## DEMOCRATIC PRESIDENTIAL CANDIDATES/PRESIDENTIAL TRIAL HEATS

Interviewing Date: 3/2–6/84
Special Telephone Survey

*Asked of Democrats: Which one of these persons would you like to see nominated as the Democratic party's candidate for president this year?*

|  | Mar. 2–6 | Mar. 1–2* | Jan. 30–Feb. 6 |
|---|---|---|---|
| Walter Mondale | 33% | 40% | 54% |
| Gary Hart | 30 | 33 | 2 |
| Jesse Jackson | 9 | 5 | 10 |
| John Glenn | 5 | 8 | 16 |
| George McGovern | 3 | 1 | 3 |
| Other; don't know | 20 | 13 | 15 |

*Special Gallup/*Newsweek* survey

*Asked of Democrats and independents: Suppose the choice for president in the Democratic convention this year narrows down to Walter Mondale and Gary Hart. Which one would you prefer to have the Democratic convention select?*

### Choice of Democrats

Mondale . . . . . . . . . . . . . . . . . . . . . . . . . . .49%
Hart . . . . . . . . . . . . . . . . . . . . . . . . . . . . .39
Undecided . . . . . . . . . . . . . . . . . . . . . . . .12

### Choice of Independents

Mondale . . . . . . . . . . . . . . . . . . . . . . . . . . .25%
Hart . . . . . . . . . . . . . . . . . . . . . . . . . . . . .55
Undecided . . . . . . . . . . . . . . . . . . . . . . . .20

*Asked of registered voters: Suppose the 1984 presidential election were being held today. If President Ronald Reagan were the Republican candidate and Walter Mondale were the Democratic candidate, which would you like to see win? [Those who were undecided were then asked: As of today, do you lean more to Reagan, the Republican, or to Mondale, the Democrat?]*

|                       | Mar. 2–6 | Mar. 1–2 |
| --------------------- | -------- | -------- |
| Reagan . . . . . . . . . . . . . . . . . | 50% | 54% |
| Mondale . . . . . . . . . . . . . . . | 45 | 42 |
| Other; undecided . . . . . . . . | 5 | 4 |

*Asked of registered voters: Suppose the 1984 presidential election were being held today. If President Ronald Reagan were the Republican candidate and Gary Hart were the Democratic candidate, which would you like to see win? [Those who were undecided were then asked: As of today, do you lean more to Reagan, the Republican, or to Hart, the Democrat?]*

|                       | Mar. 2–6 | Mar. 1–2 |
| --------------------- | -------- | -------- |
| Reagan . . . . . . . . . . . . . . . . . | 43% | 49% |
| Hart . . . . . . . . . . . . . . . . . . . | 52 | 46 |
| Other; undecided . . . . . . . . | 5 | 5 |

*Asked of registered voters: Suppose the 1984 presidential election were being held today. If President Ronald Reagan were the Republican candidate and John Glenn were the Democratic candidate, which would you like to see win? [Those who were undecided were then asked: As of today, do you lean more to Reagan, the Republican, or to Glenn, the Democrat?]*

|                       | Mar. 2–6 | Mar. 1–2 |
| --------------------- | -------- | -------- |
| Reagan . . . . . . . . . . . . . . . | 52% | 60% |
| Glenn . . . . . . . . . . . . . . . . . | 41 | 36 |
| Other; undecided . . . . . . . . | 7 | 4 |

Note: Senator Gary Hart, now virtually tied with Walter Mondale as the nomination choice of Democrats nationwide, has moved into a 52%-to-43% lead over President Ronald Reagan in national test races conducted in the aftermath of Hart's victories in New Hampshire, Maine, and Vermont. Mondale and John Glenn, on the other hand, continue to trail the president; Mondale falls behind by the margin of 45% to 50% and Glenn by 41% to 52%. Hart has picked up strength against Reagan among the nation's voters in only the last few days; in a March 1–2 Gallup/*Newsweek* survey, he was edged out by Reagan 49% to 46%.

Hart and Mondale are now in a statistical tie for first place as the nomination choice of Democratic voters nationwide, with Hart winning 30% of the vote and Mondale 33%. Glenn's fortunes, however, continue to ebb, and, with the support of only 5% of the nation's Democrats, he now places fourth behind Jesse Jackson. George McGovern wins 3% of the vote and is last among the five men still in the race.

Hart trails Mondale in a head-to-head showdown test for the nomination among Democrats— 39% to 49%—but fares better against Reagan in presidential trial heats because of his far greater appeal to voters who classify themselves as independents. Hart's meteoric rise is reflected in his dramatic gain in name recognition over the last two months. In mid-January fewer than one-half of the electorate (45%) had heard or read about him. Today at 90% the percentage is twice as high, representing a figure comparable to the name awareness scores of Glenn, McGovern, Jackson, and Mondale.

## SATISFACTION INDEX

Interviewing Date: 2/10–13/84
Survey #231-G

*In general, are you satisfied or dissatisfied with the way things are going in the United States at this time?*

Satisfied ............................50%
Dissatisfied .........................46
No opinion ......................... 4

### By Sex
#### Male

Satisfied ............................55%
Dissatisfied .........................42
No opinion ......................... 3

#### Female

Satisfied ............................45%
Dissatisfied .........................50
No opinion ......................... 5

### By Ethnic Background
#### White

Satisfied ............................54%
Dissatisfied .........................42
No opinion ......................... 4

#### Nonwhite

Satisfied ............................24%
Dissatisfied .........................71
No opinion ......................... 5

#### Black

Satisfied ............................20%
Dissatisfied .........................76
No opinion ......................... 4

### By Education
#### College Graduate

Satisfied ............................64%
Dissatisfied .........................33
No opinion ......................... 3

#### College Incomplete

Satisfied ............................54%
Dissatisfied .........................44
No opinion ......................... 2

#### High-School Graduate

Satisfied ............................52%
Dissatisfied .........................45
No opinion ......................... 3

#### Less Than High-School Graduate

Satisfied ............................35%
Dissatisfied .........................58
No opinion ......................... 7

### By Region
#### East

Satisfied ............................46%
Dissatisfied .........................48
No opinion ......................... 6

#### Midwest

Satisfied ............................46%
Dissatisfied .........................51
No opinion ......................... 3

#### South

Satisfied ............................57%
Dissatisfied .........................40
No opinion ......................... 3

#### West

Satisfied ............................50%
Dissatisfied .........................45
No opinion ......................... 5

### By Age
#### 18–29 Years

Satisfied ............................48%
Dissatisfied .........................49
No opinion ......................... 3

### 30–49 Years

Satisfied ............................49%
Dissatisfied .........................47
No opinion ......................... 4

### 50 Years and Over

Satisfied ............................52%
Dissatisfied .........................44
No opinion ......................... 4

## By Politics
### Republicans

Satisfied ...........................71%
Dissatisfied ........................26
No opinion ......................... 3

### Democrats

Satisfied ...........................31%
Dissatisfied ........................66
No opinion ......................... 3

### Independents

Satisfied ...........................54%
Dissatisfied ........................42
No opinion ......................... 4

## Selected National Trend

|  | Satisfied | Dis-satisfied | No opinion |
|---|---|---|---|
| **1984** | | | |
| February ............ | 50% | 46% | 4% |
| **1983** | | | |
| August .............. | 35 | 59 | 6 |
| **1982** | | | |
| November ........... | 24 | 72 | 4 |
| April ............... | 25 | 71 | 4 |
| **1981** | | | |
| December ........... | 27 | 67 | 6 |
| June ................ | 33 | 61 | 6 |

### 1979

| | | | |
|---|---|---|---|
| November ........... | 19 | 77 | 4 |
| July ............... | 12 | 84 | 4 |
| February ............ | 26 | 69 | 5 |

*In general, are you satisfied or dissatisfied with the way things are going in your own personal life?*

Satisfied ...........................79%
Dissatisfied ........................19
No opinion ......................... 2

## By Sex
### Male

Satisfied ...........................79%
Dissatisfied ........................18
No opinion ......................... 3

### Female

Satisfied ...........................79%
Dissatisfied ........................20
No opinion ......................... 1

## By Ethnic Background
### White

Satisfied ...........................82%
Dissatisfied ........................16
No opinion ......................... 2

### Nonwhite

Satisfied ...........................61%
Dissatisfied ........................36
No opinion ......................... 3

### Black

Satisfied ...........................58%
Dissatisfied ........................39
No opinion ......................... 3

## By Education
### College Graduate

Satisfied ...........................89%
Dissatisfied ........................ 9
No opinion ......................... 2

### College Incomplete

Satisfied ...........................84%
Dissatisfied .........................14
No opinion .......................... 2

### High-School Graduate

Satisfied ...........................77%
Dissatisfied .........................22
No opinion .......................... 1

### Less Than High-School Graduate

Satisfied ...........................70%
Dissatisfied .........................27
No opinion .......................... 3

## By Region
### East

Satisfied ...........................79%
Dissatisfied .........................19
No opinion .......................... 2

### Midwest

Satisfied ...........................77%
Dissatisfied .........................21
No opinion .......................... 2

### South

Satisfied ...........................79%
Dissatisfied .........................19
No opinion .......................... 2

### West

Satisfied ...........................82%
Dissatisfied .........................16
No opinion .......................... 2

## By Age
### 18–29 Years

Satisfied ...........................80%
Dissatisfied .........................19
No opinion .......................... 1

### 30–49 Years

Satisfied ...........................78%
Dissatisfied .........................21
No opinion .......................... 1

### 50 Years and Over

Satisfied ...........................79%
Dissatisfied .........................19
No opinion .......................... 2

## By Politics
### Republicans

Satisfied ...........................88%
Dissatisfied .........................11
No opinion .......................... 1

### Democrats

Satisfied ...........................72%
Dissatisfied .........................25
No opinion .......................... 3

### Independents

Satisfied ...........................79%
Dissatisfied .........................20
No opinion .......................... 1

### Selected National Trend

|  | Satisfied | Dis-satisfied | No opinion |
|---|---|---|---|
| **1984** | | | |
| February 10–13 ........ | 79% | 19% | 2% |
| **1983** | | | |
| August .............. | 77 | 20 | 3 |
| **1982** | | | |
| November ............ | 75 | 23 | 2 |
| April ............... | 76 | 22 | 2 |
| **1981** | | | |
| December ............ | 81 | 17 | 2 |
| June ................ | 81 | 16 | 3 |
| **1979** | | | |
| November ............ | 79 | 19 | 2 |
| July ................ | 73 | 23 | 4 |
| February ............ | 77 | 21 | 2 |

Note: The mood of the country today is the brightest it has been in five years, with 50% now saying they are satisfied with the way things are going in the nation, compared to only 26% who felt this way in 1979. The current satisfaction figure tops the previous high of 35% recorded last August. The percentage who are satisfied with trends in the nation has fluctuated between a low point of 12% in July 1979 and today's 50%. The current figure also is 33 percentage points higher than the 17% satisfaction score recorded in 1981 at the beginning of President Ronald Reagan's tenure.

The increasingly upbeat mood of the electorate is enhancing President Reagan's political standing. His job performance rating is well above 50%, and he leads the current Democratic front-runners—Walter Mondale, Gary Hart, and John Glenn—in recent test elections for the presidency. At the same time, however, an examination of the mood of the public today shows a solid majority of Democrats (66%) saying they are dissatisfied with the way things are going in the nation.

The percentage of Americans who are satisfied with the way things are going in their personal lives continues at a high level, with 79% expressing satisfaction. Fewer Democrats than Republicans express satisfaction, but nevertheless a solid majority among both parties does so.

## MARCH 15
## MOST IMPORTANT PROBLEM

Interviewing Date: 2/10–13/84
Survey #231-G

*What do you think is the most important problem facing this country today?*

| | Feb. 10–13, 1984 | Oct. 1983 | Oct. 1982 |
|---|---|---|---|
| Threat of war; international tensions | 28% | 23% | 6% |
| Unemployment; recession | 28 | 42 | 62 |
| Excessive government spending | 12 | 4 | 4 |
| Inflation; high cost of living | 10 | 12 | 18 |
| Moral decline in society | 7 | 5 | 3 |
| Reagan budget cuts | 7 | 3 | 3 |
| Economy (general) | 5 | 4 | 11 |
| All others | 11 | 13 | 15 |
| Don't know | 5 | 4 | 2 |
| | 113%* | 110%* | 124%* |

*Total adds to more than 100% due to multiple responses.

*All persons who named a problem were then asked: Which political party do you think can do a better job of handling the problem you have just mentioned—the Republican party or the Democratic party?*

|  | Feb. 10–13 |
|---|---|
| Republican | 30% |
| Democratic | 32 |
| No difference (volunteered) | 26 |
| No opinion | 12 |

Note: Almost equal proportions of Americans cite unemployment (32%) and international tensions including threat of war (37%) as the most important problems facing the country today. This latter percentage represents the highest figure recorded since the Vietnam War.

Many factors can alter the political outlook, but at this point the Gallup Poll issue barometer points to a close race in November. In the current survey, 32% say the Democratic party is better able to handle the problem they consider most urgent, while 30% credit the Republican party, 26% see no difference between the parties, and 12% are undecided.

For nearly four decades the Gallup Poll has asked Americans what they consider to be the most important problem facing the nation and which political party can better deal with these issues. The results have proved to be a good barometer of the outcome of presidential elections. In October 1980, for example, the Republican party had a 40% to 31% lead on this question, pointing to Ronald Reagan's victory over President Jimmy Carter in the November election. Similarly, the Democratic party was the choice of 43% to 23% for the Republican party in October 1976, presaging Carter's win over incumbent Gerald Ford.

## MARCH 18
## COST OF LIVING

Interviewing Date: 1/27–30/84
Survey #230-G

*Have there been times during the last year when you did not have enough money to buy food your family needed?*

|  | 1984 Yes | 1974 Yes |
|---|---|---|
| National | 20% | 14% |

**By Race**

|  |  |  |
|---|---|---|
| White | 17% | 10% |
| Black | 51 | 40 |

*Have there been times during the last year when you did not have enough money to buy clothing your family needed?*

|  | 1984 Yes | 1974 Yes |
|---|---|---|
| National | 26% | 19% |

**By Race**

|  |  |  |
|---|---|---|
| White | 24% | 14% |
| Black | 50 | 49 |

*Have there been times during the last year when you did not have enough money to pay for medical or health care?*

|  | 1984 Yes | 1974 Yes |
|---|---|---|
| National | 25% | 15% |

**By Race**

|  |  |  |
|---|---|---|
| White | 22% | 11% |
| Black | 47 | 36 |

*How often do you worry that your total family income will not be enough to meet your family's expenses and bills—all of the time, most of the time, some of the time, or almost never?*

|  | 1984 | 1974 |
|---|---|---|
| All of the time | 20% | 13% |
| Most of the time | 15 | 12 |
| Some of the time | 30 | 36 |
| Almost never | 34 | 38 |
| No opinion | 1 | 1 |

The following table shows the proportions saying they worry about their expenses either all of the time or most of the time:

|  | 1984 Yes | 1974 Yes |
|---|---|---|
| National | 35% | 25% |

**By Race**

|  |  |  |
|---|---|---|
| White | 33% | 20% |
| Black | 59 | 51 |

Note: Amid the current debate a new Gallup survey sheds light on the extent of hunger and deprivation in the United States, revealing that many Americans did not have enough money during the last year to buy food, clothing, or medical care for their families:

1) Twenty percent of adults, including 17% of whites and 51% of blacks, say there were times during the last year when they did not have enough money to buy food.

2) Twenty-six percent overall—24% of whites and 50% of blacks—report they were sometimes unable to buy clothing needed by their families.

3) Twenty-five percent nationwide—22% of whites and 47% of blacks—say there were times during the last twelve months when they could not afford to pay for family members' health care.

4) Finally, 35% of all persons surveyed (33% of whites and 59% of blacks) say they worry all of the time or most of the time that their total household income will not be enough to meet family expenses and to pay the bills.

A comparison of the current findings with those recorded in a survey ten years ago, in the recession year of 1974, shows that the situation actually may have grown worse, at least in the public's perceptions.

## MARCH 22
## SAFER WORLD/PERSONAL FINANCES

Interviewing Date: 2/10–13/84
Survey #231-G

*Do you think we live in a safer world now than we did three years ago?*

Yes ................................24%
No ..................................68
Don't know ........................ 8

### By Sex
#### Male

Yes ................................28%
No ..................................64
Don't know ........................ 8

#### Female

Yes ................................19%
No ..................................73
Don't know ........................ 8

### By Ethnic Background
#### White

Yes ................................25%
No ..................................67
Don't know ........................ 8

#### Nonwhite

Yes ................................15%
No ..................................79
Don't know ........................ 6

#### Black

Yes ................................14%
No ..................................79
Don't know ........................ 7

### By Education
#### College Graduate

Yes ................................23%
No ..................................66
Don't know ........................11

#### College Incomplete

Yes ................................30%
No ..................................64
Don't know ........................ 6

#### High-School Graduate

Yes ................................23%
No ..................................69
Don't know ........................ 8

#### Less Than High-School Graduate

Yes ................................20%
No ..................................73
Don't know ........................ 7

### By Region
#### East

Yes ................................24%
No ..................................68
Don't know ........................ 8

#### Midwest

Yes ................................20%
No ..................................75
Don't know ........................ 5

#### South

Yes ................................27%
No ..................................62
Don't know ........................:11

#### West

Yes ................................23%
No ..................................70
Don't know ........................ 7

### By Age
#### 18–29 Years

Yes ................................23%
No ..................................72
Don't know ........................ 5

### 30–49 Years

Yes ............................... 25%
No ................................ 67
Don't know ....................... 8

### 50 Years and Over

Yes ............................... 24%
No ................................ 67
Don't know ....................... 9

## By Politics
### Republicans

Yes ............................... 38%
No ................................ 52
Don't know ....................... 10

### Democrats

Yes ............................... 15%
No ................................ 79
Don't know ....................... 6

### Independents

Yes ............................... 21%
No ................................ 72
Don't know ....................... 7

Interviewing Date: 2/13–19/84
Special Telephone Survey

*Would you say you and your family are better off now than you were three years ago, or worse off?*

Better ............................ 45%
Worse ............................ 27
Same (volunteered) ................. 24
No opinion ........................ 4

## By Politics
### Republicans

Better ............................ 72%
Worse ............................ 11
Same (volunteered) ................. 16
No opinion ........................ 1

### Democrats

Better ............................ 23%
Worse ............................ 43
Same (volunteered) ................. 30
No opinion ........................ 4

### Independents

Better ............................ 51%
Worse ............................ 22
Same (volunteered) ................. 23
No opinion ........................ 4

Note: President Ronald Reagan and the U.S. public do not see eye to eye on the question of whether Americans live in a safer world now than three years ago. In his State of the Union address in January, Reagan said that "restoration of economic growth and military deterrence" meant the "United States is safer, stronger, and more secure in 1984 than before." However, the public, by almost a 3-to-1 margin, believes we live in a world that is less safe today than it was in 1981 when Reagan took office.

While the president does not fare well on the safety index, he does better on a campaign theme he used successfully against incumbent Jimmy Carter during the 1980 presidential race: "Are you better off now than you were four years ago?" For every person who says that he is worse off today than three years ago there are two who say they are better off. As many as one-fourth of survey respondents, however, say there has been little change in their situation. Respondents' views are largely dependent on their political persuasion, with Republicans, by 72% to 11%, saying they are better rather than worse off, and Democrats leaning 43% to 23% the other way. Independents, by a 2-to-1 ratio, hold the view they are better off now.

## DEMOCRATIC PRESIDENTIAL CANDIDATES/PRESIDENTIAL TRIAL HEATS

Interviewing Date: 3/16–19/84
Survey #232-G

*Asked of Democrats and independents: Which one of these persons would you like to see nominated as the Democratic party's candidate for president this year?*

### Choice of Democrats

|  | Mar. 16–19 | Mar. 2–6 |
|---|---|---|
| Walter Mondale ........ | 44% | 33% |
| Gary Hart ............ | 38 | 30 |
| Jesse Jackson ......... | 10 | 9 |
| Other; don't know ...... | 8 | 28 |

### Choice of Independents

|  | Mar. 16–19 | Mar. 2–6 |
|---|---|---|
| Mondale ............. | 27% | 13% |
| Hart ................ | 48 | 40 |
| Jackson ............. | 7 | 4 |
| Other; don't know ...... | 18 | 43 |

*Asked of Democrats and independents: Suppose the choice for president in the Democratic convention this year narrows down to Walter Mondale and Gary Hart. Which one would you prefer to have the Democratic convention select? Do you strongly support him or do you only moderately support him?*

### Choice of Democrats

Mondale ..........................49%
  Strongly support .................23
  Moderately support ..............26
Hart ................................44
  Strongly support ...............16
  Moderately support ..............28
Undecided ......................... 7

### Choice of Independents

Mondale ..........................31%
  Strongly support .............. 5
  Moderately support ..............26
Hart ................................55
  Strongly support ...............10
  Moderately support ..............45
Undecided ........................14

*Asked of registered voters: Suppose the 1984 presidential election were being held today. If President Ronald Reagan were the Republican candidate and Walter Mondale were the Democratic candidate, which would you like to see win? [Those who were undecided were then asked: As of today, do you lean more to Reagan, the Republican, or to Mondale, the Democrat?]*

|  | Mar. 16–19 | Mar. 2–6 |
|---|---|---|
| Reagan .............. | 52% | 50% |
| Mondale ............. | 44 | 45 |
| Other; undecided ...... | 4 | 5 |

### By Politics

#### Republicans

Reagan ..........................92%
Mondale .......................... 5
Other; undecided ................... 3

#### Democrats

Reagan ..........................23%
Mondale ..........................74
Other; undecided ................... 3

#### Independents

Reagan ..........................60%
Mondale ..........................34
Other; undecided ................... 6

*Asked of registered voters: Suppose the 1984 presidential election were being held today. If President Ronald Reagan were the Republican candidate and Gary Hart were the Democratic candidate, which would you like to see win? [Those who were undecided were then asked: As of today, do you lean more to Reagan, the Republican, or to Hart, the Democrat?]*

|  | Mar. 16–19 | Mar. 2–6 |
|---|---|---|
| Reagan .............. | 47% | 43% |
| Hart ................. | 49 | 52 |
| Other; undecided ...... | 4 | 5 |

### By Politics
#### *Republicans*

| | |
|---|---|
| Reagan ........................... | 88% |
| Hart ............................... | 11 |
| Other; undecided .................... | 1 |

#### *Democrats*

| | |
|---|---|
| Reagan ........................... | 20% |
| Hart ............................... | 77 |
| Other; undecided .................... | 3 |

#### *Independents*

| | |
|---|---|
| Reagan ........................... | 49% |
| Hart ............................... | 43 |
| Other; undecided .................... | 8 |

Note: The race between Walter Mondale and Gary Hart for the Democratic presidential nomination remains a standoff, with the two rivals statistically tied for first place. In the latest nationwide Gallup survey, Mondale is the choice of 44% of Democrats to 38% for Hart; the Reverend Jesse Jackson is a distant third, with 10% of the vote.

Among political independents, however, Hart holds a decisive 48% to 27% lead over Mondale, with Jackson at 7%. Hart's strong advantage among independents is reflected in his relatively better showing against President Ronald Reagan in simulated elections for the presidency. Reagan leads Hart 49% to 43%, while he leads Mondale 60% to 34%.

Hart has lost some ground against Reagan since a survey conducted March 2–6 shortly after the New Hampshire primary when he led the president 52% to 43%. Mondale also has lost some ground to Reagan in the latest survey. In the post-New Hampshire poll, the former vice-president lost to the president by a narrow 5 percentage points, 45% to 50%.

When the simulated nomination contest is narrowed to only the front-runners, Mondale receives 49% of Democrats' votes to 44% for Hart. Support for each of the two rivals leans toward moderate rather than strong. Among independent voters, however, very little of either man's support is strong. Hart easily beats Mondale in the nomination showdown test—55% to 31%—but only 10% of Hart's backers and 5% of Mondale's describe their support as strong.

### MARCH 29
### FEDERAL BUDGET

Interviewing Date: 2/10–13/84
Survey #231-G

*Have you heard or read about the Reagan administration's proposed budget for fiscal year 1985, which begins October 1?*

| | |
|---|---|
| Yes ................................. | 48% |
| No; not sure ....................... | 52 |

*Asked of those who responded in the affirmative: In general, do you feel the size of the administration's budget for 1985 is too large, too small, or about the right amount?*

| | |
|---|---|
| Too large ......................... | 69% |
| Too small ......................... | 4 |
| About right ........................ | 17 |
| No opinion ........................ | 10 |

### By Politics
#### *Republicans*

| | |
|---|---|
| Too large ......................... | 67% |
| Too small ......................... | 3 |
| About right ........................ | 24 |
| No opinion ........................ | 6 |

#### *Democrats*

| | |
|---|---|
| Too large ......................... | 68% |
| Too small ......................... | 5 |
| About right ........................ | 12 |
| No opinion ........................ | 15 |

### Independents

Too large .......................... 74%
Too small .......................... 4
About right ........................ 14
No opinion ......................... 8

*Also asked of the aware group: If reductions are made in the administration's proposed 1985 budget, which would you prefer—cuts in spending for military and defense programs or cuts in spending for social programs?*

Military and defense ................. 57%
Social programs ..................... 22
Both (volunteered) .................. 11
Neither (volunteered) ............... 7
No opinion ......................... 3

### By Politics

#### Republicans

Military and defense ................. 43%
Social programs ..................... 32
Both (volunteered) .................. 15
Neither (volunteered) ............... 7
No opinion ......................... 3

#### Democrats

Military and defense ................. 69%
Social programs ..................... 15
Both (volunteered) .................. 8
Neither (volunteered) ............... 6
No opinion ......................... 2

#### Independents

Military and defense ................. 57%
Social programs ..................... 19
Both (volunteered) .................. 11
Neither (volunteered) ............... 9
No opinion ......................... 4

*Also asked of the aware group: As you may know, the administration's 1985 budget projects a deficit of about $180 billion—that is, the federal government would spend about $180 billion more than it takes in. Do you*

*feel that budget deficits of this size are or are not likely to cut the economic recovery short?*

Are likely ......................... 65%
Are not likely ..................... 21
No opinion ......................... 14

### By Politics

#### Republicans

Are likely ......................... 67%
Are not likely ..................... 21
No opinion ......................... 12

#### Democrats

Are likely ......................... 66%
Are not likely ..................... 20
No opinion ......................... 14

#### Independents

Are likely ......................... 63%
Are not likely ..................... 22
No opinion ......................... 15

Note: A two-thirds' majority (69%) of the informed public, including equal proportions of Republicans (67%) and Democrats (68%), believes the projected $180-to-$200 billion annual federal budget deficits for fiscal 1985 and beyond may jeopardize the economic recovery. By a 55%-to-29% vote the public favors a constitutional amendment requiring the federal government to balance the budget each year.

The Congress and the Reagan administration currently are considering at least four different deficit-reducing packages, ranging from $150 to $285 billion in new taxes and budget cuts over the next three years. There is little doubt that budget cuts will be made; only the size and sources of the cuts have yet to be decided.

The survey also found a surprising consensus among Republicans, Democrats, and independents on the major elements in the 1985 budget and the projected deficits. Somewhat greater disagreement between Republicans and Democrats is found on where budget cuts should be made.

Nevertheless, a 43% plurality of Republicans prefers reductions in military spending compared to 32% who want cuts in social programs.

## APRIL 1
## PRESIDENT REAGAN

Interviewing Date: 3/16–19/84
Survey #232-G

*Do you approve or disapprove of the way Ronald Reagan is handling his job as president?*

Approve ............................54%
Disapprove ........................39
No opinion ........................ 7

### Reagan Performance Ratings
#### (Four-Survey Average January-March 1984)*

Approve ............................54%
Disapprove ........................37
No opinion ........................ 9

#### By Sex
##### Male

Approve ............................59%
Disapprove ........................34
No opinion ........................ 7

##### Female

Approve ............................50%
Disapprove ........................39
No opinion ........................11

#### By Ethnic Background
##### White

Approve ............................59%
Disapprove ........................32
No opinion ........................ 9

*Responses are based upon interviews with approximately 6,000 people.

##### Black

Approve ............................15%
Disapprove ........................76
No opinion ........................ 9

##### Hispanic

Approve ............................48%
Disapprove ........................39
No opinion ........................13

#### By Education
##### College Graduate

Approve ............................63%
Disapprove ........................33
No opinion ........................ 4

##### College Incomplete

Approve ............................60%
Disapprove ........................33
No opinion ........................ 7

##### High-School Graduate

Approve ............................57%
Disapprove ........................34
No opinion ........................ 9

##### Less Than High-School Graduate

Approve ............................41%
Disapprove ........................46
No opinion ........................13

#### By Region
##### East

Approve ............................53%
Disapprove ........................39
No opinion ........................ 8

##### Midwest

Approve ............................53%
Disapprove ........................38
No opinion ........................ 9

### South

Approve ...........................58%
Disapprove ........................32
No opinion ........................10

### West

Approve ...........................54%
Disapprove ........................40
No opinion ........................ 6

## By Age
### 18–29 Years

Approve ...........................57%
Disapprove ........................34
No opinion ........................ 9

### 30–49 Years

Approve ...........................56%
Disapprove ........................36
No opinion ........................ 8

### 50 Years and Over

Approve ...........................50%
Disapprove ........................40
No opinion ........................10

## By Income
### $40,000 and Over

Approve ...........................69%
Disapprove ........................27
No opinion ........................ 4

### $30,000–$39,999

Approve ...........................64%
Disapprove ........................28
No opinion ........................ 8

### $20,000–$29,999

Approve ...........................63%
Disapprove ........................31
No opinion ........................ 6

### $10,000–$19,999

Approve ...........................49%
Disapprove ........................40
No opinion ........................11

### Under $10,000

Approve ...........................39%
Disapprove ........................49
No opinion ........................12

## By Politics
### Republicans

Approve ...........................86%
Disapprove ........................ 9
No opinion ........................ 5

### Democrats

Approve ...........................32%
Disapprove ........................59
No opinion ........................ 9

### Independents

Approve ...........................57%
Disapprove ........................33
No opinion ........................10

## By Religion
### Protestants

Approve ...........................57%
Disapprove ........................35
No opinion ........................ 8

### Catholics

Approve ...........................55%
Disapprove ........................36
No opinion ........................ 9

## By Occupation
### Professional and Business

Approve ...........................64%
Disapprove ........................30
No opinion ........................ 6

### Clerical and Sales

Approve ............................56%
Disapprove ..........................38
No opinion ......................... 6

### Manual Workers

Approve ............................51%
Disapprove ..........................38
No opinion ..........................11

### Skilled Workers

Approve ............................59%
Disapprove ..........................32
No opinion ......................... 9

### Unskilled Workers

Approve ............................46%
Disapprove ..........................42
No opinion ..........................12

### Labor Union Households Only

Approve ............................52%
Disapprove ..........................42
No opinion ......................... 6

### Nonlabor Union Households Only

Approve ............................55%
Disapprove ..........................35
No opinion ..........................10

Note: President Ronald Reagan's generally strong standing with the American people, now in its sixth consecutive month, shows no sign of weakening. In the latest Gallup survey (mid-March), 54% approve of Reagan's handling of his presidential duties, while 39% disapprove.

Not since last October when 45% approved has less than a majority of the public given Reagan a positive score for his handling of his presidential duties. Since then his ratings have moved within a narrow range, varying by only 2 or 3 points from survey to survey. Reagan's overall standing is as high today as it has been at any point in over two years. The last time he had a significantly higher job performance rating was in August 1981, when 60% approved and 29% disapproved.

Reagan continues to enjoy greater popularity among up-scale population groups: persons from upper-income households and those headed by people employed in the professions and business, as well as among men, whites, and Republicans. Conversely, the president is less popular with blacks, those whose formal education stopped short of high-school graduation, persons whose family income is less than $20,000 per year, unskilled workers, and Democrats. Perhaps, surprisingly, labor union households and Hispanics are not far below the general public in their appraisal of President Reagan's performance in office.

The now familiar "gender gap"—the tendency of a smaller proportion of women than men to approve of Reagan's job performance—is found in the latest surveys. Currently, 59% of men compared to 50% of women give Reagan a favorable rating for his handling of his duties. The 9-percentage point difference between the sexes is the average gender gap recorded throughout Reagan's tenure.

## APRIL 5
## PERSONAL FINANCES

Interviewing Date: 3/16–19/84
Survey #232-G

*Do you expect that at this time next year you will be financially better off than now, or worse off than now?*

Better ............................54%
Worse ............................11
Same (volunteered) ..................28
No opinion ......................... 7

### Selected National Trend

|  | Better | Worse | Same | No opinion |
|---|---|---|---|---|
| *1983* | | | | |
| June 24–27 | 43% | 19% | 28% | 10% |
| *1982* | | | | |
| November 2–8 | 41 | 22 | 27 | 10 |
| February 5–8 | 42 | 31 | 21 | 6 |

*We are interested in how people's financial situation may have changed. Would you say that you are financially better off now than you were a year ago, or are you financially worse off now?*

Better .............................36%
Worse .............................26
Same (volunteered) ..................37
No opinion .........................1

## Selected National Trend

| | Better | Worse | Same | No opinion |
|---|---|---|---|---|
| **1983** | | | | |
| June 24–27 | 28% | 39% | 32% | 1% |
| **1982** | | | | |
| November 2–8 | 28 | 37 | 34 | 1 |
| February 5–8 | 28 | 47 | 24 | 1 |

The following shows the trend in optimists and pessimists, based on a combination of the two questions:

Optimists ...........................46%
Pessimists ..........................14
Neutral ............................33
No opinion .........................7

## Selected National Trend

| | Optimists | Pessimists | Neutral | No opinion |
|---|---|---|---|---|
| **1983** | | | | |
| June 24–27 | 34% | 24% | 32% | 10% |
| **1982** | | | | |
| November | 32 | 25 | 33 | 10 |
| September | 32 | 28 | 31 | 9 |

Note: A solid majority of Americans (54%) expects to be financially better off one year from now, reflecting a higher level of economic optimism than found at any other time since Gallup started this measurement in 1976. In addition, the proportion saying they are better off today than a year ago is higher than at any other time since 1977.

The two questions—looking ahead and looking back—should be examined in combination since expectations about being "better" or "worse" in the future are related to how one views the present.

When this is done, those whose views indicate an overall optimistic trend outnumber pessimists by the widest margin to date.

Since June 1983 there has been a strong rise in the proportion of "super optimists"—from 20% to 28%. Studies have shown that the people who say that they are both better off (past) and expect to be still better off (future) are particularly likely to be heavy buyers of big-ticket discretionary items like cars, houses, and appliances.

## APRIL 8
## WALTER MONDALE AND GARY HART

Interviewing Date: 3/16–19/84
Survey #232-G

*Asked of Democrats: Here is a list of terms—shown as pairs of opposites—that have been used to describe political candidates. [Respondents were handed a card listing twenty-one terms.] Now, from each pair of opposites, would you please select the term that best describes Walter Mondale?*

*Now, from each pair of opposites, would you please select the term that best describes Gary Hart?*

| Style | Mondale | Hart |
|---|---|---|
| Brings a feeling of excitement to election campaign | 35% | 59% |
| Does not generate much excitement | 40 | 17 |
| The kind of man you can be enthusiastic about | 35 | 51 |
| Not someone you can feel much enthusiasm for | 39 | 21 |
| A colorful, interesting personality | 48 | 65 |
| A dull, uninteresting personality | 27 | 10 |
| Reminds one of President John Kennedy | 20 | 40 |
| Not much different from other Democratic presidential candidates | 54 | 32 |

| Basic Character Traits | Mondale | Hart |
|---|---|---|
| A man of exceptional abilities | 34% | 40% |
| A man of average abilities | 46 | 34 |
| Bright, intelligent | 67 | 69 |
| Not too bright | 13 | 8 |
| Intelligent, cerebral | 49 | 55 |
| Not particularly intellectual | 23 | 14 |
| A man of high moral principles | 64 | 57 |
| Not particularly moral | 13 | 13 |
| A religious person · | 39 | 39 |
| Not particularly religious | 27 | 26 |
| Likable | 62 | 67 |
| Not particularly likable | 16 | 8 |
| Friendly, outgoing, personable | 62 | 62 |
| Aloof, distant, humorless | 15 | 10 |
| Strong leadership qualities | 56 | 56 |
| Lacks strong leadership qualities | 22 | 18 |

| Country's Interests vs. Politics | Mondale | Hart |
|---|---|---|
| Puts country's interests ahead of politics | 47% | 51% |
| Too much of a politician | 32 | 22 |
| Independent of pressure groups | 33 | 55 |
| Too closely connected with labor unions and other pressure groups | 40 | 14 |

| Traditional Democratic Issues | Mondale | Hart |
|---|---|---|
| Cares about needs and problems of women | 54% | 51% |
| Does not really care about needs and problems of women | 17 | 17 |
| Sympathetic to problems of the poor | 54 | 51 |
| Not particularly sympathetic to problems of the poor | 22 | 19 |
| Cares about needs and problems of black people | 54 | 48 |
| Does not really care about needs and problems of black people | 16 | 20 |

| New Approach vs. Old Approach | Mondale | Hart |
|---|---|---|
| Presents fresh new ideas and approaches | 33% | 51% |
| Presents nothing especially new or different | 40 | 23 |

| | Mondale | Hart |
|---|---|---|
| Addresses critical issues of 1980s and 1990s | 36 | 55 |
| Addresses traditional issues | 39 | 18 |
| Has modern up-to-date solutions to national problems | 34 | 46 |
| Has old-fashioned solutions to national problems | 40 | 27 |
| Speaks for the younger generation of Americans | 29 | 59 |
| Speaks for older Americans | 43 | 15 |

Note: Gary Hart leads Walter Mondale on matters related to style, for presenting fresh ideas, speaking for the younger generation, and for injecting excitement into the race for the Democratic nomination. As determined by the latest Gallup Poll, Hart is also viewed by the nation's Democratic voters as the more colorful and interesting of the two candidates, and to at least four in ten Democrats he is reminiscent of President John Kennedy.

Despite Hart's clear advantage over Mondale on style, the two men fare about equally well in Democrats' perceptions of their basic character traits—leadership, intelligence, friendliness, morality—and their commitment to traditional Democratic values. Mondale, however, is perceived as substantially more likely to be tied to special interest groups such as labor unions.

Hart leads Mondale as a person with new ideas who addresses the critical issues and has modern solutions, as well as speaking for younger Americans. At the same time, however, it should be noted that 42% of the nation's Democrats do not know where Hart stands on issues. Fewer (33%) reported not knowing where Mondale stands on issues.

## APRIL 12
## COST OF LIVING

Interviewing Date: 1/13–16; 27–30/84
Survey #229-G; 230-G

> On the average, about how much does your family spend on food, including milk, each week?

|  | *Median average** |
|---|---|
| National | $70 |

## By Region

| | |
|---|---|
| East | $80 |
| Midwest | $60 |
| South | $70 |
| West | $75 |

## By Income

| | |
|---|---|
| $20,000 and over | $80 |
| Under $20,000 | $60 |

## By Size of Household

| | |
|---|---|
| Single person | $40 |
| Two-person family | $60 |
| Three-person family | $75 |
| Four-person family | $80 |
| Five-person family | $100 |

*Farm families were excluded from the survey because many farmers raise their own food.

## Selected National Trend

|  | *Median average* |
|---|---|
| 1984 | $70 |
| 1983 | $69 |
| 1982 | $70 |
| 1981 | $62 |
| 1980 | $59 |
| 1979 | $53 |
| 1978 | $50 |
| 1977 | $48 |
| 1976 | $48 |
| 1975 | $47 |
| 1974 | $42 |
| 1973 | $37 |
| 1971 | $35 |
| 1970 | $34 |
| 1969 | $33 |
| 1959 | $29 |
| 1949 | $25 |
| 1937 | $11 |

Note: Americans are currently spending about the same amount to feed their families as they did in 1983 and 1982, reflecting the sharply lower inflation rate experienced during this period. The 1984 Gallup audit of food expenditures shows the median amount spent by nonfarm U.S. households is now about $70 per week, statistically unchanged from the $69 recorded last year and the figure of $70 in 1982.

Since the Gallup Poll began charting food expenditures in 1937, the weekly amount has increased more than sixfold, from $11 in the first audit to the current $70. During the twenty-year period between 1949 and 1969, the figure grew from $25 per week to $33 per week, an increase of only 32%. However, from 1970 to the present—a span of only fifteen years—food expenditures have doubled, from $34 per week to $70.

As in the past, food expenses take a smaller bite out of the family budgets of midwesterners and southerners than of those living elsewhere in the nation. Persons in the survey whose annual family income is $20,000 or more report spending almost half again as much on food as do those with lower incomes. However, food bills represent a larger portion of total expenditures of families in the lower-income category than is true of upper-income households.

## APRIL 15
## WOMAN FOR VICE-PRESIDENT

Interviewing Date: 1/27–30/84
Survey #230-G

> Can you think of the names of any women who you think are well qualified to serve as vice-president of the United States?

One-fourth of all survey respondents (24%) named one or more women they considered well qualified for the vice-presidency. Respondents were asked to give their choices without a list of names. This procedure, while opening the field to all possible choices, tends to favor women who are prominent in political affairs or who recently have been in the news.

Supreme Court Justice Sandra Day O'Connor, former Texas Congresswoman Barbara Jordan, and Transportation Secretary Elizabeth Dole are named most often by the American people as women well qualified to serve as vice-president of the United States. They are followed closely in the voting by U.S. Ambassador to the United Nations Jeane Kirkpatrick, former Democratic Representative Shirley Chisholm, San Francisco Mayor Dianne Feinstein, Kansas Senator Nancy Kassebaum, Governor Martha Collins of Kentucky, Florida Senator Paula Hawkins, and Jane Byrne, former mayor of Chicago.

In another recent Gallup Poll, about one-half of respondents (52%) say that a woman vice-presidential candidate on the Democratic ticket would not affect their vote one way or the other. Of those who say it would make a difference, a higher proportion (26%) says they would be more likely rather than less likely (16%) to vote for a Democratic ticket with a woman in the number two spot. Among Democrats of both sexes, 33% say they would be more likely and 13% less likely to vote for a ticket that included a woman. Among women Democrats the comparable percentages are 40% to 14% and among men 26% to 12%.

Many Americans believe that the vice-presidency is the first logical step toward electing a woman president. In a 1983 Gallup survey on the subject, 80% said they would be willing to vote for a woman for president. The growth in the percentage of Americans who accept the concept of a woman president is one of the most dramatic in polling annals. In a 1937 Gallup Poll only 31% said they would vote for a woman for the highest office.

## APRIL 19

### DEMOCRATIC PRESIDENTIAL CANDIDATES/PRESIDENTIAL TRIAL HEATS

Interviewing Date: 4/11–15/84
Special Telephone Survey

*Asked of Democrats and independents: Which one of these persons would you like to see nominated as the Democratic party's candidate for president this year?*

### Choice of Democrats

|  | Apr. 11–15 | Mar. 16–19 | Mar. 2–6 |
|---|---|---|---|
| Walter Mondale | 51% | 44% | 33% |
| Gary Hart | 28 | 38 | 30 |
| Jesse Jackson | 9 | 10 | 9 |
| Other; don't know | 12 | 8 | 28 |

### Choice of Independents

|  | Apr. 11–15 | Mar. 16–19 | Mar. 2–6 |
|---|---|---|---|
| Mondale | 29% | 27% | 13% |
| Hart | 39 | 48 | 40 |
| Jackson | 8 | 7 | 4 |
| Other; don't know | 24 | 18 | 43 |

*Asked of Democrats and independents: Suppose the choice for president in the Democratic convention this year narrows down to Walter Mondale and Gary Hart. Which one would you prefer to have the Democratic convention select? Do you strongly support him or do you only moderately support him?*

### Choice of Democrats

|  |  | Apr. 11–15 | Mar. 16–19 |
|---|---|---|---|
| Mondale . . . . . . . . . . . . . |  | 57% | 49% |
| Strongly support | 29 | 23 |
| Moderately support | 28 | 26 |
| Hart . . . . . . . . . . . . . . . . . |  | 33 | 44 |
| Strongly support | 10 | 16 |
| Moderately support | 23 | 28 |
| Undecided . . . . . . . . . . . |  | 10 | 7 |

## Choice of Independents

|  | Apr. 11–15 | Mar. 16–19 |
|---|---|---|
| Mondale ............. | 36% | 31% |
| Strongly support | 8 | 5 |
| Moderately support | 28 | 26 |
| Hart ................ | 48 | 55 |
| Strongly support | 10 | 10 |
| Moderately support | 38 | 45 |
| Undecided ........... | 16 | 14 |

*Asked of registered voters: Suppose the 1984 presidential election were being held today. If President Ronald Reagan were the Republican candidate and Walter Mondale were the Democratic candidate, which would you like to see win? [Those who were undecided were then asked: As of today, do you lean more to Reagan, the Republican, or to Mondale, the Democrat?]*

|  | Apr. 11–15 | Mar. 16–19 | Mar. 2–6 |
|---|---|---|---|
| Reagan | 52% | 52% | 50% |
| Mondale | 44 | 44 | 45 |
| Other; undecided | 4 | 4 | 5 |

*Asked of registered voters: Suppose the 1984 presidential election were being held today. If President Ronald Reagan were the Republican candidate and Gary Hart were the Democratic candidate, which would you like to see win? [Those who were undecided were then asked: As of today, do you lean more to Reagan, the Republican, or to Hart, the Democrat?]*

|  | Apr. 11–15 | Mar. 16–19 | Mar. 2–6 |
|---|---|---|---|
| Reagan | 49% | 47% | 43% |
| Hart | 46 | 49 | 52 |
| Other; undecided | 5 | 4 | 5 |

Note: Walter Mondale's lead over Gary Hart for the Democratic presidential nomination has reached its widest point since February; yet, Hart continues to fare marginally better than Mondale in test elections against President Ronald Reagan. In the latest Gallup survey, former Vice-President Mondale is the choice of 51% of Democrats for the nomination to 28% for Hart; the Reverend Jesse Jackson receives 9% of the vote. The 23-point gulf now separating Mondale and Hart is the widest observed since Hart became a credible contender following the February 28 New Hampshire primary.

In mid-March, Hart trailed Mondale by only 6 percentage points, and among Democrats during the first few days of March there was no significant difference in the relative position of the two men. In test elections for the presidency, Reagan is statistically tied with Hart 49% to 46%, while the president beats Mondale 52% to 44%.

Not only has Hart's position with Democrats weakened perceptibly during the past six weeks, but also there are current signs of erosion in Hart's principal power base, the political independents. In the immediate aftermath of New Hampshire, Hart enjoyed a 27-point lead over Mondale for the nomination among independents—40% to 13%. By mid-March, Hart's lead had shrunk to 48% to 27%; in the current survey he tops Mondale by 39% to 29%.

When the nomination contest is narrowed to only the front-runners, Mondale receives 57% of Democrats' votes to 33% for Hart. Support for Mondale is evenly divided between those who describe their support as strong and moderate, while Hart's backing is 2-to-1 moderate. Among independent voters, however, very little of either man's support is strong. Hart beats Mondale in the current nomination showdown test 48% to 36%, but only 10% of Hart's backers and 8% of Mondale's describe their support as strong.

Despite Hart's current loss of momentum among Democrats and independents, the outcome of test elections for the presidency next fall has changed remarkably little from earlier surveys, with Hart still showing slightly greater strength than Mondale against Reagan. The early March (post-New Hampshire) survey recorded a 9-point Hart victory over Reagan—52% to 43%. The mid-March and mid-April contests between the two resulted in statistical standoffs.

## APRIL 22
## CENTRAL AMERICA

Interviewing Date: 4/11–15/84
Special Telephone Interview

*Some people say the United States should give military assistance to governments in Central America that are friendly to us. Others say we should not get involved in the internal affairs of these nations. Which point of view comes closer to the way you feel—that we should give military assistance to these nations or that we should not get involved?*

Military assistance . . . . . . . . . . . . . . . . . . . .39%
Not get involved . . . . . . . . . . . . . . . . . . . .49
No opinion . . . . . . . . . . . . . . . . . . . . . . . . .12

### By Sex
#### Male

Military assistance . . . . . . . . . . . . . . . . . . . .46%
Not get involved . . . . . . . . . . . . . . . . . . . .44
No opinion . . . . . . . . . . . . . . . . . . . . . . . . .10

#### Female

Military assistance . . . . . . . . . . . . . . . . . . . .33%
Not get involved . . . . . . . . . . . . . . . . . . . .54
No opinion . . . . . . . . . . . . . . . . . . . . . . . . .13

### By Education
#### College Graduate

Military assistance . . . . . . . . . . . . . . . . . . . .49%
Not get involved . . . . . . . . . . . . . . . . . . . .43
No opinion . . . . . . . . . . . . . . . . . . . . . . . . . 8

#### College Incomplete

Military assistance . . . . . . . . . . . . . . . . . . . .49%
Not get involved . . . . . . . . . . . . . . . . . . . .46
No opinion . . . . . . . . . . . . . . . . . . . . . . . . . 5

#### High-School Graduate

Military assistance . . . . . . . . . . . . . . . . . . . .37%
Not get involved . . . . . . . . . . . . . . . . . . . .50
No opinion . . . . . . . . . . . . . . . . . . . . . . . . .13

#### Less Than High-School Graduate

Military assistance . . . . . . . . . . . . . . . . . . . .25%
Not get involved . . . . . . . . . . . . . . . . . . . .56
No opinion . . . . . . . . . . . . . . . . . . . . . . . . .19

### By Age
#### 18–29 Years

Military assistance . . . . . . . . . . . . . . . . . . . .45%
Not get involved . . . . . . . . . . . . . . . . . . . .49
No opinion . . . . . . . . . . . . . . . . . . . . . . . . . 6

#### 30–49 Years

Military assistance . . . . . . . . . . . . . . . . . . . .43%
Not get involved . . . . . . . . . . . . . . . . . . . .46
No opinion . . . . . . . . . . . . . . . . . . . . . . . . .11

#### 50 Years and Over

Military assistance . . . . . . . . . . . . . . . . . . . .32%
Not get involved . . . . . . . . . . . . . . . . . . . .52
No opinion . . . . . . . . . . . . . . . . . . . . . . . . .16

### By Politics
#### Republicans

Military assistance . . . . . . . . . . . . . . . . . . . .55%
Not get involved . . . . . . . . . . . . . . . . . . . .34
No opinion . . . . . . . . . . . . . . . . . . . . . . . . .11

#### Democrats

Military assistance . . . . . . . . . . . . . . . . . . . .29%
Not get involved . . . . . . . . . . . . . . . . . . . .59
No opinion . . . . . . . . . . . . . . . . . . . . . . . . .12

#### Independents

Military assistance . . . . . . . . . . . . . . . . . . . .39%
Not get involved . . . . . . . . . . . . . . . . . . . .50
No opinion . . . . . . . . . . . . . . . . . . . . . . . . .11

*Do you approve or disapprove of the way President Ronald Reagan is handling the situation in Central America?*

Approve . . . . . . . . . . . . . . . . . . . . . . . . . . . .29%
Disapprove . . . . . . . . . . . . . . . . . . . . . . . . .48
No opinion . . . . . . . . . . . . . . . . . . . . . . . . .23

## Selected National Trend

| | Approve | Dis-approve | No opinion |
|---|---|---|---|
| *1984* | | | |
| February 10–13 ...... | 29% | 48% | 23% |
| January 13–16 ....... | 28 | 49 | 23 |
| *1983* | | | |
| December ........... | 36 | 44 | 20 |
| October ............ | 27 | 49 | 24 |
| August ............. | 24 | 51 | 25 |
| June ............... | 25 | 46 | 29 |
| April ............... | 21 | 49 | 30 |

Note: Amid debate over U.S. involvement in planting mines in Nicaraguan harbors, the public opposes, by a margin of 49% to 39%, providing military assistance to Central American governments, believing that we should not get involved in the internal affairs of these nations. The current survey was undertaken after disclosure of the Central Intelligence Agency's involvement in the mining.

Opinion on this issue divides sharply along political lines, with Republicans, in a just completed survey, preferring military aid over non-involvement 55% to 34%. Democrats, on the other hand, favor a hands-off approach over increased arms aid by 59% to 29%. Voters who describe themselves as independents mirror the national findings, with 50% saying the United States should not get involved and 39% favoring military aid.

Consistent with the trend over the past year, the survey shows approval (29%) of President Ronald Reagan's handling of the Central American situation greatly outweighed by disapproval (48%). The poor marks Reagan receives for his actions in Central America stand in marked contrast to the 52%-to-37% approval rating currently accorded the president for his overall performance in office.

Two key features of Reagan's Central American policy are to provide military support for the El Salvador government against leftist guerrillas and to aid rightist rebels seeking to overthrow the Nicaraguan government. American officials have said the purpose of the mining of Nicaraguan harbors was to interdict military supplies intended for the Salvadoran guerrillas.

## APRIL 26
## COST OF LIVING

Interviewing Date: 1/13–16; 27–30/84
Survey #229-G; 230-G

*Asked of nonfarm families: What is the smallest amount of money a family of four (husband, wife, and two children) needs each week to get along in this community?*

| | Median average |
|---|---|
| National ......................... | $300 |

### Selected National Trend

| | |
|---|---|
| 1983 ............................. | $296 |
| 1982 ............................. | $296 |
| 1981 ............................. | $277 |
| 1980 ............................. | $250 |
| 1979 ............................. | $223 |
| 1978 ............................. | $201 |
| 1977 ............................. | $199 |
| 1976 ............................. | $177 |
| 1975 ............................. | $161 |
| 1974 ............................. | $152 |
| 1973 ............................. | $149 |
| 1971 ............................. | $127 |
| 1970 ............................. | $126 |
| 1969 ............................. | $120 |
| 1967 ............................. | $101 |
| 1966 ............................. | $ 99 |
| 1964 ............................. | $ 81 |
| 1961 ............................. | $ 84 |
| 1959 ............................. | $ 79 |
| 1957 ............................. | $ 72 |
| 1954 ............................. | $ 60 |
| 1953 ............................. | $ 60 |
| 1952 ............................. | $ 60 |
| 1951 ............................. | $ 50 |
| 1950 ............................. | $ 50 |
| 1949 ............................. | $ 50 |
| 1948 ............................. | $ 50 |
| 1947 ............................. | $ 43 |
| 1937 ............................. | $ 30 |

*Asked of nonfarm families: What is the smallest amount of money your family needs each week to get along in this community?*

|  | Median average |
|---|---|
| National | $252 |

## By Size of Household

| | |
|---|---|
| Single person | $174 |
| Two-person family | $248 |
| Three-person family | $299 |
| Four-person family | $300 |
| Five-person family | $302 |

Note: Americans believe it now takes a minimum of $300 per week for a husband, wife, and two children to make ends meet, representing the highest figure recorded in Gallup surveys since 1937. In both the 1983 and 1982 audits, the median amount cited was $296, not significantly different from that in 1984. The annual Gallup audits of perceptions of living costs have tended to conform closely to the Consumer Price Index (CPI) compiled by the U.S. Bureau of Labor Statistics. According to the CPI, living costs during 1983 were only 3.8% more than during the comparable 1982 period.

In 1937, when the Gallup Poll first surveyed Americans' perception of weekly living costs for a family of four, the median response was $30, or one-tenth the current amount. By 1947 the figure had climbed to $43. It did not hit three-digit proportions until 1967 when the median estimate was $101. It took only twelve years, until 1978, for living costs to pass $200. Notwithstanding the small recent increases, the $300 mark was reached in merely six years.

Americans' own life-styles tend to be reflected in their estimates of the minimum cost of living in their communities. The median amount cited by college-educated respondents, for instance, is $352 per week, while the comparable figures for persons with a high-school education and for those with even less formal education are $299 and $250, respectively.

## APRIL 29
## PARTY BETTER FOR PEACE AND PROSPERITY

Interviewing Date: 4/6–9/84
Survey #233-G

*Which political party do you think would be more likely to keep the United States out of World War III—the Republican party or the Democratic party?*

| | |
|---|---|
| Republican | 30% |
| Democratic | 42 |
| No difference; no opinion | 28 |

### Selected National Trend

| | Republican | Democratic | No difference; no opinion |
|---|---|---|---|
| Sept. 1983 | 26% | 39% | 35% |
| Oct. 1982 | 29 | 38 | 33 |
| Apr. 1981 | 29 | 34 | 37 |
| Sept. 1980 | 25 | 42 | 33 |
| Aug. 1976 | 29 | 32 | 39 |
| Sept. 1972 | 32 | 28 | 40 |
| Oct. 1968 | 37 | 24 | 39 |
| Oct. 1964 | 22 | 45 | 33 |
| Oct. 1960 | 40 | 25 | 35 |
| Oct. 1956 | 46 | 16 | 38 |
| Jan. 1952 | 36 | 15 | 49 |
| Sept. 1951 | 28 | 21 | 51 |

*Which political party—the Republican party or the Democratic party—do you think will do a better job of keeping the country prosperous?*

| | |
|---|---|
| Republican | 44% |
| Democratic | 36 |
| No difference; no opinion | 20 |

### By Politics
#### Republicans

| | |
|---|---|
| Republican | 81% |
| Democratic | 7 |
| No difference; no opinion | 12 |

### Democrats

Republican ........................19%
Democratic .........................65
No difference; no opinion .............16

### Independents

Republican ........................47%
Democratic .........................23
No difference; no opinion .............30

### Selected National Trend

| | Repub- lican | Demo- cratic | No difference; no opinion |
|---|---|---|---|
| Sept. 1983 ........... | 33% | 40% | 27% |
| Oct. 1982 ............ | 34 | 43 | 23 |
| Oct. 1981 ............ | 40 | 31 | 29 |
| Sept. 1980 ........... | 35 | 36 | 29 |
| Aug. 1976 ........... | 23 | 47 | 30 |
| Sept. 1972 ........... | 38 | 35 | 27 |
| Oct. 1968 ............ | 34 | 37 | 29 |
| Oct. 1964 ............ | 21 | 53 | 26 |
| Oct. 1960 ............ | 31 | 46 | 23 |
| Oct. 1956 ............ | 39 | 39 | 22 |
| Jan. 1952 ............ | 31 | 35 | 34 |
| Nov. 1951 ........... | 29 | 37 | 34 |

Note: The Republican party now enjoys the politically important advantage of being seen by the electorate as more likely than the Democratic party to keep the nation prosperous. Not since October 1981 has the GOP led the Democrats as the "party of prosperity." The latest Gallup Poll shows 44%—the highest figure since these measurements were begun in 1951—saying the Republican party will do a better job of keeping the United States prosperous, while 36% name the Democratic party and 20% see little difference between the parties in this respect or do not offer an opinion. The Republicans have had a clear advantage over the Democrats on only two other occasions, both during the early months of the Reagan administration.

The Republican party's advantage on the prosperity issue is offset by the Democratic party's substantial lead as being more likely to keep the nation at peace. Currently, 42% say the Democratic party is stronger in this regard, 30% name the GOP, and 28% see no difference or have no opinion. With only a few exceptions the Democrats have held an edge on the peace issue for over a decade, with the lead changing hands at intervals before then.

Women are less likely (27%) than men (33%) to view the GOP as being better able to keep the country out of war. Women's views on this issue, other surveys have shown, contribute strongly to President Ronald Reagan's "gender gap."

The GOP's current claim as the party of prosperity is strengthened by the fact that a substantial proportion of Democrats in the survey (19%) desert their party to vote for the Republican party as superior in this respect, compared to only 7% of Republicans who cite the Democratic party as better. Also, proportionately more Republicans are steadfast to the GOP (81%) than Democrats are loyal to their party (65%) as doing a better job of keeping the country prosperous.

## MAY 3

### DEMOCRATIC PRESIDENTIAL CANDIDATES/PRESIDENTIAL TRIAL HEATS

Interviewing Date: 4/6–9/84
Survey #233-G

*Asked of Democrats: Which candidate— Walter Mondale or Gary Hart—do you think is waging a "cleaner" campaign with less "mudslinging"?*

### All Democrats

Walter Mondale ......................26%
Gary Hart ..........................38
No difference (volunteered) ...........25
No opinion .........................11

### Democrats for Mondale

Mondale ...........................37%
Hart ..............................21
No difference (volunteered) ...........23
No opinion .........................19

### Democrats for Hart

Mondale . . . . . . . . . . . . . . . . . . . . . . . . . 7%
Hart . . . . . . . . . . . . . . . . . . . . . . . . . . . . .67
No difference (volunteered) . . . . . . . . . . .19
No opinion . . . . . . . . . . . . . . . . . . . . . . . 7

Interviewing Date: 4/11–15/84
Special Telephone Survey

*Asked of registered voters: Suppose the 1984
presidential election were being held today.
If the Republican ticket of Ronald Reagan
and George Bush were running against the
Democratic ticket of Walter Mondale and
Gary Hart, which would you like to see win?
[Those who were undecided or who named
other candidates were then asked: As of today,
do you lean more to the Republican ticket of
Reagan and Bush or to the Democratic ticket
of Mondale and Hart?]*

Reagan–Bush . . . . . . . . . . . . . . . . . . . . . . .49%
Mondale–Hart . . . . . . . . . . . . . . . . . . . . . .49
Other; undecided . . . . . . . . . . . . . . . . . . . 2

Note: If the November election were being held
today, a Democratic ticket of Walter Mondale as
president and Gary Hart as vice-president would
run evenly with a Ronald Reagan-George Bush
Republican ticket, with each ticket receiving 49%
of the vote and 2% undecided.

In the latest Gallup test elections, when Mondale alone is pitted against Reagan, he trails the
president 44% to 52%. Mondale is currently the
top nomination choice of Democrats, winning 51%
of their vote to 28% for Hart and 9% for the
Reverend Jesse Jackson. Hart and Reagan are in
a statistical tie, with Reagan receiving 49% and
Hart 46% of the support of registered voters
nationwide.

At present, Hart is seen by Democrats as waging a cleaner campaign than Mondale. Despite his
underdog status in the nomination contest, 38%
of Democrats currently credit Hart with indulging
in less mudslinging, while 26% think Mondale
has waged a cleaner campaign.

Some observers think that Mondale and Hart
would be unlikely to run on the same ticket in
view of the sharp exchanges between the two during the primary period. However, recent history
offers examples of erstwhile rivals effectively
joining forces; for example, Reagan and Bush in
1980 and John Kennedy and Lyndon Johnson in
1960.

## MAY 6
## VOTER REGISTRATION

Seven Surveys Conducted Between November 1983
and April 1984

*Is your name now recorded in the registra-
tion book of the precinct or election district
where you now live?*

| | Total Yes | Whites Yes | Blacks Yes |
|---|---|---|---|
| National . . . . . . . . . . . . . . .72% | 72% | 73% |

### By Sex

| | | | |
|---|---|---|---|
| Male . . . . . . . . . . . . . . . . . .72% | 72% | 70% |
| Female . . . . . . . . . . . . . . .72 | 72 | 76 |

### By Education

| | | | |
|---|---|---|---|
| College graduate . . . . . . . . . .79% | 79% | 80% |
| High-school graduate . . . . . .70 | 69 | 75 |
| Less than high-school graduate . . . . . . . . . . . . . .64 | 63 | 68 |

### By Region

| | | | |
|---|---|---|---|
| East . . . . . . . . . . . . . . . . . . .73% | 74% | 64% |
| Midwest . . . . . . . . . . . . . . .78 | 77 | 81 |
| South . . . . . . . . . . . . . . . . . .68 | 67 | 76 |
| West . . . . . . . . . . . . . . . . . .69 | 70 | 63 |

### By Age

| | | | |
|---|---|---|---|
| 18–29 years . . . . . . . . . . . .53% | 52% | 64% |
| 30–49 years . . . . . . . . . . . .74 | 75 | 74 |
| 50 years and over . . . . . . . .84 | 85 | 83 |

## By Income

$20,000 and over ........77% 78% 74%
Under $20,000 ..........67  67  73

## By Politics

Republicans .............79% 79% 80%
Democrats ...............76  76  78
Independents ............64  65  58

## By Labor Union Household

Labor union members .....78% 78% 80%
Nonlabor union
   members ............71  71  71

Note: For the first time in the nation's history, proportionately as many blacks and whites say they are registered to vote—a fact which, if accompanied by high turnout, could spell the difference in a close presidential election this fall. In personal interviews with over 10,000 adult Americans conducted from November through April, 72% of whites and 73% of blacks said they were registered to vote. During the same period in the 1979–80 presidential campaign, 70% of whites and 67% of blacks claimed to be registered.

Registration is only the first step toward voting. If blacks are to make a difference in the election, their turnout record will also have to improve. In the 1980 presidential election, 84% of registered blacks reported having voted, compared to 89% of registered whites.

One of the key reasons black voters can be the deciding factor in close elections is their traditional allegiance to the Democratic party. As shown below, the current division of registered white voters leans only narrowly to the Democratic over the Republican party, 39% to 33%, with 28% saying they are independents. Among registered blacks, however, Democrats outnumber Republicans by an overwhelming 81% to 4% margin, with 15% independents. Registered Hispanics, though predominantly Democratic in affiliation, are closer to the political profile of whites than of blacks.

## Political Affiliation

### Based on Registered Voters
### (November 1983–April 1984)

|  | National | Whites | Blacks | Hispanics |
|---|---|---|---|---|
| Republicans | 30% | 33% | 4% | 23% |
| Democrats | 43 | 39 | 81 | 56 |
| Independents | 27 | 28 | 15 | 21 |

Significantly higher proportions of southern blacks, those 18 to 29 years of age, and blacks from households with a total annual income of less than $20,000 say they are registered to vote than do their white counterparts. On the other hand, a greater percentage of eastern whites than eastern blacks report they are registered to vote. In all other groups, the difference between the races in reported registration is not large enough to be statistically meaningful.

## MAY 10
## PRESIDENT REAGAN

Interviewing Date: 4/6–9/84
Survey #233-G

> Suppose you were trying to convince a friend of yours to vote for President Ronald Reagan. Regardless of your own political views, what would you give as the best reason for voting for President Reagan?

Improved economy ...................36%
  in general ....................23
  lower inflation ................. 8
  lower unemployment ........... 4
  lower interest rates ............. 3
  reduced federal spending ........ 2
Doing a good job ..................11
Personality .........................10
Defense policy ..................... 7
Foreign policy ..................... 5
Experience ........................ 5
Religious person ................... 3
Position on school prayer ............. 2
Deserves a second term ............... 2

Other .............................. 5
Nothing ........................... 13
No opinion ........................ 11
                              110%*

## By Politics

### Republicans

Improved economy ..................51%
  in general ...................33
  lower inflation ................12
  lower unemployment ............ 6
  lower interest rates ............. 3
  reduced federal spending ........ 4
Doing a good job ...................16
Personality ........................11
Defense policy ..................... 8
Foreign policy ..................... 5
Experience ........................ 3
Religious person ................... 4
Position on school prayer ............. 1
Deserves a second term .............. 2
Other ............................. 6
Nothing ........................... 2
No opinion ........................ 4
                              113%*

### Democrats

Improved economy ..................25%
  in general ...................14
  lower inflation ................ 7
  lower unemployment ............ 4
  lower interest rates ............. 2
  reduced federal spending ........ 1
Doing a good job ................... 8
Personality ........................ 7
Defense policy ..................... 6
Foreign policy ..................... 5
Experience ........................ 4
Religious person ................... 3
Position on school prayer ............. 1
Deserves a second term .............. 1
Other ............................. 6
Nothing ........................... 23
No opinion ........................ 16
                              105%*

### Independents

Improved economy ..................37%
  in general ...................26
  lower inflation ................ 7
  lower unemployment ............ 4
  lower interest rates ............. 3
  reduced federal spending ........ 2
Doing a good job ...................11
Personality ........................14
Defense policy ..................... 5
Foreign policy ..................... 3
Experience ........................ 7
Religious person ................... 2
Position on school prayer ............. 3
Deserves a second term .............. 2
Other ............................. 5
Nothing ........................... 9
No opinion ........................ 10
                              108%*

*Total adds to more than 100% due to multiple responses.

*Regardless of your own political views, what would you give as the best reason for voting against President Reagan?*

Foreign policy (including fear of war) ....21%
"Fairness" issue ......................18
  Favors rich ................... 8
  Unfair to poor ................ 7
  Unfair to average person ......... 4
  Insensitive to women's issues ..... 2
  Unfair to elderly ............... 1
Too old ............................ 8
High unemployment .................. 6
Cuts in social programs ............... 5
Excess defense spending .............. 5
Inflation ........................... 5
Cuts in Social Security .............. 4
Budget deficits ..................... 4
He's a Republican ................... 1
Other .............................14
Nothing ...........................10
No opinion ......................... 9
                              110%*

## By Politics

### Republicans

Foreign policy (including fear of war) . . . . 23%
"Fairness" issue . . . . . . . . . . . . . . . . . . . . . 11
   Favors rich . . . . . . . . . . . . . . . . . . 6
   Unfair to poor . . . . . . . . . . . . . . . . 5
   Unfair to average person . . . . . . . . . 1
   Insensitive to women's issues . . . . . 2
   Unfair to elderly . . . . . . . . . . . . . . **
Too old . . . . . . . . . . . . . . . . . . . . . . . . . . 11
High unemployment . . . . . . . . . . . . . . . . . 2
Cuts in social programs . . . . . . . . . . . . . . 3
Excess defense spending . . . . . . . . . . . . . . 6
Inflation . . . . . . . . . . . . . . . . . . . . . . . . . . 2
Cuts in Social Security . . . . . . . . . . . . . . 3
Budget deficits . . . . . . . . . . . . . . . . . . . . . 6
He's a Republican . . . . . . . . . . . . . . . . . . **
Other . . . . . . . . . . . . . . . . . . . . . . . . . . . . 11
Nothing . . . . . . . . . . . . . . . . . . . . . . . . . . 17
No opinion . . . . . . . . . . . . . . . . . . . . . . . . 10
                                       105%*

### Democrats

Foreign policy (including fear of war) . . . . 19%
"Fairness" issue . . . . . . . . . . . . . . . . . . . . . 25
   Favors rich . . . . . . . . . . . . . . . . . . 12
   Unfair to poor . . . . . . . . . . . . . . . . 11
   Unfair to average person . . . . . . . . . 6
   Insensitive to women's issues . . . . . 2
   Unfair to elderly . . . . . . . . . . . . . . 1
Too old . . . . . . . . . . . . . . . . . . . . . . . . . . 4
High unemployment . . . . . . . . . . . . . . . . . 9
Cuts in social programs . . . . . . . . . . . . . . 8
Excess defense spending . . . . . . . . . . . . . . 5
Inflation . . . . . . . . . . . . . . . . . . . . . . . . . . 5
Cuts in Social Security . . . . . . . . . . . . . . 4
Budget deficits . . . . . . . . . . . . . . . . . . . . . 3
He's a Republican . . . . . . . . . . . . . . . . . . 2
Other . . . . . . . . . . . . . . . . . . . . . . . . . . . . 15
Nothing . . . . . . . . . . . . . . . . . . . . . . . . . . 6
No opinion . . . . . . . . . . . . . . . . . . . . . . . . 8
                                       113%*

### Independents

Foreign policy (including fear of war) . . . . 25%
"Fairness" issue . . . . . . . . . . . . . . . . . . . . . 13
   Favors rich . . . . . . . . . . . . . . . . . . 5
   Unfair to poor . . . . . . . . . . . . . . . . 5
   Unfair to average person . . . . . . . . . 3
   Insensitive to women's issues . . . . . 1
   Unfair to elderly . . . . . . . . . . . . . . 2
Too old . . . . . . . . . . . . . . . . . . . . . . . . . . 10
High unemployment . . . . . . . . . . . . . . . . . 4
Cuts in social programs . . . . . . . . . . . . . . 4
Excess defense spending . . . . . . . . . . . . . . 4
Inflation . . . . . . . . . . . . . . . . . . . . . . . . . . 7
Cuts in Social Security . . . . . . . . . . . . . . 3
Budget deficits . . . . . . . . . . . . . . . . . . . . . 3
He's a Republican . . . . . . . . . . . . . . . . . . 1
Other . . . . . . . . . . . . . . . . . . . . . . . . . . . . 14
Nothing . . . . . . . . . . . . . . . . . . . . . . . . . . 11
No opinion . . . . . . . . . . . . . . . . . . . . . . . . 10
                                       109%*

*Total adds to more than 100% due to multiple responses.
**Less than 1%

Note: Voters of all political stripes see President Ronald Reagan as politically most vulnerable on foreign policy and on fairness to minority groups. About one voter in five (21%) says he would cite foreign policy (including fear of war) if he were trying to convince a friend to vote against Reagan. This issue is named by 23% of Republicans, 19% of Democrats, and 25% of independents.

A similar proportion (18%) says they would cite the fairness issue ("Reagan favors the rich and is unfair to the poor and elderly") if they try to convince a friend to vote against Reagan. As many as 11% of Republicans, 25% of Democrats, and 15% of independents would mention the fairness issue, as well.

Clearly Reagan's strong suit among all voters is the improved national economy, with 23% specifically naming this and an additional 8% noting lower inflation, 4% lower unemployment, and 3% lower interest rates. In all, 36% mention a reason relating to economic factors. Democrats, Republicans, and independents all are in agreement that the improved economy is the best reason to give a friend for voting for Reagan next fall.

## MAY 13
## DEMOCRATIC PRESIDENTIAL CANDIDATES/PRESIDENTIAL TRIAL HEATS

Interviewing Date: 5/3–5/84
Special Telephone Survey

*Asked of Democrats and independents: Which one of these persons would you like to see nominated as the Democratic party's candidate for president this year?*

### Choice of Democrats

|  | May 3–5 | Apr. 11–15 | Apr. 6–9 |
|---|---|---|---|
| Mondale ...... | 53% | 51% | 40% |
| Hart ......... | 27 | 28 | 35 |
| Jackson ....... | 9 | 9 | 13 |
| Other; don't know ...... | 11 | 12 | 12 |

### Choice of Independents

|  | May 3–5 | Apr. 11–15 | Apr. 6–9 |
|---|---|---|---|
| Mondale ...... | 33% | 29% | 30% |
| Hart ......... | 35 | 39 | 42 |
| Jackson ....... | 9 | 9 | 7 |
| Other; don't know ...... | 23 | 24 | 21 |

*Asked of Democrats and independents: Suppose the choice for president in the Democratic convention this year narrows down to Walter Mondale and Gary Hart. Which one would you prefer to have the Democratic convention select? Do you strongly support him or do you only moderately support him?*

### Choice of Democrats

|  | May 3–5 | Apr. 11–15 |
|---|---|---|
| Mondale ........... | 59% | 57% |
| Strongly support | 26 | 29 |
| Moderately support | 33 | 28 |
| Hart .............. | 33 | 33 |
| Strongly support | 9 | 10 |
| Moderately support | 24 | 23 |
| Undecided ......... | 8 | 10 |

### Choice of Independents

|  | May 3–5 | Apr. 11–15 |
|---|---|---|
| Mondale ........... | 39% | 36% |
| Strongly support | 8 | 8 |
| Moderately support | 31 | 28 |
| Hart .............. | 45 | 48 |
| Strongly support | 7 | 10 |
| Moderately support | 38 | 38 |
| Undecided ......... | 16 | 16 |

*Asked of registered voters: Suppose the 1984 presidential election were being held today. If Walter Mondale were the Democratic candidate and President Ronald Reagan were the Republican candidate, which would you like to see win? [Those who were undecided were then asked: As of today, do you lean more to Mondale, the Democrat, or to Reagan, the Republican?]*

|  | May 3–5 | Apr. 11–15 |
|---|---|---|
| Mondale ........... | 46% | 44% |
| Reagan ............. | 50 | 52 |
| Other; undecided ...... | 4 | 4 |

*Asked of registered voters: Suppose the 1984 presidential election were being held today. If Gary Hart were the Democratic candidate and President Ronald Reagan were the Republican candidate, which would you like to see win? [Those who were undecided were then asked: As of today, do you lean more to Hart, the Democrat, or to Reagan, the Republican?]*

|              | May 3–5 | Apr. 11–15 |
|--------------|---------|------------|
| Hart ................ | 45% | 46% |
| Reagan .............. | 49 | 49 |
| Other; undecided ...... | 6 | 5 |

Note: New Gallup test election results show President Ronald Reagan narrowly leading both Democratic challengers Walter Mondale and Gary Hart by identical 4-point margins. This finding not only accentuates the closeness of the presidential race at this time, but also belies Hart's claim, based on earlier surveys, that he is more electable than Mondale.

In a Gallup Poll just completed, Reagan led Mondale 50% to 46%, while the president edged Hart 49% to 45%. In mid-April, Reagan was an 8-point leader over Mondale, 52% to 44%, while the Reagan-Hart contest resulted in a statistical draw, 49% to 46%. Hart enjoyed his largest lead over Reagan soon after the February New Hampshire primary, when the Colorado senator held a 52% to 43% advantage.

In this latest survey, Mondale is the choice of 53% of Democrats for the nomination to 27% for Hart and 9% for Jesse Jackson. By comparison, in a survey conducted in the immediate aftermath of Hart's stunning victory in New Hampshire, the two Democrats were effectively tied for the nomination.

When the nomination contest is narrowed to only the front-runners, Mondale receives 59% of Democrats' votes to 33% for Hart. Support for Mondale is fairly evenly divided between those who describe their support as strong (26%) and moderate (33%), while Hart's backing is more than 2-to-1 moderate. Hart receives 45% of independents' votes to 39% for Mondale, but only 7% of Hart's backers and 8% of Mondale's say they strongly support their man.

Senator Hart's strength with political independents, which has been a hallmark of his campaign for the Democratic nomination, is now showing signs of erosion. In the post-New Hampshire survey, Hart garnered 40% of independents' nomination votes to 13% for Mondale, a 3-to-1 advantage. In the current survey, Hart is selected by 35% of independents and Mondale by 33%, a statistically insignificant difference.

## MAY 17
## CONGRESSIONAL ELECTIONS

Interviewing Date: 4/6–9/84
Survey #233-G

*Asked of registered voters: If the elections for Congress were being held today, which party would you like to see win in this congressional district—the Democratic party or the Republican party? [Those who were undecided or named another party were asked: As of today, do you lean more to the Democratic party or to the Republican party?]*

|              | 1984 Gallup estimate* | 1982 election results |
|--------------|---------|------------|
| Democratic party ........ | 55% | 56.1% |
| Republican party ......... | 45 | 43.9 |

*The undecided vote was allocated to the two parties.

Note: President Ronald Reagan, if reelected in November, likely will have to work with a Democratic House of Representatives, judging by the latest Gallup Poll. This survey shows 55% of registered voters nationwide stating a preference for Democratic congressional candidates, compared to 45% who choose Republicans.

The current figures represent little gain for the GOP since the 1982 congressional contests, when 56.1% of the popular two-party vote went to Democratic candidates and 43.9% to Republicans. These percentages translated into 269 seats for the Democrats and 166 for the Republicans.

If Reagan wins in November and the Democratic party retains its present wide advantage, the pattern of a Republican president with a Democratic House will be continued. In only two years during the last half-century—in 1953–54, during Dwight Eisenhower's first term as president—has the GOP held the White House and control of both houses of Congress at the same time.

## MAY 17
## SINO-AMERICAN RELATIONS

Interviewing Date: 4/23–5/6/84
Special Telephone Survey

> Have you heard or read about President Ronald Reagan's trip to the People's Republic of China?

Yes ................................89%
No ..................................11

> Asked of those who replied in the affirmative: Do you think the president's trip will improve the relationship between the People's Republic of China and the United States a great deal, a fair amount, not very much, or not at all?

Great deal ..........................16%
Fair amount ........................49
Not very much ......................20
Not at all ..........................8
No opinion ..........................7

### By Politics
#### Republicans

Great deal ..........................23%
Fair amount ........................55
Not very much ......................12
Not at all ..........................4
No opinion ..........................6

#### Democrats

Great deal ..........................11%
Fair amount ........................47
Not very much ......................23
Not at all ..........................11
No opinion ..........................8

#### Independents

Great deal ..........................16%
Fair amount ........................46
Not very much ......................22
Not at all ..........................9
No opinion ..........................7

## MAY 20
## WALTER MONDALE AND GARY HART

Interviewing Date: 4/23–5/6/84
Special Telephone Survey

> I am going to read off some issues facing the country today. Regardless of whom you happen to prefer, please tell me which Democratic candidate, Walter Mondale or Gary Hart, you feel would do a better job of dealing with each of the following:

> Handling foreign affairs?

Mondale ...........................54%
Hart ................................23
No difference; no opinion ..............23

> Keeping the United States out of war?

Mondale ...........................38%
Hart ................................31
No difference; no opinion ..............31

> Improving the economy?

Mondale ...........................38%
Hart ................................33
No difference; no opinion ..............29

> Reducing unemployment?

Mondale ...........................39%
Hart ................................30
No difference; no opinion ..............31

> Keeping the inflation rate down?

Mondale ...........................36%
Hart ................................33
No difference; no opinion ..............31

> Improving conditions for blacks, Hispanics, and other minorities?

Mondale ...........................39%
Hart ................................29
No difference; no opinion ..............32

*Dealing with women's rights?*

Mondale .......................... 32%
Hart ............................... 35
No difference; no opinion ............. 33

*Dealing with the situation in Central America?*

Mondale .......................... 41%
Hart ............................... 26
No difference; no opinion ............. 33

*Handling disarmament negotiations with the Soviet Union?*

Mondale .......................... 45%
Hart ............................... 23
No difference; no opinion ............. 32

*Handling environmental problems?*

Mondale .......................... 33%
Hart ............................... 38
No difference; no opinion ............. 29

Note: With attention now focusing on which of the two leading Democratic candidates is more electable, a just completed Gallup Poll shows Walter Mondale with a wide lead over Gary Hart among voters of all political persuasions on issues relating to foreign affairs. On many domestic issues, however, a narrower margin separates the two Democratic presidential contenders.

In the survey, Mondale enjoys a 31-percentage point lead over Hart in terms of his perceived ability to handle foreign affairs. The former vice-president is the choice of 54% to 23% for Senator Hart. The remaining 23% see no difference between the two candidates on this issue or have no opinion.

On two other international issues studied, Mondale has a smaller but decisive edge. For his potential handling of disarmament negotiations with the Soviet Union, Mondale leads Hart 45% to 23%. Mondale also is thought to be the better man for dealing with the situation in Central America, by a 41% to 26% vote.

On four other issues, Mondale has a slim edge over the Colorado senator. He is seen by 39% of respondents as better able to improve conditions for blacks, Hispanics, and other minorities, compared to 29% for Hart. Mondale also leads Hart as better able to reduce unemployment, 39% to 30%; better able to keep the United States out of war, 38% to 31%; better able to improve the economy, 38% to 33%.

Consistent with his western background, Hart leads on the issue of handling environmental problems by 38% to 33% for Mondale. On two other issues—dealing with women's rights and keeping the inflation rate down—the differences between the two men are not statistically meaningful.

Although Mondale has an advantage on most of the issues covered, another recent Gallup Poll found Hart leading Mondale on questions of style and for presenting fresh ideas. On the other hand, both men fared about equally well in terms of their perceived character traits.

## MAY 24
## PERSONALITY FACTOR AND ELECTION RESULTS

Interviewing Date: 4/6–9/84
Survey #233–G

*You will notice that the ten boxes on this card go from the highest position of +5 for a person you have a very favorable opinion of all the way down to the lowest position of −5 for a person you have a very unfavorable opinion of. How far up the scale or how far down the scale would you rate Ronald Reagan/Walter Mondale/Gary Hart?*

The following table compares the highly favorable ratings given candidates in the early months of presidential years and the actual election results:

|  | Highly favorable ratings (+4, +5) | Election results |
|---|---|---|
| *April 1984* | | |
| Reagan ............. | 29% | — |
| Hart .............. | 21 | — |
| Mondale .......... | 18 | — |

*August 1980*

| | | |
|---|---|---|
| Reagan . . . . . . . . . . . | 31% | 51%* |
| Carter . . . . . . . . . . . . | 20 | 41 |

*May 1976*

| | | |
|---|---|---|
| Carter . . . . . . . . . . . . | 25% | 50%* |
| Ford . . . . . . . . . . . . . | 22 | 48 |

*August 1972*

| | | |
|---|---|---|
| Nixon . . . . . . . . . . . . | 40% | 62% |
| McGovern . . . . . . . . | 23 | 38 |

*May 1968*

| | | |
|---|---|---|
| Nixon . . . . . . . . . . . . | 28% | 43%* |
| Humphrey . . . . . . . . | 27 | 43 |

*August 1964*

| | | |
|---|---|---|
| Johnson . . . . . . . . . . | 55% | 61% |
| Goldwater . . . . . . . . | 21 | 39 |

*May 1960*

| | | |
|---|---|---|
| Kennedy . . . . . . . . . . | 38% | 50% |
| Nixon . . . . . . . . . . . . | 41 | 50 |

*July 1956*

| | | |
|---|---|---|
| Eisenhower . . . . . . . . | 66% | 58% |
| Stevenson . . . . . . . . . | 28 | 42 |

*Total adds to less than 100% because of third party candidates.

Note: President Ronald Reagan leads potential Democratic rivals Walter Mondale and Gary Hart on the personality factor, with three in ten voters (29%) indicating they have a highly favorable opinion of the president compared to 21% for Hart and 18% for Mondale. This factor, together with issues and party loyalty, has proved to be an important barometer of presidential election results as determined by Gallup surveys over the last three decades.

In each of the last seven presidential elections, the personality ratings given the leading candidates in the months preceding the election have pointed to the division of the vote in November. For example, personality ratings early in 1960, 1968, and 1976 pointed to the extremely close contests in November. President Reagan's current "highly favorable" rating of 29% is slightly higher than that given President Jimmy Carter (25%) at a comparable point in the 1980 campaign, but far below that accorded candidates in 1956, 1960, and 1964.

## MAY 27
## DEMOCRATIC PRESIDENTIAL CANDIDATES

Interviewing Date: 5/18–21/84
Survey #234-G

*Asked of Democrats and independents: Which one of these persons would you like to see nominated as the Democratic party's candidate for president this year?*

### Choice of Democrats

| | |
|---|---|
| Walter Mondale . . . . . . . . . . . . . . . . . . . . . . . | 46% |
| Gary Hart . . . . . . . . . . . . . . . . . . . . . . . . . . . | 34 |
| Jesse Jackson . . . . . . . . . . . . . . . . . . . . . . . | 10 |
| Other; don't know . . . . . . . . . . . . . . . . . . . . | 10 |

### Selected National Trend

| | Mondale | Hart | Jackson | Other; don't know |
|---|---|---|---|---|
| May 3–5 | 53% | 27% | 9% | 11% |
| Apr. 11–15 | 51 | 28 | 9 | 12 |
| Apr. 6–9 | 40 | 35 | 13 | 12 |
| Mar. 16–19 | 44 | 38 | 10 | 8 |
| Mar. 2–6 | 33 | 30 | 9 | 28 |

### Choice of Independents

| | |
|---|---|
| Mondale . . . . . . . . . . . . . . . . . . . . . . . . . . . . | 31% |
| Hart . . . . . . . . . . . . . . . . . . . . . . . . . . . . . . . . | 46 |
| Jackson . . . . . . . . . . . . . . . . . . . . . . . . . . . . | 5 |
| Other; don't know . . . . . . . . . . . . . . . . . . . . | 18 |

## Selected National Trend

|  | Mondale | Hart | Jackson | Other; don't know |
|---|---|---|---|---|
| May 3–5 | 33% | 35% | 9% | 23% |
| Apr. 11–15 | 29 | 39 | 8 | 24 |
| Apr. 6–9 | 30 | 42 | 7 | 21 |
| Mar. 16–19 | 27 | 48 | 7 | 18 |
| Mar. 2–6 | 13 | 40 | 4 | 43 |

*Asked of Democrats and independents: Suppose the choice for president in the Democratic convention this year narrows down to Walter Mondale and Gary Hart. Which one would you prefer to have the Democratic convention select?*

### Choice of Democrats

Mondale . . . . . . . . . . . . . . . . . . . . . . . . . .57%
Hart . . . . . . . . . . . . . . . . . . . . . . . . . . . . .35
Undecided . . . . . . . . . . . . . . . . . . . . . . . 8

### Selected National Trend

|  | Mondale | Hart | Undecided |
|---|---|---|---|
| May 3–5 . . . . . . . . . | 59% | 33% | 8% |
| April 11–15 . . . . . . . . | 57 | 33 | 10 |
| April 6–9 . . . . . . . . . | 52 | 39 | 9 |
| March 16–19 . . . . . . . | 49 | 44 | 7 |
| March 2–6 . . . . . . . . | 49 | 39 | 12 |

### Choice of Independents

Mondale . . . . . . . . . . . . . . . . . . . . . . . . . .37%
Hart . . . . . . . . . . . . . . . . . . . . . . . . . . . . .53
Undecided . . . . . . . . . . . . . . . . . . . . . . . .10

### Selected National Trend

|  | Mondale | Hart | Undecided |
|---|---|---|---|
| May 3–5 . . . . . . . . . | 39% | 45% | 16% |
| April 11–15 . . . . . . . . | 36 | 48 | 16 |
| April 6–9 . . . . . . . . . | 38 | 47 | 15 |
| March 16–19 . . . . . . . | 31 | 55 | 14 |
| March 2–6 . . . . . . . . | 25 | 55 | 20 |

Note: Senator Gary Hart's campaign for the Democratic presidential nomination appears to have received a much-needed boost following his recent victories in the Nebraska and Oregon primaries. He still trails rival Walter Mondale for the nomination among Democrats nationwide by 34% to 46%, with 10% for Jesse Jackson. However, a Gallup Poll conducted after the two primaries reveals that Hart has stalled Mondale's momentum, at least for the time being. Earlier this month, Hart was the 27% to 53% loser to the former vice-president, the high point of Mondale's post-New Hampshire campaign for the nomination.

Hart's recent primary victories served to revive the independents' flagging support. In the current poll, he beats Mondale among this group 46% to 31%, almost identical to the competitive situation in mid-March. In Gallup's early May survey Mondale has almost drawn even with Hart, 33% to 35%, among independents. Hart's strength with this group, who represent about three voters in ten, has been a hallmark of his campaign for the nomination.

Hart's current competitive standing with independents, however, is measurably improved. For the first time since March, following his New Hampshire primary triumph, the Colorado senator enjoys majority support among independents, with 53% of their votes to 37% for Mondale—a 16 point margin of victory. Earlier this month merely 6 points separated the two nomination rivals, 45% for Hart to 39% for Mondale.

When the nomination contest is narrowed to only the two front-runners, Mondale receives 57% of Democrats' votes to 35% for Hart. While this is statistically unchanged from the 59% to 33% Mondale victory recorded in early May, it again signals a halt to the Mondale tide.

## MAY 31
## PRESIDENTIAL TRIAL HEATS

Interviewing Date: 5/18–21/84
Survey #234-G

*Asked of registered voters: Suppose the 1984 presidential election were being held today. If Walter Mondale were the Democratic candidate and President Ronald Reagan were the Republican candidate, which would you like to see win? [Those who were undecided were then asked: As of today, do you lean more to Mondale, the Democrat, or to Reagan, the Republican?]*

Mondale . . . . . . . . . . . . . . . . . . . . . . . . .43%
Reagan . . . . . . . . . . . . . . . . . . . . . . . . .53
Other; undecided . . . . . . . . . . . . . . . . . . 4

### By Sex
#### Male

Mondale . . . . . . . . . . . . . . . . . . . . . . . . .40%
Reagan . . . . . . . . . . . . . . . . . . . . . . . . .56
Other; undecided . . . . . . . . . . . . . . . . . . 4

#### Female

Mondale . . . . . . . . . . . . . . . . . . . . . . . . .45%
Reagan . . . . . . . . . . . . . . . . . . . . . . . . .50
Other; undecided . . . . . . . . . . . . . . . . . . 5

### By Ethnic Background
#### White

Mondale . . . . . . . . . . . . . . . . . . . . . . . . .38%
Reagan . . . . . . . . . . . . . . . . . . . . . . . . .58
Other; undecided . . . . . . . . . . . . . . . . . . 4

#### Nonwhite

Mondale . . . . . . . . . . . . . . . . . . . . . . . . .83%
Reagan . . . . . . . . . . . . . . . . . . . . . . . . . 8
Other; undecided . . . . . . . . . . . . . . . . . . 9

#### Black

Mondale . . . . . . . . . . . . . . . . . . . . . . . . .86%
Reagan . . . . . . . . . . . . . . . . . . . . . . . . . 4
Other; undecided . . . . . . . . . . . . . . . . . .10

### By Education
#### College Graduate

Mondale . . . . . . . . . . . . . . . . . . . . . . . . .33%
Reagan . . . . . . . . . . . . . . . . . . . . . . . . .65
Other; undecided . . . . . . . . . . . . . . . . . . 2

#### College Incomplete

Mondale . . . . . . . . . . . . . . . . . . . . . . . . .33%
Reagan . . . . . . . . . . . . . . . . . . . . . . . . .64
Other; undecided . . . . . . . . . . . . . . . . . . 3

#### High-School Graduate

Mondale . . . . . . . . . . . . . . . . . . . . . . . . .44%
Reagan . . . . . . . . . . . . . . . . . . . . . . . . .51
Other; undecided . . . . . . . . . . . . . . . . . . 5

#### Less Than High-School Graduate

Mondale . . . . . . . . . . . . . . . . . . . . . . . . .60%
Reagan . . . . . . . . . . . . . . . . . . . . . . . . .33
Other; undecided . . . . . . . . . . . . . . . . . . 7

### By Region
#### East

Mondale . . . . . . . . . . . . . . . . . . . . . . . . .42%
Reagan . . . . . . . . . . . . . . . . . . . . . . . . .52
Other; undecided . . . . . . . . . . . . . . . . . . 6

#### Midwest

Mondale . . . . . . . . . . . . . . . . . . . . . . . . .47%
Reagan . . . . . . . . . . . . . . . . . . . . . . . . .50
Other; undecided . . . . . . . . . . . . . . . . . . 3

#### South

Mondale . . . . . . . . . . . . . . . . . . . . . . . . .44%
Reagan . . . . . . . . . . . . . . . . . . . . . . . . .50
Other; undecided . . . . . . . . . . . . . . . . . . 6

#### West

Mondale . . . . . . . . . . . . . . . . . . . . . . . . .35%
Reagan . . . . . . . . . . . . . . . . . . . . . . . . .61
Other; undecided . . . . . . . . . . . . . . . . . . 4

### By Age
#### 18–29 Years

Mondale . . . . . . . . . . . . . . . . . . . . . . . . .44%
Reagan . . . . . . . . . . . . . . . . . . . . . . . . .53
Other; undecided . . . . . . . . . . . . . . . . . . 3

### 30–49 Years

Mondale . . . . . . . . . . . . . . . . . . . . . . . .43%
Reagan . . . . . . . . . . . . . . . . . . . . . . . .52
Other; undecided . . . . . . . . . . . . . . . . . 5

### 50 Years and Over

Mondale . . . . . . . . . . . . . . . . . . . . . . . .42%
Reagan . . . . . . . . . . . . . . . . . . . . . . . .53
Other; undecided . . . . . . . . . . . . . . . . . 5

## By Income
### $40,000 and Over

Mondale . . . . . . . . . . . . . . . . . . . . . . . .28%
Reagan . . . . . . . . . . . . . . . . . . . . . . . .71
Other; undecided . . . . . . . . . . . . . . . . . *

### $30,000–$39,999

Mondale . . . . . . . . . . . . . . . . . . . . . . . .39%
Reagan . . . . . . . . . . . . . . . . . . . . . . . .56
Other; undecided . . . . . . . . . . . . . . . . . 5

### $20,000–$29,999

Mondale . . . . . . . . . . . . . . . . . . . . . . . .40%
Reagan . . . . . . . . . . . . . . . . . . . . . . . .54
Other; undecided . . . . . . . . . . . . . . . . . 6

### $10,000–$19,999

Mondale . . . . . . . . . . . . . . . . . . . . . . . .45%
Reagan . . . . . . . . . . . . . . . . . . . . . . . .51
Other; undecided . . . . . . . . . . . . . . . . . 4

### Under $10,000

Mondale . . . . . . . . . . . . . . . . . . . . . . . .56%
Reagan . . . . . . . . . . . . . . . . . . . . . . . .37
Other; undecided . . . . . . . . . . . . . . . . . 7

## By Politics
### Republicans

Mondale . . . . . . . . . . . . . . . . . . . . . . . . 6%
Reagan . . . . . . . . . . . . . . . . . . . . . . . .91
Other; undecided . . . . . . . . . . . . . . . . . 3

*Less than 1%

### Democrats

Mondale . . . . . . . . . . . . . . . . . . . . . . . .71%
Reagan . . . . . . . . . . . . . . . . . . . . . . . .25
Other; undecided . . . . . . . . . . . . . . . . . 4

### Independents

Mondale . . . . . . . . . . . . . . . . . . . . . . . .34%
Reagan . . . . . . . . . . . . . . . . . . . . . . . .59
Other; undecided . . . . . . . . . . . . . . . . . 7

*Asked of registered voters: Suppose the 1984 presidential election were being held today. If Gary Hart were the Democratic candidate and President Ronald Reagan were the Republican candidate, which would you like to see win? [Those who were undecided were then asked: As of today, do you lean more to Hart, the Democrat, or to Reagan, the Republican?]*

Hart . . . . . . . . . . . . . . . . . . . . . . . . . . . .44%
Reagan . . . . . . . . . . . . . . . . . . . . . . . .51
Other; undecided . . . . . . . . . . . . . . . . . 5

## By Sex
### Male

Hart . . . . . . . . . . . . . . . . . . . . . . . . . . . .43%
Reagan . . . . . . . . . . . . . . . . . . . . . . . .53
Other; undecided . . . . . . . . . . . . . . . . . 4

### Female

Hart . . . . . . . . . . . . . . . . . . . . . . . . . . . .44%
Reagan . . . . . . . . . . . . . . . . . . . . . . . .49
Other; undecided . . . . . . . . . . . . . . . . . 7

## By Ethnic Background
### White

Hart . . . . . . . . . . . . . . . . . . . . . . . . . . . .40%
Reagan . . . . . . . . . . . . . . . . . . . . . . . .55
Other; undecided . . . . . . . . . . . . . . . . . 5

### Nonwhite

Hart . . . . . . . . . . . . . . . . . . . . . . . . . . . .75%
Reagan . . . . . . . . . . . . . . . . . . . . . . . .13
Other; undecided . . . . . . . . . . . . . . . . . 12

### Black

Hart . . . . . . . . . . . . . . . . . . . . . . . . . . . . . . . .81%
Reagan . . . . . . . . . . . . . . . . . . . . . . . . . . 8
Other; undecided . . . . . . . . . . . . . . . . . . . . .11

## By Education
### College Graduate

Hart . . . . . . . . . . . . . . . . . . . . . . . . . . . . . . .35%
Reagan . . . . . . . . . . . . . . . . . . . . . . . . . .62
Other; undecided . . . . . . . . . . . . . . . . . . . . 3

### College Incomplete

Hart . . . . . . . . . . . . . . . . . . . . . . . . . . . . . .40%
Reagan . . . . . . . . . . . . . . . . . . . . . . . . . .57
Other; undecided . . . . . . . . . . . . . . . . . . . . 3

### High-School Graduate

Hart . . . . . . . . . . . . . . . . . . . . . . . . . . . . . .40%
Reagan . . . . . . . . . . . . . . . . . . . . . . . . . .53
Other; undecided . . . . . . . . . . . . . . . . . . . . 7

### Less Than High-School Graduate

Hart . . . . . . . . . . . . . . . . . . . . . . . . . . . . . .63%
Reagan . . . . . . . . . . . . . . . . . . . . . . . . . .29
Other; undecided . . . . . . . . . . . . . . . . . . . . 8

## By Region
### East

Hart . . . . . . . . . . . . . . . . . . . . . . . . . . . . . .43%
Reagan . . . . . . . . . . . . . . . . . . . . . . . . . .53
Other; undecided . . . . . . . . . . . . . . . . . . . . 4

### Midwest

Hart . . . . . . . . . . . . . . . . . . . . . . . . . . . . . .47%
Reagan . . . . . . . . . . . . . . . . . . . . . . . . . .48
Other; undecided . . . . . . . . . . . . . . . . . . . . 5

### South

Hart . . . . . . . . . . . . . . . . . . . . . . . . . . . . . .45%
Reagan . . . . . . . . . . . . . . . . . . . . . . . . . .46
Other; undecided . . . . . . . . . . . . . . . . . . . . 9

### West

Hart . . . . . . . . . . . . . . . . . . . . . . . . . . . . . .40%
Reagan . . . . . . . . . . . . . . . . . . . . . . . . . .57
Other; undecided . . . . . . . . . . . . . . . . . . . . 3

## By Age
### 18–29 Years

Hart . . . . . . . . . . . . . . . . . . . . . . . . . . . . . .45%
Reagan . . . . . . . . . . . . . . . . . . . . . . . . . .49
Other; undecided . . . . . . . . . . . . . . . . . . . . 6

### 30–49 Years

Hart . . . . . . . . . . . . . . . . . . . . . . . . . . . . . .44%
Reagan . . . . . . . . . . . . . . . . . . . . . . . . . .52
Other; undecided . . . . . . . . . . . . . . . . . . . . 4

### 50 Years and Over

Hart . . . . . . . . . . . . . . . . . . . . . . . . . . . . . .43%
Reagan . . . . . . . . . . . . . . . . . . . . . . . . . .50
Other; undecided . . . . . . . . . . . . . . . . . . . . 7

## By Income
### $40,000 and Over

Hart . . . . . . . . . . . . . . . . . . . . . . . . . . . . . .33%
Reagan . . . . . . . . . . . . . . . . . . . . . . . . . .64
Other; undecided . . . . . . . . . . . . . . . . . . . . 3

### $30,000–$39,999

Hart . . . . . . . . . . . . . . . . . . . . . . . . . . . . . .44%
Reagan . . . . . . . . . . . . . . . . . . . . . . . . . .55
Other; undecided . . . . . . . . . . . . . . . . . . . . *

### $20,000–$29,999

Hart . . . . . . . . . . . . . . . . . . . . . . . . . . . . . .41%
Reagan . . . . . . . . . . . . . . . . . . . . . . . . . .54
Other; undecided . . . . . . . . . . . . . . . . . . . . 5

### $10,000–$19,999

Hart . . . . . . . . . . . . . . . . . . . . . . . . . . . . . .46%
Reagan . . . . . . . . . . . . . . . . . . . . . . . . . .47
Other; undecided . . . . . . . . . . . . . . . . . . . . 7

*Less than 1%

### Under $10,000

Hart . . . . . . . . . . . . . . . . . . . . . . . . . . . . . .53%
Reagan . . . . . . . . . . . . . . . . . . . . . . . . . .37
Other; undecided . . . . . . . . . . . . . . . . . . . .10

### By Politics

#### Republicans

Hart . . . . . . . . . . . . . . . . . . . . . . . . . . . . . .10%
Reagan . . . . . . . . . . . . . . . . . . . . . . . . . .87
Other; undecided . . . . . . . . . . . . . . . . . . . . 3

#### Democrats

Hart . . . . . . . . . . . . . . . . . . . . . . . . . . . . . .68%
Reagan . . . . . . . . . . . . . . . . . . . . . . . . . .25
Other; undecided . . . . . . . . . . . . . . . . . . . . 7

#### Independents

Hart . . . . . . . . . . . . . . . . . . . . . . . . . . . . . .40%
Reagan . . . . . . . . . . . . . . . . . . . . . . . . . .55
Other; undecided . . . . . . . . . . . . . . . . . . . . 5

*Asked of those who voted for each Democrat in the test elections: Would you say your vote is more a vote for Walter Mondale (Gary Hart) or more a vote against Ronald Reagan?*

|  | Mondale voters | Hart voters |
|---|---|---|
| Pro-Democratic candidate | 53% | 40% |
| Anti-Reagan | 44 | 56 |
| No opinion | 3 | 4 |

*Asked of registered voters: Suppose the 1984 presidential election were being held today. If the Republican ticket of Ronald Reagan and George Bush were running against the Democratic ticket of Walter Mondale and Gary Hart, which would you like to see win? [Those who were undecided or who named other candidates were then asked: As of today, do you lean more to the Republican ticket of Reagan and Bush or to the Democratic ticket of Mondale and Hart?]*

|  | May 18–21 | April 6–9 |
|---|---|---|
| Reagan-Bush . . . . . . . . . . . . | 50% | 49% |
| Mondale-Hart . . . . . . . . . . . . | 47 | 49 |
| Other; undecided . . . . . . . . | 3 | 2 |

Note: President Ronald Reagan currently leads Democratic challengers Walter Mondale and Gary Hart in test elections for the presidency. In the latest Gallup Poll, Reagan is the choice of 53% of registered voters to 43% for Mondale. The president now leads Senator Hart by a 51% to 44% vote.

In the previous survey, conducted early this month before Hart's victories in the Nebraska and Oregon primaries, President Reagan was statistically tied with both Mondale and Hart. Hart enjoyed his largest lead over Reagan soon after the February New Hampshire primary, when the Colorado senator held a 52% to 43% advantage. Mondale has trailed or been tied with Reagan in each of the six Gallup test elections conducted since February.

Hart's campaign for the Democratic nomination received a boost from his recent primary victories, especially among independents. Mondale, however, remains the favorite of Democrats for the nomination.

Voters in the latest test elections who chose Mondale or Hart over President Reagan were asked whether theirs was more a vote for their candidate or more a vote against Reagan. The findings reveal a large anti-Reagan vote, with this sentiment more pronounced among Hart's supporters than among Mondale's. A 56% majority of those who vote for Hart in the Reagan-Hart contest say their vote is more a vote against Reagan, while 40% say it is a pro-Hart vote. In the Reagan-Mondale race, 44% describe their vote for Mondale as anti-Reagan and 53% as pro-Mondale.

The survey also tested the voter appeal of a Democratic ticket with Mondale as president and Hart as vice-president, against the Republican slate of Reagan and George Bush. The findings suggest that the Mondale-Hart ticket would have slightly more appeal against the Reagan-Bush ticket than Mondale has on his own against Reagan alone. An April survey in which the same question was asked also showed the Mondale-Hart team to fare better than Mondale alone.

## JUNE 1
## PRESIDENT REAGAN

Interviewing Date: 5/18–21/84
Survey #234-G

*Do you approve or disapprove of the way Ronald Reagan is handling his job as president?*

Approve ............................54%
Disapprove .........................38
No opinion ......................... 8

### Selected National Trend

| | Approve | Disapprove | No opinion |
|---|---|---|---|
| *1984* | | | |
| May 3–5 ........ | 52% | 37% | 11% |
| April 11–15 ..... | 52 | 37 | 11 |
| April 6–9 ....... | 54 | 36 | 10 |
| March 16–19 .... | 54 | 39 | 7 |
| February 10–13 .. | 55 | 36 | 9 |
| January 27–30 ... | 55 | 37 | 8 |
| January 13–16 ... | 52 | 38 | 10 |
| *1983* | | | |
| November ....... | 53 | 37 | 10 |
| August ......... | 43 | 46 | 11 |
| April .......... | 41 | 49 | 10 |
| January ........ | 37 | 54 | 9 |

*Now let me ask you about some specific problems. As I read off each problem, would you tell me whether you approve or disapprove of the way President Ronald Reagan is handling that problem:*

*Economic conditions in this country?*

Approve ............................49%
Disapprove .........................43
No opinion ......................... 8

### By Politics
#### Republicans

Approve ............................81%
Disapprove .........................13
No opinion ......................... 6

#### Democrats

Approve ............................28%
Disapprove .........................66
No opinion ......................... 6

#### Independents

Approve ............................51%
Disapprove .........................37
No opinion ......................12

### Selected National Trend

| | Approve |
|---|---|
| *1984* | |
| May 3–5 ............................. | 48% |
| February 10–13 ...................... | 49 |
| January 13–16 ....................... | 48 |
| *1983* | |
| November ........................... | 48 |
| August ............................. | 37 |
| April ............................... | 34 |
| January ............................. | 29 |

*Foreign policy?*

Approve ............................37%
Disapprove .........................48
No opinion ......................15

### By Politics
#### Republicans

Approve ............................63%
Disapprove .........................25
No opinion ......................12

#### Democrats

Approve ............................23%
Disapprove .........................63
No opinion ......................14

#### Independents

Approve ............................37%
Disapprove .........................45
No opinion ......................18

## Selected National Trend

|  | *Approve* |
| --- | --- |
| *1984* | |
| May 3–5 | 42% |
| February 10–13 | 40 |
| January 13–16 | 38 |
| *1983* | |
| November | 46 |
| August | 31 |
| April | 32 |
| January | 36 |

### *Situation in Central America?*

| | |
| --- | --- |
| Approve | 28% |
| Disapprove | 49 |
| No opinion | 23 |

## By Politics

### *Republicans*

| | |
| --- | --- |
| Approve | 49% |
| Disapprove | 31 |
| No opinion | 20 |

### *Democrats*

| | |
| --- | --- |
| Approve | 18% |
| Disapprove | 62 |
| No opinion | 20 |

### *Independents*

| | |
| --- | --- |
| Approve | 26% |
| Disapprove | 45 |
| No opinion | 29 |

## Selected National Trend

|  | *Approve* |
| --- | --- |
| *1984* | |
| February 10–13 | 29% |
| January 13–16 | 28 |
| *1983* | |
| November | 36 |
| August | 24 |
| April | 21 |

### *Our relations with the Soviet Union?*

| | |
| --- | --- |
| Approve | 46% |
| Disapprove | 40 |
| No opinion | 14 |

## By Politics

### *Republicans*

| | |
| --- | --- |
| Approve | 71% |
| Disapprove | 21 |
| No opinion | 8 |

### *Democrats*

| | |
| --- | --- |
| Approve | 30% |
| Disapprove | 53 |
| No opinion | 17 |

### *Independents*

| | |
| --- | --- |
| Approve | 48% |
| Disapprove | 36 |
| No opinion | 16 |

## Selected National Trend

|  | *Approve* |
| --- | --- |
| *1984* | |
| February 10–13 | 43% |
| *1983* | |
| November | 46 |
| August | 41 |
| April | 37 |
| January | 41 |

Note: President Ronald Reagan's approval ratings have remained remarkably stable for the last seven months, with the proportion of the public approving his overall job performance neither exceeding 55% nor dropping below 52% during this period. A trend of this duration in presidential election years is unprecedented in Gallup history.

In the latest Gallup Poll, 54% say they approve of the way Reagan is handling the duties of his office, while 38% disapprove and 8% withhold their opinion. The last time significantly more Americans approved than now was in August 1981, when 60% gave the president a positive rating and 24% disapproved. Reagan received lower job ratings throughout most of 1983, topping the 50%

level only in the last two months of the year. Reagan's upward trend during 1983, however, ran counter to another Gallup norm: in the third year of their initial term, presidents almost invariably lose in the public's esteem. For example, at this same point in past election years, Presidents Jimmy Carter and Gerald Ford had lower job approval scores, 38% and 47%, respectively, and lost their elections. On the other hand, Presidents Richard Nixon (62%), Lyndon Johnson (74%), and Dwight Eisenhower (69%) had higher approval ratings and won their reelection bids.

President Reagan's weakest point at present is his handling of foreign policy, with about one-third of the public (37%) approving and 48% disapproving. This positive rating falls about midway between the 46% approval rating the president receives for his handling of relations with the Soviet Union and the 28% approval for dealing with the situation in Central America.

With few exceptions, presidents who have made state visits abroad have subsequently been rewarded by enhanced popularity here at home. However, any positive effect Reagan's late-April trip to the People's Republic of China might have had on his overall popularity may have been offset by the public's generally low assessment of his handling of the Central American situation.

In the public's view, Reagan fares best for his handling of the national economy, with 49% currently approving. This assessment has not varied by more than 1 percentage point in the last six months.

## JUNE 7
## ECONOMIC SITUATION

Interviewing Date: 5/18–21/84
Survey #234-G

*As you know, the economy has begun to recover from recession this year, with increased production, employment, and profits. Of course, no one knows for sure, but what is your best guess as to how long this recovery will last before the economy turns down again—will the recovery end this year, early next year, later next year, or later than that?*

|  | May 1984 | Sept. 1983 |
|---|---|---|
| This year . . . . . . . . . . . . . . | 11% | 6% |
| Early next year . . . . . . . . | 15 | 12 |
| Later next year . . . . . . . . | 21 | 20 |
| Later than that . . . . . . . . . | 34 | 38 |
| Never end (volunteered) . . | 3 | 5 |
| No opinion . . . . . . . . . . . | 16 | 19 |

### By Politics
#### Republicans

| | |
|---|---|
| This year . . . . . . . . . . . . . . . . . . . . . . . . . | 7% |
| Early next year . . . . . . . . . . . . . . . . . . . . . | 14 |
| Later next year . . . . . . . . . . . . . . . . . . . . . | 21 |
| Later than that . . . . . . . . . . . . . . . . . . . . . | 43 |
| Never end (volunteered) . . . . . . . . . . . . . . | 3 |
| No opinion . . . . . . . . . . . . . . . . . . . . . . . | 12 |

#### Democrats

| | |
|---|---|
| This year . . . . . . . . . . . . . . . . . . . . . . . | 13% |
| Early next year . . . . . . . . . . . . . . . . . . . . | 15 |
| Later next year . . . . . . . . . . . . . . . . . . . . | 21 |
| Later than that . . . . . . . . . . . . . . . . . . . . | 29 |
| Never end (volunteered) . . . . . . . . . . . . . | 4 |
| No opinion . . . . . . . . . . . . . . . . . . . . . . . | 18 |

#### Independents

| | |
|---|---|
| This year . . . . . . . . . . . . . . . . . . . . . . . | 13% |
| Early next year . . . . . . . . . . . . . . . . . . . . | 14 |
| Later next year . . . . . . . . . . . . . . . . . . . . | 21 |
| Later than that . . . . . . . . . . . . . . . . . . . . | 33 |
| Never end (volunteered) . . . . . . . . . . . . . | 3 |
| No opinion . . . . . . . . . . . . . . . . . . . . . . . | 16 |

*For each item on this list, please tell me whether you think it will be a great threat, somewhat of a threat, or not much of a threat to continued recovery in the economy. The federal government's budget deficit? High interest rates? The amount of taxes people pay? The rate of inflation? International trade problems such as the high value of the dollar, debts owed by countries like Brazil, Poland, etc.?*

| | Those Saying Great Threat | |
|---|---|---|
| | May 1984 | Sept. 1983 |
| Budget deficit .......... | 50% | 43% |
| High interest rates ....... | 65 | 62 |
| Personal taxes .......... | 41 | 38 |
| Inflation rate .......... | 51 | 52 |
| International problems ... | 42 | 44 |

Note: President Ronald Reagan's chances for re-election in November will be enhanced greatly if the voters then have as optimistic an outlook about the economy as they do now. In the latest Gallup survey, about three persons in four (74%) say they expect the recovery to last at least until the end of this year, with 37% predicting the recovery will extend into 1986, or beyond. The current findings are only slightly less bullish than those recorded last September, when 43% saw the recovery lasting beyond the year ahead.

High interest rates are considered a great threat to the recovery by 65% of the public. Cited next most often are the inflation rate (51%) and the federal budget deficit (50%). International trade problems, such as the high value of the dollar and debts owed by developing nations, follow at 42%. Finally, 41% say the amount of taxes people pay greatly threatens the economy.

In the current survey, the responses to four of the five parts to this question are statistically unchanged from last year's findings; the exception is the budget deficit, mentioned by 50% now compared to 43% last year.

## JUNE 10
## CENTRAL AMERICA

Interviewing Date: 5/18–21/84
Survey #234-G

*Have you heard or read about the situation in Central America?*

| | Yes |
|---|---|
| National ........................... | 78% |

*Asked of those who replied in the affirmative: How likely do you think it is that the U.S. involvement in Central America could turn into a situation like Vietnam—that is, that the United States would become more and more deeply involved as time goes on? Would you say this is very likely, fairly likely, not very likely, or not at all likely?*

| | |
|---|---|
| Very likely ......................... | 39% |
| Fairly likely ....................... | 33 |
| Not very likely ..................... | 19 |
| Not at all likely ................... | 5 |
| No opinion ......................... | 4 |

### By Politics
#### Republicans

| | |
|---|---|
| Very likely ......................... | 29% |
| Fairly likely ....................... | 32 |
| Not very likely ..................... | 26 |
| Not at all likely ................... | 10 |
| No opinion ......................... | 3 |

#### Democrats

| | |
|---|---|
| Very likely ......................... | 44% |
| Fairly likely ....................... | 35 |
| Not very likely ..................... | 14 |
| Not at all likely ................... | 3 |
| No opinion ......................... | 4 |

#### Independents

| | |
|---|---|
| Very likely ......................... | 40% |
| Fairly likely ....................... | 32 |
| Not very likely ..................... | 21 |
| Not at all likely ................... | 4 |
| No opinion ......................... | 3 |

Note: The situation in Central America could be a political liability for President Ronald Reagan in November, with many Republicans as well as Democrats and independents critical of his handling of that area of foreign policy and fearful that it could lead to another Vietnam. In the latest Gallup survey, 72% of aware Americans think it is either very or fairly likely that our involvement in Central America could escalate into a Vietnam—that the United States would become more and more deeply committed as time goes on. A total of 61% of Republicans, 79% of Democrats, and 72% of independents share these views. The current figures closely match those recorded in four surveys conducted over the last fifteen months in which the question focused on U.S. involvement in El Salvador.

Although concern over Central America is not currently one of the American public's principal worries, with only about one-fifth of respondents saying they have followed the situation there very closely, it is a key element in the public's generally negative assessment of Reagan's handling of foreign policy. Recent surveys show that the president's prime area of vulnerability, in terms of voter support, lies in the area of foreign policy.

## JUNE 14
## DEMOCRATIC PRESIDENTIAL CANDIDATES/PRESIDENTIAL TRIAL HEATS

Interviewing Date: 6/6–8/84
Special Telephone Survey

*Asked of registered voters: Suppose the 1984 presidential election were being held today. If the Democratic ticket of Walter Mondale and Gary Hart were running against the Republican ticket of Ronald Reagan and George Bush, which would you like to see win? [Those who were undecided or who named other candidates were then asked: As of today, do you lean more to the Democratic ticket of Mondale and Hart or to the Republican ticket of Reagan and Bush?]*

|  | June 6–8 | May 18–21 | April 11–15 |
|---|---|---|---|
| Mondale-Hart | 47% | 47% | 49% |
| Reagan-Bush | 51 | 50 | 49 |
| Other; undecided | 2 | 3 | 2 |

*Presidential Candidates Only*

| | | | |
|---|---|---|---|
| Mondale | 44% | 43% | 44% |
| Reagan | 53 | 53 | 52 |
| Other; undecided | 3 | 4 | 4 |
| | | | |
| Hart | 43% | 44% | 46% |
| Reagan | 54 | 51 | 49 |
| Other; undecided | 3 | 5 | 5 |

*Asked of Democrats and independents: Which one of the following persons would you like to see nominated as the Democratic party's candidate for president this year?*

### Choice of Democrats

|  | June 6–8 | May 18–21 | April 11–15 |
|---|---|---|---|
| Mondale .... | 48% | 46% | 51% |
| Hart ........ | 35 | 34 | 28 |
| Jackson ..... | 6 | 10 | 9 |
| Other; don't know ..... | 11 | 10 | 12 |

### Choice of Independents

|  | June 6–8 | May 18–21 | April 11–15 |
|---|---|---|---|
| Mondale .... | 34% | 31% | 29% |
| Hart ........ | 41 | 46 | 39 |
| Jackson ..... | 5 | 5 | 8 |
| Other; don't know ..... | 20 | 18 | 24 |

*Asked of Democrats and independents: Suppose the choice for president in the Democratic convention this year narrows down to Walter Mondale and Gary Hart. Which one would you prefer to have the Democratic convention select?*

### Choice of Democrats

|  | June 6–8 | May 18–21 | April 11–15 |
|---|---|---|---|
| Mondale .... | 54% | 57% | 57% |
| Hart ........ | 39 | 35 | 33 |
| Undecided ... | 7 | 8 | 10 |

## Choice of Independents

|            | June 6–8 | May 18–21 | April 11–15 |
|------------|----------|-----------|-------------|
| Mondale .... | 39% | 37% | 36% |
| Hart ........ | 49 | 53 | 48 |
| Undecided ... | 12 | 10 | 16 |

*Asked of Democrats and independents: Would you like to see Gary Hart run as the vice-presidential candidate on a Democratic ticket headed by Walter Mondale, or not?*

### Choice of Democrats

Yes, would . . . . . . . . . . . . . . . . . . . . . . . . .59%
No, would not . . . . . . . . . . . . . . . . . . . . . .27
No opinion . . . . . . . . . . . . . . . . . . . . . . .14

### Choice of Independents

Yes, would . . . . . . . . . . . . . . . . . . . . . . . . .42%
No, would not . . . . . . . . . . . . . . . . . . . . . .43
No opinion . . . . . . . . . . . . . . . . . . . . . . .15

Note: Although Senator Gary Hart appears to have lost the Democratic presidential nomination, a majority of Democrats surveyed says they would like to see him run as the vice-presidential candidate on a ticket headed by Walter Mondale. In a special Gallup survey conducted after the final June primaries, Hart wins the vice-presidential endorsement of 59% of Democrats to 27% who are opposed and 14% who do not express an opinion.

This survey also bears out the findings of earlier Gallup polls showing that the Mondale-Hart ticket (47%) would have slightly greater appeal against the Reagan-Bush incumbency (51%) than Mondale alone (44%) has against Ronald Reagan alone (53%).

## JUNE 17
## PRESIDENTIAL TRIAL HEATS

Interviewing Date: 5/18–21; 6/6–8/84
Survey #234-G; Special Telephone Survey

*Asked of registered voters: Suppose the 1984 presidential election were being held today.*

*If Walter Mondale were the Democratic candidate and President Ronald Reagan were the Republican candidate, which would you like to see win? [Those who were undecided or named other candidates were then asked: As of today, do you lean more to Mondale, the Democrat, or to Reagan, the Republican?]*

Mondale . . . . . . . . . . . . . . . . . . . . . . . . .43%
Reagan . . . . . . . . . . . . . . . . . . . . . . . . .53
Undecided . . . . . . . . . . . . . . . . . . . . . . . 4

### By Region
#### East

Mondale . . . . . . . . . . . . . . . . . . . . . . . . .44%
Reagan . . . . . . . . . . . . . . . . . . . . . . . . .51
Undecided . . . . . . . . . . . . . . . . . . . . . . . 5

#### Midwest

Mondale . . . . . . . . . . . . . . . . . . . . . . . . .45%
Reagan . . . . . . . . . . . . . . . . . . . . . . . . .52
Undecided . . . . . . . . . . . . . . . . . . . . . . . 3

#### South

Mondale . . . . . . . . . . . . . . . . . . . . . . . . .44%
Reagan . . . . . . . . . . . . . . . . . . . . . . . . .52
Undecided . . . . . . . . . . . . . . . . . . . . . . . 4

#### West

Mondale . . . . . . . . . . . . . . . . . . . . . . . . .37%
Reagan . . . . . . . . . . . . . . . . . . . . . . . . .60
Undecided . . . . . . . . . . . . . . . . . . . . . . . 3

*Asked of registered voters: Suppose the 1984 presidential election were being held today. If the Democratic ticket of Walter Mondale and Gary Hart were running against the Republican ticket of Ronald Reagan and George Bush, which ticket would you like to see win? [Those who were undecided or who named other candidates were then asked: As of today, do you lean more to the Democratic ticket of Mondale and Hart or to the Republican ticket of Reagan and Bush?]*

Mondale-Hart . . . . . . . . . . . . . . . . . . . . . . .47%
Reagan-Bush . . . . . . . . . . . . . . . . . . . . . . .50
Undecided . . . . . . . . . . . . . . . . . . . . . . . . 3

## By Region

### East

Mondale-Hart . . . . . . . . . . . . . . . . . . . . . . .49%
Reagan-Bush . . . . . . . . . . . . . . . . . . . . . . .47
Undecided . . . . . . . . . . . . . . . . . . . . . . . . 4

### Midwest

Mondale-Hart . . . . . . . . . . . . . . . . . . . . . . .51%
Reagan-Bush . . . . . . . . . . . . . . . . . . . . . . .47
Undecided . . . . . . . . . . . . . . . . . . . . . . . . 2

### South

Mondale-Hart . . . . . . . . . . . . . . . . . . . . . . .47%
Reagan-Bush . . . . . . . . . . . . . . . . . . . . . . .50
Undecided . . . . . . . . . . . . . . . . . . . . . . . . 3

### West

Mondale-Hart . . . . . . . . . . . . . . . . . . . . . . .37%
Reagan-Bush . . . . . . . . . . . . . . . . . . . . . . .60
Undecided . . . . . . . . . . . . . . . . . . . . . . . . 3

By way of background, the national and regional vote for the three major party candidates in the 1980 presidential election was as follows:

### 1980 National and Regional Vote

Reagan . . . . . . . . . . . . . . . . . . . . . . . . . . .51%
Carter . . . . . . . . . . . . . . . . . . . . . . . . . . .41
Anderson . . . . . . . . . . . . . . . . . . . . . . . . . 7

## By Region

### East

Reagan . . . . . . . . . . . . . . . . . . . . . . . . . . .47%
Carter . . . . . . . . . . . . . . . . . . . . . . . . . . .43
Anderson . . . . . . . . . . . . . . . . . . . . . . . . . 9

### Midwest

Reagan . . . . . . . . . . . . . . . . . . . . . . . . . . .51%
Carter . . . . . . . . . . . . . . . . . . . . . . . . . . .41
Anderson . . . . . . . . . . . . . . . . . . . . . . . . . 7

### South

Reagan . . . . . . . . . . . . . . . . . . . . . . . . . . .52%
Carter . . . . . . . . . . . . . . . . . . . . . . . . . . .44
Anderson . . . . . . . . . . . . . . . . . . . . . . . . . 3

### West

Reagan . . . . . . . . . . . . . . . . . . . . . . . . . . .54%
Carter . . . . . . . . . . . . . . . . . . . . . . . . . . .35
Anderson . . . . . . . . . . . . . . . . . . . . . . . . . 9

Note: President Ronald Reagan holds a 53% to 43% lead over Walter Mondale in the latest national test election and has an edge in all four regions of the country. Adding Gary Hart's name as the vice-presidential candidate on a ticket headed by Mondale, however, pushes the Democratic ticket slightly ahead of the Reagan-Bush Republican slate in the East and Midwest. Also, Reagan's substantial lead over Mondale in the South is reduced when the Republican ticket is pitted against Mondale and Hart.

Reagan's current lead over Mondale closely matches those recorded in six earlier test elections conducted since March. When the last two surveys are combined—in order to build up the regional sample base—Reagan leads Mondale 53% to 43% nationally. In the ticket matchup, though, Reagan loses his advantage, with the Republican ticket winning 50% of the vote (based on the two surveys) to 47% for Mondale and Hart.

In the East the figures for Reagan and Mondale alone are 51% to 44%. With Hart added, the Democrats gain a thin 49% to 47% margin over Reagan and Bush, a difference that is not statistically meaningful.

In the Midwest, Reagan leads Mondale by 7 percentage points, 52% to 45%. When the tickets are pitted against each other, the Mondale-Hart ticket pulls even, with 51% of the vote to 47% for Reagan-Bush.

In the South, the Mondale-Hart ticket also picks up strength and turns a substantial 52% to 44% Reagan lead over Mondale into a 50% (GOP) to 47% (Democratic) statistical tie.

In the West, the race is not changed by adding Hart to the Democratic ticket. In the single matchup, Reagan leads Mondale 60% to 37%. In the contest between the tickets, the Republicans retain virtually the same advantage.

## JUNE 21
## UNESCO

Interviewing Date: 5/18–21/84
Survey #234-G

*Have you heard or read about UNESCO— the United Nations Educational, Scientific, and Cultural Organization?*

|  | Yes |
|---|---|
| National | 36% |

*Asked of those who replied in the affirmative: Do you think the United States should or should not withdraw from this organization?*

| | |
|---|---|
| Should | 34% |
| Should not | 48 |
| No opinion | 18 |

### By Politics
#### Republicans

| | |
|---|---|
| Should | 42% |
| Should not | 36 |
| No opinion | 22 |

#### Democrats

| | |
|---|---|
| Should | 26% |
| Should not | 55 |
| No opinion | 19 |

#### Independents

| | |
|---|---|
| Should | 36% |
| Should not | 50 |
| No opinion | 14 |

Note: The weight of opinion among Americans who have heard or read about UNESCO—the United Nations Educational, Scientific, and Cultural Organization—is against our withdrawing from this world body, as the Reagan administration has threatened to do. Of the nearly four respondents in ten (36%) who are aware of UNESCO, 48% think the United States should not withdraw, while 34% say they favor such a move.

Last December, the United States announced its decision to resign unless the organization curtails activities the Reagan administration considers politically objectionable. Great Britain also has said it will review its membership if major changes are not made in UNESCO's operation.

Supporters of continuing U.S. membership in UNESCO, while acknowledging problems, maintain that its programs generally have been valuable and reasonably well managed, and that the United States has more to lose than gain by withdrawing. Reports now indicate that the U.S. stand already has sparked some UNESCO reform efforts, yet the Reagan administration wants to see more concrete action.

## JUNE 24
## DEMOCRATIC VICE-PRESIDENTIAL CANDIDATES

Interviewing Date: 6/6–8/84
Special Telephone Survey

*Asked of Democrats and independents: If the Democratic presidential nominee selected a woman to be his vice-presidential running mate, would this make you more likely or less likely to vote for the Democratic ticket?*

### Views of Democrats

| | |
|---|---|
| More likely | 32% |
| Less likely | 18 |
| No difference (volunteered) | 41 |
| No opinion | 9 |

### Views of Independents

| | |
|---|---|
| More likely | 27% |
| Less likely | 24 |
| No difference (volunteered) | 43 |
| No opinion | 6 |

*Asked of Democrats and independents: If the Democratic presidential nominee selected a black to be his vice-presidential running mate, would this make you more likely or less likely to vote for the Democratic ticket?*

### Views of Democrats

More likely . . . . . . . . . . . . . . . . . . . . . . . .25%
Less likely . . . . . . . . . . . . . . . . . . . . . . . .23
No difference (volunteered) . . . . . . . . . . .45
No opinion . . . . . . . . . . . . . . . . . . . . . . . . 7

### Views of Independents

More likely . . . . . . . . . . . . . . . . . . . . . . . .20%
Less likely . . . . . . . . . . . . . . . . . . . . . . . .26
No difference (volunteered) . . . . . . . . . . .49
No opinion . . . . . . . . . . . . . . . . . . . . . . . . 5

Note: The Democratic ticket would gain in appeal among rank-and-file party members if likely presidential nominee Walter Mondale were to select a woman as his running mate. About four in ten Democratic voters nationwide (41%) say that a woman as the vice-presidential candidate would not affect their vote one way or the other. But of those to whom it would make a difference, nearly twice as many say they would be more likely (32%) rather than less likely (18%) to vote for such a ticket. These findings closely parallel those recorded in a survey conducted last September. Interestingly, Democratic men are nearly as likely as women to say they would be more likely to back a slate that included a woman.

Among the crucial bloc of independent voters, who represent almost one-third of the electorate, the addition of a woman to the Democratic ticket would probably hurt as much as it would help. About four in ten (43%) say a woman in the number-two spot would not affect their vote, while 27% say it would increase their likelihood of voting for the Democratic ticket and 24% say it would reduce their attraction to it.

If the Democratic presidential nominee were to select a black, any additional support might be offset by those who would be less likely to vote for this slate. A total of 25% of Democrats says they would be more likely and 23% less likely to

vote for a black in the second slot. Among independents, the situation is almost a standoff, statistically speaking, with 20% saying they would be more likely to vote for a Democratic ticket with a black and 26% saying they would be less likely. These findings also parallel those recorded last September.

### JUNE 28
### JOGGING/EXERCISE

Interviewing Date: 5/7–13/84
Special Telephone Survey

*Aside from any work you do, here at home or at a job, do you do anything regularly— that is, on a daily basis—that helps you keep physically fit?*

|  | Exercise daily |
|---|---|
| National | 59% |

### Selected National Trend

1982 . . . . . . . . . . . . . . . . . . . . . . . . . . . . .47%
1980 . . . . . . . . . . . . . . . . . . . . . . . . . . . . .46
1977 . . . . . . . . . . . . . . . . . . . . . . . . . . . . .47
1961 . . . . . . . . . . . . . . . . . . . . . . . . . . . . .24

*Do you happen to jog, or not?*

|  | Yes |
|---|---|
| National | 18% |

### Selected National Trend

1982 . . . . . . . . . . . . . . . . . . . . . . . . . . . . .14%
1980 . . . . . . . . . . . . . . . . . . . . . . . . . . . . .12
1977 . . . . . . . . . . . . . . . . . . . . . . . . . . . . .11
1961 . . . . . . . . . . . . . . . . . . . . . . . . . . . . . 6

*Asked of joggers: On the average, how far do you usually jog, in terms of miles or fractions of miles?*

Less than two miles . . . . . . . . . . . . . . . . . .32%
Two to three miles . . . . . . . . . . . . . . . . . .29
Three miles or more . . . . . . . . . . . . . . . . .39
Not sure . . . . . . . . . . . . . . . . . . . . . . . . . . *

*Less than 1%

*Also asked of joggers: About how often do you jog?*

Less than once a week ................5%
Once or twice a week .................25
Three or four times a week ............35
Every day or almost every day .........34
Not sure ..........................1

Note: One of the most remarkable lifestyle trends in a half-century of polling has been the increase in the percentage of Americans who follow some kind of daily exercise regimen to help them keep fit. Today, six in ten U.S. adults (59%) exercise on a daily basis, a full 12 percentage points higher than in 1982 and more than double the 24% recorded in 1961 when the measurement was started. The growing interest in exercise is national in scope, with similar uptrends noted in each of the four regions of the nation. Large gains also are recorded on the basis of sex, age, education, and other demographic factors.

Jogging continues to be one of the nation's most popular recreational activities, with 18% in the latest survey saying they jog on a regular basis; this is three times higher than the 6% recorded in 1961. The percentage of adults who jog has risen steadily—the figure was 14% in 1982—and the average distance covered also has increased. In the latest survey, 39% of joggers say they usually run three miles or more, while two years ago 24% ran this far on average and in 1977, 14% did so. In the current survey, joggers average 2.5 miles per outing, compared to 1.6 miles in 1977.

Sex and education play important roles in the popularity of jogging. There are substantially more men (22%) than women (14%) joggers, and persons who attended college (22%) are more apt to take up the sport than are those with less formal education (15%). But the most important factor related to jogging is age. From a peak of 33% among 18 to 24 year olds, participation falls off to merely 3% among those 65 and older. Among those in the 30 to 49 year age bracket, 18%, or the national average, are joggers.

# JULY 1
# PRESIDENTIAL TRIAL HEATS

Interviewing Date: 6/22–25/84
Survey #235-G

*Asked of registered voters: Suppose the 1984 presidential election were being held today. If President Ronald Reagan were the Republican candidate and Walter Mondale were the Democratic candidate, which would you like to see win? [Those who were undecided were then asked: As of today, do you lean more to Reagan, the Republican, or to Mondale, the Democrat?]*

|  | June 22–25 | June 6–8 |
|---|---|---|
| Reagan ............... | 56% | 53% |
| Mondale ............. | 38 | 44 |
| Other; undecided ....... | 6 | 3 |

*Asked of registered voters: Suppose the 1984 presidential election were being held today. If President Ronald Reagan were the Republican candidate and Gary Hart were the Democratic candidate, which would you like to see win? [Those who were undecided were then asked: As of today, do you lean more to Reagan, the Republican, or to Hart, the Democrat?]*

|  | June 22–25 | June 6–8 |
|---|---|---|
| Reagan ............... | 52% | 54% |
| Hart ................. | 41 | 43 |
| Other; undecided ....... | 7 | 3 |

Note: President Ronald Reagan has widened his lead over Walter Mondale, receiving 56% of the test election vote to 38% for his Democratic rival. In the previous Gallup survey conducted in early June, the race was a closer 53% for Reagan, 44% for Mondale.

Although Reagan currently holds a substantial lead over Mondale, this may narrow in the aftermath of the Democratic convention in mid-July, when many supporters of Senator Gary Hart can be expected to close ranks with other Democrats behind Mondale, the almost certain nominee.

## JULY 5
## LEGAL DRINKING AGE

Interviewing Date: 6/22–25/84
Survey #235-G

*Would you favor or oppose a national law that would raise the legal drinking age in all states to 21?*

Favor ............................79%
Oppose ...........................18
No opinion ........................ 3

### By Age
### *18–24 Years*

Favor ............................61%
Oppose ...........................37
No opinion ........................ 2

### *25–29 Years*

Favor ............................80%
Oppose ...........................18
No opinion ........................ 2

### *30–49 Years*

Favor ............................81%
Oppose ...........................17
No opinion ........................ 2

### *50 Years and Over*

Favor ............................83%
Oppose ...........................12
No opinion ........................ 5

### States Where Drinking
### Age Is 21

Favor ............................85%
Oppose ...........................12
No opinion ........................ 3

### States Where Drinking
### Age Is Below 21

Favor ............................73%
Oppose ...........................23
No opinion ........................ 4

*Asked of those who replied in the affirmative: Would you favor or oppose a law that would withhold some federal highway funds from states with minimum drinking ages below 21?*

Favor ............................66%
Oppose ...........................26
No opinion ........................ 8

### By Age
### *18–24 Years*

Favor ............................61%
Oppose ...........................33
No opinion ........................ 6

### *25–29 Years*

Favor ............................72%
Oppose ...........................21
No opinion ........................ 7

### *30–49 Years*

Favor ............................66%
Oppose ...........................26
No opinion ........................ 8

### *50 Years and Over*

Favor ............................65%
Oppose ...........................26
No opinion ........................ 9

### States Where Drinking
### Age Is 21

Favor ............................56%
Oppose ...........................32
No opinion ........................12

### States Where Drinking
### Age Is Below 21

Favor ............................66%
Oppose ...........................26
No opinion ........................ 8

Note: If the American people were voting today in a nationwide referendum making 21 the minimum drinking age, the overwhelming majority—including a substantial majority of young adults—

would vote "yes." In a new survey, 79% say they favor a national law raising the legal drinking age in all states to 21. Even in the age group that would be most affected, 18 to 24 year olds, 61% back the proposed law.

Among residents of states where 21 is already the legal minimum drinking age, 85% would like to see the law apply to the nation as a whole, while 73% of residents of other states support the proposed legislation. The latest findings are virtually the same as those recorded in 1983, when 77% favored and 20% opposed a national 21-year legal drinking age.

Two-thirds (66%) of persons favoring the national drinking age proposal also approve withholding some federal highway funds from states with minimum drinking ages below 21. A bill that would reduce federal highway aid to states that refuse to raise their drinking age to 21 in the next two years is now awaiting President Ronald Reagan's signature.

The bill's passage in the House and Senate is largely the result of a national lobbying campaign against drunk driving. Backers of the bill point out that drivers under 21 account for a disproportionately large number of alcohol-related traffic accidents and fatalities. Opposition to the measure has been led by restaurant owners fearing a loss of business and by student groups which contend the bill discriminates on the basis of age. Twenty-seven states currently allow drinking before age 21.

After a two-year grace period ending October 1, 1986, the government would withhold 5% of a noncomplying state's federal highway aid in fiscal 1987 and 10% in 1988. With the program estimated at $13 billion or more per year, large sums are at stake.

## JULY 8
## AUTOMOBILE SAFETY

Interviewing Date: 5/18–21; 6/29–7/2/84
Survey #234-G; 236-G

*Thinking about the last time you got into a car, did you use a seat belt, or not?*

|  | Yes, used belt |
|---|---|
| National | 25% |

### Selected National Trend

| 1982 | 17% |
|---|---|
| 1977 | 22 |
| 1973 | 28 |

*Would you favor or oppose a law that would require all new cars to be equipped with air bags that would inflate to protect the occupants of the front seats on impact in an accident?*

| Favor | 60% |
|---|---|
| Oppose | 31 |
| No opinion | 9 |

*Would you favor or oppose a law that would require all new cars to be equipped with seat belts that, without any action on the part of the driver, would lock automatically in place when the doors are closed?*

| Favor | 50% |
|---|---|
| Oppose | 44 |
| No opinion | 6 |

*Would you favor or oppose a law that would fine drivers and front seat passengers $50 if they did not wear seat belts when riding in a car?*

| Favor | 30% |
|---|---|
| Oppose | 65 |
| No opinion | 5 |

### By Region
#### East

| Favor | 33% |
|---|---|
| Oppose | 61 |
| No opinion | 6 |

#### Midwest

| Favor | 29% |
|---|---|
| Oppose | 66 |
| No opinion | 5 |

### South

Favor .............................30%
Oppose ...........................64
No opinion ........................ 6

### West

Favor .............................29%
Oppose ...........................69
No opinion ........................ 2

Note: The enormous attention recently given to drunken driving may have caused many Americans to become concerned about the hazards of driving and more attentive to safety measures. More people today are buckling up, with 25% now saying they used a seat belt the last time they got into a car. This figure compares to 17% two years ago.

A growing number of Americans favors a law that would fine nonseat belt users, with 30% in the latest survey in favor of hitting offenders with a $50 fine, a law now in effect in New York State. By a 2-to-1 ratio, Americans favor another law that would require all new cars to be equipped with air bags. Also, support slightly outweighs opposition by 50% to 44% on a law that would require all new cars to have automatic seat belts.

The concern of Americans about auto safety is reflected in the fact that 79% favor a national law that would raise the legal drinking age to 21 in all states. In addition, Gallup surveys over the last decade have shown that majorities of 70% or more consistently have favored keeping the present 55-mile-per-hour national speed limit.

## JULY 12
## ELECTORAL REFORMS

Interviewing Date: 6/22–25/84
Survey #235-G

*It has been suggested that presidential candidates be chosen by the voters in a nationwide primary election instead of by political party conventions as at present. Would you favor or oppose this?*

Favor .............................67%
Oppose ...........................21
No opinion ........................12

### By Politics
#### Republicans

Favor .............................62%
Oppose ...........................28
No opinion ........................10

#### Democrats

Favor .............................68%
Oppose ...........................18
No opinion ........................14

#### Independents

Favor .............................70%
Oppose ...........................19
No opinion ........................11

### Selected National Trend

|  | Favor | Oppose | No opinion |
|---|---|---|---|
| 1980 ........... | 66% | 24% | 10% |
| 1976 ........... | 68 | 21 | 11 |
| 1968 ........... | 76 | 13 | 11 |
| 1964 ........... | 62 | 25 | 13 |
| 1956 ........... | 58 | 27 | 15 |
| 1952 ........... | 73 | 12 | 15 |

*It has been proposed that four individual regional primaries be held in different weeks of June during a presidential election year. Does this sound to you like a good idea or a poor idea?*

Good idea .........................45%
Poor idea .........................30
No opinion ........................25

### By Politics
#### Republicans

Good idea .........................44%
Poor idea .........................37
No opinion ........................19

### Democrats

Good idea . . . . . . . . . . . . . . . . . . . . . . . . . 45%
Poor idea . . . . . . . . . . . . . . . . . . . . . . . . 29
No opinion . . . . . . . . . . . . . . . . . . . . . . . 26

### Independents

Good idea . . . . . . . . . . . . . . . . . . . . . . . 49%
Poor idea . . . . . . . . . . . . . . . . . . . . . . . 26
No opinion . . . . . . . . . . . . . . . . . . . . . . . 25

### National Trend

|  | Good idea | Poor idea | No opinion |
|---|---|---|---|
| 1982 . . . . . . . . . . . | 44% | 33% | 23% |

Note: If American voters had their way, this year's Democratic and Republican conventions would be the last. Two-thirds of persons interviewed recently said that presidential candidates should be chosen in a nationwide primary election instead of by political party conventions as at present. In the latest Gallup survey, 67% favor such a plan, while 21% are opposed and 12% are undecided, figures that closely parallel those recorded in 1980.

The proposal for a nationwide primary election has had the backing of the public for more than three decades. As early as 1952, Americans gave their support to such a plan by an overwhelming 6-to-1 margin. In each of eight national Gallup surveys since then, a heavy majority has voted in favor.

The plan has had bipartisan backing each time it has been put to the public. Currently 62% of Republicans, 68% of Democrats, and 70% of independents vote in favor of a nationwide presidential primary.

The chief argument given by those who favor a nationwide presidential primary are:

1) Under the present system, many Americans are denied the opportunity to vote directly for the candidate of their choice.

2) Current primaries frequently do not give a true measure of a party's strongest candidate because not all candidates enter each state primary.

3) The American people become jaded with presidential campaigns, which now stretch over the better part of a year. Surveys have found the public to favor shorter campaigns, such as those conducted in England.

4) The present primary system is a grueling process leaving the candidates physically exhausted and their funds depleted.

5) Crossover voting confuses the true support for candidates. In certain states, for example, Republican voters are able to vote in Democratic primaries and Democratic voters in Republican primaries.

Those opposed to the idea of a national presidential primary offer these arguments:

1) Under the present system a candidate has to face up to many trying situations, and the public can size him up better.

2) The generally low voter turnout for the state primaries suggests that if there were a runoff in a nationwide primary, voter participation would be lower than it is now—that voters would resist having to go to the polls a second time. This would result in an even smaller proportion of the electorate selecting the candidates than is now the case.

3) A nationwide primary would tend to favor nominees who are well known to voters and have large financial resources, excluding "dark horses" who can gradually work their way into public familiarity under the state primary system and thus gain financial support.

Voters also favor, but by a smaller 45%-to-30% ratio, changing the present primary election system to one in which four individual regional primaries would be held in different weeks of June during a presidential election year.

## JULY 15
## MOST IMPORTANT PROBLEM

Interviewing Date: 6/22–25/84
Survey #235-G

*What do you think is the most important problem facing this country today?*

|  | June 22–25, 1984 | Feb. 1984 | Nov. 1983 |
|---|---|---|---|
| Threat of war; international tensions | 27% | 28% | 37% |
| Unemployment | 26 | 28 | 32 |
| High cost of living; high interest rates | 14 | 10 | 11 |
| Excessive government spending; budget deficits | 11 | 12 | 5 |
| Moral decline in society | 5 | 7 | 6 |
| Reagan budget cuts | 4 | 7 | 4 |
| Economy (general) | 3 | 5 | 3 |
| All others | 14 | 11 | 8 |
| Don't know | 2 | 5 | 3 |
|  | 106%* | 113%* | 109%* |

## By Politics

### Republicans

Threat of war; international tensions . . . . . 26%
Unemployment . . . . . . . . . . . . . . . . . . . . . . . 18
High cost of living; high interest rates . . . . 16
Excessive government spending; budget
    deficits . . . . . . . . . . . . . . . . . . . . . . . . . . 14
Moral decline in society . . . . . . . . . . . . . . 7
Reagan budget cuts . . . . . . . . . . . . . . . . . . 3
Economy (general) . . . . . . . . . . . . . . . . . . . 3
All others . . . . . . . . . . . . . . . . . . . . . . . . . . 14
Don't know . . . . . . . . . . . . . . . . . . . . . . . . . 3
                                          104%*

### Democrats

Threat of war; international tensions . . . . . 25%
Unemployment . . . . . . . . . . . . . . . . . . . . . . . 35
High cost of living; high interest rates . . . . 14
Excessive government spending; budget
    deficits . . . . . . . . . . . . . . . . . . . . . . . . . . . 9
Moral decline in society . . . . . . . . . . . . . . 2
Reagan budget cuts . . . . . . . . . . . . . . . . . . 6

Economy (general) . . . . . . . . . . . . . . . . . . . 4
All others . . . . . . . . . . . . . . . . . . . . . . . . . .12
Don't know . . . . . . . . . . . . . . . . . . . . . . . . . 2
                                         109%*

### Independents

Threat of war; international tensions . . . . . 33%
Unemployment . . . . . . . . . . . . . . . . . . . . . . .21
High cost of living; high interest rates . . . .13
Excessive government spending; budget
    deficits . . . . . . . . . . . . . . . . . . . . . . . . . .11
Moral decline in society . . . . . . . . . . . . . . 8
Reagan budget cuts . . . . . . . . . . . . . . . . . . 2
Economy (general) . . . . . . . . . . . . . . . . . . . 4
All others . . . . . . . . . . . . . . . . . . . . . . . . . .15
Don't know . . . . . . . . . . . . . . . . . . . . . . . . . 2
                                         109%*

*Total adds to more than 100% due to multiple responses.

*All persons who named a problem were then asked: Which political party do you think can do a better job of handling the problem you have just mentioned—the Republican party or the Democratic party?*

|  | June 22–25, 1984 | Feb. 1984 | Nov. 1983 |
|---|---|---|---|
| Republican . . . . . . . . | 33% | 30% | 28% |
| Democratic . . . . . . . . | 35 | 32 | 35 |
| No difference (volunteered) . . . . . | 20 | 26 | 24 |
| No opinion . . . . . . . . | 12 | 12 | 13 |

Note: The top concerns of the nation's voters as the Democratic delegates convene in San Francisco to select their candidates and determine the party platform are international unrest (27%), including the fear of war, and joblessness (26%). These problems are followed by the high cost of living, including high interest rates (14% collectively), and excessive government spending, including the federal budget deficit (11%). Earning single-digit mentions are a perceived moral decline in American society (5%), President Ronald Reagan's budget cuts (4%), and the economy in general (3%).

The latest figures are similar to those recorded in a February survey, when the threat of war and unemployment also shared the spotlight as the most serious problems. The current findings are quite different, however, from last November, when international tensions reached the highest level (37%) recorded since the end of the Vietnam War.

One year earlier in October 1982, joblessness claimed an overwhelming share of the public's concerns and was named by 62%, followed by inflation and the high cost of living cited by 18%. International problems were mentioned by merely 6%, one-fourth the current level.

There is general agreement about the major problems facing the nation on the part of voters of different political persuasions, with one important exception: unemployment is thought by far more Democrats (35%) than either Republicans (18%) or independents (21%) to constitute the top national concern at present.

Many factors can alter the political outlook, but at this point the Gallup Poll issue barometer points to a close race in November. In the current survey, 35% say the Democratic party is better able to handle the problem they consider most urgent, while 33% credit the Republican party, 20% see no difference between the two, and 12% are undecided.

For four decades the Gallup Poll has asked Americans what they consider to be the most important problem facing the nation and which political party can better deal with these problems. The results have proved to be a good barometer of the outcome of presidential elections. In October 1980, for example, the Republican party had a 40% to 31% lead on this question, pointing to Reagan's victory over President Jimmy Carter in the November election. Similarly, the Democratic party was the choice of 43% to 23% for the Republican party in October 1976, presaging Carter's win over incumbent Gerald Ford. In October 1960, the Democratic party was considered by 29%, compared to the Republican party's 27%, as better able to deal with the top problems. John Kennedy won a narrow victory over Richard Nixon in that year.

## JULY 16
## PRESIDENTIAL TRIAL HEATS

Interviewing Date: 7/13–16/84
Survey #238-G

*Asked of registered voters: Suppose the 1984 presidential election were being held today. If the Republican ticket of Ronald Reagan and George Bush were running against the Democratic ticket of Walter Mondale and Geraldine Ferraro, which would you like to see win? [Those who were undecided were asked: As of today, do you lean more to the Republican ticket of Reagan and Bush, or to the Democratic ticket of Mondale and Ferraro?]*

Reagan-Bush . . . . . . . . . . . . . . . . . . . . . . .53%
Mondale-Ferraro . . . . . . . . . . . . . . . . . . . .39
Other; undecided . . . . . . . . . . . . . . . . . . . . 8

### By Politics
#### Republicans

Reagan-Bush . . . . . . . . . . . . . . . . . . . . . . .88%
Mondale-Ferraro . . . . . . . . . . . . . . . . . . . . 8
Other; undecided . . . . . . . . . . . . . . . . . . . . 4

#### Democrats

Reagan-Bush . . . . . . . . . . . . . . . . . . . . . . .25%
Mondale-Ferraro . . . . . . . . . . . . . . . . . . . .67
Other; undecided . . . . . . . . . . . . . . . . . . . . 8

#### Independents

Reagan-Bush . . . . . . . . . . . . . . . . . . . . . . .59%
Mondale-Ferraro . . . . . . . . . . . . . . . . . . . .32
Other; undecided . . . . . . . . . . . . . . . . . . . . 9

### Selected National Trend

| | Reagan | Mondale | Undecided |
|---|---|---|---|
| June 29–July 2 | 51% | 43% | 6% |
| June 22–25 | 55 | 38 | 7 |
| June 6–8 | 53 | 44 | 3 |
| May 18–21 | 53 | 43 | 4 |
| May 3–5 | 50 | 46 | 4 |
| April 11–15 | 52 | 44 | 4 |

| | | | |
|---|---|---|---|
| April 6–9 | 54 | 41 | 5 |
| March 16–19 | 52 | 44 | 4 |
| March 2–6 | 50 | 45 | 5 |

Note: The GOP ticket of Ronald Reagan and George Bush holds a wide lead over the Democratic ticket of Walter Mondale and Geraldine Ferraro, although the addition of the New York congresswoman to the Democratic ticket makes it a slightly closer race. Based on in-person interviews with a national sample of registered voters, the Republican slate wins 53% of the vote to 39% for the Democratic one. When Reagan and Mondale alone are pitted against each other, Reagan's margin is a greater 54% to 37%.

If only women were voting at this time, the contest would be a virtual toss-up, with 46% choosing Reagan and Bush, and 46% choosing Mondale and Ferraro. Among men, the GOP ticket prevails by a larger 60% to 32% margin. The "gender gap" is more apparent in this latest set of findings than in any test race during the last six months.

## JULY 17
## WOMAN FOR PRESIDENT

Interviewing Date: 7/13–16/84
Survey #238-G

*Assuming that both were equally well qualified for the job, do you think that a male president or a female president of the United States would do a better job of:*

*Handling economic conditions in this country?*

Male better . . . . . . . . . . . . . . . . . . . . . . . . .41%
Female better . . . . . . . . . . . . . . . . . . . . . .17
No difference . . . . . . . . . . . . . . . . . . . . . .35
No opinion . . . . . . . . . . . . . . . . . . . . . . . . 7

### By Sex
### Male

Male better . . . . . . . . . . . . . . . . . . . . . . . . .40%
Female better . . . . . . . . . . . . . . . . . . . . . .13
No difference . . . . . . . . . . . . . . . . . . . . . .40
No opinion . . . . . . . . . . . . . . . . . . . . . . . . 7

### Female

Male better . . . . . . . . . . . . . . . . . . . . . . . . .41%
Female better . . . . . . . . . . . . . . . . . . . . . .22
No difference . . . . . . . . . . . . . . . . . . . . . .29
No opinion . . . . . . . . . . . . . . . . . . . . . . . . 8

*Dealing with unemployment?*

Male better . . . . . . . . . . . . . . . . . . . . . . . . .40%
Female better . . . . . . . . . . . . . . . . . . . . . .18
No difference . . . . . . . . . . . . . . . . . . . . . .35
No opinion . . . . . . . . . . . . . . . . . . . . . . . . 7

### By Sex
### Male

Male better . . . . . . . . . . . . . . . . . . . . . . . . .41%
Female better . . . . . . . . . . . . . . . . . . . . . .12
No difference . . . . . . . . . . . . . . . . . . . . . .40
No opinion . . . . . . . . . . . . . . . . . . . . . . . . 7

### Female

Male better . . . . . . . . . . . . . . . . . . . . . . . . .39%
Female better . . . . . . . . . . . . . . . . . . . . . .23
No difference . . . . . . . . . . . . . . . . . . . . . .31
No opinion . . . . . . . . . . . . . . . . . . . . . . . . 7

*Handling foreign policy?*

Male better . . . . . . . . . . . . . . . . . . . . . . . . .58%
Female better . . . . . . . . . . . . . . . . . . . . . . 8
No difference . . . . . . . . . . . . . . . . . . . . . .26
No opinion . . . . . . . . . . . . . . . . . . . . . . . . 8

### By Sex
### Male

Male better . . . . . . . . . . . . . . . . . . . . . . . . .57%
Female better . . . . . . . . . . . . . . . . . . . . . . 7
No difference . . . . . . . . . . . . . . . . . . . . . .28
No opinion . . . . . . . . . . . . . . . . . . . . . . . . 8

### Female

Male better . . . . . . . . . . . . . . . . . . . . . . . . .59%
Female better . . . . . . . . . . . . . . . . . . . . . . 9
No difference . . . . . . . . . . . . . . . . . . . . . .25
No opinion . . . . . . . . . . . . . . . . . . . . . . . . 7

*Dealing with the situation in Central America?*

| | |
|---|---|
| Male better | 56% |
| Female better | 9 |
| No difference | 26 |
| No opinion | 9 |

### By Sex
#### Male

| | |
|---|---|
| Male better | 56% |
| Female better | 8 |
| No difference | 27 |
| No opinion | 9 |

#### Female

| | |
|---|---|
| Male better | 56% |
| Female better | 11 |
| No difference | 24 |
| No opinion | 9 |

*Handling our relations with the Soviet Union?*

| | |
|---|---|
| Male better | 57% |
| Female better | 11 |
| No difference | 25 |
| No opinion | 7 |

### By Sex
#### Male

| | |
|---|---|
| Male better | 57% |
| Female better | 10 |
| No difference | 26 |
| No opinion | 7 |

#### Female

| | |
|---|---|
| Male better | 57% |
| Female better | 13 |
| No difference | 24 |
| No opinion | 6 |

*Improving the quality of life in America?*

| | |
|---|---|
| Male better | 30% |
| Female better | 32 |
| No difference | 31 |
| No opinion | 7 |

### By Sex
#### Male

| | |
|---|---|
| Male better | 29% |
| Female better | 27 |
| No difference | 36 |
| No opinion | 8 |

#### Female

| | |
|---|---|
| Male better | 29% |
| Female better | 37 |
| No difference | 36 |
| No opinion | 8 |

Note: With Geraldine Ferraro's selection as the Democratic vice-presidential candidate ushering in a new era in politics, attention focuses on the comparative abilities of men and women to handle the presidency. In a just completed Gallup survey, voters think that a female president would stack up to a male in just one of six major areas of presidential responsibility. The greatest reservation about the qualifications of a female president is in foreign affairs.

Men come out ahead on dealing with economic conditions and unemployment. Only on improving the quality of life are women seen as more able than men. In the new survey, 32% say a female president would do more to enhance the quality of American life, 30% say a male president would be superior, and 31% perceive no difference in this respect based on the sex of the president.

The mid-range in terms of the public's perceptions of the relative competency of presidents of different sexes centers on the twin domestic responsibilities of dealing with economic conditions and unemployment. About one person in three (35%) thinks there is parity between the sexes in this area. But of the six in ten who believe there would be a difference, twice as many say a man, rather than a woman, would be more capable.

The public's greatest concern about the qualifications of a female president is in the area of foreign affairs: specifically, handling foreign policy, dealing with the situation in Central America, and handling our relations with the Soviet Union. Although about one-fourth of the public maintains the president's sex is immaterial to his or her competence in foreign affairs, those who say a male president would be superior outnumber those choosing a woman by a 5-to-1 ratio. Again, little difference is found in the views of men and women in the survey.

## JULY 26
## ELECTORAL REFORMS

Interviewing Date: 7/6–9/84
Survey #237-G

*It has been suggested that the federal government provide a fixed amount of money for the election campaign of candidates for Congress and that all private contributions from other sources be prohibited. Do you think this is a good idea or a poor idea?*

Good idea .......................... 52%
Poor idea .......................... 36
No opinion ......................... 12

### By Politics
#### Republicans

Good idea .......................... 45%
Poor idea .......................... 43
No opinion ......................... 12

#### Democrats

Good idea .......................... 56%
Poor idea .......................... 32
No opinion ......................... 12

#### Independents

Good idea .......................... 54%
Poor idea .......................... 34
No opinion ......................... 12

### Selected National Trend

|  | Good idea | Poor idea | No opinion |
|---|---|---|---|
| 1982 ............... | 55% | 31% | 14% |
| 1979 ............... | 57 | 30 | 13 |
| 1977 ............... | 57 | 32 | 11 |
| 1973 (Sept.) .......... | 65 | 24 | 11 |
| 1973 (June) .......... | 58 | 29 | 13 |

Note: With spending for this year's House and Senate election campaigns expected to top previous records, it is noteworthy that a majority of Americans would like to see the federal government provide a fixed amount of money to fund the campaigns of congressional candidates and prohibit contributions from all other sources. The latest Gallup Poll shows 52% supporting this plan and 36% opposed, consistent with the findings of Gallup surveys conducted for over a decade.

The Federal Election Commission reported that during the 1981–82 political season, candidates for the House and Senate spent almost $350 million in trying to get elected, the most in history and 44% over campaign spending in 1979–80. Political action committees (PACs) contributed more than $80 million to the 1982 campaigns, up 50% from two years earlier. Under the terms of the proposal reported today, PAC contributions would be barred.

The latest findings represent some loss in public support from earlier levels. In 1982, Republicans and Democrats shared the same beliefs about the proposed election reform. As the table below reveals, the loss in support from 1982 to 1984 can be traced to defection on the part of Republicans and independents, while Democratic backing currently is as strong as it was two years ago. This comparison of the 1984 and 1982 surveys is based on political affiliation, with "no opinion" omitted:

### Government Funding of Congressional Campaigns

|  | Good idea | | Poor idea | |
|---|---|---|---|---|
|  | 1984 | 1982 | 1984 | 1982 |
| National ........ | 52% | 55% | 36% | 31% |

## By Politics

| | | | | |
|---|---|---|---|---|
| Republicans ..... | 45% | 54% | 43% | 33% |
| Democrats ...... | 56 | 54 | 32 | 34 |
| Independents .... | 54 | 61 | 34 | 26 |

## JULY 29

## MAJOR SWINGS IN POLL FINDINGS REFLECT POLITICAL ENVIRONMENT*

Compared with previous elections, there has been little consistency in the findings of opinion polls in the past month. In Gallup surveys alone, presidential preference results have ranged from a 17-percentage point advantage for Ronald Reagan to a 2-percentage point margin for Walter Mondale. When the findings of other polling organizations are considered along with Gallup's, an even more bewildering array of test election results emerges.

Opinion surveys are sending back very mixed signals about the presidential election race. Some would interpret this as a measure of their unreliability. From a pollster's vantage point, the apparently ambiguous results of presidential preference surveys reflect the nature of opinion about the contest itself, and when the results are examined in perspective, they tell a revealing story about how voters are reacting to unfolding campaign events.

Ironically, the sheer frequency of surveys also plays a role in the seeming increase in poll variability. Since the first of June, Gallup has conducted seven national surveys measuring presidential preference. Add to that number the polls taken by other major survey organizations, and the result is enough surveys to produce a few exceptional findings by chance alone.

Considering the full Gallup trend, which includes regular Gallup Polls and Gallup surveys

*This Gallup analysis was written by Andrew Kohut, president of the Gallup Organization Inc.

for *Newsweek*, a fair amount of consistency in presidential preference is found until convention time—with one exception. In late June (June 22–25), Gallup showed a 17-percentage point margin for Reagan over Mondale rather than the 8 to 10 points it had been indicating. The next Gallup Poll, June 29–July 2, reverted to a more typical 8-percentage point Reagan margin.

However, from that point on Gallup results began to move around in reaction to the Democratic National Convention. The next Gallup survey for *Newsweek* was conducted on the Thursday and Friday nights prior to the San Francisco convention as Geraldine Ferraro was being announced as Mondale's running mate. It showed one of the smallest Reagan margins over Mondale in three months (+6 percentage points), which was mostly accounted for by a widening of the "gender gap" in response to Ms. Ferraro. Reagan's lead opened up again over the next few days as the Bert Lance affair dominated the news and the emotional response to the historic Ferraro announcement subsided.

Gallup's most recent survey for *Newsweek* was taken at the end of the Democratic convention, and it showed registered voters dividing their support about equally between Reagan-Bush (46%) and Mondale-Ferraro (48%). Following is the recent trend:

## Reagan-Bush vs. Mondale-Ferraro
### (Based on Registered Voters)

| | Reagan-Bush | Mondale-Ferraro | Other; undecided |
|---|---|---|---|
| July 27–29 | 52% | 42% | 6% |
| July 19–20* | 46 | 48 | 6 |

### Democratic Convention

| | | | |
|---|---|---|---|
| July 13–16 | 53% | 39% | 8% |
| July 12–13* | 49 | 43 | 8 |

| | | | |
|---|---|---|---|
| June 29–July 2** | 51% | 43% | 6% |
| June 22–25** | 55 | 38 | 7 |
| June 6–8** | 53 | 44 | 3 |
| May 18–21** | 53 | 43 | 4 |

*For *Newsweek*
**Reagan vs. Mondale

That the Mondale ticket would gain some ground after a successful convention is not surprising. That it would draw even with Reagan-Bush after trailing consistently for almost six months was a surprise to many. Most probably, the Reagan-Bush lead will reappear as the effect of the Democratic convention wears off.

What is significant, however, is not that the Reagan-Bush and Mondale-Ferraro tickets drew equal levels of support at the end of a big Democratic week, but rather that opinions could shift back and forth as much as they did in a two-week period. Such variability suggests the potential for a close election in November.

A close race has not been the conventional wisdom. Mondale's electability was a major issue in the nomination contest, and the news media believe that Reagan will be reelected. A Gallup survey of senior reporters and editors in the spring found the vast majority predicting that President Reagan would be elected to a second term.

The way poll results have been varying in recent weeks does not suggest a runaway election, although a strong economy, public confidence in Reagan's handling of the economy, and his leadership abilities in general argue for a Republican victory in the fall. At the same time, the polls show that Reagan has some major handicaps that can be exploited by the Democrats. The most recent *Newsweek* poll by Gallup indicates that more voters think Mondale, rather than Reagan, can do a better job of keeping the United States out of war. The president also trails Mondale on such important points as caring about "people like me," "coming close to my way of thinking," and in being fair in his policies.

Voters hold conflicting views about Mondale and Reagan. The contrast in candidate perceptions is very sharp, as are the demographic patterns of support. Responses to test election questions vary by race, income, region of the country, size of community, and gender.

The variability of candidate preference results is really an indicator of the conflicting opinions of the candidates and the crosscurrents that will shape this election campaign. If the polls were not showing any public reaction to the naming of the first female to a major party ticket, when gender was already a key factor, or to the culmination of a long nomination contest, a lack of sensitivity would be evident. The results of polls are unstable when the properties they measure—opinions—are unstable.

The general election campaign is just beginning. The current poll results answer only one question: did the Democrats help themselves at their national convention? The answer is yes, but it says little about where the race might go over the course of the next two months. Until voter attitudes crystalize and people resolve their dissonant views of the candidates, their opinions are subject to change. It is hoped that these polls will accurately reflect that change.

## JULY 29
## PERSONAL FINANCES

Interviewing Date: 7/6–9/84
Survey #237-G

*We are interested in how people's financial situation may have changed. Would you say that you are financially better off now than you were a year ago, or are you financially worse off now?*

| | |
|---|---|
| Better | 40% |
| Worse | 25 |
| Same (volunteered) | 34 |
| No opinion | 1 |

### Selected National Trend

| | Better | Worse | Same | No opinion |
|---|---|---|---|---|
| Mar. 1984 | 36% | 26% | 37% | 1% |
| June 1983 | 28 | 39 | 32 | 1 |
| Mar. 1983 | 25 | 46 | 28 | 1 |

| | | | | |
|---|---|---|---|---|
| Nov. 1982 | 28 | 37 | 34 | 1 |
| July/Aug. 1982 | 25 | 46 | 26 | 3 |
| Feb. 1982 | 28 | 47 | 24 | 1 |
| Oct. 1981 | 28 | 43 | 28 | 1 |

*Now looking ahead, do you expect that at this time next year you will be financially better off than now, or worse off than now?*

Better ............................52%
Worse .............................12
Same (volunteered) ..................28
No opinion .......................... 8

## By Sex
### Male

Better ............................55%
Worse .............................11
Same (volunteered) ..................27
No opinion .......................... 7

### Female

Better ............................50%
Worse .............................13
Same (volunteered) ..................29
No opinion .......................... 8

## By Ethnic Background
### White

Better ............................52%
Worse .............................12
Same (volunteered) ..................29
No opinion .......................... 7

### Black

Better ............................51%
Worse .............................13
Same (volunteered) ..................24
No opinion .........................12

## By Education
### College Graduate

Better ............................61%
Worse ............................. 9
Same (volunteered) ..................27
No opinion .......................... 3

### College Incomplete

Better ............................60%
Worse .............................12
Same (volunteered) ..................24
No opinion .......................... 4

### High-School Graduate

Better ............................55%
Worse .............................11
Same (volunteered) ..................25
No opinion .......................... 9

### Less Than High-School Graduate

Better ............................35%
Worse .............................16
Same (volunteered) ..................37
No opinion .........................12

## By Region
### East

Better ............................53%
Worse .............................12
Same (volunteered) ..................28
No opinion .......................... 7

### Midwest

Better ............................53%
Worse .............................12
Same (volunteered) ..................28
No opinion .......................... 7

### South

Better ............................51%
Worse .............................12
Same (volunteered) ..................26
No opinion .........................11

### West

Better ............................52%
Worse .............................14
Same (volunteered) ..................30
No opinion .......................... 4

## By Age

### 18–29 Years

Better ............................71%
Worse ......................... 8
Same (volunteered) ..................16
No opinion ........................ 5

### 30–49 Years

Better ............................60%
Worse .........................11
Same (volunteered) ..................22
No opinion ........................ 7

### 50–64 Years

Better ............................43%
Worse .........................12
Same (volunteered) ..................39
No opinion ........................ 6

### 65 Years and Over

Better ............................18%
Worse .........................21
Same (volunteered) ..................48
No opinion ........................13

## By Income

### $20,000 and Over

Better ............................60%
Worse .........................10
Same (volunteered) ..................26
No opinion ........................ 4

### Under $20,000

Better ............................44%
Worse .........................15
Same (volunteered) ..................30
No opinion ........................11

## By Politics

### Republicans

Better ............................62%
Worse ......................... 8
Same (volunteered) ..................27
No opinion ........................ 3

### Democrats

Better ............................43%
Worse .........................14
Same (volunteered) ..................33
No opinion ........................10

### Independents

Better ............................55%
Worse .........................15
Same (volunteered) ..................23
No opinion ........................ 7

## Selected National Trend

| | Better | Worse | Same | No opinion |
|---|---|---|---|---|
| Mar. 1984 | 54% | 11% | 28% | 7% |
| June 1983 | 43 | 19 | 28 | 10 |
| Mar. 1983 | 45 | 22 | 24 | 9 |
| Nov. 1982 | 41 | 22 | 27 | 10 |
| July/Aug. 1982 | 37 | 29 | 24 | 10 |
| Feb. 1982 | 42 | 31 | 21 | 6 |
| Oct. 1981 | 40 | 31 | 21 | 8 |

Note: Government reports of soaring economic growth are paralleled by booming financial optimism on the part of the American people. In the latest Gallup survey, 40% say they are financially better off now than they were a year ago, compared to 25% who say they are worse off now and 34% who see no change in their economic condition. This level of financial well-being is unsurpassed since the survey series began in 1976.

Looking ahead, a 52% majority thinks they will be better off a year from now than they are now, 28% foresee no change, and 12% see worse times on their economic horizon. These figures are not significantly different from those recorded in a March survey and, like the response to the first question, no higher degree of optimism about the future was found in earlier surveys.

When the answers of both questions are combined into an overall index, optimists are found to outnumber pessimists by a 3-to-1 ratio, 47% to 15%. Since June 1983, there has been a sharp rise in the proportion of "super optimists" from 20% to 31%. Studies have shown that these people—who say they are better off than in the past and expect to be still better off in the future—are likely to be buyers of big-ticket items such as cars, houses, and major appliances. The findings reported today according to Jay Schmiedeskamp, director of the Gallup Organization Economic Service, suggest that the economic recovery will continue to be supported by a high level of consumer demand.

Not surprisingly, the degree to which people are optimistic about their economic future is influenced by demographic factors such as age, education, and family income. For example, 71% of 18 to 29 year olds expect to be better off a year from now, while only 18% of those 65 and over share this optimism. Similarly, greater optimism is found among those with at least a high-school diploma and persons whose annual family income is $20,000 or more.

While many of these same background characteristics are related to the public's political preference, the survey found a political coloration to Americans' economic outlook over and above demographic factors alone, with Republicans more likely than Democrats to have an optimistic outlook. Nevertheless, a strong 43% plurality of Democrats, compared to 62% of Republicans, thinks they will be better off next year than they are now.

No significant difference is found by race: blacks in the survey are as likely as whites to say they expect to be better off next year. Also, financial optimism is national in scope, with similar proportions from each region optimistic about the coming year.

## JULY 30
## PRESIDENTIAL TRIAL HEATS

Interviewing Date: 7/27–30/84
Survey #239-G

*Asked of registered voters: Now I'd like to get your honest opinion on this next question. It doesn't make any difference to me how you vote; I only want to record your opinion accurately. If the presidential election were being held today, which would you vote for— the Republican candidates, Reagan and Bush, or the Democratic candidates, Mondale and Ferraro? [Those who were undecided or who named other candidates were then asked: As of today, do you lean more to Reagan and Bush, or to Mondale and Ferraro?]*

Reagan-Bush ........................53%
Mondale-Ferraro ....................41
Undecided .......................... 6

### By Sex
#### Male

Reagan-Bush ........................53%
Mondale-Ferraro ....................41
Undecided .......................... 6

#### Female

Reagan-Bush ........................54%
Mondale-Ferraro ....................41
Undecided .......................... 5

### By Ethnic Background
#### White

Reagan-Bush ........................54%
Mondale-Ferraro ....................41
Undecided .......................... 5

#### Nonwhite

Reagan-Bush ........................11%
Mondale-Ferraro ....................85
Undecided .......................... 4

#### Black

Reagan-Bush ........................ 6%
Mondale-Ferraro ....................90
Undecided .......................... 4

### By Education
#### College Graduate

Reagan-Bush ........................59%
Mondale-Ferraro ....................38
Undecided .......................... 3

### College Incomplete

Reagan-Bush ........................62%
Mondale-Ferraro ....................34
Undecided .......................... 4

### High-School Graduate

Reagan-Bush ........................53%
Mondale-Ferraro ....................40
Undecided .......................... 7

### Less Than High-School Graduate

Reagan-Bush ........................38%
Mondale-Ferraro ....................54
Undecided .......................... 8

## By Region
### East

Reagan-Bush ........................48%
Mondale-Ferraro ....................42
Undecided ..........................10

### Midwest

Reagan-Bush ........................55%
Mondale-Ferraro ....................42
Undecided .......................... 3

### South

Reagan-Bush ........................55%
Mondale-Ferraro ....................40
Undecided .......................... 5

### West

Reagan-Bush ........................56%
Mondale-Ferraro ....................40
Undecided .......................... 4

## By Age
### 18–24 Years

Reagan-Bush ........................53%
Mondale-Ferraro ....................43
Undecided .......................... 4

### 25–29 Years

Reagan-Bush ........................54%
Mondale-Ferraro ....................42
Undecided .......................... 4

### 30–49 Years

Reagan-Bush ........................56%
Mondale-Ferraro ....................37
Undecided .......................... 7

### 50–64 Years

Reagan-Bush ........................54%
Mondale-Ferraro ....................41
Undecided .......................... 5

### 65 Years and Over

Reagan-Bush ........................48%
Mondale-Ferraro ....................46
Undecided .......................... 6

## By Income
### $40,000 and Over

Reagan-Bush ........................67%
Mondale-Ferraro ....................32
Undecided .......................... 1

### $30,000–$39,999

Reagan-Bush ........................62%
Mondale-Ferraro ....................26
Undecided ..........................12

### $20,000–$29,999

Reagan-Bush ........................58%
Mondale-Ferraro ....................39
Undecided .......................... 3

### $10,000–$19,999

Reagan-Bush ........................47%
Mondale-Ferraro ....................47
Undecided .......................... 6

### Under $10,000

Reagan-Bush ........................36%
Mondale-Ferraro ....................60
Undecided .......................... 4

## By Politics
### Republicans

Reagan-Bush ........................91%
Mondale-Ferraro ....................  6
Undecided ..........................  3

### Democrats

Reagan-Bush ........................19%
Mondale-Ferraro ....................78
Undecided ..........................  3

### Independents

Reagan-Bush ........................60%
Mondale-Ferraro ....................30
Undecided ..........................10

## By Religion
### Protestants

Reagan-Bush ........................59%
Mondale-Ferraro ....................38
Undecided ..........................  3

### Catholics

Reagan-Bush ........................47%
Mondale-Ferraro ....................44
Undecided ..........................  9

## By Occupation
### Professional and Business

Reagan-Bush ........................61%
Mondale-Ferraro ....................35
Undecided ..........................  4

### Clerical and Sales

Reagan-Bush ........................49%
Mondale-Ferraro ....................50
Undecided ..........................  1

### Manual Workers

Reagan-Bush ........................49%
Mondale-Ferraro ....................43
Undecided ..........................  8

### Nonlabor Force

Reagan-Bush ........................50%
Mondale-Ferraro ....................43
Undecided ..........................  7

## Selected National Trend

| | Reagan-Bush | Mondale-Ferraro | Undecided |
|---|---|---|---|
| July 19–20* | 46% | 48% | 6% |

### Democratic Convention

| | | | |
|---|---|---|---|
| July 13–16 | 53% | 39% | 8% |
| July 12–13* | 49 | 43 | 8 |

### Ferraro Announcement

| | | | |
|---|---|---|---|
| June 29–July 2** | 51% | 43% | 6% |
| June 22–25** | 55 | 38 | 7 |

*For *Newsweek*
**Reagan vs. Mondale

*Asked of registered voters: Do you strongly support (candidates) or do you only moderately support them?*

*Vote in trial heat*
Reagan-Bush ........................53%
  Strongly support ................31
  Moderately support ..............22
Mondale-Ferraro ....................41
  Strongly support ................18
  Moderately support ..............23
Other; undecided ...................  6

## By Politics
### Republicans

Reagan-Bush ........................91%
  Strongly support ................65
  Moderately support ..............26
Mondale-Ferraro ....................  6
  Strongly support ................  2
  Moderately support ..............  4
Other; undecided ...................  3

Reagan-Bush ........................19%
 Strongly support ............... 9
 Moderately support ..............10
Mondale-Ferraro ....................78
 Strongly support ...............39
 Moderately support ..............39
Other; undecided ................... 3

*Independents*

Reagan-Bush ........................60%
 Strongly support ...............26
 Moderately support ..............34
Mondale-Ferraro ....................30
 Strongly support ............... 8
 Moderately support ..............22
Other; undecided ...................10

*All persons who voted for one of the tickets were then asked: Would you say your vote is more a vote for (Ticket A) or more a vote against (Ticket B)?*

| | Reagan-Bush | Mondale-Ferraro |
|---|---|---|
| *Vote in test election* | | |
| More "pro" candidates .... | 82% | 49% |
| More "anti" opponents .... | 14 | 46 |
| Not sure ............... | 4 | 5 |

Note: For a brief period following the Democratic convention, the Republican and Democratic tickets were effectively tied. The Reagan-Bush ticket has now regained the lead and holds a 12-point advantage over Mondale-Ferraro. Prior to the convention, in a test election on July 13–16, the GOP slate led the Democrats, 53% to 39%.

As many political observers expected, the Republican ticket has recovered some, but not all, of the ground it lost as a result of the highly acclaimed Democratic convention on July 16–19 in San Francisco. In the current Gallup Poll, Ronald Reagan and George Bush are the choice of 53% of registered voters to 41% for Walter Mondale and Geraldine Ferraro, with 6% undecided. In a *Newsweek* poll conducted by the Gallup Organization on July 19 and 20 as the convention was winding down, the rival tickets were statistically deadlocked, with the Democrats receiving 48% of the vote to 46% for the Republicans.

Most of the Reagan ticket's 7-point gain and the Mondale ticket's identical loss since the convention can be traced to women. In the July 19–20 survey, 52% of men and 41% of women voted for Reagan-Bush (a fairly typical 11-point "gender gap"). In the current survey, the GOP ticket is the choice of 53% of men and 54% of women. Thus, men's votes for the Reagan ticket went up 1 point, compared to 13 points for women.

In addition to greater numerical support, the Reagan team presently enjoys considerably stronger support than does the Mondale-Ferraro ticket. Among all registered voters, the GOP slate boasts three strong supporters for every two moderate ones, while the Democratic ticket has about equal numbers of strong and moderate backers. Republicans strongly favor their party's choice by a 5-to-2 ratio, while the Mondale-Ferraro ticket has equal proportions of strong and moderate Democratic backing.

Backers of the Democratic ticket, the survey found, are about equally divided between those who are motivated by positive feelings about Mondale-Ferraro (49%) and those who are negatively disposed toward Reagan-Bush (46%). Almost all who choose the Reagan-Bush ticket, however, say they do so because they are for the GOP slate (82%) rather than against Mondale-Ferraro (14%).

## AUGUST 1
## OLYMPIC GAMES

Interviewing Date: 6/25–7/2/84
Special Telephone Survey

*Which would you prefer for future Olympic games—a permanent site to be established in Greece, or that the Olympic games continue to move from country to country?*

Permanent site ......................37%
Continue to move ...................54
No opinion ......................... 9

## By Sex

### Male

Permanent site ...................... 41%
Continue to move ................... 53
No opinion ......................... 6

### Female

Permanent site ...................... 34%
Continue to move ................... 55
No opinion ......................... 11

## By Education

### College Graduate

Permanent site ...................... 52%
Continue to move ................... 43
No opinion ......................... 5

### College Incomplete

Permanent site ...................... 41%
Continue to move ................... 54
No opinion ......................... 5

### High-School Graduate

Permanent site ...................... 35%
Continue to move ................... 58
No opinion ......................... 7

### Less Than High-School Graduate

Permanent site ...................... 26%
Continue to move ................... 55
No opinion ......................... 19

## By Region

### East

Permanent site ...................... 41%
Continue to move ................... 54
No opinion ......................... 5

### Midwest

Permanent site ...................... 36%
Continue to move ................... 58
No opinion ......................... 6

### South

Permanent site ...................... 34%
Continue to move ................... 54
No opinion ......................... 12

### West

Permanent site ...................... 41%
Continue to move ................... 47
No opinion ......................... 12

## By Age

### 18–24 Years

Permanent site ...................... 29%
Continue to move ................... 69
No opinion ......................... 2

### 25–29 Years

Permanent site ...................... 36%
Continue to move ................... 59
No opinion ......................... 5

### 30–49 Years

Permanent site ...................... 41%
Continue to move ................... 53
No opinion ......................... 6

### 50 Years and Over

Permanent site ...................... 39%
Continue to move ................... 46
No opinion ......................... 15

The following are the international results for the question:

| | Permanent site | Continue to move | No opinion |
|---|---|---|---|
| Turkey | 2% | 95% | 3% |
| Korea (South) | 9 | 87 | 4 |
| Uruguay | 10 | 79 | 11 |
| Brazil | 12 | 79 | 9 |
| France | 23 | 66 | 11 |
| Japan | 31 | 66 | 3 |
| Canada | 26 | 65 | 9 |
| Italy | 27 | 62 | 11 |
| Austria | 25 | 61 | 14 |
| Germany (West) | 37 | 61 | 2 |

| | | | |
|---|---|---|---|
| Argentina | 26 | 55 | 19 |
| Australia | 41 | 53 | 6 |
| Norway | 34 | 52 | 14 |
| Switzerland | 33 | 50 | 17 |
| Netherlands | 45 | 45 | 10 |
| Belgium | 37 | 42 | 21 |
| Great Britain | 52 | 41 | 7 |
| Greece | 91 | 8 | 1 |

Note: Most respondents in the United States and in eighteen other nations say the Olympic games should be moved from country to country every four years, as at present, rather than adopt a permanent site in Greece, as has been proposed. In the United States, 54% favor retaining the present system, while 37% prefer the proposed permanent home in Greece where the ancient games and two of the early modern Olympics were held.

The present system is also preferred by the citizens of all but two of the eighteen other countries participating in the international survey. Not surprisingly, the Greeks vote overwhelmingly to hold the games permanently in their country, 91% to 8%; after the American boycott of the 1980 Moscow games, the Greek government offered a site for this purpose, which it would cede to an international committee. The other country is Great Britain. Taking the opposite view most strongly are Turkey and South Korea: the Turks, long-time foes of Greece, vote 95% to 2% to retain the present system of moving the Olympics, while the Koreans are scheduled to host the 1988 games.

The Munich games massacre in 1972, the American boycott in 1980, and the Soviet reprisal boycott of the Los Angeles Olympics this year have heightened demands for reform, including the proposal—endorsed by President Ronald Reagan, among others—for a permanent base in Greece. Aside from the politicization of the games, many critics believe the amateur ideal has become a sham.

In the United States, college graduates represent the only major population group in which a majority favors a permanent site for future Olympics, 52% to 43%. On the other hand, young adults, 18 to 24 years old, are least receptive to that proposal, with 69% choosing to keep the present system and 29% opting for a permanent site.

## AUGUST 5
## PRESIDENT REAGAN

Interviewing Date: 7/27–30/84
Survey #239-G

*Do you approve or disapprove of the way Ronald Reagan is handling his job as president?*

Approve . . . . . . . . . . . . . . . . . . . . . . . . . . .52%
Disapprove . . . . . . . . . . . . . . . . . . . . . . . .37
No opinion . . . . . . . . . . . . . . . . . . . . . . . .11

### Reagan Approval Ratings*
### *(Four-Survey Average: June–July 1984)*

| | Approve | Dis- approve | No opinion |
|---|---|---|---|
| National | 54% | 36% | 10% |

#### By Sex

| | | | |
|---|---|---|---|
| Male | 59% | 32% | 9% |
| Female | 49 | 39 | 12 |

#### By Ethnic Background

| | | | |
|---|---|---|---|
| White | 59% | 31% | 10% |
| Black | 14 | 76 | 10 |
| Hispanic | 46 | 38 | 16 |

#### By Education

| | | | |
|---|---|---|---|
| College graduate | 62% | 33% | 5% |
| College incomplete | 63 | 30 | 7 |
| High-school graduate | 54 | 34 | 12 |
| Less than high-school graduate | 41 | 45 | 14 |

#### By Region

| | | | |
|---|---|---|---|
| East | 49% | 39% | 12% |
| Midwest | 56 | 36 | 8 |
| South | 56 | 33 | 11 |
| West | 56 | 35 | 9 |

*Based on more than 6,000 interviews

### By Age

| | | | |
|---|---|---|---|
| 18–29 years | 55% | 34% | 11% |
| 30–49 years | 57 | 34 | 9 |
| 50 years and over | 51 | 38 | 11 |

### By Income

| | | | |
|---|---|---|---|
| $20,000 and over | 62% | 29% | 9% |
| Under $20,000 | 45 | 43 | 12 |

### By Politics

| | | | |
|---|---|---|---|
| Republicans | 88% | 8% | 4% |
| Democrats | 29 | 61 | 10 |
| Independents | 57 | 30 | 13 |

### By Religion

| | | | |
|---|---|---|---|
| Protestants | 57% | 34% | 9% |
| Catholics | 53 | 36 | 11 |

### By Labor Union Household

| | | | |
|---|---|---|---|
| Labor union members | 44% | 44% | 12% |
| Nonlabor union members | 56 | 34 | 10 |

## Reagan Performance Ratings

### (Percent Approval)

| | Both sexes | Men | Women | Difference in points |
|---|---|---|---|---|
| Tenure to date | 50% | 54% | 45% | 9 |
| 1984 | 54 | 58 | 50 | 8 |
| 1983 | 44 | 49 | 39 | 10 |
| 1982 | 44 | 48 | 40 | 8 |
| 1981 | 58 | 62 | 53 | 9 |

## Presidential Performance Ratings

### (Percent Approval)

| | Both sexes | Men | Women | Difference in points |
|---|---|---|---|---|
| Reagan | 50% | 54% | 45% | 9 |
| Carter | 47 | 46 | 47 | 1 |
| Ford | 46 | 45 | 46 | 1 |
| Nixon | 49 | 50 | 47 | 3 |
| Johnson | 55 | 56 | 54 | 1 |
| Kennedy | 70 | 70 | 70 | — |
| Eisenhower | 64 | 63 | 65 | 2 |

Note: In the latest Gallup Poll, 52% of adult Americans approve of the way Ronald Reagan is handling his job as president, while 37% disapprove and 11% have no opinion. This statement, or one very much like it, could have been made at any time during the past nine months.

Since last November, Reagan's job performance rating has averaged 54% approval and 36% disapproval in sixteen Gallup surveys. During this period, the proportion of the public approving of Reagan's overall performance in office has not fallen below 52% or topped 55%. A trend of this duration during presidential years is unprecedented in Gallup history.

The president's remarkably stable approval ratings are very unlike the results of test elections pitting Reagan against potential Democratic rivals, and the Reagan-Bush ticket against the Mondale-Ferraro ticket, which have been characterized by extreme volatility. These swings stand out even more vividly against the backdrop of Reagan's static job ratings. In twelve test election matches between Reagan and Walter Mondale, the president's lead varied from 1 percentage point in January to 17 points in late June. And in four test elections, the Reagan-Bush ticket, at one time, has been on the short end of a 46%-to-48% split and has led Mondale-Ferraro, 53% to 39%, at another.

Despite President Reagan's efforts to minimize his "gender gap"—the tendency of proportionately fewer women than men to approve of his job performance and programs and to support him in test elections—there is little evidence of progress toward this end. In the fourteen surveys conducted so far this year, Reagan's approval rating from men has averaged 58% compared to 50% from women, an 8-percentage point gender gap. Women have given Reagan lower competency ratings than have men in every Gallup survey conducted since he took office in 1981. The smallest discrepancy between the sexes this year has been 2 percentage points in the most recent survey, and the largest was 14 points in June and July.

Reagan continues to enjoy greater popularity in upper-income households, as well as among men, those who attended college, whites, and Republicans. Conversely, the president is less popular with blacks, those whose formal education stopped short of high-school graduation, persons whose family income is less than $20,000 per year, and Democrats.

The president continues to have relatively little support among black Americans. Perhaps surprisingly, labor union households and Hispanics are not far below the general public in their appraisal of Reagan's performance in office.

## AUGUST 12
## POLITICAL AFFILIATION

Interviewing Date: June–July 1984
Various Surveys*

> In politics, as of today, do you consider yourself a Republican, a Democrat, or an independent?

Republican ........................29%
Democrat .........................41
Independent ......................30

### By Sex
#### Male

Republican ........................30%
Democrat .........................38
Independent ......................32

#### Female

Republican ........................28%
Democrat .........................43
Independent ......................29

### By Ethnic Background
#### White

Republican ........................32%
Democrat .........................36
Independent ......................32

*Based on more than 6,000 interviews

#### Black

Republican ........................5%
Democrat .........................81
Independent ......................14

#### Hispanic

Republican ........................24%
Democrat .........................49
Independent ......................27

### By Education
#### College Graduate

Republican ........................38%
Democrat .........................32
Independent ......................30

#### College Incomplete

Republican ........................31%
Democrat .........................34
Independent ......................35

#### High-School Graduate

Republican ........................28%
Democrat .........................41
Independent ......................31

#### Less Than High-School Graduate

Republican ........................22%
Democrat .........................53
Independent ......................25

### By Region
#### East

Republican ........................28%
Democrat .........................43
Independent ......................29

#### Midwest

Republican ........................31%
Democrat .........................34
Independent ......................35

### South

Republican . . . . . . . . . . . . . . . . . . . . . . . . 26%
Democrat . . . . . . . . . . . . . . . . . . . . . . . . 46
Independent . . . . . . . . . . . . . . . . . . . . . . 28

### West

Republican . . . . . . . . . . . . . . . . . . . . . . . . 33%
Democrat . . . . . . . . . . . . . . . . . . . . . . . . 40
Independent . . . . . . . . . . . . . . . . . . . . . . 27

## By Age
### 18–29 Years

Republican . . . . . . . . . . . . . . . . . . . . . . . . 27%
Democrat . . . . . . . . . . . . . . . . . . . . . . . . 36
Independent . . . . . . . . . . . . . . . . . . . . . . 37

### 30–49 Years

Republican . . . . . . . . . . . . . . . . . . . . . . . . 28%
Democrat . . . . . . . . . . . . . . . . . . . . . . . . 38
Independent . . . . . . . . . . . . . . . . . . . . . . 34

### 50 Years and Over

Republican . . . . . . . . . . . . . . . . . . . . . . . . 32%
Democrat . . . . . . . . . . . . . . . . . . . . . . . . 46
Independent . . . . . . . . . . . . . . . . . . . . . . 22

## By Income
### $40,000 and Over

Republican . . . . . . . . . . . . . . . . . . . . . . . . 39%
Democrat . . . . . . . . . . . . . . . . . . . . . . . . 30
Independent . . . . . . . . . . . . . . . . . . . . . . 31

### $30,000–$39,999

Republican . . . . . . . . . . . . . . . . . . . . . . . . 33%
Democrat . . . . . . . . . . . . . . . . . . . . . . . . 36
Independent . . . . . . . . . . . . . . . . . . . . . . 31

### $20,000–$29,999

Republican . . . . . . . . . . . . . . . . . . . . . . . . 32%
Democrat . . . . . . . . . . . . . . . . . . . . . . . . 35
Independent . . . . . . . . . . . . . . . . . . . . . . 33

### $10,000–$19,999

Republican . . . . . . . . . . . . . . . . . . . . . . . . 25%
Democrat . . . . . . . . . . . . . . . . . . . . . . . . 45
Independent . . . . . . . . . . . . . . . . . . . . . . 30

### Under $10,000

Republican . . . . . . . . . . . . . . . . . . . . . . . . 21%
Democrat . . . . . . . . . . . . . . . . . . . . . . . . 53
Independent . . . . . . . . . . . . . . . . . . . . . . 26

## By Occupation
### Professional and Business

Republican . . . . . . . . . . . . . . . . . . . . . . . . 37%
Democrat . . . . . . . . . . . . . . . . . . . . . . . . 33
Independent . . . . . . . . . . . . . . . . . . . . . . 30

### Clerical and Sales

Republican . . . . . . . . . . . . . . . . . . . . . . . . 28%
Democrat . . . . . . . . . . . . . . . . . . . . . . . . 35
Independent . . . . . . . . . . . . . . . . . . . . . . 37

### Blue-Collar Workers

Republican . . . . . . . . . . . . . . . . . . . . . . . . 23%
Democrat . . . . . . . . . . . . . . . . . . . . . . . . 43
Independent . . . . . . . . . . . . . . . . . . . . . . 34

### Skilled Workers

Republican . . . . . . . . . . . . . . . . . . . . . . . . 24%
Democrat . . . . . . . . . . . . . . . . . . . . . . . . 39
Independent . . . . . . . . . . . . . . . . . . . . . . 37

### Unskilled Workers

Republican . . . . . . . . . . . . . . . . . . . . . . . . 22%
Democrat . . . . . . . . . . . . . . . . . . . . . . . . 46
Independent . . . . . . . . . . . . . . . . . . . . . . 32

### Farmers

Republican . . . . . . . . . . . . . . . . . . . . . . . . 42%
Democrat . . . . . . . . . . . . . . . . . . . . . . . . 32
Independent . . . . . . . . . . . . . . . . . . . . . . 26

## By Religion

### Protestants

Republican . . . . . . . . . . . . . . . . . . . . . . . .33%
Democrat . . . . . . . . . . . . . . . . . . . . . .40
Independent . . . . . . . . . . . . . . . . . . . . . .27

### Catholics

Republican . . . . . . . . . . . . . . . . . . . . . . . .24%
Democrat . . . . . . . . . . . . . . . . . . . . . . . .44
Independent . . . . . . . . . . . . . . . . . . . . . .32

### Jews

Republican . . . . . . . . . . . . . . . . . . . . . . . .15%
Democrat . . . . . . . . . . . . . . . . . . . . . . . .57
Independent . . . . . . . . . . . . . . . . . . . . . .28

## By Labor Union Household

### Labor Union Members

Republican . . . . . . . . . . . . . . . . . . . . . . . .21%
Democrat . . . . . . . . . . . . . . . . . . . . . . . .49
Independent . . . . . . . . . . . . . . . . . . . . . .30

### Nonlabor Union Members

Republican . . . . . . . . . . . . . . . . . . . . . . . .31%
Democrat . . . . . . . . . . . . . . . . . . . . . . . .39
Independent . . . . . . . . . . . . . . . . . . . . . .30

The following table shows political party affiliation by quarters since 1980:

|  | Republican | Democrat | Independent |
| --- | --- | --- | --- |
| 1984 (to date) | 28% | 42% | 30% |
| 2nd quarter | 28 | 42 | 30 |
| 1st quarter | 28 | 41 | 31 |
| | | | |
| 1983 | 25% | 44% | 31% |
| 4th quarter | 27 | 42 | 31 |
| 3rd quarter | 26 | 44 | 30 |
| 2nd quarter | 23 | 46 | 31 |
| 1st quarter | 24 | 46 | 30 |
| | | | |
| 1982 | 26% | 45% | 29% |
| 4th quarter | 26 | 45 | 29 |
| 3rd quarter | 27 | 45 | 28 |
| 2nd quarter | 26 | 46 | 28 |
| 1st quarter | 26 | 44 | 30 |
| | | | |
| 1981 | 28% | 42% | 30% |
| 4th quarter | 26 | 43 | 31 |
| 3rd quarter | 28 | 41 | 31 |
| 2nd quarter | 28 | 42 | 30 |
| 1st quarter | 27 | 42 | 31 |
| | | | |
| 1980 | 24% | 46% | 30% |
| 4th quarter | 26 | 43 | 31 |
| 3rd quarter | 25 | 48 | 27 |
| 2nd quarter | 23 | 47 | 30 |
| 1st quarter | 21 | 47 | 32 |

## Selected National Trend

### (Prior to 1980)

|  | Republican | Democrat | Independent |
| --- | --- | --- | --- |
| 1979 . . . . . . . . . | 22% | 45% | 33% |
| 1975 . . . . . . . . . | 22 | 45 | 33 |
| 1972 . . . . . . . . . | 28 | 43 | 29 |
| 1968 . . . . . . . . . | 27 | 46 | 27 |
| 1964 . . . . . . . . . | 25 | 53 | 22 |
| 1960 . . . . . . . . . | 30 | 47 | 23 |
| 1954 . . . . . . . . . | 34 | 46 | 20 |
| 1950 . . . . . . . . . | 33 | 45 | 22 |
| 1946 . . . . . . . . . | 40 | 39 | 21 |

Note: Riding the wave of economic recovery, Republican party affiliation is currently as high as it has been at any time during Ronald Reagan's presidency. In fact, not since the White House tenure of Dwight Eisenhower has a larger proportion of the electorate claimed the GOP label. Republicans remain the minority party, however, which points to the need for GOP presidential candidates to gain the support of Democrats and independents in order to win.

In the latest Gallup surveys, comprising over 6,000 interviews, 29% of adults classify themselves as Republicans, 41% as Democrats, and 30% as independents. As recently as the spring of 1983, when the nation was starting to recover from the recession, there were twice as many self-described Democrats (46%) as Republicans (23%).

The period between President Richard Nixon's resignation in August 1974 and the 1980 presidential campaign marked the Republican party's nadir since World War II. Except in isolated instances, GOP affiliation did not top the 23% level, while the Democrats neared 50%.

The Democrats' postwar high of 53% affiliation occurred in 1964, the year of President Lyndon Johnson's landslide victory over Senator Barry Goldwater. The GOP's postwar zenith was recorded in 1946, when about equal numbers of voters said they were Republicans (40%) and Democrats (39%).

The ascendancy of independent voters as an important political factor is a comparatively recent phenomenon. Far fewer than 30% claimed to be independents in surveys conducted in 1968 and earlier. Since then, independent status has been claimed by about three voters in ten.

Currently, the GOP is the minority party in most major demographic groups, with the exception of such traditional Republican bastions as college graduates, persons living in households in which the chief wage earner is employed in business or the professions, those whose total family income is $40,000 or more per year, and farmers. Conversely, proportionately more Democrats are found among blacks, Hispanics, those age 50 and older, persons whose education ended before graduating from high school, those from lower-income families, Jews, and unskilled workers.

President Reagan's "gender gap"—the propensity of fewer women than men to approve of his policies and programs—is reflected in their political allegiance. Not only does a larger proportion of women (43%) than men (38%) claim affiliation with the Democratic party, but slightly fewer women than men say they are Republicans.

## AUGUST 16
## WOMEN IN POLITICS

Interviewing Date: 7/27–30/84
Survey #239-G

*If your party nominated a woman to run for mayor or top official of your city or community, would you vote for her if she were qualified for the job?*

Yes ............................... 90%
No ................................. 7
No opinion ......................... 3

### By Sex
### *Male*

Yes ............................... 92%
No ................................. 6
No opinion ......................... 2

### *Female*

Yes ............................... 89%
No ................................. 8
No opinion ......................... 3

### National Trend
### *1975*

Yes ............................... 83%
No ................................. 14
No opinion ......................... 3

*If your party nominated a woman to run for governor of your state, would you vote for her if she were qualified for the job?*

Yes ............................... 87%
No ................................. 10
No opinion ......................... 3

### By Sex
### *Male*

Yes ............................... 89%
No ................................. 8
No opinion ......................... 3

### *Female*

Yes ............................... 86%
No ................................. 11
No opinion ......................... 3

### National Trend
### *1975*

Yes ............................... 81%
No ................................. 16
No opinion ......................... 3

*If your party nominated a woman to run for Congress from your district, would you vote for her if she were qualified for the job?*

Yes ................................91%
No ................................ 6
No opinion ........................ 3

### By Sex
#### Male

Yes ................................92%
No ................................ 5
No opinion ........................ 3

#### Female

Yes ................................91%
No ................................ 6
No opinion ........................ 3

### National Trend
#### 1975

Yes ................................88%
No ................................ 9
No opinion ........................ 3

*If your party nominated a woman for president, would you vote for her if she were qualified for the job?*

Yes ................................78%
No ................................17
No opinion ........................ 5

### By Sex
#### Male

Yes ................................77%
No ................................18
No opinion ........................ 5

#### Female

Yes ................................78%
No ................................17
No opinion ........................ 5

### Selected National Trend

|       | Yes | No | No opinion |
|-------|-----|-----|-----------|
| 1983 ............. | 80% | 16% | 4% |
| 1978 ............. | 76 | 19 | 5 |
| 1975 ............. | 73 | 23 | 4 |
| 1971 ............. | 66 | 29 | 5 |
| 1969 ............. | 54 | 39 | 7 |
| 1967 ............. | 57 | 39 | 4 |
| 1955 ............. | 52 | 44 | 4 |
| 1949 ............. | 48 | 48 | 4 |
| 1937 ............. | 31 | 65 | 4 |

*Do you think the country would be governed better or governed worse if more women held political office?*

Better ............................28%
Worse .............................15
No difference (volunteered) ...........46
No opinion ........................11

### By Sex
#### Male

Better ............................24%
Worse .............................15
No difference (volunteered) ...........48
No opinion ........................13

#### Female

Better ............................32%
Worse .............................14
No difference (volunteered) ...........44
No opinion ........................10

### National Trend
#### 1975

Better ............................33%
Worse .............................18
No difference (volunteered) ...........38
No opinion ........................11

Note: Geraldine Ferraro's selection as the Democratic vice-presidential candidate comes at a time of growing public willingness to vote for women for political office at the local, state, and national levels. In a just completed national survey, nine in ten Americans (90%) say they would vote for a qualified woman for top official or mayor of their city or community, an increase of 7 percentage points since a 1975 survey. A similar percentage, 87%, would vote for a woman for governor of their state, if she were qualified for the job; in 1975, the comparable figure was 81%. And today, 91% say they would vote for a woman from their district for Congress; in the earlier survey, 88% expressed a willingness to do so.

Public support for a woman for president also has increased from the high level recorded in 1975. Currently 78%, compared to 73% in 1975, say they would vote for a qualified woman. These recent findings represent a dramatic change from 1937, when the measurement was started, and only 31% would be willing to vote for a female president.

While support for a woman president today is two and one-half times as high as it was in 1937, nearly one-fourth of the electorate opposes the idea of a woman in the Oval Office or is undecided. A Gallup survey last month shed light on this opposition: voters think that a female president would stack up to a male in only one of six major areas of presidential responsibility, that of improving the quality of life. The public's greatest reservations about the qualifications of a female president are in foreign affairs, including dealing with the situation in Central America and handling our relations with the Soviet Union.

The growth since 1975 in willingness to vote for women has occurred about equally among both sexes, and, as in the earlier survey, the current support for women in political office is just as strong among men as among women. This uptrend in public support parallels an increase in the number of women actually holding office. Ten years ago, there were only sixteen women serving in Congress, all in the House. This year there are twenty-four women on Capitol Hill: twenty-two in the House and two in the Senate.

In governors' mansions, statehouses, and city halls, the rise in the number of female office holders has been even more impressive. In 1974 there were no female governors (Ella Grasso was elected governor of Connecticut that year but did not take office until 1975), 519 state representatives, and only 91 state senators. This year, one governor, 816 state representatives, and 177 state senators are women. Also, eighty-six cities with population over 30,000 have female mayors, in contrast with twelve a decade ago.

## AUGUST 19
## PRESIDENTIAL TRIAL HEATS

Interviewing Date: 8/10–13/84
Survey #240-G

*Asked of registered voters: Now I'd like to get your honest opinion on this next question. It doesn't make any difference to me how you vote; I only want to record your opinion accurately. If the presidential election were being held today, which would you vote for— the Republican candidates, Reagan and Bush, or the Democratic candidates, Mondale and Ferraro? [Those who were undecided or who named other candidates were then asked: As of today, do you lean more to Reagan and Bush, or to Mondale and Ferraro?]*

Reagan-Bush ........................52%
Mondale-Ferraro ....................41
Undecided ......................... 7

### By Sex
#### Male

Reagan-Bush ........................57%
Mondale-Ferraro ....................38
Undecided ......................... 5

#### Female

Reagan-Bush ........................46%
Mondale-Ferraro ....................45
Undecided ......................... 9

Note: When the Republican National Convention is called to order in Dallas, party members can take comfort in the knowledge that Ronald Reagan and George Bush, the GOP incumbents, hold an 11-percentage point lead over Democratic challengers Walter Mondale and Geraldine Ferraro. In the latest Gallup test election, the Reagan-Bush ticket is the choice of 52% of registered voters to 41% for Mondale-Ferraro, with 7% undecided. These findings are statistically unchanged from those of a Gallup survey conducted two weeks earlier in which the Republican ticket let the Democrats, 53% to 41%.

For a brief period following the July 16–19 Democratic convention in San Francisco, the Republican and Democratic slates were effectively tied for the lead. The latest findings, therefore, tend to confirm the tentative conclusion reached earlier that the GOP ticket has recovered some, but not all, of the ground it lost in the impact of the Democratic convention. Some political observers expect the Republican convention to boost the standings of Reagan-Bush, thereby widening the gap between the two tickets.

Most of Reagan-Bush's temporary loss to the Mondale ticket after the Democratic convention can be traced to the votes of women. In the July 19–20 survey, 52% of men and 41% of women voted for Reagan-Bush, a typical Reagan "gender gap." In the July 27–30 survey, the Reagan ticket was the choice, atypically, of equal proportions of men and women.

In the current survey, the gender gap has reappeared with 46% of women, compared to 57% of men—an 11-point gap—voting for the Reagan-Bush ticket. Similarly, 45% of women and 38% of men choose the Mondale-Ferraro slate. Thus on the basis of women's votes alone, the Republican and Democratic tickets are in a statistical deadlock, 46% to 45%. On the other hand, among men only, Reagan-Bush is a 19-point favorite over Mondale-Ferraro, 57% to 38%.

## AUGUST 23
## PARTY BETTER FOR PEACE AND PROSPERITY

Interviewing Date: 8/10–13/84
Survey #240-G

*Which political party do you think would be more likely to keep the United States out of World War III—the Republican party or the Democratic party?*

Republican ........................36%
Democratic ........................40
No difference (volunteered) ...........15
No opinion ........................ 9

### By Politics
#### *Republicans*

Republican ........................71%
Democratic ........................ 8
No difference (volunteered) ...........13
No opinion ........................ 8

#### *Democrats*

Republican ........................11%
Democratic ........................71
No difference (volunteered) ...........10
No opinion ........................ 8

#### *Independents*

Republican ........................33%
Democratic ........................35
No difference (volunteered) ...........23
No opinion ........................ 9

### Selected National Trend

|  | Republican party | Democratic party | No difference; no opinion |
|---|---|---|---|
| Apr. 1984 | 30% | 42% | 28% |
| Sept. 1983 | 26 | 39 | 35 |
| Oct. 1982 | 29 | 38 | 33 |
| Apr. 1981 | 29 | 34 | 37 |
| Sept. 1980 | 25 | 42 | 33 |
| Aug. 1976 | 29 | 32 | 39 |
| Sept. 1972 | 32 | 28 | 40 |
| Oct. 1968 | 37 | 24 | 39 |
| Oct. 1964 | 22 | 45 | 33 |
| Oct. 1960 | 40 | 25 | 35 |
| Oct. 1956 | 46 | 16 | 38 |
| Jan. 1952 | 36 | 15 | 49 |
| Sept. 1951 | 28 | 21 | 51 |

*Which political party—the Republican party or the Democratic party—do you think will do a better job of keeping the country prosperous?*

Republican . . . . . . . . . . . . . . . . . . . . . . . . 48%
Democratic . . . . . . . . . . . . . . . . . . . . . . . 36
No difference (volunteered) . . . . . . . . . . . 8
No opinion . . . . . . . . . . . . . . . . . . . . . . . . 8

## By Politics

### *Republicans*

Republican . . . . . . . . . . . . . . . . . . . . . . . . 87%
Democratic . . . . . . . . . . . . . . . . . . . . . . . 4
No difference (volunteered) . . . . . . . . . . . 4
No opinion . . . . . . . . . . . . . . . . . . . . . . . . 5

### *Democrats*

Republican . . . . . . . . . . . . . . . . . . . . . . . . 17%
Democratic . . . . . . . . . . . . . . . . . . . . . . . 69
No difference (volunteered) . . . . . . . . . . . 7
No opinion . . . . . . . . . . . . . . . . . . . . . . . . 7

### *Independents*

Republican . . . . . . . . . . . . . . . . . . . . . . . . 49%
Democratic . . . . . . . . . . . . . . . . . . . . . . . 26
No difference (volunteered) . . . . . . . . . . . 14
No opinion . . . . . . . . . . . . . . . . . . . . . . . . 11

### Selected National Trend

| | Republican party | Democratic party | No difference; no opinion |
|---|---|---|---|
| Apr. 1984 | 44% | 36% | 20% |
| Sept. 1983 | 33 | 40 | 27 |
| Oct. 1982 | 34 | 43 | 23 |
| Oct. 1981 | 40 | 31 | 29 |
| Apr. 1981 | 41 | 28 | 31 |
| Sept. 1980 | 35 | 36 | 29 |
| Aug. 1976 | 23 | 47 | 30 |
| Sept. 1972 | 38 | 35 | 27 |
| Oct. 1968 | 34 | 37 | 29 |
| Oct. 1964 | 21 | 53 | 26 |
| Oct. 1960 | 31 | 46 | 23 |
| Oct. 1956 | 39 | 39 | 22 |
| Jan. 1952 | 31 | 35 | 34 |
| Nov. 1951 | 29 | 37 | 34 |

Note: The Republican party not only is widely perceived as more likely than the Democratic party to keep the nation prosperous, but also it is now challenging the Democrats as the party more likely to keep the nation at peace. The significance of these findings is that the political party that leads on both these issues at election time has always won that election.

The latest Gallup Poll shows 48% of the public—the highest figure since these measurements began in 1951—saying the Republican party will do a better job of keeping the United States prosperous, while 36% name the Democratic party and 16% see little difference between the parties or do not offer an opinion. The Republicans have had a clear advantage over the Democrats on only three other occasions: twice during the early months of the Reagan administration in 1981, and again last April.

The GOP's current claim to the title, "party of prosperity," is strengthened by the fact that substantial numbers of Democrats in the survey (17%) desert their own party to vote for the Republican party as superior in this respect, compared to only 4% of Republicans who cite the Democratic party as better. Also, proportionately more Republicans are steadfast to the GOP (87%) than are Democrats loyal to their own party (69%), on doing a better job of keeping the country prosperous. Independents express a strong preference for the Republican party.

The Republican party's advantage on the prosperity issue earlier this year was offset by the Democratic party's substantial lead as being more likely to keep the nation at peace. In the latest survey, however, the GOP has moved to a position of statistical parity with the Democrats as the "party of peace." Currently, 40% say the Democratic party is stronger in this regard, 36% name the GOP, and 24% see no difference or have no opinion. (The 4 percentage points separating the two parties is not a statistically meaningful difference.) With only a few exceptions, the Democrats have held an edge on the peace issue for over a decade, with the lead changing hands at intervals before then.

Women are less likely (32%) than men (41%) to view the GOP as being better able to keep the country out of war. Women's views on this issue, other surveys have shown, contribute strongly to President Ronald Reagan's "gender gap."

## AUGUST 26
## SAFER WORLD/PERSONAL FINANCES

Interviewing Date: 6/29–7/2/84
Survey #236-G

*Do you think we live in a safer world now than we did four years ago, or not?*

Yes ................................20%
No ..................................68
Don't know ........................12

### By Politics
#### Republicans

Yes ................................37%
No ..................................50
Don't know ........................13

#### Democrats

Yes ................................12%
No ..................................78
Don't know ........................10

#### Independents

Yes ................................16%
No ..................................72
Don't know ........................12

*Would you say you and your family are better off now than you were four years ago, or worse off?*

Better ..............................48%*
Worse ..............................25
Same (volunteered) ................26

### By Sex
#### Male

Better ..............................51%
Worse ..............................23
Same (volunteered) ................25

*"No opinion," which adds to 1% nationally, is omitted.

#### Female

Better ..............................45%
Worse ..............................26
Same (volunteered) ................28

### By Ethnic Background
#### White

Better ..............................51%
Worse ..............................22
Same (volunteered) ................26

#### Nonwhite

Better ..............................24%
Worse ..............................48
Same (volunteered) ................27

#### Black

Better ..............................23%
Worse ..............................50
Same (volunteered) ................27

### By Education
#### College Graduate

Better ..............................58%
Worse ..............................16
Same (volunteered) ................25

#### College Incomplete

Better ..............................57%
Worse ..............................20
Same (volunteered) ................22

#### High-School Graduate

Better ..............................42%
Worse ..............................29
Same (volunteered) ................28

#### Less Than High-School Graduate

Better ..............................40%
Worse ..............................30
Same (volunteered) ................29

## By Region

### East

| | |
|---|---|
| Better | 43% |
| Worse | 27 |
| Same (volunteered) | 29 |

### Midwest

| | |
|---|---|
| Better | 43% |
| Worse | 28 |
| Same (volunteered) | 28 |

### South

| | |
|---|---|
| Better | 52% |
| Worse | 21 |
| Same (volunteered) | 25 |

### West

| | |
|---|---|
| Better | 55% |
| Worse | 25 |
| Same (volunteered) | 20 |

## By Age

### 18–29 Years

| | |
|---|---|
| Better | 59% |
| Worse | 17 |
| Same (volunteered) | 23 |

### 30–49 Years

| | |
|---|---|
| Better | 53% |
| Worse | 27 |
| Same (volunteered) | 19 |

### 50–64 Years

| | |
|---|---|
| Better | 36% |
| Worse | 33 |
| Same (volunteered) | 29 |

### 65 Years and Over

| | |
|---|---|
| Better | 34% |
| Worse | 23 |
| Same (volunteered) | 41 |

## By Income

### $40,000 and Over

| | |
|---|---|
| Better | 66% |
| Worse | 17 |
| Same (volunteered) | 16 |

### $30,000–$39,999

| | |
|---|---|
| Better | 57% |
| Worse | 15 |
| Same (volunteered) | 27 |

### $20,000–$29,999

| | |
|---|---|
| Better | 55% |
| Worse | 20 |
| Same (volunteered) | 23 |

### $10,000–$19,999

| | |
|---|---|
| Better | 42% |
| Worse | 27 |
| Same (volunteered) | 30 |

### Under $10,000

| | |
|---|---|
| Better | 29% |
| Worse | 42 |
| Same (volunteered) | 28 |

## By Politics

### Republicans

| | |
|---|---|
| Better | 66% |
| Worse | 10 |
| Same (volunteered) | 23 |

### Democrats

| | |
|---|---|
| Better | 33% |
| Worse | 37 |
| Same (volunteered) | 29 |

### Independents

| | |
|---|---|
| Better | 52% |
| Worse | 21 |
| Same (volunteered) | 25 |

Note: One of Ronald Reagan's most effective weapons during the 1980 campaign was to ask voters whether they were better off than they had been four years earlier. Their answer helped turn incumbent Jimmy Carter out of the White House.

Four years later, a strong 48% plurality says they are better off now than when President Reagan took office. In contrast, 25% state they are worse off, and 26% say their financial condition has not changed in the last four years. These figures are similar to those found in surveys earlier this year.

Although the public's overall appraisal of Reagan's record on the economy is favorable, the survey found wide disparities in the responses of people from different social, economic, and political backgrounds. The most obvious is politics. A 66% majority of Republicans thinks they are better off now than four years ago, while only half that proportion of Democrats (33%) agrees. A smaller majority of independents (52%) says they are better off.

Striking differences are also found on the basis of age, race, education, income, and sex. Almost twice the proportion of adults under 30 (59%) as those 65 and older (34%) says they are better off now than four years ago. Also, whites, men, persons who attended college, and those whose family income is $20,000 or more per year are more apt to return a favorable economic verdict than are persons with different backgrounds.

President Reagan's strong vote of confidence on the economic front may be at least partially offset by the public's perception that little progress has been made in the last four years to foster peace in the world. In his State of the Union address last January, the president said "restoration of economic growth and military deterrence" meant that the "United States is safer, stronger, and more secure in 1984 than before." But the public, by more than a 3-to-1 ratio, believes we live in a world that is less safe today than it was when Reagan took office.

Nationally, one voter in five (20%) says he or she lives in a safer world now, while 68% think the world is not any safer than it was in 1980. Even among Republicans, 50% believe the world is not safer, while 37% say it is. Small numbers of Democrats (12%) and independents (16%) state they live in a safer world than four years ago. Women's outlook, moreover, is somewhat more bleak than men's.

## AUGUST 30
## MOST IMPORTANT PROBLEM

Interviewing Date: 8/10–13/84
Survey #240-G

*What do you think is the most important problem facing this country today?*

| | Aug. 1–13, 1984 | June 1984 | Nov. 1983 |
|---|---|---|---|
| Unemployment . . . . . . | 23% | 26% | 32% |
| Threat of war; international tensions . . . . . . . . | 22 | 27 | 37 |
| High cost of living; taxes; high interest rates . . . . . . . . . . . | 18 | 14 | 11 |
| Excessive government spending; budget deficits . . . . . . . . . | 16 | 11 | 5 |
| Economy (general) . . | 8 | 3 | 3 |
| Crime . . . . . . . . . . . . | 4 | 3 | 2 |
| Moral decline in society . . . . . . . . . | 3 | 5 | 6 |
| Poverty; hunger . . . . . | 3 | 1 | * |
| Dissatisfaction with government . . . . . . | 3 | 2 | 3 |
| All others . . . . . . . . . . | 11 | 12 | 7 |
| Don't know . . . . . . . . | 3 | 2 | 3 |
| | 114%** | 106%** | 109%** |

*Less than 1%
**Total adds to more than 100% due to multiple responses.

*All persons who named a problem were then asked: Which political party do you think can do a better job of handling the problem you have just mentioned—the Republican party or the Democratic party?*

| | Aug. 10–13, 1984 | June 1984 | Nov. 1983 |
|---|---|---|---|
| Republican ......... | 39% | 33% | 28% |
| Democratic ......... | 37 | 35 | 35 |
| No difference (volunteered) ..... | 16 | 20 | 24 |
| No opinion ......... | 8 | 12 | 13 |

Note: Unemployment and international unrest, including the fear of war, continue to be the dominant concerns of the American people. But these problems have receded somewhat in recent months while high living costs and excessive government spending, including the federal budget deficit, have moved up among the nation's most urgent problems.

In the latest (mid-August) Gallup Poll, 23% cite unemployment, followed by 22% who mention international tensions and the threat of war. The high cost of living, including high interest rates and taxes, is cited by 18%, while government spending and the budget deficit are mentioned by 16%. Receiving single-digit tallies are the economy in general (8%), crime (4%), a perceived moral and religious decline in American society (3%), poverty and hunger (3%), and dissatisfaction with government (3%).

The latest figures are similar to those recorded in surveys in February and June, when the threat of war and unemployment also shared the spotlight as the nation's most serious problems. The current findings, however, are quite different from last November, when international tensions reached the highest level (37%) recorded since the end of the Vietnam War.

As was the case in the February and June surveys, the public is now evenly divided in their perceptions of which political party can do a better job of solving the problem they consider paramount. Only two percentage points separate the parties in each of the surveys this year—a statistically insignificant margin.

As shown in the table below, this question of the better party has been asked in Gallup surveys conducted in October in each of the last seven presidential election years. The results have invariably pointed to the winning candidate's party.

In October 1980, for example, the Republican party had a 40% to 31% lead, pointing to Ronald Reagan's victory over President Jimmy Carter in the November election. Similarly, the Democratic party was the choice of 43% to 23% for the Republican party in October 1976, presaging Carter's win over incumbent Gerald Ford. Although the Democrats' 2-point edge over the GOP in 1960 is not statistically meaningful, John Kennedy, the Democratic candidate, beat his Republican challenger Richard Nixon by merely two-tenths of one percent of the popular vote.

## October Survey Results

### (Party Better Able To Handle Top Problem)

| Election year | Winning candidate | Republican | Democratic | No difference; no opinion |
|---|---|---|---|---|
| 1980 | Reagan (R) | 40% | 31% | 29% |
| 1976 | Carter (D) | 23 | 43 | 34 |
| 1972 | Nixon (R) | 39 | 29 | 32 |
| 1968 | Nixon (R) | 34 | 29 | 37 |
| 1964 | Johnson (D) | 23 | 49 | 28 |
| 1960 | Kennedy (D) | 27 | 29 | 44 |
| 1956 | Eisenhower (R) | 33 | 25 | 42 |

## SEPTEMBER 2
## REAGAN VS. MONDALE

Interviewing Date: 8/10–13/84
Survey #240-G

*Regardless of which man you happen to prefer for president—Ronald Reagan or Walter Mondale—please tell me which you feel would do a better job of handling each of these problems?*

| | Ronald Reagan | Walter Mondale | No difference; no opinion |
|---|---|---|---|
| Keeping the country prosperous | 53% | 33% | 14% |
| Keeping inflation down | 53 | 32 | 15 |
| Improving the economy | 52 | 36 | 12 |

| | | | |
|---|---|---|---|
| Making people proud to be Americans | 51 | 28 | 21 |
| Handling foreign relations | 50 | 33 | 17 |
| Dealing with Soviet Union | 48 | 34 | 18 |
| Increasing respect for United States overseas | 48 | 34 | 18 |
| Reducing unemployment | 45 | 41 | 14 |
| Building trust in government | 41 | 36 | 23 |
| Dealing with situation in Central America | 41 | 35 | 24 |
| Reducing federal budget deficit | 39 | 35 | 26 |
| Spending taxpayers' money wisely | 38 | 37 | 25 |
| Keeping the country out of war | 35 | 47 | 18 |
| Improving the environment and dealing with environmental issues | 31 | 47 | 22 |
| Helping the poor and needy | 25 | 60 | 15 |
| Improving things for minorities, including blacks and Hispanics | 25 | 54 | 21 |
| Improving women's rights | 20 | 63 | 17 |

Note: As the 1984 presidential campaign gets under way, President Ronald Reagan holds an advantage over Democratic challenger Walter Mondale among voters as better able to deal with seven of seventeen key issues. In addition, the two men are not far apart on five, and Mondale is given the edge on the remaining five issues.

On economic issues—paramount in the minds of voters at present—Reagan holds big leads, since he is perceived by voters as better able to keep the country prosperous, keep the inflation rate down, and improve the economy in general. Reagan leads his Democratic opponent, though by smaller margins, on "making people proud to be Americans," handling foreign relations, dealing with the Soviet Union, and increasing respect for the United States overseas.

The two rivals are in close contention in their perceived ability to deal with the situation in Central America, reduce unemployment, build trust in the government, reduce the federal budget deficit, and spend taxpayers' money wisely. However, Mondale rises to the fore on these voter issues: keeping the country out of war, improving the environment, improving things for minorities, helping the needy, and improving women's rights.

## SEPTEMBER 6
## PRESIDENTIAL TRIAL HEATS

Interviewing Date: 7/27–30; 8/10–13/84
Survey #239-G; 240-G

*Asked of registered voters: Now I'd like to get your honest opinion on this next question. It doesn't make any difference to me how you vote; I only want to record your opinion accurately. If the presidential election were being held today, which would you vote for— the Republican candidates, Reagan and Bush, or the Democratic candidates, Mondale and Ferraro? [Those who were undecided or who named other candidates were then asked: As of today, do you lean more to Reagan and Bush, or to Mondale and Ferraro?]*

Reagan–Bush ........................53%
Mondale–Ferraro ....................41
Undecided ......................... 6

### By Sex
#### Male

Reagan–Bush ........................55%
Mondale–Ferraro ....................40
Undecided ......................... 5

### Female

Reagan–Bush ........................50%
Mondale–Ferraro ....................43
Undecided ........................ 7

## By Ethnic Background
### White

Reagan–Bush ........................58%
Mondale–Ferraro ....................36
Undecided ........................ 6

### Black

Reagan–Bush ........................ 7%
Mondale–Ferraro ....................87
Undecided ........................ 6

## By Education
### College Graduate

Reagan–Bush ........................58%
Mondale–Ferraro ....................38
Undecided ........................ 4

### College Incomplete

Reagan–Bush ........................62%
Mondale–Ferraro ....................33
Undecided ........................ 5

### High-School Graduate

Reagan–Bush ........................50%
Mondale–Ferraro ....................43
Undecided ........................ 7

### Less Than High-School Graduate

Reagan–Bush ........................39%
Mondale–Ferraro ....................52
Undecided ........................ 9

## By Region
### East

Reagan–Bush ........................48%
Mondale–Ferraro ....................43
Undecided ........................ 9

### Midwest

Reagan–Bush ........................53%
Mondale–Ferraro ....................42
Undecided ........................ 5

### South

Reagan–Bush ........................54%
Mondale–Ferraro ....................40
Undecided ........................ 6

### West

Reagan–Bush ........................55%
Mondale–Ferraro ....................41
Undecided ........................ 4

## By Age
### 18–29 Years

Reagan–Bush ........................53%
Mondale–Ferraro ....................44
Undecided ........................ 3

### 30–49 Years

Reagan–Bush ........................53%
Mondale–Ferraro ....................40
Undecided ........................ 7

### 50–64 Years

Reagan–Bush ........................54%
Mondale–Ferraro ....................41
Undecided ........................ 5

### 65 Years and Over

Reagan–Bush ........................48%
Mondale–Ferraro ....................43
Undecided ........................ 9

## By Income
### $40,000 and Over

Reagan–Bush ........................66%
Mondale–Ferraro ....................32
Undecided ........................ 2

### $30,000–$39,999

Reagan–Bush ........................59%
Mondale–Ferraro ....................32
Undecided .......................... 9

### $20,000–$29,999

Reagan–Bush ........................57%
Mondale–Ferraro ....................39
Undecided .......................... 4

### $10,000–$19,999

Reagan–Bush ........................50%
Mondale–Ferraro ....................43
Undecided .......................... 7

### Under $10,000

Reagan–Bush ........................34%
Mondale–Ferraro ....................59
Undecided .......................... 7

## By Politics
### Republicans

Reagan–Bush ........................93%
Mondale–Ferraro .................... 5
Undecided .......................... 2

### Democrats

Reagan–Bush ........................18%
Mondale–Ferraro ....................77
Undecided .......................... 5

### Independents

Reagan–Bush ........................55%
Mondale–Ferraro ....................33
Undecided .........................12

## By Religion
### Protestants

Reagan–Bush ........................56%
Mondale–Ferraro ....................39
Undecided .......................... 5

### Catholics

Reagan–Bush ........................48%
Mondale–Ferraro ....................43
Undecided .......................... 9

## By Occupation
### Professional and Business

Reagan–Bush ........................62%
Mondale–Ferraro ....................34
Undecided .......................... 4

### Clerical and Sales

Reagan–Bush ........................51%
Mondale–Ferraro ....................45
Undecided .......................... 4

### Blue Collar

Reagan–Bush ........................48%
Mondale–Ferraro ....................44
Undecided .......................... 8

### Blue Collar—Skilled

Reagan–Bush ........................52%
Mondale–Ferraro ....................41
Undecided .......................... 7

### Blue Collar—Unskilled

Reagan–Bush ........................43%
Mondale–Ferraro ....................48
Undecided .......................... 9

## By Labor Union Household
### Labor Union Members

Reagan–Bush ........................42%
Mondale–Ferraro ....................52
Undecided .......................... 6

### Nonlabor Union Members

Reagan–Bush ........................55%
Mondale–Ferraro ....................39
Undecided .......................... 6

Note: One of the key factors underlying the strength of the Republican slate is the broad diversity of its appeal to voters from widely varying backgrounds. In the latest two Gallup Polls, the Reagan-Bush ticket holds a 53%-to-41% lead over the Mondale-Ferraro ticket, a 12-percentage point advantage nationwide. Not only does the Reagan-Bush ticket prevail among such traditional Republican bastions as professional and business people, the college educated, and those with high incomes, but voters in many traditionally Democratic groups also prefer the GOP.

Such interparty appeal is necessary for Republican candidates for national office because of the GOP's numerical minority in the electorate. Not only must these candidates win the votes of the great majority of their own party members, but they must appeal to a majority of independents and significant numbers of Democrats as well. At present, the Reagan-Bush ticket qualifies on each of these points. Some 93% of Republicans say they would vote for their party's nominees if the election were being held today. This sentiment is expressed by a 55% majority of independents and by about one Democratic voter in five (18%).

As reported recently, approximately 28% of adults age 18 and older currently claim allegiance to the Republican party, while 42% say they are Democrats and 30%, independents. The diversity of the Republican ticket's appeal is reflected in the fact that the Mondale-Ferraro team is presently favored in only a handful of population groups: blacks (87%), persons whose formal education ended before graduation from high school (52%), those whose family income is less than $10,000 per year (59%), members of labor union households (52%), and, not surprisingly, Democrats (77%).

## SEPTEMBER 9
## REAGAN VS. MONDALE—
## PUBLIC IMAGES

Interviewing Date: 8/10–13/84
Survey #240-G

*Here is a list of terms—shown as pairs of opposites—that have been used to describe Ronald Reagan (Walter Mondale). From each pair of opposites, would you select the term which you feel best describes Reagan (Mondale)?*

|  | Reagan | Mondale |
|---|---|---|
| Has strong leadership qualities | 64% | 42% |
| Colorful, interesting personality | 63 | 36 |
| Says what he believes even if unpopular | 51 | 36 |
| Puts country's interests ahead of politics | 46 | 34 |
| Cares about needs and problems of women | 68 | 42 |
| Cares about needs and problems of blacks | 60 | 41 |
| Sides with average citizen | 49 | 32 |
| Likable person | 67 | 57 |
| Religious person | 52 | 43 |
| Offers imaginative, innovative solutions to national problems | 47 | 39 |
| Man of high moral principles | 68 | 62 |
| Bright, intelligent | 66 | 63 |
| Addresses critical issues of 1980s and 1990s | 46 | 43 |

Note: Dramatic differences are noted in the public images of the presidential candidates, with President Ronald Reagan winning on perceived leadership qualities and Walter Mondale leading on the "fairness" issue. Both men score about equally on basic character traits and on dealing with emerging issues.

The president has a clear lead over Mondale on demonstrating strong leadership qualities and the related issues of "saying what he believes even if unpopular" and "putting the country's interests ahead of politics." Former Vice-President Mondale holds wide leads over his rival on attributes related to the fairness issue: caring about the needs and problems of women and blacks, and siding with the average citizen.

On basic personality or character traits, the two men are not far apart. These include being a "likable person," a "religious person," a "man of high moral principles," and bright and intelligent. The two candidates are also close on issues related to moving the nation ahead: "offering imaginative, innovative solutions to national problems" and "addressing the critical issues of the 1980s and 1990s."

Issues as well as personality factors will play a key role in the outcome on November 6. As reported earlier, President Reagan is perceived as better able to handle key economic issues, such as keeping the country prosperous and keeping inflation down. But Reagan is perceived as little more able than Mondale to reduce the federal budget deficit and to spend tax money wisely, and as substantially less able than Mondale to reduce unemployment. Mondale scores heavily on helping the needy and improving women's rights.

## SEPTEMBER 13
## PERSONALITY FACTOR OF CANDIDATES

Interviewing Date: 7/27–30/84
Survey #239-G

> All persons in the survey were handed a card and asked: You will note that the ten boxes on this scale go from the highest position of +5 for someone you have a very favorable opinion of all the way down to the lowest position of −5 for someone you have a very unfavorable opinion of. How far up or down the scale would you rate Ronald Reagan and Walter Mondale?

|  | Highly favorable ratings ( +5, +4) |
| --- | --- |
| *July 27–30, 1984* | |
| Reagan | 42% |
| Mondale | 26 |
| *August 1980* | |
| Reagan | 31% |
| Carter | 20 |
| *September 1976* | |
| Carter | 41% |
| Ford | 28 |
| *August 1972* | |
| Nixon | 40% |
| McGovern | 23 |
| *September 1968* | |
| Nixon | 38% |
| Humphrey | 25 |
| *August 1964* | |
| Johnson | 55% |
| Goldwater | 21 |
| *August 1960* | |
| Nixon | 38% |
| Kennedy | 39 |
| *August 1956* | |
| Eisenhower | 66% |
| Stevenson | 28 |

Note: President Ronald Reagan leads his Democratic rival Walter Mondale on the personality factor, with four in ten voters (42%) indicating they have a highly favorable opinion of the president, compared to 26% for Mondale. The president is running 11 percentage points ahead of his pace in August 1980, when he received a highly favorable vote of 31% on this key election barometer. Mondale is running slightly ahead of the 1980 Democratic candidate, President Jimmy Carter, who had a rating of 20% four years ago.

The personality factor, together with issues and party loyalty, has proved to be a key barometer of presidential election results, as determined by Gallup surveys over the last three decades. In each of the last seven presidential elections, the personality ratings given the leading candidates in the months preceding the election have pointed to the division of the popular vote in November.

## SEPTEMBER 16
## PRESIDENTIAL TRIAL HEATS

Interviewing Date: 9/7–10/84
Survey #241-G

> Asked of registered voters: Now I'd like to get your honest opinion on this next question. It doesn't make any difference to me how you vote; I only want to record your opinion accurately. If the presidential election were being held today, which would you vote for— the Republican candidates, Reagan and Bush, or the Democratic candidates, Mondale and Ferraro? [Those who were undecided or who

*named other candidates were then asked: As
of today, do you lean more to Reagan and
Bush, or to Mondale and Ferraro?]*

Reagan-Bush ........................56%
Mondale-Ferraro ...................37
Other; undecided ................. 7

### By Sex
#### Male

Reagan-Bush ........................59%
Mondale-Ferraro ...................33
Other; undecided ................. 8

#### Female

Reagan-Bush ........................53%
Mondale-Ferraro ...................41
Other; undecided ................. 6

### By Ethnic Background
#### White

Reagan-Bush ........................61%
Mondale-Ferraro ...................33
Other; undecided ................. 6

#### Nonwhite

Reagan-Bush ........................20%
Mondale-Ferraro ...................70
Other; undecided ..................10

#### Black

Reagan-Bush ........................14%
Mondale-Ferraro ...................75
Other; undecided ..................11

### By Education
#### College Graduate

Reagan-Bush ........................56%
Mondale-Ferraro ...................38
Other; undecided ................. 6

#### College Incomplete

Reagan-Bush ........................61%
Mondale-Ferraro ...................32
Other; undecided ................. 7

#### High-School Graduate

Reagan-Bush ........................61%
Mondale-Ferraro ...................32
Other; undecided ................. 7

#### Less Than High-School Graduate

Reagan-Bush ........................43%
Mondale-Ferraro ...................49
Other; undecided ................. 8

### By Region
#### East

Reagan-Bush ........................55%
Mondale-Ferraro ...................37
Other; undecided ................. 8

#### Midwest

Reagan-Bush ........................57%
Mondale-Ferraro ...................37
Other; undecided ................. 6

#### South

Reagan-Bush ........................54%
Mondale-Ferraro ...................38
Other; undecided ................. 8

#### West

Reagan-Bush ........................61%
Mondale-Ferraro ...................34
Other; undecided ................. 5

### By Age
#### 18–24 Years

Reagan-Bush ........................57%
Mondale-Ferraro ...................37
Other; undecided ................. 6

#### 25–29 Years

Reagan-Bush ........................65%
Mondale-Ferraro ...................26
Other; undecided ................. 9

### 30–49 Years

Reagan-Bush ........................59%
Mondale-Ferraro ....................36
Other; undecided ................... 5

### 50–64 Years

Reagan-Bush ........................53%
Mondale-Ferraro ....................40
Other; undecided ................... 7

### 65 Years and Over

Reagan-Bush ........................50%
Mondale-Ferraro ....................40
Other; undecided ....................10

## By Income

### $40,000 and Over

Reagan-Bush ........................62%
Mondale-Ferraro ....................31
Other; undecided ................... 7

### $30,000–$39,999

Reagan-Bush ........................61%
Mondale-Ferraro ....................36
Other; undecided ................... 3

### $20,000–$29,999

Reagan-Bush ........................65%
Mondale-Ferraro ....................31
Other; undecided ................... 4

### $10,000–$19,999

Reagan-Bush ........................51%
Mondale-Ferraro ....................40
Other; undecided ................... 9

### Under $10,000

Reagan-Bush ........................43%
Mondale-Ferraro ....................49
Other; undecided ................... 8

## By Politics

### Republicans

Reagan-Bush ........................93%
Mondale-Ferraro .................... 4
Other; undecided ................... 3

### Democrats

Reagan-Bush ........................21%
Mondale-Ferraro ....................71
Other; undecided ................... 8

### Independents

Reagan-Bush ........................62%
Mondale-Ferraro ....................31
Other; undecided ................... 7

## By Religion

### Protestants

Reagan-Bush ........................60%
Mondale-Ferraro ....................35
Other; undecided ................... 5

### Catholics

Reagan-Bush ........................54%
Mondale-Ferraro ....................39
Other; undecided ................... 7

## By Occupation

### Professional and Business

Reagan-Bush ........................64%
Mondale-Ferraro ....................31
Other; undecided ................... 5

### Clerical and Sales

Reagan-Bush ........................63%
Mondale-Ferraro ....................32
Other; undecided ................... 5

### Manual Workers

Reagan-Bush ........................55%
Mondale-Ferraro ....................38
Other; undecided ................... 7

### Nonlabor Force

Reagan-Bush .........................44%
Mondale-Ferraro .....................46
Other; undecided ....................10

## By Community Size
### One Million and Over

Reagan-Bush .........................48%
Mondale-Ferraro .....................41
Other; undecided ....................11

### 500,000–999,999

Reagan-Bush .........................53%
Mondale-Ferraro .....................45
Other; undecided .................... 2

### 50,000–499,999

Reagan-Bush .........................58%
Mondale-Ferraro .....................40
Other; undecided .................... 2

### 2,500–49,999

Reagan-Bush .........................60%
Mondale-Ferraro .....................34
Other; undecided .................... 6

### Under 2,500; Rural

Reagan-Bush .........................67%
Mondale-Ferraro .....................27
Other; undecided .................... 6

## By Labor Union Household
### Labor Union Members

Reagan-Bush .........................48%
Mondale-Ferraro .....................49
Other; undecided .................... 3

### Nonlabor Union Members

Reagan-Bush .........................58%
Mondale-Ferraro .....................34
Other; undecided .................... 8

## Selected National Trend

|  | Reagan-Bush | Mondale-Ferraro | Other; undecided |
|---|---|---|---|
| **Republican Convention** | | | |
| Aug. 10–13 ...... | 52% | 41% | 7% |
| July 27–30 ....... | 53 | 41 | 6 |
| July 19–20* ...... | 46 | 48 | 6 |
| **Democratic Convention** | | | |
| July 13–16 ....... | 53% | 39% | 8% |
| July 12–13* ...... | 49 | 43 | 8 |
| **Ferraro Announcement**\*\* | | | |
| July 6–9 ......... | 54% | 38% | 8% |
| June 29–July 2 ... | 51 | 43 | 6 |
| June 22–25 ...... | 55 | 38 | 7 |

*For *Newsweek*
**Test elections prior to the Ferraro announcement (July 11) placed the heads of the tickets, Reagan and Mondale, against each other.

*Also asked of the sample: Right now, how strongly do you feel about your choice—very strongly, fairly strongly, or not at all strongly?*

Total Reagan-Bush ...................56%
  Very strongly .................38
  Fairly strongly .................12
  Not at all strongly ............. 6
Total Mondale-Ferraro .................37
  Very strongly .................22
  Fairly strongly .................10
  Not at all strongly ............. 5
Other; undecided .................... 7

## By Sex
### Male

Total Reagan-Bush ...................59%
  Very strongly .................42
  Fairly strongly .................12
  Not at all strongly ............. 5

Total Mondale-Ferraro . . . . . . . . . . . . . . . .32
   Very strongly . . . . . . . . . . . . . . . .20
   Fairly strongly . . . . . . . . . . . . . . . 9
   Not at all strongly . . . . . . . . . . . . . 3
Other; undecided . . . . . . . . . . . . . . . . . . . 9

### Female

Total Reagan-Bush . . . . . . . . . . . . . . . . . . .53%
   Very strongly . . . . . . . . . . . . . . . .34
   Fairly strongly . . . . . . . . . . . . . . . .13
   Not at all strongly . . . . . . . . . . . . 6
Total Mondale-Ferraro . . . . . . . . . . . . . . . .41
   Very strongly . . . . . . . . . . . . . . . .22
   Fairly strongly . . . . . . . . . . . . . . . .12
   Not at all strongly . . . . . . . . . . . . . 7
Other; undecided . . . . . . . . . . . . . . . . . . . 6

## By Ethnic Background
### White

Total Reagan-Bush . . . . . . . . . . . . . . . . . . .61%
   Very strongly . . . . . . . . . . . . . . . .41
   Fairly strongly . . . . . . . . . . . . . . . .14
   Not at all strongly . . . . . . . . . . . . . 6
Total Mondale-Ferraro . . . . . . . . . . . . . . . .33
   Very strongly . . . . . . . . . . . . . . . .18
   Fairly strongly . . . . . . . . . . . . . . . .10
   Not at all strongly . . . . . . . . . . . . . 5
Other; undecided . . . . . . . . . . . . . . . . . . . 6

### Nonwhite

Total Reagan-Bush . . . . . . . . . . . . . . . . . . .20%
   Very strongly . . . . . . . . . . . . . . . .14
   Fairly strongly . . . . . . . . . . . . . . . 4
   Not at all strongly . . . . . . . . . . . . . 2
Total Mondale-Ferraro . . . . . . . . . . . . . . . .70
   Very strongly . . . . . . . . . . . . . . . .53
   Fairly strongly . . . . . . . . . . . . . . . .12
   Not at all strongly . . . . . . . . . . . . . 5
Other; undecided . . . . . . . . . . . . . . . . . . .10

### Black

Total Reagan-Bush . . . . . . . . . . . . . . . . . . .14%
   Very strongly . . . . . . . . . . . . . . . .11
   Fairly strongly . . . . . . . . . . . . . . . 3
   Not at all strongly . . . . . . . . . . . . . *

Total Mondale-Ferraro . . . . . . . . . . . . . . . .75
   Very strongly . . . . . . . . . . . . . . . .59
   Fairly strongly . . . . . . . . . . . . . . . .11
   Not at all strongly . . . . . . . . . . . . . 5
Other; undecided . . . . . . . . . . . . . . . . . . .11

*Less than 1%

## By Education
### College Graduate

Total Reagan-Bush . . . . . . . . . . . . . . . . . . .56%
   Very strongly . . . . . . . . . . . . . . . .42
   Fairly strongly . . . . . . . . . . . . . . . 8
   Not at all strongly . . . . . . . . . . . . . 6
Total Mondale-Ferraro . . . . . . . . . . . . . . . .38
   Very strongly . . . . . . . . . . . . . . . .27
   Fairly strongly . . . . . . . . . . . . . . . 7
   Not at all strongly . . . . . . . . . . . . . 4
Other; undecided . . . . . . . . . . . . . . . . . . . 6

### College Incomplete

Total Reagan-Bush . . . . . . . . . . . . . . . . . . .61%
   Very strongly . . . . . . . . . . . . . . . .42
   Fairly strongly . . . . . . . . . . . . . . . .13
   Not at all strongly . . . . . . . . . . . . . 6
Total Mondale-Ferraro . . . . . . . . . . . . . . . .32
   Very strongly . . . . . . . . . . . . . . . .19
   Fairly strongly . . . . . . . . . . . . . . . 8
   Not at all strongly . . . . . . . . . . . . . 5
Other; undecided . . . . . . . . . . . . . . . . . . . 7

### High-School Graduate

Total Reagan-Bush . . . . . . . . . . . . . . . . . . .61%
   Very strongly . . . . . . . . . . . . . . . .38
   Fairly strongly . . . . . . . . . . . . . . . .17
   Not at all strongly . . . . . . . . . . . . . 6
Total Mondale-Ferraro . . . . . . . . . . . . . . . .32
   Very strongly . . . . . . . . . . . . . . . .18
   Fairly strongly . . . . . . . . . . . . . . . 9
   Not at all strongly . . . . . . . . . . . . . 5
Other; undecided . . . . . . . . . . . . . . . . . . . 7

### Less Than High-School Graduate

Total Reagan-Bush . . . . . . . . . . . . . . . . . . .43%
   Very strongly . . . . . . . . . . . . . . . .30
   Fairly strongly . . . . . . . . . . . . . . . .10
   Not at all strongly . . . . . . . . . . . . . 3

Total Mondale-Ferraro . . . . . . . . . . . . . . . .49
   Very strongly . . . . . . . . . . . . . . . .26
   Fairly strongly . . . . . . . . . . . . . . . .18
   Not at all strongly . . . . . . . . . . . . . 5
Other; undecided . . . . . . . . . . . . . . . . . . 8

## By Region

### East

Total Reagan-Bush . . . . . . . . . . . . . . . . . .55%
   Very strongly . . . . . . . . . . . . . . . .39
   Fairly strongly . . . . . . . . . . . . . . . 9
   Not at all strongly . . . . . . . . . . . . . 7
Total Mondale-Ferraro . . . . . . . . . . . . . . . .37
   Very strongly . . . . . . . . . . . . . . . .24
   Fairly strongly . . . . . . . . . . . . . . . .10
   Not at all strongly . . . . . . . . . . . . . 3
Other; undecided . . . . . . . . . . . . . . . . . . 8

### Midwest

Total Reagan-Bush . . . . . . . . . . . . . . . . . .57%
   Very strongly . . . . . . . . . . . . . . . .38
   Fairly strongly . . . . . . . . . . . . . . .14
   Not at all strongly . . . . . . . . . . . . . 5
Total Mondale-Ferraro . . . . . . . . . . . . . . . .37
   Very strongly . . . . . . . . . . . . . . . .22
   Fairly strongly . . . . . . . . . . . . . . . 9
   Not at all strongly . . . . . . . . . . . . . 6
Other; undecided . . . . . . . . . . . . . . . . . . 6

### South

Total Reagan-Bush . . . . . . . . . . . . . . . . . .54%
   Very strongly . . . . . . . . . . . . . . . .36
   Fairly strongly . . . . . . . . . . . . . . .13
   Not at all strongly . . . . . . . . . . . . . 5
Total Mondale-Ferraro . . . . . . . . . . . . . . . .38
   Very strongly . . . . . . . . . . . . . . . .21
   Fairly strongly . . . . . . . . . . . . . . .13
   Not at all strongly . . . . . . . . . . . . . 4
Other; undecided . . . . . . . . . . . . . . . . . . 8

### West

Total Reagan-Bush . . . . . . . . . . . . . . . . . .61%
   Very strongly . . . . . . . . . . . . . . . .41
   Fairly strongly . . . . . . . . . . . . . . .14
   Not at all strongly . . . . . . . . . . . . . 6

Total Mondale-Ferraro . . . . . . . . . . . . . . . .34
   Very strongly . . . . . . . . . . . . . . . .20
   Fairly strongly . . . . . . . . . . . . . . . 8
   Not at all strongly . . . . . . . . . . . . . 6
Other; undecided . . . . . . . . . . . . . . . . . . 5

## By Age

### 18–24 Years

Total Reagan-Bush . . . . . . . . . . . . . . . . . .57%
   Very strongly . . . . . . . . . . . . . . . .31
   Fairly strongly . . . . . . . . . . . . . . .20
   Not at all strongly . . . . . . . . . . . . . 6
Total Mondale-Ferraro . . . . . . . . . . . . . . . .37
   Very strongly . . . . . . . . . . . . . . . .20
   Fairly strongly . . . . . . . . . . . . . . .13
   Not at all strongly . . . . . . . . . . . . . 4
Other; undecided . . . . . . . . . . . . . . . . . . 6

### 25–29 Years

Total Reagan-Bush . . . . . . . . . . . . . . . . . .65%
   Very strongly . . . . . . . . . . . . . . . .44
   Fairly strongly . . . . . . . . . . . . . . .15
   Not at all strongly . . . . . . . . . . . . . 6
Total Mondale-Ferraro . . . . . . . . . . . . . . . .26
   Very strongly . . . . . . . . . . . . . . . .11
   Fairly strongly . . . . . . . . . . . . . . .12
   Not at all strongly . . . . . . . . . . . . . 3
Other; undecided . . . . . . . . . . . . . . . . . . 9

### 30–49 Years

Total Reagan-Bush . . . . . . . . . . . . . . . . . .59%
   Very strongly . . . . . . . . . . . . . . . .40
   Fairly strongly . . . . . . . . . . . . . . .13
   Not at all strongly . . . . . . . . . . . . . 6
Total Mondale-Ferraro . . . . . . . . . . . . . . . .36
   Very strongly . . . . . . . . . . . . . . . .24
   Fairly strongly . . . . . . . . . . . . . . . 9
   Not at all strongly . . . . . . . . . . . . . 3
Other; undecided . . . . . . . . . . . . . . . . . . 5

### 50–64 Years

Total Reagan-Bush . . . . . . . . . . . . . . . . . .53%
   Very strongly . . . . . . . . . . . . . . . .38
   Fairly strongly . . . . . . . . . . . . . . .10
   Not at all strongly . . . . . . . . . . . . . 5

Total Mondale-Ferraro . . . . . . . . . . . . . . . 40
   Very strongly . . . . . . . . . . . . . . . . . 24
   Fairly strongly . . . . . . . . . . . . . . . . 11
   Not at all strongly . . . . . . . . . . . . . 5
Other; undecided . . . . . . . . . . . . . . . . . . . 7

### 65 Years and Over

Total Reagan-Bush . . . . . . . . . . . . . . . . . . 50%
   Very strongly . . . . . . . . . . . . . . . . . 35
   Fairly strongly . . . . . . . . . . . . . . . . 9
   Not at all strongly . . . . . . . . . . . . . 6
Total Mondale-Ferraro . . . . . . . . . . . . . . . 40
   Very strongly . . . . . . . . . . . . . . . . . 22
   Fairly strongly . . . . . . . . . . . . . . . . 11
   Not at all strongly . . . . . . . . . . . . . 7
Other; undecided . . . . . . . . . . . . . . . . . . . 10

## By Income

### $40,000 and Over

Total Reagan-Bush . . . . . . . . . . . . . . . . . . 62%
   Very strongly . . . . . . . . . . . . . . . . . 44
   Fairly strongly . . . . . . . . . . . . . . . . 12
   Not at all strongly . . . . . . . . . . . . . 6
Total Mondale-Ferraro . . . . . . . . . . . . . . . 31
   Very strongly . . . . . . . . . . . . . . . . . 21
   Fairly strongly . . . . . . . . . . . . . . . . 8
   Not at all strongly . . . . . . . . . . . . . 2
Other; undecided . . . . . . . . . . . . . . . . . . . 7

### $30,000–$39,999

Total Reagan-Bush . . . . . . . . . . . . . . . . . . 61%
   Very strongly . . . . . . . . . . . . . . . . . 45
   Fairly strongly . . . . . . . . . . . . . . . . 12
   Not at all strongly . . . . . . . . . . . . . 4
Total Mondale-Ferraro . . . . . . . . . . . . . . . 36
   Very strongly . . . . . . . . . . . . . . . . . 23
   Fairly strongly . . . . . . . . . . . . . . . . 8
   Not at all strongly . . . . . . . . . . . . . 5
Other; undecided . . . . . . . . . . . . . . . . . . . 3

### $20,000–$29,999

Total Reagan-Bush . . . . . . . . . . . . . . . . . . 65%
   Very strongly . . . . . . . . . . . . . . . . . 45
   Fairly strongly . . . . . . . . . . . . . . . . 11
   Not at all strongly . . . . . . . . . . . . . 9

Total Mondale-Ferraro . . . . . . . . . . . . . . . 31
   Very strongly . . . . . . . . . . . . . . . . . 17
   Fairly strongly . . . . . . . . . . . . . . . . 10
   Not at all strongly . . . . . . . . . . . . . 4
Other; undecided . . . . . . . . . . . . . . . . . . . 4

### $10,000–$19,999

Total Reagan-Bush . . . . . . . . . . . . . . . . . . 51%
   Very strongly . . . . . . . . . . . . . . . . . 33
   Fairly strongly . . . . . . . . . . . . . . . . 13
   Not at all strongly . . . . . . . . . . . . . 5
Total Mondale-Ferraro . . . . . . . . . . . . . . . 40
   Very strongly . . . . . . . . . . . . . . . . . 23
   Fairly strongly . . . . . . . . . . . . . . . . 12
   Not at all strongly . . . . . . . . . . . . . 5
Other; undecided . . . . . . . . . . . . . . . . . . . 9

### Under $10,000

Total Reagan-Bush . . . . . . . . . . . . . . . . . . 43%
   Very strongly . . . . . . . . . . . . . . . . . 27
   Fairly strongly . . . . . . . . . . . . . . . . 13
   Not at all strongly . . . . . . . . . . . . . 3
Total Mondale-Ferraro . . . . . . . . . . . . . . . 49
   Very strongly . . . . . . . . . . . . . . . . . 28
   Fairly strongly . . . . . . . . . . . . . . . . 13
   Not at all strongly . . . . . . . . . . . . . 8
Other; undecided . . . . . . . . . . . . . . . . . . . 8

## By Politics

### Republicans

Total Reagan-Bush . . . . . . . . . . . . . . . . . . 93%
   Very strongly . . . . . . . . . . . . . . . . . 73
   Fairly strongly . . . . . . . . . . . . . . . . 17
   Not at all strongly . . . . . . . . . . . . . 3
Total Mondale-Ferraro . . . . . . . . . . . . . . . 4
   Very strongly . . . . . . . . . . . . . . . . . 2
   Fairly strongly . . . . . . . . . . . . . . . . 1
   Not at all strongly . . . . . . . . . . . . . 1
Other; undecided . . . . . . . . . . . . . . . . . . . 3

### Democrats

Total Reagan-Bush . . . . . . . . . . . . . . . . . . 21%
   Very strongly . . . . . . . . . . . . . . . . . 10
   Fairly strongly . . . . . . . . . . . . . . . . 6
   Not at all strongly . . . . . . . . . . . . . 5

Total Mondale-Ferraro . . . . . . . . . . . . . . . .71
  Very strongly . . . . . . . . . . . . . . . .45
  Fairly strongly . . . . . . . . . . . . . . . .19
  Not at all strongly . . . . . . . . . . . . . 7
Other; undecided . . . . . . . . . . . . . . . . . . . 8

### Independents

Total Reagan-Bush . . . . . . . . . . . . . . . . . .62%
  Very strongly . . . . . . . . . . . . . . . .34
  Fairly strongly . . . . . . . . . . . . . . . .17
  Not at all strongly . . . . . . . . . . . . . .11
Total Mondale-Ferraro . . . . . . . . . . . . . . . .31
  Very strongly . . . . . . . . . . . . . . . .13
  Fairly strongly . . . . . . . . . . . . . . . .11
  Not at all strongly . . . . . . . . . . . . . 7
Other; undecided . . . . . . . . . . . . . . . . . . . 7

## By Religion
### Protestants

Total Reagan-Bush . . . . . . . . . . . . . . . . . .60%
  Very strongly . . . . . . . . . . . . . . . .40
  Fairly strongly . . . . . . . . . . . . . . . .13
  Not at all strongly . . . . . . . . . . . . . 7
Total Mondale-Ferraro . . . . . . . . . . . . . . . .35
  Very strongly . . . . . . . . . . . . . . . .23
  Fairly strongly . . . . . . . . . . . . . . . . 8
  Not at all strongly . . . . . . . . . . . . . 4
Other; undecided . . . . . . . . . . . . . . . . . . . 5

### Catholics

Total Reagan-Bush . . . . . . . . . . . . . . . . . .54%
  Very strongly . . . . . . . . . . . . . . . .39
  Fairly strongly . . . . . . . . . . . . . . . .12
  Not at all strongly . . . . . . . . . . . . . 3
Total Mondale-Ferraro . . . . . . . . . . . . . . . .39
  Very strongly . . . . . . . . . . . . . . . .20
  Fairly strongly . . . . . . . . . . . . . . . .14
  Not at all strongly . . . . . . . . . . . . . 5
Other; undecided . . . . . . . . . . . . . . . . . . . 7

## By Occupation
### Professional and Business

Total Reagan-Bush . . . . . . . . . . . . . . . . . .64%
  Very strongly . . . . . . . . . . . . . . . .49
  Fairly strongly . . . . . . . . . . . . . . . .10
  Not at all strongly . . . . . . . . . . . . . 5

Total Mondale-Ferraro . . . . . . . . . . . . . . . .31
  Very strongly . . . . . . . . . . . . . . . .19
  Fairly strongly . . . . . . . . . . . . . . . . 9
  Not at all strongly . . . . . . . . . . . . . 3
Other; undecided . . . . . . . . . . . . . . . . . . . 5

### Clerical and Sales

Total Reagan-Bush . . . . . . . . . . . . . . . . . .63%
  Very strongly . . . . . . . . . . . . . . . .45
  Fairly strongly . . . . . . . . . . . . . . . .10
  Not at all strongly . . . . . . . . . . . . . 8
Total Mondale-Ferraro . . . . . . . . . . . . . . . .32
  Very strongly . . . . . . . . . . . . . . . .14
  Fairly strongly . . . . . . . . . . . . . . . .11
  Not at all strongly . . . . . . . . . . . . . 7
Other; undecided . . . . . . . . . . . . . . . . . . . 5

### Manual Workers

Total Reagan-Bush . . . . . . . . . . . . . . . . . .55%
  Very strongly . . . . . . . . . . . . . . . .33
  Fairly strongly . . . . . . . . . . . . . . . .16
  Not at all strongly . . . . . . . . . . . . . 6
Total Mondale-Ferraro . . . . . . . . . . . . . . . .38
  Very strongly . . . . . . . . . . . . . . . .22
  Fairly strongly . . . . . . . . . . . . . . . .12
  Not at all strongly . . . . . . . . . . . . . 4
Other; undecided . . . . . . . . . . . . . . . . . . . 7

### Nonlabor Force

Total Reagan-Bush . . . . . . . . . . . . . . . . . .44%
  Very strongly . . . . . . . . . . . . . . . .29
  Fairly strongly . . . . . . . . . . . . . . . . 9
  Not at all strongly . . . . . . . . . . . . . 6
Total Mondale-Ferraro . . . . . . . . . . . . . . . .46
  Very strongly . . . . . . . . . . . . . . . .27
  Fairly strongly . . . . . . . . . . . . . . . .12
  Not at all strongly . . . . . . . . . . . . . 7
Other; undecided . . . . . . . . . . . . . . . . . . .10

## By Community Size
### One Million and Over

Total Reagan-Bush . . . . . . . . . . . . . . . . . .48%
  Very strongly . . . . . . . . . . . . . . . .34
  Fairly strongly . . . . . . . . . . . . . . . .11
  Not at all strongly . . . . . . . . . . . . . 3

Total Mondale-Ferraro . . . . . . . . . . . . . . . . 41
   Very strongly . . . . . . . . . . . . . . . . 27
   Fairly strongly . . . . . . . . . . . . . . . . 9
   Not at all strongly . . . . . . . . . . . . . 5
Other; undecided . . . . . . . . . . . . . . . . . 11

### 500,000–999,999

Total Reagan-Bush . . . . . . . . . . . . . . . . . . 53%
   Very strongly . . . . . . . . . . . . . . . . 31
   Fairly strongly . . . . . . . . . . . . . . . . 13
   Not at all strongly . . . . . . . . . . . . . 9
Total Mondale-Ferraro . . . . . . . . . . . . . . . . 45
   Very strongly . . . . . . . . . . . . . . . . 29
   Fairly strongly . . . . . . . . . . . . . . . . 12
   Not at all strongly . . . . . . . . . . . . . 4
Other; undecided . . . . . . . . . . . . . . . . . 2

### 50,000–499,999

Total Reagan-Bush . . . . . . . . . . . . . . . . . . 58%
   Very strongly . . . . . . . . . . . . . . . . 41
   Fairly strongly . . . . . . . . . . . . . . . . 8
   Not at all strongly . . . . . . . . . . . . . 9
Total Mondale-Ferraro . . . . . . . . . . . . . . . . 40
   Very strongly . . . . . . . . . . . . . . . . 21
   Fairly strongly . . . . . . . . . . . . . . . . 13
   Not at all strongly . . . . . . . . . . . . . 6
Other; undecided . . . . . . . . . . . . . . . . . 2

### 2,500–49,999

Total Reagan-Bush . . . . . . . . . . . . . . . . . . 60%
   Very strongly . . . . . . . . . . . . . . . . 43
   Fairly strongly . . . . . . . . . . . . . . . . 13
   Not at all strongly . . . . . . . . . . . . . 4
Total Mondale-Ferraro . . . . . . . . . . . . . . . . 34
   Very strongly . . . . . . . . . . . . . . . . 15
   Fairly strongly . . . . . . . . . . . . . . . . 13
   Not at all strongly . . . . . . . . . . . . . 6
Other; undecided . . . . . . . . . . . . . . . . . 6

### Under 2,500; Rural

Total Reagan-Bush . . . . . . . . . . . . . . . . . . 67%
   Very strongly . . . . . . . . . . . . . . . . 43
   Fairly strongly . . . . . . . . . . . . . . . . 17
   Not at all strongly . . . . . . . . . . . . . 7

Total Mondale-Ferraro . . . . . . . . . . . . . . . . 27
   Very strongly . . . . . . . . . . . . . . . . 15
   Fairly strongly . . . . . . . . . . . . . . . . 9
   Not at all strongly . . . . . . . . . . . . . 3
Other; undecided . . . . . . . . . . . . . . . . . 6

## By Labor Union Household
### Labor Union Members

Total Reagan-Bush . . . . . . . . . . . . . . . . . . 48%
   Very strongly . . . . . . . . . . . . . . . . 30
   Fairly strongly . . . . . . . . . . . . . . . . 14
   Not at all strongly . . . . . . . . . . . . . 4
Total Mondale-Ferraro . . . . . . . . . . . . . . . . 49
   Very strongly . . . . . . . . . . . . . . . . 28
   Fairly strongly . . . . . . . . . . . . . . . . 15
   Not at all strongly . . . . . . . . . . . . . 6
Other; undecided . . . . . . . . . . . . . . . . . 3

### Nonlabor Union Members

Total Reagan-Bush . . . . . . . . . . . . . . . . . . 58%
   Very strongly . . . . . . . . . . . . . . . . 40
   Fairly strongly . . . . . . . . . . . . . . . . 12
   Not at all strongly . . . . . . . . . . . . . 6
Total Mondale-Ferraro . . . . . . . . . . . . . . . . 34
   Very strongly . . . . . . . . . . . . . . . . 20
   Fairly strongly . . . . . . . . . . . . . . . . 9
   Not at all strongly . . . . . . . . . . . . . 5
Other; undecided . . . . . . . . . . . . . . . . . 8

Note: As the 1984 campaign begins in earnest, the Republican ticket of Ronald Reagan and George Bush holds a 10-percentage point lead over Democrats Walter Mondale and Geraldine Ferraro. In its first test (September 7–10) since the Republican National Convention of the relative voter appeal of the rival tickets, the Gallup Poll found 56% of registered voters supporting Reagan-Bush, 37% choosing Mondale-Ferraro, and 7% undecided. In the previous, mid-August Gallup survey, the Republican ticket had held a 52% to 41% advantage.

For a brief period following the Democratic convention in mid-July, the Republican and Democratic states were tied statistically for the lead. The latest findings, therefore, show that the Reagan-Bush ticket has recovered fully the momentum it lost temporarily during the Democratic convention.

In addition to greater numerical support, the Reagan-Bush team presently enjoys considerably stronger support than Mondale-Ferraro. Most of the GOP ticket's advantage can be traced to a superior number of very strong backers, 38% and 22%, respectively. On the other hand, less ardent supporters (fairly, not at all strongly) of each ticket are very similar in number, 18% for the Republicans and 15% for the Democrats.

As noted in earlier reports, Reagan-Bush enjoys considerable support from Democrats (21%), compared to 4% of Republican voters who cross party lines to vote for Mondale-Ferraro. Also, independents come down almost 2 to 1 on the side of the GOP ticket, 62% to 31%.

## SEPTEMBER 19

## CLIMATE OF OPINION CUTS AGAINST MONDALE*

Walter Mondale is trailing Ronald Reagan by 19 percentage points in the latest Gallup Poll and by about the same margin in other polls, but a bigger problem for Mondale is that the climate of opinion is running against him by a much larger margin than 19 points. Since the outset of Reagan's administration, the press and the public attribute a political strength to the president that surpasses his demonstrated level of public support. So it is in this election campaign. Reagan has a solid lead, and Mondale's electioneering efforts so far have been ineffective. Yet Mondale must run not only against the 19-point lead but against the image of Reagan's invincibility.

Voters see Reagan winning this election by a much larger margin than they actually support the president. The September ABC/*Washington Post* Poll, which had Reagan leading Mondale 56% to 40%, asked its respondents who they thought would win. Fully 79% picked the president, while 18% chose Mondale. In July when the ABC/*Washington Post* Poll was only showing an 8-percentage point

*This Gallup analysis was written by Andrew Kohut, president of the Gallup Organization Inc.

Reagan margin, its respondents were picking the president as the winner, 66% to 28%.

Reagan's current lead over Mondale is the consequence of a very good leadership image, a strong economy, and an opponent whose own leadership image is extremely weak. But he owes his political fortunes more to an improving economy than to any other single factor. The president's political recovery from recession began just about a year ago. Prior to that his approval ratings were in the 40s, and he trailed or at best tied most Democratic challengers in test elections throughout 1983. While Reagan has held a lead over Mondale for much of 1984, it was subject to much volatility until recently.

The same polls that today give the president a big lead also continue to show him as potentially vulnerable on foreign policy issues, compassion, fairness, and a number of other dimensions. The most recent *New York Times*/CBS Poll found that "on many issues ranging from arms control to abortion, the public is closer to the Democrats' stand than to Reagan's. Yet in addition to his strong leadership image, Reagan has an intangible which Mondale is finding it difficult to run against. He is defined as a winner even by those who do not support him."

The press often talks about Reagan's magic and describes the president's personal appeal as far exceeding public evaluations of his policies and programs. Polling data do not support the notion of a president with exceptional personal appeal. Reagan's is not his personal charm but rather his image as a competent, forceful leader who has succeeded.

Gallup's personality ratings of the president show him to be a popular man, but all presidents are popular; personal popularity is a requirement of electability. At this point Reagan's personal appeal ratings do not surpass those of other elected incumbent presidents running for a second term, except for Jimmy Carter. Gallup analysis at Reagan's midterm also indicated that the president's personality ratings topped his job approval ratings by only the same margin as was found for other presidents.

An exaggerated view of Reagan's personal appeal stems from a press which is more liberal than the president and largely did not vote for him in 1980. The media see the president as not only winning the election but also winning the traditional adversarial contest between the president and the press. In April the *Gallup Press Agenda* found 96% of the 230 senior editors, writers, and publishers polled rating Reagan's chance for reelection as excellent or good. The same survey also showed 60% of media respondents saying that Reagan had the advantage in the contest between the president and the national press. Curiously, the survey also showed that the elements of the press which are most critical of him—those who write for national media and senior editors—were most apt to say that the president had the upper hand in this adversarial relationship.

The net effect is that Reagan's lead in the polls, which is substantial, may be looming even larger than it should on its own merit. The landslide leads of Richard Nixon in 1972 and Lyndon Johnson in 1964 were larger than Reagan's today. While some commentators may be foreseeing a landslide, the president's lead, as of this time, does not justify it; of the national polls, only NBC News suggests a landslide (plus 32 points). Except for the NBC poll, all other polls in early September reported about the same margin between Mondale and Reagan: Gallup, 19 points; *Newsweek*/Gallup, 18 points; *New York Times*/CBS, 21 points; ABC/ *Washington Post*, 16 points; and Harris, 13 points. These leads may well stretch with the next round of polling. In order to overcome Reagan's actual lead in the polls, Mondale will have to register positively with voters and also overcome the perception of the president's larger-than-life political appeal.

## SEPTEMBER 20
## PERSONAL FINANCES

Interviewing Date: 9/7–10/84
Survey #241-G

> *Looking ahead, do you expect at this time next year you will be financially better off than now, or worse off than now?*

Better ............................53%
Worse ............................ 9
Same (volunteered) ..............28
No opinion ......................10

### By Sex
#### Male

Better ............................54%
Worse ............................10
Same (volunteered) ..............28
No opinion ...................... 8

#### Female

Better ............................52%
Worse ............................ 8
Same (volunteered) ..............29
No opinion ......................11

### By Ethnic Background
#### White

Better ............................55%
Worse ............................ 8
Same (volunteered) ..............28
No opinion ...................... 9

#### Nonwhite

Better ............................40%
Worse ............................13
Same (volunteered) ..............30
No opinion ......................17

#### Black

Better ............................41%
Worse ............................15
Same (volunteered) ..............27
No opinion ......................17

### By Education
#### College Graduate

Better ............................56%
Worse ............................11
Same (volunteered) ..............27
No opinion ...................... 6

### College Incomplete

Better .............................58%
Worse ............................. 7
Same (volunteered) .................29
No opinion ........................ 6

### High-School Graduate

Better .............................56%
Worse ............................. 9
Same (volunteered) .................27
No opinion ........................ 8

### Less Than High-School Graduate

Better .............................43%
Worse ............................. 9
Same (volunteered) .................30
No opinion ........................18

## By Region

### East

Better .............................51%
Worse .............................10
Same (volunteered) .................31
No opinion ........................ 8

### Midwest

Better .............................56%
Worse ............................. 9
Same (volunteered) .................27
No opinion ........................ 8

### South

Better .............................50%
Worse ............................. 9
Same (volunteered) .................28
No opinion ........................13

### West

Better .............................58%
Worse ............................. 7
Same (volunteered) .................27
No opinion ........................ 8

## By Age

### 18–24 Years

Better .............................69%
Worse ............................. 7
Same (volunteered) .................15
No opinion ........................ 9

### 25–29 Years

Better .............................71%
Worse ............................. 5
Same (volunteered) .................20
No opinion ........................ 4

### 30–49 Years

Better .............................59%
Worse ............................. 9
Same (volunteered) .................24
No opinion ........................ 8

### 50–64 Years

Better .............................43%
Worse .............................10
Same (volunteered) .................38
No opinion ........................ 9

### 65 Years and Over

Better .............................23%
Worse .............................12
Same (volunteered) .................46
No opinion ........................19

## By Income

### $40,000 and Over

Better .............................63%
Worse ............................. 9
Same (volunteered) .................25
No opinion ........................ 3

### $30,000–$39,999

Better .............................54%
Worse ............................. 9
Same (volunteered) .................31
No opinion ........................ 6

### $20,000–$29,999

Better ..............................66%
Worse .............................. 6
Same (volunteered) ................22
No opinion ......................... 6

### $10,000–$19,999

Better ..............................48%
Worse .............................. 9
Same (volunteered) ................33
No opinion .........................10

### Under $10,000

Better ..............................42%
Worse ..............................12
Same (volunteered) ................27
No opinion .........................19

## By Politics

### Republicans

Better ..............................66%
Worse .............................. 3
Same (volunteered) ................26
No opinion ......................... 5

### Democrats

Better ..............................43%
Worse ..............................13
Same (volunteered) ................30
No opinion .........................14

### Independents

Better ..............................53%
Worse ..............................10
Same (volunteered) ................28
No opinion ......................... 9

## By Occupation

### Professional and Business

Better ..............................66%
Worse .............................. 6
Same (volunteered) ................21
No opinion ......................... 7

### Clerical and Sales

Better ..............................59%
Worse ..............................10
Same (volunteered) ................27
No opinion ......................... 4

### Manual Workers

Better ..............................55%
Worse .............................. 9
Same (volunteered) ................27
No opinion ......................... 9

### Nonlabor Force

Better ..............................31%
Worse ..............................12
Same (volunteered) ................41
No opinion .........................16

## Selected National Trend

|  | Better | Worse | Same | No opinion |
|---|---|---|---|---|
| **1984** | | | | |
| July ......... | 52% | 12% | 28% | 8% |
| March ....... | 54 | 11 | 28 | 7 |
| **1983** | | | | |
| June ........ | 43 | 19 | 28 | 10 |
| March ....... | 45 | 22 | 24 | 9 |
| **1982** | | | | |
| November .... | 41 | 22 | 27 | 10 |
| July/August ... | 37 | 29 | 24 | 10 |
| February ..... | 42 | 31 | 21 | 6 |
| **1981** | | | | |
| October ...... | 40 | 31 | 21 | 8 |

*We are interested in how people's financial situation may have changed. Would you say that you are financially better off now than you were a year ago, or are you financially worse off now?*

Better ..............................39%
Worse ..............................26
Same (volunteered) ................34
No opinion ......................... 1

## By Sex
### Male

Better ............................39%
Worse ...........................24
Same (volunteered) .................35
No opinion ...................... 2

### Female

Better ............................40%
Worse ...........................27
Same (volunteered) .................32
No opinion ...................... 1

## By Ethnic Background
### White

Better ............................42%
Worse ...........................23
Same (volunteered) .................34
No opinion ...................... 1

### Nonwhite

Better ............................21%
Worse ...........................49
Same (volunteered) .................28
No opinion ...................... 2

### Black

Better ............................17%
Worse ...........................53
Same (volunteered) .................28
No opinion ...................... 2

## By Education
### College Graduate

Better ............................48%
Worse ...........................19
Same (volunteered) .................32
No opinion ...................... 1

### College Incomplete

Better ............................45%
Worse ...........................19
Same (volunteered) .................36
No opinion ...................... *

*Less than 1%

### High-School Graduate

Better ............................41%
Worse ...........................27
Same (volunteered) .................30
No opinion ...................... 2

### Less Than High-School Graduate

Better ............................25%
Worse ...........................36
Same (volunteered) .................37
No opinion ...................... 2

## By Region
### East

Better ............................39%
Worse ...........................26
Same (volunteered) .................34
No opinion ...................... 1

### Midwest

Better ............................37%
Worse ...........................27
Same (volunteered) .................34
No opinion ...................... 2

### South

Better ............................35%
Worse ...........................27
Same (volunteered) .................35
No opinion ...................... 3

### West

Better ............................47%
Worse ...........................21
Same (volunteered) .................31
No opinion ...................... 1

## By Age
### 18–24 Years

Better ............................47%
Worse ...........................24
Same (volunteered) .................25
No opinion ...................... 4

### 25–29 Years

Better .............................53%
Worse ..............................21
Same (volunteered) ..................25
No opinion ..........................1

### 30–49 Years

Better .............................43%
Worse ..............................24
Same (volunteered) ..................32
No opinion ..........................1

### 50–64 Years

Better .............................28%
Worse ..............................33
Same (volunteered) ..................38
No opinion ..........................1

### 65 Years and Over

Better .............................24%
Worse ..............................27
Same (volunteered) ..................47
No opinion ..........................2

## By Income
### $40,000 and Over

Better .............................56%
Worse ..............................14
Same (volunteered) ..................29
No opinion ..........................1

### $30,000–$39,999

Better .............................48%
Worse ..............................24
Same (volunteered) ..................27
No opinion ..........................1

### $20,000–$29,999

Better .............................49%
Worse ..............................15
Same (volunteered) ..................34
No opinion ..........................2

### $10,000–$19,999

Better .............................34%
Worse ..............................29
Same (volunteered) ..................36
No opinion ..........................1

### Under $10,000

Better .............................19%
Worse ..............................44
Same (volunteered) ..................35
No opinion ..........................2

## By Politics
### Republicans

Better .............................53%
Worse ..............................15
Same (volunteered) ..................31
No opinion ..........................1

### Democrats

Better .............................26%
Worse ..............................38
Same (volunteered) ..................34
No opinion ..........................2

### Independents

Better .............................42%
Worse ..............................19
Same (volunteered) ..................37
No opinion ..........................2

## By Occupation
### Professional and Business

Better .............................55%
Worse ..............................18
Same (volunteered) ..................26
No opinion ..........................1

### Clerical and Sales

Better .............................42%
Worse ..............................23
Same (volunteered) ..................34
No opinion ..........................1

### Manual Workers

Better ............................36%
Worse ............................28
Same (volunteered) .................34
No opinion ........................ 2

### Nonlabor Force

Better ............................22%
Worse ............................30
Same (volunteered) .................47
No opinion ........................ 1

### Selected National Trend

|  | Better | Worse | Same | No opinion |
|---|---|---|---|---|
| **1984** | | | | |
| July ......... | 40% | 25% | 34% | 1% |
| March ....... | 36 | 26 | 37 | 1 |
| **1983** | | | | |
| June ........ | 28 | 39 | 32 | 1 |
| March ....... | 25 | 46 | 28 | 1 |
| **1982** | | | | |
| November .... | 28 | 37 | 34 | 1 |
| July/August ... | 25 | 46 | 26 | 3 |
| February ..... | 28 | 47 | 24 | 1 |
| **1981** | | | | |
| October ...... | 28 | 43 | 28 | 1 |

Note: The public continues to be bullish in its financial outlook, with more persons at present than at any time since 1976 saying they expect to be better off a year from now. Also, more say they are better off now than they were at this time next year.

In the latest Gallup Poll, 53% say they expect to be better off one year from now, compared to 9% who say worse and another 28% who foresee little change in their financial status. These percentages reflect the highest level of optimism recorded since September 1976, when the measurements began. In a comparison to one year ago, 39% of Americans are financially better off today, while 2% say worse and 34% see little change.

## SEPTEMBER 23
## PARTY BETTER FOR PEACE AND PROSPERITY

Interviewing Date: 9/7–10/84
Survey #241-G

*Looking ahead for the next few years, which political party do you think would be more likely to keep the United States out of World War III—the Republican party or the Democratic party?*

Republican ........................38%
Democratic ........................38
No difference (volunteered) ...........15
No opinion ........................ 9

### By Sex
#### Male

Republican ........................40%
Democratic ........................38
No difference (volunteered) ...........16
No opinion ........................ 6

#### Female

Republican ........................36%
Democratic ........................38
No difference (volunteered) ...........14
No opinion ........................12

### By Ethnic Background
#### White

Republican ........................42%
Democratic ........................34
No difference (volunteered) ...........15
No opinion ........................ 9

#### Nonwhite

Republican ........................12%
Democratic ........................67
No difference (volunteered) ...........13
No opinion ........................ 8

### Black

Republican ........................ 9%
Democratic ....................... 75
No difference (volunteered) ........... 11
No opinion ........................ 5

## By Education
### College Graduate

Republican ........................ 36%
Democratic ....................... 41
No difference (volunteered) ........... 17
No opinion ........................ 6

### College Incomplete

Republican ........................ 39%
Democratic ....................... 37
No difference (volunteered) ........... 16
No opinion ........................ 8

### High-School Graduate

Republican ........................ 43%
Democratic ....................... 33
No difference (volunteered) ........... 15
No opinion ........................ 9

### Less Than High-School Graduate

Republican ........................ 31%
Democratic ....................... 44
No difference (volunteered) ........... 13
No opinion ........................ 12

## By Region
### East

Republican ........................ 38%
Democratic ....................... 40
No difference (volunteered) ........... 16
No opinion ........................ 6

### Midwest

Republican ........................ 42%
Democratic ....................... 34
No difference (volunteered) ........... 13
No opinion ........................ 11

### South

Republican ........................ 35%
Democratic ....................... 39
No difference (volunteered) ........... 15
No opinion ........................ 11

### West

Republican ........................ 38%
Democratic ....................... 38
No difference (volunteered) ........... 17
No opinion ........................ 7

## By Age
### 18–24 Years

Republican ........................ 45%
Democratic ....................... 37
No difference (volunteered) ........... 11
No opinion ........................ 7

### 25–29 Years

Republican ........................ 34%
Democratic ....................... 39
No difference (volunteered) ........... 15
No opinion ........................ 12

### 30–49 Years

Republican ........................ 38%
Democratic ....................... 38
No difference (volunteered) ........... 16
No opinion ........................ 8

### 50 Years and Over

Republican ........................ 36%
Democratic ....................... 38
No difference (volunteered) ........... 17
No opinion ........................ 9

## By Politics
### Republicans

Republican ........................ 74%
Democratic ....................... 8
No difference (volunteered) ........... 12
No opinion ........................ 6

### Democrats

Republican ......................... 9%
Democratic .......................72
No difference (volunteered) ...........12
No opinion ......................... 7

### Independents

Republican .........................35%
Democratic .......................28
No difference (volunteered) ...........24
No opinion .........................13

### Selected National Trend

| | Republican party | Democratic party | No difference; no opinion |
|---|---|---|---|
| August 1984 ....... | 36% | 40% | 24% |
| April 1984 ......... | 30 | 42 | 28 |
| September 1983 ..... | 26 | 39 | 35 |
| October 1982 ...... | 29 | 38 | 33 |
| April 1981 ........ | 29 | 34 | 37 |
| September 1980 ..... | 25 | 42 | 33 |
| August 1976 ....... | 29 | 32 | 39 |
| September 1972 ..... | 32 | 28 | 40 |
| October 1968 ....... | 37 | 24 | 39 |
| October 1964 ....... | 22 | 45 | 33 |
| October 1960 ....... | 40 | 25 | 35 |
| October 1956 ....... | 46 | 16 | 38 |
| January 1952 ....... | 36 | 15 | 49 |
| September 1951 ..... | 28 | 21 | 51 |

*Which political party—the Republican party or the Democratic party—do you think will do a better job of keeping the country prosperous?*

Republican .........................49%
Democratic .......................33
No difference (volunteered) ...........10
No opinion ......................... 8

### By Sex
#### Male

Republican .........................50%
Democratic .......................33
No difference (volunteered) ...........10
No opinion ......................... 7

### Female

Republican .........................47%
Democratic .......................33
No difference (volunteered) ...........10
No opinion .........................10

### By Ethnic Background
#### White

Republican .........................53%
Democratic .......................28
No difference (volunteered) ...........10
No opinion ......................... 9

#### Nonwhite

Republican .........................15%
Democratic .......................69
No difference (volunteered) ...........11
No opinion ......................... 6

#### Black

Republican ......................... 8%
Democratic .......................79
No difference (volunteered) ...........10
No opinion ......................... 3

### By Education
#### College Graduate

Republican .........................58%
Democratic .......................26
No difference (volunteered) ........... 8
No opinion ......................... 8

#### College Incomplete

Republican .........................51%
Democratic .......................28
No difference (volunteered) ...........13
No opinion ......................... 8

#### High-School Graduate

Republican .........................50%
Democratic .......................32
No difference (volunteered) ...........10
No opinion ......................... 8

### Less Than High-School Graduate

Republican ..........................38%
Democratic ..........................44
No difference (volunteered) ........... 8
No opinion ..........................10

## By Region
### East

Republican ..........................48%
Democratic ..........................34
No difference (volunteered) ...........11
No opinion ......................... 7

### Midwest

Republican ..........................48%
Democratic ..........................33
No difference (volunteered) ........... 9
No opinion ..........................10

### South

Republican ..........................46%
Democratic ..........................34
No difference (volunteered) ...........11
No opinion ......................... 9

### West

Republican ..........................54%
Democratic ..........................29
No difference (volunteered) ........... 9
No opinion ......................... 8

## By Age
### 18–24 Years

Republican ..........................49%
Democratic ..........................35
No difference (volunteered) ........... 9
No opinion ......................... 7

### 25–29 Years

Republican ..........................53%
Democratic ..........................29
No difference (volunteered) ........... 9
No opinion ......................... 9

### 30–49 Years

Republican ..........................51%
Democratic ..........................30
No difference (volunteered) ...........12
No opinion ......................... 7

### 50 Years and Over

Republican ..........................45%
Democratic ..........................36
No difference (volunteered) ........... 9
No opinion ..........................10

## By Politics
### Republicans

Republican ..........................89%
Democratic ......................... 5
No difference (volunteered) ........... 3
No opinion ......................... 3

### Democrats

Republican ..........................16%
Democratic ..........................66
No difference (volunteered) ........... 9
No opinion ......................... 9

### Independents

Republican ..........................47%
Democratic ..........................23
No difference (volunteered) ...........18
No opinion ..........................12

## Selected National Trend

|  | Republican party | Democratic party | No difference; no opinion |
|---|---|---|---|
| August 1984 ....... | 48% | 36% | 16% |
| April 1984 ........ | 44 | 36 | 20 |
| September 1983 ..... | 33 | 40 | 27 |
| October 1982 ....... | 34 | 43 | 23 |
| October 1981 ....... | 40 | 31 | 29 |
| April 1981 ........ | 41 | 28 | 31 |
| September 1980 ..... | 35 | 36 | 29 |
| August 1976 ....... | 23 | 47 | 30 |
| September 1972 ..... | 38 | 35 | 27 |
| October 1968 ....... | 34 | 37 | 29 |
| October 1964 ....... | 21 | 53 | 26 |

| | | | |
|---|---|---|---|
| October 1960 . . . . . . . | 31 | 46 | 23 |
| October 1956 . . . . . . . | 39 | 39 | 22 |
| January 1952 . . . . . . . | 31 | 35 | 34 |
| November 1951 . . . . . | 29 | 37 | 34 |

Note: The Republican party not only is widely perceived as more likely than the Democratic party to keep the nation prosperous, but also it is now tied with the Democrats as the party more likely to keep the nation at peace. The latest Gallup Poll shows 49% of the public—the highest figure since these measurements were begun in 1951—saying the Republicans will do a better job of keeping the United States prosperous, while 33% name the Democrats, and 18% say they see little difference or do not offer an opinion.

Bread and butter issues have always outranked the fear of war as determinants of presidential elections. Since 1952, in each election in which the Republican party has led or been tied with the Democratic party as the "party of prosperity," the Republican presidential candidate has won. The GOP's current claim to the title is strengthened by the fact that a substantial proportion of Democrats in the survey (16%) deserts their own party to vote for the other as superior in this respect, compared to only 5% of Republicans who cite the Democratic party as better. Also, proportionately more Republicans are steadfast to the GOP (89%) on the prosperity issue than Democrats are loyal to their own party (66%). Independents express a strong preference for the Republicans (47%).

The GOP has had a clear advantage over the Democrats on only four other occasions, twice during the early months of the Reagan administration in 1981, and twice earlier this year. Then its advantage was offset by the Democratic party's substantial lead as being thought of as more likely to keep the nation at peace. In the latest survey, however, the GOP has moved into a tie with the Democrats as the "party of peace."

Currently, 38% say the Republican party is stronger in this regard, 38% name the Democrats, and 24% see no difference or have no opinion. With only a few exceptions, the Democratic party has held an edge on the peace issue for over a decade, with the lead changing hands at intervals before then. The last time the GOP held an outright advantage as better able to keep the nation out of war was during the closing months of President Richard Nixon's successful reelection campaign in 1972.

## SEPTEMBER 25
## PRESIDENTIAL TRIAL HEATS

Interviewing Date: 9/21–24/84
Survey #242-G

*Asked of registered voters: If the 1984 presidential election were being held today, which would you vote for—the Republican candidates, Reagan and Bush, or the Democratic candidates, Mondale and Ferraro? [Those who were undecided or named other candidates were then asked: As of today, do you lean more to Reagan and Bush, or to Mondale and Ferraro?]*

Reagan-Bush . . . . . . . . . . . . . . . . . . . . . . .58%
Mondale-Ferraro . . . . . . . . . . . . . . . . . .37
Other; undecided . . . . . . . . . . . . . . . . . . . 5

### By Sex
#### Male

Reagan-Bush . . . . . . . . . . . . . . . . . . . . . . .60%
Mondale-Ferraro . . . . . . . . . . . . . . . . . .36
Other; undecided . . . . . . . . . . . . . . . . . . . 4

#### Female

Reagan-Bush . . . . . . . . . . . . . . . . . . . . . . .56%
Mondale-Ferraro . . . . . . . . . . . . . . . . . .39
Other; undecided . . . . . . . . . . . . . . . . . . . 5

### By Ethnic Background
#### White

Reagan-Bush . . . . . . . . . . . . . . . . . . . . . . .62%
Mondale-Ferraro . . . . . . . . . . . . . . . . . .33
Other; undecided . . . . . . . . . . . . . . . . . . . 5

#### Nonwhite

Reagan-Bush . . . . . . . . . . . . . . . . . . . . . . .24%
Mondale-Ferraro . . . . . . . . . . . . . . . . . .69
Other; undecided . . . . . . . . . . . . . . . . . . . 7

### Black

Reagan-Bush ........................18%
Mondale-Ferraro .....................75
Other; undecided ..................... 7

## By Education
### College Graduate

Reagan-Bush ........................59%
Mondale-Ferraro .....................38
Other; undecided ..................... 3

### College Incomplete

Reagan-Bush ........................66%
Mondale-Ferraro .....................30
Other; undecided ..................... 4

### High-School Graduate

Reagan-Bush ........................57%
Mondale-Ferraro .....................38
Other; undecided ..................... 5

### Less Than High-School Graduate

Reagan-Bush ........................48%
Mondale-Ferraro .....................46
Other; undecided ..................... 6

## By Region
### East

Reagan-Bush ........................49%
Mondale-Ferraro .....................45
Other; undecided ..................... 6

### Midwest

Reagan-Bush ........................56%
Mondale-Ferraro .....................37
Other; undecided ..................... 7

### South

Reagan-Bush ........................61%
Mondale-Ferraro .....................35
Other; undecided ..................... 4

### West

Reagan-Bush ........................64%
Mondale-Ferraro .....................33
Other; undecided ..................... 3

## By Age
### 18–24 Years

Reagan-Bush ........................57%
Mondale-Ferraro .....................40
Other; undecided ..................... 3

### 25–29 Years

Reagan-Bush ........................56%
Mondale-Ferraro .....................39
Other; undecided ..................... 5

### 30–49 Years

Reagan-Bush ........................61%
Mondale-Ferraro .....................35
Other; undecided ..................... 4

### 50–64 Years

Reagan-Bush ........................57%
Mondale-Ferraro .....................37
Other; undecided ..................... 6

### 65 Years and Over

Reagan-Bush ........................54%
Mondale-Ferraro .....................41
Other; undecided ..................... 5

## By Income
### $40,000 and Over

Reagan-Bush ........................69%
Mondale-Ferraro .....................27
Other; undecided ..................... 4

### $30,000–$39,999

Reagan-Bush ........................65%
Mondale-Ferraro .....................30
Other; undecided ..................... 5

### $20,000–$29,999

Reagan-Bush ........................62%
Mondale-Ferraro ...................34
Other; undecided .................. 4

### $10,000–$19,999

Reagan-Bush ........................51%
Mondale-Ferraro ...................46
Other; undecided ................. 3

### Under $10,000

Reagan-Bush ........................42%
Mondale-Ferraro ...................50
Other; undecided ................. 8

## By Politics
### Republicans

Reagan-Bush ........................94%
Mondale-Ferraro ................... 4
Other; undecided ................. 2

### Democrats

Reagan-Bush ........................24%
Mondale-Ferraro ...................71
Other; undecided ................. 5

### Independents

Reagan-Bush ........................60%
Mondale-Ferraro ...................31
Other; undecided ................. 9

## By Religion
### Protestants

Reagan-Bush ........................60%
Mondale-Ferraro ...................35
Other; undecided ................. 5

### Catholics

Reagan-Bush ........................57%
Mondale-Ferraro ...................38
Other; undecided ................. 5

## By Occupation
### Professional and Business

Reagan-Bush ........................68%
Mondale-Ferraro ...................28
Other; undecided ................. 4

### Clerical and Sales

Reagan-Bush ........................52%
Mondale-Ferraro ...................43
Other; undecided ................. 5

### Manual Workers

Reagan-Bush ........................52%
Mondale-Ferraro ...................44
Other; undecided ................. 4

### Nonlabor Force

Reagan-Bush ........................53%
Mondale-Ferraro ...................42
Other; undecided ................. 5

## By Community Size
### One Million and Over

Reagan-Bush ........................49%
Mondale-Ferraro ...................46
Other; undecided ................. 5

### 500,000–999,999

Reagan-Bush ........................64%
Mondale-Ferraro ...................33
Other; undecided ................. 3

### 50,000–499,999

Reagan-Bush ........................65%
Mondale-Ferraro ...................32
Other; undecided ................. 3

### 2,500–49,999

Reagan-Bush ........................59%
Mondale-Ferraro ...................36
Other; undecided ................. 5

### Under 2,500; Rural

Reagan-Bush ........................62%
Mondale-Ferraro ....................32
Other; undecided ...................  6

## By Labor Union Household

### Labor Union Members

Reagan-Bush ........................46%
Mondale-Ferraro ....................51
Other; undecided ...................  3

### Nonlabor Union Members

Reagan-Bush ........................61%
Mondale-Ferraro ....................34
Other; undecided ...................  5

## Selected National Trend

|              | Reagan-Bush | Mondale-Ferraro | Other; undecided |
|--------------|-------------|-----------------|------------------|
| Sept. 7–10 .......  | 56% | 37% | 7% |

### Republican Convention

| Aug. 10–13 ......  | 52% | 41% | 7% |
| July 27–30 .......  | 53 | 41 | 6 |

### Democratic Convention

| July 13–16 .......  | 53% | 39% | 8% |

### Ferraro Announcement

| July 6–9 ........  | 54% | 38% | 8%* |

*Test election was between Reagan and Mondale.

*Asked of those who chose a ticket: Right now, how strongly do you feel about your choice— very strongly, fairly strongly, or not at all strongly?*

Total Reagan-Bush ....................58%
  Very strongly .................40
  Fairly strongly ...............13
  Not at all strongly ...........  5

Total Mondale-Ferraro ................37
  Very strongly ..................21
  Fairly strongly .................13
  Not at all strongly .............  3
Other; undecided ....................  5

## By Sex

### Male

Total Reagan-Bush ....................60%
  Very strongly ..................43
  Fairly strongly .................12
  Not at all strongly .............  5
Total Mondale-Ferraro ................36
  Very strongly ..................22
  Fairly strongly .................12
  Not at all strongly .............  2
Other; undecided ....................  4

### Female

Total Reagan-Bush ....................56%
  Very strongly ..................38
  Fairly strongly .................13
  Not at all strongly .............  5
Total Mondale-Ferraro ................39
  Very strongly ..................21
  Fairly strongly .................14
  Not at all strongly .............  4
Other; undecided ....................  5

## By Ethnic Background

### White

Total Reagan-Bush ....................62%
  Very strongly ..................44
  Fairly strongly .................13
  Not at all strongly .............  5
Total Mondale-Ferraro ................33
  Very strongly ..................19
  Fairly strongly .................11
  Not at all strongly .............  3
Other; undecided ....................  5

### Nonwhite

Total Reagan-Bush ....................24%
  Very strongly ..................12
  Fairly strongly .................  7
  Not at all strongly .............  5

Total Mondale-Ferraro . . . . . . . . . . . . . . . .69
  Very strongly . . . . . . . . . . . . . . . .40
  Fairly strongly . . . . . . . . . . . . . . . .26
  Not at all strongly . . . . . . . . . . . . . 3
Other; undecided . . . . . . . . . . . . . . . . . 7

### Black

Total Reagan-Bush . . . . . . . . . . . . . . . . . .18%
  Very strongly . . . . . . . . . . . . . . . . 8
  Fairly strongly . . . . . . . . . . . . . . . 7
  Not at all strongly . . . . . . . . . . . . . 3
Total Mondale-Ferraro . . . . . . . . . . . . . . .75
  Very strongly . . . . . . . . . . . . . . . .44
  Fairly strongly . . . . . . . . . . . . . . . .28
  Not at all strongly . . . . . . . . . . . . . 3
Other; undecided . . . . . . . . . . . . . . . . . 7

## By Education

### College Graduate

Total Reagan-Bush . . . . . . . . . . . . . . . . . .59%
  Very strongly . . . . . . . . . . . . . . . .45
  Fairly strongly . . . . . . . . . . . . . . . 9
  Not at all strongly . . . . . . . . . . . . . 5
Total Mondale-Ferraro . . . . . . . . . . . . . . .38
  Very strongly . . . . . . . . . . . . . . . .21
  Fairly strongly . . . . . . . . . . . . . . . .13
  Not at all strongly . . . . . . . . . . . . . 4
Other; undecided . . . . . . . . . . . . . . . . . 3

### College Incomplete

Total Reagan-Bush . . . . . . . . . . . . . . . . . .66%
  Very strongly . . . . . . . . . . . . . . . .49
  Fairly strongly . . . . . . . . . . . . . . . .14
  Not at all strongly . . . . . . . . . . . . . 3
Total Mondale-Ferraro . . . . . . . . . . . . . . .30
  Very strongly . . . . . . . . . . . . . . . .14
  Fairly strongly . . . . . . . . . . . . . . . .12
  Not at all strongly . . . . . . . . . . . . . 4
Other; undecided . . . . . . . . . . . . . . . . . 4

### High-School Graduate

Total Reagan-Bush . . . . . . . . . . . . . . . . . .57%
  Very strongly . . . . . . . . . . . . . . . .36
  Fairly strongly . . . . . . . . . . . . . . . .15
  Not at all strongly . . . . . . . . . . . . . 6

Total Mondale-Ferraro . . . . . . . . . . . . . . . .38
  Very strongly . . . . . . . . . . . . . . . .25
  Fairly strongly . . . . . . . . . . . . . . . .10
  Not at all strongly . . . . . . . . . . . . . 3
Other; undecided . . . . . . . . . . . . . . . . . 5

### Less Than High-School Graduate

Total Reagan-Bush . . . . . . . . . . . . . . . . . .48%
  Very strongly . . . . . . . . . . . . . . . .32
  Fairly strongly . . . . . . . . . . . . . . . .11
  Not at all strongly . . . . . . . . . . . . . 5
Total Mondale-Ferraro . . . . . . . . . . . . . . .46
  Very strongly . . . . . . . . . . . . . . . .26
  Fairly strongly . . . . . . . . . . . . . . . .18
  Not at all strongly . . . . . . . . . . . . . 2
Other; undecided . . . . . . . . . . . . . . . . . 6

## By Region

### East

Total Reagan-Bush . . . . . . . . . . . . . . . . . .49%
  Very strongly . . . . . . . . . . . . . . . .33
  Fairly strongly . . . . . . . . . . . . . . . .11
  Not at all strongly . . . . . . . . . . . . . 5
Total Mondale-Ferraro . . . . . . . . . . . . . . .45
  Very strongly . . . . . . . . . . . . . . . .20
  Fairly strongly . . . . . . . . . . . . . . . .20
  Not at all strongly . . . . . . . . . . . . . 5
Other; undecided . . . . . . . . . . . . . . . . . 6

### Midwest

Total Reagan-Bush . . . . . . . . . . . . . . . . . .56%
  Very strongly . . . . . . . . . . . . . . . .37
  Fairly strongly . . . . . . . . . . . . . . . .16
  Not at all strongly . . . . . . . . . . . . . 3
Total Mondale-Ferraro . . . . . . . . . . . . . . .37
  Very strongly . . . . . . . . . . . . . . . .24
  Fairly strongly . . . . . . . . . . . . . . . .10
  Not at all strongly . . . . . . . . . . . . . 3
Other; undecided . . . . . . . . . . . . . . . . . 7

### South

Total Reagan-Bush . . . . . . . . . . . . . . . . . .61%
  Very strongly . . . . . . . . . . . . . . . .44
  Fairly strongly . . . . . . . . . . . . . . . .11
  Not at all strongly . . . . . . . . . . . . . 6

Total Mondale-Ferraro . . . . . . . . . . . . . . . . 35
  Very strongly . . . . . . . . . . . . . . . . . 21
  Fairly strongly . . . . . . . . . . . . . . . . . 11
  Not at all strongly . . . . . . . . . . . . . . 3
Other; undecided . . . . . . . . . . . . . . . . . 4

### West

Total Reagan-Bush . . . . . . . . . . . . . . . . . . 64%
  Very strongly . . . . . . . . . . . . . . . . . 49
  Fairly strongly . . . . . . . . . . . . . . . . . 11
  Not at all strongly . . . . . . . . . . . . . . 4
Total Mondale-Ferraro . . . . . . . . . . . . . . . 33
  Very strongly . . . . . . . . . . . . . . . . . 21
  Fairly strongly . . . . . . . . . . . . . . . . . 10
  Not at all strongly . . . . . . . . . . . . . . 2
Other; undecided . . . . . . . . . . . . . . . . . 3

### By Age
#### 18–24 Years

Total Reagan-Bush . . . . . . . . . . . . . . . . . . 57%
  Very strongly . . . . . . . . . . . . . . . . . 33
  Fairly strongly . . . . . . . . . . . . . . . . . 19
  Not at all strongly . . . . . . . . . . . . . . 5
Total Mondale-Ferraro . . . . . . . . . . . . . . . 40
  Very strongly . . . . . . . . . . . . . . . . . 12
  Fairly strongly . . . . . . . . . . . . . . . . . 23
  Not at all strongly . . . . . . . . . . . . . . 5
Other; undecided . . . . . . . . . . . . . . . . . 3

#### 25–29 Years

Total Reagan-Bush . . . . . . . . . . . . . . . . . . 56%
  Very strongly . . . . . . . . . . . . . . . . . 33
  Fairly strongly . . . . . . . . . . . . . . . . . 18
  Not at all strongly . . . . . . . . . . . . . . 5
Total Mondale-Ferraro . . . . . . . . . . . . . . . 39
  Very strongly . . . . . . . . . . . . . . . . . 25
  Fairly strongly . . . . . . . . . . . . . . . . . 11
  Not at all strongly . . . . . . . . . . . . . . 3
Other; undecided . . . . . . . . . . . . . . . . . 5

#### 30–49 Years

Total Reagan-Bush . . . . . . . . . . . . . . . . . . 61%
  Very strongly . . . . . . . . . . . . . . . . . 43
  Fairly strongly . . . . . . . . . . . . . . . . . 12
  Not at all strongly . . . . . . . . . . . . . . 6

Total Mondale-Ferraro . . . . . . . . . . . . . . . . 35
  Very strongly . . . . . . . . . . . . . . . . . 21
  Fairly strongly . . . . . . . . . . . . . . . . . 11
  Not at all strongly . . . . . . . . . . . . . . 3
Other; undecided . . . . . . . . . . . . . . . . . 4

### 50–64 Years

Total Reagan-Bush . . . . . . . . . . . . . . . . . . 57%
  Very strongly . . . . . . . . . . . . . . . . . 41
  Fairly strongly . . . . . . . . . . . . . . . . . 12
  Not at all strongly . . . . . . . . . . . . . . 4
Total Mondale-Ferraro . . . . . . . . . . . . . . . 37
  Very strongly . . . . . . . . . . . . . . . . . 24
  Fairly strongly . . . . . . . . . . . . . . . . . 9
  Not at all strongly . . . . . . . . . . . . . . 4
Other; undecided . . . . . . . . . . . . . . . . . 6

### 65 Years and Over

Total Reagan-Bush . . . . . . . . . . . . . . . . . . 54%
  Very strongly . . . . . . . . . . . . . . . . . 41
  Fairly strongly . . . . . . . . . . . . . . . . . 10
  Not at all strongly . . . . . . . . . . . . . . 3
Total Mondale-Ferraro . . . . . . . . . . . . . . . 41
  Very strongly . . . . . . . . . . . . . . . . . 23
  Fairly strongly . . . . . . . . . . . . . . . . . 15
  Not at all strongly . . . . . . . . . . . . . . 3
Other; undecided . . . . . . . . . . . . . . . . . 5

### By Income
#### $40,000 and Over

Total Reagan-Bush . . . . . . . . . . . . . . . . . . 69%
  Very strongly . . . . . . . . . . . . . . . . . 49
  Fairly strongly . . . . . . . . . . . . . . . . . 12
  Not at all strongly . . . . . . . . . . . . . . 8
Total Mondale-Ferraro . . . . . . . . . . . . . . . 27
  Very strongly . . . . . . . . . . . . . . . . . 16
  Fairly strongly . . . . . . . . . . . . . . . . . 7
  Not at all strongly . . . . . . . . . . . . . . 4
Other; undecided . . . . . . . . . . . . . . . . . 4

#### $30,000–$39,999

Total Reagan-Bush . . . . . . . . . . . . . . . . . . 65%
  Very strongly . . . . . . . . . . . . . . . . . 51
  Fairly strongly . . . . . . . . . . . . . . . . . 9
  Not at all strongly . . . . . . . . . . . . . . 5

Total Mondale-Ferraro ................30
  Very strongly .................16
  Fairly strongly ................10
  Not at all strongly ............. 4
Other; undecided ................... 5

### $20,000–$29,999

Total Reagan-Bush ..................62%
  Very strongly .................46
  Fairly strongly ................12
  Not at all strongly ............. 4
Total Mondale-Ferraro ................34
  Very strongly .................18
  Fairly strongly ................13
  Not at all strongly ............. 3
Other; undecided ................... 4

### $10,000–$19,999

Total Reagan-Bush ..................51%
  Very strongly .................31
  Fairly strongly ................15
  Not at all strongly ............. 5
Total Mondale-Ferraro ................46
  Very strongly .................28
  Fairly strongly ................15
  Not at all strongly ............. 3
Other; undecided ................... 3

### Under $10,000

Total Reagan-Bush ..................42%
  Very strongly .................28
  Fairly strongly ................12
  Not at all strongly ............. 2
Total Mondale-Ferraro ................50
  Very strongly .................28
  Fairly strongly ................18
  Not at all strongly ............. 4
Other; undecided ................... 8

## By Politics

### Republicans

Total Reagan-Bush ..................94%
  Very strongly .................75
  Fairly strongly ................15
  Not at all strongly ............. 4

Total Mondale-Ferraro ................ 4
  Very strongly ................. 1
  Fairly strongly ................. 2
  Not at all strongly ............. 1
Other; undecided ................... 2

### Democrats

Total Reagan-Bush ..................24%
  Very strongly .................11
  Fairly strongly ................ 8
  Not at all strongly ............. 5
Total Mondale-Ferraro ................71
  Very strongly .................45
  Fairly strongly ................22
  Not at all strongly ............. 4
Other; undecided ................... 5

### Independents

Total Reagan-Bush ..................60%
  Very strongly .................37
  Fairly strongly ................16
  Not at all strongly ............. 7
Total Mondale-Ferraro ................31
  Very strongly .................11
  Fairly strongly ................14
  Not at all strongly ............. 6
Other; undecided ................... 9

## By Religion

### Protestants

Total Reagan-Bush ..................60%
  Very strongly .................43
  Fairly strongly ................14
  Not at all strongly ............. 3
Total Mondale-Ferraro ................35
  Very strongly .................21
  Fairly strongly ................11
  Not at all strongly ............. 3
Other; undecided ................... 5

### Catholics

Total Reagan-Bush ..................57%
  Very strongly .................38
  Fairly strongly ................12
  Not at all strongly ............. 7

Total Mondale-Ferraro . . . . . . . . . . . . . . . .38
    Very strongly . . . . . . . . . . . . . . . .24
    Fairly strongly . . . . . . . . . . . . . . . .12
    Not at all strongly . . . . . . . . . . . . . 2
Other; undecided . . . . . . . . . . . . . . . . . . . 5

Total Mondale-Ferraro . . . . . . . . . . . . . . . .42
    Very strongly . . . . . . . . . . . . . . . .26
    Fairly strongly . . . . . . . . . . . . . . . .13
    Not at all strongly . . . . . . . . . . . . . 3
Other; undecided . . . . . . . . . . . . . . . . . . . 5

## By Occupation

### Professional and Business

Total Reagan-Bush . . . . . . . . . . . . . . . . . .68%
    Very strongly . . . . . . . . . . . . . . . .48
    Fairly strongly . . . . . . . . . . . . . . . .13
    Not at all strongly . . . . . . . . . . . . . 7
Total Mondale-Ferraro . . . . . . . . . . . . . . . .28
    Very strongly . . . . . . . . . . . . . . . .14
    Fairly strongly . . . . . . . . . . . . . . . .11
    Not at all strongly . . . . . . . . . . . . . 3
Other; undecided . . . . . . . . . . . . . . . . . . . 4

### Clerical and Sales

Total Reagan-Bush . . . . . . . . . . . . . . . . . .52%
    Very strongly . . . . . . . . . . . . . . . .34
    Fairly strongly . . . . . . . . . . . . . . . .12
    Not at all strongly . . . . . . . . . . . . . 6
Total Mondale-Ferraro . . . . . . . . . . . . . . . .43
    Very strongly . . . . . . . . . . . . . . . .15
    Fairly strongly . . . . . . . . . . . . . . . .19
    Not at all strongly . . . . . . . . . . . . . 9
Other; undecided . . . . . . . . . . . . . . . . . . . 5

### Manual Workers

Total Reagan-Bush . . . . . . . . . . . . . . . . . .52%
    Very strongly . . . . . . . . . . . . . . . .35
    Fairly strongly . . . . . . . . . . . . . . . .13
    Not at all strongly . . . . . . . . . . . . . 4
Total Mondale-Ferraro . . . . . . . . . . . . . . . .44
    Very strongly . . . . . . . . . . . . . . . .28
    Fairly strongly . . . . . . . . . . . . . . . .14
    Not at all strongly . . . . . . . . . . . . . 2
Other; undecided . . . . . . . . . . . . . . . . . . . 4

### Nonlabor Force

Total Reagan-Bush . . . . . . . . . . . . . . . . . .53%
    Very strongly . . . . . . . . . . . . . . . .38
    Fairly strongly . . . . . . . . . . . . . . . .12
    Not at all strongly . . . . . . . . . . . . . 3

## By Community Size

### One Million and Over

Total Reagan-Bush . . . . . . . . . . . . . . . . . .49%
    Very strongly . . . . . . . . . . . . . . . .33
    Fairly strongly . . . . . . . . . . . . . . . .12
    Not at all strongly . . . . . . . . . . . . . 4
Total Mondale-Ferraro . . . . . . . . . . . . . . . .46
    Very strongly . . . . . . . . . . . . . . . .25
    Fairly strongly . . . . . . . . . . . . . . . .16
    Not at all strongly . . . . . . . . . . . . . 5
Other; undecided . . . . . . . . . . . . . . . . . . . 5

### 500,000–999,999

Total Reagan-Bush . . . . . . . . . . . . . . . . . .64%
    Very strongly . . . . . . . . . . . . . . . .45
    Fairly strongly . . . . . . . . . . . . . . . .16
    Not at all strongly . . . . . . . . . . . . . 3
Total Mondale-Ferraro . . . . . . . . . . . . . . . .33
    Very strongly . . . . . . . . . . . . . . . .22
    Fairly strongly . . . . . . . . . . . . . . . .10
    Not at all strongly . . . . . . . . . . . . . 1
Other; undecided . . . . . . . . . . . . . . . . . . . 3

### 50,000–499,999

Total Reagan-Bush . . . . . . . . . . . . . . . . . .65%
    Very strongly . . . . . . . . . . . . . . . .47
    Fairly strongly . . . . . . . . . . . . . . . .10
    Not at all strongly . . . . . . . . . . . . . 8
Total Mondale-Ferraro . . . . . . . . . . . . . . . .32
    Very strongly . . . . . . . . . . . . . . . .20
    Fairly strongly . . . . . . . . . . . . . . . .10
    Not at all strongly . . . . . . . . . . . . . 2
Other; undecided . . . . . . . . . . . . . . . . . . . 3

### 2,500–49,999

Total Reagan-Bush . . . . . . . . . . . . . . . . . .59%
    Very strongly . . . . . . . . . . . . . . . .40
    Fairly strongly . . . . . . . . . . . . . . . .14
    Not at all strongly . . . . . . . . . . . . . 5

Total Mondale-Ferraro . . . . . . . . . . . . . . . . 36
    Very strongly . . . . . . . . . . . . . . . . . 18
    Fairly strongly . . . . . . . . . . . . . . . . . 15
    Not at all strongly . . . . . . . . . . . . . 3
Other; undecided . . . . . . . . . . . . . . . . . . . 5

### Under 2,500; Rural

Total Reagan-Bush . . . . . . . . . . . . . . . . . . 62%
    Very strongly . . . . . . . . . . . . . . . . . .43
    Fairly strongly . . . . . . . . . . . . . . . . . 15
    Not at all strongly . . . . . . . . . . . . . 4
Total Mondale-Ferraro . . . . . . . . . . . . . . . . 32
    Very strongly . . . . . . . . . . . . . . . . . 18
    Fairly strongly . . . . . . . . . . . . . . . . . 11
    Not at all strongly . . . . . . . . . . . . . 3
Other; undecided . . . . . . . . . . . . . . . . . . . 6

### By Labor Union Household

#### Labor Union Members

Total Reagan-Bush . . . . . . . . . . . . . . . . . . 46%
    Very strongly . . . . . . . . . . . . . . . . . 32
    Fairly strongly . . . . . . . . . . . . . . . . . 8
    Not at all strongly . . . . . . . . . . . . . 6
Total Mondale-Ferraro . . . . . . . . . . . . . . . . 51
    Very strongly . . . . . . . . . . . . . . . . . 34
    Fairly strongly . . . . . . . . . . . . . . . . . 14
    Not at all strongly . . . . . . . . . . . . . 3
Other; undecided . . . . . . . . . . . . . . . . . . . 3

#### Nonlabor Union Members

Total Reagan-Bush . . . . . . . . . . . . . . . . . . 61%
    Very strongly . . . . . . . . . . . . . . . . . 42
    Fairly strongly . . . . . . . . . . . . . . . . . 14
    Not at all strongly . . . . . . . . . . . . . 5
Total Mondale-Ferraro . . . . . . . . . . . . . . . . 34
    Very strongly . . . . . . . . . . . . . . . . . 18
    Fairly strongly . . . . . . . . . . . . . . . . . 13
    Not at all strongly . . . . . . . . . . . . . 3
Other; undecided . . . . . . . . . . . . . . . . . . . 5

Note: With only six weeks remaining until election day, the Republican ticket of Ronald Reagan and George Bush holds a commanding 21-percentage point lead over Walter Mondale and Geraldine Ferraro, the Democratic challengers. Between mid-September and the election in six of the last eight presidential contests, the trailing candidates narrowed the margins separating them from the leaders, and two of the mid-September underdogs came within a point or two of scoring upset victories. Also, at this stage in the landslide elections of 1964 and 1972, the underdogs trailed by 30 and 28 points, respectively—far more than Mondale's present 21-point deficit.

In the latest Gallup Poll, the Reagan-Bush ticket is the choice of 58% of registered voters to 37% for Mondale-Ferraro, with 5% undecided. In a similar poll conducted two weeks earlier, the GOP ticket led the Democrats by a 56% to 37% margin.

The candidates' standings in test elections have ebbed and flowed since the July 11 announcement of the selection of Ferraro as Mondale's running mate. For a brief period following the Democratic convention in mid-July, the Republican and Democratic tickets were tied statistically for the lead. To attain their large majority, the Reagan-Bush ticket has made a strong appeal to Democrats, 24% of whom say they would vote for the GOP if the election were being held now. In contrast, only 4% of Republicans would cross party lines to vote for Mondale-Ferraro. Independents express almost a 2-to-1 preference for the GOP ticket over the Democratic slate, 60% to 31%.

Not only does President Reagan enjoy a solid lead over Mondale, but also 40% of voters say they very strongly support Reagan, while only 21% are very strong Mondale backers. In contrast, 18% of voters describe their support for Reagan-Bush as fairly strong or not at all strong, compared to 16% for Mondale-Ferraro.

As shown in the table below, in all but two of the last eight elections the leading candidates have seen their margins narrow between Gallup polls conducted approximately six weeks before the election and election day itself. In the 1976 contest between President Gerald Ford and challenger Jimmy Carter, for example, Carter's 11-point advantage in late September dwindled to merely a 2-percentage point edge in the popular vote in the November election. Similarly, Richard Nixon, leading Hubert Humphrey by 15 points at this time in 1968, fended off a last-minute Humphrey charge to win by only a 1-point difference in the popular vote.

In a mid-September Gallup survey in 1972, Democrat George McGovern trailed incumbent Richard Nixon by 28 points. In a similar test election in the 1964 campaign, Senator Barry Goldwater placed 30 points behind President Lyndon Johnson.

The table, based on the total popular vote, compares the difference between the vote for the leading and trailing candidates in Gallup test elections and the difference in the popular vote actually cast:

### Presidential Test Elections

#### Leader's Margin in Percentage Points

| Year | Candidates | Gallup Poll late Sept. | Election outcome* |
|------|-----------|------|------|
| 1984 | Reagan-Mondale | 21 | ? |
| 1980 | Reagan-Carter | ** | 10 |
| 1976 | Carter-Ford | 11 | 2 |
| 1972 | Nixon-McGovern | 28 | 24 |
| 1968 | Nixon-Humphrey | 15 | 1 |
| 1964 | Johnson-Goldwater | 30 | 23 |
| 1960 | Kennedy-Nixon | 3 | ** |
| 1956 | Eisenhower-Stevenson | 12 | 15 |
| 1952 | Eisenhower-Stevenson | 14 | 11 |

*Based on total popular vote
**Less than 0.5%

Reagan's now familiar "gender gap" is still evident. In the latest test election, more men than women vote for the Reagan ticket by 4 percentage points, while more women than men vote for the Mondale ticket by 3 percentage points. The gap has been found in six of the seven Gallup trial heats conducted since mid-July and has averaged 9 points more for men for Reagan and 7 points more for women for Mondale, as shown below:

#### Vote in Test Elections

| | Reagan-Bush | | Mondale-Ferraro | |
|---|---|---|---|---|
| | Men | Women | Men | Women |
| Sept. 21–24 | 60% | 56% | 36% | 39% |
| Sept. 7–10 | 59 | 53 | 33 | 41 |
| Aug. 10–13 | 57 | 46 | 38 | 45 |
| July 27–30 | 53 | 54 | 41 | 41 |
| July 19–20* | 52 | 41 | 43 | 52 |
| July 13–16 | 61 | 46 | 32 | 46 |
| July 12–13* | 58 | 41 | 36 | 49 |
| Averages | 57 | 48 | 38 | 45 |

*For *Newsweek*

## SEPTEMBER 27
## ALCOHOLIC BEVERAGES

Interviewing Date: 7/6–9/84
Survey #237-G

*Do you have occasion to use alcoholic beverages such as liquor, wine, or beer, or are you a total abstainer?*

| | Those who drink |
|---|---|
| National | 64% |

#### By Sex

| | |
|---|---|
| Male | 73% |
| Female | 57 |

#### By Education

| | |
|---|---|
| College graduate | 74% |
| College incomplete | 75 |
| High-school graduate | 66 |
| Less than high-school graduate | 44 |

#### By Region

| | |
|---|---|
| East | 70% |
| Midwest | 70 |
| South | 52 |
| West | 67 |

#### By Age

| | |
|---|---|
| 18–29 years | 73% |
| 30–49 years | 69 |
| 50 years and over | 54 |

#### By Religion

| | |
|---|---|
| Protestants | 58% |
| Catholics | 76 |

## Selected National Trend

|  | *Those who drink* |
|---|---|
| 1982 | 65% |
| 1981 | 70 |
| 1979 | 69 |
| 1978 | 71 |
| 1976 | 71 |
| 1974 | 68 |
| 1969 | 64 |
| 1966 | 65 |
| 1964 | 63 |
| 1960 | 62 |
| 1958 | 55 |
| 1957 | 58 |
| 1956 | 60 |
| 1952 | 60 |
| 1951 | 59 |
| 1950 | 60 |
| 1949 | 58 |
| 1947 | 63 |
| 1946 | 67 |
| 1945 | 67 |
| 1939 | 58 |

*Has drinking\* ever been a cause of trouble in your family?*

|  | *Yes* |
|---|---|
| National | 17% |

### By Sex

| Male | 16% |
|---|---|
| Female | 18 |

### By Education

| College graduate | 13% |
|---|---|
| College incomplete | 22 |
| High-school graduate | 15 |
| Less than high-school graduate | 20 |

\*The word "liquor" was used instead of "drinking" in surveys before 1984.

### By Region

| East | 15% |
|---|---|
| Midwest | 19 |
| South | 18 |
| West | 17 |

### By Age

| 18–29 years | 20% |
|---|---|
| 30–49 years | 20 |
| 50 years and over | 13 |

### By Religion

| Protestants | 19% |
|---|---|
| Catholics | 13 |

### Selected National Trend

| 1981 | 22% |
|---|---|
| 1978 | 24 |
| 1976 | 17 |
| 1974 | 12 |
| 1966 | 12 |
| 1950 | 14 |

*Would you favor or oppose a law forbidding the sale of all beer, wine, and liquor throughout the nation?*

|  | *Favor* |
|---|---|
| National | 17% |

### By Sex

| Male | 12% |
|---|---|
| Female | 21 |

### By Education

| College graduate | 7% |
|---|---|
| College incomplete | 13 |
| High-school graduate | 15 |
| Less than high-school graduate | 31 |

### By Region

| East | 12% |
|---|---|
| Midwest | 13 |
| South | 26 |
| West | 13 |

## By Age

| | |
|---|---|
| 18–29 years | 16% |
| 30–49 years | 12 |
| 50 years and over | 22 |

## By Religion

| | |
|---|---|
| Protestants | 20% |
| Catholics | 13 |

## Selected National Trend

| | Favor |
|---|---|
| 1979 | 19% |
| 1976 | 19 |
| 1966 | 22 |
| 1960 | 26 |
| 1957 | 28 |
| 1956 | 33 |
| 1954 | 34 |
| 1952 | 33 |
| 1948 | 38 |
| 1945 | 33 |
| 1944 | 37 |
| 1942 | 36 |
| 1940 | 32 |
| 1938 | 36 |
| 1936 | 38 |

*Recently the New Jersey Supreme Court ruled that hosts can be sued for injuries to victims of auto accidents caused by adult guests to whom the hosts have served alcoholic beverages. Would you like to see such a law in this state, or not?*

| | |
|---|---|
| Yes | 28% |
| No | 64 |
| Not sure | 8 |

## By Sex

### *Male*

| | |
|---|---|
| Yes | 26% |
| No | 68 |
| Not sure | 6 |

### *Female*

| | |
|---|---|
| Yes | 30% |
| No | 61 |
| Not sure | 9 |

## By Education

### *College Graduate*

| | |
|---|---|
| Yes | 27% |
| No | 68 |
| Not sure | 5 |

### *College Incomplete*

| | |
|---|---|
| Yes | 24% |
| No | 70 |
| Not sure | 6 |

### *High-School Graduate*

| | |
|---|---|
| Yes | 27% |
| No | 65 |
| Not sure | 8 |

### *Less Than High-School Graduate*

| | |
|---|---|
| Yes | 33% |
| No | 57 |
| Not sure | 10 |

## By Region

### *East*

| | |
|---|---|
| Yes | 26% |
| No | 65 |
| Not sure | 9 |

### *Midwest*

| | |
|---|---|
| Yes | 31% |
| No | 64 |
| Not sure | 5 |

### *South*

| | |
|---|---|
| Yes | 28% |
| No | 64 |
| Not sure | 8 |

### West

| | |
|---|---|
| Yes | 26% |
| No | 65 |
| Not sure | 9 |

### By Age
#### 18–29 Years

| | |
|---|---|
| Yes | 28% |
| No | 67 |
| Not sure | 5 |

#### 30–49 Years

| | |
|---|---|
| Yes | 26% |
| No | 67 |
| Not sure | 7 |

#### 50 Years and Over

| | |
|---|---|
| Yes | 31% |
| No | 60 |
| Not sure | 9 |

### By Religion
#### Protestants

| | |
|---|---|
| Yes | 31% |
| No | 62 |
| Not sure | 7 |

#### Catholics

| | |
|---|---|
| Yes | 22% |
| No | 69 |
| Not sure | 9 |

*The Safe Rides program is a confidential telephone network of high-school seniors and juniors who provide transportation home for teen-agers who have had too much to drink at parties. Would you like to see such a program in your community, or not?*

| | |
|---|---|
| Yes | 87% |
| No | 8 |
| Already have program | 2 |
| Not sure | 3 |

Note: The use of alcoholic beverages is at a fifteen-year low point, with 64% of adult Americans saying they at least occasionally take a drink of beer, wine, or liquor. The decline in drinking has been most pronounced among downscale population groups, women, and older persons of both sexes.

About one person in six (17%) says drinking has been a cause of trouble in his or her family; the latest figure represents a downtrend since 1978, when the figure was 24%. Considerable support is still found for a return to prohibition, with 17% of adults saying they would favor a law forbidding the sale of all beer, wine, and liquor throughout the nation. The latest figure, however, is only about half that recorded in 1936, when the measurement was started.

By a wide 64% to 28% margin, adults say they would oppose a New Jersey law under which hosts can be sued for injuries to victims of auto accidents caused by guests to whom the hosts have served alcoholic beverages. However, an overwhelming 87% of the public would like to see the Safe Rides program, which provides transportation home for teen-agers who have overindulged at parties, introduced in their community.

The latest Gallup audit of adult drinking also reveals several practices and attitudes. About one-third of all adult drinkers (34%) could be considered regular drinkers, having taken a drink within the twenty-four-hour period prior to being interviewed. Another three in ten (30%) had done so within the week prior to the interview, and 35% had their last drink longer than a week ago. The most popular beverage in the survey is beer (43% say they drink it most often), followed by wine (33%) and liquor (27%).

### OCTOBER 2
### PRESIDENTIAL TRIAL HEATS

Interviewing Date: 9/28–10/1/84
Survey #243-G

*Asked of registered voters: If the 1984 presidential election were being held today, which would you vote for—the Republican candidates, Reagan and Bush, or the Democratic candidates, Mondale and Ferraro? [Those who were undecided or named other candidates were then asked: As of today, do you lean more to Reagan and Bush, or to Mondale and Ferraro?]*

Reagan-Bush .........................55%
Mondale-Ferraro .....................39
Other; undecided ................... 6

## By Sex
### Male

Reagan-Bush .........................58%
Mondale-Ferraro .....................36
Other; undecided ................... 6

### Female

Reagan-Bush .........................52%
Mondale-Ferraro .....................42
Other; undecided ................... 6

## By Ethnic Background
### White

Reagan-Bush .........................61%
Mondale-Ferraro .....................34
Other; undecided ................... 5

### Nonwhite

Reagan-Bush ......................... 7%
Mondale-Ferraro .....................80
Other; undecided ...................13

### Black

Reagan-Bush ......................... 4%
Mondale-Ferraro .....................82
Other; undecided ...................14

## By Education
### College Graduate

Reagan-Bush .........................57%
Mondale-Ferraro .....................39
Other; undecided ................... 4

### College Incomplete

Reagan-Bush .........................60%
Mondale-Ferraro .....................35
Other; undecided ................... 5

### High-School Graduate

Reagan-Bush .........................59%
Mondale-Ferraro .....................37
Other; undecided ................... 4

### Less Than High-School Graduate

Reagan-Bush .........................38%
Mondale-Ferraro .....................50
Other; undecided ...................12

## By Region
### East

Reagan-Bush .........................48%
Mondale-Ferraro .....................47
Other; undecided ................... 5

### Midwest

Reagan-Bush .........................58%
Mondale-Ferraro .....................36
Other; undecided ................... 6

### South

Reagan-Bush .........................58%
Mondale-Ferraro .....................36
Other; undecided ................... 6

### West

Reagan-Bush .........................56%
Mondale-Ferraro .....................40
Other; undecided ................... 4

## By Age
### 18–24 Years

Reagan-Bush .........................60%
Mondale-Ferraro .....................34
Other; undecided ................... 6

### 25–29 Years

Reagan-Bush ........................58%
Mondale-Ferraro ....................39
Other; undecided ................... 3

### 30–49 Years

Reagan-Bush ........................55%
Mondale-Ferraro ....................42
Other; undecided ................... 3

### 50–64 Years

Reagan-Bush ........................52%
Mondale-Ferraro ....................42
Other; undecided ................... 6

### 65 Years and Over

Reagan-Bush ........................55%
Mondale-Ferraro ....................33
Other; undecided ..................12

## By Income

### $40,000 and Over

Reagan-Bush ........................68%
Mondale-Ferraro ....................28
Other; undecided ................... 4

### $30,000–$39,999

Reagan-Bush ........................63%
Mondale-Ferraro ....................32
Other; undecided ................... 5

### $20,000–$29,999

Reagan-Bush ........................58%
Mondale-Ferraro ....................38
Other; undecided ................... 4

### $10,000–$19,999

Reagan-Bush ........................46%
Mondale-Ferraro ....................47
Other; undecided ................... 7

### Under $10,000

Reagan-Bush ........................43%
Mondale-Ferraro ....................49
Other; undecided ................... 8

## By Politics
### Republicans

Reagan-Bush ........................92%
Mondale-Ferraro .................... 5
Other; undecided ................... 3

### Democrats

Reagan-Bush ........................21%
Mondale-Ferraro ....................74
Other; undecided ................... 5

### Independents

Reagan-Bush ........................54%
Mondale-Ferraro ....................37
Other; undecided ................... 9

## By Religion
### Protestants

Reagan-Bush ........................59%
Mondale-Ferraro ....................36
Other; undecided ................... 5

### Catholics

Reagan-Bush ........................49%
Mondale-Ferraro ....................46
Other; undecided ................... 5

## By Occupation
### Professional and Business

Reagan-Bush ........................63%
Mondale-Ferraro ....................34
Other; undecided ................... 3

### Clerical and Sales

Reagan-Bush ........................57%
Mondale-Ferraro ....................42
Other; undecided ................... 1

### Manual Workers

Reagan-Bush ........................52%
Mondale-Ferraro ....................42
Other; undecided ................... 6

### Nonlabor Force

Reagan-Bush ........................48%
Mondale-Ferraro ....................42
Other; undecided ...................10

## By Community Size
### One Million and Over

Reagan-Bush ........................48%
Mondale-Ferraro ....................46
Other; undecided ................... 6

### 500,000–999,999

Reagan-Bush ........................60%
Mondale-Ferraro ....................34
Other; undecided ................... 6

### 50,000–499,999

Reagan-Bush ........................48%
Mondale-Ferraro ....................42
Other; undecided ...................10

### 2,500–49,999

Reagan-Bush ........................70%
Mondale-Ferraro ....................29
Other; undecided ................... 1

### Under 2,500; Rural

Reagan-Bush ........................62%
Mondale-Ferraro ....................33
Other; undecided ................... 5

## By Labor Union Household
### Labor Union Members

Reagan-Bush ........................40%
Mondale-Ferraro ....................56
Other; undecided ................... 4

### Nonlabor Union Members

Reagan-Bush ........................59%
Mondale-Ferraro ....................35
Other; undecided ................... 6

## Selected National Trend

|            | Reagan-Bush | Mondale-Ferraro | Other; undecided |
|------------|-------------|-----------------|------------------|
| Sept. 21–24 | 58%        | 37%             | 5%               |
| Sept. 7–10  | 56         | 37              | 7                |

### Republican Convention

| Aug. 10–13 | 52% | 41% | 7% |
|------------|-----|-----|----|
| July 27–30 | 53  | 41  | 6  |
| July 19–20* | 46 | 8   | 6  |

### Democratic Convention

| July 13–16 | 53% | 39% | 8% |
|------------|-----|-----|----|
| July 12–13* | 49 | 43  | 8  |

### Ferraro Announcement

| July 6–9       | 54% | 38% | 8%** |
|----------------|-----|-----|------|
| June 29–July 2 | 51  | 43  | 6**  |

*For *Newsweek*
**Test election between Reagan and Mondale

*Also asked of the sample: Do you strongly support them, or do you only moderately support them?*

Total Reagan-Bush ...................55%
  Strongly support ...............35
  Moderately support .............20
  Can't say ..................... *
Total Mondale-Ferraro ................39
  Strongly support ...............21
  Moderately support .............18
  Can't say ..................... *
Other; undecided ..................... 6

## By Politics
### Republicans

Total Reagan-Bush ...................92%
  Strongly support ...............69
  Moderately support .............23
  Can't say ..................... *

Total Mondale-Ferraro . . . . . . . . . . . . . . . . . 5
  Strongly support . . . . . . . . . . . . . . . 1
  Moderately support . . . . . . . . . . . . 4
  Can't say . . . . . . . . . . . . . . . . . . . . . *
Other; undecided . . . . . . . . . . . . . . . . . . . 3

### Democrats

Total Reagan-Bush . . . . . . . . . . . . . . . . . . 21%
  Strongly support . . . . . . . . . . . . . . . 9
  Moderately support . . . . . . . . . . . . 12
  Can't say . . . . . . . . . . . . . . . . . . . . . *
Total Mondale-Ferraro . . . . . . . . . . . . . . . . 74
  Strongly support . . . . . . . . . . . . . . . 44
  Moderately support . . . . . . . . . . . . 29
  Can't say . . . . . . . . . . . . . . . . . . . . . 1
Other; undecided . . . . . . . . . . . . . . . . . . . 5

### Independents

Total Reagan-Bush . . . . . . . . . . . . . : . . . 54%
  Strongly support . . . . . . . . . . . . . . . 25
  Moderately support . . . . . . . . . . . . 27
  Can't say . . . . . . . . . . . . . . . . . . . . . 2
Total Mondale-Ferraro . . . . . . . . . . . . . . . . 37
  Strongly support . . . . . . . . . . . . . . . 14
  Moderately support . . . . . . . . . . . . 22
  Can't say . . . . . . . . . . . . . . . . . . . . . 1
Other; undecided . . . . . . . . . . . . . . . . . . . 9

*Less than 1%

*Also asked of the sample: Would you say your vote is more a vote for (candidates) or more a vote against (other candidates)?*

Total Reagan-Bush . . . . . . . . . . . . . . . . . . 55%
  For this ticket . . . . . . . . . . . . . . . . 42
  Against other ticket . . . . . . . . . . . . 10
  Not sure . . . . . . . . . . . . . . . . . . . . . 3
Total Mondale-Ferraro . . . . . . . . . . . . . . . . 39
  For this ticket . . . . . . . . . . . . . . . . 17
  Against other ticket . . . . . . . . . . . . 19
  Not sure . . . . . . . . . . . . . . . . . . . . . 3
Other; undecided . . . . . . . . . . . . . . . . . . . 6

### By Sex
#### Male

Total Reagan-Bush . . . . . . . . . . . . . . . . . . 58%
  For this ticket . . . . . . . . . . . . . . . . 43
  Against other ticket . . . . . . . . . . . . 12
  Not sure . . . . . . . . . . . . . . . . . . . . . 3
Total Mondale-Ferraro . . . . . . . . . . . . . . . . 36
  For this ticket . . . . . . . . . . . . . . . . 15
  Against other ticket . . . . . . . . . . . . 18
  Not sure . . . . . . . . . . . . . . . . . . . . . 3
Other; undecided . . . . . . . . . . . . . . . . . . . 6

#### Female

Total Reagan-Bush . . . . . . . . . . . . . . . . . . 52%
  For this ticket . . . . . . . . . . . . . . . . 42
  Against other ticket . . . . . . . . . . . . 8
  Not sure . . . . . . . . . . . . . . . . . . . . . 2
Total Mondale-Ferraro . . . . . . . . . . . . . . . . 42
  For this ticket . . . . . . . . . . . . . . . . 19
  Against other ticket . . . . . . . . . . . . 21
  Not sure . . . . . . . . . . . . . . . . . . . . . 2
Other; undecided . . . . . . . . . . . . . . . . . . . 6

### By Ethnic Background
#### White

Total Reagan-Bush . . . . . . . . . . . . . . . . . . 61%
  For this ticket . . . . . . . . . . . . . . . . 47
  Against other ticket . . . . . . . . . . . . 11
  Not sure . . . . . . . . . . . . . . . . . . . . . 3
Total Mondale-Ferraro . . . . . . . . . . . . . . . . 34
  For this ticket . . . . . . . . . . . . . . . . 15
  Against other ticket . . . . . . . . . . . . 17
  Not sure . . . . . . . . . . . . . . . . . . . . . 2
Other; undecided . . . . . . . . . . . . . . . . . . . 5

#### Nonwhite

Total Reagan-Bush . . . . . . . . . . . . . . . . . . 7%
  For this ticket . . . . . . . . . . . . . . . . 5
  Against other ticket . . . . . . . . . . . . 2
  Not sure . . . . . . . . . . . . . . . . . . . . . *
Total Mondale-Ferraro . . . . . . . . . . . . . . . . 80
  For this ticket . . . . . . . . . . . . . . . . 36
  Against other ticket . . . . . . . . . . . . 40
  Not sure . . . . . . . . . . . . . . . . . . . . . 4
Other; undecided . . . . . . . . . . . . . . . . . . . 13

### Black

Total Reagan-Bush . . . . . . . . . . . . . . . . . 4%
  For this ticket . . . . . . . . . . . . . . . . 2
  Against other ticket . . . . . . . . . . . . 2
  Not sure . . . . . . . . . . . . . . . . . . . . *
Total Mondale-Ferraro . . . . . . . . . . . . . .82
  For this ticket . . . . . . . . . . . . . . . .39
  Against other ticket . . . . . . . . . . . .38
  Not sure . . . . . . . . . . . . . . . . . . . . 5
Other; undecided . . . . . . . . . . . . . . . . .14

### Less Than High-School Graduate

Total Reagan-Bush . . . . . . . . . . . . . . . . .38%
  For this ticket . . . . . . . . . . . . . . . .31
  Against other ticket . . . . . . . . . . . . 5
  Not sure . . . . . . . . . . . . . . . . . . . . 2
Total Mondale-Ferraro . . . . . . . . . . . . . .50
  For this ticket . . . . . . . . . . . . . . . .30
  Against other ticket . . . . . . . . . . . .18
  Not sure . . . . . . . . . . . . . . . . . . . . 2
Other; undecided . . . . . . . . . . . . . . . . .12

## By Education

### College Graduate

Total Reagan-Bush . . . . . . . . . . . . . . . . .57%
  For this ticket . . . . . . . . . . . . . . . .44
  Against other ticket . . . . . . . . . . . .12
  Not sure . . . . . . . . . . . . . . . . . . . . .1
Total Mondale-Ferraro . . . . . . . . . . . . . .39
  For this ticket . . . . . . . . . . . . . . . .16
  Against other ticket . . . . . . . . . . . .22
  Not sure . . . . . . . . . . . . . . . . . . . . 1
Other; undecided . . . . . . . . . . . . . . . . . 4

## By Region

### East

Total Reagan-Bush . . . . . . . . . . . . . . . . .48%
  For this ticket . . . . . . . . . . . . . . . .38
  Against other ticket . . . . . . . . . . . . 8
  Not sure . . . . . . . . . . . . . . . . . . . . 2
Total Mondale-Ferraro . . . . . . . . . . . . . .47
  For this ticket . . . . . . . . . . . . . . . .17
  Against other ticket . . . . . . . . . . . .28
  Not sure . . . . . . . . . . . . . . . . . . . . 2
Other; undecided . . . . . . . . . . . . . . . . . 5

### College Incomplete

Total Reagan-Bush . . . . . . . . . . . . . . . . .60%
  For this ticket . . . . . . . . . . . . . . . .47
  Against other ticket . . . . . . . . . . . .11
  Not sure . . . . . . . . . . . . . . . . . . . . 2
Total Mondale-Ferraro . . . . . . . . . . . . . .35
  For this ticket . . . . . . . . . . . . . . . .12
  Against other ticket . . . . . . . . . . . .19
  Not sure . . . . . . . . . . . . . . . . . . . . 4
Other; undecided . . . . . . . . . . . . . . . . . 5

### Midwest

Total Reagan-Bush . . . . . . . . . . . . . . . . .58%
  For this ticket . . . . . . . . . . . . . . . .41
  Against other ticket . . . . . . . . . . . .12
  Not sure . . . . . . . . . . . . . . . . . . . . 5
Total Mondale-Ferraro . . . . . . . . . . . . . .36
  For this ticket . . . . . . . . . . . . . . . .17
  Against other ticket . . . . . . . . . . . .17
  Not sure . . . . . . . . . . . . . . . . . . . . 2
Other; undecided . . . . . . . . . . . . . . . . . 6

### High-School Graduate

Total Reagan-Bush . . . . . . . . . . . . . . . . .59%
  For this ticket . . . . . . . . . . . . . . . .43
  Against other ticket . . . . . . . . . . . .11
  Not sure . . . . . . . . . . . . . . . . . . . . 5
Total Mondale-Ferraro . . . . . . . . . . . . . .37
  For this ticket . . . . . . . . . . . . . . . .16
  Against other ticket . . . . . . . . . . . .19
  Not sure . . . . . . . . . . . . . . . . . . . . 2
Other; undecided . . . . . . . . . . . . . . . . . 4

### South

Total Reagan-Bush . . . . . . . . . . . . . . . . .58%
  For this ticket . . . . . . . . . . . . . . . .45
  Against other ticket . . . . . . . . . . . .10
  Not sure . . . . . . . . . . . . . . . . . . . . 3
Total Mondale-Ferraro . . . . . . . . . . . . . .36
  For this ticket . . . . . . . . . . . . . . . .19
  Against other ticket . . . . . . . . . . . .14
  Not sure . . . . . . . . . . . . . . . . . . . . 3
Other; undecided . . . . . . . . . . . . . . . . . 6

### West

Total Reagan-Bush ...................56%
   For this ticket ..................44
   Against other ticket ............11
   Not sure ......................1
Total Mondale-Ferraro ................40
   For this ticket ..................16
   Against other ticket ............21
   Not sure ......................3
Other; undecided ....................4

## By Age
### 18–24 Years

Total Reagan-Bush ...................60%
   For this ticket ..................44
   Against other ticket ............9
   Not sure ......................7
Total Mondale-Ferraro ................34
   For this ticket ..................12
   Against other ticket ............19
   Not sure ......................3
Other; undecided ....................6

### 25–29 Years

Total Reagan-Bush ...................58%
   For this ticket ..................46
   Against other ticket ............8
   Not sure ......................4
Total Mondale-Ferraro ................39
   For this ticket ..................15
   Against other ticket ............21
   Not sure ......................3
Other; undecided ....................3

### 30–49 Years

Total Reagan-Bush ...................55%
   For this ticket ..................41
   Against other ticket ............12
   Not sure ......................2
Total Mondale-Ferraro ................42
   For this ticket ..................19
   Against other ticket ............20
   Not sure ......................3
Other; undecided ....................3

### 50–64 Years

Total Reagan-Bush ...................52%
   For this ticket ..................41
   Against other ticket ............9
   Not sure ......................2
Total Mondale-Ferraro ................42
   For this ticket ..................19
   Against other ticket ............21
   Not sure ......................2
Other; undecided ....................6

### 65 Years and Over

Total Reagan-Bush ...................55%
   For this ticket ..................43
   Against other ticket ............9
   Not sure ......................3
Total Mondale-Ferraro ................33
   For this ticket ..................17
   Against other ticket ............14
   Not sure ......................2
Other; undecided ....................12

## By Income
### $40,000 and Over

Total Reagan-Bush ...................68%
   For this ticket ..................48
   Against other ticket ............15
   Not sure ......................5
Total Mondale-Ferraro ................28
   For this ticket ..................10
   Against other ticket ............17
   Not sure ......................1
Other; undecided ....................4

### $30,000–$39,999

Total Reagan-Bush ...................63%
   For this ticket ..................49
   Against other ticket ............12
   Not sure ......................2
Total Mondale-Ferraro ................32
   For this ticket ..................12
   Against other ticket ............18
   Not sure ......................2
Other; undecided ....................5

### $20,000–$29,999

Total Reagan-Bush ................58%
   For this ticket ...............44
   Against other ticket ..........12
   Not sure ..................... 2
Total Mondale-Ferraro ..............38
   For this ticket ...............17
   Against other ticket ..........17
   Not sure ..................... 4
Other; undecided ................. 4

### $10,000–$19,999

Total Reagan-Bush ................46%
   For this ticket ...............35
   Against other ticket .......... 8
   Not sure ..................... 3
Total Mondale-Ferraro ..............47
   For this ticket ...............21
   Against other ticket ..........24
   Not sure ..................... 2
Other; undecided ................. 7

### Under $10,000

Total Reagan-Bush ................43%
   For this ticket ...............37
   Against other ticket .......... 5
   Not sure ..................... 1
Total Mondale-Ferraro ..............49
   For this ticket ...............25
   Against other ticket ..........21
   Not sure ..................... 3
Other; undecided ................. 8

### By Politics
#### Republicans

Total Reagan-Bush ................92%
   For this ticket ...............80
   Against other ticket ..........10
   Not sure ..................... 2
Total Mondale-Ferraro .............. 5
   For this ticket ............... 2
   Against other ticket .......... 3
   Not sure ..................... *
Other; undecided ................. 3

### Democrats

Total Reagan-Bush ................21%
   For this ticket ...............11
   Against other ticket .......... 7
   Not sure ..................... 2
Total Mondale-Ferraro ..............74
   For this ticket ...............37
   Against other ticket ..........33
   Not sure ..................... 4
Other; undecided ................. 5

### Independents

Total Reagan-Bush ................54%
   For this ticket ...............35
   Against other ticket ..........15
   Not sure ..................... 4
Total Mondale-Ferraro ..............37
   For this ticket ...............10
   Against other ticket ..........23
   Not sure ..................... 4
Other; undecided ................. 9

### By Religion
#### Protestants

Total Reagan-Bush ................59%
   For this ticket ...............45
   Against other ticket ..........11
   Not sure ..................... 3
Total Mondale-Ferraro ..............36
   For this ticket ...............16
   Against other ticket ..........18
   Not sure ..................... 2
Other; undecided ................. 5

### Catholics

Total Reagan-Bush ................49%
   For this ticket ...............36
   Against other ticket .......... 9
   Not sure ..................... 3
Total Mondale-Ferraro ..............46
   For this ticket ...............21
   Against other ticket ..........22
   Not sure ..................... 3
Other; undecided ................. 5

## By Occupation

### Professional and Business

Total Reagan-Bush ................63%
  For this ticket ................51
  Against other ticket ...........11
  Not sure .......................1
Total Mondale-Ferraro ............34
  For this ticket ................14
  Against other ticket ...........18
  Not sure .......................2
Other; undecided .................3

### Clerical and Sales

Total Reagan-Bush ................57%
  For this ticket ................44
  Against other ticket ...........9
  Not sure .......................4
Total Mondale-Ferraro ............42
  For this ticket ................10
  Against other ticket ...........25
  Not sure .......................7
Other; undecided .................1

### Manual Workers

Total Reagan-Bush ................52%
  For this ticket ................35
  Against other ticket ...........13
  Not sure .......................4
Total Mondale-Ferraro ............42
  For this ticket ................20
  Against other ticket ...........20
  Not sure .......................2
Other; undecided .................6

### Nonlabor Force

Total Reagan-Bush ................48%
  For this ticket ................40
  Against other ticket ...........6
  Not sure .......................2
Total Mondale-Ferraro ............42
  For this ticket ................21
  Against other ticket ...........18
  Not sure .......................3
Other; undecided .................10

## By Community Size

### One Million and Over

Total Reagan-Bush ................48%
  For this ticket ................35
  Against other ticket ...........10
  Not sure .......................3
Total Mondale-Ferraro ............46
  For this ticket ................20
  Against other ticket ...........23
  Not sure .......................3
Other; undecided .................6

### 500,000–999,999

Total Reagan-Bush ................60%
  For this ticket ................43
  Against other ticket ...........15
  Not sure .......................2
Total Mondale-Ferraro ............34
  For this ticket ................15
  Against other ticket ...........17
  Not sure .......................2
Other; undecided .................6

### 50,000–499,999

Total Reagan-Bush ................48%
  For this ticket ................41
  Against other ticket ...........6
  Not sure .......................1
Total Mondale-Ferraro ............42
  For this ticket ................16
  Against other ticket ...........24
  Not sure .......................2
Other; undecided .................10

### 2,500–49,999

Total Reagan-Bush ................70%
  For this ticket ................50
  Against other ticket ...........13
  Not sure .......................7
Total Mondale-Ferraro ............29
  For this ticket ................12
  Against other ticket ...........15
  Not sure .......................2
Other; undecided .................1

Total Reagan-Bush . . . . . . . . . . . . . . . . . .62%
    For this ticket . . . . . . . . . . . . . . . . .50
    Against other ticket . . . . . . . . . . . .10
    Not sure . . . . . . . . . . . . . . . . . . . . . 2
Total Mondale-Ferraro . . . . . . . . . . . . . . . .33
    For this ticket . . . . . . . . . . . . . . . . .17
    Against other ticket . . . . . . . . . . . .14
    Not sure . . . . . . . . . . . . . . . . . . . . . 2
Other; undecided . . . . . . . . . . . . . . . . . . . . 5

## By Labor Union Household

### Labor Union Members

Total Reagan-Bush . . . . . . . . . . . . . . . . . .40%
    For this ticket . . . . . . . . . . . . . . . . .24
    Against other ticket . . . . . . . . . . . .11
    Not sure . . . . . . . . . . . . . . . . . . . . . 5
Total Mondale-Ferraro . . . . . . . . . . . . . . . .56
    For this ticket . . . . . . . . . . . . . . . . .23
    Against other ticket . . . . . . . . . . . .29
    Not sure . . . . . . . . . . . . . . . . . . . . . 4
Other; undecided . . . . . . . . . . . . . . . . . . . . 4

### Nonlabor Union Members

Total Reagan-Bush . . . . . . . . . . . . . . . . . .59%
    For this ticket . . . . . . . . . . . . . . . . .47
    Against other ticket . . . . . . . . . . . .10
    Not sure . . . . . . . . . . . . . . . . . . . . . 2
Total Mondale-Ferraro . . . . . . . . . . . . . . . .35
    For this ticket . . . . . . . . . . . . . . . . .16
    Against other ticket . . . . . . . . . . . .17
    Not sure . . . . . . . . . . . . . . . . . . . . . 2
Other; undecided . . . . . . . . . . . . . . . . . . . . 6

*Less than 1%

Note: With only five weeks remaining until election day, the Republican ticket of Ronald Reagan and George Bush holds a commanding 16-percentage point lead over Walter Mondale and Geraldine Ferraro, the Democratic challengers. The latest findings show the GOP ticket leading 55% to 39% with 6% undecided, statistically unchanged from two earlier September readings.

The Reagan-Bush ticket not only enjoys a substantial lead at this time, but its backers, by a 42% to 10% margin, describe their support in positive (pro-Reagan) rather than negative (anti-Mondale) terms. On the other hand, supporters of the Democratic ticket are divided fairly evenly between those who are voting for their ticket (17%) and those voting against the GOP (19%). Of particularly bad news to Democrats is the tendency of independents, who currently support Mondale and Ferraro (37%), to express what is largely a negative vote: far more say they are voting against the GOP ticket (23%) than for the Democratic one (10%).

## OCTOBER 4
## PRESIDENTIAL/VICE-PRESIDENTIAL DEBATES

Interviewing Date: 9/7–10/84
Survey #241-G

> As you may know, the presidential and vice-presidential candidates will hold televised debates later this fall. First, how likely are you to watch the debates between Ronald Reagan and Walter Mondale? Would you say you are very likely, fairly likely, or not at all likely to watch them?

Very likely . . . . . . . . . . . . . . . . . . . . . . . . .38%
Fairly likely . . . . . . . . . . . . . . . . . . . . . . .31
Not at all likely . . . . . . . . . . . . . . . . . . . . .29
Don't know . . . . . . . . . . . . . . . . . . . . . . . . 2

### By Sex
### Male

Very likely . . . . . . . . . . . . . . . . . . . . . . . . .40%
Fairly likely . . . . . . . . . . . . . . . . . . . . . . .27
Not at all likely . . . . . . . . . . . . . . . . . . . . .31
Don't know . . . . . . . . . . . . . . . . . . . . . . . . 2

### Female

Very likely . . . . . . . . . . . . . . . . . . . . . . . . .37%
Fairly likely . . . . . . . . . . . . . . . . . . . . . . .34
Not at all likely . . . . . . . . . . . . . . . . . . . . .27
Don't know . . . . . . . . . . . . . . . . . . . . . . . . 2

## By Ethnic Background

### White

| | |
|---|---|
| Very likely | 37% |
| Fairly likely | 31 |
| Not at all likely | 30 |
| Don't know | 2 |

### Nonwhite

| | |
|---|---|
| Very likely | 52% |
| Fairly likely | 27 |
| Not at all likely | 17 |
| Don't know | 4 |

### Black

| | |
|---|---|
| Very likely | 54% |
| Fairly likely | 31 |
| Not at all likely | 13 |
| Don't know | 2 |

## By Education

### College Graduate

| | |
|---|---|
| Very likely | 48% |
| Fairly likely | 34 |
| Not at all likely | 16 |
| Don't know | 2 |

### College Incomplete

| | |
|---|---|
| Very likely | 35% |
| Fairly likely | 34 |
| Not at all likely | 29 |
| Don't know | 2 |

### High-School Graduate

| | |
|---|---|
| Very likely | 35% |
| Fairly likely | 30 |
| Not at all likely | 33 |
| Don't know | 2 |

### Less Than High-School Graduate

| | |
|---|---|
| Very likely | 38% |
| Fairly likely | 27 |
| Not at all likely | 33 |
| Don't know | 2 |

## By Region

### East

| | |
|---|---|
| Very likely | 37% |
| Fairly likely | 30 |
| Not at all likely | 30 |
| Don't know | 3 |

### Midwest

| | |
|---|---|
| Very likely | 36% |
| Fairly likely | 32 |
| Not at all likely | 31 |
| Don't know | 1 |

### South

| | |
|---|---|
| Very likely | 40% |
| Fairly likely | 31 |
| Not at all likely | 26 |
| Don't know | 3 |

### West

| | |
|---|---|
| Very likely | 42% |
| Fairly likely | 28 |
| Not at all likely | 29 |
| Don't know | 1 |

## By Age

### 18–29 Years

| | |
|---|---|
| Very likely | 30% |
| Fairly likely | 29 |
| Not at all likely | 38 |
| Don't know | 3 |

### 30–49 Years

| | |
|---|---|
| Very likely | 36% |
| Fairly likely | 36 |
| Not at all likely | 26 |
| Don't know | 2 |

### 50 Years and Over

| | |
|---|---|
| Very likely | 47% |
| Fairly likely | 27 |
| Not at all likely | 24 |
| Don't know | 2 |

## By Income

### $40,000 and Over

Very likely . . . . . . . . . . . . . . . . . . . . . . . . .45%
Fairly likely . . . . . . . . . . . . . . . . . . . . .29
Not at all likely . . . . . . . . . . . . . . . . . . . .25
Don't know . . . . . . . . . . . . . . . . . . . . . . . 1

### $30,000–$39,999

Very likely . . . . . . . . . . . . . . . . . . . . . . . . .39%
Fairly likely . . . . . . . . . . . . . . . . . . . . .36
Not at all likely . . . . . . . . . . . . . . . . . . . .23
Don't know . . . . . . . . . . . . . . . . . . . . . . . 2

### $20,000–$29,999

Very likely . . . . . . . . . . . . . . . . . . . . . . . . .35%
Fairly likely . . . . . . . . . . . . . . . . . . . . .35
Not at all likely . . . . . . . . . . . . . . . . . . . .27
Don't know . . . . . . . . . . . . . . . . . . . . . . . 3

### $10,000–$19,999

Very likely . . . . . . . . . . . . . . . . . . . . . . . . .35%
Fairly likely . . . . . . . . . . . . . . . . . . . . .29
Not at all likely . . . . . . . . . . . . . . . . . . . .34
Don't know . . . . . . . . . . . . . . . . . . . . . . . 2

### Under $10,000

Very likely . . . . . . . . . . . . . . . . . . . . . . . . .39%
Fairly likely . . . . . . . . . . . . . . . . . . . . .27
Not at all likely . . . . . . . . . . . . . . . . . . . .31
Don't know . . . . . . . . . . . . . . . . . . . . . . . 3

## By Politics

### Republicans

Very likely . . . . . . . . . . . . . . . . . . . . . . . . .45%
Fairly likely . . . . . . . . . . . . . . . . . . . . .27
Not at all likely . . . . . . . . . . . . . . . . . . . .27
Don't know . . . . . . . . . . . . . . . . . . . . . . . 1

### Democrats

Very likely . . . . . . . . . . . . . . . . . . . . . . . . .41%
Fairly likely . . . . . . . . . . . . . . . . . . . . .33
Not at all likely . . . . . . . . . . . . . . . . . . . .23
Don't know . . . . . . . . . . . . . . . . . . . . . . . 3

### Independents

Very likely . . . . . . . . . . . . . . . . . . . . . . . . .28%
Fairly likely . . . . . . . . . . . . . . . . . . . . .32
Not at all likely . . . . . . . . . . . . . . . . . . . .39
Don't know . . . . . . . . . . . . . . . . . . . . . . . 1

## By Occupation

### Professional and Business

Very likely . . . . . . . . . . . . . . . . . . . . . . . . .43%
Fairly likely . . . . . . . . . . . . . . . . . . . . .30
Not at all likely . . . . . . . . . . . . . . . . . . . .26
Don't know . . . . . . . . . . . . . . . . . . . . . . . 1

### Clerical and Sales

Very likely . . . . . . . . . . . . . . . . . . . . . . . . .43%
Fairly likely . . . . . . . . . . . . . . . . . . . . .25
Not at all likely . . . . . . . . . . . . . . . . . . . .26
Don't know . . . . . . . . . . . . . . . . . . . . . . . 6

### Manual Workers

Very likely . . . . . . . . . . . . . . . . . . . . . . . . .30%
Fairly likely . . . . . . . . . . . . . . . . . . . . .36
Not at all likely . . . . . . . . . . . . . . . . . . . .31
Don't know . . . . . . . . . . . . . . . . . . . . . . . 3

### Nonlabor Force

Very likely . . . . . . . . . . . . . . . . . . . . . . . . .47%
Fairly likely . . . . . . . . . . . . . . . . . . . . .27
Not at all likely . . . . . . . . . . . . . . . . . . . .24
Don't know . . . . . . . . . . . . . . . . . . . . . . . 2

*How about a televised debate between the vice-presidential candidates, George Bush and Geraldine Ferraro? Would you say you are very likely, fairly likely, or not very likely to watch it?*

Very likely . . . . . . . . . . . . . . . . . . . . . . . . .35%
Fairly likely . . . . . . . . . . . . . . . . . . . . .26
Not very likely . . . . . . . . . . . . . . . . . . . .36
Don't know . . . . . . . . . . . . . . . . . . . . . . . 3

## By Sex
### Male

Very likely . . . . . . . . . . . . . . . . . . . . . . . . 34%
Fairly likely . . . . . . . . . . . . . . . . . . . . . . . .24
Not very likely . . . . . . . . . . . . . . . . . . . . .40
Don't know . . . . . . . . . . . . . . . . . . . . . . . 2

### Female

Very likely . . . . . . . . . . . . . . . . . . . . . . . . 36%
Fairly likely . . . . . . . . . . . . . . . . . . . . . . . .28
Not very likely . . . . . . . . . . . . . . . . . . . . .33
Don't know . . . . . . . . . . . . . . . . . . . . . . . 3

## By Ethnic Background
### White

Very likely . . . . . . . . . . . . . . . . . . . . . . . . 33%
Fairly likely . . . . . . . . . . . . . . . . . . . . . . . .26
Not very likely . . . . . . . . . . . . . . . . . . . . .38
Don't know . . . . . . . . . . . . . . . . . . . . . . . 3

### Nonwhite

Very likely . . . . . . . . . . . . . . . . . . . . . . . . 50%
Fairly likely . . . . . . . . . . . . . . . . . . . . . . . .24
Not very likely . . . . . . . . . . . . . . . . . . . . .22
Don't know . . . . . . . . . . . . . . . . . . . . . . . 4

### Black

Very likely . . . . . . . . . . . . . . . . . . . . . . . . 52%
Fairly likely . . . . . . . . . . . . . . . . . . . . . . . .30
Not very likely . . . . . . . . . . . . . . . . . . . . .16
Don't know . . . . . . . . . . . . . . . . . . . . . . . 2

## By Education
### College Graduate

Very likely . . . . . . . . . . . . . . . . . . . . . . . . 45%
Fairly likely . . . . . . . . . . . . . . . . . . . . . . . .29
Not very likely . . . . . . . . . . . . . . . . . . . . .24
Don't know . . . . . . . . . . . . . . . . . . . . . . . 2

### College Incomplete

Very likely . . . . . . . . . . . . . . . . . . . . . . . . 33%
Fairly likely . . . . . . . . . . . . . . . . . . . . . . . .26
Not very likely . . . . . . . . . . . . . . . . . . . . .40
Don't know . . . . . . . . . . . . . . . . . . . . . . . 1

### High-School Graduate

Very likely . . . . . . . . . . . . . . . . . . . . . . . .29%
Fairly likely . . . . . . . . . . . . . . . . . . . . . . . .27
Not very likely . . . . . . . . . . . . . . . . . . . . .40
Don't know . . . . . . . . . . . . . . . . . . . . . . . 4

### Less Than High-School Graduate

Very likely . . . . . . . . . . . . . . . . . . . . . . . .37%
Fairly likely . . . . . . . . . . . . . . . . . . . . . . . .23
Not very likely . . . . . . . . . . . . . . . . . . . . .38
Don't know . . . . . . . . . . . . . . . . . . . . . . . 2

## By Region
### East

Very likely . . . . . . . . . . . . . . . . . . . . . . . .36%
Fairly likely . . . . . . . . . . . . . . . . . . . . . . . .24
Not very likely . . . . . . . . . . . . . . . . . . . . .37
Don't know . . . . . . . . . . . . . . . . . . . . . . . 3

### Midwest

Very likely . . . . . . . . . . . . . . . . . . . . . . . .31%
Fairly likely . . . . . . . . . . . . . . . . . . . . . . . .27
Not very likely . . . . . . . . . . . . . . . . . . . . .40
Don't know . . . . . . . . . . . . . . . . . . . . . . . 2

### South

Very likely . . . . . . . . . . . . . . . . . . . . . . . .37%
Fairly likely . . . . . . . . . . . . . . . . . . . . . . . .27
Not very likely . . . . . . . . . . . . . . . . . . . . .33
Don't know . . . . . . . . . . . . . . . . . . . . . . . 3

### West

Very likely . . . . . . . . . . . . . . . . . . . . . . . .35%
Fairly likely . . . . . . . . . . . . . . . . . . . . . . . .26
Not very likely . . . . . . . . . . . . . . . . . . . . .37
Don't know . . . . . . . . . . . . . . . . . . . . . . . 2

## By Age
### 18–29 Years

Very likely . . . . . . . . . . . . . . . . . . . . . . . .27%
Fairly likely . . . . . . . . . . . . . . . . . . . . . . . .24
Not very likely . . . . . . . . . . . . . . . . . . . . .46
Don't know . . . . . . . . . . . . . . . . . . . . . . . 3

### 30–49 Years

Very likely . . . . . . . . . . . . . . . . . . . . . . . .32%
Fairly likely . . . . . . . . . . . . . . . . . . . . . .29
Not very likely . . . . . . . . . . . . . . . . . . . .36
Don't know . . . . . . . . . . . . . . . . . . . . . . . 3

### 50 Years and Over

Very likely . . . . . . . . . . . . . . . . . . . . . . . .45%
Fairly likely . . . . . . . . . . . . . . . . . . . . . .24
Not very likely . . . . . . . . . . . . . . . . . . . .29
Don't know . . . . . . . . . . . . . . . . . . . . . . . 2

## By Income
### $40,000 and Over

Very likely . . . . . . . . . . . . . . . . . . . . . . . .39%
Fairly likely . . . . . . . . . . . . . . . . . . . . . .26
Not very likely . . . . . . . . . . . . . . . . . . . .34
Don't know . . . . . . . . . . . . . . . . . . . . . . . 1

### $30,000–$39,999

Very likely . . . . . . . . . . . . . . . . . . . . . . . .37%
Fairly likely . . . . . . . . . . . . . . . . . . . . . .24
Not very likely . . . . . . . . . . . . . . . . . . . .37
Don't know . . . . . . . . . . . . . . . . . . . . . . . 2

### $20,000–$29,999

Very likely . . . . . . . . . . . . . . . . . . . . . . . .34%
Fairly likely . . . . . . . . . . . . . . . . . . . . . .25
Not very likely . . . . . . . . . . . . . . . . . . . .39
Don't know . . . . . . . . . . . . . . . . . . . . . . . 2

### $10,000–$19,999

Very likely . . . . . . . . . . . . . . . . . . . . . . . .32%
Fairly likely . . . . . . . . . . . . . . . . . . . . . .26
Not very likely . . . . . . . . . . . . . . . . . . . .38
Don't know . . . . . . . . . . . . . . . . . . . . . . . 4

### Under $10,000

Very likely . . . . . . . . . . . . . . . . . . . . . . . .34%
Fairly likely . . . . . . . . . . . . . . . . . . . . . .28
Not very likely . . . . . . . . . . . . . . . . . . . .35
Don't know . . . . . . . . . . . . . . . . . . . . . . . 3

## By Politics
### Republicans

Very likely . . . . . . . . . . . . . . . . . . . . . . . .35%
Fairly likely . . . . . . . . . . . . . . . . . . . . . .25
Not very likely . . . . . . . . . . . . . . . . . . . .39
Don't know . . . . . . . . . . . . . . . . . . . . . . . 1

### Democrats

Very likely . . . . . . . . . . . . . . . . . . . . . . . .42%
Fairly likely . . . . . . . . . . . . . . . . . . . . . .28
Not very likely . . . . . . . . . . . . . . . . . . . .26
Don't know . . . . . . . . . . . . . . . . . . . . . . . 4

### Independents

Very likely . . . . . . . . . . . . . . . . . . . . . . . .26%
Fairly likely . . . . . . . . . . . . . . . . . . . . . .24
Not very likely . . . . . . . . . . . . . . . . . . . .48
Don't know . . . . . . . . . . . . . . . . . . . . . . . 2

## By Occupation
### Professional and Business

Very likely . . . . . . . . . . . . . . . . . . . . . . . .36%
Fairly likely . . . . . . . . . . . . . . . . . . . . . .28
Not very likely . . . . . . . . . . . . . . . . . . . .35
Don't know . . . . . . . . . . . . . . . . . . . . . . . 1

### Clerical and Sales

Very likely . . . . . . . . . . . . . . . . . . . . . . . .42%
Fairly likely . . . . . . . . . . . . . . . . . . . . . .22
Not very likely . . . . . . . . . . . . . . . . . . . .31
Don't know . . . . . . . . . . . . . . . . . . . . . . . 5

### Manual Workers

Very likely . . . . . . . . . . . . . . . . . . . . . . . .28%
Fairly likely . . . . . . . . . . . . . . . . . . . . . .27
Not very likely . . . . . . . . . . . . . . . . . . . .41
Don't know . . . . . . . . . . . . . . . . . . . . . . . 4

### Nonlabor Force

Very likely . . . . . . . . . . . . . . . . . . . . . . . .46%
Fairly likely . . . . . . . . . . . . . . . . . . . . . .23
Not very likely . . . . . . . . . . . . . . . . . . . .29
Don't know . . . . . . . . . . . . . . . . . . . . . . . 2

*What issues would you most like to have the presidential candidates debate?*

Economic issues . . . . . . . . . . . . . . . . . . . . . .45%
  Unemployment . . . . . . . . . . . . . . .18
  Economy . . . . . . . . . . . . . . . . . . . . .16
  High cost of living . . . . . . . . . . . . . 6
  Hunger, poverty . . . . . . . . . . . . . . . 2
  High interest rates . . . . . . . . . . . . . 2
  Other . . . . . . . . . . . . . . . . . . . . . . . 1
Domestic problems . . . . . . . . . . . . . . . . . .23
  Problems of elderly . . . . . . . . . . . . 6
  Education . . . . . . . . . . . . . . . . . . . . 4
  Abortion . . . . . . . . . . . . . . . . . . . . . 2
  Other . . . . . . . . . . . . . . . . . . . . . . .11
Political problems . . . . . . . . . . . . . . . . . .35
  Federal budget deficit . . . . . . . . . . .13
  Taxation . . . . . . . . . . . . . . . . . . . . .11
  Excessive defense spending . . . . . . . 3
  Cuts in social spending . . . . . . . . . 2
  Excessive government spending . . . 2
  Other . . . . . . . . . . . . . . . . . . . . . . . 4
War, defense . . . . . . . . . . . . . . . . . . . . . .27
  Threat of war . . . . . . . . . . . . . . . . .10
  Arms race . . . . . . . . . . . . . . . . . . . . 7
  Arms talks . . . . . . . . . . . . . . . . . . . . 4
  National security . . . . . . . . . . . . . . . 3
  Defense capability . . . . . . . . . . . . . . 2
  Other . . . . . . . . . . . . . . . . . . . . . . . 1
International, foreign affairs . . . . . . . . . . .13
  Relations with Soviet Union . . . . . . 2
  Foreign affairs . . . . . . . . . . . . . . . . . 9
  Other . . . . . . . . . . . . . . . . . . . . . . . 2
All others . . . . . . . . . . . . . . . . . . . . . . . . 5
No opinion . . . . . . . . . . . . . . . . . . . . . . .15
                              163%*

*Total adds to more than 100% due to multiple responses.

*Asked of registered voters: Who do you think is likely to do a better job in the presidential debates—Ronald Reagan or Walter Mondale?*

| | Choice in Test Election | | |
| | Reagan-Bush (55%) | Mondale-Ferraro (40%) | Other; undecided (5%) |
|---|---|---|---|
| Reagan | 61% | 83% | 33% | 34% |
| Mondale | 22 | 6 | 45 | 25 |
| No difference | 7 | 5 | 9 | 15 |
| No opinion | 10 | 6 | 13 | 26 |

*Asked of registered voters: And who do you think is likely to do a better job in a debate between the vice-presidential candidates—George Bush or Geraldine Ferraro?*

| | Choice in Test Election | | |
| | Reagan-Bush (55%) | Mondale-Ferraro (40%) | Other; undecided (5%) |
|---|---|---|---|
| Bush | 36% | 52% | 15% | 20% |
| Ferraro | 38 | 22 | 64 | 25 |
| No difference | 9 | 8 | 7 | 25 |
| No opinion | 17 | 18 | 14 | 30 |

Note: Although Walter Mondale badly needs a strong showing in the presidential debates to boost his sagging campaign, the public heavily favors President Ronald Reagan to outperform Mondale in the debates, the first of which will be televised on October 7. One element that should work in Mondale's favor is also the top item on the public's agenda: unemployment, an issue on which Reagan does not have a strong advantage.

The public expressed considerable interest in the debates, with seven in ten saying they are "very likely" (38%) or "fairly likely" (31%) to watch them.

Six in ten registered voters (61%) in a Gallup Poll conducted in early September said they thought Reagan was likely to do a better job in the debates than Mondale, the choice of 22%. The balance thought the contests would be a stand-off (7%) or did not express an opinion (10%). Not surprisingly, the public's assessment of who will win the debates is closely related to their choice for president. In a test election conducted in the same survey, Reagan enjoyed a 55% to 40% lead over Mondale, with 5% undecided.

President Reagan's reputation as a communicator is amply illustrated by the survey findings.

Among his partisans in the test election, Reagan is the overwhelming (83%) choice to outperform Mondale in the debates. However, only a 45% plurality of Mondale's test election supporters thinks he will best the president, while almost as many, 33%, think that Mondale will lose to Reagan.

Unemployment is the leading topic the public would like to see addressed in the debates; it is mentioned by 18% of all respondents (and 26% of Democrats). Cited next most often is the economy in general (16%), followed by the federal budget deficit (13%) and foreign affairs (13%). Taxes are mentioned by 11%, and the threat of war by 10%. Other frequently named issues include the arms race (7%), the high cost of living (6%), problems of the elderly (6%), national defense (5%), and education (4%).

Only slightly fewer say they are likely to watch the vice-presidential candidates debate than expect to watch the Reagan-Mondale debates, with 61% and 69%, respectively, saying they are at least fairly likely to do so. The public is evenly divided on the probable outcome, with Democrat Geraldine Ferraro the choice of 38% of registered voters to 36% for the GOP incumbent, George Bush. The 2-percentage point difference is within the statistical margin of error for polls of this size and design. Backers of the Mondale-Ferraro ticket are on much firmer ground with regard to the winner of the Bush-Ferraro debate, with a 64% majority picking their party's vice-presidential nominee and only 15%, Bush. And, although a slim 52% majority of Reagan-Bush supporters favors Bush as the likely winner of his debate with Ferraro, she is chosen by 22% of those who say they would vote for the GOP ticket if the election were being held now.

The importance of the candidate debates is well illustrated by the experience of past elections. President Reagan's sweeping victory in the 1980 election reflected one of the most dramatic shifts ever recorded in voter preferences in the last week of a presidential campaign. Incumbent President Jimmy Carter led Reagan prior to their debate on October 28, but Carter's momentum stalled as a result, and he never regained his predebate level of support.

In 1976, the second Ford-Carter debate, on foreign policy, appeared to have dealt a fatal blow to President Gerald Ford's comeback in that race. In early September, Ford had trailed Carter by 18 points. The president then moved into a virtual tie with Carter on the eve of the second debate. That contest brought Ford's momentum to a halt, and the Democratic challenger began to recoup some of his earlier losses. The 1976 election became one of the closest in history, with Carter winning 51.1% of the popular vote for the major party candidates, to 48.9% for Ford.

In 1960, Vice-President Richard Nixon led Senator John Kennedy prior to the first televised debate. Following this contest, which the public by a 2-to-1 margin thought was won by Kennedy, Nixon lost the lead and never regained it. His loss to Kennedy in that election was even closer than the 1976 contest: Kennedy won 50.1% of the popular vote for the major party candidates, to 49.9% for Nixon.

## OCTOBER 8
## FIRST PRESIDENTIAL DEBATE

Special *Newsweek* Poll*

*Viewers of all or most of the debate (84%), about half of it (9%), or only some of it (7%) were asked: Regardless of which candidate you happen to support, who do you think did a better job in the debate—Ronald Reagan or Walter Mondale?*

*For the *Newsweek* Poll, the Gallup Organization on Sunday night, October 7, telephoned 379 registered voters who watched the debate. They were drawn from a pool of respondents in the latest Gallup Poll who said there was a chance they would watch, and who closely reflected the national sample of registered voters in demographics, party affiliation, and candidate support. The margin of error is plus or minus 7 percentage points.

Reagan ...........................35%
Mondale ..........................54
Neither (volunteered) ................ 8
No opinion ....................... 3

*The same viewers were then asked: Regardless of which man you happen to prefer, please tell me whether you feel each phrase applies more to Ronald Reagan or more to Walter Mondale in the debate:*

*Seemed thoughtful, well informed?*

Reagan ...........................37%
Mondale ..........................45
Neither; no opinion .................18

*Seemed confident, self-assured?*

Reagan ...........................33%
Mondale ..........................55
Neither; no opinion .................12

*Came closer to reflecting your point of view on the issues?*

Reagan ...........................57%
Mondale ..........................38
Neither; no opinion ................. 5

*Seemed more capable of dealing with the problems facing this country?*

Reagan ...........................58%
Mondale ..........................36
Neither; no opinion ................. 6

*Came across as more likable?*

Reagan ...........................50%
Mondale ..........................40
Neither; no opinion .................10

*Presented better ideas for keeping the country prosperous?*

Reagan ...........................55%
Mondale ..........................36
Neither; no opinion ................. 9

Note: The American public's overwhelming expectation that President Ronald Reagan would outperform Walter Mondale in their two debates this month was confounded at least temporarily by the Democratic challenger's strong showing in the first debate, televised on Sunday, October 7. As reported, almost three times as many voters (61%) in a September Gallup Poll said they expected the president to do a better job in the debates, than the 22% who chose Mondale.

A *Newsweek* Poll conducted by the Gallup Organization after the first debate, however, indicates that viewers thought that Mondale, rather than Reagan, had done a better job by a vote of 54% to 35%, very close to a reversal of the two candidates' relative standings in the latest presidential test elections. (The Gallup Poll's September 28–October 1 reading showed Reagan leading Mondale, 55% to 39%). Mondale's strong showing was ascribed to the greater confidence and self-assurance he displayed, and he also outscored Reagan on appearing "thoughtful and well informed." Ironically, Mondale appears in the debate to have beaten the president at his own game, by better displaying the qualities of presentation so closely identified with Reagan.

President Reagan, on the other hand, succeeded in convincing debate viewers that he was "more capable of dealing with the problems facing this country," and that he "presented better ideas for keeping the country prosperous." He also "came closer to reflecting (the audience's) point of view on the issues" and "came across as more likable."

A major portion of the debate focused on the federal budget deficit and Mondale's plan for tax increases to reduce it. In a late September Gallup Poll, 40% of those aware of the Mondale tax plan favored it, while 48% were opposed. Public opinion closely followed party lines.

Perhaps the strongest evidence of the debate's power as a campaign device is that among viewers who had not firmly decided on their presidential choice—including moderate supporters of either man and undecideds—63% said they were more likely to vote for Mondale because of the debate, compared to 29% who expressed greater support for Reagan.

## OCTOBER 8
## MONDALE'S TAX PLAN

Interviewing Date: 9/21–24/84
Survey #242-G

*Have you heard or read about Walter Mondale's proposed plan to reduce the federal budget deficit by increasing personal income taxes, especially for middle and upper income families, and by increasing taxes on corporations?*

| | Yes |
|---|---|
| National | 84% |

*Asked of those who replied in the affirmative: Do you favor or oppose this plan?*

| | |
|---|---|
| Favor | 40% |
| Oppose | 48 |
| No opinion | 12 |

### By Sex
#### Male

| | |
|---|---|
| Favor | 41% |
| Oppose | 50 |
| No opinion | 9 |

#### Female

| | |
|---|---|
| Favor | 39% |
| Oppose | 46 |
| No opinion | 15 |

### By Ethnic Background
#### White

| | |
|---|---|
| Favor | 37% |
| Oppose | 51 |
| No opinion | 12 |

#### Nonwhite

| | |
|---|---|
| Favor | 63% |
| Oppose | 23 |
| No opinion | 14 |

#### Black

| | |
|---|---|
| Favor | 67% |
| Oppose | 19 |
| No opinion | 14 |

### By Education
#### College Graduate

| | |
|---|---|
| Favor | 39% |
| Oppose | 54 |
| No opinion | 7 |

#### College Incomplete

| | |
|---|---|
| Favor | 36% |
| Oppose | 54 |
| No opinion | 10 |

#### High-School Graduate

| | |
|---|---|
| Favor | 41% |
| Oppose | 45 |
| No opinion | 14 |

#### Less Than High-School Graduate

| | |
|---|---|
| Favor | 45% |
| Oppose | 39 |
| No opinion | 16 |

### By Region
#### East

| | |
|---|---|
| Favor | 37% |
| Oppose | 50 |
| No opinion | 13 |

#### Midwest

| | |
|---|---|
| Favor | 45% |
| Oppose | 43 |
| No opinion | 12 |

#### South

| | |
|---|---|
| Favor | 39% |
| Oppose | 48 |
| No opinion | 13 |

### West

Favor . . . . . . . . . . . . . . . . . . . . . . . . . . . . 40%
Oppose . . . . . . . . . . . . . . . . . . . . . . . . . . 51
No opinion . . . . . . . . . . . . . . . . . . . . . . . 9

### By Age

#### 18–24 Years

Favor . . . . . . . . . . . . . . . . . . . . . . . . . . . 41%
Oppose . . . . . . . . . . . . . . . . . . . . . . . . . 44
No opinion . . . . . . . . . . . . . . . . . . . . . . 15

#### 25–29 Years

Favor . . . . . . . . . . . . . . . . . . . . . . . . . . . 46%
Oppose . . . . . . . . . . . . . . . . . . . . . . . . . 43
No opinion . . . . . . . . . . . . . . . . . . . . . . 11

#### 30–49 Years

Favor . . . . . . . . . . . . . . . . . . . . . . . . . . . 39%
Oppose . . . . . . . . . . . . . . . . . . . . . . . . . 51
No opinion . . . . . . . . . . . . . . . . . . . . . . 10

#### 50–64 Years

Favor . . . . . . . . . . . . . . . . . . . . . . . . . . . 39%
Oppose . . . . . . . . . . . . . . . . . . . . . . . . . 49
No opinion . . . . . . . . . . . . . . . . . . . . . . 12

#### 65 Years and Over

Favor . . . . . . . . . . . . . . . . . . . . . . . . . . . 40%
Oppose . . . . . . . . . . . . . . . . . . . . . . . . . 46
No opinion . . . . . . . . . . . . . . . . . . . . . . 14

### By Income

#### $40,000 and Over

Favor . . . . . . . . . . . . . . . . . . . . . . . . . . . 35%
Oppose . . . . . . . . . . . . . . . . . . . . . . . . . 57
No opinion . . . . . . . . . . . . . . . . . . . . . . 8

#### $30,000–$39,999

Favor . . . . . . . . . . . . . . . . . . . . . . . . . . . 32%
Oppose . . . . . . . . . . . . . . . . . . . . . . . . . 54
No opinion . . . . . . . . . . . . . . . . . . . . . . 14

### $20,000–$29,999

Favor . . . . . . . . . . . . . . . . . . . . . . . . . . . 40%
Oppose . . . . . . . . . . . . . . . . . . . . . . . . . 52
No opinion . . . . . . . . . . . . . . . . . . . . . . 8

### $10,000–$19,999

Favor . . . . . . . . . . . . . . . . . . . . . . . . . . . 47%
Oppose . . . . . . . . . . . . . . . . . . . . . . . . . 40
No opinion . . . . . . . . . . . . . . . . . . . . . . 13

### Under $10,000

Favor . . . . . . . . . . . . . . . . . . . . . . . . . . . 48%
Oppose . . . . . . . . . . . . . . . . . . . . . . . . . 37
No opinion . . . . . . . . . . . . . . . . . . . . . . 15

### By Politics

#### Republicans

Favor . . . . . . . . . . . . . . . . . . . . . . . . . . . 13%
Oppose . . . . . . . . . . . . . . . . . . . . . . . . . 75
No opinion . . . . . . . . . . . . . . . . . . . . . . 12

#### Democrats

Favor . . . . . . . . . . . . . . . . . . . . . . . . . . . 65%
Oppose . . . . . . . . . . . . . . . . . . . . . . . . . 24
No opinion . . . . . . . . . . . . . . . . . . . . . . 11

#### Independents

Favor . . . . . . . . . . . . . . . . . . . . . . . . . . . 41%
Oppose . . . . . . . . . . . . . . . . . . . . . . . . . 47
No opinion . . . . . . . . . . . . . . . . . . . . . . 12

### By Occupation

#### Professional and Business

Favor . . . . . . . . . . . . . . . . . . . . . . . . . . . 30%
Oppose . . . . . . . . . . . . . . . . . . . . . . . . . 57
No opinion . . . . . . . . . . . . . . . . . . . . . . 13

#### Clerical and Sales

Favor . . . . . . . . . . . . . . . . . . . . . . . . . . . 44%
Oppose . . . . . . . . . . . . . . . . . . . . . . . . . 46
No opinion . . . . . . . . . . . . . . . . . . . . . . 10

### Manual Workers

Favor .................................49%
Oppose ...............................41
No opinion ...........................10

### Nonlabor Force

Favor .................................38%
Oppose ...............................48
No opinion ...........................14

*Also asked of the aware group (84% of the sample): Do you think Mondale's plan would, in general, help or hurt the overall U.S. economy?*

Help .................................39%
Hurt .................................43
No opinion ...........................18

## By Sex
### Male

Help .................................38%
Hurt .................................46·
No opinion ...........................16

### Female

Help .................................39%
Hurt .................................41
No opinion ...........................20

## By Ethnic Background
### White

Help .................................36%
Hurt .................................46
No opinion ...........................18

### Nonwhite

Help .................................61%
Hurt .................................19
No opinion ...........................20

### Black

Help .................................67%
Hurt .................................14
No opinion ...........................19

## By Education
### College Graduate

Help .................................37%
Hurt .................................50
No opinion ...........................13

### College Incomplete

Help .................................30%
Hurt .................................52
No opinion ...........................18

### High-School Graduate

Help .................................43%
Hurt .................................40
No opinion ...........................17

### Less Than High-School Graduate

Help .................................43%
Hurt .................................33
No opinion ...........................24

## By Region
### East

Help .................................38%
Hurt .................................43
No opinion ...........................19

### Midwest

Help .................................40%
Hurt .................................40
No opinion ...........................20

### South

Help .................................39%
Hurt .................................43
No opinion ...........................18

### West

Help .................................38%
Hurt .................................49
No opinion ...........................13

## By Age

### 18–24 Years

Help ................................. 39%
Hurt ................................. 39
No opinion .......................... 22

### 25–29 Years

Help ................................. 45%
Hurt ................................. 41
No opinion .......................... 14

### 30–49 Years

Help ................................. 40%
Hurt ................................. 45
No opinion .......................... 15

### 50–64 Years

Help ................................. 36%
Hurt ................................. 45
No opinion .......................... 19

### 65 Years and Over

Help ................................. 35%
Hurt ................................. 42
No opinion .......................... 23

## By Income

### $40,000 and Over

Help ................................. 32%
Hurt ................................. 52
No opinion .......................... 16

### $30,000–$39,999

Help ................................. 34%
Hurt ................................. 49
No opinion .......................... 17

### $20,000–$29,999

Help ................................. 40%
Hurt ................................. 45
No opinion .......................... 15

### $10,000–$19,999

Help ................................. 42%
Hurt ................................. 41
No opinion .......................... 17

### Under $10,000

Help ................................. 48%
Hurt ................................. 31
No opinion .......................... 21

## By Politics

### Republicans

Help ................................. 11%
Hurt ................................. 69
No opinion .......................... 20

### Democrats

Help ................................. 67%
Hurt ................................. 18
No opinion .......................... 15

### Independents

Help ................................. 35%
Hurt ................................. 45
No opinion .......................... 20

## By Occupation

### Professional and Business

Help ................................. 29%
Hurt ................................. 52
No opinion .......................... 19

### Clerical and Sales

Help ................................. 43%
Hurt ................................. 44
No opinion .......................... 13

### Manual Workers

Help ................................. 48%
Hurt ................................. 36
No opinion .......................... 16

### Nonlabor Force

Help .............................35%
Hurt .............................42
No opinion ........................23

Note: Prior to the first presidential debate, public reaction to Walter Mondale's tax plan was linked to a great extent to political affiliation. Democrats backed the plan 65% to 24%, while Republicans voted 75% to 13% in opposition. Opinion was much more evenly divided among independents, who voted 47% to 41% against it.

Opinion also was closely divided on whether Mondale's plan would help or hurt the overall U.S. economy, with 39% saying it would help and 43% holding the opposite view. Democrats believed it would help, by a 67% to 18% ratio, while Republicans said it would hurt, by a 69% to 11% margin. The views of independents again fell between those belonging to the major parties, with 35% saying the plan would help the economy and 45% disagreeing.

## OCTOBER 14
## VOTER REGISTRATION

Interviewing Date: 7/27–30; 8/10–13; 9/7–10/84*
Survey #239-G; 240-G; 241-G

*Is your name now recorded in the registration book of the precinct or election district where you now live?*

*The analysis is based on comparable data from six surveys conducted in 1984 and 1980. The 1984 data are based on in-person interviews with 4,685 adults, age 18 and older, in three separate surveys conducted between July 27 and September 10. The 1980 data are based on 4,686 in-person interviews conducted between July 11 and August 18. Although the 1984 data were collected somewhat later in the year than the 1980 data, which might have affected registration and intent to vote, examination of the individual surveys showed the time difference had no appreciable effect on the findings.

|  | 1984 Yes | 1980 Yes | Point difference |
|---|---|---|---|
| National .......... | 74% | 70% | +4 |

### By Sex

|  | 1984 Yes | 1980 Yes | Point difference |
|---|---|---|---|
| Male ............. | 74% | 71% | +3 |
| Female ........... | 73 | 69 | +4 |

### By Ethnic Background

|  | 1984 Yes | 1980 Yes | Point difference |
|---|---|---|---|
| White ............ | 74% | 71% | +3 |
| Black ............ | 76 | 66 | +10 |

### By Education

|  | 1984 Yes | 1980 Yes | Point difference |
|---|---|---|---|
| College graduate .... | 83% | 81% | +2 |
| College incomplete .. | 78 | 77 | +1 |
| High-school graduate ........ | 70 | 67 | +3 |
| Less than high-school graduate ... | 67 | 65 | +2 |

### By Region

|  | 1984 Yes | 1980 Yes | Point difference |
|---|---|---|---|
| East ............. | 73% | 72% | +1 |
| Midwest .......... | 77 | 75 | +2 |
| South ............ | 71 | 68 | +3 |
| West ............. | 74 | 65 | +9 |

### By Age

|  | 1984 Yes | 1980 Yes | Point difference |
|---|---|---|---|
| 18–29 years ........ | 54% | 49% | +5 |
| 30–49 years ........ | 75 | 74 | +1 |
| 50–64 years ........ | 87 | 83 | +4 |
| 65 years and over ... | 87 | 84 | +3 |

### By Politics

|  | 1984 Yes | 1980 Yes | Point difference |
|---|---|---|---|
| Republicans ........ | 80% | 78% | +2 |
| Democrats ......... | 78 | 74 | +4 |
| Independents ....... | 64 | 62 | +2 |

*Do you, yourself, plan to vote in the presidential election this November, or not? [If yes: How certain are you that you will vote—absolutely certain, fairly certain, or not certain?]*

*Here is a picture of a ladder. Suppose we say the top of the ladder, marked 10, represents a person who definitely will vote in the election this November, and the bottom of the ladder, marked 1, represents a person who definitely will not vote in the election. How far up or down the ladder would you place yourself?*

## Voting Intentions

|  | 1984 | 1980 | Point differ- ence |
|---|---|---|---|
| Absolutely certain | 69% | 61% | +8 |
| Ten on ladder scale | 60 | 55 | +5 |

Following is a comparison of the three voting indicators combined: registered voters who say they are "absolutely certain" to go to the polls and who indicate on the ladder scale that they plan to vote:

## Turnout Index*

|  | 1984 | 1980 | Point differ- ence |
|---|---|---|---|
| National | 53% | 49% | +4 |

### By Sex

|  | | | |
|---|---|---|---|
| Male | 53% | 50% | +3 |
| Female | 43 | 47 | +6 |

### By Ethnic Background

|  | | | |
|---|---|---|---|
| White | 53% | 50% | +3 |
| Black | 57 | 40 | +17 |

### By Education

|  | | | |
|---|---|---|---|
| College graduate | 69% | 65% | +4 |
| College incomplete | 55 | 55 | — |
| High-school graduate | 47 | 46 | +1 |
| Less than high-school graduate | 48 | 40 | +8 |

*Although this index measures the relative likelihood of different population groups to go to the polls, the figures should not be interpreted as indicating the percentage of each group that will vote.

### By Region

|  | | | |
|---|---|---|---|
| East | 54% | 50% | +4 |
| Midwest | 53 | 50 | +3 |
| South | 48 | 45 | +3 |
| West | 59 | 50 | +9 |

### By Age

|  | | | |
|---|---|---|---|
| 18–29 years | 32% | 30% | +2 |
| 30–49 years | 55 | 52 | +3 |
| 50–64 years | 68 | 62 | +6 |
| 65 years and over | 66 | 56 | +10 |

### By Politics

|  | | | |
|---|---|---|---|
| Republicans | 60% | 60% | — |
| Democrats | 58 | 51 | +7 |
| Independents | 42 | 40 | +2 |

As shown in the table below, participation rose from 59.3% in the 1956 Dwight Eisenhower reelection race to 62.8% in the tightly fought 1960 contest between John Kennedy and Richard Nixon. Since then, turnout steadily has deteriorated, culminating in the 1980 election, when merely 52.6% of eligible Americans exercised their franchise. A steep decline occurred in the 1972 election, when Republican incumbent Richard Nixon won his bid for reelection in a landslide victory over Democrat George McGovern.

## Voter Turnout*

| | |
|---|---|
| 1980 | 52.6% |
| 1976 | 53.5 |
| 1972 | 55.2 |
| 1968 | 60.9 |
| 1964 | 61.9 |
| 1960 | 62.8 |
| 1956 | 59.3 |
| 1952 | 61.6 |
| 1948 | 51.1 |

*Census Bureau, Elections Research Center

Note: Despite a twenty-four-year downtrend in voter participation, the stage may be set for an increase in voter turnout in this year's presidential election. Four key factors contribute to this possibility:

1) The latest polls clearly reflect the political parties' successful efforts to register new voters. Nationally, 74% of eligible Americans report they are now registered, up from 70% at this time in 1980. Gains are recorded in almost all population groups, especially among blacks.

2) A higher proportion now (69%) than four years ago (61%) says not only that they plan to vote, but also that they are "absolutely certain" to do so, with gains found in all major segments of the population.

3) On a Gallup scale designed to determine voter interest in elections, significantly more now (60%) than in 1980 (55%) place themselves at the scale's highest point, indicating that they definitely will vote in the election this November.

4) Democratic candidate Walter Mondale's upset victory over Ronald Reagan in the first presidential debate (October 7) may have breathed new vitality into a campaign that had become so lopsided as to cause some voters to lose interest. Many political analysts now expect the contest to become closer than the 16-point chasm separating the two tickets in the Gallup Poll's late September assessment.

These favorable signs notwithstanding, if the 1984 presidential election produces a voter turnout higher than that of 1980, it will be the first election since 1960 to have topped its predecessor.

## OCTOBER 18

## REAGAN VS. MONDALE—PUBLIC IMAGES

Interviewing Date: 9/21–24/84
Survey #242-G

*Here is a list of terms—shown as pairs of opposites—that have been used to describe Ronald Reagan (Walter Mondale). From each pair of opposites, would you select the term which you feel best describes Reagan (Mondale)?*

## Candidates' Perceived Sympathy for Groups

### (Percent Rating Each Candidate Positively)

| Cares about needs and problems of | Reagan | Mondale | Reagan advantage |
|---|---|---|---|
| Business executives | 67% | 46% | +21 |
| Wealthy people | 66 | 37 | +29 |
| Unemployed people | 51 | 63 | −12 |
| Farmers | 50 | 55 | −5 |
| Middle-income people | 50 | 58 | −8 |
| Young people | 49 | 55 | −6 |
| Elderly | 49 | 60 | −11 |
| People like yourself | 48 | 53 | −5 |
| Poor people | 46 | 65 | −19 |
| Small-business people | 46 | 53 | −7 |
| Average citizen | 43 | 52 | −9 |
| Black people | 43 | 58 | −15 |
| Manual workers | 43 | 60 | −17 |
| Women | 43 | 66 | −23 |

Note: Partisans of both President Ronald Reagan and his Democratic rival, Walter Mondale, will find good news in the results of a recent Gallup survey. Asked to rate each candidate's concern for the needs and problems of people in fourteen different population categories, the public bestows more positive ratings on Mondale than on Reagan for twelve of the groups tested.

On the other hand, although losing to Mondale, Reagan is given a positive grade by at least 43% of the public for his concern for the average citizen, blacks, women, and manual workers, groups on which he scores least well. Reagan outscores Mondale on caring for the needs and problems of business executives, 67% and 46%, respectively. He also prevails on caring for wealthy people, with 66% positive votes to 37% for Mondale.

The charge that Reagan is unsympathetic to some groups finds its greatest expression with regard to women's needs, with Mondale receiving a positive rating of 66% to Reagan's 43%. Others include poor people, on whom Mondale is positively rated by 65% to 46% for Reagan; manual workers, 60% to 43%; and blacks, 58% to 43%.

For the most part, survey respondents in each population category tend to agree with the general public's assessment of the presidential candidates.

For example, the public gives Reagan and Mondale positive grades of 49% and 60%, respectively, for their concern for the elderly; among persons in the survey age 65 and older, the figures are 46% and 59%. Similarly, Reagan and Mondale receive positive ratings of 66% and 37% for their concern about the wealthy; those in the survey with annual family incomes of $40,000 or more assign Reagan a 71% positive score to 33% for Mondale. This observation holds true for most of the groups in the survey, including women, poor people, and business executives. The two major exceptions are blacks and young people.

As shown on the table, 43% of the public give Reagan a positive rating for his concern about blacks' needs and problems, while 58% rate Mondale positively in this regard. Among blacks themselves, however, only 13% rate Reagan's concern for people of their race positively, while 65% give Mondale a favorable grade. Similarly, among the general public, Reagan (49%) is outscored by Mondale (55%) on his concern about the needs and problems of young people. Among 18 to 24 year olds in the survey, the score is 48% for Reagan to 44% for Mondale, a statistical draw.

## OCTOBER 18
## PRESIDENTIAL TRIAL HEATS

Interviewing Date: 10/15–17/84
Special Telephone Survey

*Asked of registered voters: If the 1984 presidential election were being held today, which would you vote for—the Republican candidates, Reagan and Bush, or the Democratic candidates, Mondale and Ferraro? [Those who were undecided or named other candidates were then asked: As of today, do you lean more to Reagan and Bush, or to Mondale and Ferraro?]*

Reagan-Bush ........................58%
Mondale-Ferraro ....................38
Other; undecided ................... 4

### Selected National Trend

|  | Reagan-Bush | Mondale-Ferraro | Other; undecided |
|---|---|---|---|
| Sept. 28–Oct. 1 | 55% | 39% | 6% |
| Sept. 21–24 | 58 | 37 | 5 |
| Sept. 7–10 | 56 | 37 | 7 |

*Also asked of the sample: Do you strongly support them, or do you only moderately support them?*

|  | Oct. 15–17 | Sept. 28–Oct. 1 |
|---|---|---|
| Total Reagan-Bush ....... | 58% | 55% |
| Strongly support | 36 | 35 |
| Moderately support | 22 | 20 |
| Total Mondale-Ferraro .... | 38 | 39 |
| Strongly support | 22 | 21 |
| Moderately support | 16 | 18 |
| Other; undecided ........ | 4 | 6 |

*Also asked of the sample: Would you say your vote is more a vote for (candidates) or more a vote against (other candidates)?*

|  | Oct. 15–17 | Sept. 28–Oct. 1 |
|---|---|---|
| Total Reagan-Bush ....... | 58% | 55% |
| For this ticket | 43 | 42 |
| Against other ticket | 11 | 10 |
| Not sure | 4 | 3 |
| Total Mondale-Ferraro .... | 38 | 39 |
| For this ticket | 18 | 17 |
| Against other ticket | 16 | 19 |
| Not sure | 4 | 3 |
| Other; undecided ........ | 4 | 6 |

*Ronald Reagan is now 73—is his age a factor in your decision as to how to vote, or not?*

|  | Oct. 15–17 | September survey* |
|---|---|---|
| Is a factor .............. | 19% | 20% |
| Is not; no opinion ....... | 81 | 80 |

*Conducted for *Newsweek*. The first presidential debate was held on October 7.

Note: In its first postdebate test election, the Gallup Poll finds no narrowing of the Reagan-Bush ticket's wide lead over the Mondale-Ferraro Democratic ticket. The latest survey shows the GOP slate leading 58% to 38%, with 4% undecided. In the preceding survey, conducted at the end of last month, Ronald Reagan and George Bush held a 55% to 39% lead over Walter Mondale and Geraldine Ferraro. The difference between the present 20-point spread between the two tickets and the previous 16-point spread is statistically inconclusive.

President Reagan's relatively poor performance in the first debate was attributed to an uncharacteristic lack of self-assurance, in a *Newsweek* survey conducted by the Gallup Organization after the debate. This gave rise to speculation—absent earlier during the campaign—that Reagan's age had caused some loss of mental acuity. When questioned in the new Gallup survey, however, only 19% of respondents said the president's age was a factor that would influence their vote, while 81% said it was not or they had no opinion. When the same question was asked in a September *Newsweek* survey by Gallup, virtually identical responses were recorded, with 20% saying Reagan's age would be a factor in their voting decision and 80% saying it would not.

## OCTOBER 18
## VOTER REGISTRATION

Interviewing Date: 9/21–24/84
Survey #242-G

*Has anyone contacted you this year to encourage or to help you register to vote?*

|  | Yes |
| --- | --- |
| National | 20% |

### By Ethnic Background

| | |
| --- | --- |
| White | 19% |
| Black | 24 |

### By Age

| | |
| --- | --- |
| 18–24 years | 25% |
| 25–29 years | 24 |
| 30–49 years | 23 |
| 50–64 years | 16 |
| 65 years and over | 10 |

### By Politics

| | |
| --- | --- |
| Republicans | 20% |
| Democrats | 23 |
| Independents | 16 |

*Have you, yourself, been contacted within the last six months by anyone representing a candidate for president—either in person, by phone, by mail, or in some other way?*

| | Sept. 1984 | Sept. 1980 |
| --- | --- | --- |
| Contacted | 32% | 17% |
| Mail | 23 | 11 |
| Phone | 8 | 3 |
| In person | 4 | 2 |
| Other | 1 | 1 |
| Not contacted | 68 | 83 |

Note: Amid the hubbub raised by the presidential and vice-presidential debates, it is easy to overlook the growth of other kinds of political activity. A comparison of survey results, however, presents evidence of almost twice as much at the grassroots' level this fall as during the same period in 1980. In a mid-September Gallup Poll, nearly one-third (32%) of the public said they had been contacted on behalf of a presidential candidate during the preceding six months; the comparable figure for 1980 was 17%.

Direct mail was the principal contact medium in both periods, with 23% this year and 11% in 1980 saying they were the recipients of one or more pieces of political advertising. Phone messages were received by 8% this year, compared to 3% four years ago. In-person contacts were cited by 4% and 2% during the 1984 and 1980 campaigns, respectively.

So far this year, Republicans (36%) have been contacted more than either Democrats (28%) or independents (24%). Virtually all of the difference in the greater number of contacts made with

Republicans than Democrats can be traced to mail solicitations, with 28% of the former and 20% of the latter saying they had received at least one piece of mail boosting their party's presidential candidate.

As many as one adult in five (20%) claims he or she has been encouraged to register to vote this year or has been offered help in doing so. Citizens under 50 years are far more likely than those 50 or older to have been offered this assistance. Also, blacks are somewhat more likely than whites to report being asked to register.

## OCTOBER 21
## MOST IMPORTANT PROBLEM

Interviewing Date: 9/30–10/1/84
Survey #243-G

*What do you think is the most important problem facing this country today?*

| | |
|---|---|
| Threat of war; international tensions | 30% |
| Unemployment | 22 |
| High cost of living; taxes; high interest rates | 12 |
| Excessive government spending; budget deficits | 10 |
| Economy (general) | 4 |
| Moral decline in society | 4 |
| Poverty; hunger | 4 |
| Crime | 3 |
| Dissatisfaction with government | 3 |
| All others | 22 |
| Don't know | 1 |
| | 115%* |

*Total adds to more than 100% due to multiple responses.

*All persons who named a problem were then asked: Which presidential candidate do you think can do a better job of handling the problem you have just mentioned—Ronald Reagan or Walter Mondale?*

| | |
|---|---|
| Reagan | 43% |
| Mondale | 36 |
| No difference (volunteered) | 12 |
| No opinion | 9 |

*Which man, if elected president in November, do you think would be more likely to keep the United States out of World War III— Ronald Reagan or Walter Mondale?*

| | |
|---|---|
| Reagan | 42% |
| Mondale | 37 |
| No difference (volunteered) | 12 |
| No opinion | 9 |

### Selected National Trend

| | Reagan | Mondale | No difference | No opinion |
|---|---|---|---|---|
| June 1984 | 38% | 38% | 15% | 9% |
| Jan. 1984 | 35 | 44 | 11 | 10 |

*Now, which man would do a better job of keeping the country prosperous—Ronald Reagan or Walter Mondale?*

| | |
|---|---|
| Reagan | 54% |
| Mondale | 30 |
| No difference (volunteered) | 8 |
| No opinion | 8 |

### Selected National Trend

| | Reagan | Mondale | No difference | No opinion |
|---|---|---|---|---|
| June 1984 | 51% | 32% | 8% | 9% |
| Jan. 1984 | 50 | 34 | 6 | 10 |

*Do you think the Reagan administration's defense policies have brought the United States closer to war or closer to peace?*

| | |
|---|---|
| War | 38% |
| Peace | 39 |
| No difference (volunteered) | 13 |
| No opinion | 10 |

## Selected National Trend

| | War | Peace | No difference | No opinion |
|---|---|---|---|---|
| June–July 1984 | 46% | 28% | 16% | 10% |
| November 1983 | 47 | 28 | 15 | 17 |
| August 1983 | 43 | 26 | 17 | 14 |

*Which man, if elected president in November, would be better able to work with the leaders of the Soviet Union to achieve world peace— Ronald Reagan or Walter Mondale?*

Reagan ............................45%
Mondale ...........................35
No difference (volunteered) ...........9
No opinion ........................11

Interviewing Date: 9/21–24/84
Survey #242-G

*In general, are you satisfied or dissatisfied with the way things are going in the United States at this time?*

Satisfied .............................48%
Dissatisfied ..........................45
No opinion ........................ 7

### By Sex
#### Male

Satisfied .............................53%
Dissatisfied ..........................41
No opinion ........................ 6

#### Female

Satisfied .............................44%
Dissatisfied ..........................49
No opinion ........................ 7

### By Ethnic Background
#### White

Satisfied .............................52%
Dissatisfied ..........................42
No opinion ........................ 6

#### Nonwhite

Satisfied ............................21%
Dissatisfied .........................69
No opinion .........................10

#### Black

Satisfied ............................16%
Dissatisfied .........................74
No opinion .........................10

### By Education
#### College Graduate

Satisfied .............................55%
Dissatisfied ..........................41
No opinion ........................ 4

#### College Incomplete

Satisfied .............................56%
Dissatisfied ..........................37
No opinion ........................ 7

#### High-School Graduate

Satisfied .............................48%
Dissatisfied ..........................46
No opinion ........................ 6

#### Less Than High-School Graduate

Satisfied .............................36%
Dissatisfied ..........................55
No opinion ........................ 9

### By Region
#### East

Satisfied .............................47%
Dissatisfied ..........................46
No opinion ........................ 7

#### Midwest

Satisfied .............................49%
Dissatisfied ..........................45
No opinion ........................ 6

### South

Satisfied . . . . . . . . . . . . . . . . . . . . . . . . . . .47%
Dissatisfied . . . . . . . . . . . . . . . . . . . . . . . .46
No opinion . . . . . . . . . . . . . . . . . . . . . . . 7

### West

Satisfied . . . . . . . . . . . . . . . . . . . . . . . . . . .51%
Dissatisfied . . . . . . . . . . . . . . . . . . . . . . . .43
No opinion . . . . . . . . . . . . . . . . . . . . . . . 6

## By Age
### 18–24 Years

Satisfied . . . . . . . . . . . . . . . . . . . . . . . . . . .51%
Dissatisfied . . . . . . . . . . . . . . . . . . . . . . . .40
No opinion . . . . . . . . . . . . . . . . . . . . . . . 9

### 25–29 Years

Satisfied . . . . . . . . . . . . . . . . . . . . . . . . . . .47%
Dissatisfied . . . . . . . . . . . . . . . . . . . . . . . .44
No opinion . . . . . . . . . . . . . . . . . . . . . . . 9

### 30–49 Years

Satisfied . . . . . . . . . . . . . . . . . . . . . . . . . . .50%
Dissatisfied . . . . . . . . . . . . . . . . . . . . . . . .46
No opinion . . . . . . . . . . . . . . . . . . . . . . . 4

### 50–64 Years

Satisfied . . . . . . . . . . . . . . . . . . . . . . . . . . .47%
Dissatisfied . . . . . . . . . . . . . . . . . . . . . . . .45
No opinion . . . . . . . . . . . . . . . . . . . . . . . 8

### 65 Years and Over

Satisfied . . . . . . . . . . . . . . . . . . . . . . . . . . .46%
Dissatisfied . . . . . . . . . . . . . . . . . . . . . . . .49
No opinion . . . . . . . . . . . . . . . . . . . . . . . 5

## By Income
### $40,000 and Over

Satisfied . . . . . . . . . . . . . . . . . . . . . . . . . . .56%
Dissatisfied . . . . . . . . . . . . . . . . . . . . . . . .37
No opinion . . . . . . . . . . . . . . . . . . . . . . . 7

### $30,000–$39,999

Satisfied . . . . . . . . . . . . . . . . . . . . . . . . . . .61%
Dissatisfied . . . . . . . . . . . . . . . . . . . . . . . .36
No opinion . . . . . . . . . . . . . . . . . . . . . . . 3

### $20,000–$29,999

Satisfied . . . . . . . . . . . . . . . . . . . . . . . . . . .52%
Dissatisfied . . . . . . . . . . . . . . . . . . . . . . . .41
No opinion . . . . . . . . . . . . . . . . . . . . . . . 7

### $10,000–$19,999

Satisfied . . . . . . . . . . . . . . . . . . . . . . . . . . .42%
Dissatisfied . . . . . . . . . . . . . . . . . . . . . . . .51
No opinion . . . . . . . . . . . . . . . . . . . . . . . 7

### Under $10,000

Satisfied . . . . . . . . . . . . . . . . . . . . . . . . . . .35%
Dissatisfied . . . . . . . . . . . . . . . . . . . . . . . .57
No opinion . . . . . . . . . . . . . . . . . . . . . . . 8

## By Politics
### Republicans

Satisfied . . . . . . . . . . . . . . . . . . . . . . . . . . .76%
Dissatisfied . . . . . . . . . . . . . . . . . . . . . . . .19
No opinion . . . . . . . . . . . . . . . . . . . . . . . 5

### Democrats

Satisfied . . . . . . . . . . . . . . . . . . . . . . . . . . .25%
Dissatisfied . . . . . . . . . . . . . . . . . . . . . . . .68
No opinion . . . . . . . . . . . . . . . . . . . . . . . 7

### Independents

Satisfied . . . . . . . . . . . . . . . . . . . . . . . . . . .48%
Dissatisfied . . . . . . . . . . . . . . . . . . . . . . . .45
No opinion . . . . . . . . . . . . . . . . . . . . . . . 7

## By Occupation
### Professional and Business

Satisfied . . . . . . . . . . . . . . . . . . . . . . . . . . .59%
Dissatisfied . . . . . . . . . . . . . . . . . . . . . . . .35
No opinion . . . . . . . . . . . . . . . . . . . . . . . 6

### Clerical and Sales

Satisfied ............................52%
Dissatisfied .........................46
No opinion ......................... 2

### Manual Workers

Satisfied ............................43%
Dissatisfied .........................49
No opinion ......................... 8

### Nonlabor Force

Satisfied ............................42%
Dissatisfied .........................52
No opinion ......................... 6

### Selected National Trend

|  | Satisfied | Dis-satisfied | No opinion |
|---|---|---|---|
| *1984* | | | |
| February ......... | 50% | 46% | 4% |
| *1983* | | | |
| August ........... | 35 | 59 | 6 |
| *1982* | | | |
| November ........ | 24 | 72 | 4 |
| September ........ | 24 | 72 | 4 |
| April ............ | 25 | 71 | 4 |
| *1981* | | | |
| December ........ | 27 | 67 | 6 |
| June ............. | 33 | 61 | 6 |
| January .......... | 17 | 78 | 5 |
| *1979* | | | |
| November ........ | 19 | 77 | 4 |
| July ............. | 12 | 84 | 4 |
| February ......... | 26 | 69 | 5 |

Note: The second presidential debate this fall takes on great political significance, with fear of war at the highest point in Gallup surveys in a year and voters closely divided on whether Ronald Reagan or Walter Mondale would be more likely to keep the United States out of war. The twin issues of peace and prosperity have been the most important in most presidential campaigns during the last half century. The candidate or political party seen as better able to keep the nation both at peace and prosperous invariably has been the winner at the polls.

At present, 42% say Reagan would be better able to keep the country at peace, while nearly as many, 37%, credit Mondale in this respect. On the other key issue, however, Reagan far outstrips his rival, with 54% saying the president would do a better job of keeping the country prosperous, compared to 30% who say Mondale. President Reagan has registered gains on both issues since the beginning of the year when he led Mondale, 50% to 34%, on prosperity and trailed his Democratic challenger, 35% to 44%, on the peace issue.

Paralleling the findings on peace, an increasing number of Americans now believes the Reagan administration's defense policies have brought the United States closer to peace than to war. In a survey conducted this summer, 46% said Reagan's policies had brought the nation closer to war, while 28% said peace. Currently—in a survey conducted shortly after Soviet Foreign Minister Andrei Gromyko's September visit to the United States—38% believe the president's policies have increased the chances for war, while 39% say the chances for peace have been enhanced.

Reagan also has gained ground since the Gromyko visit in the public's perception that he would be better able than Mondale to work with the leaders of the Soviet Union to achieve world peace. In the latest survey, 45% of voters credit Reagan in this respect, while 35% think Mondale would do a better job.

As the presidential candidates meet in Kansas City to debate foreign policy matters, international strife and the threat of war are the dominant concerns of the American electorate. Nearly one-third of voters (30%) name these as the most important problem facing the country; named next most often by 22% is unemployment. Interestingly, an issue that received considerable attention in the first debate, the federal budget deficit, was mentioned by relatively few (10%). President Reagan is given a slight edge over Mondale as the candidate who can better handle the problems of greatest concern to voters, 43% to 36%.

Despite the many and pressing concerns of the American people today, their mood continues to be far more upbeat than at any time over the last five years, with nearly half (48%) saying they are satisfied with the way things are going in the United States at this time. In August 1983, far fewer (35%) expressed satisfaction, although the figure was the highest since the measurement began in 1979. While satisfaction continues at the highest level to date (the figure was statistically the same in February at 50%), for every person who expresses satisfaction, another expresses dissatisfaction. The current dissatisfaction rating is highest among blacks (74%).

## OCTOBER 22
## SECOND PRESIDENTIAL DEBATE

Special *Newsweek* Poll*

*Asked of those who watched the second debate: Does the following phrase apply more to Reagan or to Mondale?*

*Seemed thoughtful, well informed?*

|  | After first debate | After second debate |
|---|---|---|
| Reagan ........... | 37% | 44% |
| Mondale .......... | 45 | 38 |
| Both; not sure ...... | 18 | 18 |

*Seemed confident, self-assured?*

|  | After first debate | After second debate |
|---|---|---|
| Reagan ........... | 33% | 46% |
| Mondale .......... | 55 | 36 |
| Both; not sure ...... | 12 | 18 |

*Came closer to reflecting your point of view on the issues?*

*These findings are based on telephone interviews with a national sample of registered voters who watched the second debate on October 21. The sample was drawn from a pool of those in a pre-debate Gallup Poll who said they might watch the contest.

|  | After first debate | After second debate |
|---|---|---|
| Reagan ........... | 57% | 57% |
| Mondale .......... | 38 | 38 |
| Both; not sure ...... | 5 | 5 |

### Perceptions of Candidates on Foreign Policy Issues

#### (Second Debate Only)

*Came closer to reflecting your point of view on foreign policy issues?*

Reagan ........................... 57%
Mondale .......................... 38
Both; neither; not sure ................ 5

*Seemed more capable of handling relations with the Soviet Union?*

Reagan ........................... 55%
Mondale .......................... 38
Both; neither; not sure ................ 7

*Has best judgment on needed defense expenditures?*

Reagan ........................... 53%
Mondale .......................... 39
Both; neither; not sure ................ 8

*Seemed more likely to keep the United States out of war?*

Reagan ........................... 49%
Mondale .......................... 39
Both; neither; not sure ................ 12

*Also asked of those who watched the second debate: Regardless of which candidate you happen to support, who do you think did a better job in the debate—Ronald Reagan or Walter Mondale?*

|  | After first debate | After second debate |
|---|---|---|
| Reagan ........... | 35% | 43% |
| Mondale .......... | 54 | 40 |
| Neither; not sure .... | 11 | 17 |

*Also asked of those who watched the second debate: Did the debate make you more likely to vote for Ronald Reagan (Walter Mondale) or against him?*

|  | After First Debate | | After Second Debate | |
|  | Reagan | Mondale | Reagan | Mondale |
|---|---|---|---|---|
| More likely to: | | | | |
| Vote for | | | | |
| candidate | 48% | 46% | 47% | 37% |
| Vote against | | | | |
| candidate | 37 | 41 | 33 | 44 |
| Had no | | | | |
| effect | 13 | 11 | 18 | 16 |
| No opinion | 2 | 2 | 2 | 3 |

*Also asked of those who watched the second debate: How concerned are you that Ronald Reagan may not be able to meet the demands of a second term as president?*

|  | After first debate | After second debate |
|---|---|---|
| Very concerned ........ | 23% | 22% |
| Fairly concerned ........ | 22 | 20 |
| Not concerned ......... | 51 | 57 |
| No opinion ........... | 4 | 1 |

Note: Neither presidential candidate scored a decisive victory in the second televised debate on October 21, according to registered voters who viewed it. However, President Ronald Reagan's performance represented a marked improvement over his showing in the first debate on October 7.

In a *Newsweek* survey conducted by the Gallup Organization after the recent Kansas City debate, 43% of viewers said Reagan had done a better job, while 40% thought Walter Mondale was the winner; the balance believed neither candidate had prevailed (14%) or did not express an opinion (3%). In the first debate, Reagan had trailed Mondale, 35% to 54%.

A major factor in Reagan's improved overall showing was that viewers of the second debate gave him a 44% to 38% edge over Mondale for seeming thoughtful and well informed. In the October 7 confrontation, Reagan had been the 37% to 45% underdog in this regard. Similarly, the president succeeded in reversing the public's

earlier judgment that Mondale was more confident and self-assured. By a vote of 46% to 36%, Reagan was judged superior to Mondale in this respect after the second debate. He had trailed Mondale, 33% to 55%, after the first one.

The president also was perceived by many viewing voters as having the edge on foreign policy issues, as he had on domestic issues in the first debate. These included coming "closer to reflecting your point of view on foreign policy issues," 57% for Reagan to 38% for Mondale; seeming "more capable of handling relations with the Soviet Union," 55% to 38%; having the "best judgment on needed defense expenditures," 53% to 39%; and seeming "more likely to keep the United States out of war," 49% to 39%.

In addition to the president's improved performance overall and on perceived personal characteristics—confidence, thoughtfulness, self-assurance—the second debate survey showed no increase in the proportion who said they were concerned that Reagan "may not be able to meet the demands of a second term": 45% after the first debate to 42% after the second one.

## OCTOBER 28
## CONGRESSIONAL ELECTIONS

Interviewing Date: 9/7–10; 21–24; 28–10/1/84
Survey #241-G; 242-G; 243-G

*Asked of likely voters: If the elections for Congress were being held today, which party would you like to see win in this congressional district—the Democratic party or the Republican party? [Those who were undecided or named another party were asked: As of today, do you lean more to the Democratic party, or to the Republican party?]*

The following are the findings, based on the choices of likely voters, and the 1980 results at a comparable period:

|  | 1984 | 1980 |
|---|---|---|
| Democratic ............... | 48% | 51% |
| Republican ............... | 46 | 42 |
| Other .................... | 1 | 2 |
| Undecided ................ | 5 | 5 |

After dividing the other and undecided vote evenly between the major parties, the division of the vote is as follows:

|  | 1984 | 1980 |
|---|---|---|
| Democratic | 51% | 55% |
| Republican | 49 | 45 |

The following shows the division of the 1984 congressional test election vote by key groups:

Democratic candidates . . . . . . . . . . . . . . . .48%
Republican candidates . . . . . . . . . . . . . . . .46
Other; undecided . . . . . . . . . . . . . . . . . . . 6

## By Sex
### Male

Democratic candidates . . . . . . . . . . . . . . . .46%
Republican candidates . . . . . . . . . . . . . . . .49
Other; undecided . . . . . . . . . . . . . . . . . . . 5

### Female

Democratic candidates . . . . . . . . . . . . . . . .50%
Republican candidates . . . . . . . . . . . . . . . .44
Other; undecided . . . . . . . . . . . . . . . . . . . 6

## By Ethnic Background
### White

Democratic candidates . . . . . . . . . . . . . . . .44%
Republican candidates . . . . . . . . . . . . . . . .50
Other; undecided . . . . . . . . . . . . . . . . . . . 6

### Black

Democratic candidates . . . . . . . . . . . . . . . .86%
Republican candidates . . . . . . . . . . . . . . . .10
Other; undecided . . . . . . . . . . . . . . . . . . . 4

### Hispanic*

Democratic candidates . . . . . . . . . . . . . . . .64%
Republican candidates . . . . . . . . . . . . . . . .29
Other; undecided . . . . . . . . . . . . . . . . . . . 7

## By Education
### College Graduate

Democratic candidates . . . . . . . . . . . . . . . .46%
Republican candidates . . . . . . . . . . . . . . . .48
Other; undecided . . . . . . . . . . . . . . . . . . . 6

### College Incomplete

Democratic candidates . . . . . . . . . . . . . . . .42%
Republican candidates . . . . . . . . . . . . . . . .53
Other; undecided . . . . . . . . . . . . . . . . . . . 5

### High-School Graduate

Democratic candidates . . . . . . . . . . . . . . . .47%
Republican candidates . . . . . . . . . . . . . . . .48
Other; undecided . . . . . . . . . . . . . . . . . . . 5

### Less Than High-School Graduate

Democratic candidates . . . . . . . . . . . . . . . .59%
Republican candidates . . . . . . . . . . . . . . . .34
Other; undecided . . . . . . . . . . . . . . . . . . . 7

## By Region
### East

Democratic candidates . . . . . . . . . . . . . . . .51%
Republican candidates . . . . . . . . . . . . . . . .43
Other; undecided . . . . . . . . . . . . . . . . . . . 6

### Midwest

Democratic candidates . . . . . . . . . . . . . . . .46%
Republican candidates . . . . . . . . . . . . . . . .48
Other; undecided . . . . . . . . . . . . . . . . . . . 6

### South

Democratic candidates . . . . . . . . . . . . . . . .49%
Republican candidates . . . . . . . . . . . . . . . .45
Other; undecided . . . . . . . . . . . . . . . . . . . 6

### West

Democratic candidates . . . . . . . . . . . . . . . .45%
Republican candidates . . . . . . . . . . . . . . . .51
Other; undecided . . . . . . . . . . . . . . . . . . . 4

## By Age
### 18–29 Years

Democratic candidates ................47%
Republican candidates ................46
Other; undecided ................ 7

### 30–49 Years

Democratic candidates ................50%
Republican candidates ................45
Other; undecided ................ 5

### 50 Years and Over

Democratic candidates ................47%
Republican candidates ................47
Other; undecided ................ 6

## By Income
### $20,000 and Over

Democratic candidates................43%
Republican candidates ................51
Other; undecided ................ 6

### Under $20,000

Democratic candidates ................55%
Republican candidates ................40
Other; undecided ................ 5

## By Politics
### Republicans

Democratic candidates ................87%
Republican candidates ................10
Other; undecided ................ 3

### Democrats

Democratic candidates ................ 9%
Republican candidates ................88
Other; undecided ................ 3

### Independents

Democratic candidates ................42%
Republican candidates ................44
Other; undecided ................14

## By Religion
### Protestants

Democratic candidates ................44%
Republican candidates ................51
Other; undecided ................ 5

### Catholics

Democratic candidates ................54%
Republican candidates ................41
Other; undecided ................ 5

### Jews*

Democratic candidates ................68%
Republican candidates ................24
Other; undecided ................ 8

## By Occupation
### Professional and Business

Democratic candidates ................41%
Republican candidates ................54
Other; undecided ................ 5

### Clerical and Sales

Democratic candidates ................43%
Republican candidates ................52
Other; undecided ................ 5

### Manual Workers

Democratic candidates ................55%
Republican candidates ................39
Other; undecided ................ 6

### Manual Workers—Skilled

Democratic candidates ................51%
Republican candidates ................44
Other; undecided ................ 5

### Manual Workers—Unskilled

Democratic candidates ................59%
Republican candidates ................35
Other; undecided ................ 6

### Farmers*

Democratic candidates . . . . . . . . . . . . . . . . .28%
Republican candidates . . . . . . . . . . . . . . . .68
Other; undecided . . . . . . . . . . . . . . . . . . . 4

## By Labor Union Household
### Labor Union Members

Democratic candidates . . . . . . . . . . . . . . . .61%
Republican candidates . . . . . . . . . . . . . . . .34
Other; undecided . . . . . . . . . . . . . . . . . . . 5

### Nonlabor Union Members

Democratic candidates . . . . . . . . . . . . . . . .44%
Republican candidates . . . . . . . . . . . . . . . .50
Other; undecided . . . . . . . . . . . . . . . . . . . 6

*Small samples

Note: With election day only about one week away, the race for popular vote for seats in the House of Representatives is virtually deadlocked. Gallup surveys indicate that Democratic candidates for the House would receive about 51% of the popular vote, if the election were held now, to 49% for Republican candidates, much closer than the 55% to 45% split observed at this point in the 1980 elections.

Although the national vote for Congress cannot be translated directly into House seats, based on past experience these findings suggest a considerable increase in Republican congressional representation. If present voter sentiment persists, 1984 could resemble the 1980 congressional elections. At that time, Democratic candidates won 51% of the two-party popular vote to 49% for GOP candidates, as Ronald Reagan wrested the presidency from incumbent Jimmy Carter. The Democratic party lost 34 seats in that election, with a resulting House composition of 243 Democrats and 192 Republicans.

The 1982 off-year congressional elections resulted in a loss of 26 Republican seats; the present House makeup is 269 Democrats and 166 Republicans. The popular two-party vote in 1982 was 56.2% Democratic and 43.8% Republican.

In the 1980 presidential and congressional elections many persons from traditionally Democratic groups—including blue-collar workers, labor union members, persons whose education ended at the high-school level or earlier—abandoned their usual election behavior to vote for Reagan. With few exceptions, the present voting intentions of people in these groups, as well as those in regular Republican strongholds, show at least as much affinity for GOP congressional candidates as in 1980.

## OCTOBER 29
## PRESIDENTIAL TRIAL HEATS—
## SEMIFINAL TEST

Interviewing Date: 10/26–29/84
Survey #244-G

*Asked of registered voters: If the 1984 presidential election were being held today, which would you vote for—the Republican candidates, Reagan and Bush, or the Democratic candidates, Mondale and Ferraro? [Those who were undecided or named other candidates were then asked: As of today, do you lean more to Reagan and Bush, or to Mondale and Ferraro?]*

Reagan-Bush . . . . . . . . . . . . . . . . . . . . . . .56%
Mondale-Ferraro . . . . . . . . . . . . . . . . . . .39
Other; undecided . . . . . . . . . . . . . . . . . . . 5

## By Sex
### Male

Reagan-Bush . . . . . . . . . . . . . . . . . . . . . . .57%
Mondale-Ferraro . . . . . . . . . . . . . . . . . . .39
Other; undecided . . . . . . . . . . . . . . . . . . . 4

### Female

Reagan-Bush . . . . . . . . . . . . . . . . . . . . . . .55%
Mondale-Ferraro . . . . . . . . . . . . . . . . . . .40
Other; undecided . . . . . . . . . . . . . . . . . . . 5

## By Ethnic Background

### White

Reagan-Bush .........................62%
Mondale-Ferraro ....................33
Other; undecided ................. 5

### Nonwhite

Reagan-Bush .........................20%
Mondale-Ferraro ....................78
Other; undecided ................. 2

### Black

Reagan-Bush .........................14%
Mondale-Ferraro ....................85
Other; undecided ................. 1

## By Education

### College Graduate

Reagan-Bush .........................59%
Mondale-Ferraro ....................37
Other; undecided ................. 4

### College Incomplete

Reagan-Bush .........................62%
Mondale-Ferraro ....................35
Other; undecided ................. 3

### High-School Graduate

Reagan-Bush .........................56%
Mondale-Ferraro ....................39
Other; undecided ................. 5

### Less Than High-School Graduate

Reagan-Bush .........................46%
Mondale-Ferraro ....................49
Other; undecided ................. 5

## By Region

### East

Reagan-Bush .........................53%
Mondale-Ferraro ....................41
Other; undecided ................. 6

### Midwest

Reagan-Bush .........................54%
Mondale-Ferraro ....................41
Other; undecided ................. 5

### South

Reagan-Bush .........................58%
Mondale-Ferraro ....................38
Other; undecided ................. 4

### West

Reagan-Bush .........................62%
Mondale-Ferraro ....................36
Other; undecided ................. 2

## By Age

### 18–24 Years

Reagan-Bush .........................51%
Mondale-Ferraro ....................41
Other; undecided ................. 8

### 25–29 Years

Reagan-Bush .........................50%
Mondale-Ferraro ....................48
Other; undecided ................. 2

### 30–49 Years

Reagan-Bush .........................52%
Mondale-Ferraro ....................43
Other; undecided ................. 5

### 50–64 Years

Reagan-Bush .........................67%
Mondale-Ferraro ....................29
Other; undecided ................. 4

### 65 Years and Over

Reagan-Bush .........................56%
Mondale-Ferraro ....................39
Other; undecided ................. 5

## By Income

### $40,000 and Over

Reagan-Bush ........................60%
Mondale-Ferraro .....................36
Other; undecided ................... 4

### $30,000–$39,999

Reagan-Bush ........................56%
Mondale-Ferraro .....................37
Other; undecided ................... 7

### $20,000–$29,999

Reagan-Bush ........................57%
Mondale-Ferraro .....................39
Other; undecided ................... 4

### $10,000–$19,999

Reagan-Bush ........................59%
Mondale-Ferraro .....................37
Other; undecided ................... 4

### Under $10,000

Reagan-Bush ........................45%
Mondale-Ferraro .....................51
Other; undecided ................... 4

## By Politics

### Republicans

Reagan-Bush ........................93%
Mondale-Ferraro ..................... 5
Other; undecided ................... 2

### Democrats

Reagan-Bush ........................20%
Mondale-Ferraro .....................76
Other; undecided ................... 4

### Independents

Reagan-Bush ........................65%
Mondale-Ferraro .....................27
Other; undecided ................... 8

## By Religion

### Protestants

Reagan-Bush ........................57%
Mondale-Ferraro .....................39
Other; undecided ................... 4

### Catholics

Reagan-Bush ........................58%
Mondale-Ferraro .....................37
Other; undecided ................... 5

## By Occupation

### Professional and Business

Reagan-Bush ........................63%
Mondale-Ferraro .....................32
Other; undecided ................... 5

### Clerical and Sales

Reagan-Bush ........................70%
Mondale-Ferraro .....................25
Other; undecided ................... 5

### Manual Workers

Reagan-Bush ........................52%
Mondale-Ferraro .....................44
Other; undecided ................... 4

### Nonlabor Force

Reagan-Bush ........................48%
Mondale-Ferraro .....................47
Other; undecided ................... 5

## By Community Size

### One Million and Over

Reagan-Bush ........................49%
Mondale-Ferraro .....................44
Other; undecided ................... 7

### 500,000–999,999

Reagan-Bush ........................51%
Mondale-Ferraro .....................48
Other; undecided ................... 1

### 50,000–499,999

Reagan-Bush ........................65%
Mondale-Ferraro ....................33
Other; undecided ................... 2

### 2,500–49,999

Reagan-Bush ........................72%
Mondale-Ferraro ....................25
Other; undecided ................... 3

### Under 2,500; Rural

Reagan-Bush ........................55%
Mondale-Ferraro ....................40
Other; undecided ................... 5

## By Labor Union Household
### Labor Union Members

Reagan-Bush ........................40%
Mondale-Ferraro ....................56
Other; undecided ................... 4

### Nonlabor Union Members

Reagan-Bush ........................60%
Mondale-Ferraro ....................35
Other; undecided ................... 5

## Selected National Trend

|  | Reagan-Bush | Mondale-Ferraro | Other; undecided |
|---|---|---|---|
| Oct. 15–17 | 58% | 38% | 4% |
| Sept. 28–Oct. 1 | 55 | 39 | 6 |
| Sept. 21–24 | 58 | 37 | 5 |
| Sept. 7–10 | 56 | 37 | 7 |

### Republican Convention

| Aug. 10–13 | 52% | 41% | 7% |
|---|---|---|---|
| July 27–30 | 53 | 41 | 6 |
| July 19–20* | 46 | 48 | 6 |

### Democratic Convention

| July 13–16 | 53% | 39% | 8% |
|---|---|---|---|
| July 12–13* | 49 | 43 | 8 |

*For *Newsweek*

*Also asked of the sample: Do you strongly support them, or do you only moderately support them?*

Total Reagan-Bush ...................56%
  Strongly support ...............36
  Moderately support .............20
Total Mondale-Ferraro ...............39
  Strongly support ...............24
  Moderately support .............15
Other; undecided ................... 5

## By Sex
### Male

Total Reagan-Bush ...................57%
  Strongly support ...............38
  Moderately support .............19
Total Mondale-Ferraro ...............39
  Strongly support ...............25
  Moderately support .............14
Other; undecided ................... 4

### Female

Total Reagan-Bush ...................55%
  Strongly support ...............35
  Moderately support .............20
Total Mondale-Ferraro ...............40
  Strongly support ...............23
  Moderately support .............17
Other; undecided ................... 5

## By Ethnic Background
### White

Total Reagan-Bush ...................62%
  Strongly support ...............40
  Moderately support .............22
Total Mondale-Ferraro ...............33
  Strongly support ...............19
  Moderately support .............14
Other; undecided ................... 5

### Nonwhite

Total Reagan-Bush ...................20%
  Strongly support ............... 9
  Moderately support ............. 10*

Total Mondale-Ferraro . . . . . . . . . . . . . . . . 78
  Strongly support . . . . . . . . . . . . . . 57
  Moderately support . . . . . . . . . . . . . 21
Other; undecided . . . . . . . . . . . . . . . . . . 2

### Black

Total Reagan-Bush . . . . . . . . . . . . . . . . 14%
  Strongly support . . . . . . . . . . . . . . 4
  Moderately support . . . . . . . . . . . . 8**
Total Mondale-Ferraro . . . . . . . . . . . . . . . . 85
  Strongly support . . . . . . . . . . . . . . 62
  Moderately support . . . . . . . . . . . . 23
Other; undecided . . . . . . . . . . . . . . . . . . 1

### By Education
#### College Graduate

Total Reagan-Bush . . . . . . . . . . . . . . . . 59%
  Strongly support . . . . . . . . . . . . . . 39
  Moderately support . . . . . . . . . . . . 20
Total Mondale-Ferraro . . . . . . . . . . . . . . . . 37
  Strongly support . . . . . . . . . . . . . . 23
  Moderately support . . . . . . . . . . . . 14
Other; undecided . . . . . . . . . . . . . . . . . . 4

#### College Incomplete

Total Reagan-Bush . . . . . . . . . . . . . . . . 62%
  Strongly support . . . . . . . . . . . . . . 41
  Moderately support . . . . . . . . . . . . 21
Total Mondale-Ferraro . . . . . . . . . . . . . . . . 35
  Strongly support . . . . . . . . . . . . . . 18
  Moderately support . . . . . . . . . . . . 17
Other; undecided . . . . . . . . . . . . . . . . . . 3

#### High-School Graduate

Total Reagan-Bush . . . . . . . . . . . . . . . . 56%
  Strongly support . . . . . . . . . . . . . . 36
  Moderately support . . . . . . . . . . . . 20
Total Mondale-Ferraro . . . . . . . . . . . . . . . . 39
  Strongly support . . . . . . . . . . . . . . 24
  Moderately support . . . . . . . . . . . . 15
Other; undecided . . . . . . . . . . . . . . . . . . 3

#### Less Than High-School Graduate

Total Reagan-Bush . . . . . . . . . . . . . . . . 46%
  Strongly support . . . . . . . . . . . . . . 26
  Moderately support . . . . . . . . . . . . 20

Total Mondale-Ferraro . . . . . . . . . . . . . . . . 49
  Strongly support . . . . . . . . . . . . . . 33
  Moderately support . . . . . . . . . . . . 16
Other; undecided . . . . . . . . . . . . . . . . . . 5

### By Region
#### East

Total Reagan-Bush . . . . . . . . . . . . . . . . 53%
  Strongly support . . . . . . . . . . . . . . 33
  Moderately support . . . . . . . . . . . . 19*
Total Mondale-Ferraro . . . . . . . . . . . . . . . . 41
  Strongly support . . . . . . . . . . . . . . 26
  Moderately support . . . . . . . . . . . . 15
Other; undecided . . . . . . . . . . . . . . . . . . 5

#### Midwest

Total Reagan-Bush . . . . . . . . . . . . . . . . 54%
  Strongly support . . . . . . . . . . . . . . 29
  Moderately support . . . . . . . . . . . . 25
Total Mondale-Ferraro . . . . . . . . . . . . . . . . 41
  Strongly support . . . . . . . . . . . . . . 23
  Moderately support . . . . . . . . . . . . 18
Other; undecided . . . . . . . . . . . . . . . . . . 5

#### South

Total Reagan-Bush . . . . . . . . . . . . . . . . 58%
  Strongly support . . . . . . . . . . . . . . 44
  Moderately support . . . . . . . . . . . . 14
Total Mondale-Ferraro . . . . . . . . . . . . . . . . 38
  Strongly support . . . . . . . . . . . . . . 26
  Moderately support . . . . . . . . . . . . 12
Other; undecided . . . . . . . . . . . . . . . . . . 4

#### West

Total Reagan-Bush . . . . . . . . . . . . . . . . 62%
  Strongly support . . . . . . . . . . . . . . 39
  Modcratcly support . . . . . . . . . . . . 23
Total Mondale-Ferraro . . . . . . . . . . . . . . . . 36
  Strongly support . . . . . . . . . . . . . . 19
  Moderately support . . . . . . . . . . . . 16*
Other; undecided . . . . . . . . . . . . . . . . . . 2

## By Age

### 18–24 Years

Total Reagan-Bush ...................51%
  Strongly support ...............39
  Moderately support .............12
Total Mondale-Ferraro .................41
  Strongly support ...............20
  Moderately support .............21
Other; undecided ....................  8

### 25–29 Years

Total Reagan-Bush ...................50%
  Strongly support ...............40
  Moderately support ...........  8**
Total Mondale-Ferraro .................48
  Strongly support ...............26
  Moderately support .............21*
Other; undecided ....................  2

### 30–49 Years

Total Reagan-Bush ...................52%
  Strongly support ...............33
  Moderately support .............19
Total Mondale-Ferraro .................43
  Strongly support ...............31
  Moderately support .............12
Other; undecided ....................  5

### 50–64 Years

Total Reagan-Bush ...................67%
  Strongly support ...............41
  Moderately support .............26
Total Mondale-Ferraro .................29
  Strongly support ...............17
  Moderately support .............12
Other; undecided ....................  4

### 65 Years and Over

Total Reagan-Bush ...................56%
  Strongly support ...............35
  Moderately support .............21
Total Mondale-Ferraro .................39
  Strongly support ...............23
  Moderately support .............16
Other; undecided ....................  5

## By Income

### $40,000 and Over

Total Reagan-Bush ...................60%
  Strongly support ...............43
  Moderately support .............17
Total Mondale-Ferraro .................36
  Strongly support ...............20
  Moderately support .............16
Other; undecided ....................  4

### $30,000–$39,999

Total Reagan-Bush ...................56%
  Strongly support ...............36
  Moderately support .............20
Total Mondale-Ferraro .................37
  Strongly support ...............23
  Moderately support .............13*
Other; undecided ....................  7

### $20,000–$29,999

Total Reagan-Bush ...................57%
  Strongly support ...............37
  Moderately support .............20
Total Mondale-Ferraro .................39
  Strongly support ...............24
  Moderately support .............15
Other; undecided ....................  4

### $10,000–$19,999

Total Reagan-Bush ...................59%
  Strongly support ...............35
  Moderately support .............24
Total Mondale-Ferraro .................37
  Strongly support ...............21
  Moderately support .............16
Other; undecided ....................  4

### Under $10,000

Total Reagan-Bush ...................45%
  Strongly support ...............28
  Moderately support ...........  16*
Total Mondale-Ferraro .................51
  Strongly support ...............35
  Moderately support .............16
Other; undecided ....................  4

## By Politics

### Republicans

Total Reagan-Bush  . . . . . . . . . . . . . . . . .93%
  Strongly support  . . . . . . . . . . . . . .72
  Moderately support  . . . . . . . . . . . .21
Total Mondale-Ferraro . . . . . . . . . . . . . . . 5
  Strongly support  . . . . . . . . . . . . . . 2
  Moderately support  . . . . . . . . . . . . 3
Other; undecided  . . . . . . . . . . . . . . . . . . 2

### Democrats

Total Reagan-Bush  . . . . . . . . . . . . . . . . .20%
  Strongly support  . . . . . . . . . . . . . . 6
  Moderately support  . . . . . . . . . . . .14
Total Mondale-Ferraro . . . . . . . . . . . . . . .76
  Strongly support  . . . . . . . . . . . . . .51
  Moderately support  . . . . . . . . . . . .25
Other; undecided  . . . . . . . . . . . . . . . . . . 4

### Independents

Total Reagan-Bush  . . . . . . . . . . . . . . . . .65%
  Strongly support  . . . . . . . . . . . . . .36
  Moderately support  . . . . . . . . . . . . 28*
Total Mondale-Ferraro . . . . . . . . . . . . . . .27
  Strongly support  . . . . . . . . . . . . . .11
  Moderately support  . . . . . . . . . . . .16
Other; undecided  . . . . . . . . . . . . . . . . . . 8

## By Religion

### Protestants

Total Reagan-Bush  . . . . . . . . . . . . . . . . .57%
  Strongly support  . . . . . . . . . . . . . .38
  Moderately support  . . . . . . . . . . . .19
Total Mondale-Ferraro . . . . . . . . . . . . . . .39
  Strongly support  . . . . . . . . . . . . . .26
  Moderately support  . . . . . . . . . . . .13
Other; undecided  . . . . . . . . . . . . . . . . . . 4

### Catholics

Total Reagan-Bush  . . . . . . . . . . . . . . . . .58%
  Strongly support  . . . . . . . . . . . . . .35
  Moderately support  . . . . . . . . . . . 22*

Total Mondale-Ferraro . . . . . . . . . . . . . . . .37
  Strongly support  . . . . . . . . . . . . . .20
  Moderately support  . . . . . . . . . . . .17
Other; undecided  . . . . . . . . . . . . . . . . . . 5

## By Occupation

### Professional and Business

Total Reagan-Bush  . . . . . . . . . . . . . . . . .63%
  Strongly support  . . . . . . . . . . . . . .41
  Moderately support  . . . . . . . . . . . .22
Total Mondale-Ferraro . . . . . . . . . . . . . . .32
  Strongly support  . . . . . . . . . . . . . .20
  Moderately support  . . . . . . . . . . . 11*
Other; undecided  . . . . . . . . . . . . . . . . . . 5

### Clerical and Sales

Total Reagan-Bush  . . . . . . . . . . . . . . . . .70%
  Strongly support  . . . . . . . . . . . . . .42
  Moderately support  . . . . . . . . . . . 27*
Total Mondale-Ferraro . . . . . . . . . . . . . . .25
  Strongly support  . . . . . . . . . . . . . .11
  Moderately support  . . . . . . . . . . . .14
Other; undecided  . . . . . . . . . . . . . . . . . . 5

### Manual Workers

Total Reagan-Bush  . . . . . . . . . . . . . . . . .52%
  Strongly support  . . . . . . . . . . . . . .30
  Moderately support  . . . . . . . . . . . 21*
Total Mondale-Ferraro . . . . . . . . . . . . . . .44
  Strongly support  . . . . . . . . . . . . . .28
  Moderately support  . . . . . . . . . . . .16
Other; undecided  . . . . . . . . . . . . . . . . . . 4

### Nonlabor Force

Total Reagan-Bush  . . . . . . . . . . . . . . . . .48%
  Strongly support  . . . . . . . . . . . . . .36
  Moderately support  . . . . . . . . . . . .12
Total Mondale-Ferraro . . . . . . . . . . . . . . .47
  Strongly support  . . . . . . . . . . . . . .27
  Moderately support  . . . . . . . . . . . .20
Other; undecided  . . . . . . . . . . . . . . . . . . 5

## By Community Size
### One Million and Over

Total Reagan-Bush . . . . . . . . . . . . . . . . . . .49%
   Strongly support . . . . . . . . . . . . . . .30
   Moderately support . . . . . . . . . . . . 18*
Total Mondale-Ferraro . . . . . . . . . . . . . . . .44
   Strongly support . . . . . . . . . . . . . . .29
   Moderately support . . . . . . . . . . . . .15
Other; undecided . . . . . . . . . . . . . . . . . . . 7

### 500,000–999,999

Total Reagan-Bush . . . . . . . . . . . . . . . . . .51%
   Strongly support . . . . . . . . . . . . . . .38
   Moderately support . . . . . . . . . . . . .13
Total Mondale-Ferraro . . . . . . . . . . . . . . . .48
   Strongly support . . . . . . . . . . . . . . .26
   Moderately support . . . . . . . . . . . . 21*
Other; undecided . . . . . . . . . . . . . . . . . . . 1

### 50,000–499,999

Total Reagan-Bush . . . . . . . . . . . . . . . . . . .65%
   Strongly support . . . . . . . . . . . . . . .42
   Moderately support . . . . . . . . . . . . .23
Total Mondale-Ferraro . . . . . . . . . . . . . . . .33
   Strongly support . . . . . . . . . . . . . . .19
   Moderately support . . . . . . . . . . . . .14
Other; undecided . . . . . . . . . . . . . . . . . . . 2

### 2,500–49,999

Total Reagan-Bush . . . . . . . . . . . . . . . . . . .72%
   Strongly support . . . . . . . . . . . . . . .51
   Moderately support . . . . . . . . . . . . .21
Total Mondale-Ferraro . . . . . . . . . . . . . . . .25
   Strongly support . . . . . . . . . . . . . . .16
   Moderately support . . . . . . . . . . . . . 9
Other; undecided . . . . . . . . . . . . . . . . . . . 3

### Under 2,500; Rural

Total Reagan-Bush . . . . . . . . . . . . . . . . . . .55%
   Strongly support . . . . . . . . . . . . . . .33
   Moderately support . . . . . . . . . . . . .22

Total Mondale-Ferraro . . . . . . . . . . . . . . . .40
   Strongly support . . . . . . . . . . . . . . .23
   Moderately support . . . . . . . . . . . . .17
Other; undecided . . . . . . . . . . . . . . . . . . . 5

## By Labor Union Households
### Labor Union Members

Total Reagan-Bush . . . . . . . . . . . . . . . . . . .40%
   Strongly support . . . . . . . . . . . . . . .23
   Moderately support . . . . . . . . . . . . .17
Total Mondale-Ferraro . . . . . . . . . . . . . . . .56
   Strongly support . . . . . . . . . . . . . . .34
   Moderately support . . . . . . . . . . . . .22
Other; undecided . . . . . . . . . . . . . . . . . . . 4

### Nonlabor Union Members

Total Reagan-Bush . . . . . . . . . . . . . . . . . . .60%
   Strongly support . . . . . . . . . . . . . . .39
   Moderately support . . . . . . . . . . . . .21
Total Mondale-Ferraro . . . . . . . . . . . . . . . .35
   Strongly support . . . . . . . . . . . . . . .22
   Moderately support . . . . . . . . . . . . .13
Other; undecided . . . . . . . . . . . . . . . . . . . 5

### Selected National Trend

|  | Oct. 15–17 | Sept. 28– Oct. 1 |
|---|---|---|
| Total Reagan-Bush . . . . . . . | 58% | 55% |
| Strongly support | 36 | 35 |
| Moderately support | 22 | 20 |
| Total Mondale-Ferraro . . . . | 38 | 39 |
| Strongly support | 22 | 21 |
| Moderately support | 16 | 18 |
| Other; undecided . . . . . . . . | 4 | 6 |

*1% responded "don't know."
**2% responded "don't know."

*Also asked of the sample: Would you say your vote is more a vote for (candidates) or more a vote against (other candidates)?*

Total Reagan-Bush . . . . . . . . . . . . . . . . . .56%
    For this ticket . . . . . . . . . . . . . . . .44
    Against other ticket . . . . . . . . . . . .10
    Not sure . . . . . . . . . . . . . . . . . . . . . 2
Total Mondale-Ferraro . . . . . . . . . . . . . . .39
    For this ticket . . . . . . . . . . . . . . . .19
    Against other ticket . . . . . . . . . . . .18
    Not sure . . . . . . . . . . . . . . . . . . . . . 2
Other; undecided . . . . . . . . . . . . . . . . . . 5

## By Sex
### *Male*

Total Reagan-Bush . . . . . . . . . . . . . . . . . .57%
    For this ticket . . . . . . . . . . . . . . . .44
    Against other ticket . . . . . . . . . . . .10
    Not sure . . . . . . . . . . . . . . . . . . . . . 3
Total Mondale-Ferraro . . . . . . . . . . . . . . .39
    For this ticket . . . . . . . . . . . . . . . .18
    Against other ticket . . . . . . . . . . . .18
    Not sure . . . . . . . . . . . . . . . . . . . . . 3
Other; undecided . . . . . . . . . . . . . . . . . . 4

### *Female*

Total Reagan-Bush . . . . . . . . . . . . . . . . . .55%
    For this ticket . . . . . . . . . . . . . . . .43
    Against other ticket . . . . . . . . . . . . 9
    Not sure . . . . . . . . . . . . . . . . . . . . . 3
Total Mondale-Ferraro . . . . . . . . . . . . . . .40
    For this ticket . . . . . . . . . . . . . . . .20
    Against other ticket . . . . . . . . . . . .18
    Not sure . . . . . . . . . . . . . . . . . . . . . 2
Other; undecided . . . . . . . . . . . . . . . . . . 5

## By Ethnic Background
### *White*

Total Reagan-Bush . . . . . . . . . . . . . . . . . .62%
    For this ticket . . . . . . . . . . . . . . . .49
    Against other ticket . . . . . . . . . . . .10
    Not sure . . . . . . . . . . . . . . . . . . . . . 3
Total Mondale-Ferraro . . . . . . . . . . . . . . .33
    For this ticket . . . . . . . . . . . . . . . .14
    Against other ticket . . . . . . . . . . . .17
    Not sure . . . . . . . . . . . . . . . . . . . . . 2
Other; undecided . . . . . . . . . . . . . . . . . . 5

### *Nonwhite*

Total Reagan-Bush . . . . . . . . . . . . . . . . . .20%
    For this ticket . . . . . . . . . . . . . . . .11
    Against other ticket . . . . . . . . . . . . 7
    Not sure . . . . . . . . . . . . . . . . . . . . . 2
Total Mondale-Ferraro . . . . . . . . . . . . . . .78
    For this ticket . . . . . . . . . . . . . . . .51
    Against other ticket . . . . . . . . . . . .25
    Not sure . . . . . . . . . . . . . . . . . . . . . 2
Other; undecided . . . . . . . . . . . . . . . . . . 2

### *Black*

Total Reagan-Bush . . . . . . . . . . . . . . . . . .14%
    For this ticket . . . . . . . . . . . . . . . . 7
    Against other ticket . . . . . . . . . . . . 4
    Not sure . . . . . . . . . . . . . . . . . . . . . 3
Total Mondale-Ferraro . . . . . . . . . . . . . . .85
    For this ticket . . . . . . . . . . . . . . . .55
    Against other ticket . . . . . . . . . . . .28
    Not sure . . . . . . . . . . . . . . . . . . . . . 2
Other; undecided . . . . . . . . . . . . . . . . . . 1

## By Education
### *College Graduate*

Total Reagan-Bush . . . . . . . . . . . . . . . . . .59%
    For this ticket . . . . . . . . . . . . . . . .46
    Against other ticket . . . . . . . . . . . . 9
    Not sure . . . . . . . . . . . . . . . . . . . . . 4
Total Mondale-Ferraro . . . . . . . . . . . . . . .37
    For this ticket . . . . . . . . . . . . . . . .14
    Against other ticket . . . . . . . . . . . .22
    Not sure . . . . . . . . . . . . . . . . . . . . . 1
Other; undecided . . . . . . . . . . . . . . . . . . 4

### *College Incomplete*

Total Reagan-Bush . . . . . . . . . . . . . . . . . .62%
    For this ticket . . . . . . . . . . . . . . . .49
    Against other ticket . . . . . . . . . . . .11
    Not sure . . . . . . . . . . . . . . . . . . . . . 2
Total Mondale-Ferraro . . . . . . . . . . . . . . .35
    For this ticket . . . . . . . . . . . . . . . .14
    Against other ticket . . . . . . . . . . . .20
    Not sure . . . . . . . . . . . . . . . . . . . . . 1
Other; undecided . . . . . . . . . . . . . . . . . . 3

### High-School Graduate

Total Reagan-Bush ..................56%
   For this ticket .................44
   Against other ticket ............10
   Not sure ......................  2
Total Mondale-Ferraro ................39
   For this ticket .................18
   Against other ticket ............18
   Not sure ......................  3
Other; undecided ...................  3

### Less Than High-School Graduate

Total Reagan-Bush ..................46%
   For this ticket .................35
   Against other ticket ............  8
   Not sure ......................  3
Total Mondale-Ferraro ................49
   For this ticket .................31
   Against other ticket ............14
   Not sure ......................  4
Other; undecided ...................  5

## By Region

### East

Total Reagan-Bush ..................53%
   For this ticket .................40
   Against other ticket ............  9
   Not sure ......................  4
Total Mondale-Ferraro ................41
   For this ticket .................21
   Against other ticket ............18
   Not sure ......................  2
Other; undecided ...................  5

### Midwest

Total Reagan-Bush ..................54%
   For this ticket .................42
   Against other ticket ............11
   Not sure ......................  1
Total Mondale-Ferraro ................41
   For this ticket .................21
   Against other ticket ............17
   Not sure ......................  3
Other; undecided ...................  5

### South

Total Reagan-Bush ..................58%
   For this ticket .................45
   Against other ticket ............10
   Not sure ......................  3
Total Mondale-Ferraro ................38
   For this ticket .................22
   Against other ticket ............13
   Not sure ......................  3
Other; undecided ...................  4

### West

Total Reagan-Bush ..................62%
   For this ticket .................49
   Against other ticket ............12
   Not sure ......................  1
Total Mondale-Ferraro ................36
   For this ticket .................  8
   Against other ticket ............27
   Not sure ......................  1
Other; undecided ...................  2

## By Age

### 18–24 Years

Total Reagan-Bush ..................51%
   For this ticket .................41
   Against other ticket ............  7
   Not sure ......................  3
Total Mondale-Ferraro ................41
   For this ticket .................15
   Against other ticket ............24
   Not sure ......................  2
Other; undecided ...................  8

### 25–29 Years

Total Reagan-Bush ..................50%
   For this ticket .................41
   Against other ticket ............  3
   Not sure ......................  6
Total Mondale-Ferraro ................48
   For this ticket .................24
   Against other ticket ............19
   Not sure ......................  6
Other; undecided ...................  2

### 30–49 Years

Total Reagan-Bush . . . . . . . . . . . . . . . . . . .52%
    For this ticket . . . . . . . . . . . . . . . .40
    Against other ticket . . . . . . . . . . . . 8
    Not sure . . . . . . . . . . . . . . . . . . . . 4
Total Mondale-Ferraro . . . . . . . . . . . . . . . .43
    For this ticket . . . . . . . . . . . . . . . .21
    Against other ticket . . . . . . . . . . . . .21
    Not sure . . . . . . . . . . . . . . . . . . . . 1
Other; undecided . . . . . . . . . . . . . . . . . . 5

### 50–64 Years

Total Reagan-Bush . . . . . . . . . . . . . . . . . . .67%
    For this ticket . . . . . . . . . . . . . . . .53
    Against other ticket . . . . . . . . . . . . .11
    Not sure . . . . . . . . . . . . . . . . . . . . 3
Total Mondale-Ferraro . . . . . . . . . . . . . . . .29
    For this ticket . . . . . . . . . . . . . . . .15
    Against other ticket . . . . . . . . . . . . .14
    Not sure . . . . . . . . . . . . . . . . . . . . *
Other; undecided . . . . . . . . . . . . . . . . . . 4

### 65 Years and Over

Total Reagan-Bush . . . . . . . . . . . . . . . . . . .56%
    For this ticket . . . . . . . . . . . . . . . .44
    Against other ticket . . . . . . . . . . . . .11
    Not sure . . . . . . . . . . . . . . . . . . . . 1
Total Mondale-Ferraro . . . . . . . . . . . . . . . .39
    For this ticket . . . . . . . . . . . . . . . .20
    Against other ticket . . . . . . . . . . . . .17
    Not sure . . . . . . . . . . . . . . . . . . . . 2
Other; undecided . . . . . . . . . . . . . . . . . . 5

## By Income

### $40,000 and Over

Total Reagan-Bush . . . . . . . . . . . . . . . . . . .60%
    For this ticket . . . . . . . . . . . . . . . .47
    Against other ticket . . . . . . . . . . . . .10
    Not sure . . . . . . . . . . . . . . . . . . . . 3
Total Mondale-Ferraro . . . . . . . . . . . . . . . .36
    For this ticket . . . . . . . . . . . . . . . .15
    Against other ticket . . . . . . . . . . . . .21
    Not sure . . . . . . . . . . . . . . . . . . . . *
Other; undecided . . . . . . . . . . . . . . . . . . 4

### $30,000–$39,999

Total Reagan-Bush . . . . . . . . . . . . . . . . . . .56%
    For this ticket . . . . . . . . . . . . . . . .47
    Against other ticket . . . . . . . . . . . . 8
    Not sure . . . . . . . . . . . . . . . . . . . . 1
Total Mondale-Ferraro . . . . . . . . . . . . . . . .37
    For this ticket . . . . . . . . . . . . . . . .17
    Against other ticket . . . . . . . . . . . . .18
    Not sure . . . . . . . . . . . . . . . . . . . . 2
Other; undecided . . . . . . . . . . . . . . . . . . 7

### $20,000–$29,999

Total Reagan-Bush . . . . . . . . . . . . . . . . . . .57%
    For this ticket . . . . . . . . . . . . . . . .44
    Against other ticket . . . . . . . . . . . . .11
    Not sure . . . . . . . . . . . . . . . . . . . . 2
Total Mondale-Ferraro . . . . . . . . . . . . . . . .39
    For this ticket . . . . . . . . . . . . . . . .17
    Against other ticket . . . . . . . . . . . . .20
    Not sure . . . . . . . . . . . . . . . . . . . . 2
Other; undecided . . . . . . . . . . . . . . . . . . 4

### $10,000–$19,999

Total Reagan-Bush . . . . . . . . . . . . . . . . . . .59%
    For this ticket . . . . . . . . . . . . . . . .45
    Against other ticket . . . . . . . . . . . . .11
    Not sure . . . . . . . . . . . . . . . . . . . . 3
Total Mondale-Ferraro . . . . . . . . . . . . . . . .37
    For this ticket . . . . . . . . . . . . . . . .16
    Against other ticket . . . . . . . . . . . . .17
    Not sure . . . . . . . . . . . . . . . . . . . . 4
Other; undecided . . . . . . . . . . . . . . . . . . 4

### Under $10,000

Total Reagan-Bush . . . . . . . . . . . . . . . . . . .45%
    For this ticket . . . . . . . . . . . . . . . .35
    Against other ticket . . . . . . . . . . . . 8
    Not sure . . . . . . . . . . . . . . . . . . . . 2
Total Mondale-Ferraro . . . . . . . . . . . . . . . .51
    For this ticket . . . . . . . . . . . . . . . .32
    Against other ticket . . . . . . . . . . . . .17
    Not sure . . . . . . . . . . . . . . . . . . . . 2
Other; undecided . . . . . . . . . . . . . . . . . . 4

## By Politics

### Republicans

Total Reagan-Bush .................93%
  For this ticket ................81
  Against other ticket ...........10
  Not sure ......................2
Total Mondale-Ferraro ...............5
  For this ticket ................2
  Against other ticket ...........2
  Not sure ......................1
Other; undecided ...................2

### Democrats

Total Reagan-Bush .................20%
  For this ticket ................12
  Against other ticket ...........6
  Not sure ......................2
Total Mondale-Ferraro ..............76
  For this ticket ................40
  Against other ticket ...........33
  Not sure ......................3
Other; undecided ...................4

### Independents

Total Reagan-Bush .................65%
  For this ticket ................44
  Against other ticket ...........16
  Not sure ......................5
Total Mondale-Ferraro ..............27
  For this ticket ................8
  Against other ticket ...........16
  Not sure ......................3
Other; undecided ...................8

## By Religion

### Protestants

Total Reagan-Bush .................57%
  For this ticket ................45
  Against other ticket ...........9
  Not sure ......................3
Total Mondale-Ferraro ..............39
  For this ticket ................20
  Against other ticket ...........17
  Not sure ......................2
Other; undecided ...................4

### Catholics

Total Reagan-Bush .................58%
  For this ticket ................46
  Against other ticket ...........9
  Not sure ......................3
Total Mondale-Ferraro ..............37
  For this ticket ................18
  Against other ticket ...........17
  Not sure ......................2
Other; undecided ...................5

## By Occupation

### Professional and Business

Total Reagan-Bush .................63%
  For this ticket ................50
  Against other ticket ...........11
  Not sure ......................2
Total Mondale-Ferraro ..............32
  For this ticket ................13
  Against other ticket ...........18
  Not sure ......................1
Other; undecided ...................5

### Clerical and Sales

Total Reagan-Bush .................70%
  For this ticket ................51
  Against other ticket ...........14
  Not sure ......................5
Total Mondale-Ferraro ..............25
  For this ticket ................11
  Against other ticket ...........13
  Not sure ......................1
Other; undecided ...................5

### Manual Workers

Total Reagan-Bush .................52%
  For this ticket ................41
  Against other ticket ...........8
  Not sure ......................3
Total Mondale-Ferraro ..............44
  For this ticket ................22
  Against other ticket ...........20
  Not sure ......................2
Other; undecided ...................4

### Nonlabor Force

Total Reagan-Bush ...................48%
   For this ticket ..................41
   Against other ticket ............ 5
   Not sure ...................... 2
Total Mondale-Ferraro ................47
   For this ticket ..................25
   Against other ticket ............17
   Not sure ...................... 5
Other; undecided ................... 5

## By Community Size

### One Million and Over

Total Reagan-Bush ...................49%
   For this ticket ..................39
   Against other ticket ............ 7
   Not sure ...................... 3
Total Mondale-Ferraro ................44
   For this ticket ..................24
   Against other ticket ............19
   Not sure ...................... 1
Other; undecided ................... 7

### 500,000–999,999

Total Reagan-Bush ...................51%
   For this ticket ..................35
   Against other ticket ............14
   Not sure ...................... 2
Total Mondale-Ferraro ................48
   For this ticket ..................21
   Against other ticket ............26
   Not sure ...................... 1
Other; undecided ................... 1

### 50,000–499,999

Total Reagan-Bush ...................65%
   For this ticket ..................55
   Against other ticket ............ 8
   Not sure ...................... 2
Total Mondale-Ferraro ................33
   For this ticket ..................15
   Against other ticket ............17
   Not sure ...................... 1
Other; undecided ................... 2

### 2,500–49,999

Total Reagan-Bush ...................72%
   For this ticket ..................57
   Against other ticket ............12
   Not sure ...................... 3
Total Mondale-Ferraro ................25
   For this ticket ..................10
   Against other ticket ............14
   Not sure ...................... 1
Other; undecided ................... 3

### Under 2,500; Rural

Total Reagan-Bush ...................55%
   For this ticket ..................41
   Against other ticket ............13
   Not sure ...................... 2
Total Mondale-Ferraro ................40
   For this ticket ..................18
   Against other ticket ............17
   Not sure ...................... 5
Other; undecided ................... 5

## By Labor Union Household

### Labor Union Members

Total Reagan-Bush ...................40%
   For this ticket ..................30
   Against other ticket ............ 8
   Not sure ...................... 2
Total Mondale-Ferraro ................56
   For this ticket ..................22
   Against other ticket ............31
   Not sure ...................... 3
Other; undecided ................... 4

### Nonlabor Union Members

Total Reagan-Bush ...................60%
   For this ticket ..................47
   Against other ticket ............10
   Not sure ...................... 3
Total Mondale-Ferraro ................35
   For this ticket ..................18
   Against other ticket ............15
   Not sure ...................... 3
Other; undecided ................... 5

*Less than 1%

## Selected National Trend

|  | Oct. 15–17 | Sept. 28–Oct. 1 |
|---|---|---|
| Total Reagan-Bush ....... | 58% | 55% |
| For this ticket | 43 | 42 |
| Against other ticket | 11 | 10 |
| Not sure | 4 | 3 |
| Total Mondale-Ferraro .... | 38 | 39 |
| For this ticket | 18 | 17 |
| Against other ticket | 16 | 19 |
| Not sure | 4 | 3 |
| Other; undecided ........ | 4 | 6 |

Note: In its semifinal preelection survey, the Gallup Poll found no statistically perceptible change in the standings of the two major party tickets. The Reagan-Bush Republican ticket is the choice of 56% of registered voters to 39% for the Mondale-Ferraro slate, with 5% undecided. In a similar survey conducted October 15–17, the Reagan ticket received 58% of the vote and the Mondale ticket, 38%.

There has been very little change in the strength of support for either slate since the mid-October assessment. However, comparison of the results of the three most recent surveys suggests some firming up of Walter Mondale's support in the last month: in the late September survey, about equal proportions of Mondale backers described their support as "strong" (21%) and "moderate" (18%). In the latest survey, strong Mondale supporters (24%) outnumber moderates (15%), a 3-to-2 ratio. Similarly, the "pro" and "anti" character of the race remains basically unchanged during the last month, although slightly more of Mondale's backers now than in September describe their support in positive (pro-Mondale) terms rather than in negative (anti-Reagan) terms.

## NOVEMBER 5
## PRESIDENTIAL TRIAL HEATS—
## FINAL TEST ELECTION

Interviewing Date: 11/2–3/84
Special Survey*

*Suppose you were voting today for president and vice-president of the United States. Here is a Gallup Poll secret ballot listing the candidates for these offices. Will you please mark that secret ballot for the candidates you favor today and then drop the folded ballot into the box?*

| | |
|---|---|
| Reagan-Bush ........................ | 57% |
| Mondale-Ferraro ..................... | 39 |
| Other;** undecided .................. | 4 |

When the undecided vote is allocated to the major party candidates on the basis of survey evidence, the final survey results become:†

| | |
|---|---|
| Reagan-Bush ........................ | 59% |
| Mondale-Ferraro ..................... | 41 |

*For the Gallup Poll's final preelection analysis this year, 3,456 adults were interviewed in person, of whom 1,985 were considered "likely voters." The interviews were conducted in more than 300 scientifically selected election precincts across the nation. For results based on the likely voter sample, one can say with 95% confidence that the error attributable to sampling and other random effects could be 3 percentage points in either direction.

**Minor party candidates received less than 1% of the vote, collectively.

†These findings should not be construed as a projection of the national popular vote in the next day's (November 6) balloting, but rather as an indication of the candidate preferences of voters, with roughly three days to go until election day.

## 1984 Presidential Vote by Key Voter Groups

### (Based on the Final Gallup Poll Preelection Test)

| | Reagan-Bush | Mondale-Ferraro |
|---|---|---|
| National ................ | 59% | 41% |

### By Sex

| | | |
|---|---|---|
| Male ................... | 64% | 36% |
| Female ................ | 55 | 45 |

## Sex by Age

**18–29 years**

| | | |
|---|---|---|
| Male | 67% | 33% |
| Female | 53 | 47 |

**30–49 years**

| | | |
|---|---|---|
| Male | 62 | 38 |
| Female | 57 | 43 |

**50 years and over**

| | | |
|---|---|---|
| Male | 61 | 39 |
| Female | 58 | 42 |

## By Ethnic Background

| | | |
|---|---|---|
| White | 66% | 34% |
| Nonwhite | 13 | 87 |
| Black | 8 | 92 |

## By Region

| | | |
|---|---|---|
| East | 54% | 46% |
| Midwest | 58 | 42 |
| South | 63 | 37 |
| West | 60 | 40 |

## By Age

| | | |
|---|---|---|
| 18–29 years | 60% | 40% |
| 30–49 years | 60 | 40 |
| 50 years and over | 59 | 41 |

## By Politics

| | | |
|---|---|---|
| Republicans | 96% | 4% |
| Democrats | 21 | 79 |
| Independents | 67 | 33 |

## By Religion

| | | |
|---|---|---|
| Protestants | 61% | 39% |
| Catholics | 61 | 39 |

## By Labor Union Households

| | | |
|---|---|---|
| Labor union members | 48% | 52% |
| Nonlabor union members | 62 | 38 |

Note: The Gallup Poll's preelection estimate of the national popular vote in the 1984 presidential election continued the high level of accuracy maintained by the Gallup Poll throughout its nearly fifty years of existence. With about 99% of the vote counted, the popular vote on Tuesday, election day, went 59% to Reagan-Bush to 41% for Mondale-Ferraro. The Gallup Poll's final preelection survey, reported on Monday, November 5, showed the same division of the vote: 59% for Reagan-Bush and 41% for Mondale-Ferraro.

The average deviation of Gallup Poll results from the actual election results for the twenty-five presidential and congressional contests between 1936 and 1984 has been 2.1 percentage points. The average deviation for the eighteen presidential and congressional elections since 1950 is 1.4 percentage points.

## NOVEMBER 7
## PRESIDENTIAL ELECTION— A SUMMARY

Remarkable shifts in the pattern of voting in President Ronald Reagan's sweeping victory are seen in the Gallup Poll's analysis of the 1984 election vote. This analysis by groups is based on the results of the final preelection Gallup survey, which exactly matched the nearly final results on election day, with about 99% of the vote counted.

1) In the November 6 contest, the vote among both Catholics and Protestants was exactly the same—61% for Reagan and 39% for Walter Mondale—in sharp contrast to the previous pattern of Catholic voting since 1952, when Gallup initiated these special vote analyses. During this three-decade period Catholics voted, on average, 20 points more Democratic than their Protestant counterparts.

2) A strong movement toward the GOP also was found among members of labor union families. In seven of the eight presidential elections between 1952 and 1980, this group voted for the Democratic candidate over the Republican one by an average of 28 percentage points. In the 1980 Carter-Reagan contest, the division was even closer, with 50% to 43% in favor of Jimmy Carter. In Tuesday's

election, unionists supported Mondale over Reagan by a narrow 52% to 48% margin.

3) After voting more Democratic than their elders in the previous five presidential elections, young voters under age 30 this year were as Republican in their preferences as persons 30 and older.

4) As in the 1980 presidential election, women voted more Democratic than men. The "gender gap" was most apparent among young adults under 30, with 67% of men but only 53% of women voting for President Reagan.

5) As in every presidential election since 1952, nonwhites voted overwhelmingly Democratic (87%). Although the Republican vote was only 13% this year among nonwhites, the figure had been lower in three earlier presidential elections.

The Gallup Poll reported on Monday, November 5, the day before the election, this division of the popular vote:

## Final Preelection Gallup Survey

Reagan-Bush . . . . . . . . . . . . . . . . . . . . . . . .59%
Mondale-Ferraro . . . . . . . . . . . . . . . . . . . .41

This compares remarkably with the latest available division of the popular vote on election day, with approximately 98% of the vote counted:

## Actual Election Results

Reagan-Bush . . . . . . . . . . . . . . . . . . . . . . . .59%
Mondale-Ferraro . . . . . . . . . . . . . . . . . . . .41

Despite the talk of volatility in voter preferences, the race throughout the final ten-week campaign period was remarkably stable, with any change between the Gallup Poll's surveys well within the normal range of sampling deviation. This was due in considerable measure to the low proportion of undecided voters. The following table shows the trend in voter preference since the opening of the campaign proper in early September, with the undecided vote allocated:

## Presidential Test Elections

|  | Reagan-Bush | Mondale-Ferraro | Other; undecided |
|---|---|---|---|
| November 2–3* | 57% | 39% | 4% |
| October 26–29 | 58 | 38 | 4 |
| October 15–17 | 58 | 38 | 4 |
| September 28– October 1 | 55 | 39 | 6 |
| September 21–24 | 58 | 37 | 5 |
| September 7–10 | 56 | 37 | 7 |

It is important to bear in mind that the current survey findings refer to the popular vote, not the electoral vote. To report the electoral vote, it would be necessary to conduct separate, full-scale polls in each of the fifty states.

Of importance too is the fact that some error is inherent in all sample surveys; no measuring instrument dealing with human behavior is perfect. Although the problems that arise in every election seem to be similar to those faced in previous elections, each contest involves unique variables and problems of measurement. The interviewing areas used constitute a probability sample of election precincts throughout the United States. Selection of households and respondents within households is not left to the discretion of interviewers but is controlled by a procedure designed to provide an objective, systematic choice of respondents.

To register their choice of candidates, respondents were handed a secret ballot by Gallup Poll interviewers and asked:

*Suppose you were voting today for the president and vice-president of the United States. Here is a Gallup Poll secret ballot listing the candidates for these offices. Will you please mark that secret ballot for the candidate you favor today—and then drop the folded ballot into the box?*

The ballot listed the names of this year's two major pairs of candidates under headings corresponding

*The final survey figures are based on likely voters. Earlier figures were based on registered voters.

to the name of the party each pair represents. Each voter marked and folded his ballot and placed it in a ballot box.

Two of the continuing problems in election polling are voter turnout and the undecided voter. First, if every adult in the nation voted, one of the most serious sources of possible polling error would be eliminated. In practice, however, far fewer eligible voters bother to cast their ballots; for example, in 1980 less than 53% of the electorate voted in the presidential election. To identify those voters most likely to go to the polls, the Gallup Poll uses a battery of screening questions designed to measure such factors as interest in politics, amount of thought given to the upcoming election, and whether or not the person is registered to vote.

Second, the undecided voter poses a major problem for polling organizations in election surveys. In the voting booth a choice has to be made, but in survey situations some respondents are actually reluctant to choose and prefer to say they are undecided. The final figures reported by the Gallup Poll reflect an allocation of this undecided vote to the major party candidates. If this step were not taken, there would be no clear way to judge how close a particular poll has come to the actual election results.

## NOVEMBER 15
## CRIME

Interviewing Date: 9/21–24/84
Survey #242-G

*During the last twelve months, have any of these happened to you? [Respondents were handed a card listing crimes.]*

|  | Yes |
|---|---|
| Money or property stolen | 12% |
| Property vandalized | 12 |
| Home broken into or attempt made | 9 |
| Car stolen | 3 |
| Personal assault | 4 |
| One or more incidents | 24 |

### By Sex
#### Male

| Money or property stolen | 13% |
|---|---|
| Property vandalized | 14 |
| Home broken into or attempt made | 10 |
| Car stolen | 4 |
| Personal assault | 5 |
| One or more incidents | 27 |

#### Female

| Money or property stolen | 11% |
|---|---|
| Property vandalized | 11 |
| Home broken into or attempt made | 8 |
| Car stolen | 2 |
| Personal assault | 3 |
| One or more incidents | 22 |

### By Ethnic Background
#### White

| Money or property stolen | 12% |
|---|---|
| Property vandalized | 13 |
| Home broken into or attempt made | 9 |
| Car stolen | 3 |
| Personal assault | 3 |
| One or more incidents | 24 |

#### Nonwhite

| Money or property stolen | 10% |
|---|---|
| Property vandalized | 9 |
| Home broken into or attempt made | 12 |
| Car stolen | 4 |
| Personal assault | 10 |
| One or more incidents | 24 |

#### Black

| Money or property stolen | 9% |
|---|---|
| Property vandalized | 8 |
| Home broken into or attempt made | 10 |
| Car stolen | 5 |
| Personal assault | 9 |
| One or more incidents | 22 |

## By Education

### College Graduate

Money or property stolen ...... .......14%
Property vandalized ........ ........14
Home broken into or attempt made .. ... 9
Car stolen ............. ............ 2
Personal assault ..................... 3
One or more incidents ................25

### College Incomplete

Money or property stolen ...... .......16%
Property vandalized ........ ........18
Home broken into or attempt made .. ... 9
Car stolen ............. ............ 3
Personal assault ..................... 3
One or more incidents ................29

### High-School Graduate

Money or property stolen ...... .......12%
Property vandalized ........ ........12
Home broken into or attempt made .. ...10
Car stolen ............. ............ 4
Personal assault ..................... 6
One or more incidents ................25

### Less Than High-School Graduate

Money or property stolen ...... ....... 6%
Property vandalized ........ ........ 5
Home broken into or attempt made .. ... 8
Car stolen ............. ............ 3
Personal assault ..................... 5
One or more incidents ................19

## By Region

### East

Money or property stolen ...... ....... 9%
Property vandalized ........ ........ 9
Home broken into or attempt made .. ... 9
Car stolen ............. ............ 4
Personal assault ..................... 3
One or more incidents ................22

### Midwest

Money or property stolen ...... .......14%
Property vandalized ........ ........12
Home broken into or attempt made .. ... 9
Car stolen ............. ............ 1
Personal assault ..................... 5
One or more incidents ................22

### South

Money or property stolen ...... .......10%
Property vandalized ........ ........11
Home broken into or attempt made .. ...10
Car stolen ............. ............ 3
Personal assault ..................... 4
One or more incidents ................24

### West

Money or property stolen ...... .......16%
Property vandalized ........ ........18
Home broken into or attempt made .. ...10
Car stolen ............. ............ 4
Personal assault ..................... 4
One or more incidents ................31

## By Age

### 18–29 Years

Money or property stolen ...... .......18%
Property vandalized ........ ........18
Home broken into or attempt made .. ...14
Car stolen ............. ............ 4
Personal assault ..................... 6
One or more incidents ................34

### 30–49 Years

Money or property stolen ...... .......13%
Property vandalized ........ ........13
Home broken into or attempt made .. ...10
Car stolen ............. ............ 2
Personal assault ..................... 5
One or more incidents ................27

### 50 Years and Over

Money or property stolen ...... ....... 7%
Property vandalized ........ ........ 7
Home broken into or attempt made .. ... 5

Car stolen ........................ 3
Personal assault ..................... 2
One or more incidents ................26

## By Income

### $40,000 and Over

Money or property stolen ...... ........14%
Property vandalized ................18
Home broken into or attempt made .. ... 5
Car stolen ................. 2
Personal assault ..................... 4
One or more incidents ................30

### $30,000–$39,999

Money or property stolen ...... .......11%
Property vandalized ................ 8
Home broken into or attempt made .. ... 4
Car stolen ................. *
Personal assault ..................... 3
One or more incidents ................22

### $20,000–$29,999

Money or property stolen ...... .......13%
Property vandalized ................12
Home broken into or attempt made .. ... 9
Car stolen ................. 2
Personal assault ..................... 2
One or more incidents ................21

### $10,000–$19,999

Money or property stolen ...... .......10%
Property vandalized ................10
Home broken into or attempt made .. ...12
Car stolen ................. 4
Personal assault ..................... 8
One or more incidents ................24

### Under $10,000

Money or property stolen ...... ....... 9%
Property vandalized ................ 9
Home broken into or attempt made .. ...13
Car stolen ................. 3
Personal assault ..................... 4
One or more incidents ................24

*Less than 1%

## Selected National Trend

| | 1983 | 1981 | 1979 | 1977 | 1972 |
|---|---|---|---|---|---|
| Money or property stolen | 12% | 11% | 11% | 8% | 8% |
| Property vandalized | 11 | 11 | 10 | 11 | 8 |
| Home broken into or attempt made | 8 | 7 | 7 | 5 | 7 |
| Car stolen | 2 | 2 | 2 | 1 | 2 |
| Personal assault | 5 | 2 | 3 | 2 | 2 |
| One or more incidents | 25 | 23 | 22 | 20 | 21 |

## International Comparisons

| | Money, property stolen | Home broken into, attempt made | Personal assault |
|---|---|---|---|
| *North America* | | | |
| United States | 12% | 9% | 4% |
| Canada | 13 | 5 | 2 |
| *South America* | | | |
| Brazil | 21% | 11% | 4% |
| Colombia | 33 | 19 | 10 |
| Uruguay | 7 | 8 | 2 |
| *Europe* | | | |
| Belgium | 5% | 2% | 1% |
| Denmark | 11 | 4 | 2 |
| France | 11 | 9 | 3 |
| Ireland | 11 | 5 | 2 |
| Italy | 9 | 4 | 2 |
| Netherlands | 14 | 4 | 1 |
| Norway | 11 | 4 | 2 |
| Spain | 11 | 6 | 3 |
| Sweden | 10 | 2 | 2 |
| United Kingdom | 13 | 7 | 2 |
| Germany (West) | 8 | 3 | 1 |
| *Asia* | | | |
| Japan | 2% | 1% | * |
| Korea (South) | 5 | 3 | 1 |
| Turkey | 6 | 3 | 4 |

*Less than 1%

*Asked of those who experienced a crime: Did you happen to report this to the police, or not?*

|  | Crime incidence | Reported to police |
|---|---|---|
| Money or property stolen | 12% | 7% |
| Property vandalized | 12 | 7 |
| Home broken into or attempt made | 9 | 7 |
| Car stolen | 3 | 3 |
| Personal assault | 4 | 3 |

Note: The latest Gallup crime audit shows that close to one-fourth (24%) of U.S. households were victimized during the twelve months preceding the survey. These were crimes either against property (money or property stolen or vandalized) or against persons (robberies or assaults). In addition, the level of victimization has changed little over the recent past; in the 1983 audit, 25% reported they had been victimized.

Despite the international reputation of the United States as a crime-ridden country, a major study recently conducted by Gallup-affiliated research companies in nineteen nations around the world showed it to be no worse than most of the other developed nations in terms of crime incidence. By comparison, in the developing nations of Brazil and Colombia higher crime rates were reported; in South Korea and Turkey the rates were lower. Based on all the nations included in the study, Japan would seem to be the safest; Colombia, the most dangerous. While the latest figures for the United States are little changed from earlier years, the current results for most of the industrialized nations represent dramatic increases in the incidence of crime from those reported in surveys conducted a decade ago.

## NOVEMBER 18
## NATIONAL REFERENDUM

Interviewing Date: 9/28–10/1/84
Survey #243-G

*This card lists various proposals being discussed in this country today. Would you tell me whether you generally favor or generally oppose each of these proposals:*

*Tax increases to reduce the federal budget deficit?*

Favor . . . . . . . . . . . . . . . . . . . . . . . . . . . . .34%
Oppose . . . . . . . . . . . . . . . . . . . . . . . . . . . .62
No opinion . . . . . . . . . . . . . . . . . . . . . . . . 4

### By Sex
#### Male

Favor . . . . . . . . . . . . . . . . . . . . . . . . . . . . .38%
Oppose . . . . . . . . . . . . . . . . . . . . . . . . . . . .59
No opinion . . . . . . . . . . . . . . . . . . . . . . . . 3

#### Female

Favor . . . . . . . . . . . . . . . . . . . . . . . . . . . . .31%
Oppose . . . . . . . . . . . . . . . . . . . . . . . . . . . .64
No opinion . . . . . . . . . . . . . . . . . . . . . . . . 5

### By Ethnic Background
#### White

Favor . . . . . . . . . . . . . . . . . . . . . . . . . . . . .33%
Oppose . . . . . . . . . . . . . . . . . . . . . . . . . . . .63
No opinion . . . . . . . . . . . . . . . . . . . . . . . . 4

#### Nonwhite

Favor . . . . . . . . . . . . . . . . . . . . . . . . . . . . .40%
Oppose . . . . . . . . . . . . . . . . . . . . . . . . . . . .53
No opinion . . . . . . . . . . . . . . . . . . . . . . . . 7

#### Black

Favor . . . . . . . . . . . . . . . . . . . . . . . . . . . . .40%
Oppose . . . . . . . . . . . . . . . . . . . . . . . . . . . .53
No opinion . . . . . . . . . . . . . . . . . . . . . . . . 7

### By Education
#### College Graduate

Favor . . . . . . . . . . . . . . . . . . . . . . . . . . . . .44%
Oppose . . . . . . . . . . . . . . . . . . . . . . . . . . . .54
No opinion . . . . . . . . . . . . . . . . . . . . . . . . 2

#### College Incomplete

Favor . . . . . . . . . . . . . . . . . . . . . . . . . . . . .34%
Oppose . . . . . . . . . . . . . . . . . . . . . . . . . . . .62
No opinion . . . . . . . . . . . . . . . . . . . . . . . . 4

### High-School Graduate

Favor . . . . . . . . . . . . . . . . . . . . . . . . . . . . 32%
Oppose . . . . . . . . . . . . . . . . . . . . . . . . . . . 65
No opinion . . . . . . . . . . . . . . . . . . . . . . 3

### Less Than High-School Graduate

Favor . . . . . . . . . . . . . . . . . . . . . . . . . . . . 31%
Oppose . . . . . . . . . . . . . . . . . . . . . . . . . . . 62
No opinion . . . . . . . . . . . . . . . . . . . . . . . 7

## By Region
### East

Favor . . . . . . . . . . . . . . . . . . . . . . . . . . . . 37%
Oppose . . . . . . . . . . . . . . . . . . . . . . . . . . . 61
No opinion . . . . . . . . . . . . . . . . . . . . . . . 2

### Midwest

Favor . . . . . . . . . . . . . . . . . . . . . . . . . . . . 29%
Oppose . . . . . . . . . . . . . . . . . . . . . . . . . . . 67
No opinion . . . . . . . . . . . . . . . . . . . . . . 4

### South

Favor . . . . . . . . . . . . . . . . . . . . . . . . . . . . 34%
Oppose . . . . . . . . . . . . . . . . . . . . . . . . . . . 61
No opinion . . . . . . . . . . . . . . . . . . . . . . 5

### West

Favor . . . . . . . . . . . . . . . . . . . . . . . . . . . . 37%
Oppose . . . . . . . . . . . . . . . . . . . . . . . . . . . 58
No opinion . . . . . . . . . . . . . . . . . . . . . . 5

## By Age
### 18–29 Years

Favor . . . . . . . . . . . . . . . . . . . . . . . . . . . . 32%
Oppose . . . . . . . . . . . . . . . . . . . . . . . . . . . 65
No opinion . . . . . . . . . . . . . . . . . . . . . . 3

### 30–49 Years

Favor . . . . . . . . . . . . . . . . . . . . . . . . . . . . 35%
Oppose . . . . . . . . . . . . . . . . . . . . . . . . . . . 61
No opinion . . . . . . . . . . . . . . . . . . . . . . 4

### 50 Years and Over

Favor . . . . . . . . . . . . . . . . . . . . . . . . . . . . 35%
Oppose . . . . . . . . . . . . . . . . . . . . . . . . . . . 60
No opinion . . . . . . . . . . . . . . . . . . . . . . 5

## By Income
### $40,000 and Over

Favor . . . . . . . . . . . . . . . . . . . . . . . . . . . . 39%
Oppose . . . . . . . . . . . . . . . . . . . . . . . . . . . 58
No opinion . . . . . . . . . . . . . . . . . . . . . . 3

### $30,000–$39,999

Favor . . . . . . . . . . . . . . . . . . . . . . . . . . . . 41%
Oppose . . . . . . . . . . . . . . . . . . . . . . . . . . . 55
No opinion . . . . . . . . . . . . . . . . . . . . . . 4

### $20,000–$29,999

Favor . . . . . . . . . . . . . . . . . . . . . . . . . . . . 32%
Oppose . . . . . . . . . . . . . . . . . . . . . . . . . . . 65
No opinion . . . . . . . . . . . . . . . . . . . . . . 3

### $10,000–$19,999

Favor . . . . . . . . . . . . . . . . . . . . . . . . . . . . 35%
Oppose . . . . . . . . . . . . . . . . . . . . . . . . . . . 61
No opinion . . . . . . . . . . . . . . . . . . . . . . 4

### Under $10,000

Favor . . . . . . . . . . . . . . . . . . . . . . . . . . . . 28%
Oppose . . . . . . . . . . . . . . . . . . . . . . . . . . . 65
No opinion . . . . . . . . . . . . . . . . . . . . . . 7

## By Politics
### Republicans

Favor . . . . . . . . . . . . . . . . . . . . . . . . . . . . 28%
Oppose . . . . . . . . . . . . . . . . . . . . . . . . . . . 68
No opinion . . . . . . . . . . . . . . . . . . . . . . 4

### Democrats

Favor . . . . . . . . . . . . . . . . . . . . . . . . . . . . 41%
Oppose . . . . . . . . . . . . . . . . . . . . . . . . . . . 55
No opinion . . . . . . . . . . . . . . . . . . . . . . 4

### Independents

Favor . . . . . . . . . . . . . . . . . . . . . . . . . . . .32%
Oppose . . . . . . . . . . . . . . . . . . . . . . . . . . .65
No opinion . . . . . . . . . . . . . . . . . . . . . . . . 3

### Prayer in public schools?

Favor . . . . . . . . . . . . . . . . . . . . . . . . . . . .69%
Oppose . . . . . . . . . . . . . . . . . . . . . . . . . . .28
No opinion . . . . . . . . . . . . . . . . . . . . . . . . 3

## By Sex
### Male

Favor . . . . . . . . . . . . . . . . . . . . . . . . . . . .66%
Oppose . . . . . . . . . . . . . . . . . . . . . . . . . . .31
No opinion . . . . . . . . . . . . . . . . . . . . . . . . 3

### Female

Favor . . . . . . . . . . . . . . . . . . . . . . . . . . . .71%
Oppose . . . . . . . . . . . . . . . . . . . . . . . . . . .26
No opinion . . . . . . . . . . . . . . . . . . . . . . . . 3

## By Ethnic Background
### White

Favor . . . . . . . . . . . . . . . . . . . . . . . . . . . .68%
Oppose . . . . . . . . . . . . . . . . . . . . . . . . . . .29
No opinion . . . . . . . . . . . . . . . . . . . . . . . . 3

### Nonwhite

Favor . . . . . . . . . . . . . . . . . . . . . . . . . . . .72%
Oppose . . . . . . . . . . . . . . . . . . . . . . . . . . .22
No opinion . . . . . . . . . . . . . . . . . . . . . . . . 6

### Black

Favor . . . . . . . . . . . . . . . . . . . . . . . . . . . .72%
Oppose . . . . . . . . . . . . . . . . . . . . . . . . . . .22
No opinion . . . . . . . . . . . . . . . . . . . . . . . . 6

## By Education
### College Graduate

Favor . . . . . . . . . . . . . . . . . . . . . . . . . . . .55%
Oppose . . . . . . . . . . . . . . . . . . . . . . . . . . .42
No opinion . . . . . . . . . . . . . . . . . . . . . . . . 3

### College Incomplete

Favor . . . . . . . . . . . . . . . . . . . . . . . . . . . .63%
Oppose . . . . . . . . . . . . . . . . . . . . . . . . . . .33
No opinion . . . . . . . . . . . . . . . . . . . . . . . . 4

### High-School Graduate

Favor . . . . . . . . . . . . . . . . . . . . . . . . . . . .72%
Oppose . . . . . . . . . . . . . . . . . . . . . . . . . . .25
No opinion . . . . . . . . . . . . . . . . . . . . . . . . 3

### Less Than High-School Graduate

Favor . . . . . . . . . . . . . . . . . . . . . . . . . . . .81%
Oppose . . . . . . . . . . . . . . . . . . . . . . . . . . .15
No opinion . . . . . . . . . . . . . . . . . . . . . . . . 4

## By Region
### East

Favor . . . . . . . . . . . . . . . . . . . . . . . . . . . .66%
Oppose . . . . . . . . . . . . . . . . . . . . . . . . . . .32
No opinion . . . . . . . . . . . . . . . . . . . . . . . . 2

### Midwest

Favor . . . . . . . . . . . . . . . . . . . . . . . . . . . .71%
Oppose . . . . . . . . . . . . . . . . . . . . . . . . . . .26
No opinion . . . . . . . . . . . . . . . . . . . . . . . . 3

### South

Favor . . . . . . . . . . . . . . . . . . . . . . . . . . . .78%
Oppose . . . . . . . . . . . . . . . . . . . . . . . . . . .19
No opinion . . . . . . . . . . . . . . . . . . . . . . . . 3

### West

Favor . . . . . . . . . . . . . . . . . . . . . . . . . . . .54%
Oppose . . . . . . . . . . . . . . . . . . . . . . . . . . .40
No opinion . . . . . . . . . . . . . . . . . . . . . . . . 6

## By Age
### 18–29 Years

Favor . . . . . . . . . . . . . . . . . . . . . . . . . . . .60%
Oppose . . . . . . . . . . . . . . . . . . . . . . . . . . .36
No opinion . . . . . . . . . . . . . . . . . . . . . . . . 4

### 30–49 Years

Favor . . . . . . . . . . . . . . . . . . . . . . . . . . . .68%
Oppose . . . . . . . . . . . . . . . . . . . . . . . . . .30
No opinion . . . . . . . . . . . . . . . . . . . . . 2

### 50 Years and Over

Favor . . . . . . . . . . . . . . . . . . . . . . . . . . . .76%
Oppose . . . . . . . . . . . . . . . . . . . . . . . . . .20
No opinion . . . . . . . . . . . . . . . . . . . . . 4

## By Income
### $40,000 and Over

Favor . . . . . . . . . . . . . . . . . . . . . . . . . . . .58%
Oppose . . . . . . . . . . . . . . . . . . . . . . . . . .40
No opinion . . . . . . . . . . . . . . . . . . . . . 2

### $30,000–$39,999

Favor . . . . . . . . . . . . . . . . . . . . . . . . . . . .68%
Oppose . . . . . . . . . . . . . . . . . . . . . . . . . .29
No opinion . . . . . . . . . . . . . . . . . . . . . 3

### $20,000–$29,999

Favor . . . . . . . . . . . . . . . . . . . . . . . . . . . .72%
Oppose . . . . . . . . . . . . . . . . . . . . . . . . . .25
No opinion . . . . . . . . . . . . . . . . . . . . . 3

### $10,000–$19,999

Favor . . . . . . . . . . . . . . . . . . . . . . . . . . . .70%
Oppose . . . . . . . . . . . . . . . . . . . . . . . . . .26
No opinion . . . . . . . . . . . . . . . . . . . . . 4

### Under $10,000

Favor . . . . . . . . . . . . . . . . . . . . . . . . . . . .72%
Oppose . . . . . . . . . . . . . . . . . . . . . . . . . .23
No opinion . . . . . . . . . . . . . . . . . . . . . 5

## By Politics
### Republicans

Favor . . . . . . . . . . . . . . . . . . . . . . . . . . . .79%
Oppose . . . . . . . . . . . . . . . . . . . . . . . . . .17
No opinion . . . . . . . . . . . . . . . . . . . . . 4

### Democrats

Favor . . . . . . . . . . . . . . . . . . . . . . . . . . . .61%
Oppose . . . . . . . . . . . . . . . . . . . . . . . . . .36
No opinion . . . . . . . . . . . . . . . . . . . . . 3

### Independents

Favor . . . . . . . . . . . . . . . . . . . . . . . . . . . .65%
Oppose . . . . . . . . . . . . . . . . . . . . . . . . . .32
No opinion . . . . . . . . . . . . . . . . . . . . . 3

### *Reduced defense spending?*

Favor . . . . . . . . . . . . . . . . . . . . . . . . . . . .50%
Oppose . . . . . . . . . . . . . . . . . . . . . . . . . .46
No opinion . . . . . . . . . . . . . . . . . . . . . 4

## By Sex
### Male

Favor . . . . . . . . . . . . . . . . . . . . . . . . . . . .51%
Oppose . . . . . . . . . . . . . . . . . . . . . . . . . .47
No opinion . . . . . . . . . . . . . . . . . . . . . 2

### Female

Favor . . . . . . . . . . . . . . . . . . . . . . . . . . . .50%
Oppose . . . . . . . . . . . . . . . . . . . . . . . . . .44
No opinion . . . . . . . . . . . . . . . . . . . . . 6

## By Ethnic Background
### White

Favor . . . . . . . . . . . . . . . . . . . . . . . . . . . .49%
Oppose . . . . . . . . . . . . . . . . . . . . . . . . . .47
No opinion . . . . . . . . . . . . . . . . . . . . . 4

### Nonwhite

Favor . . . . . . . . . . . . . . . . . . . . . . . . . . . .57%
Oppose . . . . . . . . . . . . . . . . . . . . . . . . . .36
No opinion . . . . . . . . . . . . . . . . . . . . . 7

### Black

Favor . . . . . . . . . . . . . . . . . . . . . . . . . . . .58%
Oppose . . . . . . . . . . . . . . . . . . . . . . . . . .34
No opinion . . . . . . . . . . . . . . . . . . . . . 8

## By Education

### College Graduate

Favor ..............................51%
Oppose ............................48
No opinion ........................ 1

### College Incomplete

Favor ..............................49%
Oppose ............................48
No opinion ........................ 3

### High-School Graduate

Favor ..............................47%
Oppose ............................50
No opinion ........................ 3

### Less Than High-School Graduate

Favor ..............................58%
Oppose ............................34
No opinion ........................ 8

## By Region

### East

Favor ..............................56%
Oppose ............................39
No opinion ........................ 5

### Midwest

Favor ..............................49%
Oppose ............................48
No opinion ........................ 3

### South

Favor ..............................48%
Oppose ............................48
No opinion ........................ 4

### West

Favor ..............................49%
Oppose ............................46
No opinion ........................ 5

## By Age

### 18–29 Years

Favor ..............................50%
Oppose ............................48
No opinion ........................ 2

### 30–49 Years

Favor ..............................52%
Oppose ............................46
No opinion ........................ 2

### 50 Years and Over

Favor ..............................49%
Oppose ............................43
No opinion ........................ 8

## By Income

### $40,000 and Over

Favor ..............................46%
Oppose ............................52
No opinion ........................ 2

### $30,000–$39,999

Favor ..............................48%
Oppose ............................49
No opinion ........................ 3

### $20,000–$29,999

Favor ..............................44%
Oppose ............................53
No opinion ........................ 3

### $10,000–$19,999

Favor ..............................56%
Oppose ............................41
No opinion ........................ 3

### Under $10,000

Favor ..............................56%
Oppose ............................35
No opinion ........................ 9

## By Politics
### Republicans
Favor . . . . . . . . . . . . . . . . . . . . . . . . . .40%
Oppose . . . . . . . . . . . . . . . . . . . . . . .56
No opinion . . . . . . . . . . . . . . . . . . . . 4

### Democrats
Favor . . . . . . . . . . . . . . . . . . . . . . . . . .61%
Oppose . . . . . . . . . . . . . . . . . . . . . . .35
No opinion . . . . . . . . . . . . . . . . . . . . 4

### Independents
Favor . . . . . . . . . . . . . . . . . . . . . . . . . .49%
Oppose . . . . . . . . . . . . . . . . . . . . . . .47
No opinion . . . . . . . . . . . . . . . . . . . . 4

*Tuition tax credits for children attending private or parochial schools?*

Favor . . . . . . . . . . . . . . . . . . . . . . . . . .50%
Oppose . . . . . . . . . . . . . . . . . . . . . . .45
No opinion . . . . . . . . . . . . . . . . . . . . 5

## By Sex
### Male
Favor . . . . . . . . . . . . . . . . . . . . . . . . . .52%
Oppose . . . . . . . . . . . . . . . . . . . . . . .45
No opinion . . . . . . . . . . . . . . . . . . . . 3

### Female
Favor . . . . . . . . . . . . . . . . . . . . . . . . . .49%
Oppose . . . . . . . . . . . . . . . . . . . . . . .45
No opinion . . . . . . . . . . . . . . . . . . . . 6

## By Ethnic Background
### White
Favor . . . . . . . . . . . . . . . . . . . . . . . . . .50%
Oppose . . . . . . . . . . . . . . . . . . . . . . .45
No opinion . . . . . . . . . . . . . . . . . . . . 5

### Nonwhite
Favor . . . . . . . . . . . . . . . . . . . . . . . . . .52%
Oppose . . . . . . . . . . . . . . . . . . . . . . .41
No opinion . . . . . . . . . . . . . . . . . . . . 7

### Black
Favor . . . . . . . . . . . . . . . . . . . . . . . . . .50%
Oppose . . . . . . . . . . . . . . . . . . . . . . .42
No opinion . . . . . . . . . . . . . . . . . . . . 8

## By Education
### College Graduate
Favor . . . . . . . . . . . . . . . . . . . . . . . . . .48%
Oppose . . . . . . . . . . . . . . . . . . . . . . .49
No opinion . . . . . . . . . . . . . . . . . . . . 3

### College Incomplete
Favor . . . . . . . . . . . . . . . . . . . . . . . . . .48%
Oppose . . . . . . . . . . . . . . . . . . . . . . .49
No opinion . . . . . . . . . . . . . . . . . . . . 3

### High-School Graduate
Favor . . . . . . . . . . . . . . . . . . . . . . . . . .52%
Oppose . . . . . . . . . . . . . . . . . . . . . . .43
No opinion . . . . . . . . . . . . . . . . . . . . 5

### Less Than High-School Graduate
Favor . . . . . . . . . . . . . . . . . . . . . . . . . .51%
Oppose . . . . . . . . . . . . . . . . . . . . . . .39
No opinion . . . . . . . . . . . . . . . . . . . .10

## By Region
### East
Favor . . . . . . . . . . . . . . . . . . . . . . . . . .55%
Oppose . . . . . . . . . . . . . . . . . . . . . . .40
No opinion . . . . . . . . . . . . . . . . . . . . 5

### Midwest
Favor . . . . . . . . . . . . . . . . . . . . . . . . . .44%
Oppose . . . . . . . . . . . . . . . . . . . . . . .50
No opinion . . . . . . . . . . . . . . . . . . . . 6

### South
Favor . . . . . . . . . . . . . . . . . . . . . . . . . .53%
Oppose . . . . . . . . . . . . . . . . . . . . . . .41
No opinion . . . . . . . . . . . . . . . . . . . . 6

### West

Favor ............................46%
Oppose ...........................50
No opinion ....................... 4

### By Age
#### 18–29 Years

Favor ............................51%
Oppose ...........................46
No opinion ....................... 3

#### 30–49 Years

Favor ............................50%
Oppose ...........................46
No opinion ....................... 4

#### 50 Years and Over

Favor ............................50%
Oppose ...........................43
No opinion ....................... 7

### By Income
#### $40,000 and Over

Favor ............................50%
Oppose ...........................50
No opinion ....................... *

#### $30,000–$39,999

Favor ............................47%
Oppose ...........................49
No opinion ....................... 4

#### $20,000–$29,999

Favor ............................56%
Oppose ...........................42
No opinion ....................... 2

#### $10,000–$19,999

Favor ............................50%
Oppose ...........................44
No opinion ....................... 6

### Under $10,000

Favor ............................51%
Oppose ...........................39
No opinion .......................10

### By Politics
#### Republicans

Favor ............................50%
Oppose ...........................44
No opinion ....................... 6

#### Democrats

Favor ............................49%
Oppose ...........................46
No opinion ....................... 5

#### Independents

Favor ............................53%
Oppose ...........................44
No opinion ....................... 3

*Less than 1%

*A ban on all abortions except in cases of rape, incest, or when the mother's life is endangered?*

Favor ............................50%
Oppose ...........................46
No opinion ....................... 4

### By Sex
#### Male

Favor ............................51%
Oppose ...........................45
No opinion ....................... 4

#### Female

Favor ............................49%
Oppose ...........................46
No opinion ....................... 5

## By Ethnic Background
### White
Favor . . . . . . . . . . . . . . . . . . . . . . . . . . . . .51%
Oppose . . . . . . . . . . . . . . . . . . . . . . . . . .45
No opinion . . . . . . . . . . . . . . . . . . . . . . 4

### Nonwhite
Favor . . . . . . . . . . . . . . . . . . . . . . . . . . . . .47%
Oppose . . . . . . . . . . . . . . . . . . . . . . . . . .47
No opinion . . . . . . . . . . . . . . . . . . . . . . 6

### Black
Favor . . . . . . . . . . . . . . . . . . . . . . . . . . . . .44%
Oppose . . . . . . . . . . . . . . . . . . . . . . . . . .50
No opinion . . . . . . . . . . . . . . . . . . . . . . 6

## By Education
### College Graduate
Favor . . . . . . . . . . . . . . . . . . . . . . . . . . . . .40%
Oppose . . . . . . . . . . . . . . . . . . . . . . . . . .62
No opinion . . . . . . . . . . . . . . . . . . . . . . 8

### College Incomplete
Favor . . . . . . . . . . . . . . . . . . . . . . . . . . . . .45%
Oppose . . . . . . . . . . . . . . . . . . . . . . . . . .52
No opinion . . . . . . . . . . . . . . . . . . . . . . 3

### High-School Graduate
Favor . . . . . . . . . . . . . . . . . . . . . . . . . . . . .54%
Oppose . . . . . . . . . . . . . . . . . . . . . . . . . .42
No opinion . . . . . . . . . . . . . . . . . . . . . . 4

### Less Than High-School Graduate
Favor . . . . . . . . . . . . . . . . . . . . . . . . . . . . .61%
Oppose . . . . . . . . . . . . . . . . . . . . . . . . . .31
No opinion . . . . . . . . . . . . . . . . . . . . . . 8

## By Region
### East
Favor . . . . . . . . . . . . . . . . . . . . . . . . . . . . .45%
Oppose . . . . . . . . . . . . . . . . . . . . . . . . . .50
No opinion . . . . . . . . . . . . . . . . . . . . . . 5

### Midwest
Favor . . . . . . . . . . . . . . . . . . . . . . . . . . . . .53%
Oppose . . . . . . . . . . . . . . . . . . . . . . . . . .43
No opinion . . . . . . . . . . . . . . . . . . . . . . 4

### South
Favor . . . . . . . . . . . . . . . . . . . . . . . . . . . . .57%
Oppose . . . . . . . . . . . . . . . . . . . . . . . . . .38
No opinion . . . . . . . . . . . . . . . . . . . . . . 5

### West
Favor . . . . . . . . . . . . . . . . . . . . . . . . . . . . .41%
Oppose . . . . . . . . . . . . . . . . . . . . . . . . . .56
No opinion . . . . . . . . . . . . . . . . . . . . . . 3

## By Age
### 18–29 Years
Favor . . . . . . . . . . . . . . . . . . . . . . . . . . . . .49%
Oppose . . . . . . . . . . . . . . . . . . . . . . . . . .48
No opinion . . . . . . . . . . . . . . . . . . . . . . 3

### 30–49 Years
Favor . . . . . . . . . . . . . . . . . . . . . . . . . . . . .45%
Oppose . . . . . . . . . . . . . . . . . . . . . . . . . .52
No opinion . . . . . . . . . . . . . . . . . . . . . . 3

### 50 Years and Over
Favor . . . . . . . . . . . . . . . . . . . . . . . . . . . . .55%
Oppose . . . . . . . . . . . . . . . . . . . . . . . . . .37
No opinion . . . . . . . . . . . . . . . . . . . . . . 8

## By Income
### $40,000 and Over
Favor . . . . . . . . . . . . . . . . . . . . . . . . . . . . .34%
Oppose . . . . . . . . . . . . . . . . . . . . . . . . . .64
No opinion . . . . . . . . . . . . . . . . . . . . . . 2

### $30,000–$39,999
Favor . . . . . . . . . . . . . . . . . . . . . . . . . . . . .42%
Oppose . . . . . . . . . . . . . . . . . . . . . . . . . .54
No opinion . . . . . . . . . . . . . . . . . . . . . . 4

### $20,000–$29,999

Favor ..............................53%
Oppose .............................43
No opinion .......................... 4

### $10,000–$19,999

Favor ..............................56%
Oppose .............................39
No opinion .......................... 5

### Under $10,000

Favor ..............................56%
Oppose .............................37
No opinion .......................... 7

## By Politics
### Republicans

Favor ..............................56%
Oppose .............................40
No opinion .......................... 4

### Democrats

Favor ..............................47%
Oppose .............................49
No opinion .......................... 4

### Independents

Favor ..............................47%
Oppose .............................49
No opinion .......................... 4

### Passage of the Equal Rights Amendment to the Constitution?

Favor ..............................63%
Oppose .............................31
No opinion .......................... 6

## By Sex
### Male

Favor ..............................64%
Oppose .............................31
No opinion .......................... 5

### Female

Favor ..............................62%
Oppose .............................32
No opinion .......................... 6

## By Ethnic Background
### White

Favor ..............................61%
Oppose .............................33
No opinion .......................... 6

### Nonwhite

Favor ..............................79%
Oppose .............................17
No opinion .......................... 4

### Black

Favor ..............................78%
Oppose .............................18
No opinion .......................... 4

## By Education
### College Graduate

Favor ..............................67%
Oppose .............................31
No opinion .......................... 2

### College Incomplete

Favor ..............................59%
Oppose .............................35
No opinion .......................... 6

### High-School Graduate

Favor ..............................62%
Oppose .............................34
No opinion .......................... 4

### Less Than High-School Graduate

Favor ..............................65%
Oppose .............................24
No opinion .........................11

## By Region
### East

Favor . . . . . . . . . . . . . . . . . . . . . . . . . . . . .69%
Oppose . . . . . . . . . . . . . . . . . . . . . . . . . . .27
No opinion . . . . . . . . . . . . . . . . . . . . . . 4

### Midwest

Favor . . . . . . . . . . . . . . . . . . . . . . . . . . . . .59%
Oppose . . . . . . . . . . . . . . . . . . . . . . . . . . .35
No opinion . . . . . . . . . . . . . . . . . . . . . . 6

### South

Favor . . . . . . . . . . . . . . . . . . . . . . . . . . . . .58%
Oppose . . . . . . . . . . . . . . . . . . . . . . . . . . .35
No opinion . . . . . . . . . . . . . . . . . . . . . . 7

### West

Favor . . . . . . . . . . . . . . . . . . . . . . . . . . . . .67%
Oppose . . . . . . . . . . . . . . . . . . . . . . . . . . .28
No opinion . . . . . . . . . . . . . . . . . . . . . . 5

## By Age
### 18–29 Years

Favor . . . . . . . . . . . . . . . . . . . . . . . . . . . . .69%
Oppose . . . . . . . . . . . . . . . . . . . . . . . . . . .26
No opinion . . . . . . . . . . . . . . . . . . . . . . 5

### 30–49 Years

Favor . . . . . . . . . . . . . . . . . . . . . . . . . . . . .67%
Oppose . . . . . . . . . . . . . . . . . . . . . . . . . . .31
No opinion . . . . . . . . . . . . . . . . . . . . . . 2

### 50 Years and Over

Favor . . . . . . . . . . . . . . . . . . . . . . . . . . . . .54%
Oppose . . . . . . . . . . . . . . . . . . . . . . . . . . .36
No opinion . . . . . . . . . . . . . . . . . . . . . .10

## By Income
### $40,000 and Over

Favor . . . . . . . . . . . . . . . . . . . . . . . . . . . . .64%
Oppose . . . . . . . . . . . . . . . . . . . . . . . . . . .31
No opinion . . . . . . . . . . . . . . . . . . . . . . 5

### $30,000–$39,999

Favor . . . . . . . . . . . . . . . . . . . . . . . . . . . . .62%
Oppose . . . . . . . . . . . . . . . . . . . . . . . . . . .32
No opinion . . . . . . . . . . . . . . . . . . . . . . 6

### $20,000–$29,999

Favor . . . . . . . . . . . . . . . . . . . . . . . . . . . . .60%
Oppose . . . . . . . . . . . . . . . . . . . . . . . . . . .36
No opinion . . . . . . . . . . . . . . . . . . . . . . 4

### $10,000–$19,999

Favor . . . . . . . . . . . . . . . . . . . . . . . . . . . . .65%
Oppose . . . . . . . . . . . . . . . . . . . . . . . . . . .30
No opinion . . . . . . . . . . . . . . . . . . . . . . 5

### Under $10,000

Favor . . . . . . . . . . . . . . . . . . . . . . . . . . . . .64%
Oppose . . . . . . . . . . . . . . . . . . . . . . . . . . .28
No opinion . . . . . . . . . . . . . . . . . . . . . . 8

## By Politics
### Republicans

Favor . . . . . . . . . . . . . . . . . . . . . . . . . . . . .50%
Oppose . . . . . . . . . . . . . . . . . . . . . . . . . . .43
No opinion . . . . . . . . . . . . . . . . . . . . . . 7

### Democrats

Favor . . . . . . . . . . . . . . . . . . . . . . . . . . . . .73%
Oppose . . . . . . . . . . . . . . . . . . . . . . . . . . .23
No opinion . . . . . . . . . . . . . . . . . . . . . . 4

### Independents

Favor . . . . . . . . . . . . . . . . . . . . . . . . . . . . .67%
Oppose . . . . . . . . . . . . . . . . . . . . . . . . . . .29
No opinion . . . . . . . . . . . . . . . . . . . . . . 4

*Increased spending for social programs such as education and Medicare?*

Favor . . . . . . . . . . . . . . . . . . . . . . . . . . . . .74%
Oppose . . . . . . . . . . . . . . . . . . . . . . . . . . .24
No opinion . . . . . . . . . . . . . . . . . . . . . . 2

### By Sex
#### Male

Favor ............................69%
Oppose ...........................29
No opinion ........................ 2

#### Female

Favor ............................78%
Oppose ...........................19
No opinion ........................ 3

### By Ethnic Background
#### White

Favor ............................71%
Oppose ...........................26
No opinion ........................ 3

#### Nonwhite

Favor ............................93%
Oppose ............................ 4
No opinion ........................ 3

#### Black

Favor ............................94%
Oppose ............................ 3
No opinion ........................ 3

### By Education
#### College Graduate

Favor ............................67%
Oppose ...........................32
No opinion ........................ 1

#### College Incomplete

Favor ............................72%
Oppose ...........................25
No opinion ........................ 3

#### High-School Graduate

Favor ............................74%
Oppose ...........................23
No opinion ........................ 3

#### Less Than High-School Graduate

Favor ............................80%
Oppose ...........................16
No opinion ........................ 4

### By Region
#### East

Favor ............................80%
Oppose ...........................19
No opinion ........................ 1

#### Midwest

Favor ............................70%
Oppose ...........................27
No opinion ........................ 3

#### South

Favor ............................71%
Oppose ...........................26
No opinion ........................ 3

#### West

Favor ............................73%
Oppose ...........................23
No opinion ........................ 4

### By Age
#### 18–29 Years

Favor ............................80%
Oppose ...........................17
No opinion ........................ 3

#### 30–49 Years

Favor ............................72%
Oppose ...........................27
No opinion ........................ 1

#### 50 Years and Over

Favor ............................70%
Oppose ...........................27
No opinion ........................ 3

## By Income
### $40,000 and Over
Favor ...........................65%
Oppose ..........................35
No opinion ........................ *

### $30,000–$39,999
Favor ...........................68%
Oppose ..........................30
No opinion ........................ 2

### $20,000–$29,999
Favor ...........................74%
Oppose ..........................23
No opinion ........................ 3

### $10,000–$19,999
Favor ...........................77%
Oppose ..........................19
No opinion ........................ 4

### Under $10,000
Favor ...........................79%
Oppose ..........................19
No opinion ........................ 2

## By Politics
### Republicans
Favor ...........................61%
Oppose ..........................36
No opinion ........................ 3

### Democrats
Favor ...........................84%
Oppose ..........................14
No opinion ........................ 2

### Independents
Favor ...........................73%
Oppose ..........................24
No opinion ........................ 3

*Less than 1%

*An agreement between the United States and the Soviet Union for an immediate, verifiable freeze on the testing and production of nuclear weapons?*

Favor ...........................78%
Oppose ..........................18
No opinion ........................ 4

## By Sex
### Male
Favor ...........................79%
Oppose ..........................19
No opinion ........................ 2

### Female
Favor ...........................77%
Oppose ..........................17
No opinion ........................ 6

## By Ethnic Background
### White
Favor ...........................78%
Oppose ..........................18
No opinion ........................ 4

### Nonwhite
Favor ...........................76%
Oppose ..........................20
No opinion ........................ 4

### Black
Favor ...........................76%
Oppose ..........................20
No opinion ........................ 4

## By Education
### College Graduate
Favor ...........................85%
Oppose ..........................14
No opinion ........................ 1

### College Incomplete

Favor ...............................80%
Oppose ..............................16
No opinion ........................... 4

### High-School Graduate

Favor ...............................77%
Oppose ..............................19
No opinion ........................... 4

### Less Than High-School Graduate

Favor ...............................71%
Oppose ..............................21
No opinion ........................... 8

## By Region

### East

Favor ...............................77%
Oppose ..............................20
No opinion ........................... 3

### Midwest

Favor ...............................82%
Oppose ..............................16
No opinion ........................... 2

### South

Favor ...............................74%
Oppose ..............................20
No opinion ........................... 6

### West

Favor ...............................80%
Oppose ..............................15
No opinion ........................... 5

## By Age

### 18–29 Years

Favor ...............................82%
Oppose ..............................16
No opinion ........................... 2

### 30–49 Years

Favor ...............................80%
Oppose ..............................18
No opinion ........................... 2

### 50 Years and Over

Favor ...............................74%
Oppose ..............................19
No opinion ........................... 7

## By Income

### $40,000 and Over

Favor ...............................85%
Oppose ..............................13
No opinion ........................... 2

### $30,000–$39,999

Favor ...............................78%
Oppose ..............................17
No opinion ........................... 5

### $20,000–$29,999

Favor ...............................83%
Oppose ..............................14
No opinion ........................... 3

### $10,000–$19,999

Favor ...............................76%
Oppose ..............................20
No opinion ........................... 4

### Under $10,000

Favor ...............................71%
Oppose ..............................22
No opinion ........................... 7

## By Politics

### Republicans

Favor ...............................74%
Oppose ..............................22
No opinion ........................... 4

### Democrats

Favor . . . . . . . . . . . . . . . . . . . . . . . . . . . . . 82%
Oppose . . . . . . . . . . . . . . . . . . . . . . . . . . . 14
No opinion . . . . . . . . . . . . . . . . . . . . . . . 4

### Independents

Favor . . . . . . . . . . . . . . . . . . . . . . . . . . . . . 78%
Oppose . . . . . . . . . . . . . . . . . . . . . . . . . . . 19
No opinion . . . . . . . . . . . . . . . . . . . . . . . 3

*Relaxing pollution controls to reduce costs to industry?*

Favor . . . . . . . . . . . . . . . . . . . . . . . . . . . . . 33%
Oppose . . . . . . . . . . . . . . . . . . . . . . . . . . . 64
No opinion . . . . . . . . . . . . . . . . . . . . . . . 3

### By Sex
#### Male

Favor . . . . . . . . . . . . . . . . . . . . . . . . . . . . . 32%
Oppose . . . . . . . . . . . . . . . . . . . . . . . . . . . 66
No opinion . . . . . . . . . . . . . . . . . . . . . . . 2

#### Female

Favor . . . . . . . . . . . . . . . . . . . . . . . . . . . . . 34%
Oppose . . . . . . . . . . . . . . . . . . . . . . . . . . . 62
No opinion . . . . . . . . . . . . . . . . . . . . . . . 4

### By Ethnic Background
#### White

Favor . . . . . . . . . . . . . . . . . . . . . . . . . . . . . 31%
Oppose . . . . . . . . . . . . . . . . . . . . . . . . . . . 66
No opinion . . . . . . . . . . . . . . . . . . . . . . . 3

#### Nonwhite

Favor . . . . . . . . . . . . . . . . . . . . . . . . . . . . . 46%
Oppose . . . . . . . . . . . . . . . . . . . . . . . . . . . 47
No opinion . . . . . . . . . . . . . . . . . . . . . . . 7

#### Black

Favor . . . . . . . . . . . . . . . . . . . . . . . . . . . . . 47%
Oppose . . . . . . . . . . . . . . . . . . . . . . . . . . . 46
No opinion . . . . . . . . . . . . . . . . . . . . . . . 7

### By Education
#### College Graduate

Favor . . . . . . . . . . . . . . . . . . . . . . . . . . . . . 17%
Oppose . . . . . . . . . . . . . . . . . . . . . . . . . . . 82
No opinion . . . . . . . . . . . . . . . . . . . . . . . 1

#### College Incomplete

Favor . . . . . . . . . . . . . . . . . . . . . . . . . . . . . 22%
Oppose . . . . . . . . . . . . . . . . . . . . . . . . . . . 76
No opinion . . . . . . . . . . . . . . . . . . . . . . . 2

#### High-School Graduate

Favor . . . . . . . . . . . . . . . . . . . . . . . . . . . . . 37%
Oppose . . . . . . . . . . . . . . . . . . . . . . . . . . . 59
No opinion . . . . . . . . . . . . . . . . . . . . . . . 4

#### Less Than High-School Graduate

Favor . . . . . . . . . . . . . . . . . . . . . . . . . . . . . 50%
Oppose . . . . . . . . . . . . . . . . . . . . . . . . . . . 42
No opinion . . . . . . . . . . . . . . . . . . . . . . . 8

### By Region
#### East

Favor . . . . . . . . . . . . . . . . . . . . . . . . . . . . . 34%
Oppose . . . . . . . . . . . . . . . . . . . . . . . . . . . 62
No opinion . . . . . . . . . . . . . . . . . . . . . . . 4

#### Midwest

Favor . . . . . . . . . . . . . . . . . . . . . . . . . . . . . 31.%
Oppose . . . . . . . . . . . . . . . . . . . . . . . . . . . 67
No opinion . . . . . . . . . . . . . . . . . . . . . . . 2

#### South

Favor . . . . . . . . . . . . . . . . . . . . . . . . . . . . . 39%
Oppose . . . . . . . . . . . . . . . . . . . . . . . . . . . 56
No opinion . . . . . . . . . . . . . . . . . . . . . . . 5

#### West

Favor . . . . . . . . . . . . . . . . . . . . . . . . . . . . . 24%
Oppose . . . . . . . . . . . . . . . . . . . . . . . . . . . 73
No opinion . . . . . . . . . . . . . . . . . . . . . . . 3

## By Age

### 18–29 Years

Favor .............................29%
Oppose ...........................70
No opinion ........................ 1

### 30–49 Years

Favor .............................29%
Oppose ...........................69
No opinion ........................ 2

### 50 Years and Over

Favor .............................39%
Oppose ...........................55
No opinion ........................ 6

## By Income

### $40,000 and Over

Favor .............................28%
Oppose ...........................70
No opinion ........................ 2

### $30,000–$39,999

Favor .............................30%
Oppose ...........................67
No opinion ........................ 3

### $20,000–$29,999

Favor .............................25%
Oppose ...........................72
No opinion ........................ 3

### $10,000–$19,999

Favor .............................34%
Oppose ...........................62
No opinion ........................ 4

### Under $10,000

Favor .............................44%
Oppose ...........................48
No opinion ........................ 8

## By Politics

### Republicans

Favor .............................32%
Oppose ...........................64
No opinion ........................ 4

### Democrats

Favor .............................36%
Oppose ...........................61
No opinion ........................ 3

### Independents

Favor .............................30%
Oppose ...........................68
No opinion ........................ 2

*Maintaining cost-of-living increases on Social Security benefits?*

Favor .............................88%
Oppose ...........................10
No opinion ........................ 2

## By Sex

### Male

Favor .............................88%
Oppose ...........................11
No opinion ........................ 1

### Female

Favor .............................89%
Oppose ........................... 9
No opinion ........................ 2

## By Ethnic Background

### White

Favor .............................88%
Oppose ...........................10
No opinion ........................ 2

### Nonwhite

Favor .............................90%
Oppose ........................... 7
No opinion ........................ 3

### Black

Favor ............................91%
Oppose ........................... 7
No opinion ........................ 2

### West

Favor ............................92%
Oppose ........................... 7
No opinion ........................ 1

## By Education

### College Graduate

Favor ............................89%
Oppose ........................... 9
No opinion ........................ 2

## By Age

### 18–29 Years

Favor ............................88%
Oppose ...........................10
No opinion ........................ 2

### College Incomplete

Favor ............................87%
Oppose ...........................12
No opinion ........................ 1

### 30–49 Years

Favor ............................91%
Oppose ........................... 8
No opinion ........................ 1

### High-School Graduate

Favor ............................89%
Oppose ........................... 9
No opinion ........................ 2

### 50 Years and Over

Favor ............................90%
Oppose ........................... 8
No opinion ........................ 2

### Less Than High-School Graduate

Favor ............................88%
Oppose ...........................10
No opinion ........................ 2

## By Income

### $40,000 and Over

Favor ............................87%
Oppose ...........................11
No opinion ........................ 2

## By Region

### East

Favor ............................87%
Oppose ...........................11
No opinion ........................ 2

### $30,000–$39,999

Favor ............................89%
Oppose ........................... 8
No opinion ........................ 3

### Midwest

Favor ............................90%
Oppose ........................... 9
No opinion ........................ 1

### $20,000–$29,999

Favor ............................87%
Oppose ...........................11
No opinion ........................ 2

### South

Favor ............................86%
Oppose ...........................12
No opinion ........................ 2

### $10,000–$19,999

Favor ............................89%
Oppose ...........................10
No opinion ........................ 1

### Under $10,000

Favor ............................88%
Oppose ...........................10
No opinion ........................ 2

### By Politics
#### Republicans

Favor ............................86%
Oppose ...........................11
No opinion ........................ 3

#### Democrats

Favor ............................91%
Oppose ........................... 8
No opinion ........................ 1

#### Independents

Favor ............................87%
Oppose ...........................11
No opinion ........................ 2

Note: The shape of public opinion at the outset of President Ronald Reagan's second term fails to reveal a strong endorsement of his administration's position on some key voter issues. A recent Gallup Poll shows continuing heavy public support on five important issues: a verifiable nuclear freeze, increased spending for social programs, prayer in public schools, the passage of the Equal Rights Amendment, and cost-of-living increases on Social Security benefits.

Strong opposition is expressed on two key issues: tax increases to reduce the federal budget deficit, and relaxing pollution controls. However, a close division of opinion is found on the remaining three issues: reduced defense spending, tuition tax credits, and a ban on abortion.

## NOVEMBER 22
## ILLEGAL ALIENS

Interviewing Date: 6/22–25/84
Survey #235-G

> Do you think it should or should not be against the law to employ a person who has come into the United States without proper papers?

Should ............................75%
Should not ........................20
No opinion ........................ 5

### By Region
#### East

Should ............................76%
Should not ........................18
No opinion ........................ 6

#### Midwest

Should ............................77%
Should not ........................16
No opinion ........................ 7

#### South

Should ............................76%
Should not ........................20
No opinion ........................ 4

#### West

Should ............................72%
Should not ........................25
No opinion ........................ 3

### By Politics
#### Republicans

Should ............................77%
Should not ........................17
No opinion ........................ 6

#### Democrats

Should ............................71%
Should not ........................23
No opinion ........................ 6

#### Independents

Should ............................79%
Should not ........................17
No opinion ........................ 4

**Selected National Trend**

| | Should | Should not | No opinion |
|---|---|---|---|
| 1983 | 79% | 18% | 3% |
| 1980 | 76 | 18 | 6 |
| 1977 | 72 | 23 | 5 |

*Do you believe everyone in the United States should be required to carry an identification card such as a Social Security card, or not?*

Should . . . . 63%
Should not . . . . 34
No opinion . . . . 3

**By Region**

***East***

Should . . . . 57%
Should not . . . . 38
No opinion . . . . 5

***Midwest***

Should . . . . 64%
Should not . . . . 33
No opinion . . . . 3

***South***

Should . . . . 70%
Should not . . . . 28
No opinion . . . . 2

***West***

Should . . . . 56%
Should not . . . . 40
No opinion . . . . 4

**By Politics**

***Republicans***

Should . . . . 63%
Should not . . . . 34
No opinion . . . . 3

***Democrats***

Should . . . . 67%
Should not . . . . 29
No opinion . . . . 4

***Independents***

Should . . . . 54%
Should not . . . . 43
No opinion . . . . 3

**Selected National Trend**

| | Should | Should not | No opinion |
|---|---|---|---|
| 1983 | 66% | 31% | 3% |
| 1980 | 62 | 33 | 5 |
| 1977 | 65 | 30 | 5 |

Interviewing Date: 7/13–16/84
Survey #238-G

*It has been proposed that illegal aliens who can show that they have lived continuously in the United States since 1982 be eligible for permanent resident status. Do you favor or oppose this proposal?*

Favor . . . . 35%
Oppose . . . . 55
No opinion . . . . 10

**By Ethnic Background**

***White***

Favor . . . . 34%
Oppose . . . . 56
No opinion . . . . 10

***Black***

Favor . . . . 43%
Oppose . . . . 41
No opinion . . . . 16

***Hispanic****

Favor . . . . 57%
Oppose . . . . 37
No opinion . . . . 6

**By Region**

***East***

Favor . . . . 38%
Oppose . . . . 49
No opinion . . . . 13

### Midwest

Favor . . . . . . . . . . . . . . . . . . . . . . . . . . . .30%
Oppose . . . . . . . . . . . . . . . . . . . . . . . . . .62
No opinion . . . . . . . . . . . . . . . . . . . . . . . 8

### South

Favor . . . . . . . . . . . . . . . . . . . . . . . . . . . .36%
Oppose . . . . . . . . . . . . . . . . . . . . . . . . . .54
No opinion . . . . . . . . . . . . . . . . . . . . . . . 10

### West

Favor . . . . . . . . . . . . . . . . . . . . . . . . . . . .36%
Oppose . . . . . . . . . . . . . . . . . . . . . . . . . .54
No opinion . . . . . . . . . . . . . . . . . . . . . . . 10

## By Politics

### Republicans

Favor . . . . . . . . . . . . . . . . . . . . . . . . . . . .27%
Oppose . . . . . . . . . . . . . . . . . . . . . . . . . .64
No opinion . . . . . . . . . . . . . . . . . . . . . . . 9

### Democrats

Favor . . . . . . . . . . . . . . . . . . . . . . . . . . . .37%
Oppose . . . . . . . . . . . . . . . . . . . . . . . . . .51
No opinion . . . . . . . . . . . . . . . . . . . . . . . 12

### Independents

Favor . . . . . . . . . . . . . . . . . . . . . . . . . . . .39%
Oppose . . . . . . . . . . . . . . . . . . . . . . . . . .53
No opinion . . . . . . . . . . . . . . . . . . . . . . . 8

*Small sample

Note: One of the major legislative casualties in Congress's preelection recess in October was a comprehensive immigration reform bill. When the 99th Congress convenes in January, the stalled Simpson-Mazzoli immigration bill is expected to have a high priority on the agenda. This bill, already passed by the House, would install a system of sanctions against employers who knowingly employ illegals, and would introduce a means of identifying them. It`also would grant amnesty to immigrants who have lived in the United States since 1982.

Previously unpublished Gallup Poll data show that the American public takes a hard line toward illegal aliens, with 75% favoring and 20% opposed to a law that would make it illegal to employ a person who has entered the United States without proper papers. The public also strongly supports a proposal requiring all citizens and permanent resident aliens to carry an identification card; this would make it possible for prospective employers to distinguish illegal aliens from legal job seekers. Almost two persons in three (63%) in the latest survey back such legislation, similar to the findings in 1980, when the figure was 62%.

One of the current bill's most controversial features is the plan to grant permanent resident status to aliens who have lived continuously in this country since January 1982. In the latest survey, 35% favor this, while 55% are opposed. In earlier surveys, a proposal first made by President Jimmy Carter to make illegal aliens eligible for citizenship after seven years' residency was opposed by similar majorities.

Among Hispanics in the survey, support for a law against hiring illegal aliens outweighs opposition by 56% to 33%, while 59% express approval of requiring identification cards compared to 36% who disapprove, findings similar to those for the nation as a whole. On the other hand, opinion among Hispanics is 57% to 37% in favor of granting amnesty to aliens, compared to 55% to 35% in opposition among non-Hispanics. While the sample included fewer than one hundred Hispanics and the percentages reported are subject to 10 percentage points' sampling deviation, the results indicate the majority position taken by Hispanics on these issues.

The hard-line attitude of the public undoubtedly stems in considerable measure from fear that illegal aliens will take jobs from U.S. citizens. For example, persons engaged in manual work—particularly those in unskilled jobs—are more likely to favor an identification card than are persons in white-collar jobs. Border officials estimate that between half a million and a million "illegals" cross from Mexico annually, driven by unemployment and population pressures at home.

## POLITICAL AFFILIATION

Interviewing Date: 9/7–10, 21–24, 28–10/1;
10/26–29/84
Survey #241-G; 242-G; 243-G; 244-G

*In politics, as of today, do you consider your-
self a Republican, a Democrat, or an
independent?**

Republican ........................35%
Democrat ..........................39
Independent .......................26

### By Sex
#### Male

Republican ........................35%
Democrat ..........................37
Independent .......................28

#### Female

Republican ........................35%
Democrat ..........................40
Independent .......................25

### By Ethnic Background
#### White

Republican ........................38%
Democrat ..........................34
Independent .......................28

#### Black

Republican ........................ 7%
Democrat ..........................80
Independent .......................13

### By Education
#### College

Republican ........................39%
Democrat ..........................32
Independent .......................29

#### High School

Republican ........................34%
Democrat ..........................41
Independent .......................25

#### Grade School

Republican ........................25%
Democrat ..........................56
Independent .......................19

*Those saying they have no party preference or
who name other parties (3% to 4% in the latest
surveys) are excluded.

### Political Party Affiliation
*Republican Change Compared to 1977*

|  | 1984 | 1977* | Point change |
|---|---|---|---|
| National .......... | 35% | 20% | + 15 |

#### By Sex

| | | | |
|---|---|---|---|
| Male ............. | 35% | 19% | + 16 |
| Female ........... | 35 | 22 | + 13 |

#### By Ethnic Background

| | | | |
|---|---|---|---|
| White ............ | 38% | 22% | + 16 |
| Black ............ | 7 | 8 | − 1 |

#### By Education

| | | | |
|---|---|---|---|
| College .......... | 39% | 25% | + 14 |
| High school ....... | 34 | 19 | + 15 |
| Grade school ...... | 25 | 18 | + 7 |

#### By Region

| | | | |
|---|---|---|---|
| East ............. | 32% | 23% | + 9 |
| Midwest .......... | 34 | 23 | + 11 |
| South ............ | 36 | 15 | + 21** |
| West ............. | 40 | 21 | + 19 |

#### By Age

| | | | |
|---|---|---|---|
| 18–29 years ........ | 36% | 15% | + 21** |
| 30–49 years ........ | 33 | 19 | + 14 |
| 50 years and over ... | 37 | 25 | + 12 |

#### By Income

| | | | |
|---|---|---|---|
| Upper half ........ | 38% | 22% | + 16 |
| Lower half ........ | 31 | 19 | + 12 |

### By Religion

| | | | |
|---|---|---|---|
| Protestants ........ | 38% | 26% | + 12 |
| Catholics ......... | 32 | 14 | + 18** |

### By Occupation

| | | | |
|---|---|---|---|
| Professional and busi- | | | |
| ness ............ | 42% | 27% | + 15 |
| Clerical and sales .... | 35 | 18 | + 17 |
| Blue collar ........ | 30 | 14 | + 16** |

### By Labor Union Household

| | | | |
|---|---|---|---|
| Labor union | | | |
| members ........ | 25% | 14% | + 11 |
| Nonlabor union | | | |
| members ........ | 38 | 22 | + 16 |

*Interviews were conducted between May 6 and July 25, 1977.
**Republican gains of 100% or more since 1977.

### Selected National Trend*

| | Repub-lican | Demo-crat | Inde-pendent |
|---|---|---|---|
| 1984 (to date) .. | 30% | 41% | 29% |
| 1983 ......... | 25 | 44 | 31 |
| 1982 ......... | 26 | 45 | 29 |
| 1981 ......... | 28 | 42 | 30 |
| 1980 ......... | 24 | 46 | 30 |
| 1979 ......... | 22 | 45 | 33 |
| 1978 ......... | 23 | 48 | 29 |
| 1977 ......... | 21 | 48 | 31 |
| 1976 ......... | 23 | 47 | 30 |
| 1975 ......... | 22 | 45 | 33 |
| 1972 ......... | 28 | 43 | 29 |
| 1968 ......... | 27 | 46 | 27 |
| 1964 ......... | 25 | 53 | 22 |
| 1960 ......... | 30 | 47 | 23 |
| 1954 ......... | 34 | 46 | 20 |
| 1952 ......... | 34 | 41 | 25 |
| 1950 ......... | 33 | 45 | 22 |
| 1949 ......... | 32 | 48 | 20 |
| 1946 ......... | 40 | 39 | 21 |
| 1944 ......... | 39 | 41 | 20 |
| 1940 ......... | 38 | 42 | 20 |
| 1937 ......... | 34 | 50 | 16 |

*Based on annual average

Interviewing Date: 9/21–24/84
Survey #242-G

*You will notice that the ten boxes on this card go from the highest position of +5 for something you have a very favorable opinion of all the way down to the lowest position of −5 for something you have a very unfavorable opinion of. How far up the scale or how far down the scale would you rate the Democratic party? The Republican party?*

### Highly Favorable Ratings

| | Sept. 1984 | Oct. 1980 |
|---|---|---|
| Democratic party ........ | 26% | 27% |
| Republican party ........ | 27 | 18 |

Note: The proportion of Americans claiming affiliation with the Republican party just prior to President Ronald Reagan's landslide election victory reached a level not seen since the Eisenhower era of the 1950s. Concurrently, the proportion of the electorate expressing loyalty to the Democratic party was as low as it has been at any point since the end of World War II.

In four Gallup surveys conducted from early September until the week before election day, 35% of voters classified themselves as Republicans, 39% as Democrats, and 26% as independents. Only time can tell whether the current near-parity division of party allegiance signals a basic realignment of political loyalties, or reflects a temporary setback for the Democrats induced by Reagan's stunning election victory. Nevertheless, the Democrats' present 4-percentage point advantage over the Republicans is the narrowest observed since 1946, when 40% of voters described themselves as Republicans and 39% as Democrats.

Gallup surveys during the last half century have shown that political party allegiance tends to ebb and flow with the fortunes of the party controlling the White House. Thus, Republican affiliation rose to 28% at the time of Reagan's election in 1980. After the onset of the recession, however, it declined steadily to the 23% level until mid-1983, when there was clear evidence of economic recovery. The proportion of the electorate claiming

Republican allegiance has been on a slow but steady upturn since then.

With the sole exception of blacks, the GOP's current 15-percentage point nationwide gain since 1977, from 20% affiliation to 35%, traces to every major demographic group, as shown in the table. Two such groups, for example, are women and blue-collar workers. The "gender gap" notwithstanding, in the last seven years women have turned to the Republican party to almost the same extent as men have; both sexes are now equally represented in the GOP ranks.

Although most blue-collar workers have remained true to their political roots, the proportion now calling themselves Republicans is more than double the proportion observed in 1977. Interestingly, the same holds true for Catholics (from 14% Republican in 1977 to 32% now) and southerners (15% to 36%).

Not only do the latest political affiliation figures show a numerical increase in voters classifying themselves as Republicans, but also there has been a qualitative improvement in voters' perceptions of the GOP. Using a nonverbal scaling device, with the top two positions ($+5$, $+4$) indicating "highly favorable" ratings, the two parties are now about equal. Four years ago, just as President Reagan was about to be elected to his first term, the Republican party was given only two-thirds as many highly favorable votes as the Democratic party, 18% and 27%, respectively.

## NOVEMBER 29
## SPEED LIMIT

Interviewing Date: 11/9–12/84
Survey #245-G

> Do you favor or oppose keeping the present 55-mile-per-hour speed limit on the highways of the nation?

Favor ............................71%
Oppose ...........................25
No opinion ....................... 4

### By Sex
#### Male

Favor ............................62%
Oppose ...........................35
No opinion ....................... 3

#### Female

Favor ............................80%
Oppose ...........................16
No opinion ....................... 4

### By Education
#### College Graduate

Favor ............................72%
Oppose ...........................28
No opinion ....................... *

#### College Incomplete

Favor ............................68%
Oppose ...........................29
No opinion ....................... 3

#### High-School Graduate

Favor ............................73%
Oppose ...........................23
No opinion ....................... 4

#### Less Than High-School Graduate

Favor ............................72%
Oppose ...........................21
No opinion ....................... 7

### By Region
#### East

Favor ............................74%
Oppose ...........................19
No opinion ....................... 7

#### Midwest

Favor ............................72%
Oppose ...........................25
No opinion ....................... 3

### South

Favor ............................. 71%
Oppose ........................... 26
No opinion ........................ 3

### West

Favor ............................. 66%
Oppose ........................... 31
No opinion ........................ 3

### By Age
#### 18–29 Years

Favor ............................. 68%
Oppose ........................... 30
No opinion ........................ 2

#### 30–49 Years

Favor ............................. 69%
Oppose ........................... 27
No opinion ........................ 4

#### 50 Years and Over

Favor ............................. 76%
Oppose ........................... 19
No opinion ........................ 5

*Less than 1%

### Selected National Trend

|      | Favor | Oppose | No opinion |
|------|-------|--------|------------|
| 1982 ........... | 76%   | 21%    | 3%         |
| 1981 ........... | 75    | 23     | 2          |
| 1980 ........... | 81    | 17     | 2          |
| 1979 ........... | 71    | 26     | 3          |
| 1977 ........... | 76    | 22     | 2          |
| 1974 ........... | 73    | 24     | 3          |

Note: A decade after its enactment, the statute mandating a national speed limit of 55 miles per hour continues to retain broad popular support. In the latest Gallup assessment, 71% favor keeping the 55-mph limit, while 25% would like to see it repealed.

Public opinion on the issue has been remarkably stable since the law was enacted in 1974 as an energy-saving measure. In seven national studies, support for the 55-mph limit has never fallen below 71%, the current figure, and opposition has not topped 26%. Today's findings represent a 5-percentage point decrease from the 1982 results and a decline of 10 points since 1980, when 81% favored the law's retention.

In addition to contributing to the lower rate of consumption of petroleum products, the 55-mph limit has reduced auto accidents by forcing motorists to drive more slowly. Now that there is an oversupply of oil and a reduction in gas prices at the pump, however, critics of the legal speed limit have increased their demands for its repeal. Criticism has been particularly intense in the western states, where long stretches of uncrowded, open highways are common.

A 1978 federal law requires that at least 50% of the motorists in each state comply with the law. Failure to meet this requirement could cause non-complying states to lose 5% of their federal funds for highway construction and repair. Nevertheless, some states are finding ways to circumvent the law. Nevada, for example, imposes only a $5 fine for motorists driving between 55 and 70 mph.

The legal 55-mph maximum speed is credited with having saved more than 50,000 lives since it was enacted in 1974. By some estimates, as many as 250,000 barrels of oil per day are conserved because of the lower speed limit.

## DECEMBER 2
## POLITICAL IDEOLOGY

Interviewing Date: 11/9–12/84
Survey #245-G

*People who are conservative in their political views are referred to as being right of center and people who are liberal in their political views are referred to as being left of center. Which one of these categories best describes your own/the Republican party's/the Democratic party's political position? [Respondents were handed a card listing categories.]*

Here is the trend since the presidential election year of 1976, excluding those not indicating a position:

### Personal Political Position

|  | 1984 | 1980 | 1976 |
|---|---|---|---|
| Right of center ....... | 36% | 32% | 31% |
| Middle of the road ... | 46 | 49 | 45 |
| Left of center ........ | 18 | 19 | 24 |

Here is a comparison of the current public perceptions of the two major parties with views recorded in 1982:

### Perceptions of Republican Party

|  | 1984 | 1982 |
|---|---|---|
| Right of center ............ | 50% | 49% |
| Middle of the road .......... | 20 | 17 |
| Left of center ............. | 12 | 13 |
| No opinion ................ | 18 | 21 |

### Perceptions of Democratic Party

|  | 1984 | 1982 |
|---|---|---|
| Right of center ............ | 15% | 18% |
| Middle of the road .......... | 21 | 23 |
| Left of center ............. | 44 | 39 |
| No opinion ................ | 20 | 20 |

Note: The proportion of Americans who describe their political views as right of center has grown since 1976, with a corresponding decline in those whose views are left of center. In the latest mid-November Gallup survey, 36% of respondents place themselves to the right of center on a conservative-liberal scale, 18% are left of center, while 46% indicate a middle-of-the-road position. In 1976, 31% leaned to the right, 24% to the left, and 45% embraced the middle positions on the scale. Similarly, a slightly larger proportion of the public today than in 1982 (44% to 39%) perceives the Democratic party as left of center, although there has been no corresponding shift in those viewing the Republican party in conservative terms (50% today and 49% in 1982).

The trend toward the right in the public's political philosophy parallels a substantial increase in the proportion of Americans claiming affiliation with the Republican party. This proportion, just prior to President Ronald Reagan's landslide reelection, reached a level not seen since the Eisenhower era of the 1950s. Concurrently, the proportion of the electorate expressing allegiance to the Democratic party is now as low as it has been at any time since the end of World War II. In four Gallup surveys, conducted from early September until the week before election day, 35% of voters classified themselves as Republicans, 39% as Democrats, and 26% as independents.

## DECEMBER 6
## ELECTORAL REFORMS

Interviewing Date: 11/9–12/84
Survey #245-G

*Would you like to see any changes in the way political campaigns are conducted?*

| | |
|---|---|
| Yes | 53% |
| No | 35 |
| No opinion | 12 |

### By Education
#### College Graduate

| | |
|---|---|
| Yes | 72% |
| No | 24 |
| No opinion | 4 |

#### College Incomplete

| | |
|---|---|
| Yes | 60% |
| No | 31 |
| No opinion | 9 |

#### High-School Graduate

| | |
|---|---|
| Yes | 51% |
| No | 39 |
| No opinion | 10 |

#### Less Than High-School Graduate

| | |
|---|---|
| Yes | 38% |
| No | 40 |
| No opinion | 22 |

## By Politics

### Republicans

Yes . . . . . . . . . . . . . . . . . . . . . . . . . . . . . .58%
No . . . . . . . . . . . . . . . . . . . . . . . . . . . . . . .35
No opinion . . . . . . . . . . . . . . . . . . . . . . . . 7

### Democrats

Yes . . . . . . . . . . . . . . . . . . . . . . . . . . . . . .54%
No . . . . . . . . . . . . . . . . . . . . . . . . . . . . . . .34
No opinion . . . . . . . . . . . . . . . . . . . . . . . .12

### Independents

Yes . . . . . . . . . . . . . . . . . . . . . . . . . . . . . .50%
No . . . . . . . . . . . . . . . . . . . . . . . . . . . . . . .36
No opinion . . . . . . . . . . . . . . . . . . . . . . . .14

*Asked of those who replied in the affirmative: In what ways?*

The following were mentioned frequently:

1) Search committees would be established by both major parties which would help select the best possible candidates.

2) A national primary, or regional primaries, would replace the present system of individual state primaries. Voters in each party would select a single candidate.

3) Two-thirds of persons surveyed said presidential candidates should be chosen in a nationwide primary election instead of by political party conventions as at present. In a survey reported in July, 67% favored the new plan, while 21% were opposed and 12% undecided, figures that closely parallel those recorded in 1980. If American voters had their way, the 1984 Democratic and Republican conventions would be the last.

4) Voters also favor changing the present primary election system to a regional system but by a smaller 45%-to-30% ratio than is the case for a national primary. In the regional system, individual primaries would be held in each of four regions of the country during different weeks in June of presidential election years.

5) The presidential election would be held in September instead of November, allowing incoming presidents more time to prepare legislation for the opening of Congress in January.

6) Nationally televised debates among the candidates would replace the traditional "whistle-stop" approach. Part or all of this year's presidential debates were watched by a remarkable three in four Americans.

7) With spending for the U.S. House and Senate election campaigns setting new records, it is important to note that a majority of Americans would like the federal government to provide a fixed amount of money to fund the campaigns of congressional candidates, prohibiting contributions from all other sources. A recent survey shows 52% supporting this plan and 36% opposed, consistent with the findings of previous polls on this topic.

8) The public would like to have the opportunity to vote on national issues as well as for candidates. Surveys indicate that the voter turnout even might increase substantially if voters could express their opinions on national issues.

9) The Electoral College would be abolished, with the president chosen by direct popular vote.

10) The terms of members of the House of Representatives would be changed from two to four years. The public votes 51% to 37% for such a chance, with majority backing also recorded among opinion leaders.

11) Members of the House of Representatives would be limited to three four-year terms, or a total of twelve years. The public backs this change by a 2-to-1 vote—59% to 32%.

12) Changing the term of office of the president to one six-year term with no reelection is favored by at least half of voters with views on the proposal.

## DECEMBER 9
## PRESIDENTIAL ELECTION

Interviewing Date: 11/9–12/84
Survey #245-G

*Asked of those who did not vote: What was it that kept you from voting?*

| | 1984 | 1980 | 1976 | 1972 |
|---|---|---|---|---|
| Not registered | 31% | 42% | 38% | 28% |
| Did not like candidates | 10 | 17 | 14 | 10 |
| Not interested in politics | 8 | 5 | 10 | 4 |
| Illness | 7 | 8 | 7 | 11 |
| Inconvenient | 7 | * | * | * |
| Working | 7 | 3 | 2 | 7 |
| Not an American citizen | 6 | 5 | 4 | * |
| New resident | 6 | 4 | 4 | 8 |
| Out of town | 5 | 3 | 3 | 5 |
| No way to get to polls | 3 | 1 | 2 | * |
| Did not get absentee ballot | 1 | * | 1 | 1 |
| No particular reason | 8 | 10 | 10 | 13 |
| Others; no opinion | 1 | 2 | 5 | 13 |

*Less than 1%

*Asked of those who voted for Reagan: What was the main reason why you voted for Reagan—that is, why do you think he was the best man?*

The following are the top six reasons in each of the main voter categories:*

| | |
|---|---|
| Like his economic policies | 24% |
| He tried to do good job | 22 |
| Strong leadership | 11 |
| Like his policies | 11 |
| Voted against Mondale | 7 |
| Like his defense policies | 6 |

## By Sex

### Male

| | |
|---|---|
| Like his economic policies | 25% |
| He tried to do good job | 22 |
| Strong leadership | 12 |
| Like his policies | 10 |
| Like his defense policies | 8 |
| Voted against Mondale | 6 |

*Multiple responses were given.

### Female

| | |
|---|---|
| Like his economic policies | 23% |
| He tried to do good job | 23 |
| Like his policies | 11 |
| Strong leadership | 10 |
| Voted against Mondale | 8 |
| He is an honest man | 6 |

## By Education

### College Graduate

| | |
|---|---|
| Like his economic policies | 26% |
| He tried to do good job | 21 |
| Like his policies | 11 |
| Strong leadership | 10 |
| Like his defense policies | 7 |
| His conservative values | 7 |

### College Incomplete

| | |
|---|---|
| Like his economic policies | 28% |
| He tried to do good job | 24 |
| Strong leadership | 12 |
| Like his policies | 7 |
| Like his defense policies | 6 |
| He is an honest man | 6 |

### High-School Graduate

| | |
|---|---|
| Like his economic policies | 21% |
| He tried to do good job | 21 |
| Like his policies | 16 |
| Strong leadership | 10 |
| Voted against Mondale | 9 |
| Voted against Ferraro | 6 |

### Less Than High-School Graduate

| | |
|---|---|
| He tried to do good job | 23% |
| Like his economic policies | 19 |
| Strong leadership | 13 |
| Voted against Mondale | 9 |
| Just like him | 8 |
| Like his policies | 7 |

## By Region

### East

Like his economic policies . . . . . . . . . . . . 32%
He tried to do good job . . . . . . . . . . . . . . 25
Strong leadership . . . . . . . . . . . . . . . . . . . 8
Like his policies . . . . . . . . . . . . . . . . . . . . 8
Like his defense policies . . . . . . . . . . . . . 8
Voted against Mondale . . . . . . . . . . . . . . 7

### Midwest

He tried to do good job . . . . . . . . . . . . . . 25%
Like his economic policies . . . . . . . . . . . . 20
Strong leadership . . . . . . . . . . . . . . . . . . . 15
Like his policies . . . . . . . . . . . . . . . . . . . . 9
Voted against Mondale . . . . . . . . . . . . . . 8
Mondale wants to raise taxes . . . . . . . . . . 7

### South

He tried to do good job . . . . . . . . . . . . . . 26%
Like his economic policies . . . . . . . . . . . . 22
Like his policies . . . . . . . . . . . . . . . . . . . . 12
Strong leadership . . . . . . . . . . . . . . . . . . . 11
Like his defense policies . . . . . . . . . . . . . 7
He is an honest man . . . . . . . . . . . . . . . . . 7

### West

Like his economic policies . . . . . . . . . . . . 24%
Like his policies . . . . . . . . . . . . . . . . . . . . 15
He tried to do good job . . . . . . . . . . . . . . 12
Strong leadership . . . . . . . . . . . . . . . . . . . 10
Voted against Mondale . . . . . . . . . . . . . . 7
His conservative values . . . . . . . . . . . . . . 5

## By Age

### 18–24 Years

He tried to do good job . . . . . . . . . . . . . . 25%
Like his defense policies . . . . . . . . . . . . . 21
Like his economic policies . . . . . . . . . . . . 18
Voted against Mondale . . . . . . . . . . . . . . 12
He is an honest man . . . . . . . . . . . . . . . . . 8
Like his policies . . . . . . . . . . . . . . . . . . . . 7

### 25–29 Years

Like his economic policies . . . . . . . . . . . . 30%
He tried to do good job . . . . . . . . . . . . . . 23
Strong leadership . . . . . . . . . . . . . . . . . . . 18
Like his policies . . . . . . . . . . . . . . . . . . . . 11
He is experienced . . . . . . . . . . . . . . . . . . . 5
Did not like Mondale's stand
   on some issues . . . . . . . . . . . . . . . . . . . 4

### 30–49 Years

Like his economic policies . . . . . . . . . . . . 26%
He tried to do good job . . . . . . . . . . . . . . 21
Strong leadership . . . . . . . . . . . . . . . . . . . 12
Like his policies . . . . . . . . . . . . . . . . . . . . 11
Voted against Mondale . . . . . . . . . . . . . . 8
He is an honest man . . . . . . . . . . . . . . . . . 6

### 50–64 Years

Like his economic policies . . . . . . . . . . . . 24%
He tried to do good job . . . . . . . . . . . . . . 22
Like his policies . . . . . . . . . . . . . . . . . . . . 12
Voted against Mondale . . . . . . . . . . . . . . 9
Strong leadership . . . . . . . . . . . . . . . . . . . 8
His conservative values . . . . . . . . . . . . . . 7

### 65 Years and Over

He tried to do good job . . . . . . . . . . . . . . 24%
Like his economic policies . . . . . . . . . . . . 22
Strong leadership . . . . . . . . . . . . . . . . . . . 14
Like his policies . . . . . . . . . . . . . . . . . . . . 12
Stay with my party . . . . . . . . . . . . . . . . . . 5
He is an honest man . . . . . . . . . . . . . . . . . 5

## By Politics

### Republicans

Like his economic policies . . . . . . . . . . . . 25%
He tried to do good job . . . . . . . . . . . . . . 24
Strong leadership . . . . . . . . . . . . . . . . . . . 11
Like his policies . . . . . . . . . . . . . . . . . . . . 10
Like his defense policies . . . . . . . . . . . . . 7
Voted against Mondale . . . . . . . . . . . . . . 7

### Democrats

| | |
|---|---|
| Like his economic policies | 26% |
| He tried to do good job | 23 |
| Strong leadership | 12 |
| Voted against Mondale | 9 |
| Lesser of two evils | 8 |
| Did not need a change | 7 |

### Independents

| | |
|---|---|
| Like his economic policies | 21% |
| He tried to do good job | 16 |
| Like his policies | 16 |
| Strong leadership | 11 |
| Voted against Mondale | 7 |
| Lesser of two evils | 6 |

*Asked of those who voted for Mondale: What was the main reason why you voted for Mondale—that is, why do you think he was the best man?*

The following are the top six reasons in each of the main voter categories:*

| | |
|---|---|
| Dissatisfied with Reagan | 22% |
| Like his policies | 15 |
| For the poor, the working person | 14 |
| Wanted to stay with my party | 13 |
| Need a change | 8 |
| He is an honest man | 6 |

### By Sex
#### Male

| | |
|---|---|
| Dissatisfied with Reagan | 21% |
| Like his policies | 16 |
| Wanted to stay with my party | 14 |
| For the poor, the working person | 11 |
| Need a change | 8 |
| He is an honest man | 6 |

*Multiple responses were given.

### Female

| | |
|---|---|
| Dissatisfied with Reagan | 23% |
| For the poor, the working person | 17 |
| Wanted to stay with my party | 14 |
| Like his policies | 14 |
| Need a change | 7 |
| He is an honest man | 6 |

### By Education
#### College Graduate

| | |
|---|---|
| Dissatisfied with Reagan | 33% |
| Like his policies | 27 |
| Afraid of Reagan | 8 |
| He is an honest man | 7 |
| Wanted to stay with my party | 7 |
| Like his foreign policy | 6 |

#### College Incomplete

| | |
|---|---|
| Dissatisfied with Reagan | 28% |
| Like his policies | 16 |
| Wanted to stay with my party | 11 |
| He is an honest man | 8 |
| Like his foreign policy | 8 |
| For the poor, the working person | 6 |

#### High-School Graduate

| | |
|---|---|
| For the poor, the working person | 28% |
| Dissatisfied with Reagan | 20 |
| Wanted to stay with my party | 14 |
| Need a change | 12 |
| Like his policies | 11 |
| He is an honest man | 6 |

#### Less Than High-School Graduate

| | |
|---|---|
| Wanted to stay with my party | 14% |
| For the poor, the working person | 13 |
| Like his policies | 8 |
| Dissatisfied with Reagan | 8 |
| Need a change | 7 |
| He is an honest man | 6 |

## By Region

### East

| | |
|---|---|
| Dissatisfied with Reagan | 26% |
| Like his policies | 11 |
| Need a change | 10 |
| Wanted to stay with my party | 10 |
| He is a good union man | 8 |
| Afraid of Reagan | 7 |

### Midwest

| | |
|---|---|
| Dissatisfied with Reagan | 23% |
| Wanted to stay with my party | 14 |
| For the poor, the working person | 14 |
| Like his policies | 11 |
| He is an honest man | 9 |
| He is a better leader | 8 |

### South

| | |
|---|---|
| Wanted to stay with my party | 19% |
| Like his policies | 17 |
| For the poor, the working person | 17 |
| Dissatisfied with Reagan | 15 |
| Need a change | 9 |
| He is a better leader | 5 |

### West

| | |
|---|---|
| Like his policies | 23% |
| For the poor, the working person | 23 |
| Dissatisfied with Reagan | 22 |
| Need a change | 10 |
| Like his foreign policies | 9 |
| Like his defense policies | 9 |

## By Age

### 18–24 Years

| | |
|---|---|
| For the poor, the working person | 26% |
| Like his policies | 24 |
| Dissatisfied with Reagan | 18 |
| Wanted to stay with my party | 16 |
| Like his foreign policies | 13 |
| Like his defense policies | 8 |

### 25–29 Years

| | |
|---|---|
| Dissatisfied with Reagan | 37% |
| Like his policies | 18 |
| Afraid of Reagan | 14 |
| He is an honest man | 12 |
| Wanted to stay with my party | 9 |
| For the poor, the working person | 7 |

### 30–49 Years

| | |
|---|---|
| Dissatisfied with Reagan | 23% |
| Like his policies | 16 |
| For the poor, the working person | 15 |
| Wanted to stay with my party | 9 |
| He is a better leader | 6 |
| He is a good union man | 5 |

### 50–64 Years

| | |
|---|---|
| Dissatisfied with Reagan | 20% |
| Wanted to stay with my party | 19 |
| For the poor, the working person | 15 |
| Need a change | 12 |
| Like his policies | 9 |
| He is an honest man | 6 |

### 65 Years and Over

| | |
|---|---|
| Dissatisfied with Reagan | 17% |
| Like his policies | 15 |
| Wanted to stay with my party | 15 |
| For the poor, the working person | 11 |
| Wanted a woman in office | 7 |
| Lesser of two evils | 7 |

## By Politics

### Republicans

| | |
|---|---|
| Dissatisfied with Reagan | 23% |
| Don't know | 15 |
| Need a change | 15 |
| Like his policies | 15 |
| Afraid of Reagan | 8 |
| For the poor, the working person | 8 |

### Democrats

Dissatisfied with Reagan ..............21%
For the poor, the working person .......16
Wanted to stay with my party ..........16
Like his policies .....................16
He is an honest man ..................  6
Need a change .......................  6

### Independents

Dissatisfied with Reagan ..............26%
Like his policies ....................10
He is an honest man ..................  8
Wanted a woman in office ............  6
Like his defense policies ..............  5
Need a change .....................  5

*Asked of those who voted: At any time did you intend to vote for another candidate?*

|  | Yes |
|---|---|
| National ........................... | 16% |

### Selected National Trend

|  | Yes |
|---|---|
| 1980 ........................... | 27% |
| 1976 ........................... | 21 |
| 1972 ........................... | 12 |
| 1968 ........................... | 17 |

*Also asked of those who voted: For the various political offices, did you vote for all the candidates of one party—that is, a straight ticket, or did you vote for the candidates of different parties?*

Straight ticket ........................43%
Different parties .....................54
Don't know ........................  3

### Selected National Trend

|  | Straight ticket | Different parties | Don't know |
|---|---|---|---|
| 1980 ........... | 37% | 60% | 3% |
| 1976 ........... | 41 | 56 | 3 |
| 1972 ........... | 44 | 54 | 2 |
| 1968 ........... | 37 | 60 | 3 |

Note: The pro-Reagan character of the president's recent landslide victory was markedly different from the character of his support in the 1980 election. The vote for Ronald Reagan in 1984 was decidedly for him rather than against Walter Mondale, with many voters naming his economic policies and leadership as reasons for their choice. By contrast, in 1980 Reagan voters gave anti-Carter reasons rather than pro-Reagan ones for their selection, with Jimmy Carter's perceived lack of leadership a major reason for rejecting him.

By a 6-to-1 ratio, the president's supporters said their vote was more pro-Reagan than anti-Mondale, while Mondale voters were about equally divided between those who said their vote was for their candidate and those who described theirs as an anti-Reagan vote. Those who pulled the lever for Mondale most often named dissatisfaction with Reagan, approval of Mondale's policies in general, the belief that he was for the poor and the working man, and party loyalty.

Voters tended to change their minds less this year than they did in 1980. Four years ago, 27% said that at one point in the campaign they had intended to vote for a different candidate; this year, only 16% did so.

Ticket splitting—that is, voting for candidates of different parties—was less common this year than in 1980. In the latest survey, 54% of voters said they split their vote in choosing candidates for the various political offices, while 43% voted a straight ticket.

One of the ironies of this year's presidential election was that despite an increase in the proportion of Americans who registered to vote, turnout was only marginally higher than in 1980. This is reflected in responses to the question on the reasons for not voting.

## DECEMBER 13
## RAISING CHILDREN

Interviewing Date: 10/26–29/84
Survey #244-G

*Which of these would you say is the main fault of parents in raising children nowadays? [Respondents were handed a card listing six reasons.]*

No discipline; parents too lenient;
  children have it too easy . . . . . . . . . . . . 37%
Children neglected, unattended . . . . . . . . . 24
Parents set poor example . . . . . . . . . . . . . . 8
Children not treated as persons, given too
  little responsibility . . . . . . . . . . . . . . . . . 7
Lack of understanding, sympathy . . . . . . . 6
Children have too much money . . . . . . . . 2
All others . . . . . . . . . . . . . . . . . . . . . . . . . 2
Don't know . . . . . . . . . . . . . . . . . . . . . . . . 14

Interviewing Date: April–June 1984
Special Telephone Survey

*Asked of teen-agers: What is the biggest
problem facing teen-agers today?*

|  | 1984 | 1983 | 1977 |
|---|---|---|---|
| Drug abuse . . . . . . . . . | 42% | 35% | 27% |
| Alcohol abuse . . . . . . . . | 14 | 10 | 7 |
| Unemployment . . . . . . . | 10 | 16 | 6 |
| Peer pressures . . . . . . . . | 8 | 8 | 5 |
| Fear of war . . . . . . . . . | 5 | 4 | ** |
| Growing up, finding purpose in life . . . . . . | 4 | 1 | 6 |
| Getting along with parents . . . . . . . . . . . | 3 | 5 | 20 |
| School problems . . . . . . | 3 | 5 | 3 |
| Career doubts, uncertainty . . . . . . . . | 3 | 3 | 3 |
| All others . . . . . . . . . . | 8 | 8 | 15 |
| Don't know . . . . . . . . . | 16 | 18 | 14 |
|  | 116%* | 113%* | 106%* |

*Total adds to more than 100% due to multiple
responses.
**Less than 1%

Note: Lack of discipline, child neglect, and poor
parental examples are seen as the major failures
of parents in raising children today, with the views
of women and men in close agreement. Also named
with considerable frequency are giving children
too little responsibility, not treating them as
persons, and failing to understand and sympathize
with their needs.

These findings are seen against a backdrop of
problems cited most often by teen-agers
themselves. According to a recent Gallup Youth

Survey, drug abuse is the biggest problem currently
facing young people. Concern about drugs has
risen from 27% in 1977, when teen-agers also
named it as the biggest problem facing their
generation, to 42% today. Alcohol abuse, cited
by 14% of teen-agers, ranks next, with
unemployment as the third leading cause of
concern, named by 10%, down from 16% in 1983.

## DECEMBER 16
## ENVIRONMENTAL PROTECTION

Interviewing Date: 9/28–10/1/84
Survey #243-G

*Here are two statements which people some-
times make when discussing the environment
and economic growth. Which of these statements comes closer to your own point of view?*

*1) Protection of the environment should be
given priority, even at the risk of curbing
economic growth.*

*2) Economic growth should be given prior-
ity, even if the environment suffers to some
extent.*

Protection of environment . . . . . . . . . . . . . 61%
Economic growth . . . . . . . . . . . . . . . . . . . 28
Other; no opinion . . . . . . . . . . . . . . . . . . . 11

### By Sex
#### Male

Protection of environment . . . . . . . . . . . . . 62%
Economic growth . . . . . . . . . . . . . . . . . . . 27
Other; no opinion . . . . . . . . . . . . . . . . . . . 11

#### Female

Protection of environment . . . . . . . . . . . . . 61%
Economic growth . . . . . . . . . . . . . . . . . . . 28
Other; no opinion . . . . . . . . . . . . . . . . . . . 11

### By Education
#### College Graduate

Protection of environment . . . . . . . . . . . . . 67%
Economic growth . . . . . . . . . . . . . . . . . . . 25
Other; no opinion . . . . . . . . . . . . . . . . . . . 8

### College Incomplete

Protection of environment . . . . . . . . . . . . .69%
Economic growth . . . . . . . . . . . . . . . . . . .24
Other; no opinion . . . . . . . . . . . . . . . . . 7

### High-School Graduate

Protection of environment . . . . . . . . . . . . .63%
Economic growth . . . . . . . . . . . . . . . . . . .28
Other; no opinion . . . . . . . . . . . . . . . . . 9

### Less Than High-School Graduate

Protection of environment . . . . . . . . . . . . .46%
Economic growth . . . . . . . . . . . . . . . . . . .33
Other; no opinion . . . . . . . . . . . . . . . . . .21

## By Region
### East

Protection of environment . . . . . . . . . . . . .61%
Economic growth . . . . . . . . . . . . . . . . . . .30
Other; no opinion . . . . . . . . . . . . . . . . . 9

### Midwest

Protection of environment . . . . . . . . . . . . .62%
Economic growth . . . . . . . . . . . . . . . . . . .27
Other; no opinion . . . . . . . . . . . . . . . . . .11

### South

Protection of environment . . . . . . . . . . . . .58%
Economic growth . . . . . . . . . . . . . . . . . . .30
Other; no opinion . . . . . . . . . . . . . . . . . .12

### West

Protection of environment . . . . . . . . . . . . .67%
Economic growth . . . . . . . . . . . . . . . . . . .22
Other; no opinion . . . . . . . . . . . . . . . . . .11

## By Age
### 18–29 Years

Protection of environment . . . . . . . . . . . . .69%
Economic growth . . . . . . . . . . . . . . . . . . .22
Other; no opinion . . . . . . . . . . . . . . . . . 9

### 30–49 Years

Protection of environment . . . . . . . . . . . . .65%
Economic growth . . . . . . . . . . . . . . . . . . .27
Other; no opinion . . . . . . . . . . . . . . . . . 8

### 50–64 Years

Protection of environment . . . . . . . . . . . . .54%
Economic growth . . . . . . . . . . . . . . . . . . .33
Other; no opinion . . . . . . . . . . . . . . . . . .13

### 65 Years and Over

Protection of environment . . . . . . . . . . . . .49%
Economic growth . . . . . . . . . . . . . . . . . . .32
Other; no opinion . . . . . . . . . . . . . . . . . .19

## By Income
### $20,000 and Over

Protection of environment . . . . . . . . . . . . .65%
Economic growth . . . . . . . . . . . . . . . . . . .27
Other; no opinion . . . . . . . . . . . . . . . . . 8

### Under $20,000

Protection of environment . . . . . . . . . . . . .58%
Economic growth . . . . . . . . . . . . . . . . . . .28
Other; no opinion . . . . . . . . . . . . . . . . . .14

*Where you live now, do you have reason to complain a great deal, a fair amount, not very much, or not at all about the following? If you have no reason to complain, please don't hesitate to say so:*

*Deterioration of landscape?*

Great deal . . . . . . . . . . . . . . . . . . . . . . . . .15%
Fair amount . . . . . . . . . . . . . . . . . . . . . . .18
Not very much . . . . . . . . . . . . . . . . . . . . .15
Not at all . . . . . . . . . . . . . . . . . . . . . . . .50
No opinion . . . . . . . . . . . . . . . . . . . . . . . 2

*Loss of farmland?*

Great deal . . . . . . . . . . . . . . . . . . . . . . . . .12%
Fair amount . . . . . . . . . . . . . . . . . . . . . . .14
Not very much . . . . . . . . . . . . . . . . . . . . .13
Not at all . . . . . . . . . . . . . . . . . . . . . . . .56
No opinion . . . . . . . . . . . . . . . . . . . . . . . 5

### Water purity?

Great deal ........................11%
Fair amount ......................11
Not very much ....................14
Not at all .......................63
No opinion .......................1

### Air pollution?

Great deal ........................ 9%
Fair amount ......................15
Not very much ....................20
Not at all .......................54
No opinion .......................2

### Noise?

Great deal ........................ 8%
Fair amount ......................11
Not very much ....................17
Not at all .......................63
No opinion .......................1

### No access to open spaces?

Great deal ........................ 6%
Fair amount ...................... 9
Not very much ....................16
Not at all .......................67
No opinion .......................2

*Now, concerning this country as a whole, I would like to find out how worried or concerned you are about a number of problems I am going to mention—a great deal, a fair amount, not very much, or not at all:*

### Nuclear waste disposal?

Great deal ........................69%
Fair amount ......................17
Not very much .................... 7
Not at all ....................... 4
No opinion ....................... 3

### Industrial waste disposal?

Great deal ........................64%
Fair amount ......................22
Not very much .................... 7
Not at all ....................... 4
No opinion ....................... 3

### Damage from oil spills?

Great deal ........................54%
Fair amount ......................27
Not very much ....................10
Not at all ....................... 6
No opinion ....................... 3

### Water pollution?

Great deal ........................52%
Fair amount ......................32
Not very much .................... 9
Not at all ....................... 5
No opinion ....................... 2

### Air pollution?

Great deal ........................46%
Fair amount ......................32
Not very much ....................14
Not at all ....................... 6
No opinion ....................... 2

Note: In a strong expression of the value Americans assign to preserving this country's natural resources, respondents place a far higher priority on protecting the environment than on sustained economic growth. In a recent Gallup Poll, 61% say environmental protection should have precedence even at the risk of curbing economic growth, while 28% would assign top priority to the economy; the remaining 11% give other reasons or withhold their opinions. The public's preference finds even greater expression among adults aged 18 to 49, westerners, the college educated, and those from upper-income households.

In another assessment, the public shows the most concern over disposal of hazardous wastes, with 69% saying they worry a great deal about nuclear wastes and 64% about industrial wastes.

Next comes damage to sea life and beaches by spillage or discharge from oil tankers, with 54% greatly concerned, and about the same proportion, 52%, worrying a great deal about pollution of our rivers and lakes. Slightly fewer, 46%, are greatly concerned about air pollution.

To a considerable extent, Americans complain less about environmental conditions where they live than they do about problems that are national in scope. For example, only 11% say they have a great deal to complain about the purity of their local drinking water while, as noted above, 52% are greatly concerned about the pollution of rivers and lakes throughout the United States. Similarly, merely 9% cite air pollution as a local problem of great concern, but 46% are very worried about it nationwide.

Other local problems and the proportions who see them as sources of a great deal of concern include deterioration of the landscape (15%), the loss of good farmland (12%), noise (8%), and the lack of access to open space and the countryside (6%).

## DECEMBER 17

## ENVIRONMENTAL PROTECTION—INTERNATIONAL COMPARISON

Interviewing Date: 9/28–10/1/84 (U.S.); October 1984 for Other Nations
Survey #243-G*

*Here are two statements which people sometimes make when discussing the environment and economic growth. Which of these statements comes closer to your own point of view?*

*1) Protection of the environment should be given priority, even at the risk of curbing economic growth.*

*2) Economic growth should be given priority, even if the environment suffers to some extent.*

*The European results were sponsored by the Commission of the European Communities and the OECD.

| | Protection of environment | Economic growth | Other; no opinion |
|---|---|---|---|
| Denmark . . . . . . . | 75% | 14% | 11% |
| Italy . . . . . . . . . | 67 | 20 | 13 |
| Germany (West) . . . . . . . | 64 | 21 | 15 |
| United States . . . | 61 | 28 | 11 |
| France . . . . . . . . | 58 | 30 | 12 |
| Greece . . . . . . . | 56 | 26 | 18 |
| Netherlands . . . . | 56 | 34 | 10 |
| Belgium . . . . . . . | 50 | 30 | 20 |
| Great Britain . . . | 50 | 36 | 14 |
| Ireland . . . . . . . . | 29 | 58 | 13 |

*Now, concerning this country as a whole, I would like to find out how worried or concerned you are about a number of problems I am going to mention—a great deal, a fair amount, not very much, or not at all:*

*Pollution of rivers and lakes?*

| | Those saying a great deal |
|---|---|
| United States . . . . . . . . . . . . . . . . . . . . | 52% |
| Netherlands . . . . . . . . . . . . . . . . . . . . . | 46 |
| Denmark . . . . . . . . . . . . . . . . . . . . . . . | 38 |
| France . . . . . . . . . . . . . . . . . . . . . . . . . | 34 |
| Great Britain . . . . . . . . . . . . . . . . . . . . | 27 |
| Greece . . . . . . . . . . . . . . . . . . . . . . . . . | 37 |
| Italy . . . . . . . . . . . . . . . . . . . . . . . . . . | 43 |
| Ireland . . . . . . . . . . . . . . . . . . . . . . . . | 29 |
| Germany (West) . . . . . . . . . . . . . . . . . . | 35 |
| Belgium . . . . . . . . . . . . . . . . . . . . . . . | 24 |

Average: European countries . . . . . . . . 35%

*Damage to sea life and beaches by spillage or discharge from oil tankers?*

| | Those saying a great deal |
|---|---|
| United States . . . . . . . . . . . . . . . . . . . . | 54% |
| Netherlands . . . . . . . . . . . . . . . . . . . . . | 55 |

Denmark . . . . . . . . . . . . . . . . . . . . . . . . . 48
France . . . . . . . . . . . . . . . . . . . . . . . . . . 48
Great Britain . . . . . . . . . . . . . . . . . . . . . 45
Greece . . . . . . . . . . . . . . . . . . . . . . . . . . 52
Italy . . . . . . . . . . . . . . . . . . . . . . . . . . . 46
Ireland . . . . . . . . . . . . . . . . . . . . . . . . . 33
Germany (West) . . . . . . . . . . . . . . . . . . . 39
Belgium . . . . . . . . . . . . . . . . . . . . . . . . . 29

Average: European countries . . . . . . . . 44%


### Air pollution?

| | Those saying a great deal |
|---|---|
| United States | 46% |
| Netherlands | 38 |
| Denmark | 34 |
| France | 28 |
| Great Britain | 24 |
| Greece | 32 |
| Italy | 43 |
| Ireland | 24 |
| Germany (West) | 36 |
| Belgium | 25 |

Average: European countries . . . . . . . . 32%


### Disposal of industrial wastes?

| | Those saying a great deal |
|---|---|
| United States | 64% |
| Netherlands | 59 |
| Denmark | 45 |
| France | 42 |
| Great Britain | 45 |
| Greece | 54 |
| Italy | 44 |
| Ireland | 37 |
| Germany (West) | 39 |
| Belgium | 29 |

Average: European countries . . . . . . . . 44%


### Disposal of nuclear wastes?

| | Those saying a great deal |
|---|---|
| United States | 69% |
| Netherlands | 58 |
| Denmark | 51 |
| France | 45 |
| Great Britain | 42 |
| Greece | 42 |
| Italy | 41 |
| Ireland | 40 |
| Germany (West) | 40 |
| Belgium | 35 |

Average: European countries . . . . . . . . 44%


*Where you live now, do you have reason to complain a great deal, a fair amount, not very much, or not at all about the following? If you have no reason to complain, please don't hesitate to say so.*


### Landscape deterioration?

| | A great deal or a fair amount |
|---|---|
| United States | 33% |
| Italy | 36 |
| France | 30 |
| Netherlands | 27 |
| Greece | 26 |
| Belgium | 25 |
| Germany (West) | 23 |
| Great Britain | 21 |
| Ireland | 15 |
| Denmark | 8 |

Average: European countries . . . . . . . . 23%


### Loss of farmland?

| | A great deal or a fair amount |
|---|---|
| United States | 26% |
| Italy | 31 |
| France | 26 |

Netherlands . . . . . . . . . . . . . . . . . . . . . . . 17
Greece . . . . . . . . . . . . . . . . . . . . . . . . . . 25
Belgium . . . . . . . . . . . . . . . . . . . . . . . 23
Germany (West) . . . . . . . . . . . . . . . . . . . 17
Great Britain . . . . . . . . . . . . . . . . . . . . . 17
Ireland . . . . . . . . . . . . . . . . . . . . . . . . . 10
Denmark . . . . . . . . . . . . . . . . . . . . . . . . 4

Average: European countries . . . . . . . . 19%

### Air pollution?

| | A great deal or a fair amount |
|---|---|
| United States | 24% |
| Italy | 25 |
| France | 19 |
| Netherlands | 17 |
| Greece | 26 |
| Belgium | 27 |
| Germany (West) | 35 |
| Great Britain | 18 |
| Ireland | 13 |
| Denmark | 12 |

Average: European countries . . . . . . . . 21%

### Water purity?

| | A great deal or a fair amount |
|---|---|
| United States | 22% |
| Italy | 27 |
| France | 15 |
| Netherlands | 6 |
| Greece | 15 |
| Belgium | 16 |
| Germany (West) | 25 |
| Great Britain | 9 |
| Ireland | 13 |
| Denmark | 3 |

Average: European countries . . . . . . . . 14%

### Noise?

| | A great deal or a fair amount |
|---|---|
| United States | 19% |
| Italy | 27 |
| France | 21 |
| Netherlands | 19 |
| Greece | 24 |
| Belgium | 27 |
| Germany (West) | 33 |
| Great Britain | 21 |
| Ireland | 14 |
| Denmark | 13 |

Average: European countries . . . . . . . . 22%

### No access to open country?

| | A great deal or a fair amount |
|---|---|
| United States | 15% |
| Italy | 29 |
| France | 17 |
| Netherlands | 8 |
| Greece | 30 |
| Belgium | 21 |
| Germany (West) | 19 |
| Great Britain | 12 |
| Ireland | 11 |
| Denmark | 4 |

Average: European countries . . . . . . . . 17%

Note: Although Americans are sometimes criticized by foreign observers as being overly preoccupied with protecting the environment, a similar degree of concern is found in many European nations. Studies conducted this fall in the United States and in nine European countries two years ago found basic environmental values shared by many people on both sides of the Atlantic, as well as some disparities.

Asked to choose between protecting the environment or allowing economic growth, Americans opt for protecting the environment by a 2-to-1 ratio, as reported recently. While the U.S. results represent an enthusiastic endorsement of environmental safeguards, the citizens of Italy and West Germany back environmental protection over economic growth in their countries by even greater 3-to-1 majorities. Topping the list are the Danes, whose support for preserving their environment surpasses their desire for economic growth by 75% to 14%, a 5-to-1 ratio.

In the next tier of European countries, with almost as much pro-environment sentiment recorded as in the United States, are France, Greece, and the Netherlands. Somewhat narrower divisions of opinion are found in Belgium and Great Britain. Only in the Republic of Ireland— one of the poorer nations participating in the study—does public opinion favor economic growth over environmental protection, 58% to 29%.

Although the United States ranks in the mid-range of the ten countries in terms of the overall priorities its citizens assign to environmental protection and economic growth, more Americans worry a great deal about most of the five specific forms of pollution included in the study than do residents of the European nations. In the United States, 69% and 64% say they are greatly concerned about the disposal of nuclear and industrial wastes, respectively. By comparison, the European country closest to us in this regard is the Netherlands, where 58% and 59% of the citizens share Americans' concerns; the average is 44% for all nine European countries claiming to be greatly concerned about disposal of both types of pollutant. The differences between the United States and the Europeans are less extreme in the case of oil spills and water and air pollution, but Americans also are at or near the top in their concern about these pollutants.

As was found in the United States, European respondents express less concern about environmental factors in the communities where they live than they do about pollution of natural resources on a national scale. On average, for example, 32% in the European countries say they worry about air pollution as a national problem, whereas 21% complain a lot about air pollution in their neighborhoods. Compared to the generally wide disparity between the United States and Europe on national environmental factors, however, the views of Americans and Europeans on local conditions are more attuned. On the factor of noise, 19% of Americans express dissatisfaction, while 22% of Europeans are similarly concerned; on average, complaints about noise range from a

high of 33% in West Germany to a low of 13% in Denmark. Similarly, lack of access to open spaces and the countryside is a matter of concern to 15% of Americans and 17% of Europeans; the range there extends from 30% in Greece to 4% in Denmark. As a rule, the Italians express the greatest concern about all of the local environmental problems studied—surpassing the Americans on most—while the Danes and Irish complain least.

## DECEMBER 20
## CHURCH ATTENDANCE

Interviewing Date: Five Selected Weeks During 1984
Various Surveys

*Did you, yourself, happen to attend church or synagogue in the last seven days?*

|  | Yes |
|---|---|
| National | 40% |

### By Sex

| | |
|---|---|
| Male | 35% |
| Female | 44 |

### By Ethnic Background

| | |
|---|---|
| White | 39% |
| Black | 43 |
| Hispanic | 49 |

### By Education

| | |
|---|---|
| College graduate | 41% |
| College incomplete | 40 |
| High-school graduate | 39 |
| Less than high-school graduate | 39 |
| Grade school | 46 |

### By Region

| | |
|---|---|
| East | 38% |
| Midwest | 42 |
| South | 44 |
| West | 33 |

## By Age

| | |
|---|---|
| 18–24 years | 30% |
| 25–29 years | 31 |
| 30–49 years | 40 |
| 50–64 years | 45 |
| 65 years and over | 48 |

## By Religion

| | |
|---|---|
| Protestants | 39% |
| Catholics | 51 |
| Jews | 22 |

| | |
|---|---|
| All Baptists | 41 |
| Southern Baptists | 46 |
| Methodists | 33 |
| Lutherans | 39 |
| Presbyterians | 39 |
| Episcopalians | 35 |
| Latter-Day Saints | 53 |

## Selected National Trend

| | Yes |
|---|---|
| 1983 | 40% |
| 1982 | 41 |
| 1981 | 41 |
| 1980 | 40 |
| 1979 | 40 |
| 1978 | 41 |
| 1977 | 41 |
| 1972 | 40 |
| 1969 | 42 |
| 1967 | 43 |
| 1962 | 46 |
| 1958 | 49 |
| 1957 | 47 |
| 1955 | 49 |
| 1954 | 46 |
| 1950 | 39 |
| 1940 | 37 |
| 1939 | 41 |

*Do you happen to be a member of a church or synagogue?*

| | Yes |
|---|---|
| National | 68% |

## Selected National Trend

| | Yes |
|---|---|
| 1983 | 69% |
| 1982 | 67* |
| 1981 | 68 |
| 1980 | 69 |
| 1978 | 68 |
| 1976 | 71 |
| 1965 | 73 |
| 1952 | 73 |
| 1947 | 76 |
| 1942 | 75 |
| 1939 | 72 |
| 1937 | 73 |

*Seven-survey average

Note: Four adults in every ten (40%) attended church or synagogue in a typical week in 1984, matching the figure recorded in 1983. Church-going has remained remarkably constant since 1969, after having declined from the high point of 49% recorded in 1955 and 1958. Attendance has not varied by more than two percentage points since 1969.

Since 1958, a peak year for church attendance, the decline in churchgoing has been sharpest among Catholics. Attendance at Mass fell 23 points between 1958 and 1982, while by contrast Protestant churchgoing has remained remarkably stable since 1958.

In 1984 more women (44%) attended in a typical week than men (35%), and more older persons than younger ones. Nationwide, 51% of Catholics went to church in a typical week, compared to 39% of Protestants, figures that almost exactly match those from the 1983 audit.

The proportion of adults who say they are church members also has changed little in recent years, with seven in ten Americans (68%) now claiming membership in a church or synagogue. The 1983 figure was 69%. The highest level (76%) was found in 1947, close to the 73% recorded in the first Gallup audit in 1937.

It is important to bear in mind that the membership figures reported here are self-classifications, representing the proportion of people who say they are members of a church or synagogue, and may include some who are not actually on the rolls of the local churches. It should also be stressed that adherents of certain faiths—for example, the Roman Catholic and Eastern Orthodox churches—are considered members at birth.

## DECEMBER 23
## PERSONAL FINANCES

Interviewing Date: 11/30–12/3/84
Survey #246-G

*We are interested in how people's financial situation may have changed. Would you say that you are financially better off now than you were a year ago, or are you financially worse off now?*

Better ............................ 43%
Worse ............................ 24
Same (volunteered) .................. 32
No opinion ......................... 1

### Selected National Trend

| | Better | Worse | Same | No opinion |
|---|---|---|---|---|
| *1984* | | | | |
| September | 39% | 26% | 34% | 1% |
| July | 40 | 25 | 34 | 1 |
| March | 36 | 26 | 37 | 1 |
| *1983* | | | | |
| June | 28 | 39 | 32 | 1 |
| March | 25 | 46 | 28 | 1 |
| *1982* | | | | |
| November | 28 | 37 | 34 | 1 |
| February | 28 | 47 | 24 | 1 |
| *1981* | | | | |
| October | 28 | 43 | 28 | 1 |

*Looking ahead, do you expect that at this time next year you will be financially better off than now, or worse off than now?*

Better ............................ 50%
Worse ............................ 17
Same (volunteered) .................. 28
No opinion ......................... 5

### Selected National Trend

| | Better | Worse | Same | No opinion |
|---|---|---|---|---|
| *1984* | | | | |
| September | 53% | 9% | 28% | 10% |
| July | 52 | 12 | 28 | 8 |
| March | 54 | 11 | 28 | 7 |
| *1983* | | | | |
| June | 43 | 19 | 28 | 10 |
| March | 45 | 22 | 24 | 9 |
| *1982* | | | | |
| November | 41 | 22 | 27 | 10 |
| February | 42 | 31 | 21 | 6 |
| *1981* | | | | |
| October | 40 | 31 | 21 | 8 |

Combining the results of the two questions to show the overall trend, past and future, the latest survey reveals about the same level of optimism recorded all year. Pessimism has increased somewhat, with all of this increase accounted for by a reduction in the number of those persons who are neutral or undecided about their financial prospects:

Optimists ........................... 48%
Pessimists .......................... 18
Neutral (volunteered) ................ 29
No opinion ......................... 5

### Selected National Trend

| | Opti- mists | Pessi- mists | Neutral | No opinion |
|---|---|---|---|---|
| *1984* | | | | |
| September | 47% | 11% | 32% | 10% |
| July | 47 | 15 | 30 | 8 |
| March | 46 | 14 | 33 | 7 |
| *1983* | | | | |
| June | 34 | 24 | 32 | 10 |
| March | 32 | 28 | 30 | 10 |
| *1982* | | | | |
| November | 32 | 25 | 33 | 10 |

Note: The American people are less bullish today in their financial outlook than they were in September, but optimists still outweigh pessimists by a wide margin. In the latest Gallup Poll, 50% say they expect to be financially better off a year from now, 28% think their situation will be about the same, while 17% foresee a downturn. In a comparable September survey, 53% were optimistic, 28% neutral, and 9%—or only about half the current figure—were pessimistic about the coming year.

Although the current level of pessimism is the highest measured in four surveys this year, it is markedly lower than any recorded in recent years. Surveys conducted at this time in 1982 and 1981, for example, found 22% and 31%, respectively, expecting austerity a year hence.

The recent downturn in economic expectations has occurred in all major population groups, but it is especially pronounced among the less well-to-do, older people, and blacks. Among the latter, for instance, 15% in September said they expected to be worse off next year; the current figure is 29%.

Asked to rate their current financial situation vis-à-vis one year ago, 43% of respondents say they are now better off, 32% perceive no change, while 24% claim to be worse off. Not only is the latest optimistic assessment the highest this year, but it also tops any recorded since the question was first asked in 1976.

## DECEMBER 27
## MOST ADMIRED WOMAN

Interviewing Date: 11/30–12/3/84
Survey #246-G

*What woman whom you have heard or read about, living today in any part of the world, do you admire most? Who is your second choice?*

The following are the 1984 results, based on first and second choices, combined:

Margaret Thatcher
Geraldine Ferraro
Mother Teresa of Calcutta
Nancy Reagan
Jeane Kirkpatrick
Betty Ford

Queen Elizabeth II
Coretta King
Princess Diana
Sandra Day O'Connor

## By Sex
### Male

Margaret Thatcher
Geraldine Ferraro
Mother Teresa of Calcutta
Jeane Kirkpatrick
Nancy Reagan
Queen Elizabeth II
Barbara Jordan
Farrah Fawcett
Sandra Day O'Connor ⎱ tie
Coretta King ⎰

### Female

Geraldine Ferraro
Margaret Thatcher
Mother Teresa of Calcutta
Nancy Reagan
Betty Ford
Jeane Kirkpatrick
Coretta King
Queen Elizabeth II
Princess Diana
Sandra Day O'Connor ⎱ tie
Rosalynn Carter ⎰

## By Ethnic Background
### White

Margaret Thatcher
Geraldine Ferraro
Mother Teresa of Calcutta
Nancy Reagan
Jeane Kirkpatrick
Betty Ford
Queen Elizabeth II
Princess Diana
Sandra Day O'Connor
Barbara Walters

*Nonwhite*

Geraldine Ferraro
Coretta King
Shirley Chisholm
Margaret Thatcher
Barbara Jordan
Mother Teresa of Calcutta
Rosalynn Carter
Barbara Walters
Nancy Reagan ⎫
Farrah Fawcett ⎭ tie

Note: British Prime Minister Margaret Thatcher, for the third year in a row, tops the list of women most admired by the American people. She is followed in this year's voting by the 1984 Democratic vice-presidential candidate, Geraldine Ferraro, and by Mother Teresa of Calcutta.

The nation's First Lady, Nancy Reagan, places fourth in this year's audit, followed by U.S. Ambassador to the United Nations Jeane Kirkpatrick. Sixth-place honors go to Betty Ford, followed by Queen Elizabeth II, Coretta King, Princess Diana, and Supreme Court Justice Sandra Day O'Connor.

Receiving frequent mentions in the 1984 survey, but not included in the top ten, are in alphabetical order: Rosalynn Carter, Shirley Chisholm, Farrah Fawcett, Barbara Jordan, and Barbara Walters.

Survey respondents in this study, which the Gallup Poll has conducted for more than three decades, are asked to give their choices without the aid of a prearranged list of names. This procedure, while opening the field to all possible choices, tends to favor those who are currently or have recently been in the news.

## DECEMBER 30
## MOST ADMIRED MAN

Interviewing Date: 11/30–12/3/84
Survey #246-G

*What man whom you have heard or read about, living today in any part of the world, do you admire the most? Who is your second choice?*

The following are the 1984 results, based on first and second choices, combined:

Ronald Reagan
Pope John Paul II
Jesse Jackson
Billy Graham
Walter Mondale
Edward Kennedy
Jimmy Carter
Henry Kissinger
Lee Iacocca
George Bush

Note: President Ronald Reagan, Pope John Paul II, and the Reverend Jesse Jackson top the list of men most admired by the American people. Fourth is the Reverend Billy Graham, followed by Democratic presidential candidate Walter Mondale, Senator Edward Kennedy, Jimmy Carter, and former Secretary of State Henry Kissinger. The ninth position is held by Lee Iacocca, chairman of the Chrysler Corporation, one of the few business leaders ever to appear in these audits. Rounding out the top ten is Vice-President George Bush.

President Reagan and Pope John Paul II were also number one and two in the 1983, 1982, and 1981 audits. Last year the Polish labor union leader, Lech Walesa, was in the third position. Jackson has registered steady gains since 1981, moving from tenth place to ninth in 1982, sixth in 1983, and to the number-three spot in this year's balloting.

Survey respondents in these studies, which have been conducted for more than three decades, are asked to give their choices without a list of names. This procedure, while opening the field to all possible candidates, tends to favor those who are currently in the news.

# Index

Brazil (*continued*)
    on government's hiding bad news, 36
    on hatred of others, 29
    on having peace by waging war, 32
    on poor people and lottery, 28
    on privacy, 27
    on punishment for criticism of government, 31
    on sacrifices by people but luxury for· officials, 34
    on surrendering freedom to gain security, 33
    predictions for 1984 in, 2
    vote on permanent site for Olympic games, 131
Budget (federal)
    cuts in military or in social programs, 77
    Reagan cuts, as most important problem, 71, 118
    size of administration's 1985 budget, 76-77
Budget deficit (federal)
    approval rating, of tax increases to reduce, 234-36
    handled by Reagan, 64
    as issue for presidential debates, 195
    likely to cut economic recovery short, 77
    as most important problem, 118, 144, 207
    Reagan or Mondale better at reducing, 146
    as reason for voting against Reagan, 92-93
    reduced by Mondale's tax plan, 198-200
    as threat to continued economic recovery, 106-07
Burglary (home broken into)
    incidence of, 231-33
        international comparisons, 233
        national trend, 233
    reported to police, 233-34
Bush, George
    better than Ferraro in vice-presidential debate, 195
    likely to watch debate between Ferraro and, 192-95
    as most admired man, 274
    *see also* Reagan-Bush ticket
Byrne, Jane
    as vice-president, 84

# C

Canada
    degree of freedom in, 43
        evaluated by five countries, 43
    evaluation of freedom
        in Canada, 43
        in East Germany, 41
        in France, 41
        in Great Britain, 41
        in India, 43
        in Iran, 43
        in Italy, 42
        in Japan, 42
        in Mexico, 43
        in Poland, 42
        in Red China, 42
        in Soviet Union, 42
        in United States, 41
        in West Germany, 41

    incidence of crime in, 233
    and Orwell's predictions
        on artificial insemination, 37
        on government by dictator, 38
        on government's hiding bad news, 36
        on hatred of others, 29
        on having peace by waging war, 32
        on poor people and lottery, 28
        on privacy, 27
        on punishment for criticism of government, 31
        on sacrifices by people but luxury for officials, 34
        on surrendering freedom to gain security, 33
    predictions for 1984 in, 2
    vote on permanent site for Olympic games, 131
Carter, Jimmy
    approval rating
        vs. Ford, 19, 98
        vs. Ford by personality factor, 150
        vs. Reagan, 18, 23, 98
        vs. Reagan by personality factor, 150
        vs. six presidents, 133
    margin over Ford, 178
    as most admired man, 8, 274
    national and regional vote in 1980, 110
    and party better able to handle top problem, 145
    Reagan's margin over, 178
Carter, Rosalynn
    as most admired woman, 273-74
Central America
    Mondale or Hart better at dealing with situation in, 97
    Reagan or Mondale better at dealing with situation in, 146
    should give military assistance to friendly governments in, 86
    situation in, dealt with by female president, 121
    situation in, handled by Reagan, 48-49, 65, 86, 105
        national trend, 65, 87, 105
    U.S. involvement could turn into a Vietnam, 107
Children
    main fault of parents in raising, 263-64
    *see also* Teen-agers
Chile
    predictions for 1984 in, 2
China (People's Republic)
    degree of freedom in, 42
        evaluated by five countries, 42
    Reagan's trip will improve U.S. relationship with, 96
Chisholm, Shirley
    as most admired woman, 274
    as vice-president, 84
Church attendance *see* Religion
Collins, Martha
    as vice-president, 84
Colombia
    incidence of crime in, 233
Congressional elections
    money provided by government for campaign of candidates for Congress, 122

and environmental problems of
    air pollution, 268
    damage by spillage from oil tankers, 268
    disposal of industrial wastes, 268
    disposal of nuclear wastes, 268
    pollution of rivers and lakes, 267
incidence of crime in, 233
predictions for 1984 in, 2
protection of environment as priority, or economic growth in, 267
vote on permanent site for Olympic games, 131
Freedom
    degree of
      in Canada, 43
      in East Germany, 41
      in France, 41
      in Great Britain, 41
      in India, 43
      in Iran, 43
      in Italy, 42
      in Japan, 42
      in Mexico, 43
      in Poland, 42
      in Red China, 42
      in Soviet Union, 42
      in United States, 39-41
      in West Germany, 41
    and Orwell's predictions on surrendering freedom to gain security, 32-33

# G

Gandhi, Indira
    as most admired woman, 8
Germany *see* East Germany; West Germany
Glenn, John
    degree of support for, vs. Reagan, 9
    and depth of support (analysis by Kohut), 9-10
    as most admired man, 8
    as nominee for Democratic presidential candidate, 7, 10, 52, 66
      choice with Mondale, 7, 10-11, 52
      national trend, 11, 52
    in trial heats vs. Reagan, 5-6, 13-14, 54-56, 67
      national trend, 7, 56
Goldwater, Barry
    approval rating vs. Johnson, 19, 98
    approval rating vs. Johnson by personality factor, 150
    Johnson's margin over, 178
Government
    dissatisfaction with, as most important problem, 144, 207
    and Orwell's predictions
      on country ruled by dictator, 37-38
      on punishment for criticism of, 29-31
      on sacrifices by people but luxury for officials, 33-34
    Reagan or Mondale better at building trust in, 146

Government benefits
    for one year of national service, 50-51
Government spending
    excessive, as issue for presidential debates, 195
    excessive, as most important problem, 71, 118, 144, 207
    reduced, as reason for voting for Reagan, 91-92
Graham, Billy
    as most admired man, 8, 274
Great Britain (United Kingdom)
    degree of freedom in, 41
      evaluated by five countries, 41
    and environmental complaints about
      air pollution, 269
      landscape deterioration, 268
      loss of farmland, 269
      no access to open country, 269
      noise, 269
      water purity, 269
    and environmental problems of
      air pollution, 268
      damage by spillage from oil tankers, 268
      disposal of industrial wastes, 268
      disposal of nuclear wastes, 268
      pollution of rivers and lakes, 267
    evaluation of freedom
      in Canada, 43
      in East Germany, 41
      in France, 41
      in Great Britain, 41
      in India, 43
      in Iran, 43
      in Italy, 42
      in Japan, 42
      in Mexico, 43
      in Poland, 42
      in Red China, 42
      in Soviet Union, 42
      in United States, 41
      in West Germany, 41
    and Orwell's predictions
      on artificial insemination, 37
      on government by dictator, 38
      on government's hiding bad news, 36
      on hatred of others, 29
      on having peace by waging war, 32
      on poor people and lottery, 28
      on privacy, 27
      on punishment for criticism of government, 31
      on sacrifices by people but luxury for officials, 34
      on surrendering freedom to gain security, 33
    predictions for 1984 in, 2
    protection of environment as priority, or economic growth in, 267
    vote on permanent site for Olympic games, 132
Greece
    and environmental complaints about
      air pollution, 269

Greece (*continued*)
    landscape deterioration, 268
    loss of farmland, 269
    no access to open country, 269
    noise, 269
    water purity, 269
  and environmental problems of
    air pollution, 268
    damage by spillage from oil tankers, 268
    disposal of industrial wastes, 268
    disposal of nuclear wastes, 268
    pollution of rivers and lakes, 267
  predictions for 1984 in, 2
  protection of environment as priority, or economic growth in, 267
  vote on permanent site for Olympic games, 132

# H

Hart, Gary
  approval rating, 97
  better than Mondale
    in dealing with situation in Central America, 97
    in dealing with women's rights, 97
    in handling disarmament negotiations with Soviet Union, 97
    in handling environmental problems, 97
    in handling foreign affairs, 96
    in improving conditions for minorities, 96
    in improving economy, 96
    in keeping inflation rate down, 96
    in keeping United States out of war, 96
    in reducing unemployment, 96
  cares more about problems of blacks, compared to Mondale, 82
  cares more about problems of women, compared to Mondale, 82
  choice on ticket with Mondale, 109
  as nominee for Democratic presidential candidate, 7, 10, 52, 66, 75, 84, 94, 98, 108
    choice with Mondale, 66-67, 75, 84-85, 94, 99, 108-09
    national trend, 98, 99
  perceived style, character traits, and other attributes of, compared to Mondale, 81-82
  reminds one of President Kennedy, 81
  sympathetic to problems of the poor, compared to Mondale, 82
  in trial heats vs. Reagan, 67, 75-76, 85, 94-95, 101-03, 113
  waging "cleaner" campaign than Mondale, 89-90
  your vote more for, or against Reagan, 103
  *see also* Mondale-Hart ticket
Hatred of people in other countries
  and Orwell's predictions, 28-29
Hawkins, Paula
  as vice-president, 84

Hispanics
  political affiliation of, 91
  *see also* Minorities
Hollings, Ernest
  as nominee for Democratic presidential candidate, 7, 10, 52
Humphrey, Hubert
  approval rating
    vs. Nixon, 98
    vs. Nixon by personality factor, 150
    vs. Nixon and Wallace, 19
  Nixon's margin over, 178
Hunger
  as issue for presidential debates, 195
  as most important problem, 144, 207

# I

Iacocca, Lee
  as most admired man, 274
Illegal aliens
  employ person without proper papers, 250
    national trend, 257
  everyone required to carry identification card, 251
    national trend, 251
  those in United States since 1982 be elligible for permanent status, 251-52
Independents
  affiliation of blacks with, 91
  affiliation of Hispanics with, 91
  affiliation with, 91, 134-36, 253
    national trend, 136, 254
India
  degree of freedom in, 43
    evaluated by five countries, 43
  predictions for 1984 in, 2
Inflation
  as most important problem, 71
  as reason for voting against Reagan, 92-93
Inflation rate
  lower, as reason for voting for Reagan, 91-92
  Mondale or Hart better at keeping down, 96
  Reagan or Mondale better at keeping down, 145
  by this time next year, 24-25
    misery index trend, 25
  as threat to continued economic recovery, 106-07
Interest rates
  high, as issue for presidential debates, 195
  high, as most important problem, 118, 144, 207
  high, as threat to continued economic recovery, 106-07
  lower, as reason for voting for Reagan, 91-92
International tensions
  as most important problem, 71, 118, 144, 207
International trade problems
  as threat to continued economic recovery, 106-07

Iran
  degree of freedom in, 43
    evaluated by five countries, 43
Ireland
  and environmental complaints about
    air pollution, 269
    landscape deterioration, 268
    loss of farmland, 269
    no access to open country, 269
    noise, 269
    water purity, 269
  and environmental problems of
    air pollution, 268
    damage by spillage from oil tankers, 268
    disposal of industrial wastes, 268
    disposal of nuclear wastes, 268
    pollution of rivers and lakes, 267
  incidence of crime in, 233
  predictions for 1984 in, 2
  protection of environment as priority, or economic
      growth in, 267
Italy
  degree of freedom in, 42
    evaluated by five countries, 42
  and environmental complaints about
    air pollution, 269
    landscape deterioration, 268
    loss of farmland, 268
    no access to open country, 269
    noise, 269
    water purity, 269
  and environmental problems of
    air pollution, 268
    damage by spillage from oil tankers, 268
    disposal of industrial wastes, 268
    disposal of nuclear wastes, 268
    pollution of rivers and lakes, 267
  incidence of crime in, 233
  predictions for 1984 in, 2
  protection of environment as priority, or economic
      growth in, 267
  vote on permanent site for Olympic games, 131

# J

Jackson, Jesse
  as most admired man, 8, 274
  as nominee for Democratic presidential candidate, 7,
      10, 52, 66, 75, 84, 94, 98, 108
    national trend, 98, 99
    in trial heats vs. Reagan, 14-17
Japan
  degree of freedom in, 42
    evaluated by five countries, 42
  incidence of crime in, 233
  predictions for 1984 in, 2
  vote on permanent site for Olympic games, 131

John Paul II, Pope
  as most admired man, 8, 274
Johnson, Lyndon
  approval rating
    vs. Goldwater, 19, 98
    vs. Goldwater by personality factor, 150
    vs. six presidents, 133
  margin over Goldwater, 178
  and party better able to handle top problem, 145
Jordan, Barbara
  as most admired woman, 273-74
  as vice-president, 84

# K

Kassebaum, Nancy
  as vice-president, 84
Kennedy, Edward
  as most admired man, 8, 274
Kennedy, John
  approval rating
    vs. Nixon, 19, 98
    vs. Nixon by personality factor, 150
    vs. six presidents, 133
  margin over Nixon, 178
  Mondale or Hart reminds one of, 81
  and party better able to handle top problem, 145
King, Coretta
  as most admired woman, 273-74
Kirkpatrick, Jeane
  as most admired woman, 273
  as vice-president, 84
Kissinger, Henry
  as most admired man, 8, 274
Kohut, Andrew, analysis by
  *Climate of Opinion Cuts Against Mondale*, 159-60
  *Major Swings in Poll Findings Reflect Political Environment*, 123-24
  *Reagan's Depth of Support Unmatched by Democratic Hopefuls*, 9-10
Korea *see* South Korea

# L

Landon, Alfred
  approval rating vs. Roosevelt, 19
Lebanon
  all U.S. forces should be withdrawn from, 62-63
  situation in, handled by Reagan, 47-48, 62, 66
    national trend, 66
  United States made mistake in sending marines to, 21-22, 58-60
    national trend, 22, 60
  United States should withdraw troops from, 19-21, 60-61

Lottery
  Orwell's predictions on poor people and, 27-28
Luxembourg
  predictions for 1984 in, 2

# M

McGovern, George
  approval rating
    vs. Nixon, 98
    vs. Nixon by personality factor, 150
    vs. Nixon and Wallace, 19
  Nixon's margin over, 178
  as nominee for Democratic presidential candidate, 7,
    10, 52, 66
  in trial heats vs. Reagan, 17-18
Man, most admired
  choice for, 8, 274
Medical care
  not enough money to pay for, 72
Medicare
  increased spending for, 243-45
Mexico
  degree of freedom in, 43
    evaluated by five countries, 43
Military spending
  cuts in, for reductions in budget, 77
Minorities
  Mondale or Hart better at improving conditions for, 96
  Reagan or Mondale better at improving things for, 146
Mondale, Walter
  approval rating, 97
  approval rating of his tax plan, 198-200
  approval rating vs. Reagan by personality factor, 150
  better than Hart
    in dealing with situation in Central America, 97
    in dealing with women's rights, 97
    in handling disarmament negotiations with Soviet
      Union, 97
    in handling environmental problems, 97
    in handling foreign affairs, 96
    in improving conditions for minorities, 96
    in improving economy, 96
    in keeping inflation rate down, 96
    in keeping United States out of war, 96
    in reducing unemployment, 96
  better than Reagan
    for building trust in government, 146
    for dealing with situation in Central America, 146
    for dealing with Soviet Union, 146, 208
    in first debate, 196-97
    for handling foreign relations, 146
    for handling most important problems, 207
    for helping the poor and needy, 146
    for improving economy, 145
    for improving environment, 146
    for improving things for minorities, 146

    for improving women's rights, 146
    for increasing respect for United States overseas, 146
    for keeping country prosperous, 62, 145, 207
      national trend, 207
    for keeping inflation down, 145
    for keeping United States out of war, 61-62, 146,
      207
      national trend, 207
    for making people proud to be Americans, 146
    in presidential debates, 195
    for reducing budget deficit, 146
    for reducing unemployment, 146
    in second debate, 211
    for spending taxpayers' money wisely, 146
  cares more about problems
    of blacks, compared to Hart, 82
    of blacks, compared to Reagan, 149, 204
    of the elderly, compared to Reagan, 204
    of poor people, compared to Reagan, 204
    of women, compared to Hart, 82
    of women, compared to Reagan, 149, 204
  choice on ticket with Hart, 109
  and climate of opinion against (analysis by Kohut), 159-
    60
  degree of support for, vs. Reagan, 9
  and depth of support (analysis by Kohut), 9-10
  has best judgment on needed defense expenditures,
    compared to Reagan, 211
  his tax plan a help to U.S. economy, 200-02
  likely to watch debates between Reagan and, 190-92
  main reason you voted for, 261-63
  more capable than Reagan for handling relations with
    Soviet Union, 211
  more likely than Reagan to keep United States out of
    war, 211
  more likely to vote for, after debates, 212
  as most admired man, 8, 274
  as nominee for Democratic presidential candidate, 7,
    10, 52, 66, 75, 84, 94, 98, 108
    choice with Glenn, 7, 10-11, 52
    choice with Hart, 66-67, 75, 84-85, 94, 99, 108-09
    national trend, 11, 52, 98, 99
  perceived public image and character traits of, com-
    pared to Reagan, 149
  perceived style, character traits, and other attributes of,
    compared to Hart, 81-82
  perceived sympathy for groups, compared to Reagan,
    204
  perceptions of, on foreign policy issues in second debate,
    211
  reminds one of President Kennedy, 81
  sympathetic to problems of the poor, compared to Hart,
    82
  in trial heats vs. Reagan, 3-5, 12-13, 53-54, 67, 75,
    85, 94, 99-101, 109, 113
    national trend, 5, 54
    see also Mondale-Ferraro ticket
  waging "cleaner" campaign than Hart, 89-90

# N

# O

# P

national trend, 23, 58, 104
performance ratings, 133
vs. Carter, 18
vs. Carter by personality factor, 150
vs. Mondale by personality factor, 150
vs. predecessors, 23, 98, 133
best reason for voting against, 92-93
best reason for voting for, 91-92
better than Mondale
    for building trust in government, 146
    for dealing with situation in Central America, 146
    for dealing with Soviet Union, 146, 208
    in first debate, 196-97
    for handling foreign relations, 146
    for handling most important problems, 207
    for helping the poor and needy, 146
    for improving economy, 145
    for improving environment, 146
    for improving things for minorities, 146
    for improving women's rights, 146
    for increasing respect for United States overseas, 146
    for keeping country prosperous, 62, 145, 207
        national trend, 207
    for keeping inflation down, 145
    for keeping United States out of war, 61-62, 146, 207
        national trend, 207
    for making people proud to be Americans, 146
    in presidential debates, 195
    for reducing budget deficit, 146
    for reducing unemployment, 146
    in second debate, 211
    for spending taxpayers' money wisely, 146
cares more about problems
    of blacks, compared to Mondale, 149, 204
    of the elderly, compared to Mondale, 204
    of poor people, compared to Mondale, 204
    of women, compared to Mondale, 149, 204
concern after debates that he may not meet demands of second term, 212
degree of support for, vs. Glenn, 9
degree of support for, vs. Mondale, 9
and depth of support (analysis by Kohut), 9-10
and economic conditions, 44-45, 63, 104
    national trend, 64, 104
and federal budget deficit, 64
and foreign policy, 45-47, 64, 104
    national trend, 64-65, 105
has best judgment on needed defense expenditures, compared to Mondale, 211
his age a factor (too old), 92-93, 205
likely to watch debates between Mondale and, 190-92
main reason you voted for, 259-61
margin over Carter, 178
more capable than Mondale of handling relations with Soviet Union, 211
more likely than Mondale to keep United States out of war, 211

more likely to vote for, after debates, 212
as most admired man, 8, 274
national and regional vote in 1980, 110
and party better able to handle top problem, 145
perceived public image and character traits of, compared to Mondale, 149
perceived sympathy for groups, compared to Mondale, 204
perceptions of, on foreign policy issues in second debate, 211
president's trip will improve U.S. relationship with China, 96
and relations with Soviet Union, 65, 105
    national trend, 65, 105
and situation in Central America, 48-49, 65, 86, 105
    national trend, 65, 87, 105
and situation in Lebanon, 47-48, 62, 65-66
    national trend, 66
in trial heats vs. Glenn, 5-6, 13-14, 54-56, 67
    national trend, 7, 56
in trial heats vs. Hart, 67, 75-76, 85, 94-95, 101-03, 113
    national trend, 99
in trial heats vs. Jackson, 14-17
in trial heats vs. McGovern, 17-18
in trial heats vs. Mondale, 3-5, 12-13, 53-54, 67, 75, 85, 94, 99-101, 109, 113
    national trend, 5, 54
    *see also* Reagan-Bush ticket
and unemployment, 64
    national trend, 64
your vote for Mondale because you were dissatisfied with, 261
your vote more for Hart, or against Reagan, 103
your vote more for Mondale, or against Reagan, 103
Reagan-Bush ticket
    degree of support for, 123-24, 129-30, 184-85, 205, 218-22
        national trend, 222
        vote by men and women, 178
    strength of choice, 153-58, 172-77
    in trial heats vs. Mondale-Ferraro ticket, 119, 127-29, 139, 146-48, 150-53, 169-72, 181-84, 205, 215-18, 228-29
        national trend, 119-20, 129, 153, 172, 184, 205, 218
    in trial heats vs. Mondale-Hart ticket, 90, 103, 108, 109-10
    your vote more for, or against Mondale-Ferraro, 130, 185-90, 205, 222-27
        national trend, 228
Recession
    as most important problem, 71
Religion
    church or synagogue attendance, 1, 270-71
        national trend, 1, 271
    church or synagogue membership, 1, 271
        national trend, 1, 271

Republican party
affiliation of blacks with, 91
affiliation of Hispanics with, 91
affiliation with, 91, 134-36, 253
change compared to 1977, 253-54
national trend, 136, 254
approval rating, 254
better for handling most important problem, 71, 118, 144-45
results by election year, 145
better for keeping country prosperous, 88-89, 140-41, 167-68
national trend, 89, 141, 168-69
more likely to keep United States out of war, 88, 140, 165-67
national trend, 88, 140, 167
perceived political ideology, 257-58
preference for, in congressional elections, 95, 212-15
Roosevelt, Franklin
approval rating
vs. Dewey, 19
vs. Landon, 19
vs. Willkie, 19

# S

Safer world
now than four years ago, 142
now than three years ago, 73-74
Satisfaction
with United States, 68-69
national trend, 69
with your personal life, 69-70
national trend, 70
Schools see Prayer in public schools; Tuition tax credits
Seat belts
law to equip new cars with air bags, 115
law to equip new cars with belts that would lock automatically in place, 115
law to fine drivers and passengers if they did not wear, 115-16
your use of, 115
national trend, 115
Security
and Orwell's predictions on surrendering freedom to gain security, 32-33
Social Security
approval rating, for cost-of-living increases, 248-50
cuts in, as reason for voting against Reagan, 92-93
Social spending
approval rating, for increased, 243-45
cuts in, as issue for presidential debates, 195
cuts in, as reason for voting against Reagan, 92-93
cuts in, for reductions in budget, 77
Social work
service in, in return for government benefits, 50-51

South Korea
incidence of crime in, 233
predictions for 1984 in, 2
vote on permanent site for Olympic games, 131
Soviet Union
agreement with United States for nuclear weapons freeze, 245-47
degree of freedom in, 42
evaluated by five countries, 42
Mondale or Hart better at handling disarmament negotiations with, 97
Reagan or Mondale better able to work with, 208
Reagan or Mondale better at dealing with, 146
Reagan or Mondale more capable of handling relations with, 211
relations with, handled by female president, 121
relations with, handled by Reagan, 65, 105
national trend, 65, 105
relations with, as issue for presidential debates, 195
relations with United States under new Soviet leadership, 63
Spain
incidence of crime in, 233
predictions for 1984 in, 2
Speed limit
keep present 55-mile-per-hour, 255-56
national trend, 256
Stevenson, Adlai
approval rating vs. Eisenhower, 19, 98
approval rating vs. Eisenhower by personality factor, 150
Eisenhower's margins over, 178
Sweden
incidence of crime in, 233
predictions for 1984 in, 2
Switzerland
evaluation of freedom
in Canada, 43
in East Germany, 41
in France, 41
in Great Britain, 41
in India, 43
in Iran, 43
in Italy, 42
in Japan, 42
in Mexico, 43
in Poland, 42
in Red China, 42
in Soviet Union, 42
in United States, 41
in West Germany, 41
and Orwell's predictions
on artificial insemination, 37
on government by dictator, 38
on government's hiding bad news, 36
on hatred of others, 29
on having peace by waging war, 32
on poor people and lottery, 28

on privacy, 27
on punishment for criticism of government, 31
on sacrifices by people but luxury for officials, 34
on surrendering freedom to gain security, 33
predictions for 1984 in, 2
vote on permanent site for Olympic games, 132

# T

Taxes and taxation
approval rating of increases in, to reduce federal budget deficit, 234-36
approval rating of Mondale's plan for increasing, 198-200
as issue for presidential debates, 195
as most important problem, 144, 207
Reagan or Mondale better at spending taxpayers' money wisely, 146
as threat to continued economic recovery, 106-07
Teen-agers
biggest problem facing, 264
Teresa of Calcutta, Mother
as most admired woman, 8, 273-74
Thatcher, Margaret
as most admired woman, 8, 273-74
Theft of car
incidence of, 231-33
national trend, 233
reported to police, 233-34
Theft of money or property
incidence of, 231-33
international comparisons, 233
national trend, 233
reported to police, 233-34
Truman, Harry S.
approval rating vs. Dewey and Wallace, 19
Tuition tax credits
approval rating, for children attending private or parochial schools, 239-40
Turkey
incidence of crime in, 233
vote on permanent site for Olympic games, 131

# U

Unemployment
dealt with by female president, 120
handled by Reagan, 64
national trend, 64
high, as reason for voting against Reagan, 92-93
as issue for presidential debates, 195
lower, as reason for voting for Reagan, 91-92
Mondale or Hart better at reducing, 96
as most important problem, 71, 118, 144, 207
as problem facing teen-agers, 264
Reagan or Mondale better at reducing, 146

Unemployment rate
by this time next year, 24-25
misery index trend, 25
UNESCO
United States should withdraw from, 111
United Kingdom *see* Great Britain
United States
degree of freedom in, 39-41
evaluated by five countries, 41
predictions for 1984 in, 2
national trend, 2
protection of environment as priority, or economic growth in, 267
international comparisons, 267
*see also* Environment
Reagan or Mondale better at increasing respect for overseas, 146
relations with Soviet Union under new Soviet leadership, 63
satisfaction with way things are going in, 68-69, 208-10
national trend, 69, 210
Uruguay
incidence of crime in, 233
predictions for 1984 in, 2
vote on permanent site for Olympic games, 131

# V

Vandalism of property
incidence of, 231-33
national trend, 233
reported to police, 233-34
Venezuela
predictions for 1984 in, 2
Vice-presidential candidates *see* Blacks; Women; *and by name*
Voter registration
anyone contacted you to help you register, 206
have you been contacted by anyone representing a candidate for president, 206
name recorded in precinct or election district, 90-91, 202
political affiliation, 91
plan to vote in presidential election, 202-03
turnout index, 203
voter turnout, 203

# W

Walesa, Lech
as most admired man, 8
Wallace, George
approval rating vs. Nixon and Humphrey, 19
approval rating vs. Nixon and McGovern, 19

Other Gallup Poll Publications Available from Scholarly Resources

*The Gallup Poll: Public Opinion, 1983*
ISBN 0-8420-2220-1 (1984)

*The Gallup Poll: Public Opinion, 1982*
ISBN 0-8420-2214-7 (1983)

*The Gallup Poll: Public Opinion, 1981*
ISBN 0-8420-2200-7 (1982)

*The Gallup Poll: Public Opinion, 1980*
ISBN 0-8420-2181-7 (1981)

*The Gallup Poll: Public Opinion, 1979*
ISBN 0-8420-2170-1 (1980)

*The Gallup Poll: Public Opinion, 1978*
ISBN 0-8420-2159-0 (1979)

*The Gallup Poll: Public Opinion, 1972–1977*
2 volumes ISBN 0-8420-2129-9 (1978)

*The International Gallup Polls: Public Opinion, 1979*
ISBN 0-8420-2180-9 (1981)

*The International Gallup Polls: Public Opinion, 1978*
ISBN 0-8420-2162-0 (1980)

*The Gallup International Public Opinion Polls:*
*France, 1939, 1944–1975*
2 volumes ISBN 0-394-40998-1 (1976)

*The Gallup International Public Opinion Polls:*
*Great Britain, 1937–1975*
2 volumes ISBN 0-394-40992-2 (1976)